NUMBER	FORMULA	PAGE
(7.1)	$z = \dfrac{X - \overline{X}}{s}$	124
(8.2)	$r = \dfrac{\sum(X - \overline{X})(Y - \overline{Y})}{\sqrt{SS_x \cdot SS_y}}$	145
(8.3)	$\sum(X - \overline{X})(Y - \overline{Y}) = \sum XY - \dfrac{(\sum X)(\sum Y)}{N}$	146
(8.4)	$r = \dfrac{\sum XY - \dfrac{(\sum X)(\sum Y)}{N}}{\sqrt{\left[\sum X^2 - \dfrac{(\sum X)^2}{N}\right]\left[\sum Y^2 - \dfrac{(\sum Y)^2}{N}\right]}}$	147
(8.5)	$r = \dfrac{\dfrac{\sum XY}{N} - \overline{X}\,\overline{Y}}{s_x s_y}$	148
(8.6)	$r_s = 1 - \dfrac{6\sum D^2}{N(N^2 - 1)}$	152
(9.5)	$Y' = \overline{Y} + r\dfrac{s_y}{s_x}(X - \overline{X})$	168
(9.9)	$Y' = \overline{Y} + \dfrac{N\sum XY - (\sum X)(\sum Y)}{N\sum X^2 - (\sum X)^2}(X - \overline{X})$	169

Continued on back endpaper

Random House New York

*Fundamentals
of
Behavioral
Statistics*

Fundamentals of Behavioral Statistics

RICHARD P. RUNYON

AUDREY HABER

FIFTH EDITION

Fifth Edition
9876

Copyright © 1967, 1971, 1976, 1980, 1984 by Newbery Award Records, Inc.

Library of Congress Cataloging in Publication Data

Runyon, Richard P.
  Fundamentals of behavioral statistics.

  Includes bibliographical references and index.
  1. Social sciences—Statistical methods.
2. Statistics.   1. Haber, Audrey.   II. Title.
HA29 R85   1984   519.5   83-6327
ISBN 0-394-35018-9

Manufactured in the United States of America

Preface
to the Fifth Edition

Much has happened since the publication of the first edition of *Fundamentals of Behavioral Statistics* in 1967. At that time, computers were the exclusive province of multimillion dollar corporations that could afford building-size facilities to house their elephantine babies of the transistor age. Available calculators were of the mechanical type that often took minutes to grind out the answer to a simple arithmetic problem. There was little hint that, in less than a quarter of a century, sophisticated personal computers would enter the classrooms and homes on a massive scale nor that caculators would become totally electronic and pocket sized.

Little did we, the authors, imagine that the fifth edition would be prepared by a word processor with calculations checked by computer programs we developed. The guiding light in our conceptualization and execution of this fifth edition has been the widespread availability of electronic means of conducting statistical analyses. Gone are the days when the instructor must spend hours of precious class time in tedious demonstrations of the squaring of values and the extracting of square roots. The computers and electronic calculators have given us the freedom to explore other important aspects of statistical analysis— the design of research, the relationship between that design and the strength of conclusions that may be drawn, to name but two.

With these considerations in mind, this edition features a broader emphasis on the interpretation of data. To illustrate, we have prominantly displayed

Case Examples throughout the text. These examples are excerpted from a rich and varied menu of contemporary research in the behavioral sciences. Some of the topics include women and minorities in psychology; help-giving strategies of bartenders, hairdressers, lawyers, and supervisors; the effects of mood on memory; adolescent hypertension; the relationship between endorphins and near Sudden Infant Death; the hearing of binaural beats at high frequencies; and many others.

With each of these Case Examples, raw data are presented and analyzed in terms of the topics featured in a given chapter. Later, they are subjected to more advanced analyses, culminating in the formulation of the statistical decision and the conclusions.

To illustrate, in Chapter 2 we introduce, on the descriptive level, the research of Benson, Karabenick, and Lerner on the effects of physical attractiveness, race, and sex on receiving help. Proportions and percentages are presented at this time. Later we return to this research in order to introduce and illuminate various probability concepts, including joint, marginal, and conditional probabilities. Finally, in later chapters, the students are given an opportunity to hone their inferential skills by applying the appropriate tests of significance to these data and drawing the conclusions warranted by the experimental facts. The effect of these Case Examples is to bring cohesion to statistical topics that are often perceived as separate and discrete.

The chapter on probability has undergone considerable revision, including the addition of tree and Venn diagrams, as well as conditional and joint probability tables. Moreover, many of the features have been retained that were so well received in the previous edition. For example, we have retained the marginal definitions of terms. As in the past edition, a tentative definition may be provided in an early chapter, and then elaborated on in a subsequent chapter when the student is better able to appreciate subtle nuances of meaning.

Throughout our years of teaching, we have often noted that statistical tables appearing in a textbook are not given the care and thought devoted to the text. Rather, they often seem more like afterthoughts than important elements in the educational process. We have attempted to design the tables to serve rather than to frustrate the students. Thus, where appropriate, we indicate when probability or critical values are one- or two-tailed. Moreover, we have included accompanying illustrations of the use. We have also extended some of the tables. To illustrate, we show one- and two-tailed binomial probabilities for $N < 49$ when P does not equal Q, one- and two-tailed probabilities for Ns through 50 when $P = Q$, and two-tailed critical values of the F-table.

All end-of-chapter exercises that are used to lay the groundwork for future discussions are preceded by an asterisk. It is vital that students complete these exercises so that there is a smooth transition to concepts of increasing complexity. It is thus that the contents of this textbook comes to belong, in the best sense of the word, to the students.

Acknowledgment

Although we owe a debt of gratitude to many colleagues who have made suggestions for this editon, we are particularly indebted to the following, whose contributions were both lucid and insightful: Robert Beck, Wake Forest University; James I. Chumbley, University of Massachusetts/Amherst; Dennis Cogan, Texas Technical University; Kathleen Dillon, Western New England College; Joseph D. Eubanks, San Antonio College; William Frankenberger, University of Wisconsin/Eau Claire; Willard Larkin, University of Maryland; John Reid, University of Missouri/Columbia; Wayne Velicer, University of Rhode Island.

We are grateful to the Literary Executor of the late Sir Ronald A. Fisher, F.R.S., to Dr. Frank Yates, F.R.S., and to Longman Group Ltd., London, for permission to reprint Table III from their book Statistical Tables for Biological, Agricultural and Medical Research (Sixth editon, 1974).

Tucson, Arizona   R. P. R.
Toms River, New Jersey   A. H.
November 1983

Contents

PART II Descriptive Statistics   **45**

3 *Frequency Distributions and Graphing Techniques*   **47**

4 *Percentiles*   **72**

5 *Measures of Central Tendency*   **88**

6 Measures of Dispersion 105

7 The Standard Deviation and the Standard Normal Distribution 123

8 Correlation 139

9 Regression and Prediction 162

PART III Inferential Statistics 189
Parametric Tests of Significance

10 Probability 191

11 Introduction to Statistical Inference 224

12 Statistical Inference and Continuous Variables 241

13

Statistical Inference with Two Independent Samples **274**

14

Statistical Inference with Correlated Samples **292**

15

An Introduction to the Analysis of Variance **309**

PART *IV* Inferential Statistics 337
Nonparametric Test of Significance

16 *Power and Power Efficiency of a Statistical Test* 339

17 *Statistical Inference with Categorical Variables* 355

18 *Statistical Inference with Ordinally Scaled Variables* 375

PART I

Introduction

1 Statistical Analysis

3

1.1 What Is Statistics?

Think for a moment of the thousands of incredibly complex things you do during the course of a day, and then stand in awe at the marvel you represent. You are absolutely unique. No one else possesses your features, your intellectual makeup, your personality characteristics, nor your value system. Yet, like billions of others of your species, you are the most finely tuned and enormously sophisticated statistical instrument ever devised by natural forces. Every moment of your life provides mute testimony to your ability to receive, integrate, and process a wealth of sensory data and then to act upon this information in an instant to generate a spectrum of probabilities relating to possible courses of action. To illustrate, imagine you are driving in heavy traffic. You are continuously scanning the road conditions, noting the speed of cars in front of you relative to your speed, the position and rate of approach of vehicles to your rear, and the presence of automobiles in the oncoming lane. If you are an alert driver, you are constantly summarizing this descriptive information—usually without words or awareness. Imagine next that, without warning, the car in front of you suddenly jams on its brakes. In an instant, you are summoned to act upon this prior descriptive information. You must brake the car, turn left, turn right, or pray. Your probability mechanism instantly assesses alternative courses of action: If you jam on the brakes, what is the likelihood that you will stop in time? Is the car behind you sufficiently distant to avoid a rear-end collision? Can you prevent an accident by turning into the left lane or onto the right shoulder? Most of the time, the decision made from sensory data is correct. It is for this reason that most of us grow up to reach a ripe old age. In this situation, as in many others during the course of a lifetime, you have accurately assessed the probabilities and taken the right course of action. And we make such decisions uncounted thousands of times each and every day of our lives. It is for this reason that you should regard yourself as a sublime mechanism for generating statistical decisions. In this sense, you are already a statistician.

In daily living, our statistical functioning is usually informal and loosely structured. We *behave* statistically, although we may be totally unaware of the formal laws of probability.

In this course, we shall attempt to provide you with some of the procedures for collecting and analyzing data, and making decisions or inferences based upon these analyses. Since we shall frequently be building upon your prior experiences, you will often feel you are in familiar territory: "Why, I have been calculating arithmetic means almost all my life—whenever I determine my test average in a course or the batting average of my favorite baseball player!" If you constantly draw upon your previous knowledge and relate course materials to what is familiar in daily life, statistics need not, and should not, be the bugaboo it is often painted to be.

Vital statistics: A matter of life and death

BOX 1.1

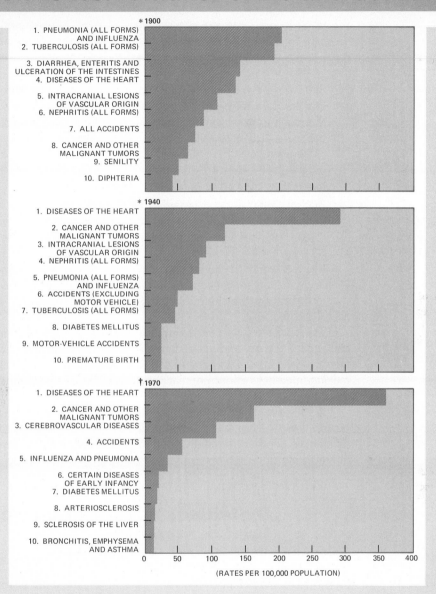

*1900

1. PNEUMONIA (ALL FORMS) AND INFLUENZA
2. TUBERCULOSIS (ALL FORMS)
3. DIARRHEA, ENTERITIS AND ULCERATION OF THE INTESTINES
4. DISEASES OF THE HEART
5. INTRACRANIAL LESIONS OF VASCULAR ORIGIN
6. NEPHRITIS (ALL FORMS)
7. ALL ACCIDENTS
8. CANCER AND OTHER MALIGNANT TUMORS
9. SENILITY
10. DIPHTERIA

*1940

1. DISEASES OF THE HEART
2. CANCER AND OTHER MALIGNANT TUMORS
3. INTRACRANIAL LESIONS OF VASCULAR ORIGIN
4. NEPHRITIS (ALL FORMS)
5. PNEUMONIA (ALL FORMS) AND INFLUENZA
6. ACCIDENTS (EXCLUDING MOTOR VEHICLE)
7. TUBERCULOSIS (ALL FORMS)
8. DIABETES MELLITUS
9. MOTOR-VEHICLE ACCIDENTS
10. PREMATURE BIRTH

†1970

1. DISEASES OF THE HEART
2. CANCER AND OTHER MALIGNANT TUMORS
3. CEREBROVASCULAR DISEASES
4. ACCIDENTS
5. INFLUENZA AND PNEUMONIA
6. CERTAIN DISEASES OF EARLY INFANCY
7. DIABETES MELLITUS
8. ARTERIOSCLEROSIS
9. SCLEROSIS OF THE LIVER
10. BRONCHITIS, EMPHYSEMA AND ASTHMA

0   50   100   150   200   250   300   350   400
(RATES PER 100,000 POPULATION)

Statistics is one of the most widely used tools in the behavioral, social, medical, and physical sciences. Statistical information is collected on virtually every aspect of life. Often, observations are made at varying times to permit the comparison of changes over time. The data presented in the accompanying figure illustrate that, since the turn of the century, the leading causes of death have changed dramatically. Note, for example, that pneumonia and tuberculosis accounted for a large number of all deaths in 1900, whereas by 1970 relatively few deaths could be attributed to these causes. Although it doesn't show in the graphs, it is interesting to note that the average life expectancy increased from 47 years in 1900 to 71 in 1970.

6

Chapter 1   Statistical Analysis

What, then, is statistics all about? Although it would be virtually impossible to obtain a consensus on the definition of statistics, it is possible to make a distinction between two definitions of **statistics.**

Statistics

Collection of numerical facts which are expressed in summarizing statements; method of dealing with data: a tool for collecting, organizing, and analyzing numerical facts or observations.

1. Statistics is commonly regarded as a *collection* of numerical facts that are expressed in terms of summarizing statements and that have been collected either from several observations or from other numerical data. From this perspective, statistics constitutes a collection of statements such as, "The average I.Q. of 8th grade children is . . . ," or "Seven out of ten people prefer Brand X to Brand Y," or "The New York Yankees hit 25 home runs over a two-week span during . . ."

2. Statistics may also be regarded as a *method* of dealing with data. This definition stresses the view that statistics is a tool concerned with the collection, organization, and analysis of numerical facts or observations.

Descriptive Statistics

Procedures employed to organize and present data in a convenient, usable, and communicable form.

It is the second definition that constitutes the subject matter of this text.

A distinction may be made between the two functions of the statistical method: **descriptive** statistical techniques and **inferential** or **inductive** statistical techniques.

Inferential or Inductive Statistics

Procedures employed to arrive at broader generalizations or inferences from sample data to populations.

The major concern of descriptive statistics is to present information in a convenient, usable, and understandable form. Inferential statistics, on the other hand, is concerned with generalizing this information or, more specifically, with making inferences about populations that are based upon samples taken from those populations.

In describing the functions of statistics, certain terms have already appeared with which you may or may not be familiar. Before elaborating on the differences between descriptive and inductive statistics, it is important to learn the meaning of certain terms that will be employed repeatedly throughout the text.

1.2 *Definitions of Terms Commonly Used in Statistics*

Variable

A characteristic or phenomenon that may take on different values.

Variable • Any characteristic of a person, environment, or experimental situation that can vary from person to person, environment to environment, or experimental situation to experimental situation. Thus weight, I.Q., and sex are variables since they will take on different values when different individuals are observed. A variable is contrasted with a constant, the value of which never changes, for example, pi.

Data • Numbers or measurements that are collected as a result of observations. They may be head counts (frequency data) as, for example, the number of individuals stating a preference for the Republican presidential candidate; or they may be scores, as on a psychological or educational test. Frequency data are also referred to as enumerative or categorical data.

Population • A complete set of individuals, objects, or measurements having some common observable characteristic. Thus all babies born in a particular year may constitute a population. However, a population may also be a *theoretical* set of *potential* observations, rather than a "complete set." For example, we may expand the above population to include *all* babies regardless of when they were born or will be born.

Some statisticians prefer to distinguish between a population and a source. They use population to refer only to numerical measurements or observations and source as the origin of these observations. According to this distinction, voters in a national election are a source and their votes are the population. We do not differentiate between population and source in this book. The slight ambiguity does not usually constitute a problem as long as we are aware of the fact that statistical statements are expressed in terms of numerical values.

Parameter • Any characteristic of a **population** which is measurable, e.g., the true proportion of registered Democrats among Americans of voting age. In this text we shall follow the generally accepted practice of employing Greek letters (i.e., μ pronounced "mew". Greek symbol for the population mean. σ pronounced sigma: Greek symbol for the population standard deviation) to represent population parameters.

Sample • A subset of a population or universe selected according to some scheme (e.g., from the population of all females or the population of all psychology majors with a grade point average of at least 3.0, etc.)

Random sample • A subset of a population or universe selected in such a way that each member of the population has a equal opportunity to be selected. Random sampling permits inferences about characteristics of the population from which the sample is selected.

Statistic • A number resulting from manipulation of sample data according to certain specified procedures or rules. For example, if we wanted to express the number of patients in a care facility diagnosed "schizophrenic" as a proportion, we follow the rule: divide the number diagnosed as schizophrenic by the total number of patients. Thus, if there are 880 patients and 356 are diagnosed schizophrenic, the proportion is $356/880 = 0.40$ (rounded to the second decimal place). Commonly, we use a statistic that is calculated from a sample in order to estimate the population parameter; e.g., a sample of Americans of voting age is employed to estimate the proportion of Democrats in the entire population of voters. It should be noted that for *every* statistic that de-

Data

Numbers or measurements that are collected as a result of observations.

Population

A complete set of individuals, objects, or measurements having some common observable characteristic, or a theoretical set of potential observations.

Parameter

Any characteristic of a population that is measurable.

Sample

A subset of a population or universe selected according to some scheme.

Random Sample

A subset of a population or universe selected in such a way that each member of the population has an equal opportunity to be selected.

Statistic

A number resulting from the manipulation of sample data according to certain specified procedures.

scribes some aspect of a sample there is a corresponding parameter that describes the same aspect of a population. Thus for the statistic "mean of a sample" there is a parameter "mean of the population." We shall employ italic letters (e.g., $\overline{X}$ sample mean; s: sample standard deviation) to represent sample statistics. Thus, by looking at statistical notation, we can distinguish between sample and populations. More will be said about the fascinating problem of sampling later in the text.

- *Example*   Imagine that you have been hired as a statistical consultant by the governing body of a large metropolitan region. Your first assignment is to obtain statistical information on a medico-psychological problem that has surfaced over the past decade or so, namely, drug addiction among newborn infants. Treatment of these innocent victims of drug abuse requires some specialized equipment and round-the-clock medical supervision. Your immediate task is to estimate the extent and types of neonatal drug addiction so that the various clinics and hospitals in the city may make informed decisions about equipment and personnel needs for the coming year. Typically, your operating budget and the availability of trained assistants are limited. Therefore there is no way you can hope to study the medical records of *all* the children born during the preceding year. At best, you can select only a small portion of the total records and subject these to intensive scrutiny. These selected records constitute the sample. If the sample is selected in such a way that each record has an equal probability of being chosen, we speak of the selection process as **random selection.** The **variable** of interest is the drug addiction status of each neonate. For our purposes we'll assume that each record reveals either the presence or the absence of drug addiction. The **data** consist of the number of drug-addicted and non-drug-addicted infants in the sample. When the data are manipulated according to certain rules to yield summary statements (such as the proportion of drug-addicted neonates), the resulting numerical value constitutes a **statistic.** The **population** to which we are interested in generalizing is all the infant births occurring in the metropolitan region during the preceding year. The "true" proportion of neonatal addicts in the population is the **parameter** (see Fig. 1.1). Note that it is highly unlikely that the parameter will ever be known for, to find it, we would require the examination of the medical records of every infant born in the region over a time period of one year. Since this is usually not feasible for economic and other reasons, it is rare that an exhaustive study of a population is undertaken. Consequently, parameters are rarely known but, as we shall see, they are commonly estimated from sample statistics.

    It is, of course, possible to define a very small population by narrowing the definition of "common observable characteristic" to something like "all students attending their Psych 91 class at Pitzer College today." In this event, calculating a parameter (such as the class mean on the examination given to-

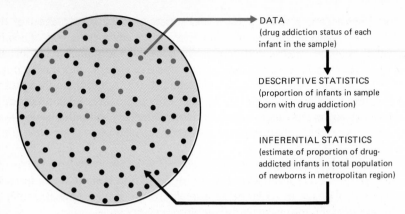

Figure 1.1   A *random sample* is selected from some population. The dots represent
all births during the year. The color dots represent the sample. *Data* are
collected and summarized, employing descriptive statistics. In *inferential
statistics,* we attempt to estimate one or more population *parameters*
(e.g., the proportion of drug-addicted infants among all newborn children
in the metropolitan region).

day) would pose no difficulty. For such small populations, there is no reason
to select samples and to calculate sample statistics.

From the point of view of the instructor, observations on the students in
Psych 91 at Pitzer College may be of supreme importance. However, such
limited populations would be of little theoretical interest. Usually, in the real
workaday world, the behavioral scientist is interested in making statements
having general validity over a wider domain and thus must *estimate* the (population) parameter. This estimate is based on the statistic that is calculated on
the sample. Thus we might use the observations on the students at Pitzer College as a basis for estimating parameters of the larger population.

Let us return to the two functions of statistical analysis for a closer look.

1.3 *Descriptive Statistics*

When a behavioral scientist conducts a study, he or she characteristically col-
lects a great deal of numerical information or data about the problem at hand.
The data may take a variety of forms: frequency data (head counts of voters
preferring various political candidates), or scale data (the weights of the contents of a popular breakfast cereal, or the I.Q. scores of a group of college
students). In their original form, as collected, these data are usually a confusing
hodge-podge of scores, frequency counts, etc. In performing the descriptive

function, statisticians formulate rules and procedures for presentation of the data in a more usable and meaningful form. Thus statisticians state rules by which data may be represented graphically. They also formulate rules for calculating various *statistics* from masses of raw data.

Let us imagine that, as a behavioral scientist, you administered a number of measuring instruments (e.g., intelligence tests, personality inventories, aptitude tests) to a group of high-school students. What are some things you may do with the resulting measurements or scores to fulfill your descriptive functions?

1. You may rearrange the scores and group them in various ways, in order to be able to see at a glance an overall picture of your data (Chapter 3, "Frequency Distributions and Graphing Techniques").

2. You may construct tables, graphs, and figures to permit visualization of the results (Section 3.3, "Graphing Techniques," in Chapter 3).

3. You may convert raw scores to other types of scores that are more useful for specific purposes. Thus you may convert these scores into either percentile ranks, standard scores, or grades. Other types of conversion will also be described in the text (Chapter 4, "Percentiles," and Chapter 7, "The Standard Deviation and the Standard Normal Distribution").

4. You may calculate averages, to learn something about the typical performances of your subjects (Chapter 5, "Measures of Central Tendency").

5. Employing the average as a reference point, you may describe the dispersion, or spread, of scores about this central point. Statistics that quantify this dispersion are known as measures of variability or measures of dispersion (Chapter 6, "Measures of Dispersion").

6. A relationship between two different measuring instruments may be obtained. The statistic for describing the extent of the relationship is referred to as a *correlation coefficient.* Such coefficients are extremely useful to the behavioral scientist. For example, you may wish to determine the relationship between intelligence and classroom grades, personality measures and aptitudes, or interests and personality measures. Once these relationships are established, you may employ scores obtained from one measuring instrument to predict performance on another (Chapter 8, "Correlation," and Chapter 9, "Regression and Prediction").

1.4 Inferential Statistics

As a behavioral scientist, your task has just begun when you have completed your descriptive function. In fact, you are often nearer to the beginning than to the end of your task. The reason for this is obvious when we consider that the purpose of your research is often to explore hypotheses of a general nature, rather than to simply compare limited samples.

Let us imagine that you are interested in determining the effects of a given drug upon the performance of a task involving psychomotor coordination. Consequently you set up a study involving two conditions, *experimental* and *control*. You administer the drug to the experimental subjects at specified time periods before they undertake the criterion task. To rule out "placebo effects," you administer a pill containing inert ingredients to the control subjects. After all subjects have been tested, you perform your descriptive function. You find that "on the average" the experimental subjects did not perform as well as the controls. In other words, the arithmetic mean of the experimental group was lower than that of the control group. You then ask the question, "Can we conclude that the drug produced the difference between the two groups?" Or, more generally, "Can we assert that the drug has an adverse effect upon the performance of the criterion task under investigation?" To answer these questions, it is not sufficient to rely solely upon *descriptive statistics*.

"After all," you reason, "even if the drug had *no effect,* it is highly improbable that the two group means would have been *identical.* Some difference would have been observed." The operation of uncontrolled variables (sometimes referred to rather imprecisely as "chance factors") is certain to produce some disparity between the group means. The critical question, from the point of view of inferential statistics, becomes: Is the difference great enough to rule out uncontrolled variation in the experiment as a sufficient explanation? Stated another way, if we were to repeat the experiment, would we be able to predict with confidence that the same differences (i.e., the control group mean greater than the experimental group mean) would systematically occur?

As soon as we raise these questions, we move into the fascinating area of statistical analysis that is known as **inductive** or **inferential statistics.** As you will see, much of the present text is devoted to procedures that the researcher employs to arrive at conclusions extending beyond the sample statistics themselves.

1.5 *The Goals of Research*

Behavioral scientists engage in a rich variety of different activities in diverse settings that involve the collection and analysis of numerical observations or data. These activities are generally subsumed under the label "research." The goals of these research activities may be classified into three broad categories: information gathering, describing relationships, and establishing causality. It should be noted that these goals are not mutually exclusive. All three are common components of many research efforts.

Information Gathering

The focus of many statistical activities is to provide accurate information about some aspect of our professional activities that arouse our interest. For example, we may wish to know if the proportion of women entering the field of psychology is changing over the years, or the average starting salary of recent Ph.D.s accepting positions at academic institutions, or the proportion of clinical psychologists using the 3rd edition of the *Diagnostic and Statistical Manual* (*DSM* III) as a means of classifying the presenting behaviors of clients. In these information gathering activities, the emphasis is to provide accurate m descriptions of the situations studied. The information is considered valuable in its own right. Therefore, there may not be any effort to relate the data to other events or situations. For example, we may make no attempt to answer the question, why is the starting salaries of new Ph.D.s in academia X dollars?

CASE EXAMPLE • 1.1
Women and Minorities in Psychology

The survey is one means of collecting information on topics of interest. If the survey includes the entire population it is called a *census*. If only a subset of the population, it is called a sample. Every year the National Research Council obtains a census on the number of doctorates awarded in various fields in the United States. Starting in 1972, a breakdown was made available in terms of the gender of the recipient. In 1977, data were also collected on the number of members of ethnic/racial groups who received the doctorate degree. The results of these annual surveys, as they pertain to the field of psychology, are summarized in Fig. 1.2.

A glance at the figure reveals a marked and steady increase in the percentage of women receiving their doctorates in psychology relative to the men receiving their doctorates. The percentage of men can be found by subtracting the percentage of women receiving doctorates from 100%. Thus, in 1972, $100\% - 26.7\% = 73.3\%$ were males among those receiving a doctorate in psychology compared to $100\% - 42.3\% = 57.7\%$ in 1980.

The minorities are also showing gains since 1977, but they are much less than those shown by women. In part, the lower percentages among minorities (black, Hispanic, Asian, and American Indian) reflect the fact that, compared to women (which are 53% of the general population), they constitute a lower percentage in the general population.

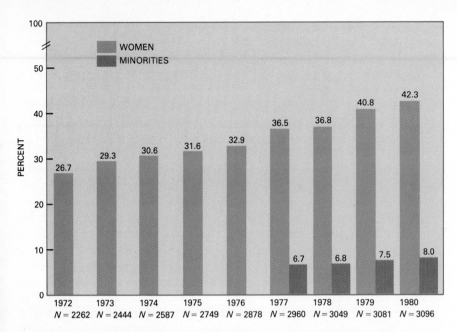

Figure 1.2 Percentages of women (1972–1980) and minority (1977–1980)
doctorate recipients in psychology. *Source:* National Research Council
(1973, 1974, 1975, 1976, 1977, 1978, 1979, 1980, 1981).

Based on "Women and Minorities in Psychology" by Nancy F. Russo, Esteban L. Olmedo, Joy
Stapp, and Robert Fulcher (1981), *American Pyschologist,* **35**(11), 1315–1363.

Describing Relationships

In the course of conducting research, we often obtain measurements on two
or more variables from each subject, and we wish to know whether or not the
variables go together or covary. Does academic performance vary in relation
to measured intelligence? Is there a relationship between temporal lobe epi-
lepsy and aggressviveness as some researchers have claimed? Does our ability
to recall childhood experiences depend on the pleasantness/unpleasantness associated with these experiences at the time they occurred?

Studies of this sort are referred to as correlational. They attempt to ascertain whether or not two variables are related (i.e. correlated—think of them as
co-related) or vary together and, if so, to measure the direction and strength
of the relationship. To illustrate, if we have measurements on two variables for
each individual, we may raise such questions as: As the values of one variable
increase (e.g., measured intelligence), do the paired measures on the second

variable also increase (e.g., academic performance)? Or are increases in one variable (e.g., anxiety) associated with decreases in a second variable (e.g., score on a complex problem solving task)? Or does there not appear to be any detectable relationship between the two variables (e.g., length of big toe and score on an intelligence test)?

It is important to note that correlations between naturally occurring variables such as intelligence, gender, racial/ethnic backgrounds, or learning scores do not, as such, permit us to claim that changes in one variable *cause* changes in a second variable. They merely establish whether or not the two variables vary together. Many serious misinterpretations of data have occurred because people have ignored this fact. Thus, at various times in our history as a nation, members of various minority groups (e.g., blacks, Italians, Poles, Jews, etc.) have labored under the label of inferiority because their low positions on the educational and socio-economic ladders have been attributed to their racial and/or ethnic backgrounds. The point is that these groups differed from each other in many other ways than their ethnic/racial backgrounds—e.g., command of the English language, educational and economic opportunities, and life styles—to name a few. To focus on a single characteristic (such as ethnic background) that distinguished each of these groups from the majority and to attribute their social and economic position to this characteristic is to ignore the wealth of other ways in which they differ.

Establishing Causality

One of the paramount goals of any science is to go beyond statements of relationships (e.g., If the value of A is high then the value of B is also high) to those of causality (e.g., increases in the values of A *cause* the values of B to increase also). In spite of hundreds of years of speculating, thinking, and writing about causality, it remains a somewhat elusive term. Not all scientists agree on the procedures for establishing cause-effect relationships. Indeed, some even doubt its feasibility while others question its necessity. However, the vast majority of scientists appear to agree that a statement such as "A causes B" is among the most powerful that a scientist can make and should be at the core of scientific inquiry.

Although there are advocates of several different strategies for establishing causality, we'll limit our discussion to the "true" experiment. In the typical true experiment, we are concerned primarily with two different types of variables—*independent* and *dependent*. The independent variable is usually some feature of the individual's external environment (type of incentive, instructional materials, pharmaceutical compound), although it may also be an internal state, such as motivational level. The purpose of the experiment is to assess the effects of variations in the independent variable on some response measure (the dependent variable). Response variables include such diverse measures as scores on a test, the time required to demonstrate mastery of a task or skill, attitudes toward a political candidate or proposed piece of legislation, electrical conductivity of the skin, or time required to react to the introduction of a visual or auditory stimulus. The key to qualifying as a true experiment is that *the independent variable must be under the control of the experimenter.* To illustrate, different types of incentives, instructional materials, or pharmaceutical compounds can all be independently manipulated and varied by an experimenter. Consequently, they can all qualify as independent variables in a true experiment. If our data analyses yield convincing evidence that variations in the independent variable lead to systematic and predictable variations in the dependent measure, we are justified in concluding that the manipulation of the independent variable caused the changes in the response variable.

This is not necessarily the case with all independent variables. Often the independent variable is a state of nature or of the organism that is not under the experimenter's control. To illustrate, we may have observed that moods of people appear to be different on cloudy days as opposed to sunny days. We design the following study: We administer a mood scale to two randomly selected groups of subjects. Half take the test on sunny days and half on cloudy days. Let's suppose we find that the moods are clearly better on the sunny days. Can we conclude that sunshine causes the favorable moods? Not necessarily. It is quite possible that mood is unaffected by sunshine, as such, but reflects the effects of variables that covary with sunshine (lower relative humidity, different barometric pressures, or better visibility). To conclude that sunshine causes better moods, we would be required to manipulate sunshine independent of these other variables. The same considerations apply when we use naturally occurring variables within the individual as independent measures. To illustrate, suppose we conducted a study in which we formed two groups—schizophrenic and normal subjects. The diagnosis would constitute the independent variable. Next, suppose we measured the levels of a particular neurotransmitter (the dependent variable) at a specific site in the central nervous system and found consistently lower levels among schizophrenics? Could we conclude that schizophrenia causes reduced levels of the neurotransmitter? As with the sunshine example, we could not. There are numerous other variables that covary with schizophrenia (e.g., dietary habits, life styles, activity levels, etc.), any number of which could cause the drop in the neurotransmitter level. It is also possible that the level of neurotransmitter is a cause of the schizophrenia, but this study would not provide the answer.

To summarize, the key to ascertaining if a study can qualify as a true experiment resides in the degree of control the researcher has over the manipulation of the independent variable. If the investigator can randomly assign the experimental conditions (the independent variable) to the subjects, the study is a true experiment and strong conclusions of causality may be drawn. If the independent variable cannot be manipulated by the researcher but is a naturally occurring variable that forms the basis for constituting the experimental groups, strong inferences of causality cannot be drawn. Although superficially resembling a true experiment, such investigations have more in common with the correlational study (see "Describing Relationships" earlier in this chapter). Moreover, they share both the assets and liabilities of correlational research.

Case Examples are to be found throughout this book. Some will be correlational research; others will be correlational studies that have the surface appearance of an experiment; and still others will be true experiments. Much emphasis will be placed on the types of conclusions that can be drawn from such research.

1.6 A Word to the Student

The study of statistics need not and should not become a series of progressive exercises in calculated tedium. If it is approached with the proper frame of mind, statistics can be one of the most exciting fields of study; it has applications in virtually all areas of human endeavor and cuts across countless fields of study. H. G. Wells, the nineteenth-century prophet, remarked, "Statistical thinking will one day be as necessary for efficient citizenship as the ability to read and write." Keep this thought constantly in mind. The course will be much more interesting and profitable to you if you develop the habit of "thinking statistically." Constantly attempt to apply statistical concepts to all daily activities, no matter how routine. When you are stopped at an intersection that you cross frequently, note the time the traffic light remains red. Obtain some estimate of the length of the green cycle. If it is red three minutes and green two, you would expect that the chances are three in five that it will be red when you reach the intersection. Start collecting data. Do you find that it is red 60 percent of the time as expected? If not, why not? Perhaps you have unconciously made some driving adjustments in order to change the statistical probabilities.

A common misconception held by laymen is that statistics is merely a rather sophisticated method for fabricating lies or falsifying our descriptions of reality. The authors do not deny that some unscrupulous individuals employ statistics for just such purposes. However, such uses of statistics are anathema to the behavioral scientist who is dedicated to the establishment of truth. From time to time, references will be made to various techniques that are used for lying with statistics. However, the purpose is not to instruct you in these techniques but to make you aware of the various *misuses* of statistical analyses so that you do not inadvertently "tell a lie," and so that you may be aware when others do.

When you see statistical information being exhibited, develop a healthy attitude of skepticism. Ask pertinent questions. When a national magazine sends a physically fit reporter to ten different diet doctors and he or she receives an unneeded prescription from each, do not jump to the conclusion that all diet doctors are frauds. Do not say, "After all, ten out of ten is a rather high proportion" and dismiss further inquiry at this point. Ask how the reporter obtained the sample. Was it at random, or is it possible that the doctors were selected on the basis of prior information indicating they were rather careless in their professional practices? Question constantly, but reserve judgment until you have the answers.

Watch commercials on television; read newspaper advertisements. When the pitchman claims, "Dodoes are more effective," ask, "More effective than what? What is the evidence?"

If you make statistical thinking an everyday habit, you will find not only that the study of statistics becomes more interesting, but also that the world you live in appears different and, perhaps, more interesting.

Chapter Summary

In this chapter, we have distinguished between two definitions of statistical analysis, one stressing statistics as a collection of numerical facts and the other emphasizing statistics as a method or tool concerned with the collection, organization, and analysis of numerical facts. The second definition constitutes the subject matter of this text.

A distinction is made between two functions of the statistical methods, descriptive and inferential statistical analyses. The former is concerned with the organization and presentation of data in a convenient, usable, and communicable form. The latter is addressed to the problem of making broader generalizations or inferences from sample data to populations.

A number of terms commonly employed in statistical analysis were defined.

Finally, it was pointed out that statistics is frequently employed for the purpose of "telling lies." Such practices are inimical to the goal of establishing a factual basis for our conclusions and statistically based decisions. However, you should be aware of the techniques for telling statistical lies, so that you do not inadvertently "tell one" yourself or fail to recognize one when someone else does.

New terms or concepts that have been introduced in a chapter will be listed at the end of each chapter as well as in the margins at the points where they first appear. Some of these terms will be more precisely defined in other chapters and consequently may appear again.

Terms to Remember

data	random sample
descriptive statistics	sample
inferential or inductive statistics	statistic
parameter	statistics
population or universe	variable

EXERCISES

1. Indicate whether each of the following constitutes a statistic, data, or inference from statistics.
    a. A sample of 250 wage earners in Carlthorp City yielded a per-capita income of $14,460.
    b. Based on a random sample of 250 wage earners in Carlthorp City, it is believed that the average income of all wage earners in this city is about $14,500.
    c. The slug from a .22 rifle can travel one mile.
    d. My tuition payment this year was $4580.
    e. The number of people viewing Monday night's television special was 23,500,000.

2. Many populations studied in experimental situations are theoretical in nature. Give some examples of theoretical populations that may be dealt with in research.

3. Indicate whether each of the following represents a variable or a constant:
    a. Number of days in the month of August.
    b. Number of shares traded on the New York Stock Exchange on various days of the year.
    c. Age of freshmen entering college.
    d. Time it takes to complete an assignment.
    e. Age at which an individual is first eligible to vote in a national election.
    f. Scores obtained on a 100-item multiple-choice examination.
    g. Maximum score possible on a 100-item multiple-choice examination.
    h. Amount of money spent on books per year by students.

4. Professor Norman Yetman of the University of Kansas has concerned himself with possible economic discrimination against black athletes by the media.* He has analyzed their opportunities to appear on commercials, make guest appearances, and obtain off-season jobs. Two of the findings follow:
    a. In 351 commercials associated with New York sporting events in the autumn of 1966, black athletes appeared in only 2.

---

*Source: Gary Lehman, AP sports writer, August 22, 1975.

b. An analysis of media advertising opportunities of athletes on a professional football team in 1971 revealed that in a sample of 11 whites, 8 had an opportunity; in contrast, only 2 of 13 black athletes had a similar opportunity.

Indicate whether these examples provide parameters, data, or inferences from statistics.

5. Football telecasters frequently point to tables like the following and offer such comments as, "Here are the half-time statistics. They really tell the story of this game!"

	Team A	Team B
First downs	6	10
Passes attempted	12	8
Passes completed	7	4
Yards passing	62	30
Yards running	78	104
Total Yards	140	134
Turnovers	2	1
Time of possession	12'04"	17'56"

Are these numbers in fact statistics? If not, what are they?

Exercises 6 though 11 are based on the following: Imagine an industrial firm engaged in the production of hardware for the space industry. Among its products are machine screws that must be maintained within fine tolerances with respect to width. As part of its quality-control procedures, a number of screws are selected from the daily output and are carefully measured.

6. The screws selected for study constitute the
   a. Population.   b. Statistic.   c. Parameter.   d. Sample.
7. The widths of all of these screws constitute the
   a. Statistic.   b. Variable.   c. Parameter.   d. Sample.
8. The measurement of each screw constitutes the
   a. Data.   b. Sample.   c. Statistic.   d. Population.
9. The average width of the screws in the sample constitutes the
   a. Parameter.   b. Statistic.   c. Variable.   d. Data.
10. We wish to generalize the output of the sample to the
    a. Data.   b. Variable.   c. Statistic.   d. Population.
11. The average width of all screws produced in a day constitutes the
    a. Parameter.   b. Variable.   c. Data.   d. Population.

2 Basic Mathematical Concepts

2.1 Introduction

"I'm not much good in math. How can I possibly pass statistics?" The authors have heard these words from the lips of countless undergraduate students. For many, this is probably a concern that legitimately stems from prior discouraging experiences with mathematics. A brief glance through the pages of this text may only serve to increase this anxiety, since many of the formulas appear quite imposing to the novice and may seem impossible to master. Therefore it is most important to set the record straight right at the beginning of the course.

You do not have to be a mathematical genius to master the statistical principles enumerated in this text. The amount of mathematical sophistication necessary for a firm grasp of the fundamentals of statistics is often exaggerated. As a matter of actual fact, statistics requires a good deal of arithmetic computation, sound logic, and a willingness to stay with a point until it is mastered. To paraphrase Carlyle, success in statistics is an infinite capacity for taking pains. Beyond these modest requirements, little is needed but the mastery of several algebraic and arithmetic procedures that most of you learned early in your high-school careers. In this chapter, we review the grammar of mathematical notation, discuss several types of numerical scales, and adopt certain conventions for the rounding of numbers.

If you wish to brush up on your basic mathematics, Appendix A contains a review of all the math necessary to master this text.

2.2 The Grammar of Mathematical Notation

Throughout this textbook, you'll be learning new mathematical symbols. For the most part, we define these symbols when they first appear. However, there are three notations that will appear so frequently that their separate treatment at this time is justified. These notations are $\sum$ (pronounced *sigma*), X, and N. However, while defining these symbols and showing their use, let's also review the grammar of mathematical notation.

It is not surprising to learn that many students become so involved in the forest of mathematical symbols, formulas, and operations, that they fail to realize that mathematics has a form of grammar which closely parallels the spoken language. Thus, mathematics has its nouns, adjectives, verbs, and adverbs.

Mathematical nouns • In mathematics, we commonly use symbols to stand for quantities. The notation we employ most commonly in statistics to represent quantity (or a score) is X, although we occasionally employ Y. In

BOX 2.1

Birth: The question of control

Respondents	Should %	Should Not %	No Opinion %
White	88	8	4
Black	77	18	5
Under 30 years	96	3	1
Over 30 years	82	12	6
Annual family income			
Under $5,000	72	20	8
Over $15,000	95	5	*
Protestant†	86	9	4
Catholic	83	12	5
Jewish†	98	0	3
No affiliation†	95	6	0
Republican	88	7	5
Democrat	84	12	4
Independent	89	8	3
Northeast	85	11	4
South	85	10	5
North Central	88	8	4
West	88	9	3
All	87	9	4

*Percent less than 0.5.
†In some categories, the percentages do not add up to exactly 100. This is due to small rounding errors.

Much of the data collected in the behavioral and social sciences consists of head counts—the number of people falling in one category as opposed to another. We commonly use percentages and proportions to describe such data. Attitude surveys on various issues represent one of many applications of the "head count" technique.

The accompanying table presents the results of a survey of over 1700 men and women, 16 years of age and older. All were asked the following question: "Do you think that information about birth control should or should not be made available by the government to all men and women who want it?"

Lipson, G., and W. Solman (1972). "Polling Americans on Birth Control and Population," *Family Planning Perspectives,* **4** (1), 39–42 (Table 1 appears on p. 39). Reprinted with permission from *Family Planning Perspective.*

addition, X and Y are employed to identify variables; for example, if weight and height were two variables in a study, X might be used to represent weight and Y to represent height. Other frequently used "nouns" are the symbol c, which represents a constant, and the symbol N, which represents the number of scores or quantities with which we are dealing. Thus, if we have ten quantities,

$$N = 10.$$

Mathematical adjectives • When we want to modify a mathematical noun, to identify it more specifically, we commonly employ subscripts. Thus if we have a series of scores or quantities, we may represent them as X_1, X_2, X_3, X_4, etc. We shall also frequently encounter X_i, in which the subscript may take on any value that we desire.

Mathematical verbs • Notations that direct the reader to do something have the same characteristics as verbs in the spoken language. One of the most important "verbs" is the symbol already alluded to as $\sum$. This notation directs us to sum all quantities or scores following the symbol. Thus

$$\sum X_1, X_2, X_3, X_4, X_5$$

indicates that we should add together all these quantities from X_1 though X_5. Other "verbs" we encounter frequently are $\sqrt{}$, which direct us to find the square root, and exponents (X^a), which tell us to raise a quantity to the indicated power. In mathematics, mathematical verbs are commonly referred to as *operators*.

Mathematical adverbs • These are notations which, as in spoken language, modify the verbs. We frequently find that the summation signs are modified by adverbial notations. Let's imagine that we want to indicate that the following quantities are to be added:

$$X_1 + X_2 + X_3 + X_4 + X_5 + \cdots + X_N.$$

Symbolically, we would represent these operations as follows:

$$\sum_{i=1}^{N} X_i.$$

The notations above and below the summation sign indicate that i takes on the successive values from 1, 2, 3, 4, 5 up to N. Stated verbally, the notation reads: We should sum all quantities of X starting with $i = 1$ (that is, X_1) and proceeding through to $i = N$ (that is, X_N).

Sometimes this form of notation may direct us to add only selected quantities; thus

$$\sum_{i=2}^{5} X_i = X_2 + X_3 + X_4 + X_5.$$

2.3 *Summation Rules*

The summation sign is one of the most frequently used operators in statistics. Let us summarize a few of the rules governing the use of the summation sign.

Generalization 1. *The sum of a constant added together N times is equal to N times that constant.* Symbolically,

$$\sum_{i=1}^{N} c = Nc.$$

Let c be a constant. Thus, if $c = 10$ and $N = 5$,

$$\sum_{i=1}^{N} c = (10 + 10 + 10 + 10 + 10) = 5(10) = 50.$$

Similarly, if $\overline{X}$ *is the constant and* $\overline{X} = 20$, $N = 15$,

$$\sum_{i=1}^{N} \overline{X} = N\overline{X} = (15)(20) = 300.$$

Generalization 2. *Multiplying each value of a variable by a constant and then summing the products yields the same result as first summing the values and then multiplying the sum by the constant.* Symbolically,

$$\sum_{i=1}^{N} cX_i = c \sum_{i=1}^{N} X_i.$$

Thus, if $c = 5$, and $X_1 = 2$, $X_2 = 3$, $X_3 = 4$,

$$\sum_{i=1}^{N} cX_i = (5)(2) + (5)(3) + (5)(4) = 45.$$

Also,

$$c\sum_{i=1}^{N} X_i = 5(2 + 3 + 4) = 45.$$

Generalization 3.   *Adding a constant to each value of a variable and then summing these new values yields the same result as first summing the values of the variable and then adding that sum to N times the constant.* Symbolically,

$$\sum_{i=1}^{N} (X_i + c) = \sum_{i=1}^{N} X_i + Nc.$$

Imagine a sample in which $N = 3$ and $X_1 = 3$, $X_2 = 4$, and $X_3 = 6$. The sum of the three values of the variable may be shown by

$$\sum_{i=1}^{N} X_i = X_1 + X_2 + X_3$$
$$= 3 + 4 + 6.$$

To show the sum of the values of a variable when a constant ($c = 2$) has been added to each,

$$\sum_{i=1}^{N} (X_i + c) = (3 + c) + (4 + c) + (6 + c)$$
$$= 3 + 4 + 6 + (c + c + c)$$
$$= 3 + 4 + 6 + (2 + 2 + 2)$$
$$= 13 + 3c = 13 + 3(2)$$
$$= 19.$$

Generalization 4.   *Subtracting a constant from each value of a variable and then summing these new values yields the same result as first summing the values of the variable and then subtracting N times the constant from that sum.* Symbolically,

$$\sum_{i=1}^{N} (X_i - c) = \sum_{i=1}^{N} X_i - Nc.$$

To show the sum of the values of a variable when a constant has been subtracted from each, let $X_1 = 3$, $X_2 = 4$, $X_3 = 6$, and $c = 2$.

$$\sum_{i=1}^{N} (X_i - c) = (3 - c) + (4 - c) + 6 - c)$$
$$= 3 + 4 + 6 - (c + c + c)$$
$$= 3 + 4 + 6 - 3c$$
$$= 13 - 3(2) = 7.$$

- *Example.*   These generalizations are often useful in statistics, particularly when we want to sum numbers with large quantitative values, for example,

$$X_1 = 100,465, \qquad X_2 = 100,467, \qquad X_3 = 100,469, \qquad X_4 = 100,472.$$

To sum these four numbers, you can subtract 100,000 from each quantity, sum the remainder, and then add 4 times 100,000. Thus

$$\sum_{i=1}^{4} X_i = 465 + 467 + 469 + 472 + 4(100,000)$$
$$= 1873 + 400,000$$
$$= 401,873.$$

2.4 *Types of Numbers and Scales*

Cultural anthropologists, psychologists, and sociologists have repeatedly called attention to the common human tendency to explore the world that is remote from our primary experiences long before we have investigated that which is closest to us. Thus, while we were probing distant stars and describing with striking accuracy their apparent movements and interrelationships, we virtually ignored the very substance that gave us life: air (which we inhale and exhale over four hundred million times a year). In the authors' experience, a similar pattern exists in relation to the student's familiarity with numbers and his or her concepts of them. In our quantitatively oriented western civilization, student Cory employs and manipulates numbers long before he is expected to calculate the batting averages of the latest baseball hero. Nevertheless, ask him to define a number, or to describe the ways in which numbers are employed, and you will likely be met with expressions of consternation and bewilderment. "I've never thought about it before," he will frequently reply. After a few minutes of soul searching and deliberation, he will probably reply something to the effect that numbers are symbols denoting amounts of things that can be added, subtracted, multiplied, and divided. These are all familiar arithmetic concepts, but do they exhaust all possible uses of numbers? At the risk of reducing our student to utter confusion, you may ask: "Is the symbol 7 on a baseball player's uniform such a number? What about your home address? Channel 2 on your television set? Do these numbers indicate amounts of things? Can they reasonably be added, subtracted, multiplied, or divided? Can you multiply the number on any football player's back by any other number and obtain a meaningful value?" A careful analysis of our use of numbers in everyday life reveals a very interesting fact: Most of the numbers we employ do not have the arithmetical properties we usually ascribe to them; they cannot be meaningfully added, subtracted, multiplied, and divided. A few examples are the serial number of a home appliance, a Zipcode number, a telephone number, a home address, an automobile registration number, and the numbers on a book in the library.

The important point is that numbers are used in a variety of ways to achieve many different ends. Much of the time, these ends do not include the representation of an amount or a quantity. In fact, there are three fundamentally different ways in which numbers are used.

1. To name **(nominal numbers)**
2. To represent position in a series **(ordinal numbers)**
3. To represent quantity **(cardinal numbers)**

Measurement is the assignment of numbers to objects or events according to sets of predetermined (or arbitrary) rules. The different levels of measurement that we shall discuss represent different levels of numerical information contained in a set of observations (data), such as a series of house numbers, the order of finish in a horse race, a set of I.Q. scores, or the price per share of various stocks. The type of scale obtained depends on the kinds of mathematical operations that can be legitimately performed on the numbers. In the social sciences, we encounter measurements at every level.

It should be noted that there are other schema for classifying numbers and the ways they are used. We use the nominal–ordinal–cardinal classification because it best handles the types of data we obtain in the behavioral sciences. As you will see, we count, we place in relative position, and we obtain quantitative scores. We should also note that assignment to categories is not always clear-cut or unambiguous. There are times when even experts cannot agree. To illustrate: Is the number in your street address nominal or ordinal? The answer depends on your need. For certain purposes it can be considered nominal, such as when used as a *name* of a dwelling. At other times it can be considered ordinal, since the numbers place your house in a position relative to other houses on the block. Thus 08 may be to the left of 12 and to the right of 04.

The fundamental requirements of observation and measurement are acknowledged by all the physical and social sciences as well as by any modern-day corporation interested in improving its competitive position. The things that we observe are often referred to as **variables** or **variates.** Any particular observation is called the *value of the variable.* Let us look at two examples. If we are studying number of days of hospitalization among different kinds of patients, our variable is number of days in the hospital. Thus, if a patient spends $8\frac{1}{2}$ days in the hospital, the value of the variable is 8.50. If we are interested in determining whether or not an employer discriminates on the basis of racial background, the racial classification of our employees is the variable. This variable may have several values, such as black, Hispanic, and white.

Nominal Numbers

Numbers used to name.

Ordinal Numbers

Numbers used to represent position, or order, in a series.

Cardinal Numbers

Numbers used to represent quantity.

Measurement

The assignment of numbers to objects or events according to sets of predetermined (or arbitrary) rules.

Variable or Variate

A characteristic or phenomenon that may take on different values.

BOX 2.2

Paradoxical percentages

Hypothetical data showing the number of male and female applicants for various categories, the number accepted, and the percent accepted.*

Job Category Teacher	No. Appl.	Male No. Accp.	% Accp.	No. Appl.	Female No. Accp.	% Accp.
Grades 13–14 (2-yr coll)	150	30	20	40	16	40
Grades 11–12	200	70	35	50	35	70
Grades 9–10	100	15	15	50	15	30
Grades K–8	50	2	4	600	48	8
Total	500	117	23	740	114	15

A common form of data collection involves the "head-count" technique, i.e., recording the number of individuals, objects, or observations that fall into various categories. To make sense of these data, the head counts are frequently converted to proportions or percentages. However, under certain circumstances, these percentages can be deceptive and misleading.

The following is an excerpt from *Winning with Statistics** that illustrates the problem of the Paradoxical Percentages.

Let me show you some hypothetical data in which the proportion of females accepted in each job category is actually higher than the proportion of males accepted in each of these categories. Nevertheless, when the proportions of males and females accepted for the various positions are combined over all of the categories, it is found, as if by magic, that the females have a much lower overall proportion of acceptances. So if you were to look at the overall figures you'd be led inexorably to the conclusion that there is discrimination against females. However, if you looked at the same evidence category by category you'd be led to precisely the opposite conclusion, namely, that there is discrimination against males. Let's look at these data in the table above.

Take a careful look at the table. It has been purposely constructed so that in every single category, the percentage of women accepted is double the percentage of men accepted. Nevertheless, when all of the applicants among the males are combined, and the number is divided into the number of males accepted, and the same thing is done with the female category, you find that in fact the overall percentage of males accepted (23%) is higher than the overall percentage of females accepted (15%). How is it possible to obtain this sort of numerical sleight-of-hand? Very simple. If you look at the table again you will find that most of the female applications, 600, were for positions in Grades K through 8. Conversely, very few of the male applicants competed for those positions. It turns out that the number of openings for grades K through 8 is the smallest. What you have then is a situation in which an overwhelming majority of the women were applying for "difficult-to-get" positions. On the other hand, most of the men were applying for positions that were more plentiful. When you combine all of these categories in which there are different numbers of applicants for different positions, the lower percentage of females in the K–8 group is devastating to the female teachers. Why? Better than 80% of the female teachers applied for the very positions where the number of openings was extremely low in relation to the number of applicants.

There is a moral here. Better to apply for a position where few are called but many (relatively speaking) are chosen than to seek entrance where many are called but few are chosen.

*Runyon, R. P., *Winning with Statistics*. Reading, Mass.: Addison-Wesley, 1977.

Nominal Scales

When the majority of people think about measurement, they probably conjure up mental images of wild-eyed men in white suits manipulating costly and incredibly complex instruments in order to obtain precise measures of the variable that they are studying. Actually, however, not all measurements are this precise or this quantitative. If we were to study the sex of the offspring of female rats that had been subjected to atomic radiation during pregnancy, sex would be the variable that we would observe. There are only two possible values of this variable: male and female (barring an unforeseen mutation which produced a third sex!). If we were using a computer to analyze our results, we might assign a number to each value of the variable. Thus male may be assigned a zero and female a one. Our data would consist of the number of observations in each of these two classes. Note that we do not think of this variable as representing an ordered series of values, such as height, weight, speed, etc. An organism that is female does not have any more of the variable, sex, than one that is male.

Observations of unordered variables constitute a very low level of measurement and are referred to as a **nominal scale** of measurement. As we have seen, we may assign numerical values to represent the various classes in a nominal scale, but these numbers have no quantitative properties. They serve only to identify the class.

Nominal Scale

Observations of unordered variables.

The data employed with nominal scales consist of frequency counts or tabulations of the number of occurrences in each class of the variable under study (see Box 2.2). In the aforementioned radiation study, our frequency counts of male and female progeny would comprise our data. Such data are often referred to interchangeably as **frequency data, enumerative data, attribute data,** or **categorical data.** The only mathematical relationships germane to nominal scales are those of equivalence ($=$) or of nonequivalence ($\neq$). Thus a particular person or object has the characteristic that defines the class ($=$) or does *not* have that characteristic ($\neq$).

Frequency Data (Attribute Data, Categorical Data, Enumerative Data)

Tabulations of the number of occurrences in each class of a given variable.

Ordinal Scales

When we move into the next higher level of measurement, we encounter variables in which the classes *do* represent an ordered series of relationships. Thus the classes in **ordinal scales** not only are different from one another (the characteristic defining nominal scales) but also stand in some kind of *relation* to one another. More specifically, the relationships are expressed in terms of the algebra of inequalities: a is less than b ($a < b$) or a is greater than b ($a > b$). Thus the relationships encountered are: greater, faster, more intelligent, more mature, more prestigious, more disturbed, etc. The numerals employed in connection with ordinal scales are nonquantitative. They indicate only position in an ordered series and not "how much" of a difference exists between successive positions on the scale.

Ordinal Scale

Scale in which the classes stand in a relationship to one another that is expressed in terms of the algebra of inequalities: a is less than b, or a is greater than b (this statement is algebraic notation is written $a < b$, or $a > b$).

CASE EXAMPLE • 2.1
Help Is Where You Find It

Psychological help and counseling is not the exclusive province of people specifically trained to give such help. Members of some occupational categories are necessarily involved in interpersonal relationships with their clients, often involving intimate revelations by the clients and attempts to render verbal assistance by the help-giver. One aspect of this study dealt with the response strategies of four different occupational groups (hairdressers, lawyers, supervisors, and bartenders) when clients sought help and advice concerning personal problems. The various strategies employed by members of each of these groups were rank arranged in an ordinal scale from most frequent to least frequent. Table 2.1 shows ordinal ranking of 11 different strategies among hairdressers and bartenders.

Table 2.1 reveals some interesting differences as well as similarities in the help-giving strategies of these two professions. Both rate offering support, trying to be lighthearted, and just listening high on their hierarchy of response strategies. The most notable disagreement involves telling the clients to count their blessings. Hairdressers are more inclined to adopt this strategy than bartenders.

Table 2.1 Ordinal position of response strategies of hairdressers and bartenders when clients seek advice and counsel. A rank of 1 corresponds to the most frequently used strategy and 11 to the least frequently strategy.

Strategy	Hairdressers	Bartenders
Offer support and sympathy	1	3
Try to be lighthearted	2	2
Just listen	3	1
Present alternatives	4	4
Tell person to count blessings	5	10
Share personal experiences	6	5
Try not to get involved	7	6
Give advice	8	7
Ask questions	9	9
Try to get person to talk to someone else	10	11
Try to change topic	11	8

Based on Emory L. Cowen's (1982), "Help Is Where You Find It," *American Psychologist,* **37**(4), 385–395.

We shall be looking at these data again in Chapter 9 when we obtain the correlation between the rankings of response strategies of these two occupational groups.

Examples of ordinal scaling include the following: rank ordering of baseball players according to their "value to the team," rank ordering of potential candidates for political office according to their "popularity" with people, and rank ordering of officer candidates in terms of their "leadership" qualities. Note that the ranks are assigned according to the ordering of individuals within the class. Thus the most popular candidate may receive the rank of 1, the next most popular may receive the rank of 2, and so on, down to the least popular candidate. It does not in fact make any difference whether or not we give the most popular candidate the highest numerical rank or the lowest, *so long as we are consistent in placing the individuals accurately with respect to their relative position in the ordered series.* By popular usage, however, the lower numerical ranks (1st, 2nd, 3rd) are usually assigned to those "highest" on the scale. Thus the winning candidate receives the rank of "first" in a Miss America or Mr. America pageant; the pennant winner is "first" in its respective league. The fact that we are not completely consistent in our ranking procedures is illustrated by such popular expressions as "first-class idiot" and "first-class scoundrel."

Interval and Ratio Scales

Finally, the highest level of measurement in science is achieved with scales employing cardinal numbers (**interval** and **ratio scales**). The numerical values associated with these scales are truly quantitative and therefore permit the use of arithmetic operations such as adding, subtracting, multiplying, and dividing. In interval and ratio scales, equal differences between points on any part of the scale are equal. Thus the difference between 4 feet and 2 feet is the same as the difference between 9231 and 9229 feet.

In ordinal scaling, as you will recall, we cannot claim that the *difference* between first and second place is the same as the *difference* between second and third place.

There are two types of scales based upon cardinal numbers: interval and ratio. The interval scale differs from the ratio scale in terms of the location of the zero point. In an interval scale the zero point is arbitrarily determined. It does not represent the complete absence of the attribute being measured. Our calendar is an example of an interval scale; the year zero does not mean that there was no time before this year. In contrast, the zero in a ratio scale does represent the complete absence of the attribute of interest. Zero length means no length. As a consequence of this difference in the location of the zero point, only the ratio scale permits us to make statements concerning the ratios of numbers in the scale; e.g., 4 feet are to 2 feet as 2 feet are to 1 foot. The difference between these scales can be clarified by examining a well-known

Interval Scale

Quantitative scale that permits the use of arithmetic operations. The zero point in this scale is arbitrary.

Ratio Scale

Same as interval scale, except that there is a true zero point.

interval scale, e.g., the Celsius scale of temperature. Incidentally, the Fahrenheit scale of temperature is also an interval scale.

The zero point on the Celsius scale does not represent the complete absence of heat. In fact, it is merely the point at which water freezes at sea level and it has, therefore, an arbitrary zero point. Actually, the true zero point is known as *absolute zero,* which is approximately −273° Celsius. Now, if we were to say that 40°C is to 20°C as 20°C is to 10°C, it would appear that we were making a correct statement. Actually, we are completely wrong since 40°C really represents 273° + 40° of temperature; 20°C represents 273° + 20° of temperature; and 10°C represents 273° + 10° of temperature. The ratio of 313:293 as 293:283, clearly does not hold. These facts may be better appreciated graphically. In Fig. 2.1 we have represented all three temperature readings as distances from the true zero point, which is −273°C. From this graph it is seen that the distance from −273°C to 40°C is not twice as long as the distance from −273°C to 20°C. Thus, 40°C is not twice as warm as 20°C, and the ratio 40°C is to 20°C as 20°C is to 10°C does not hold.

Apart from the difference in the nature of the zero point, interval and ratio scales have the same properties and will be treated alike throughout the text.

It should be clear that one of the most sought-after goals of the behavioral scientist is to achieve measurements that are at least interval in nature. Indeed, interval scaling is assumed for most of the statistical tests reported in this book. Although it is debatable that many of our scales achieve interval measurement, most behavioral scientists are willing to make the assumption that they do.

One of the characteristics of higher-order scales is that they can readily be transformed into lower-order scales. Thus the outcome of a one-mile foot race may be expressed as time scores (ratio scale), e.g., 3:56, 3:58, and 4:92. The time scores may then be transformed into an ordinal scale, e.g., first-, second-, and third-place finishers. However, the reverse transformation is not possible. If we know only the order of finishing a race, for example, we cannot express the outcome in terms of a ratio scale (time scores). Although it is permissible to transform scores from higher-level to lower-level scales, it is not usually recommended since precise quantitative information is lost in the transformation.

Figure 2.1 Relationships of various points on a Celsius scale to absolute Zero.

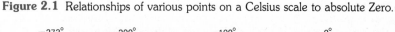
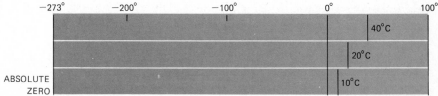

2.5 *Continuous and Discontinuous Variables*

Imagine that you are given the problem of trying to determine the number of children per American family. Your scale of measurement would start with zero (no children) and would proceed by *increments of one* to perhaps fifteen or twenty. Note that in moving from one value on the scale to the next we proceed by *whole numbers* rather than by fractional amounts. Thus a family has either 0, 1, 2, or more children. In spite of the statistical abstraction that the American family averages approximately one and three-quarters children, the authors do not know a single couple that has achieved this marvelous rate of family planning. Such variables are referred to as **discontinuous** or **discrete.** They are characterized by gaps in which no real values of the variable are found. Discrete variables are characterized by equality of *counting units.* Thus, if we are studying the number of children in a family, each child is equal with respect to providing one counting unit. Such variables involve cardinality insofar as they permit arithmetic operations such as adding, subtracting, multiplying, and dividing. Thus we can say that a family with four children has twice as many children as one with two children. Observations of discrete variables are always exact so long as the counting procedures are accurate. Examples of discontinuous variables are the pulse rate (number of beats per minute) of human adults, the number of white blood cells counted in one square centimeter, the number of alpha particles observed in a second, etc.

You should not assume from the preceding discussion that discrete variables necessarily involve *only* whole numbers. However, most of the discontinuous variables used by behavioral and social scientists are usually expressed in terms of whole numbers. For example, a psychologist tabulates the number of people with varying pulse rates, or the number of kindergarten children from family units of different sizes. In each of these examples we are clearly dealing with values that proceed by whole numbers.

In contrast, a **continuous variable** is one in which there are not gaps in which values of the variable are absent; there are an unlimited number of *possible* values between any two adjacent values on the scale. Thus, if the variable is height measured in inches, then 4 inches and 5 inches would be two adjacent values of the variable. However, there can be an infinite number of intermediate values, such as 4.5 inches or 4.7 inches. If the variable is height measured in tenths of inches, then 4.5 inches and 4.6 inches are two adjacent values of the variable, but there can be *still* be an infinite number of intermediate values such as 4.53 inches or 4.59 inches.

It is important to note that, although our measurement of discrete variables is always exact, our measurement of continuous variables is always approximate. If we are measuring the height of American males, for example, any particular measurement is inexact because it is always possible to imagine a

Discontinuous Variables (Discrete Variables)

Variables that can assume only a certain finite number of values.

Continuous Variables

Variables that can assume an unlimited number of intermediate values.

measuring stick that would provide greater accuracy. Thus, if we reported the height of a man to be 68 inches, we would mean 68 inches give or take one-half an inch. If our scale is accurate to the nearest tenth, we can always imagine another scale providing greater accuracy, say, to the nearest hundredth or thousandth of an inch. The basic characteristic of continuous variables, then, is equality of *measuring units*. Thus, if we are measuring in inches, one inch is always the same throughout the scale. Examples of continuous variables are length, velocity, time, weight, etc.

Let's consider one additional point. Often, continuous variables are expressed as whole numbers and therefore appear to be discontinuous. Thus you may say that you are 5'8" tall and weigh 150 pounds, your father is 5'9" and weighs 193 pounds, and your mother is 5'3" and weighs 123 pounds. However, the decision to express heights to the nearest inch and weights to the nearest pound was yours. You could just as easily have expressed height to the nearest fraction of an inch and weight to the nearest ounce. You do not have such a choice when reporting such things as the number of children in a family. These *must* occur as whole numbers.

Continuous Variables, Errors of Measurement, and "True Limits" of Numbers

In our preceding discussion, we pointed out that continuously distributed variables can take on an unlimited number of intermediate values. Therefore we can never specify the exact value for any particular measurement, since it is possible that a more sensitive measuring instrument can slightly increase the accuracy of our measurements. For this reason, we stated that numerical values of continuously distributed variables are always approximate. However, it is possible to specify the limits within which the true value falls; e.g., the **true limits** of a value of a continuous variable are equal to that number plus or minus one-half of the unit of measurement. Let's look at a few examples. You have a bathroom scale that is calibrated in terms of pounds. When you step on the scale the pointer will usually be a little above or below a pound marker. However, you report your weight to the nearest pound. Thus, if the pointer were approximately three quarters of the the distance between 212 pounds and 213 pounds, you would report your weight as 213 pounds. It would be understood that the "true" limit of your weight, assuming an accurate scale, falls between 212.5 pounds and 213.5 pounds. If, on the other hand, you are measuring the weight of whales, you would probably have a fairly gross unit of measurement, say 100 pounds. Thus, if you reported the weight of a whale at 32,000 pounds, you would mean that the whale weighed between 31,950 pounds and 32,050 pounds. If the scale were calibrated in terms of 1000 pounds, the true limits of the whale's weight would be between 31,500 pounds and 32,500 pounds.

True Limits of a Number

The true limits of a value of a continuous variable are equal to that number plus or minus one-half of a unit of measurement.

2.6 *Rounding*

Imagine that you have some data which, in the course of conducting a statistical analysis, require that you divide one number into another. There will be innumerable occasions in this course when you'll be required to perform this arithmetic operation. In some cases, the answer will be a value that extends to an endless number of decimal places. For example, if you were to express the fraction 1/3 in decimal form, the result would be 0.33333+. It is obvious that you cannot extend this series of numbers *ad infinitum*. You must terminate at some point and assign a value to the last number in the series that best reflects the remainder. When you do this, two problems will arise:

1. To how many decimal places do we carry the final answer?
2. How do we decide on the last number in the series?

The answer to the first question is usually given in terms of the number of significant figures. However, there are many good reasons for not following the mathematical stricture to the letter. For simplicity and convenience, we have adopted the following policy with respect to rounding:

> In obtaining the final answer, we should round to two more places than were in the original data. We should not round the intermediate steps.*

Thus, if the original data were in whole-numbered units, we would round our answer to the second decimal. If in tenths, we would round to the third decimal, and so forth.

Once we have decided the number of places to carry our final figures, we are still left with the problem of representing the last digit. Fortunately, the rule governing the determination of the last digit is perfectly simple and explicit. If the remainder beyond that digit is greater than 5, increase that digit to the next higher number. If the remainder beyond that digit is less than 5, allow that digit to remain as it is. Let's look at a few illustrations. In each case, we shall round to the second decimal place:

6.546 becomes 6.55,
6.543 becomes 6.54,
1.967 becomes 1.97,
1.534 becomes 1.53.

---

*Since many of you will be using calculators, you should be aware of minor differences that may occur in the final answer. These differences may be attributed to the fact that different calculators will carry the intermediate steps to a different number of decimal places. Thus, a calculator that carries the intermediate steps to 4 places will probably produce a slightly different final answer than one that carries to 14 places.

You may ask, "In those illustrations, what happens if the digit at the third decimal place is 5?"

You should first determine whether or not the digit is exactly 5. If it is 5 plus the slightest remainder, the above rule holds and you must add one to the digit at the second decimal place. If it is almost, but not quite 5, the digit at the second decimal place remains the same. If it is *exactly 5 with no remainder,* then an arbitrary convention that is accepted universally by mathematicians applies: Round the digit at the second decimal place to the *nearest even* number. If this digit is already even, then it is not changed. If it is odd, then *add* one to this digit to make it even. Let's look at several illustrations in which we round to the second decimal place:

$$6.545001 \text{ becomes } 6.55. \text{ Why?}$$
$$6.545000 \text{ becomes } 6.54. \text{ Why?}$$
$$1.9652 \quad \text{ becomes } 1.97. \text{ Why?}$$
$$0.00500 \text{ becomes } 0.00. \text{ Why?}$$
$$0.02500 \text{ becomes } 0.02. \text{ Why?}$$
$$16.89501 \text{ becomes } 16.90. \text{ Why?}$$

2.7 Ratios, Frequencies, Proportions, and Percentages

Of all the statistics in everyday use, perhaps the most misunderstood and misused involve the representation of ratios, proportions, and percentages. These statistics also provide the most fertile grounds for misleading and outright fraudulent statements. It is possible for a congressman, seeking to impress "the people back home" with his vital interest in consumer affairs to charge that a given drug company is making a 300% profit on its sales to retail outlets, while the drug company, looking at precisely the same statistical facts, may reply with righteous indignation that its profit is only 75%. How could this come about? Let us see.

Assume that the cost to manufacture a given drug is $2 per gross. In turn, a gross is sold to the retailer at $8. The ratio of profit ($8 − $2 = $6) to manufacturing cost is 6:2 or 3:1. Stating this ratio as a percentage (multiplying by 100), we get 300%. It would appear that the congressman is correct. But the drug company replies, "The selling price is $8 and our profit is $6, the ratio of profit to selling price is 6:8 or 0.75. Stated as a percentage, our profit is 75% of the selling price. When considering the cost of research and development and all the inherent financial risks, the profit is not excessive."

Which statement better describes the facts? Actually, both statements are correct. The confusion stems from the fact that two different values ($2 and $8) have been employed as the base, or denominator, in arriving at the final percentage figures. There is nothing wrong with either procedure *as long as it*

is made perfectly clear which base has been employed in the initial calculations. Knowing the base, we can freely move from one to the other with little
confusion. Thus, if we know that the congressman has used the production
cost as the base, we may employ elementary algebra to translate this statement
to one employing selling price as a base: Let

$$x = \text{Production cost} = \$2$$
$$y = \text{Selling price} = \$8.$$

The following equation represents the percentage of profit, employing production cost as a base:

$$\frac{y - x}{x} \times 100 = \text{Percent of profit (employing production cost as a base).}$$

Using the values above and substituting in the equation, we find that

$$\frac{y - x}{x} \times 100 = \frac{8 - 2}{2} \times 100 = 300\%.$$

The formula for calculating percentage of profit employing *selling price* as
a base is

$$\frac{y - x}{y} \times 100 = \text{Percent of profit (related to selling price).}$$

Substituting into the above formula, we obtain

$$\frac{y - x}{y} \times 100 = \frac{6}{8} \times 100 = 75\%$$

CASE EXAMPLE • 2.2
Do We Help Beauty or the Beast?

Much research has been done on the effects of physical attractiveness on various aspects of our behavior. In this field study, the objective was to ascertain
whether favoritism for the physically attractive generalizes to behavioral helping
responses. Graduate school applications, complete with mailing address, envelope, and stamps were "inadvertently" left in a number of telephone booths
at a busy metropolitan airport. Pictures of the applicant were prominently dis-

played, some chosen to be physically attractive and others to be unattractive. Thus, physical attractiveness was the independent variable. The dependent response was whether or not the subject engaged in helping behavior, defined as "mailing the application or taking the envelope to one of the airport ticket counters." Thus the dependent variable was nominal—either the subject engaged in helping behavior or he/she did not. The results of one aspect of the study are summarized in Table 2.2.

A number of different proportions and percentages can be obtained from this table. Let's look at three of them—the percentage of the total who helped regardless of the attractiveness of the applicant, the percentage who helped the attractive applicant, and the percentage who helped the unattractive candidate.

The percentage who helped regardless of the attractiveness of the candidate is $87/220 \times 100\% = 39.5\%$. The percentage not helping is $100\% - 39.5\% = 60.5\%$. Thus, approximately 6 out of every 10 in this sample chose not to help.

The percentage who chose to help the attractive female applicant is $52/114 \times 100\% = 45.6\%$. Thus $100\% - 45.6\% = 54.4\%$ did not engage in a helping response.

The percentage who helped the unattractive applicant is $35/106 \times 100\% = 33.0\%$. Therefore, 67.0% chose not to help the unattractive appliant.

Thus, in this sample of 220 males, we see that almost 13% more engaged in helping behaviors when an attractive applicant was involved. We will return to these data in Chapter 13 and raise the question, "Is this difference in 12.6% likely to be due to chance factors or does it reflect a real preference to help the attractive rather than the unattractive people in the population sampled by this study?"

Table 2.2 **Number helping when the applicant is an attractive or unattractive female (whites and blacks combined) and the subject is a male.**

Helping Response	Characteristics of Target		
	Attractive	Unattractive	Total
Helped	52	35	87
Did not help	62	71	133
Total	114	106	220

Based on Peter L. Benson, Stuart A. Karabenick, and Richard M. Lerner (1976), "Pretty Pleases: The Effects of Physical Attractiveness, Race, and Sex on Receiving Help," *Journal of Experimental Social Psychology,* **12,** 409–415.

Chapter Summary

In this chapter, we pointed out that advanced knowledge of mathematics is not a prerequisite for success in this course. A sound background in high-school mathematics plus steady application to assignments should be sufficient to permit mastery of the fundamental concepts put forth in this text.

To aid the student who may not have had recent contact with mathematics, we have attempted to review some of the basic concepts of mathematics. Included in this review are: (1) the grammar of mathematical notation, (2) types of numbers, (3) types of numerical scales, (4) continuous and discontinuous scales, (5) rounding, and (6) frequencies, proportions, and percentages. Students requiring a more thorough review of mathematics may refer to Appendix A.

Terms to Remember

cardinal numbers

continuous scales

discontinuous scales (discrete scales)

frequency data (attribute data, categorical data, enumerative data)

interval scale

nominal numbers

nominal scale

measurement

ordinal numbers

ordinal scale

ratio scale

true limits of a number

variable or variate

EXERCISES

The following exercises are based on this chapter and Appendix A.

1. It has often been speculated that Californians cope with earthquake hazards by avoidance—simply not thinking about them. Professor Ralph H. Turner, a sociologist and the director of UCLA's Institute for Social Science Research, has collected data that bear on this common belief. Shown below are the data collected on a number of survey questions concerned with media coverage of earthquake-related information.

Find the proportion and percentage of individuals responding in each category to each of the questions raised in the survey.

Do the responses appear to support the common view that Californians avoid thinking about earthquakes?

a. Do the media provide too little, too much, or sufficient coverage about what to do if an earthquake strikes?

	Number Responding
Too little	386
About right	103
Too much	8
No opinion	3

b. How about the news media's coverage on preparations for an earthquake?

	Number Responding
Too little	357
About right	121
Too much	14
No opinion	8

c. Do the media provide sufficient information about what the government is doing to prepare for an earthquake?

	Number Responding
Too little	413
About right	67
Too much	10
No opinion	10

d. How about the attention the media pay to the nonscientific earthquake predictions?

	Number Responding
Too little	126
About right	142
Too much	215
No opinion	17

2. Find a when $b = 10$, $c = 4$, and $a + b + c = 19$.

3. Find y when $N = 4$ and $20 + N = y + 2$.

4. Find $\sum X$ when $N = 20$, $\overline{X} = 60$, where $\overline{X} = \sum X/N$.

5. Find N when $\overline{X} = 90$, $\sum X = 360$, where $\overline{X} = \sum X/N$.

6. Find N when

$$\sum(X - \overline{X})^2 = 640, \qquad s^2 = 16, \qquad \text{where } s^2 = \frac{\sum(X - \overline{X})^2}{N}.$$

7. Find s^2 when

$$\sum(X - \overline{X})^2 = 240, \qquad N = 12, \qquad \text{where } s^2 = \frac{\sum(X - \overline{X})^2}{N}.$$

8. Round the following numbers to the second decimal place.
   a. 99.99500   b. 46.40501   c. 2.96500   d. 0.00501
   e. 16.46500   f. 1.05499   g. 86.2139   h. 10.0050

9. In 1973, there were 15,840 male suicides and 4625 female suicides. Find the proportion of male and female suicides (round to the second decimal).

10. In 1973, the deaths of 17,123 murder victims were caused by the following: guns, 11,249; cutting or stabbing, 2,985; strangulations or beatings, 1,445; blunt object, 848; arson, 173; other, 423. Find the proportions attributable to each cause of death (round to the second decimal).

11. In 1973, there were 20,465 suicides and 17,123 homicides. Find the proportion of the total attributable to suicide; then find the proportion attributable to homicide (round to the fourth decimal place).

12. The table below shows the number of male and female victims of homicide between the years 1968 and 1973.

Year	Number of Male Victims of Homicide	Number of Female Victims of Homicide
1968	5106	1700
1969	5215	1801
1970	5865	1938
1971	6455	2106
1972	6820	2156
1973	7411	2575

    a. Of the total number of male homicide victims during the years 1968 through 1973, find the percentage for each year.

    b. Of the total number of female homicide victims during the years 1968 through 1973, find the percentage for each year.

13. Determine the value of the following expressions in which $X_1 = 4$, $X_2 = 5$, $X_3 = 7$, $X_4 = 9$, $X_5 = 10$, $X_6 = 11$, $X_7 = 14$.

    a. $\sum_{i=1}^{4} X_i =$ b. $\sum_{i=1}^{7} X_i =$ c. $\sum_{i=3}^{6} X_i =$

    d. $\sum_{i=2}^{5} X_i =$ e. $\sum_{i=1}^{N} X_i =$ f. $\sum_{i=4}^{N} X_i =$

14. Express the following in summation notation.

    a. $X_1 + X_2 + X_3$ b. $X_1 + X_2 + \cdots + X_N$

    c. $X_3^2 + X_4^2 + X_5^2 + X_6^2$ d. $X_4^2 + X_5^2 + \cdots + X_N^2$

15. The answers to the following questionnaire items are based on what scale of measurement?

    a. What is your height?

    b. What is your weight?

    c. What is your occupation?

    d. How does this course compare with others you have taken?

16. In the following examples, identify the scale of measurement, and determine whether the italicized variable is continuous or discontinuous

    a. *Distance* traveled from home to school by 50 different students.

    b. Number of infants born at *varying times of the day.*

    c. Number of votes compiled by each of *three candidates* for a political office.

17. Determine the square roots of the following numbers to two decimal places.

    a. 160   b. 16   c. 1.60   d. 0.16   e. 0.016

18. State the true limits of the following numbers.
    a. 0   b. 0.5   c. 1.0   d. 0.49   e. −5   f. −4.5

19. Using the values of X_i given in Exercise 13 above, show that

$$\sum_{i=1}^{N} X_i^2 \neq \left(\sum_{i=1}^{N} X_i \right)^2.$$

20. Which of the following represent continuous scales and which represent discrete scales of measurement?
    a. The number of light bulbs sold each day in a hardware store.
    b. The monthly income of graduate students.
    c. The temperatures recorded every two hours in the meat department of a supermarket.
    d. The weights of pigeons recorded every 24 hours in an experimental laboratory.
    e. The lengths of newborns recorded at a hospital nursery.
    f. The number of textbooks found in the college bookstore.

21. Using the figures shown in the table below, answer the following questions:
    a. Of all the students majoring in each academic area, what percentage is female?
    b. Considering only the males, what percentages are found in each academic area?
    c. Considering only the females, what percentages are found in each academic area?
    d. Of all students majoring in the five areas, what percentage is male? What percentage is female?
    The number of students, by sex, majoring in each of five academic areas:

Academic Area	Male	Female
Business administration	400	100
Education	50	150
Humanities	150	200
Science	250	100
Social science	200	200

22. Indicate which of the following variables represent discrete or continuous scales.
    a. The time it takes you to complete these problems.
    b. The number of newspapers sold in a given city of December 19, 1979.
    c. The amount of change in weight of 5 women during a period of 4 weeks.
    d. The number of home runs hit by each of 10 randomly selected batters during the 1980 baseball season.
    e. The number of stocks on the New York Stock Exchange that increased in selling price on January 3, 1980.

Year	Males	Females
1950	1824	1731
1955	2074	1974
1960	2180	2078
1965	1927	1833
1970	1915	1816

23. At left is a list showing the number of births in the United States (expressed in thousands) between 1950 and 1970. (*Source: The World Alamanac*, 1975, adapted. Published by Newspaper Enterprise Association Inc., p. 951.) Calculate the percentage of males and females for each year.

24. Eugene J. Kanin* has studied various aspects of the behavior of sexually aggressive males. Sexually aggressive was defined as "a quest for coital access of a rejecting female during the course of which physical coercion is utilized to the degree that offended responses are elicited from the female" (p. 429). When his findings were compared with those for a sample of nonaggressive males, it was hypothesized that nonaggressive males might attempt *exploitative* rather than aggressive techniques more often than their aggressive counterparts as a means of achieving sexual access.

The data from a high-school sample of 254 nonaggressive and 87 aggressive males reveals the following frequencies with which the subjects admitted to the use of exploitative techniques.

	Nonaggressive Males[†]	Aggressive Males[†]
Attempted to get girl intoxicated	23	33
Falsely promised marriage	19	7
Falsely professed love	37	39
Threatened to terminate relationship	9	8
Total number of males interview	N = 254	N = 87

[†]The sum of the frequencies does not equal N, since some subjects admitted to employing more than one technique and others claimed never to use such techniques.

a. Find the percentages of aggressive and nonaggressive males admitting to the use of each exploitative technique.

b. Does it appear that the hypothesis is supported?

25. Shown below are the methods of suicide used by students at University of California at Berkeley (1952–1961) and at Yale (1920–1955). (*Source:* Seiden, R. H. (1966), "Campus Tragedy: A Story of Student Suicide," *Journal of Abnormal and Social Psychology,* **71**, 389–399.)

	Berkeley	Yale
Firearms	8	10
Poisioning	6	3
Asphyxiation	4	5
Hanging	2	6
Jumping from high places	2	1
Cutting instruments	1	0
Total suicides	N = 23	N = 25

Calculate the percentage of suicides in which the various means of self-destruction were employed at each institution. Round to the nearest percent.

---

*(*Source:* Kanin, E. J. (1967), "An Examination of Sexual Aggression as a Response to Sexual Frustration," *Journal of Marriage and the Family,* **29**, 428–433.) Copyright © 1967 by the National Council on Family Relations. Reprinted by permission.

26. Refer to Exercise 4, Chapter 1.
   a. What are the proportion and the percentage of black athletes appearing in media advertising in 1966?
   b. In 1971, what proportion of white and black professional football players had an opportunity to appear in advertising?

27. In the study of attractiveness and helping behavior (Case Example 2.2), the table below shows the number of female subjects choosing to help attractive and unattractive male applicants (whites and blacks combined). Calculate
   a. the percentage of females rendering help regardless of the attractiveness of the target.
   b. the percentage rendering help and not rendering help when the target is attractive.
   c. the percentage helping and not helping when the target is physically unattractive.

Helping Response	Characteristics of Target		
	Attractive	**Unattractive**	**Total**
Helped	17	13	30
Did not help	24	27	51
Total	41	40	81

28. Refer to Exercise 27 and Case Example 2.2.
   a. What is the population for this study.
   b. Is it likely to be representative of the general population?

PART *II*

Descriptive Statistics

3
Frequency Distributions and Graphing Techniques

3.1 *Grouping of Data*

Imagine that you have just accepted a position as curriculum director in a large senior high school. Your responsibility is to develop curricula that not only agree with the students' needs and motivations but also provide maximum challenges to their intellectual capacities. The total solution to such a complex and provoking problem is beyond the scope of this text. However, it is clear that no steps toward a solution can be initiated without some assessment of the intellecual capacities of the student body. Accordingly, you go to the guidance office and "pull out" at **random** (i.e., in such a way that every member of the populuation share an equal chance of being selected) 110 student folders containing a wealth of personal and scholastic information. Since your present concern is to assess intellectual ability, you focus your attention on the entry labeled "I.Q. estimate." You write these down on a piece of paper, with the results listed in Table 3.1.

As you mull over these figures, it becomes obvious to you that you cannot "make heads or tails" out of them unless you organize them in some systematic fashion. It occurs to you to list all the scores from highest to lowest and then place a slash mark alongside each score every time it occurs (Table 3.2). The number of slash marks, then, represents the frequency of occurrence of each score.

When you have done this, you have constructed an ungrouped **frequency distribution** of scores. Note that in the present example the scores are widely spread out, a number of scores have a frequency of zero, and there is no "visually" clear indication of central tendency. Under these circumstances it is customary for most researchers to *group* the scores into what is referred to as *classes* and then obtain a frequency distribution of "grouped scores."

Random

A method of selecting samples so that each sample of a given size shares an equal chance of being selected.

Frequency Distribution

When the values of a variable are arranged in order according to their magnitudes, a frequency distribution shows the number of times each seore occurs.

Table 3.1 I.Q. scores of 110 high-school students selected at random.

154	131	122	100	113	119	121	128	112	93
133	119	115	117	110	104	125	85	120	135
116	103	103	121	109	147	103	113	107	98
128	93	90	105	118	134	89	143	108	142
85	108	108	136	115	117	110	80	111	127
100	100	114	123	126	119	122	102	100	106
105	111	127	108	106	91	123	132	97	110
150	130	87	89	108	137	124	96	111	101
118	104	127	94	115	101	125	129	131	110
97	135	108	139	133	107	115	83	109	116
110	113	112	82	114	112	113	142	145	123

BOX 3.1

Just a heartbeat away

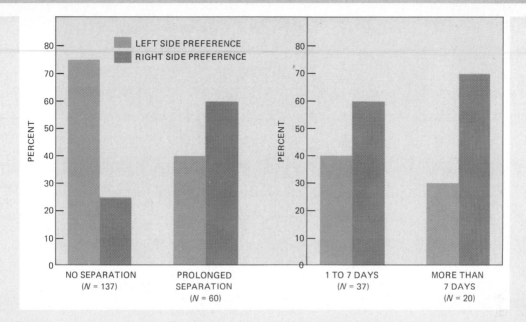

Psychologists have often speculated that the heartbeat of the mother is comforting to the infant. If a child is held on the mother's left side, the sound of the heartbeat is more pronounced. One investigator explored the various circumstances under which mothers show a preference for holding their infants on the left or right side. Some mothers have access to their infants immediately after birth (no separation), whereas others do not have their first contact for at least a period of 24 hours (prolonged separation). The graphs summarize the findings in a sample of 197 mothers.

Mothers of firstborns who were not separated from their infants at birth showed a marked preference for holding their baby on the left side. In contrast, mothers of firstborns who did not have early contact tended to prefer the right side. (See graph on the left above.)

Any separation (for a day or more) appears to lead to a right-side preference. The longer the separation, the greater is the right-side preference, as shown in the second graph. This is based on data for 57 mothers who did not have access to their infants immediately after birth.

Grouping into Classes

Grouping involves a sort of "collapsing the scale" wherein we assign scores to **mutually exclusive** classes in which the classes are defined in terms of the grouping intervals employed. The reasons for grouping are (1) Unless automatic calculators are available, it is uneconomical and unwieldy to deal with a large number of cases spread out over many scores. (2) Some of the scores

Mutually Exclusive

Events *A* and *B* are said to be mutually exclusive if both cannot occur simultaneously.

Table 3.2 **Frequency distribution of I.Q. scores of 110 high-school students selected at random.**

X	f	X	f	X	f	X	f
154	I	135	II	116	II	97	II
153		134	I	115	IIII	96	I
152		133	II	114	II	95	
151		132	I	113	IIII	94	I
150	I	131	II	112	III	93	II
149		130	I	111	III	92	
148		129	I	110	IIIII	91	I
147	I	128	II	109	II	90	I
146		127	III	108	IIIIII	89	II
145	I	126	I	107	II	88	
144		125	II	106	II	87	I
143	I	124	I	105	II	86	
142	II	123	III	104	II	85	II
141		122	II	103	III	84	
140		121	II	102	I	83	I
139	I	120	I	101	II	82	I
138		119	III	100	IIII	81	
137	I	118	II	99		80	I
136	I	117	II	98	I		

have such low frequency counts that we are not justified in maintaining these scores as separate and distinct entities. (3) Grouping makes the display more comprehensible; that is, there is less information to overwhelm the reader.

On the negative side, of course, is the fact that grouping inevitably results in the loss of information. For example, individual scores lose their identity when we group into classes and some small errors in statistics based upon grouped scores are unavoidable.

The question now becomes, "On what basis do we decide upon the grouping intervals that we will employ?" Obviously, the interval selected must not be so wide that we lose the discrimination provided by our original measurement. For example, if we were to divide the previously collected I.Q. scores into two classes, those below 100 and those 100 and above, practically all the information inherent in the original scores would be lost. On the other hand, the width of the classes should not be so narrow that the purposes served by grouping are defeated. In answer to our question there is unfortunately no general prescription that can be applied to all data. Much of the time the choice of the number of classes must represent a judgment based on a consideration of the relative effects of grouping upon discriminability and presentational economy. However, it is generally agreed that most data in the behavioral sciences can be accomodated by 10 to 20 classes. For uniformity, we aim for approximately 15 classes for the data that we discuss in this textbook.

Having decided upon the number of classes that is appropriate for a set of data, we find that the procedures for assigning scores to classes are quite straightforward. Although any of several different techniques may be used, we employ only one, for the sake of consistency. The procedures to be employed are as follows:

Step 1. Find the difference between the highest and the lowest score values contained in the original data. Add 1 to obtain the total number of scores or potential scores. In the present example, this result is $(154 - 80) + 1 = 75$.

Step 2. Divide this figure by 15 to obtain the number of scores or poential scores in each class. If the resulting value is not a whole number, and it usually is not, we prefer to round the nearest odd number so that a whole number will be at the middle of the interval. However, this practice is far from universal and you would not be wrong if you rounded to the *nearest number.* In the present example, the number of scores for each class is 75/15, or 5. We designate the width of the class by the symbol i. In this example, $i = 5$.

Step 3. Take the lowest score in the original data as the minimum value in the lowest class. Add to this $i - 1$ to obtain the maximum score of the lowest class. Thus the lowest class of the data on hand is 80–84.

Step 4. The next higher class begins at the integer following the maximum score of the lower class. In the present example, the next integer is 85. Follow the same steps as in (3) to obtain the maximum score of the second class. Follow these procedures for each successive higher class until all the scores are included in their appropriate classes.

Step 5. Assign each obtained score to the class within which it is included. The **grouped frequency distribution** of Table 3.3 was obtained by employing the preceding steps.

Grouped Frequency Distribution

A frequency distribution in which the values of the variable have been grouped into classes.

You will note that by grouping we may obtain an immediate "picture" of the distribution of I.Q. scores among our high-school students. For example, note that there is a clustering of frequencies in the classes between the scores of 100 and 119. It is also apparent that the number of scores in the extremes tends to dwindle off. Thus we have achieved one of our objectives in grouping: To provide an economical and manageable array of scores.

One word of caution: Most scores with which the behavioral scientist deals are expressed as whole numbers rather than as decimals. It is for this reason that our examples employ integers. However, occasionally scores are expressed in decimal form (e.g., reaction time). The simplest procedure is to treat

Table 3.3 Grouped frequency distribution of I.Q. scores based upon data appearing in Table 3.2.

Class	f	Class	f	Class	f
150–154	2	125–129	9	100–104	12
145–149	2	120–124	9	95–99	4
140–144	3	115–119	13	90–94	5
135–139	5	110–114	17	85–89	5
130–134	7	105–109	14	80–84	3

$N = 110$

the scores as if the decimals did not exist. In other words, treat each score as a whole number. The decimals can then be reinserted at the final step. If, in the preceding example, the highest score had been 1.54 and the lowest 0.80, the calculations would have been exactly the same. At the last step, however, the highest would have been changed to 1.50–1.54 and the lowest to 0.80–0.84, with corresponding changes in between. The width of the class would have been 0.05.

The True Limits of a Class

In our prior discussion of the "true limits" of a number (Section 2.5.1), we pointed out that the "true" value of a number is equal to its apparent value plus and minus one-half of the unit of measurement. Of course, the same is true of these values even after they have been grouped into classes. Thus, although we write the limits of the lowest class as 80–84, the true limits of the class are 79.5–84.5 (i.e, the lower real limit of 80 and the upper real limit of 84, respectively).

It is important to keep in mind that the true limits of a class are not the same as the *apparent limits*. Later, when calculating the median and percentile ranks for grouped data, we shall make use of the *true limits* of the class.

3.2 Cumulative Frequency and Cumulative Percentage Distributions

Cumulative Frequency

The number of cases (frequencies) at and below a given point.

It is often desirable to arrange the data from a frequency distribution into a **cumulative frequency** distribution. Besides aiding in the interpretation of the frequency distribution, a **cumulative frequency distribution** is of great value in obtaining the median and the various percentile ranks of scores, as we shall see in Chapter 4. A cumulative frequency distribution shows the cumulative frequency below the upper real limit of the corresponding class. If, for example, we want the people with the fastest reaction times to be our champions at the PACMAN tournament, we select those in the bottom 10 percent of the reaction time distribution.

The cumulative frequency distribution is obtained in a very simple and straightforward manner. Look at the data in Table 3.4. The entries in the frequency distribution indicate the number of high-school students falling within each of the classses. Each entry within the cumulative frequency distribution indicates the number of all cases or frequencies *below the upper, real limit* of that class. Thus, in the third class from the bottom in Table 3.4, the entry "13" in the cumulative frequency distribution indicates that a total of 13 students scored lower than the upper real limit of that class, which is 94.5. The entries in the cumulative frequency distribution are obtained by a simple process of successive addition of the entries in the frequency column. Thus the cumulative frequency corresponding to the upper real limit of the class 104.5–109.5 is obtained by successive addition of $3 + 5 + 5 + 4 + 12 + 14 = 43$. Note that the top entry in the cumulative frequency column is always equal to N. If you fail to obtain this result, you know that you have made an error in cumulating frequencies and should check your work.

The **cumulative proportion distribution** also shown in Table 3.4, is obtained by dividing each entry in the cumulative frequency column by N. When each cumulative proportion is multiplied by 100, we obtain a **cumulative percentage distribution.** Note that the top entry must be 100%, since all cases fall below the upper real limit of the highest class.

Cumulative Frequency Distribution

A distribution that shows the cumulative frequency below the upper real limit of the corresponding class.

Cumulative Proportion

The proportion of cases (frequencies) at and below a given point.

Cumulative Proportion Distribution

A distribution that shows the cumulative proportion below the upper real limit of the corresponding class.

Cumulative Percentage

The percentage of cases (frequencies) at and below a given point.

Cumulative Percentage Distribution

A distribution that shows the cumulative percentage below the upper real limit of the corresponding class.

Table 3.4 **Grouped frequency distribution and cumulative frequency distribution based upon data appearing in Table 3.3 $N = 110$.**

Class	f	Cumulative f	Cumulative Proportion	Cumulative %
150–154	2	110	1.00	100
145–149	2	108	0.98	98
140–144	3	106	0.96	96
135–139	5	103	0.94	94
130–134	7	98	0.89	89
125–129	9	91	0.83	83
120–124	9	82	0.75	75
115–119	13	73	0.66	66
110–114	17	60	0.55	55
105–109	14	43	0.39	39
100–104	12	29	0.26	26
95–99	4	17	0.15	15
90–94	5	13	0.12	12
85–89	5	8	0.07	7
80–84	3	3	0.03	3

3.3 *Graphing Techniques*

We have just examined some of the procedures involved in making sense out of a mass of unorganized data. As we pointed out, your work is usually just beginning when you have constructed frequency distributions of data. The next step usually is to present the data in pictorial form so that readers may readily apprehend the essential features of a frequency distribution and compare one with another if they desire. Such pictures, called graphs, should *not* be thought of as substitutes for statistical treatment of data but rather as *visual aids* for thinking about and discussing statistical problems.

3.4 *Misuse of Graphing Techniques*

Y-axis

Vertical axis of a graph.

X-axis

Horizontal axis of a graph.

As you are well aware, graphs are often employed in the practical world of commerce to mislead the reader. For example, by the astute manipulation of the vertical **(Y-axis)** and horizontal **(X-axis)** axes of a graph, it is possible to convey almost any impression that is desired. Figure 3.1 illustrates this misapplication of graphing techniques. In it are shown two bar graphs (based on the same data) in which the X- and Y-axes are respectively elongated to produce two distinctly different impressions.

Figure 3.1 Bar graphs representing the same data but producing different impressions by varying the relative lengths of Y- and X-axes.

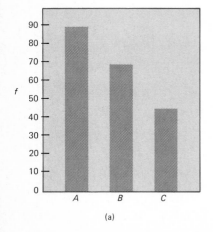

(a)

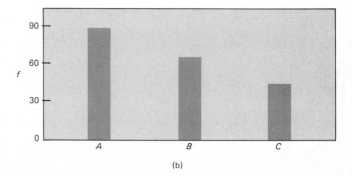

(b)

Note that Graph (a) tends to exaggerate the difference in frequency counts among the three classes, whereas Graph (b) tends to minimize these differences.

The differences might be further exaggerated by use of a device called the "Gee Whiz!" chart by Darrell Huff and Irving Geis in their excellent book, *How to Lie with Statistics.* This procedure consists of eliminating the zero frequency from the vertical axis and beginning with a frequency count greater than zero. Figure 3.2 is borrowed from the *How to Lie* book and illustrates quite dramatically the way in which graphs may be employed for purposes of deception.

It is obvious that the use of such devices is inimical to the aim of the statistician, which is to present data with such clarity that misinterpretations are reduced to a minimum. We may overcome the second source of error illustrated in Figure 3.2 by making the initial entry on the Y-axis a zero frequency. The first problem, however, remains: the selection of scale units to represent the horizontal and vertical axes. Clearly, the choice of these units is an arbitrary affair, and anyone who decides to make the Y-axis twice the length of the X-axis is just as correct as one who decides upon the opposite representation. In order to avoid graphic anarchy, however, it is necessary to adopt a convention designed to minimize bias. Most statisticians agree that the height of the vertical axis should be approximately 0.75 the length of the horizontal axis, with any proportion between 0.70 and 0.80 being acceptable.

The advantage of this convention is that it prevents subjective factors and, possibly, personal biases from influencing decisions concerning the relative proportion of the X-axis and the Y-axis in graphic representations. The use of this convention is illustrated in the forthcoming section dealing with bar graphs.

Figure 3.2 The use of the "Gee Whiz!" chart to exaggerate differences along the Y-axis. (Reprinted from D. Huff and I. Geis, *How To Lie with Statistics;* New York: W. W. Norton, 1954, with permission.)

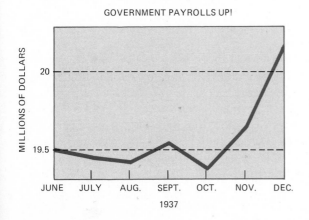
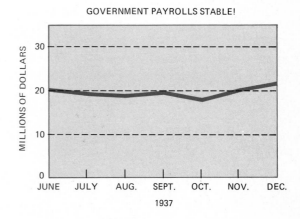

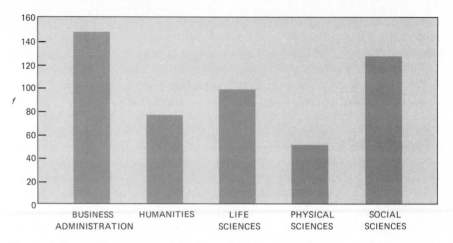

Figure 3.3 Number of students who are enrolled in introductory economics courses and are majoring in the various academic fields (hypothetical data).

This rule has also been applied to all the graphs appearing in the remainder of the chapter.

3.5 *Nominally Scaled Variables*

Bar Graph

A form of graph that employs bars to indicate the frequency of occurrence of observations within each nominal or ordinal category.

The **bar graph,** illustrated in Fig. 3.3, is a graphic device employed to represent data that are either nominally or ordinally scaled. A vertical bar is drawn* for each category, and the *height* of the bar represents the number of members of that class. If we arbitrarily set the width of each bar at one unit, the *area* of each bar may be used to represent the frequency for that category. Thus the total area of all the bars is equal to N.

In preparing frequency distributions of nominally scaled variables, you must keep two things in mind:

1. No order is assumed to underlie nominally scaled variables. Thus the various categories can be represented along the abscissa in any order you choose. The authors prefer to arrange the categories alphabetically, in keeping with their desire to eliminate any possibility of personal factors entering into the decision.

---

*Bar graphs are sometimes drawn horizontally (this has an advantage in cases where the number of cases [or classes] is large and the list may occupy a full page in length). Nevertheless, the vertical array (as shown in Fig. 3.3) is more often used (and more easily understood at sight) because of its adaptability to a histogram or a frequency curve (see Figs. 3.6 and 3.7).

2. The bars should be separated rather than touching, so that any implication of continuity among the categories is avoided.

3.6 *Ordinally Scaled Variables*

It will be recalled that the scale values of ordinal scales carry the implication of an ordering that is expressible in terms of the algebra of inequalities (greater than, less than). In terms of our preceding discussion, ordinally scaled variables should be treated in the same way as nominally scaled variables, except that the categories should be placed in their naturally occurring order along the X-axis. Figure 3.4 illustrates the use of the bar graph with an ordinally scaled variable.

3.7 *Interval- and Ratio-Scaled Variables*

Histogram

Recall the fact that interval- and ratio-scaled variables differ from ordinally scaled variables in one important way: Equal differences in scale values are equal. This means that we may permit the vertical bars to touch one another

Figure 3.4 Wins accrued on a circular track by horses from eight post positions. (From S. Siegel, *Non-Parametric Statistics*. New York: McGraw-Hill, 1956. Adapted with permission.)

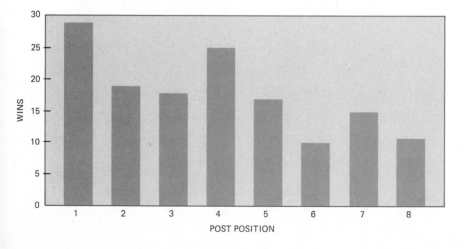

Histogram

A form of bar graph used with interval- or ratio-scaled frequency distributions.

in graphic representations of interval- and ratio-scaled frequency distributions. Such a graph is referred to as a **histogram** and replaces the bar graph employed with nominal and ordinal variables. Figure 3.5 illustrates the use of the histogram with a discretely distributed ratio-scaled variable.

We previously noted (Section 3.5) that frequency may be represented either by the area of a bar or by its height. However, there are many graphic applications in which the height of the bar may give misleading information concerning frequency. Consider Fig. 3.6, which shows the resulting histogram when the data are grouped into classes with unequal widths. The use of unequal class widths is most commonly found when there are relatively few scores at one or another extreme end of a distribution. For example, income figures commonly contain a few very extreme cases, such as annual incomes in the upper hundreds of thousands to millions of dollars. It is common to lump these extreme values into a single broad category.

If you think of frequency in terms of the height of the ordinate, you might erroneously conclude that the class 15–25 includes only two cases. However, if we represent each score by one unit on the scale of frequency and an equal unit on the scale of scores, the total area for each score is equal to one. In the class 15–25 there are 22 frequency units distributed over 11 score units; thus for this class the height of the ordinate will be 22/11 or 2 score units. Similarly, in the class 6–8 there are 24 frequency units distributed over 3 score units. Thus the height of the ordinate must equal 8 units.

This problem with classes of unequal widths can readily be avoided by using equal widths wherever possible. Figure 3.7 shows the days-absent-from-work graph when equal widths of classes are used.

Figure 3.5 Frequency distribution of the number of children per family among 389 familes surveyed in a small suburban community (hypothetical data).

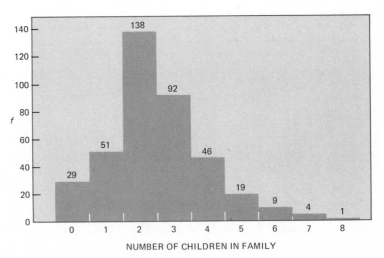

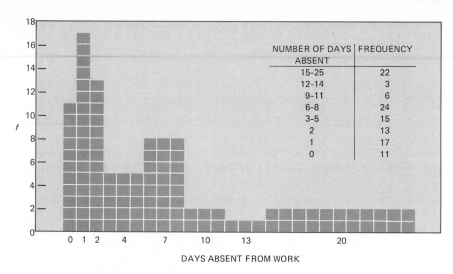

NUMBER OF DAYS ABSENT	FREQUENCY
15–25	22
12–14	3
9–11	6
6–8	24
3–5	15
2	13
1	17
0	11

Figure 3.6 Histogram employing unequal class widths (hypothetical data). The squares have been added for illustrative purposes. Each square represents one frequency at a given score. The total number of squares equals N (the sum of all the frequencies).

Figure 3.7 Histogram based on Fig. 3.6, but employing equal class widths.

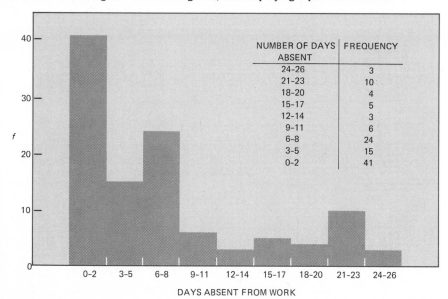

NUMBER OF DAYS ABSENT	FREQUENCY
24–26	3
21–23	10
18–20	4
15–17	5
12–14	3
9–11	6
6–8	24
3–5	15
0–2	41

In general, it is advisable that we consider frequency in terms of area whenever we are dealing with variables in which an underlying continuity may be assumed.

Frequency Curve

Frequency Curve

A form of graph representing a frequency distribution, in which a continuous line is used to indicate the frequency of the corresponding scores.

We can readily convert the histogram into another commonly employed form of graphic representation, the **frequency curve,** by joining the midpoints of the bars with straight lines. However, it is not necessary to construct a histogram prior to the construction of a frequency curve. All you need to do is place a dot where the tops of the bars would have been, and join these dots. In practice, we prefer to reserve the use of the histogram for discrete distributions and the frequency curve for distributions in which underlying continuity is explicit or may be assumed. When two or more frequency distributions are compared, the frequency curve provides a clearer picture. Figure 3.8 shows a frequency curve based upon the grouped frequency distribution appearing in Table 3.3.

Cumulative Frequency Curve

In Section 3.2, we demonstrated the procedures for constructing cumulative frequency and cumulative percentage distributions. The corresponding graphic representations are the cumulative frequency curve and the cumulative per-

Figure 3.8 Frequency curve based on the data in Table 3.3

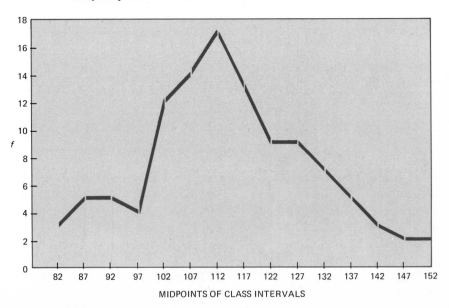

MIDPOINTS OF CLASS INTERVALS

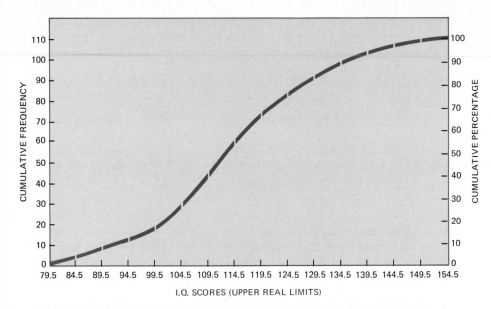

Figure 3.9 Cumulative frequency and cumulative percentage curve based on the cumulative frequency and cumulative percentage distributions in Table 3.4.

centage curve. These are combined in Fig. 3.9, with the left-hand Y-axis showing cumulative frequencies and the right-hand axis showing cumulative percentages.

There are three important points to remember: (1) The cumulative frequencies are plotted against the *upper real limit* of each class; (2) the maximum value on the Y-axis in the cumulative-frequency curve is N, and in the cumulative-percentage curve it is 100%; and (3) the cumulative frequency curve never decreases as you read from left to right.

 Forms of Frequency Curves

Frequency curves may take on an unlimited number of forms. However, many of the statistical procedures discussed in the text assume a particular form of distribution, namely, the "bell-shaped" **normal curve.**

In Fig. 3.10, several forms of bell-shaped distributions are shown. Curve (a), which is characterized by a piling up of scores in the center of the distribution, is referred to as a **leptokurtic distribution.** In curve (c), where the opposite condition prevails, the distribution is referred to as **platykurtic.** And

Normal Curve

A frequency curve with a characteristic bell-shaped form.

Leptokurtic Distribution

Bell-shaped distribution characterized by a piling up of scores in the center of the distribution.

Platykurtic Distribution

Frequency distribution characterized by a flattening in the central portion.

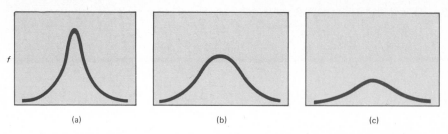

(a)   (b)   (c)

Figure 3.10   Three forms of bell-shaped distributions: (a) leptokurtic, (b) mesokurtic, and (c) platykuric.

Mesokurtic Distribution

Bell-shaped distribution: "ideal" form of normal curve.

Skewed Distribution

Distribution that departs from symmetry and tails off at one end.

Positively Skewed Distribution

Distribution that has relatively fewer frequencies at the high end of the horizontal axis.

Negatively Skewed Distribution

Distribution which has relatively fewer frequecies at the low end of the horizontal axis.

finally, curve (b) takes on the ideal form of the normal curve and is referred to as a **mesokurtic distribution.**

The normal curve is referred to as a symmetrical distribution, since, if it is folded in half, the two sides will coincide. Not all symmetrical curves are bell-shaped, however. A number of different symmetrical curves are shown in Fig. 3.11.

Certain distributions have been given names; that in Fig. 3.11(a) is called a *rectangular distribution* and that in Fig. 3.11(b) a U-*distribution.* Incidently, a *bimodal distribution,* for example, such as appears in Fig. 3.11(c), is often found when the frequency distributions of two different populations are represented in a single graph. For example, a frequency distribution of male and female adults of the same age would probably yield a curve similar to Fig. 3.11(c) on a strength-of-grip task.

When a distribution is not symmetrical, it is said to be **skewed.** If we say that a distribution is **positively skewed,** we mean that the distribution tails off at the high end of the horizontal axis and there are relatively fewer frequencies at this end. If, on the other hand, we say that the distribution is **negatively skewed,** we mean that there are relatively fewer scores associated with the left-hand, or low, side of the horizontal axis. Figure 3.12 presents several forms of skewed distributions.

Figure 3.12(a) is referred to as a J-curve and Fig. 3.12(b) is referred to as an **ogive.** A cumulative frequency distribution of data that are distributed in a

Figure 3.11   Illustrations of several nonnormal symmetrical frequency curves.

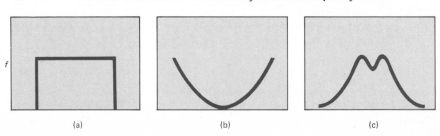

(a)   (b)   (c)

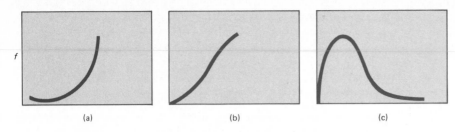

Figure 3.12 Illustration of skewed frequency curves.

bell-shaped fashion will yield an ogive or S-shaped distribution. Note that, even though the data in Table 3.4 only approximate a bell-shaped distribution, the cumulative curve takes on the form of an ogive (see Fig. 3.9).

    Figure 3.12(c) is positively skewed. Incidentally, Fig. 3.12(a) illustrates an extreme *negative skew.*

    It is not always possible to determine by inspection whether or not a distribution is skewed. There is a precise mathematical method for determining both direction and magnitude of skew. It is beyond the scope of this book to go into a detailed discussion of this topic. In Chapter 5, however, we outline a procedure for determining the *direction,* if not the magnitude, of skew.

Ogive

A cumulative frequency distribution of bell-shaped data.

3.9 *Other Graphic Representations*

As we noted in Section 1.5, we are often interested in comparing various groups or conditions with respect to a given characteristic. The groups or conditions are defined by the independent variable that is administered to them, whereas the characteristic we measure in order to judge the impact of the independent variable is called the dependent measure. Case Example 3.1 shows the use of graphic representations to illuminate the results of an experiment. Note that the independent variable is represented along the X-axis (horizontal) and the dependent variable along the Y-axis (vertical).

CASE EXAMPLE • 3.1
Mood and Memory

"Mood and Memory," an article in *American Psychologist,* describes a series of studies in which hypnosis was used to induce moods in subjects in order to ascertain the influence of emotions on learning and memory. In one part of the investigation, the subjects were asked to keep a diary in which they re-

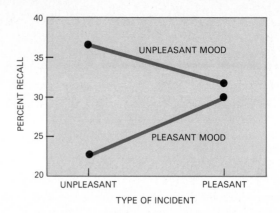

Figure 3.13 Percentage recall of incidents from an emotional diary depending on whether the incident was pleasant or unpleasant and whether the subject was in a pleasant or unpleasant mood during recall.

corded emotional incidents: time, place, participants, the gist of what happened, and a rating of each incident as pleasant or unpleasant on a 10-point scale. One week after submitting the diaries, the subjects returned to the laboratory. Hypnosis was used to induce a pleasant mood in half the subjects and an unpleasant mood in the remaining half. They were then asked to recall all the incidents they could that were reported in their diaries. The results are graphically displayed in Fig. 3.13.

A glance at Fig. 3.13 suggests a complex effect of mood on the recall of pleasant and unpleasant experiences. Specifically, when the mood is unpleasant a greater percentage of unpleasant incidents is recalled. In contrast, when the mood is pleasant, the percentage of recall of pleasant incidents is greater than the recall of unpleasant incidents. However, a note of caution is in order. The graph does not, in and of itself, prove the effects of mood on recall. It merely summarizes, in a readily grasped form, the findings for the sample used in the study. To draw broad inferences about the data requires the use of inferential statistical analyses.

Based on Gordon H. Bower (1981), "Mood and Memory," *American Psychologist,* **36**(2), 129–148.

Chapter Summary

This chapter was concerned with the techniques employed in "making sense" out of a mass of data. We demonstrated the construction of frequency distributions of scores and presented various graphing techniques. When the scores are widely spread out, many have a frequency of zero; and when there is no clear indication of central tendency, it is customary to group scores into classes. The resulting distribution is referred to as a grouped frequency distribution.

The basis for arriving at a decision concerning the grouping units to employ and the procedures for constructing a grouped frequency distribution were discussed and demonstrated. We saw that the true limits of a class are obtained in the same way as the true limits of a score. We also demonstrated procedures for converting a frequency distribution into a cumulative frequency percentage distribution.

We reveiwed the various graphing techniques employed in the behavioral sciences. The basic purpose of graphical representation is to provide visual aids for thinking about and discussing statistical problems. The primary objective is to present data in a clear, unambiguous fashion so that the reader may apprehend at a glance the relationships that you want to portray.

1. Devices employed by unscrupulous individuals to mislead the unsophisticated reader.
2. The use of the bar graph with nominally and ordinally scaled variables.
3. The use of the histogram and the frequency curve with continuous and discontinuous ratio- or interval-scaled variables.
4. Various forms of normally distributed data, nonnormal symmetrical distributions, and asymmetrical or skewed distributions.
5. Graphic representations of data, other than frequency distributions, commonly employed in the behavioral sciences.

Terms to Remember

bar graph

cumulative frequency

cumulative frequency distribution

cumulative percentage

cumulative percentage distribution

cumulative proportion

cumulative proportion distribution

frequency curve

frequency distribution

grouped frequency distribution

histogram

leptokurtic distribution

mesokurtic distribution

mutually exclusive

negatively skewed distribution

normal curve

ogive

platykurtic distribution

positively skewed distribution

random	*X*-axis
skewed distribution	*Y*-axis

EXERCISES

1. Give the true limits; the midpoints, and the width of the class for each of the following classes.

   a. 8–12   b. 6–7   c. 0–2   d. 5–14
   e. (−8)(−2) f. 2.5–3.5   g. 1.50–1.75 h. (−3)–(+3)

2. For each of the following sets of measurements, state (a) the best width of the class, *(i)*, (b) the apparent limits of the lowest class, (c) the true limits of that class, (d) the midpoint of that class.

   i. 0 to 106   ii. 29 to 41   iii. 18 to 48
   iv. −30 to +30   v. 0.30 to 0.47   vi. 0.206 to 0.293

3. Given the following list of scores in a statistics examination, use $i = 5$ for the classes and (a) set up a frequency distribution; (b) list the true limits and the midpoint of each class; (c) prepare a cumulative frequency distribution; and (d) prepare a cumulative percentage distribution.

Scores on a Statistics Examination									
63	88	79	92	86	87	83	78	40	67
68	76	46	81	92	77	84	76	70	66
77	75	98	81	82	81	87	78	70	60
94	79	52	82	77	81	77	70	74	61

4. Using the data in Exercise 3, set up frequency distributions with the following:

   a. $i = 1$ (ungrouped frequency distribution)   b. $i = 3$
   c. $i = 10$ d. $i = 20$
   Discuss the advantages and the disadvantages of employing these widths.

5. Given the following list of numbers, (a) construct a grouped frequency distribution; (b) list the true limits and the midpoint of each class (indicate the width employed); and (c) compare the results with those of Exercises 3 and 4.

6.3	8.8	7.9	9.2	8.6	8.7	8.3	7.8	4.0	6.7
6.8	7.6	4.6	8.1	9.2	7.7	8.4	7.6	7.0	6.6
7.7	7.5	9.8	8.1	8.2	8.1	8.7	7.8	7.0	6.0
9.4	7.9	5.2	8.2	7.7	8.1	7.7	7.0	7.4	6.1

6. Several entries in a frequency distribution showing the yield of corn per acre of land are 15–21, 8–14, 1–7.

   a. What is the width of the class?   b. What are the lower and
   c. What are the midpoints of   upper real limits of each
      each class?   of these three classes?

7. Construct a grouped frequency distribution, using 5–9 as the lowest class for the following list of numbers. List the width, midpoint, and real limits of the highest class.

67	63	64	57	56	55	53	53	54	54
45	45	46	47	37	23	34	44	27	44
45	34	34	15	23	43	16	44	36	36
35	37	24	24	14	43	37	27	36	26
25	36	26	5	44	13	33	33	17	33

8. Do Exercise 7 again, using 3–7 as the lowest class. Compare the resulting frequency distribution with those of Exercises 7, 9, and 10.

9. Repeat Exercise 7, using 4–5 as the lowest class.

10. Repeat Exercise 7 using 0–9 as the lowest class.

11. Give an example of each of the following distributions
   a. normal distribution
   b. U-shaped distribution
   c. positively skewed distribution
   d. negatively skewed distribution
   e. rectangular distribution
   f. bimodal distribution

12. Given the following frequency distribution of the weights of 96 students, draw a histogram.

Class	f	Class	f
160–164	1	130–134	17
155–159	3	125–129	11
150–154	10	120–124	8
145–149	6	115–119	3
140–144	14	110–114	1
135–139	22		

13. Take a pair of dice, toss 100 times, and record the sum (on the face of the two dice) for each toss. Prepare a bar graph, showing the number of times each sum occurs.

14. Given the following monthly sales by five salespeople in a large appliance store, draw graphs to perpetrate lies or distort facts to accomplish the following:
   a. The sales manager wants to impress upon the owner of the store that all members of his sales force are functioning at a uniformly high level.
   b. The sales manager wants to spur Mr. Richard to greater efforts.
   c. The store owner wants to spur the sales manager to greater efforts.

Sales Person	Sales, $	Sales Person	Sales, $
Ms. Amy	22,500	Mr. Tommy	22,100
Mr. Richard	17,900	Ms. Maribeth	20,700
Ms. Nancy	21,400		

15. Draw a graph of the data representing the true state of affairs in Exercise 14.

16. Below are the scores of two groups of fourth-grade students on a test of reading ability.

Class	Group A f	Group B f	Class	Group A f	Group B f
50–52	5	2	29–31	9	22
47–49	12	3	26–28	6	11
44–46	18	5	23–25	4	9
41–43	19	8	20–22	3	6
38–40	26	12	17–19	1	4
35–37	19	24	14–16	2	2
32–34	13	35			
				137	143

    a. Construct a frequency curve for each of these groups on the same axis.

    b. Describe and compare each distribution.

17. Describe the types of distributions you would expect if you were to graph each of the following:

    a. Annual incomes of U.S. families.

    b. The heights of adult U.S. males.

    c. The heights of adult U.S. females.

    d. The heights of U.S. males and females combined in one graph.

Class	f	Class	f
95–99	2	65–69	11
90–94	2	60–64	6
85–89	5	55–59	3
80–84	9	50–54	0
75–79	16	45–49	1
70–74	18		

18. Consider the table to the left. Given this frequency distribution of the score results of 73 students on a midterm exam, draw a frequency curve.

19. For the data in Exercise 18, draw a cumulative frequency curve.

20. A team of researchers at New York Metropolitan Medical Center (Zelon, Rubio, and Wasserman, 1971) has been collecting data on the incidence of drug addiction among mothers of newborn infants as well as among the infants themselves. The following table shows the total live births over a ten-year period as well as the number of mothers found to be drug addicted. Calculate the percentage of drug-addicted mothers for each year. Graph the percent incidence over the ten-year period. Does there appear to be any change in the incidence of drug addiction of mothers over this ten-year period?

Year	Total Live Births	Total Drug-Addicted Mothers
1960	4284	26
1961	4396	36
1962	4290	43
1963	4335	44
1964	3923	31
1965	3615	28
1966	3089	31
1967	2688	47
1968	2283	46
1969	2367	50

21. In addition to being addicted at birth, many infants of drug-addicted mothers appear to display other physical deviations from infants born to nonaddicted mothers. The table below shows the percentage of drug-addicted infants whose birth weight was less then 2500 grams. The hospital incidence of weights less than 2500 grams is also shown. Prepare a graph showing the percent of incidence of infants with low weight among neonates of drug-addicted mothers and among all children born in the hospital during the ten-year period. Does there appear to be any consistent difference in the two rates of incidence?

Year	Percent of Neonates with Birth Weight under 2500 Grams	
	Infants of Drug-Addicted Mothers	Hospital Incidence*
1960	69.0	13.9
1961	52.7	15.9
1962	56.8	15.8
1963	40.9	15.1
1964	29.0	14.4
1965	50.0	12.6
1966	54.8	14.2
1967	52.0	14.7
1968	45.6	14.6
1969	48.0	12.7

*Includes drug-addicted infants.

22. Following are the number of quarts of milk sold at a supermarket on 52 consecutive Saturdays.

67	75	63	71	65	73	71	88	61
65	56	62	58	72	66	76	77	75
61	70	64	71	63	61	63	64	62
69	60	66	78	92	64	64	69	64
65	75	72	67	88	74	65	73	
78	62	68	69	67	57	65	58	

a. The manager of the dairy department decides to limit the number of quarts of milk on sale each Saturday to 70. Assuming that the sales figures will be the same the following year, what is the likelihood (i.e., the percentage of time) that the department will be caught short?

b. Group the sales figures into a frequency distribution with the lower class limits of 56–58.

c. Prepare a cumulative frequency distribution and cumulative percentage distribution based on the above frequency distribution.

d. Group the sales figures into a frequency distribution with the lower class limit of 55–59. Prepare a cumulative frequency distribution and cumulative percentage distribution based on this frequency distribution. Compare the resulting distributions with those obtained above.

23. Draw a frequency curve for the frequency distribution obtained in Exercise 7.

24. Draw a frequency curve for the frequency distribution obtained in Exercise 8. Compare this distribution with that of Exercise 23.

25. Draw a cumulative frequency curve for the frequency distribution of Exercise 7.

26. Draw a cumulative frequency curve for the frequency distribution obtained in Exercise 8. Compare this distribution with that of Exercise 25.

27. Figures on birthrates are usually given in terms of the number of births per thousand in the population. This table shows the birthrate data at the end of each

Year	Number of Births per 1000 Population
1900	32
1910	30
1920	28
1930	21
1940	19
1950	24
1960	24
1970	18

decade since the turn of the century, rounded to the nearest whole number. (*Source*: Commission on Population Growth and the American Future.)

    a. Plot these data on a line chart.

    b. Is any general trend in birthrate discernible?

*28. Imagine that you have a population consisting of severn scores: 0, 1, 2, 3, 4, 5, 6. You write each of these numbers on a paper tab and place them in a hat. Then you draw a number, record it, place it back in the hat, and draw a second number. You add the second number to the first to obtain a sum. You continue drawing pairs of scores and obtaining their sums until you have obtained all possible combinations of these seven scores, taken two at a time.

    The following table shows all possible results from drawiung samples of $N = 2$ from this population of seven scores. The values within each cell show the sum of the two scores.

		First Draw						
		0	**1**	**2**	**3**	**4**	**5**	**6**
Second Draw	0	0 + 0 = 0	1 + 0 = 1	2 + 0 = 2	3 + 0 = 3	4 + 0 = 4	5 + 0 = 5	6 + 0 = 6
	1	0 + 1 = 1	1 + 1 = 2	2 + 1 = 3	3 + 1 = 4	4 + 1 = 5	5 + 1 = 6	6 + 1 = 7
	2	0 + 2 = 2	1 + 2 = 3	2 + 2 = 4	3 + 2 = 5	4 + 2 = 6	5 + 2 = 7	6 + 2 = 8
	3	0 + 3 = 3	1 + 3 = 4	2 + 3 = 5	3 + 3 = 6	4 + 3 = 7	5 + 3 = 8	6 + 3 = 9
	4	0 + 4 = 4	1 + 4 = 5	2 + 4 = 6	3 + 4 = 7	4 + 4 = 8	5 + 4 = 9	6 + 4 = 10
	5	0 + 5 = 5	1 + 5 = 6	2 + 5 = 7	3 + 5 = 8	4 + 5 = 9	5 + 5 = 10	6 + 5 = 11
	6	0 + 6 = 6	1 + 6 = 7	2 + 6 = 8	3 + 6 = 9	4 + 6 = 10	5 + 6 = 11	6 + 6 = 12

    a. Obtain an ungrouped frequency distribution of the 49 sums.

    b. Construct a histogram from the frequency distribution.

    c. Note that the original distribution of scores was rectangular since each score occurred with the same frequency. Compare the form of the original distribution with the form of the frequency distribution of sums.

29. Refer to Exercise 24 in Chapter 2. Prepare a bar graph to show the percentages of aggressive and nonaggressive males who employ exploitive techniques in order to gain "coital access to a female."

30. In another aspect of the study reported in Case Example 3.1, the subjects were asked to recall events from childhood when they were in a neutral mood and to classify each incident as pleasant, unpleasant, or neutral. At a later time, they were induced into either a happy or a sad mood and were asked to recall incidents from their childhood. When their mood was happy, they recalled approximately 1 unpleasant event, on the average, and approximately 26 pleasant incidents. When their mood was sad, they recalled about 10 unpleasant events, on the average, and 8 pleasant events. Construct a graph to summarize these findings.

31. Paradoxically, hyperactive children are often treated with a stimulant in order to *reduce* their activity. In one study, 20 hyperactive boys were treated with a stimulant (methylphenidate). A number of behaviors were then studied, including activity levels and interactions with their mothers (R.A. Barkley and C.E. Cunningham

---

*All exercises that are used to lay the groundwork for future discussion are preceded by an asterisk.

(1979), "The Effects of Methylphenidate on the Mother-Child Interactions of Hyperactive Children," *Arch. Gen. Psychiatry*, **36**, 201–208). In one facet of the study, wrist and ankle actometers recorded the time that wrist and ankles were active. Under the placebo condition, the wrist activity was approximately 1600 minutes, on the average, and the ankle activity was about 1700. Under the drug, the average number of minutes were about 900 for the wrist and 1000 for the ankle. Prepare a graph to show these findings.

4

Percentiles

4.1 Introduction

Suppose a younger brother or sister came home from school and announced, "I received a score of 127 on my scholastic aptitude test." What would be your reaction? Commend him for obtaining such a fine score? Criticize him for not getting a higher one? Or reserve judgment until you learned more about the distribution of scores within your sibling's class or group? If you have passed the course up to this point, you have undoubtedly selected the last of these three alternatives.

It should be clear that a score by itself is meaningless. It takes on meaning only when it can be compared to some standard scale or base. Thus, if your younger sibling were to volunteer the information, "Seventy nine percent of the students scored lower than I," he would be providing some frame of reference for interpreting the score. Indeed, he would have been citing the **percentile rank** of his score. The *percentile rank* of a score, then, *represents the percent of cases in a comparison group that achieved scores at or lower than the one cited.* Thus to say that a score of 127 has a percentile rank of 79 is to indicate that 79% of the comparison group scored at or below 127. Incidentally, each score is considered to be a hypothetical point without dimension, so that it would be equally meaningful to say that 21% of the comparison group scored higher than 127.

Percentiles

Numbers that divide a distribution into 100 equal parts.

Percentile Rank

A number that represents the percent of cases in a comparison group that achieved scores equal to or lower than the one cited.

4.2 Cumulative Percentiles and Percentile Rank

Obtaining the Percentile Rank of Scores from a Cumulative Percentage Graph

In Chapter 3 we constructed cumulative frequency and cumulative percentage distributions. If we were to graph a cumulative percentage distribution, we could read the percentile ranks directly from the graph, since the cumulative percentage corresponding to a given score is the same as the percentile rank of that score. Note that the reverse is also true; that is, given a percentile rank, we could read the corresponding scores. Figure 4.1 displays a graphic form of the cumulative percentage distribution presented in Table 3.4.

To illustrate, let's imagine that we want to determine the percentile rank of a score of 127. We locate 127 along the horizontal axis and construct a perpendicular line at the point that intercepts the curve. From that point on the curve, we read directly across the scale to the left, and see that the percen-

BOX 4.1

The stress of the beginning

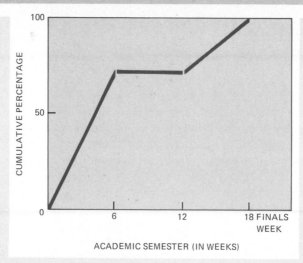

A cumulative percentage graph shows the percentages of cases falling below any selected value of the variable of interest. The accompanying graph shows that almost two-thirds of student suicides occur by the sixth week of the semester.

It has frequently been maintained that suicides among college students result from the stresses of final examinations. A long-term study at the University of California, Berkeley, investigated various factors related to student suicides. The figure above shows that the percentage of suicides was greatest in the opening weeks of the semester, leveled off at mid-semester, and showed a moderate increase during the last third of the semester. Thus, contrary to popular opinion, the period of greatest danger appears to be the beginning, rather than the end of the semester.

Seiden, R. H. (1966). "Campus Tragedy: A Story of Student Suicide," *Journal of Abnormal Social Psychology,* **71**, 389–399, Copyright © by the American Psychological Association, Reprinted by permission.

tile rank is approximately 79. On the other hand, if we wanted to know the score at a given *percentile,* we could reverse the procedure. For example, what is the score at the 90th percentile? We locate the 90th percentile on the vertical axis, then read directly to the right until we meet the curve; at this point, we construct a line perpendicular to the horizontal axis, and read the value on the scale of scores. In the present example, it can be seen that the score at the 90th percentile is approximately 135.

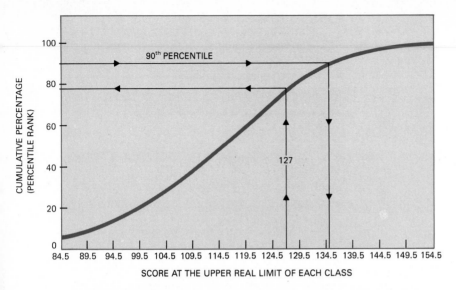

Figure 4.1 Graphic representation of a cumulative percentage distribution. (*Note:* The cumulative percentage corresponding to a given score is the same as the percentile rank of that score.)

Obtaining the Percentile Rank of Scores Directly

We are often called upon to determine the percentile rank of scores without the assistance of a cumulative percentage curve, or with greater precision than is possible with a graphical representation. To do this, it is usually necessary to interpolate within the cumulative frequency column to determine the precise cumulative frequency corresponding to a given score.

Using the grouped frequency distribution found in Table 4.1, let us determine directly the percentile rank of a score of 127 that we previously approximated by the use of the cumulative percentage curve. The first thing we should note is that a score of 127 falls within the class 125–129. The total cumulative frequency below that class is 82. Since a percentile rank of a score is defined symbolically as

$$\text{Percentile rank} = \frac{\text{cum } f}{N} \times 100, \tag{4.1}$$

it is necessary to find the precise cumulative frequency corresponding to a score of 127. It is clear that the cumulative frequency corresponding to a score of 127 lies somewhere between the 82nd and the 91st cases, the cumulative frequencies at both extremes of the class. We must now interpolate within the class 124.5–129.5 to find the exact cumulative frequency of a score of 127. In

Table 4.1 **Grouped frequency distribution and cumulative frequency distribution of scores in an educational test (hypothetical data).**

Class	f	Cumulative f
150–154	2	110
145–149	2	108
140–144	3	106
135–139	5	103
130–134	7	98
125–129	9	91
120–124	9	82
115–119	13	73
110–114	17	60
105–109	14	43
100–104	12	29
95–99	4	17
90–94	5	13
85–89	5	8
80–84	3	3

N = 110

doing this, we are actually trying to determine the proportion of distance that we must move into the class in order to find the number of cases included up to a score of 127.

A score of 127 is 2.5 score units above the lower real limit of the class (that is, $127 - 124.5 = 2.5$). Since there are 5 score units within the class, a score of 127 is 2.5/5 of the distance through the class. We now make a very important assumption: *The cases or frequencies within a particular class are evenly distributed throughout that class.* Since there are 9 cases within the class, we may now calculate that a score of 127 is $(2.5/5) \times 9$, or the 4.5th case within the class. In other words, the frequency 4.5 in the class corresponds exactly to a score of 127. We have already seen, however, that 82 cases fall at or below the lower real limit of the class. Adding the two together, we find that the score of 127 has a cumulative frequency of exactly 86.5. Substituting 86.5 into Formula (4.1), we obtain the following:

$$\text{Percentile rank of } 127 = \frac{86.5}{110} \times 100 = 78.64.$$

Note that this answer, when rounded to the nearest percentile, agrees with the approximation obtained by the use of the graphical representation of a cumulative percentage distribution (Fig. 4.1).

Figure 4.2 summarizes graphically the procedures involved in finding the cumulative frequency of a given score. You will note that the class 124.5–129.5 is divided into 5 equal units corresponding to the scores within that class, whereas the frequency scale is divided into 9 equal units corresponding to the 9 frequencies within that class. What we are accomplishing, in effect, in finding the frequency corresponding to a score, is a *linear transformation* from a scale of scores to a scale of frequencies; this is analogous to converting Fahrenheit readings to values on a Celsius scale, and the converse.

Formula (4.2) presents a generalized formula for calculating the percentile rank of a given score.

$$\text{Percentile rank} = \frac{\text{cum } f_{ll} + \left(\dfrac{X - X_{ll}}{i}\right)(f_i)}{N} \times 100, \qquad (4.2)$$

where

$\qquad$ cum f_{ll} = cumulative frequency at the lower real limit of the class containing X,
$\qquad\quad X$ = given score,
$\qquad\; X_{ll}$ = score at lower real limit of the class containing X,
$\qquad\quad\; i$ = width of class,
$\qquad\quad f_i$ = number of cases within the class containing X.

Finding the Score Corresponding to a Given Percentile Value

Imagine that your younger brother, instead of apprising you of his score, reported, instead, his percentile rank. He tells you his score was at the 96th percentile. What was his score?

To obtain the answer, we must interpolate in the reverse direction, from the cumulative frequency scale to the scale of scores. The first thing we must learn is the cumulative frequency corresponding to the 96th percentile. It fol-

Figure 4.2 Graphic representation of the procedures involved in finding the cumulative frequency corresponding to a given score.

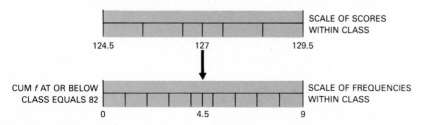

SCALE OF SCORES WITHIN CLASS

124.5   127   129.5

CUM *f* AT OR BELOW CLASS EQUALS 82

SCALE OF FREQUENCIES WITHIN CLASS

0   4.5   9

lows algebraically from Formula (4.1) that

$$\text{cum } f = \frac{\text{percentile rank} \times N}{100}. \tag{4.3}$$

Since we are interested in a score at the 96th percentile and our N is 110, the cumulative frequency of a score at the 96th percentile is

$$\text{cum } f = \frac{96 \times 110}{100} = 105.6.$$

Referring to Table 4.1, we see that the frequency 105.6 is in the class with the real limits of 139.5–144.5. Indeed, it is 2.6 frequencies into the class, since the cum f at the lower real limit of the class is 103, which is 2.6 less than 105.6. There are three cases in all within the class. Thus the frequency 105.6 is 2.6/3 of the way through a class with a lower real limit of 139.5 and an upper real limit of 144.5. In other words, it is 2.6/3 of the way through 5 score units. Expressed in terms of score units, then, it is (2.6/3) × 5 or 4.33 score units above the lower real limit of the class. By adding 4.33 to 139.5, we obtain the score at the 96th percentile, which is 143.83.

Figure 4.3 represents graphically the procedures involved in the linear transformation from units of the frequency scale to units of the scale of scores. For those of you who desire a generalized method for determining scores corresponding to a given percentile, Formula (4.4) should be helpful:

$$\text{Score at a given percentile} = X_{ll} + \frac{i(\text{cum } f - \text{cum } f_{ll})}{f_i}, \tag{4.4}$$

where

X_{ll} = score at lower real limit of the class containing cum f,
i = width of the class,
cum f = cumulative frequency of the score,
cum f_{ll} = cumulative frequency at the lower real limit of the class containing cum f,
f_i = number of cases within the class containing cum f.

Figure 4.3 Graphic representation of the procedures involved in finding the score corresponding to a given frequency within the class.

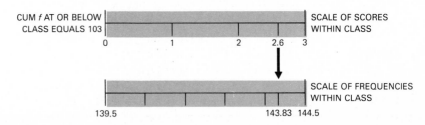

To illustrate the use of the formula, let's employ an example with which we are already familiar. What score is at the 78.64th percentile? First, by employing Formula (4.3), we obtain

$$\text{cum } f = \frac{78.64 \times 110}{100} = 86.50.$$

The score at the lower real limit of the class containing the frequency 86.50 is 124.5; i is 5; cum f to the lower real limit of the class is 82, and the number of cases within the class is 9. Substituting the above values into Formula (4.4), we obtain:

$$\text{Score at 78.64 percentile} = 124.5 + \frac{5(86.50 - 82)}{9}$$
$$= 124.5 + 2.50 = 127.00.$$

Note that this is the score from which we previously obtained the percentile rank 78.64 and that this formula illustrates, incidentally, a good procedure for checking the accuracy of our calculations. In other words, whenever you find the percentile rank of a score, you may take that answer and determine the score corresponding to that percentile value. You should obtain the original score. Similarly, whenever you obtain a score corresponding to a given percentile rank, you may take that answer and determine the percentile rank of that score. You should always come back to the original percentile rank. Failure to do so indicates that you have made an error. It is preferable to repeat the solution without reference to your prior answer rather than to attempt to find the mistake in your prior solution. Such errors are frequently of the "proofreader" type that defy detection, are time-consuming to locate, and are highly frustrating.

4.3 Percentile Rank and Reference Group

Just as a score is meaningless in the abstract, so also is a percentile rank. A percentile rank must always be expressed in relation to some reference group. Thus if a friend claims that she obtained a percentile rank of 93 in a test of mathematical aptitude, you might not be terribly impressed if the reference group were made up of individuals who completed only the eighth grade. On the other hand, if the reference group consisted of individuals holding a doctorate in mathematics, your attitude would unquestionably be quite different.

Many standardized tests employed in psychology, education, and industry publish separate norms for various reference groups. Table 4.2 shows the raw-score equivalents for selected percentile points on a test widely employed for graduate-school admissions. You will note that a person obtaining a raw score

Table 4.2 **Raw-score equivalents of selected percentile points on the Miller Analogies Test for eight graduate and professional school groups. (Reproduced by permission. Copyright by the Psychological Corporation, New York, N.Y.)**

Percentile	Physical Sciences	Agriculture	Medical Science	Biological Sciences	Social Sciences	Social Work	Languages and Literature	Law-School Freshmen	Percentile
99	93	89	92	88	90	81	87	84	99
95	91	86	83	87	85	76	84	79	95
90	88	77	78	86	82	67	80	73	90
85	85	72	76	80	79	64	76	66	85
80	82	67	74	76	76	61	74	63	80
75	80	64	71	70	74	60	73	60	75
70	78	61	67	68	69	58	68	58	70
65	76	59	64	67	67	57	66	55	65
60	74	57	60	65	64	54	65	53	60
55	70	56	58	63	63	52	61	51	55
50	68	54	57	61	61	50	59	49	50
45	65	51	55	58	58	47	56	47	45
40	63	50	53	55	56	46	53	45	40
35	60	48	50	53	53	45	51	42	35
30	58	43	47	52	51	41	46	40	30
25	55	40	45	50	49	39	43	37	25
20	51	37	43	48	46	37	41	35	20
15	47	34	41	47	44	32	38	32	15
10	43	31	34	41	39	27	35	30	10
5	39	26	30	37	32	22	29	25	5
1	28	5	24	28	18	9	7	18	1
N	251	125	103	84	229	116	145	558	N
Mean	66.7	53.6	57.6	61.5	60.2	49.4	57.7	49.6	Mean
SD	16.6	17.3	16.2	15.6	16.0	15.2	17.4	16.1	SD

of 50 on this test would obtain a percentile rank of 25, 35, 40, and 50 when compared successively with reference groups in the biological sciences, medical science, agriculture, and social work.

CASE EXAMPLE • 4.1
One Person's Normal Is Another's Hypertension

Hypertension is a condition in which the blood pressure—either systolic (when the heart pumps blood through the arteries) and/or diastolic (when the heart is at rest between beats)—is chronically elevated. In about two-thirds of all cases, the cause of the condition is unknown, giving rise to speculation that psychological factors (work pressures, anxiety, etc.) may be involved. What is not widely known is that many adolescent boys and girls have abnormally high systolic and/or diastolic blood pressures for their age.

In "Adolescent Hypertention," Klein presents blood pressure (BP) readings (systolic/diastolic) at the 50th percentile (the median) and the 95th percentile for boys and girls from ages 10 through 18. Three readings at or above the 95th percentile, taken at least a week apart at a single health clinic, are sufficient for a diagnosis of adolescent hypertension.

Note that, as the subject's age increases, the BP reading at the 95th percentile also increases. Thus, an 18 year old female with BP readings of, say, 135/88 would be considered within the high "normal" range. For a female of 10 years of age, however, these readings would be above the 95th percentile on both systolic and diastolic measures.

Table 4.3 **Percentiles of blood pressure (mm Hg) taken from the right arm, with the subject seated.**

	Male		Female	
Age	50th %ile	95th %ile	50th %ile	95th %ile
10	109/72	130/86	110/73	132/87
11	112/73	134/87	113/74	134/88
12	115/74	137/87	115/75	136/89
13	117/75	137/89	117/76	138/89
14	120/76	143/91	119/76	140/90
15	122/76	146/92	120/77	142/91
16	124/77	148/93	121/77	143/91
17	126/78	150/94	122/78	144/92
18	128/79	153/95	123/79	145/92

Based on Arthur Klein (1981), "Adolescent Hypertension," *Therapaeia,* Sept., 37–41.

Chapter Summary

In this chapter, we saw that a score, by itself, is meaningless unless is it compared to a standard base or scale. Scores are often converted into units of the percentile-rank scale in order to provide a readily understandable basis for their interpretation and comparison.

We saw that

1. Percentile ranks of scores and scores corresponding to a given percentile may be approximated from a cumulative percentage graph.

2. Direct computational methods permit a more precise location of the percentile rank of a score and the score corresponding to a given percentile. These methods were discussed and demonstrated in the text. (See Tables 4.4 and 4.5.)

Table 4.4 Summary procedures: Obtaining the score corresponding to a given percentile rank.

Class	f	Cum f	
			Problem: Find the score corresponding to a percentile rank of 75.17.
			STEPS:
			1. Sum f column to obtain N. $N = 98$.
41–43	1	98	**2.** Cumulate frequencies by successive addition of frequencies from lowest to highest classes. Last cumulative frequency must equal N.
38–40	2	97	
35–37	4	95	**3.** Multiply 75.17 by N and divide by 100. Thus,
32–34	9	91	$$\frac{75.17 \times 98}{100} = 73.67.$$
29–31	10	82	
26–28	13	72	This represents the cumulative frequency corresponding to the unknown score.
23–25	18	59	**4.** Find the class containing the 73.67th cumulative frequency.
20–22	14	41	**5.** Subtract from the value obtained in step 4 the cumulative frequency at the upper real limit of the *adjacent lower class;* i.e., $73.67 - 72 = 1.67$. This value shows that the desired score is 1.67 frequencies within the class 28.5–31.5.
17–19	11	27	
14–16	8	16	
11–13	5	8	
8–10	2	3	**6.** Divide the value found in step 5 by the frequency within the class and multiply by the width of the class ($i = 3$). Thus, $(1.67/10) \times 3 = 0.50$.
5–7	1	1	
$i = 3$	98		**7.** Add the value found in step 6 to the score at the lower real limit of the class containing the 73.67th cumulative frequency. Thus, $28.5 + 0.5 = 29.0$ (answer).

Table 4.5 Summary procedures: Obtaining percentile rank of a score.

Problem: Find the percentile rank of a score of 29.

Class	f	Cum f
41–43	1	98
38–40	2	97
35–37	4	95
32–34	9	91
29–31	10	82
26–28	13	72
23–25	18	59
20–22	14	41
17–19	11	27
14–16	8	16
11–13	5	8
8–10	2	3
5–7	1	1
$i = 3$	98	

STEPS:

1. Sum f column to obtain N. $N = 98$.
2. Cumulate frequencies by successive addition of frequencies from lowest to highest classes. Last cumulative frequency must equal N.
3. Identify the class containing the score: 29.
4. Subtract the score at the *lower real limit* of that class from 29: $29 - 28.5 = 0.5$.
5. Note the frequency within that class: 10.
6. Divide the value found in step 4 by the width of the class and multiply by the frequency found in step 5. Thus, $(0.5/3) \times 10 = 1.67$. This value represents the frequency within the class $28.5 - 31.5$ corresponding to a score of 29.
7. Note the cumulative frequency appearing in the *adjacent lower class*. Cum $f = 72$.
8. Add the value found in step 6 to the value found in step 7. Thus, $1.67 + 72 = 73.67$.
9. Divide the value found in step 8 by N and multiply by 100. Thus $(73.67/98) \times 100 = 75.17$ (answer).

3. A percentile rank is meaningless in the abstract. It must always be expressed in relation to some reference group.

Terms to Remember

percentile rank   percentiles

EXERCISES

1. Estimate the percentile rank of the following scores, employing Fig. 4.1.
   a. 104.5   b. 112   c. 134
2. Calculate the percentile rank of the scores in Exercise 1, employing Table 4.1.
3. Estimate the scores corresponding to the following percentiles, employing Fig. 4.1.
   a. 25   b. 50   c. 75

4. Calculate the scores corresponding to the percentiles in Exercise 3, employing Table 4.1.

5. A younger sibling claims to have obtained a score of 130 on a standard vocabulary test. What additional information might you seek in order to interpret this score?

6. Refer to Chapter 3, Exercise 18.

   a. A student in group A obtained a score of 45 on the test of reading ability. What is his or her percentile rank in the group?
   b. What is the percentile rank of a student in group *B* who also obtained a score of 45?
   c. Combine both groups into an overall frequency distribution and obtain the percentile rank of a score of 45. What happens to the percentile rank of the student in group *A*? group *B*? Why?

7. If we were to place all the scores shown in Table 4.1 into a hat, what is the likelihood that, selecting at random, we would obtain
   a. A score equal to or higher than 131?
   b. A score equal to or lower than 131?
   c. A score equal to or below 84?
   d. A score equal to or above 154?
   e. A score between 117 and 133?
   f. A score equal to or greater than 148, or equal to or less than 82?

8. The following questions are based on Table 4.2.
   a. John H. proudly proclaims that he obtained a "higher" percentile ranking than his friend Howard. Investigation of the fact reveals that his score on the test was actually lower. Must it be concluded that John H. was mistaken, or is some other explanation possible? Explain.
   b. Jean H. obtained a percentile rank of 65 on the social-work scale. What was her score? What score would she have had to obtain to achieve the same percentile rank on the physical sciences scale?
   c. World Law School employs the Miller Analogies Test as an element of the admissions procedure. No applicants obtaining percentile ranks below 75 are considered for admission, regardless of their other qualifications. Thus the 75th percentile might be called a "cutoff" point. Which reference group is most likely involved in the decision? What score constitutes the cutoff point for this distribution?
   d. Foster Medical School also employs the 75th percentile as a cutoff point. Lee F. obtained a raw score of 62. What are Lee's chances of being considered for admission?

The following table shows a frequency distribution of the Environmental Protection Agency's estimates of miles-per-gallon ratings of 60 automobiles. In Exercises 9–14, we provide the miles-per-gallon ratings of six models. Determine the percentile rank of each car.

9. Chevette, 22 mpg.   10. Hornet wagon, 16 mpg.

Table 4.6

Class				Class			
Apparent Limits	Real Limits	f	Cum f	Apparent Limits	Real Limits	f	Cum f
28–29	27.5–29.5	1	60	18–19	17.5–19.5	6	46
26–27	25.5–27.5	1	59	16–17	15.5–17.5	10	40
24–25	23.5–25.5	2	58	14–15	13.5–15.5	6	30
22–23	21.5–23.5	3	56	12–13	11.5–13.5	10	24
20–21	19.5–21.5	7	53	10–11	9.5–11.5	14	14
					$\sum f = 60$		

11. Audi Fox, 24 mpg.

12. Vega Kammback, 19 mpg.

13. Cadillac Eldorado, 11 mpg.

14. Toyota Corolla, 20 mpg.

Using the same table, find the miles-per-gallon scores corresponding to the percentile ranks provided in Exercises 15–20.

15. Percentile rank of 10.

16. Percentile rank of 75.

17. Percentile rank of 25.

18. Percentile rank of 18.

19. Percentile rank of 84.

20. Percentile rank of 16.

21. Suppose a manager were interested in comparing the scores of 25 employees on a mathematical test. Assigning one person to each letter, he records the following scores:

A. 55	F. 40	K. 50	P. 40	U. 40
B. 50	G. 60	L. 45	Q. 35	V. 30
C. 25	H. 45	M. 25	R. 25	W. 45
D. 45	I. 50	N. 35	S. 20	X. 35
E. 40	J. 30	O. 55	T. 30	Y. 40

Calculate the percentile rank for each person, employing $i = 5$ and assuming that the lowest class is 20–24.

22. In addition, the manager studies the number of mathematical problems the employees solve per day. He finds the following number of units completed per day for the same 25 employees (the employees were designated by the same letters as above):

A. 45	F. 30	K. 40	P. 30	U. 30
B. 40	G. 50	L. 35	Q. 25	V. 20
C. 25	H. 35	M. 15	R. 15	W. 34
D. 35	I. 40	N. 25	S. 10	X. 25
E. 30	J. 20	O. 45	T. 20	Y. 30

Calculate the percentile rank for each person and compare it to the ranks in Exercise 21. Employ $i = 5$ and a lowest class of 10–14.

*23. Refer to Exercise 28, Chapter 3, and construct both a cumulative frequency and cumulative percentage distribution of the 49 sums.

*24. Review the sampling experiment demonstrated in Exercise 28, Chapter 3. Then return to the cumulative percentage distribution in Exercise 23, above. Answer the following questions:

   a. What is the likelihood (what is the percentage of times?) that a sum equal to or less than 11 would have been drawn in a sample of $N = 2$ from the original population of seven numbers?
   b. What is the likelihood (what percentage of times?) that a sum greater than 5 or less than 10 would have been obtained? [Hint: The cumulative percentage to the upper real limit of 9 is 88; below the upper limit of 5 is 43.]
   c. What percentage of times would a sum equal to or less than 2 be obtained?
   d. What percentage of times would a sum equal to or greater than 10 be obtained?
   e. What percentage of times would a sum equal to or less than 2 or equal to or greater than 10 be obtained.

25. Refer to Case Example 4.1, and answer the following. Which of the following systolic blood pressures would be at or above the 95th percentile?

   a. Charles, age 15: 99.   b. Maria, age 13: 139.
   c. Matthew, age 10: 133.   d. Ali, age 18: 145.
   e. Alicia, age 14: 140.   f. Karen, age 17: 143.

26. Given the accompanying table, calculate the percentile rank for the following size families:

   a. 3   b. 5   c. 7

In what way does this table violate the procedures outlined for constructing a grouped frequency distribution

Size of U.S. families of Spanish origin in 1977.

Size	Number (in thousands)
2	662
3	636
4	625
5	408
6	218
7 or more persons	216

Source: U.S. Bureau of Census. Current Population Reports, Series P-20, No. 339, U.S. Government Printing Office.

27. The percentile bands corresponding to systolic and diastolic blood pressures of boys and girls between 2 and 18 years of age are shown on p. 87. Using these figures, find the approximate percentile rank of each of the following:

   a. boy, age 6, systolic BP = 90.   b. girl, age 6, systolic BP = 90.
   c. boy, age 18, systolic BP = 130.   d. girl, age 18, systolic BP = 130.
   e. girl, age 8, diastolic BP = 78.   f. girl, age 17, diastolic BP = 78.

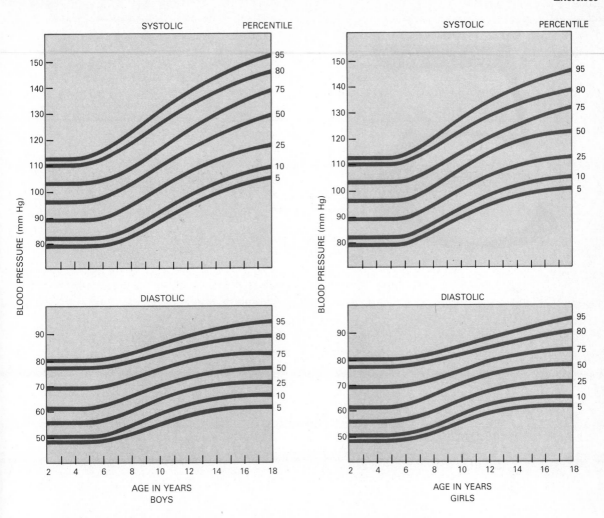

Percentiles of distribution of blood pressure measurements (taken at the right arm, subject seated) are shown plotted against age for boys and for girls. (From National Heart, Lung, and Blood Institute: Report of the Task Force on Blood Pressure Control in Children. *Pediatrics* **59**(2), 797–820, 1977. Reprinted with permission.)

5

Measures of Central Tendency

5.1 *Introduction*

One of the greatest sources of confusion among lay people, and perhaps a cause for their suspicion that statistics is more of an art than a science, revolves about the ambiguity in the use of the term "average." Unions and management speak of average salaries and frequently cite numerical values in sharp disagreement with each other; television programs and commercials are said to be prepared with the average viewer in mind; politicians are deeply concerned about the views of the average voter; the average family size is frequently given as a fractional value, a statistical abstraction which is ludicrous to some and absurd to others; the term "average" is commonly used as a synonym for the term "normal"; the TV meteorologist tells us we had an average day or that rainfall for the month is above or below average. Indeed, the term "average" has so many popular connotations that many statisticians prefer to drop it from the technical vocabulary and refer, instead, to **measure of central tendency.** We define a measure of central tendency as an *index of central location employed in the description of frequency distributions.* Since the center of a distribution may be defined in different ways, there will be a number of different measures of central tendency. In this chapter, we shall concern ourselves with three of the most frequently employed measures of central tendency: the mean, the median, and the mode.

Measure of Central Tendency

Index of central location employed in the description of frequency distributions.

Why Describe Central Tendency?

Through the first four chapters of the book, we concerned ourselves primarily with organizing data into a meaningful and useful form. Beyond this, however, we want to describe our data in such ways that quantitative statements can be made. A frequency distribution represents an organization of data but it does not, in itself, permit us to make quantitative statements either describing the distribution or comparing two or more distributions.

There are two features of many frequency distributions that statisticians have noted and have developed quantitative methods for describing: (1) Data often cluster around a central value that lies between the two extreme values of the variable under study; (2) data may tend to be dispersed and distributed about the central value in a way that can be specified quantitatively. The first of these features—central tendency—is the topic of the present chapter; the second—dispersion—will be discussed in Chapter 6.

The ability to locate a point of central tendency, particularly when coupled with a description of the disperson of scores about that point, can be very useful to behavioral scientists. For example, they may be able to reduce a mass of data to a simple quantitative value that can be communicated to and understood by other scientists.

BOX 5.1

The ambiguity of "average"

Annual Salaries of XYZ Company (In dollars)	
30,000	
24,000	
14,000	
10,000	←——— Mean
9,000	
9,000	
9,000	
7,000	←——— Median
6,000	
6,000	
6,000	
5,000	
5,000	
5,000	←——— Mode
5,000	

The term "average" is frequently used by mass media, labor unions, corporations, hucksters, politicians, and students to describe scores or numerical values in the central part of a distribution. Unfortunately, there are three different measures of central tendency, which, for a given distribution, may deviate substantially from one another. This disparity often gives rise to heated disagreements among individuals who focus their attention upon one or another measure of central tendency. Many people are confused by all this bickering and the endless citation of conflicting statistics. They may conclude, in dismay, "Statistics are meaningless. You can do anything you want with them."

In the accompanying table we show an array of annual salaries of a hypothetical small business that employs fifteen individuals, including the president and the vice-president. The company has recently gone on strike. The leader of the strike cites the poor wages—pointing to the most frequently occurring wage (the mode). "The average salary is five thousand dollars," shouts the leader, in a controlled rage. Management, looking at the arithmetic average (mean) of all the salaries, replies with righteous indignation, "Nonsense! The average salary is ten thousand dollars." A mediator, looking at exactly the same data but concentrating on the middle salary (the median), expostulates contemptuously, "Balderdash! Both of you are wrong. The average salary is seven thousand dollars."

Thus doth statistics make liars of us all!

We have already stated that the behavioral scientist is frequently called upon to compare the measurements obtained from two or more groups of subjects for the purpose of drawing inferences about the effects of an independent variable. Measures of central tendency greatly simplify the task of drawing conclusions.

5.2 The Arithmetic Mean

Methods of Calculation

Mean

Sum of the scores or values of a variable divided by their number.

You are probably intimately familiar with the arithmetic mean, for whenever you obtain an "average" of grades by summing the grades and dividing by the number of grades, you are calculating the arithmetic **mean**. In short, *the mean is the sum of the scores or values of a variable divided by their number.* Stated in algebraic form:

$$\overline{X} = \frac{X_1 + X_2 + \cdots + X_N}{N} = \frac{\sum X}{N},$$ (5.1)

where

$\overline{X}$ = the mean and is referred to as X bar,*
N = the number of scores, and
$\sum$ = the mathematical verb directing us to sum all the measurements.

Thus the arithmetic mean of the scores 8, 12, 15, 19, 24 is $\overline{X}$ = 78/5 = 15.60.

Obtaining the mean from an ungrouped frequency distribution • You will recall that we constructed a frequency distribution as a means of eliminating the constant repetition of scores that occur with varying frequency, in order to permit a single entry in the frequency column to represent the number of times a given score occurs. Thus, in Table 5.1, we know from the column headed f that the score of 8 occurred 6 times. In calculating the mean, then, it is not necessary to add 8 six times since we may multiply the score by its frequency and obtain the same value of 48. Since each score is multiplied by its corresponding frequency prior to summing, we may represent the mean for frequency distributions as follows:

$$\overline{X} = \frac{\sum fX}{N}$$ (5.2)

Table 5.1 **Computational procedures for calculating the mean with ungrouped frequency distributions.**

X	f	fX	Computation
12	1	12	
11	2	22	$\overline{X} = \dfrac{\sum fx}{N}$
10	5	50	
9	4	36	
8	6	48	$\overline{X} = \dfrac{232}{29}$
7	4	28	
6	3	18	
5	2	10	$\overline{X} = 8.00$
4	2	8	
	N = 29	$\sum fX$ = 232	

---

*In Section 1.2, we indicated that italic letters would be employed to represent sample statistics and Greek letters to represent population parameters. The Greek letter μ will be used to represent the population mean.

Endorphins and Sudden Infant Death: A Link?

The occurrence of sudden, unexplained deaths in infants (SID or Sudden Infant Death Syndrome) has been a source of great concern in the health-care professions. Mental health professionals are specifically concerned with SID because the death of a child often leaves a deep residue of guilt in the parents. Compounding this problem is the fact that one parent often blames the other for the catastrophe.

A seemly unrelated series of developments in physiological research might provide a clue to the cause of at least some SIDs. In recent years, it has been discovered that the body produces its own narcotic-like substances, endorphins and enkephalins. In the Orlowski study, the research team obtained the β-endorphin levels in the cerebrospinal fluid of 8 infants who had experienced near-SIDs (a cessation of breathing for more than 20 seconds). These levels were as follows: 52, 52, 66, 54, 47, 66, 90, 50. The β-endorphin levels of two control infants were 10 and 1.

The mean of the experimental subjects is $\overline{X} = 477/8 = 59.62$. The mean of the two control subjects is $\overline{X} = 11/2 = 5.5$. The difference between these two means is $59.62 - 5.5 = 54.12$. We shall reexamine these data in Chapter 13 to see if this large a difference in means could reasonably be attributed to chance. Note, however, that this study is not a true experiment. The high endorphin levels were not randomly assigned to the near-SID infants. Rather, they occurred naturally. It is altogether possible that the elevated endorphin levels were a bodily reaction to the cessation of breathing rather than a cause of the cessation.

Based on James P. Orlowski (1982), "Endorphins in Infant Apnea," *New England Journal of Medicine*, **307**(3), 186–187.

Properties of the Arithmetic Mean

One of the most important properties of the mean is that *it is the point in a distribution of measurements or scores about which the summed deviations are equal to zero*. In other words, if we were to subtract the mean from each score and then sum or add the resulting deviations from the mean, this sum would equal zero. Symbolically,

$$\sum (X - \overline{X}) = 0. \tag{5.3}$$

The algebraic proof of this statement is

$$\sum (X - \overline{X}) = \sum X - \sum \overline{X}$$
$$= N\overline{X} - N\overline{X}$$
$$= 0.$$

In following this algebraic proof, it is important to note (1) that since

$$\overline{X} = \frac{\sum X}{N},$$

it follows that $\sum X = N\overline{X}$ and (2) that summing the mean over all the scores, $(\sum \overline{X})$ is the same as multiplying $\overline{X}$ by N—that is, $N\overline{X}$ (see Generalization 1, Chapter 2).

Therefore the mean is a score or a potential score that balances all the scores on either side of it. In this sense it is analogous to the fulcrum of a seesaw. In playing on seesaws you may have noticed that it is possible for a small individual to balance a heavy individual if the latter moves closer to the fulcrum. Thus, if you wanted to balance a younger brother or sister (presumably lighter than you) on a seesaw, you would move yourself toward the center of the board. This analogy leads to a second important characteristic of the mean; that is, *the mean is very sensitive to extreme measurements when these measurements are not balanced on both sides of it.*

Observe the two **arrays** of scores in Table 5.2. An *array is an arrangement of data according to their magnitude from the smallest to the largest value.* Note that all the scores in both distributions are the same except for the very large score of 33 in column X_2. This one extreme score is sufficient to double the size of the mean. The sensitivity of the mean to extreme scores is a characteristic that has important implications governing our use of it. These implica-

Array

Arrangement of data according to their magnitude, from the smallest to the largest value.

Table 5.2 **Comparison of the means of two arrays of scores, one of which contains an extreme value.**

Group 1 Score, X_1	Group 2 Score, X_2
2	2
3	3
5	5
7	7
8	33
$\sum X_1 = 25$	$\sum X_2 = 50$
$\overline{X}_1 = 5.00$	$\overline{X}_2 = 10.00$

Sum of Squares

Deviations from the mean, squared and summed.

tions will be discussed in Section 5.5, when we compare the three measures of central tendency.

A third important characteristic of the mean is that *the **sum of squares** of deviations from the arithmetic mean is less than the **sum of squares** of deviations about any other score or potential score.*

To illustrate this characteristic of the mean, Table 5.3 shows the squares and the sum of squares when deviations are taken from the mean and various other scores in a distribution. It can be seen that the sum of squares is smallest in column 4, when deviations are taken from the mean.

This property of the mean provides us with another definition; i.e., *the mean is that measure of central tendency that makes the sum of squared deviations around it minimal.* The method of locating the mean by finding the minimum sum of squares is referred to as the **least-squares method.** The least-squares method is of considerable value in statistics, particularly when it is applied to curve fitting.

Least-Squares Method

Method of locating the mean by finding the minimum sum of squares.

The Weighted Mean

Let's imagine that four classes in introductory sociology obtained the following mean scores on the final examination: 75, 78, 72, and 80. Could you sum these four means together and divide by four, to obtain an overall mean for all four classes? This could be done *only if* the N in each class is identical. What if, as a matter of fact, the mean of 75 is based on an N of 30, the second mean is based on 40 observations, the third on $N = 25$, and the fourth on $N = 50$?

The total sum of scores may be obtained by multiplying each mean by its respective N and summing.

Thus

$$\sum (N \cdot \overline{X}) = 30(75) + 40(78) + 25(72) + 50(80)$$
$$= 11,170.$$

Table 5.3 **The squares and sum of squares of deviations taken from various scores in a distribution.**

1 X	2 $(X - 2)^2$	3 $(X - 3)^2$	4 $(X - \overline{X})^2$	5 $(X - 5)^2$	6 $(X - 6)^2$
2	0	1	4	9	16
3	1	0	1	4	9
4	4	1	0	1	4
5	9	4	1	0	1
6	16	9	4	1	0
Totals $N = 5$ $\overline{X} = 4$	30	15	10	15	30

The **weighted mean,** $\bar{X}_w$, can be expressed as the sum of the mean of each group multiplied by its respective weight (the N in each group) divided by the sum of the weights (i.e., $\Sigma w = \Sigma N_i = N$).

Weighted Mean

Sum of the mean of each group multiplied by its respective weight (the N in each group), divided by the sum of the weights (total N).

$$\bar{X}_w = \frac{\sum(w \cdot \bar{X})}{\sum w} = \frac{\sum(N_i \cdot \bar{X})}{N}$$

$$\bar{X}_w = \frac{30(75) + 40(78) + 25(72) + 50(80)}{145}$$

$$= \frac{11,170}{145} = 77.03.$$

5.3 *The Median*

With grouped frequency distributions, the **median** is defined as *that score or potential score in a distribution of scores that divides the distribution so that the same number of scores lie on each side of it*. If this definition sounds vaguely familiar to you, it isn't surprising. The median is merely a special case of a percentile rank. Indeed, the median is the score at the 50th percentile. It should be clear that the generalized procedures discussed in Chapter 4 for determining the score at various percentile ranks may be applied to the calculation of the median.

Median

Score or potential score in a distribution of scores that divides the distribution so that the same number of scores lie on each side of it.

Modifying Formula (4.4) for application to the special case of the median, we obtain the following:

$$\text{Median} = X_{ll} + i\frac{(N/2) - \text{cum } f_{ll}}{f_i}. \qquad (5.4)$$

Applied to the data in Table 4.1, the median becomes

$$\text{Median} = 109.5 + 5\frac{(110/2) - 43}{17}$$

$$= 109.5 + 5\frac{(55 - 43)}{17} = 109.5 + 5\left(\frac{12}{17}\right)$$

$$= 109.5 + 3.53 = 113.03.$$

The Median of an Array of Scores

Occasionally it will be necessary to obtain the median when the N is not sufficient to justify casting the data into the form of a frequency distribution or a grouped frequency distribution. Consider the following array of scores: 5, 19, 37, 39, 45. Note that the scores are arranged in order of magnitude and that N is an odd number. A score of 37 is the median, since two scores fall above it and two scores fall below it.* If N is an *even* number, the median is the arithmetic mean of the *two middle values*. The two middle values in the array of scores 8, 26, 35, 43, 47, 73 are 35 and 43. The arithmetic mean of these two values is (35 + 43)/2, or 39. Therefore the median is 39.

Occasionally the middle score in an array of scores is tied with other scores. How do we specify the median when we encounter tied scores?

Consider the following array of 20 scores: 2, 3, 3, 4, 5, 7, 7, 8, 8, 8, 8, 9, 10, 12, 14, 15, 17, 19, 19, 20. The easiest procedure to convert the array to an ungrouped frequency distribution and apply Formula (5.4). However, the i in the numerator may be eliminated since it is equal to 1.

X	f	Cum f	X	f	Cum f
20	1	20	10	1	13
19	2	19	9	1	12
18	0	17	8	4	11
17	1	17	7	2	7
16	0	16	6	0	5
15	1	16	5	1	5
15	1	15	4	1	4
13	0	14	3	2	3
12	1	14	2	1	1
11	0	13			

$$\text{Median} = X_{ll} + \frac{(N/2 - \text{cum } f_{ll})}{f_1}$$

$$= 7.5 + \frac{(20/2 - 7)}{4}$$

$$= 7.5 + \frac{3}{4} = 8.25$$

Characteristics of the Median

An outstanding characteristic of the median is its *insensitivity* to extreme scores. Consider the following set of scores: 2, 5, 8, 11, 48. The median is 8. This is true in spite of the fact that the set contains one extreme score of 48. Had the 48 been a score of 97, the median would *remain the same*. This characteristic of the median makes it valuable for describing central tendency in certain types of distributions in which the *mean* is an unacceptable measure of central tendency due to its sensitivity to extreme scores. This point will be further elaborated in Section 5.5 when the uses of the three measures of central tendency are discussed.

---

*When you work with an array of numbers where N is odd, the definition of the median does not quite hold; i.e., in the example above, in which the median is 37, two scores lie below it and two above it, as opposed to one-half of N. If the score of 37 is regarded as falling one-half on either side of the median, this disparity is reconciled.

5.4 The Mode

Of all measures of central tendency, the **mode** is the most easily determined since it is obtained by inspection rather than by computation. The mode is simply *the score that occurs with greatest frequency*. For grouped data, the mode is designated as the mid-point of the interval containing the highest frequency count. In Table 4.1 the mode is a score of 112, since it is the midpoint of the class (110–114) containing the greatest frequency.

In some distributions, which we shall not consider here, there will be two high points, which produce the appearance of two humps, as on a camel's back. Such distributions are referred to as being *bimodal.* A distribution containing more than two humps is referred to as being *multimodal.*

Mode

Score that occurs with the greatest frequency.

5.5 Comparison of Mean, Median, and Mode

We have seen that the mean is a measure of central tendency in which the *sum* of the deviations on one side equals the sum of the deviations on the other side. The median, on the other hand, divides the area under the curve into halves so that the *number* of scores below the median equals the *number* of scores above the median.

In general, the arithmetic mean is the preferred statistic for representing central tendency because its function is more versatile. To begin with, the mean is a member of a mathematical system that permits its use in more advanced statistical analyses. We have used deviations from the mean to demonstrate two of its most important characteristics: i.e., the sum of deviations is zero and the sum of squares is minimal. Deviations of scores from the mean provide valuable information about any distribution. We shall be making frequent use of deviation scores throughout the remainder of the text. In contrast, deviation scores from the median and the corresponding squared deviations have only limited applications to more advanced statistical considerations. Another important feature of the mean is that it is the most stable or reliable measure of central tendency. If we were to take repeated samples from a given population, the mean would usually show less fluctuation than either the median or the mode. In other words, the mean generally provides a better estimate of the corresponding population parameter.

On the other hand, there are certain situations in which the median is preferred as the measure of central tendency. When the distribution is symmetrical, the mean and the median are identical. Under these circumstances, the mean should be employed. However, as we have seen, when the distribution is markedly skewed, the mean will provide a misleading estimate of central tendency. In column X_2 of Table 5.2, the mean is 10, even though four of the five scores are below this value. Annual family income is a commonly studied variable in which the median is preferred over the mean, since the distribution of this variable is distinctly skewed in the direction of high salaries, with the result that the mean overestimates the income obtained by most families.

The median is also the measure of choice in distributions in which there are *indeterminate values*. Consider this illustration: When an experimenter tries to run rats in a maze, there will be occasions when one or more rats will simply not run. Their time scores are therefore indeterminate. Their "scores" cannot simply be thrown out, since the fact of their not running may be of considerable significance in evaluating the effects of the independent variable. Under these circumstances, the median should be employed as the measure of central tendency.

The mode is the appropriate statistic whenever a quick, rough estimate of central tendency is desired or when we are interested in the typical case only. It is rarely used in the behavioral sciences.

5.6 *The Mean, Median, and Skewness*

In Chapter 3, we demonstrated several forms of skewed distributions. We pointed out, however, that skew cannot always be determined by inspection. If you have understood the differences between the mean and the median, you should be able to suggest a method for determining whether or not a distribution is skewed and to determine the direction of the skew, if one exists. The basic fact to keep in mind is that the mean is pulled in the direction of the skew whereas the median, unaffected by extreme scores, is not. Thus, when the mean is higher than the median, the distribution may be said to be positively skewed; when the mean is lower than the median, the distribution is negatively skewed. Figure 5.1 demonstrates the relation between the mean

Figure 5.1 The relation between the mean and median in (a) positively and (b) negatively skewed distributions.

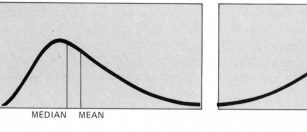
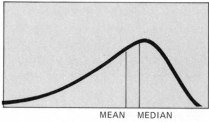

(a)   (b)

and the median in positively and negatively skewed distributions. In Chapter 6, we present a useful index of skew.

Chapter Summary

In this chapter, we discussed, demonstrated the calculation of, and compared three indices of central tendency that are frequently employed in the description of frequency distributions: the mean, the median, and the mode.

We saw that the mean may be defined variously as the sum of scores divided by their number, the point in a distribution about which the summed deviations are equal to zero, or the point in the distribution that makes the sum of the squared deviations around it minimal. The median divides the area under the curve into halves, so that the number of scores below the median equals the number of scores above it. Finally, the mode is defined as the most frequently occurring score. We demonstrated the method for obtaining the weighted mean of a set of means when each of the individual means is based on a different N.

Because it possesses special properties, the mean is the most frequently employed measure of central tendency. However, the sensitivity of the mean to extreme scores that are not balanced on both sides of the distribution makes the median the usual measure of choice when distributions are markedly skewed. The mode is rarely employed in the behavioral sciences.

Finally, we demonstrated the relationship between the mean and the median in negatively and positively skewed distributions.

Terms to Remember

array	**median**
least-squares method	**mode**
mean	**sum of squares**
measure of central tendency	**weighted mean**

EXERCISES

1. Find the mean, the median, and the mode for each of the following sets of measurements. Show that $\sum(X - \overline{X}) = 0$.
   a. 10, 8, 6, 0, 8, 3, 2, 5, 8, 0   b. 1, 3, 3, 5, 5, 5, 7, 7, 9
   c. 119, 5, 4, 4, 4, 3, 1, 0

2. In which of the sets of measurements in Exercise 1 is the mean a poor measure of central tendency? Why?

3. For each of the sets of measurements in Exercise 1, show that *the sum of squares of deviations from the arithmetic mean is less than the sum of squares of deviations about any other score or potential score.*

4. You have calculated the maximum speed of various automobiles. You later discover that all the speedometers were set 5 miles per hour too fast. How will the measures of central tendency based on the corrected data compare with those calculated from the original data?

5. You have calculated measures of central tendency on the weights of barbells, expressing your data in terms of ounces. You decide to recompute after you have divided all the weights by 16 to convert them to pounds. How will this affect the measures of central tendency?

6. Calculate the median and mode for the data in Chapter 3, Exercises 12 and 18.

7. In Exercise 1(c), if the score of 119 were changed to a score of 19, how would the various measures of central tendency be affected?

8. On the basis of the following measures of central tendency, indicate whether or not there is evidence of skew and, if so, what its direction is.

    a. $\bar{X} = 56$ Median = 62   Mode = 68
    b. $\bar{X} = 68$ Median = 62   Mode = 56
    c. $\bar{X} = 62$ Median = 62   Mode = 62
    d. $\bar{X} = 62$ Median = 62   Mode = 30, Mode = 94

9. What is the nature of the distributions in Exercise 8(c) and (d)?

10. Calculate the mean of the following array of scores: 3, 4, 5, 5, 6, 7.
    a. Add a constant, say 2, to each score. Recalculate the mean.

        Generalize: What is the effect on the mean of adding a constant to all scores?

    b. Subtract the same constant from each score. Recalculate the mean.

        Generalize: What is the effect on the mean of subtracting a constant from all scores?

    c. Alternately add and subtract the same constant, say 2, from the array of scores that is, 3 + 2, 4 − 2, 5 + 2, etc). Recalculate the mean.

        Generalize: What is the effect on the mean of adding and subtracting the same constant an equal number of times from an array of scores?

    d. Multiply each score by a constant, say 2. Recalculate the mean.

        Generalize: What is the effect on the mean of multiplying each score by a constant?

    e. Divide each score by the same constant. Recalculate the mean.

        Generalize: What is the effect on the mean of dividing each score by a constant?

11. Refer to Exercise 18, Chapter 3. Which measure of central tendency might best be used to describe group *A?* group *B?* Why?

12. In Section 5.5 we stated that the mean is usually *more reliable* than the median, i.e., less subject to fluctuations. Suppose we conduct an experiment consisting of 30 tosses of three dice, obtaining the following results:

6, 6, 2	5, 4, 3	4, 3, 2	2, 1, 1	6, 5, 3	6, 5, 4
4, 1, 1	4, 4, 3	6, 4, 1	5, 4, 3	5, 1, 1	6, 2, 1
6, 5, 5	6, 6, 4	6, 4, 2	5, 4, 4	6, 5, 2	5, 4, 3
6, 4, 3	5, 3, 2	5, 1, 1	4, 3, 1	6, 3, 3	5, 4, 1
4, 2, 1	6, 3, 3	6, 5, 4	4, 2, 2	6, 6, 5	6, 3, 1

   a. Calculate the 30 means and 30 medians.
   b. Starting with the real limits of the lower interval 0.5–1.5, group the means and medians into separate frequency distributions.
   c. Draw histograms for the two distributions. Do they support the contention that the mean is a more stable estimator of central tendency? Explain.
   d. Assume that we place the medians and means into two separate hats and draw one at random from each. What is the likelihood that
     i. a statistic greater than 5.5 would be obtained?
    ii. a statistic less than 1.5 would be obtained?
   iii. a statistic greater than 5.5 or less than 1.5 would be obtained?

13. If we know that the mean and median of a set of scores are equal, what can we say about the form of the distribution?

14. Give examples of data in which the preferred measure of central tendency would be the
   a. mean,   **b.** median,   **c.** mode.

15. In a study by Grinspoon (1969), nine naive subjects were tested on the Digit Symbol Substitution Test. The scores were considered the baseline measures. The subjects were tested 15 minutes after smoking a heavy dose of marijuana in one test session, and 15 minutes after smoking a placebo in another session. The scores made in these sessions were subtracted from the baseline scores. The resulting difference scores are shown below. A negative sign means that the test score was lower than the baseline score.

Subject	1	2	3	4	5	6	7	8	9
Placebo	−3	10	−3	3	4	−3	2	−1	−1
Heavy dose	5	−17	−7	−3	−7	−9	−6	1	−3

   Find the mean difference scores under (a) the placebo condition and (b) the heavy-dose condition.

16. In the same study cited in Exercise 15, eight chronic users were tested 15 minutes after a heavy-dose session. The difference scores are shown below:

Subject	1	2	3	4	5	6	7	8
Difference score	−4	1	11	3	−2	−6	−4	3

   Find the mean difference score for this group.

17. In a study on the effects of operant conditioning on systolic blood pressure (Benson et al., 1971), the investigators recorded the following blood pressures* of seven subjects during control sessions (no feedback or reinforcement given).

Subject	1	2	3	4	5	6	7
Systolic blood pressure	139.6	213.3	162.3	166.9	157.8	165.7	149.0

Calculate the mean blood pressure of these seven subjects during the control session.

18. In the same study cited in Exercise 17, the blood pressure of these same subjects was recorded during conditioning sessions (feedback and rewards given for lowering systolic blood pressure).

Subject	1	2	3	4	5	6	7
Systolic blood pressure	136.1	179.5	133.1	150.4	141.7	166.6	131.7

Calculate the mean blood pressure of these seven subjects during the conditioning sessions.

19. The difference scores (control minus conditioning sessions) for each subject are given below:

Subject	1	2	3	4	5	6	7
Difference score	−3.5	−33.8	−29.2	−16.5	−16.1	0.9	−17.3

   a. Calculate the mean difference scores for the seven subjects.
   b. Find the difference between the means in Exercise 17 and Exercise 18, and compare this to the mean difference found here. What do you discover?

20. On the basis of examination performance, an instructor identifies the following groups of students:
   a. Those with a percentile rank of 90 or higher.
   b. Those with a percentile rank of 10 or less.
   c. Those with percentile ranks between 40 and 49.
   d. Those with percentile ranks between 51 and 60.
      Which group would the instructor work with if he wished to raise most easily the *median* performance of the total group? Which group would he work with if he wished to raise most easily the *mean* performance of the total group?

21. Which of the measures of central tendency is most affected by the degree of skew in the distribution? Explain.

22. What can we say about the relationships between the mean and median in a negatively skewed distribution? In a positively skewed distribution?

23. Shown at the end of this exercise are the population and the annual rate of growth for six geographical regions. (*Source:* L. Rocks and R. P. Runyon, *The Energy*

---

*The measures were actually the median blood pressure during the last five control and last five conditioning sessions.

Crisis. New York: Crown Publishers, 1972.) Calculate the weighted percent of growth over all six regions.

Region	Present Population (in millions)	Annual Rate of Growth (Percent)
North America	225	1.1
South America	276	2.9
Europe	456	0.8
USSR	241	1.0
Africa	344	2.4
Asia	1990	2.0

24. What is the mean number of cleaners sold per sales agent per day?
Mr. A sells a mean of 1.75 vacuum cleaners per day in 4 days.
Ms. B sells a mean of 2.0 per day in 5 days.
Mr. C sells a mean of 2.4 per day in 5 days.
Ms. D sells a mean of 2.5 per day in 4 days.
Mr. E sells a mean of 2.0 per day in 3 days.
Ms. F sells a mean of 1.67 per day in 3 days.

25. Suppose that a given merchant sells the following number of apples from Monday through Saturday.

a. 30,   30,   30,   30,   30,   30
What are the mean, median, and mode?

b. 25,   30,   35,   30,   35,   25
What are the mean, median, and mode?

c. 10,   25,   30,   36,   25,   30
Calculate the mean, median, and mode.

26. Work the following problems:
a. In Exercise 25(c) show that $\Sigma(X - \bar{X}) = 0$.
b. Show that the sum of the deviations from the median and from the mode do not equal zero.
c. Why do the deviations from the mean equal zero, whereas the deviations from the median and mode do not?

27. Determine the mean, median, and mode for the following array:

4, 4, 5, 5, 6, 7, 7, 7, 8, 8

28. A freelance writer earns a mean of $15.00 per hour for 4 hours of work, $17.50 per hour for 2 hours of work, $13.33 per hour for 3 hours, and $14.00 per hour for 1 hour. What are the writer's mean earnings per hour?

29. Two manufacturers state that the "average" life of their refrigerators is seven years. However, upon drawing a random sample of durations, a person finds that the life (in years) of 20 machines from manufacturer A is as follows:

5, 5, 5, 6, 6, 6, 6, 7, 7, 7, 7, 7, 7, 8, 8, 8, 8, 9, 9, 9

A sample of machines from manufacturer B shows durations of:

2, 3, 4, 5, 5, 5, 5, 6, 6, 6, 7, 7, 7, 7, 7, 8, 8, 20, 20, 20

What measurement of "average" was each manufacturer reporting? Which machine would probably be the best investment? With which machine would you feel more confident in stating that the "average" life is 7 years?

30. At the beginning of 1972, there were 27 nuclear power plants in the U.S., with a mean output of 436.5 megawatts. An additional 54 plants, with a mean output of 847.8 megawatts, were being built. Finally, 52 additional plants were planned, with a mean output of 991.7 megawatts.
    a. What is the anticipated mean output, in megawatts, of all 133 nuclear power plants?
    b. What will be the total output of all 133 power plants?

*31. In Chapter 3, Exercise 28, we described a sampling experiment in which samples of $N = 2$ were drawn from a population of seven scores. We constructed a table of sums of all possible combinations of seven scores, taken two at a time. Since $N = 2$ in each sample, that sum can be converted to a mean by dividing by 2. Construct a table showing all 49 means.

*32. Construct a frequency distribution of the means calculated in Exercise 31, above.

*33. Selecting samples of $N = 2$ as we did in Exercise 28 of Chapter 3, what percentage of the time would we expect to obtain (round to nearest percent)?
    a. A mean equal to 6.
    b. A mean of 5.5 or greater.
    c. A mean of 2.5 or less.
    d. A mean equal to or greater than 5.5, or equal to or less than 0.5.

*34. Calculate the mean of the sample means in Exercise 33, above. (*Hint:* Treat each mean as a score, and follow the computational procedures for calculating the mean with ungrouped frequency distributions.) How does the mean of the sample means compare with the original population mean?

6

Measures of Dispersion

6.1 Introduction

In the introduction to Chapter 4, we saw that a score by itself is meaningless, and takes on meaning only when it is compared with other scores or other statistics. Thus, if we know the mean of the distribution of a given variable, we can determine whether a particular score is higher or lower than the mean. But how much higher or lower? It is clear at this point that a measure of central tendency such as the mean provides only a limited amount of information. To more fully describe a distribution, or to more fully interpret a score, we require additional information concerning the **dispersion** of scores about our measure of central tendency.

Consider Fig. 6.1, parts (a) and (b). In both examples of frequency curves, the mean of the distribution is exactly the same. However, note the difference in the interpretations of a score of 128. In (a), because the scores are widely dispersed about the mean, a score of 128 may be considered only moderately high. Quite a few individuals in the distribution scored above 128, as indicated by the area to the right of 128. In (b), on the other hand, the scores are compactly distributed about the same mean. This is a more *homogeneous* distribution. Consequently the score of 128 is now virtually at the top of the distribution and it may therefore be considered a very high score.

It can be seen, then, that in interpreting individual scores, we must find a companion to the mean or the median. This companion must in some way express the degree of dispersion of scores about the measure of central tendency. We shall discuss five such measures of disperson or variability: the **range,** the **semi-interquartile range,** the **mean deviation,** the **vari-**

Dispersion

The spread or variability of scores about the measure of central tendency.

Figure 6.1 Two frequency curves with identical means but different dispersion or variability.

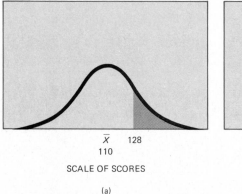

$\overline{X}$ 128
110

SCALE OF SCORES

(a)

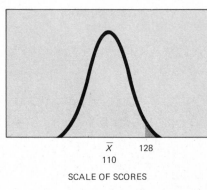

$\overline{X}$ 128
110

SCALE OF SCORES

(b)

106

Shaving peak is reducing variability

BOX 6.1

When we have found a measure of central tendency, we have taken a first and important step in describing a distribution. To complete our description, we must find some comparison measure that tells us something about how widely the scores are dispersed or spread about the central value. Interest in dispersion is more than a mere academic exercise engaged in by statisticians during their leisure hours. The following excerpt from *Winning with Statistics* makes the point that a consideration of variability is of fundamental importance in the everyday affairs of the real world.

────────────

At times our preoccupation with averages can cause us to lose sight of the fact that many of the most important workaday decisions are based on considerations of the extremes, rather than on the middle of a distribution. Imagine what life would be like if:

- Our highways were constructed to accommodate the average traffic load of vehicles of average weight.
- Mass transit systems were designed to move only the average number of passengers (i.e., total passengers per day divided by 24 hours) during each hour of the day.
- Bridges, homes, and industrial and commercial buildings were constructed to withstand the average wind or the average earthquake.
- Telephone lines and switchboards were sufficient in number to accommodate only the average number of phone calls per hour.
- Your friendly local electric utility calculated the year-round average electrical demand and constructed facilities to provide only this average demand.
- Emergency services provided average personnel and facilities during all hours of the day and all seasons of the year.

- Our space program provided emergency procedures for only the average type of failure.

Chaos is the word for it. Utter chaos. The fact of the matter is that virtually all of human endeavor must gear itself to meet the extreme conditions known as peak load. If you don't mind my digressing a bit, let me say that the peak load problem is, at once, one of the great challenges and monumental opportunities that we face today. It is because of peak load that many community facilities and services are barely used during certain time periods and are swamped at others. Assuming that the years ahead are sure to place a continued stress on resources, both natural and human, we shall not long be able to sustain the luxury of "gearing up to peak."

The alternative is to raise the valleys and lower the peaks of demand. In statistical terms, the goal is to obtain the same average while reducing the variability. By doing so, we are able to increase and improve our use of existing facilities. To illustrate, some years ago my family and I visited Paris to plug the publication of the French edition of *The Energy Crisis*. We spent a great deal of our time riding the wonderful Metro (Paris subway system). Besides the quietness of the ride and the attractiveness of the stations (the one at the Louvre actually has faithful reproductions of great works of art and sculpture), we marveled at the relatively uncrowded condition of the subways during rush hours. A few inquiries elicited an explanation—commerce and industry in Paris operate on a staggered system of opening and closing hours. While Jean-Paul still sleeps, Jacques is on his way to work. The result of this "peak-shaving" strategy is to spread the morning and evening rush more evenly, thereby permitting a more efficient use of rolling stock and sparing many frayed nerves.

Look for the utilities to solve their present dilemma of perpetual rate increases by finding ways to even out both the diurnal and seasonal demand for electricity.

Excerpted from R. P. Runyon, *Winning with Statistics.* Reading, Mass.: Addison-Wesley, 1977.

ance, and the **standard deviation.** Of the five, we will find the standard deviation to be our most useful measure of disperson in both descriptive and inferential statistics. In advanced inferential statistics, as in analysis of variance (Chapter 15), the variance will become a most useful measure of variability.

6.2 *The Range*

When we calculated the various measures of central tendency, we located a *single point* along the scale of scores and identified it as the mean, the median, or the mode. When our interest shifts to measures of dispersion, however, we must look for an index of variability which indicates the *distance* along the scale of scores.

One of the first measures of distance that comes to mind is the so-called **crude range.** The range is by far the simplest and the most straightforward measure of dispersion. It consists simply of the scale distance between the largest and the smallest score. Thus, if the highest score is 140 and the lowest is 30, the range is 110.

Although the range is meaningful, it is of little use because of its marked instability. Note that if there is one extreme score in a distribution, the dispersion of scores will appear to be large when in fact the removal of that score may reveal an otherwise "compact" distribution. Several years ago, an inmate of an institution for retarded persons was found to have an I.Q. score in the 140s. Imagine the erroneous impression that would result if the range of scores for the inmates was reported as, say, 140–20 or 120! Stated another way, the range reflects only the two most extreme scores in a distribution.

Crude Range

Measure of dispersion: The scale distance between the largest and the smallest score.

6.3 *The Semi-interquartile Range*

In order to overcome the instability of the crude range as a measure of dispersion, the **semi-interquartile range** is sometimes employed. The semi-interquartile range is calculated simply by subtracting the score at the 25th percentile (referred to as the first quartile or Q_1) from the score at the 75th percentile (the third quartile or Q_3) and dividing by 2 (see Fig. 6.2). This measure of variability is most frequently used in conjunction with the median when extreme skew rules out the use of the mean as the measure of central tendency and the standard deviation as the measure of dispersion. In the behavioral sciences we find that reaction-time scores, heart-rate measures, and income figures are typically sufficiently skewed to justify the use of the median and the

Semi-interquartile Range

A measure of variability obtained by subtracting the score at the 25th percentile from the score at the 75th percentile and dividing by 2.

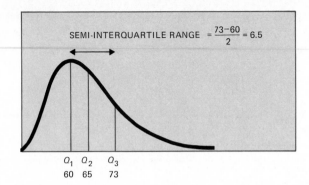

Figure 6.2 The semi-interquartile range and a skewed distribution. Like the median (Q_2), the semi-interquartile range is not sensitive to extreme scores at one or the other end of the distribution.

semi-interquartile range as measures of central tendency and dispersion, respectively. In addition, both are often used with ordinally scaled data. Although this measure of variability of scores is far more meaningful than the crude range, it has two significant shortcomings: (1) like the crude range, it does not by itself permit the precise interpretation of a score within a distribution, and (2) like the median, it does not enter into any of the "higher" mathematical relationships that are basic to inferential statistics. Consequently we shall not devote any more discussion to the semi-interquartile range.

6.4 *The Mean Deviation*

In Chapter 5, we pointed out that, when we are dealing with data from normally distributed populations, the mean is our most useful measure of central tendency. We obtained the mean by adding together all the scores and dividing them by N. If we carried these procedures one step further, we could subtract the mean from each score, sum the deviations from the mean, and thereby obtain an estimate of the typical amount of deviation from the mean. By dividing by N, we would have a measure that would be analogous to the arithmetic mean except that it would represent the dispersion of scores from the arithmetic mean.

If you think for a moment about the characteristics of the mean, which we discussed in the preceding chapter, you will encounter one serious difficulty. The sum of the deviations of all scores from the mean must add up to zero. Thus if we defined the **mean deviation** (M.D.) as this sum divided by N, the

Mean Deviation (Average Deviation)

Sum of the deviations of each score from the mean, without regard to sign, divided by the number of scores.

mean deviation would have to be zero. You will recall that we employed the fact that $\Sigma(X - \overline{X}) = 0$ to arrive at one of several definitions of the mean.

Now, if we were to add all the deviations *without regard to sign* and divide by N, we would still have a measure reflecting the mean deviation from the arithmetic mean. The resulting statistic would, of course, be based upon the **absolute value** of the deviations. The absolute value of a positive number or of zero is the number itself. The absolute value of a negative number can be found by changing the sign to a positive one. Thus the absolute value of $+3$ or -3 is 3. The symbol for an absolute value is $|\ \ |$. Thus $|-3| = 3$.

The calculation of the mean deviation is shown in Table 6.1.

As a basis for comparison of the disperson of several distributions, the mean deviation has some value. For example, the greater the mean deviation, the greater the dispersion of scores. However, for interpreting scores within a distribution, the mean deviation is less useful, since there is no precise mathematical relationship between the mean deviation, as such, and the location of scores within a distribution.

Absolute Value of a Number

The value of a number without regard to sign.

Table 6.1 Computational procedures for calculating the M.D. from an array of scores.

X	$(\lvert X - \overline{X}\rvert)$	Computation
9	$\lvert +4 \rvert$	$\text{M.D.} = \dfrac{\Sigma(\lvert X - \overline{X}\rvert)^*}{N}$ (6.1)
8	$\lvert +3 \rvert$	
7	$\lvert +2 \rvert$	
7	$\lvert +2 \rvert$	$\text{M.D.} = \dfrac{26}{15} = 1.73$
7	$\lvert +2 \rvert$	
5	$\lvert\ 0\ \rvert$	
5	$\lvert\ 0\ \rvert$	
5	$\lvert\ 0\ \rvert$	
5	$\lvert\ 0\ \rvert$	
4	$\lvert -1 \rvert$	
4	$\lvert -1 \rvert$	
3	$\lvert -2 \rvert$	
3	$\lvert -2 \rvert$	
2	$\lvert -3 \rvert$	
1	$\lvert -4 \rvert$	
$\Sigma X = 75$	$\Sigma(\lvert X - \overline{X}\rvert) = 26$	$N = 15$ $\overline{X} = 5$

*For scores arranged in the form of a frequency distribution, the following formula for the mean deviation should be used:

$$\text{M.D.} = \Sigma f(\lvert X - \overline{X}\rvert)/N.$$

You may wonder why we bother demonstrating the mean deviation when it is of so little use in statistical analysis. As we shall see, the standard deviation and the variance, which have great value in statistical analysis, are very close relatives of the mean deviation.

6.5 The Variance (s^2) and Standard Deviation (s)*

Following a perusal of Table 6.1, you might be tempted to make this speculation: "We had to treat the values in the column headed ($X - \overline{X}$) as absolute numbers because their sum was equal to zero. Why could we not square each ($X - \overline{X}$) and then add the squared deviations? In this way we would legitimately rid ourselves of the minus signs, while still preserving the information that is inherent in these deviation scores."

The answer: We could, if by so doing we arrived at a statistic of greater value in judging dispersion than those we have already discussed. It is most fortunate that the standard deviation, based on the squaring of these deviation scores, is of immense value in three different respects.

1. The standard deviation reflects dispersion of scores, so that the variability of different distributions may be compared in terms of the standard deviation (s).

2. The standard deviation permits the *precise* interpretation of scores within a distribution.

3. The standard deviation, like the mean, is a member of a *mathematical system* that permits its use in more advanced statistical considerations. Thus we employ measures based on s when we advance into inferential statistics.

4. An understanding of the meaning of the standard deviation hinges on a knowledge of the relationship between the standard deviation and the normal distribution. Thus, in order to be able to interpret the standard deviations that are calculated in this chapter, it will be necessary to explore the relationship between the raw scores, the standard deviation, and the normal distribution. This material is presented in the following chapter.

---

*We remind you that italic letters are used to represent sample statistics, and Greek letters to represent population parameters; e.g., σ^2 represents the population variance and σ represents the population standard deviation. The problem of estimating population parameters from sample values will be discussed in Chapter 12.

Calculation of Variance and Standard Deviation, Mean-Deviation Method, with Ungrouped Scores

Variance

Sum of the squared deviations from the mean, divided by N.

The **variance** is defined verbally as *the sum of the squared deviations from the mean divided by N.* Symbolically, it is represented as

$$s^2 = \frac{\sum(X - \bar{X})^2}{N}. \qquad (6.2)*$$

Sum of Squares

Deviation of each score from the mean, squared and then summed. Represented as SS.

You will recall that the sum of the $(X - \bar{X})^2$ column, that is $\sum(X - \bar{X})^2$, is known as the **sum of squares** and that this sum is minimal when deviations are taken about the mean. From this point on in the course, we encounter the sum of squares with regularity. It will take on a number of different forms, depending on the procedures that we elect for calculating it. However, it is important to remember that, whatever the form, the sum of squares represents the *sum of the squared deviations from the mean.* Since it is more convenient, we use the symbol SS to represent $\sum(X - \bar{X})^2$. Thus

$$SS = \sum(X - \bar{X})^2. \qquad (6.3)$$

The variance then becomes

$$s^2 = \frac{SS}{N}. \qquad (6.4)$$

Standard Deviation

Extremely useful measure of dispersion defined as the square root of the sum of the squared deviations from the mean, divided by N.

The **standard deviation** is the *square root* of the variance and is defined as

$$s = \sqrt{\frac{SS}{N}}. \qquad (6.5)$$

The computational procedures for calculating the standard deviation, utilizing the mean deviation method, are shown in Table 6.2.

The mean deviation method was shown only to impress you with the fact that the standard deviation is based on the deviation of scores from the mean. This method is extremely unwieldy for use in calculation, particularly when the mean is a fractional value, which is usually the case. Consequently in the suc-

---

*The important distinction between biased $\sum(X - \bar{X})^2/N$ and unbiased $\sum(X - \bar{X})^2/(N - 1)$ estimates of the population variance will be discussed in Chapter 12.

Table 6.2 Computational procedures for calculation s, mean-deviation method, from an array of scores.

X	$X - \overline{X}$	$(X - \overline{X})^2$	Computation
9	+4	16	
8	+3	9	$s = \sqrt{\dfrac{\sum(X - \overline{X})^2}{N}} = \sqrt{\dfrac{SS}{N}}$
7	+2	4	
7	+2	4	
7	+2	4	$= \sqrt{72/15}$
5	0	0	$= \sqrt{4.80}$
5	0	0	
5	0	0	$= 2.19$
5	0	0	
4	−1	1	
4	−1	1	
3	−2	4	
3	−2	4	
2	−3	9	
1	−4	16	
$\sum X = 75$	$\sum(X - \overline{X}) = 0$	$\sum(X - \overline{X})^2 = 72$	$N = 15$ $\overline{X} = 5$

ceeding paragraphs, we will examine a number of alternative ways of calculating the sum of squares.

Calculation of Standard Deviation, Raw-Score Method, with Ungrouped Scores

It can be shown mathematically that

$$SS = \sum X^2 - \frac{(\sum X)^2}{N}, \qquad (6.6)$$

where

$$SS = \sum (X - \overline{X})^2 = \sum X^2 - 2\sum X\overline{X} + \sum \overline{X}^2.$$

However, $\sum X = N\overline{X}$,* and summing the mean square over all values of $\overline{X}$ is

---

*Since $\overline{X} = \sum X/N$, it follows that $\sum X = N\overline{X}$.

the same as multiplying by N (see Generalization 1, Chapter 2). Thus

$$SS = \sum X^2 - 2N\bar{X}^2 + N\bar{X}^2$$

$$= \sum X^2 - N\bar{X}^2 = \sum X^2 - N\left(\frac{\sum X}{N}\right)^2$$

$$= \sum X^2 - \frac{N(\sum X)^2}{N^2}$$

$$= \sum X^2 - \frac{(\sum X)^2}{N}.$$

Dividing the sum of squares by N yields the variance

$$s^2 = \frac{SS}{N}.$$

In turn, extracting the square root of the variance yields the standard deviation

$$s = \sqrt{\frac{SS}{N}}.$$

Table 6.3   **Computational procedures for calculating
s, raw-score method, from an array of
scores.**

X	X^2	Computation
9	81	
8	64	$SS = \sum X^2 - \dfrac{(\sum X)^2}{N}$
7	49	
7	49	
7	49	$= 447 - \dfrac{(75)^2}{15}$
5	25	
5	25	$= 447 - 375 = 72$
5	25	
5	25	$s^2 = \dfrac{SS}{N}$
4	16	
4	16	
3	9	$= \dfrac{72}{15} = 4.80$
3	9	
2	4	$s = \sqrt{4.80} = 2.19$
1	1	
$\sum X = 75$	$\sum X^2 = 447$	$N = 15$ $\bar{X} = 5$

Table 6.3 summarizes the computational procedures. You will note that the result agrees with the answer we obtained by the mean deviation method.

CASE EXAMPLE • 6.1
The Beat of a Different Tone

If an individual hears two fundamental tones in each ear but with the frequency of one of the two tones in one ear modified slightly, the subject will report a beat that appears to originate in the central nervous system. Table 6.4 shows the data for one subject. For one ear, the fundamental tone was 3,550 Hz with the lower tone differing by the amount shown in the table. For the other ear, the lower tone was either the same or two hertz higher. The subject was asked to report when a beat was heard.

The mean percentage of correct discriminations is $\overline{X} = 560/7 = 80\%$. The sum of squares is

$$SS = 45,638 - \frac{(560)^2}{7}$$
$$= 45,638 - 44,800$$
$$= 838.$$

Table 6.4 **Correct discrimination, expressed as a percentage, between beat and no-beat conditions for a single subject.**

Frequency Separation of Fundamental Tone (in hertz)	Correct Discriminations (%)	
	X	X^2
25	94	8,836
75	85	7,225
125	84	7,056
175	92	8,464
225	74	5,476
275	65	4,225
325	66	4,356
	$\sum X = 560$	$\sum X^2 = 45,638$

Therefore, the variance (s^2) is $838/7 = 119.7143$, and the standard deviation (s) is $\sqrt{119.7143} = 10.94$.

Calculation of Standard Deviation, Raw-Score Method, from an Ungrouped Frequency Distribution

If we take the data in Table 6.2 and arrange them into an ungrouped frequency distribution, we obtain

X	f	X	f
9	1	4	2
8	1	3	2
7	3	2	1
6	0	1	1
5	4		

To calculate SS, multipy each score by its corresponding frequency and then sum. This yields $\sum fX$. Next, to find $\sum fX^2$, square each score, multiply by its corresponding frequency, and sum. Place these values in the formula for sum of squares:

$$SS = \sum fX^2 - \frac{\left(\sum fX\right)^2}{N}.$$

Finally, substitute this value in the formula for the standard deviation:

$$s = \sqrt{\frac{SS}{N}}.$$

Table 6.5 summarizes the procedure for obtaining the standard deviation from an ungrouped frequency distribution.

Errors to Avoid

In using the raw-score method to calculate the standard deviation, it is common for students to confuse the similar-appearing terms $\sum X^2$ (or $\sum fX^2$) and $(\sum X)^2$ (or $[\sum fX]^2$). It is important to remember that the former represents the *sum of the squares* of each of the individual scores, whereas the latter represents the *square of the sum* of the scores. By definition, it is impossible to

Table 6.5 **Procedures for calculating the standard deviation of scores from an ungrouped frequency distribution.**

X	f	fX	X²	fX²	Computation
9	1	9	81	81	$SS = \sum fX^2 - \dfrac{(\sum fX)^2}{N}$
8	1	8	64	64	
7	3	21	49	147	$= 447 - \dfrac{(75)^2}{N}$
6	0	0	36	0	
5	4	20	25	100	$= 447 - 375 = 72$
4	2	8	16	32	
3	2	6	9	18	$s^2 = \dfrac{SS}{N} = \dfrac{72}{15} = 4.80$
2	1	2	4	4	
1	1	1	1	1	$s = \sqrt{4.80} = 2.19$
	$N = 15$	$\sum fX = 75$		$\sum fX^2 = 447$	

obtain a negative sum of squares or a negative standard deviation. In the event that you obtain a negative value under the square-root sign, you have probably confused these two terms.

A rule of thumb for estimating the standard deviation is that the ratio of the range to the standard deviation is rarely smaller than 2 or greater than 6. In our preceding example, the ratio is $9/2.19 = 4.11$. If we obtain a standard deviation that yields a ratio greater than 6 or smaller than 2, we have almost certainly made an error.

The Mean, Median, Standard Deviation, and Pearson's Coefficient of Skew

In Section 5.6, we noted that the direction of skew can be judged by the position of the mean relative to the median. When the mean is higher than the median, i.e., when $[\overline{X} - \text{Mdn}]$ is a positive value, the distribution of scores is positively skewed. Conversely, when $[\overline{X} - \text{Mdn}]$ is a negative value, the scores are negatively skewed. However, these indices of *direction* of skew tell us little about the amount of skew. E. S. Pearson, whom many consider the founder of modern statistics, proposed the following coefficient of skew (sk):

$$sk = \frac{3(\overline{X} - \text{Median})}{s} \qquad (6.7)$$

Let's apply this formula to the data presented in Case Example 6.1, where we found the mean to be 80, the standard deviation to be 10.94, and the median to be 84. Thus, the index of skew is

$$sk = \frac{3(80 - 84)}{10.95}$$
$$= -1.10$$

The negative sign indicates that the scores are negatively skewed. If the distribution is symmetrical, the mean and median are the same. Therefore, $sk = 0$. However, it is widely accepted that data sets with indices of skew ranging between ± 0.50 may be considered sufficiently symmetrical for most practical applications. Since the skew of the data in Case Example 6.1 exceeds $|0.50|$, the distribution of scores are not regarded as symmetrical.

Chapter Summary

We have seen that to fully describe a distribution of scores we require more than a measure of central tendency. We must be able to describe how these scores are dispersed about central tendency. In this connection we discussed five measures of dispersion: the range, the semi-interquartile range, the mean deviation, the standard deviation, and the variance. (See Table 6.6.)

For normally distributed variables, the two measures based on the squaring of deviations about the mean (the variance and the standard deviation) are maximally useful. We discussed and demonstrated the procedures for calculating the standard deviation employing the mean-deviation method and the raw-

Table 6.6 Summary procedures: Calculating the variance and the standard deviation from an array of scores.

X	X^2	Steps
7	49	**1.** Count the number of scores to obtain N. $N = 12$.
6	36	**2.** Sum the scores in the X column to obtain $\sum X$. $\sum X = 48$.
6	36	
5	25	**3.** Square each score and place it in the adjacent column.
5	25	**4.** Sum the X^2 column to obtain $\sum X^2 = 242$.
5	25	
4	16	**5.** Substitute the values found in steps 2 and 4 in the formula for sum
4	16	of squares.
3	9	
2	4	$$SS = \sum X^2 - \frac{(\sum X)^2}{N} = 242 - \frac{2304}{12} = 50$$
1	1	
0	0	**6.** Substitute SS in the formulas for s^2 and s.

$\sum X = 48$ $\sum X^2 = 242$

$(\sum X)^2 = 48^2$

$= 2304$

$$s^2 = \frac{SS}{N} = \frac{50}{12} = 4.17, \qquad s = \sqrt{4.17} = 2.04$$

score method with ungrouped frequency distributions. We also pointed out several of the errors commonly made in calculating standard deviations.

Terms to Remember

absolute value of a number

dispersion

mean deviation (average deviation)

range

semi-interquartile range

standard deviation

sum of squares

variance

EXERCISES

1. Calculate s^2 and s for the following array of scores: 3, 4, 5, 5, 6, 7.

   a. Add a constant, say, 2, to each score. Recalculate s^2 and s. Would the results be any different if you had added a larger constant, say, 200?

      Generalize: What is the effect on s and s^2 of adding a constant to an array of scores? Does the variability increase as we increase the magnitude of the scores?

   b. Subtract the same constant from each score. Recalculate s^2 and s. Would the results be any different if you had subtracted a larger constant, say, 200?

      Generalize: What is the effect on s and s^2 of subtracting a constant from an array of scores?

   c. Alternately add and subtract the same constant from each score (i.e., 3 + 2, 4 − 2, 5 + 2, etc.). Recalculate s and s^2. Would the results be any different if you had added and subtracted a larger constant?

      Generalize: What is the effect on s and s^2 of adding and subtracting a constant from an array of scores? (*Note:* This generalization is extremely important with relation to subsequent chapters where we discuss the effect of random errors on measures of variability.)

   d. Multiply each score by a constant, say, 2. Recalculate s and s^2.

      Generalize: What is the effect on s and s^2 of multiplying each score by a constant?

   e. Divide each score by the same constant. Recalculate s and s^2.

      Generalize: What is the effect on s and s^2 of dividing each score by a constant?

2. Compare your generalizations with those you made in relation to the mean (see Exercise 10, Chapter 5).

3. A rigorous definition of a measure of variation as a descriptive statistic would involve the following properties: (a) if a constant is added to or subtracted from each score or observation, the measure of variation remains unchanged; (b) if each score is multiplied or divided by a constant, the measure of variation is also multiplied or divided by that number. Check the following for the satisfaction of these conditions:

   i. the mean,   **ii.** the median,   **iii.** the mode,
   iv. the mean deviation,   **v.** the standard deviation,   **vi.** the variance.

   If the properties defining measures of dispersion were extended to include *powers* of the constant by which each score is multiplied, would the variance qualify as a measure of dispersion?

4. How would the standard deviation be affected by the situations described in Exercises 4 and 5, Chapter 5?

5. What is the nature of the distribution if $s = 0$?

6. Calculate the standard deviations for the following sets of measurements.
   a. 10, 8, 6, 0, 8, 3, 2, 2, 8, 0   **b.** 1, 3, 3, 5, 5, 5, 7, 7, 9
   c. 20, 1, 2, 5, 4, 4, 4, 0   **d.** 5, 5, 5, 5, 5, 5, 5, 5, 5, 5

7. Why is the standard deviation in part (c) of Exercise 6 so large? Describe the effect of extreme deviations on *s*.

8. Determine the range for the sets of measurements in Exercise 6. For which of these is the range a misleading index of variability, and why?

9. In Exercises 15 and 16, Chapter 5, find the variances and standard deviations of the difference scores made by the naive subjects, (a) placebo and (b) heavy dose, and those made by the (c) chronic users in the marijuana study by Grinspoon. (*Hint:* To expedite calculations when there are negative scores, add a constant to all scores that is equal to or greater than the absolute value of the largest negative score.)

10. Calculate the mean and standard deviation for the set of 40 scores found in Exercise 5, Chapter 3.

11. A comparison shopper compares prices of plums at a number of different supermarkets. She finds the following prices per pound (in cents): 56, 65, 48, 73, 59, 72, 63, 65, 60, 63, 44, 79, 63, 61, 66, 69, 64, 71, 58, 63.
   a. Find the mean.
   b. Find the range, semi-interquartile range, and mean deviation.
   c. Find the standard deviation and variance.

12. Give one advantage of the standard deviation over the variance. Give an example.

13. Referring to Exercise 22 Chapter 3, find the mean and standard deviation of the number of quarts of milk sold at the supermarket.

14. List at least three specific instances in which a measure of variability was important in describing a group.

15. List at least three specific instances in which a measure of variability was important in comparing a group of people.

16. The following data list the maximum daily temperature recorded for New York City for the months of January and May, 1965 and 1966.* For each month and year, do (a)–(c).

Date	Jan. 1965	Jan. 1966	May 1965	May 1966	Date	Jan. 1965	Jan. 1966	May 1965	May 1966
1	35	62	71	66	17	16	39	83	68
2	29	52	77	60	18	25	38	73	66
3	32	46	71	68	19	25	35	70	64
4	39	45	90	59	20	38	44	80	84
5	43	53	62	70	21	36	42	72	85
6	44	47	78	83	22	50	39	80	75
7	44	47	52	66	23	47	37	79	85
8	49	44	60	61	24	32	38	70	80
9	55	30	78	52	25	38	32	79	76
10	40	48	92	57	26	44	26	94	84
11	35	42	88	63	27	42	36	92	82
12	36	27	78	57	28	38	19	83	73
13	41	32	80	67	29	27	23	68	82
14	37	42	74	64	30	20	38	67	73
15	19	41	82	74	31	30	28	74	68
16	17	26	87	71					

    a. Find the mean.   **b.** Find the range and mean deviation.
    c. Find the standard deviation and variance.

17. Suppose merchant A sold a quart of milk for $0.40 and the standard deviation of this price was 0 during the last month. What was the price on the third day of the month? on the fifteenth day?

18. Calculate the crude range, variance, and standard deviation for both manufacturers in Exercise 29, Chapter 5.

19. Monthly normal precipitation (in inches)† for 4 urban areas. Determine the yearly variance and standard deviation for each.

Stations	Jan	Feb	Mar	Apr	May	June	July	Aug	Sept	Oct	Nov	Dec
Barrow, Alaska	0.2	0.2	0.1	0.1	0.1	0.4	0.8	0.9	0.6	0.5	0.2	0.2
Burlington, Vt.	2.0	1.8	2.1	2.6	3.0	3.5	3.9	3.4	3.3	3.0	2.6	2.1
Honolulu, Hawaii	3.8	3.3	2.9	1.3	1.0	0.3	0.4	0.9	1.0	1.8	2.2	3.0
Seattle-Tacoma, Washington	5.7	4.2	3.8	2.4	1.7	1.6	0.8	1.0	2.1	4.0	5.4	6.3

****20.** Refer to Exercise 32, Chapter 5. Calculate the standard deviation of the frequency distribution of sample means. (*Hint:* Treat each mean as a score, and employ the raw-score method for obtaining the standard deviation from an ungrouped frequency distribution.)

---

*The data for this problem were extracted from *The World Almanac*, pp. 558–559, New York: Newspaper Enterprise Association, Inc. 1967. Reprinted by permission.
†*Source:* National Climatic Center, NOAA, U.S. Department of Commerce.

21. Find the variance and standard deviations of the systolic blood pressure scores (Benson *et al.,* 1971) appearing in Exercises 17–19, Chapter 5:
    a. Control sessions.
    b. Conditioning sessions.
    c. Difference scores.

22. Refer to Case Example 5.1. Calculate the standard deviation of the
    a. β-endorphin levels of the near-SID infants.
    b. Control infants.

23. Refer to Case Example 5.1. Calculate *sk* for the β-endorphin levels of the near-SID infants.

7

Standard Deviation/ Standard Normal Distribution

7.1 Introduction

We previously noted that to the behavioral scientist scores derived from scales are generally meaningless by themselves. To take on meaning they must be compared to the distribution of scores from some reference group. Indeed, the scores derived from any scale, including those employed by the physical scientists, become more meaningful when they are compared to some reference group of objects or persons. Thus, if we were to learn that a Canadian fisherman caught a northern pike weighing 50 pounds, we might or might not be impressed, depending upon the extent of our knowledge concerning the usual weight of this type of fish. However, once a reference group is established, the measurement becomes meaningful. Since most northern pike weigh under 10 pounds and only rarely achieve weights as high as 20 pounds, the achievement of our apocryphal fisherman must be considered Bunyanesque.

7.2 The Concept of z-Scores

In interpreting a single score, we want to place it in some position with respect to a collection of scores from some reference group. In Chapter 4, you learned to place a score by determining its percentile rank. It will be recalled that the percentile rank of a score tells us the percentage of scores that are of lower scale value. Another approach for interpretation of a single score might be to view it with reference to some central point, such as the mean. Thus a score of 20 in a distribution with a mean of 23 might be reported as -3. Finally, we might express this deviation score in terms of standard deviation units. Thus, if our standard deviation is 1.5, the score of 20 would be two standard deviations below the mean (that is, $-3/1.5 = -2$). This process of dividing a deviation of a score from the mean by the standard deviation is known as the transformation to **z-scores.** Symbolically, z is defined as

z-Score

A score that represents the deviation of a specific score from the mean and is expressed in standard deviation units.

$$z = \frac{X - \overline{X}}{s}.^*$$

(7.1)

Note that *every* score in the distribution may be transformed into a z-score, in which case each z will represent the *deviation of a specific score from the mean, expressed in standard deviation units.*

---

*It is sometimes useful to go from a z-score to a raw score: $X = zs + \overline{X}$.

So you want to interpret a test score?

BOX 7.1

As we previously noted, a score in and of itself is meaningless. In this chapter, we see that the z-score transformation provides a precise means of interpreting any value of a variable when the scores are normally distributed. The following excerpt from *Winning with Statistics* illustrates the use of the z-score transformation in the interpretation of test scores on standard psychological and educational tests.

Here are the step-by-step procedures for taking all of the mystery out of the interpretation of test scores on standard psychological and educational tests.

1. Determine the mean and the standard deviation of the test. Sometimes different means and standard deviations are given for different age groups. Be sure to find these two measures for the age group in which you are interested. Sources of this information are the Administration Booklet for the particular test and the Buros Mental Measurement Yearbook. Since the Administration Booklets are not usually available to nonprofessionals, the Mental Measurement Yearbook is your best bet. If it is not found in your local library, it is almost certain to be in the collection of your nearest college and university library.

2. Transform the score you are interested in interpreting to a z-score using the following formula:

$$z = \frac{Score - Mean}{Standard\ deviation}.$$

If you are interested in interpreting a score of 40 and you know that the mean and standard deviation are 30 and 9, respectively, you would have

$$z = \frac{40 - 30}{9} = \frac{10}{9} = 1.1$$

3. Look up a positive value of 1.1 under column B of the accompanying table. Here we find an entry of 86. This means that 86 percent of a comparison group with which this score is being compared obtained scores lower than 86. Only 14 percent (column C) scored higher.

There it is. It's as easy as that.

Percent of Scores Above and Below a Given z-Score

A	B	C
z	Percent of Cases Below	Percent of Cases Above
−2.2	1	99
−2.1	2	98
−2.0	2	98
−1.9	3	97
−1.8	4	96
−1.7	4	96
−1.6	5	95
−1.5	7	93
−1.4	8	92
−1.3	9	91
−1.2	12	88
−1.1	14	86
−1.0	16	84
−0.9	18	82
−0.8	21	79
−0.7	24	76
−0.6	27	73
−0.5	31	69
−0.4	34	66
−0.3	38	62
−0.2	42	58
−0.1	46	54
0.00	50	50
0.1	54	46
0.2	58	42
0.3	62	38
0.4	66	34
0.5	69	31
0.6	73	27
0.7	76	24
0.8	79	21
0.9	82	18
1.0	84	16
1.1	86	14
1.2	88	12
1.3	91	9
1.4	92	8
1.5	93	7
1.6	95	5
1.7	96	4
1.8	96	4
1.9	97	3
2.0	98	2
2.1	98	2
2.2	99	1

Excerpted from R. P. Runyon, *Winning with Statistics*. Reading, Mass.: Addison-Wesley, 1977.

1. The sum of the z-scores is zero. Symbolically stated,

$$\sum z = 0. \tag{7.2}$$

2. The mean of z-scores is zero. Thus

$$\bar{z} = \frac{\sum z}{N} = 0. \tag{7.3}$$

3. The sum of the squared z-scores equals N.* Thus

$$\sum z^2 = N. \tag{7.4}$$

This characteristic may be demonstrated mathematically:

$$\sum z^2 = \frac{\sum (X - \bar{X})^2}{s^2} = \frac{1}{s^2} \cdot \sum (X - \bar{X})^2$$

$$= \frac{N}{\sum (X - \bar{X})^2} \cdot \sum (X - \bar{X})^2$$

$$= N.$$

4. The standard deviation and the variance of z-scores is one. Thus

$$s_z = s_z^2 = 1. \tag{7.5}$$

To demonstrate,

$$s_z^2 = \frac{\sum (z - \bar{z})^2}{N}.$$

Since $\bar{z} = 0$, then

$$s_z^2 = \frac{\sum z^2}{N}.$$

Since $\sum z^2 = N$, then

$$s_z^2 = \frac{N}{N} = 1.$$

What is the value of transforming to a z-score? The conversion to z-scores

---

*This property of z-scores is important for understanding one of many alternative formulas for calculating the Pearson correlation coefficient r (see Section 8.2).

always yields a mean of 0 and a standard deviation of 1, but it does not "normalize" a nonnormal distribution. However, if the *population of scores* on a given variable is normal, we may express any score as a percentile rank by referring our z to the *standard normal distribution*. In addition, since z-scores represent abstract numbers as opposed to the concrete values of the original scores (inches, pounds, I.Q. scores, etc.), we may compare an individual's position on one variable with his or her position on a second. To understand these two important characteristics of z-scores, we must make reference to the *standard normal distribution*.

7.3 *The Standard Normal Distribution*

The **standard normal distribution** has a μ of 0, a σ of 1, and a total area equal to 1.00.* There is a fixed proportion of cases between a vertical line (ordinate) erected at any one point and an ordinate erected at any other point. Taking a few reference points along the normal curve, we can make the following statements:

Standard Normal Distribution

A normal distribution that has a mean of 0, a standard deviation of 1, and a total area equal to 1.00.

1. Between the mean and 1 standard deviation above the mean are found 34.13% of all cases. Similarly, 34.13% of all cases fall between the mean and 1 standard deviation below the mean. Stated in another way, 34.13% of the *area* under the curve is found between the mean and 1 standard deviation above the mean, and 34.13% of the *area* falls between the mean and −1 standard deviation.

2. Between the mean and 2 standard deviations above the mean are found 47.72% of all cases. Since the normal curve is symmetrical, 47.72% of the area also falls between the mean and −2 standard deviations.

---

*It will be recalled that the Greek letters μ and σ represent the population mean and the standard deviation, respectively. The equation of the normal curve is

$$Y = \frac{Ni}{\sigma\sqrt{2\pi}}\, e^{\frac{-(X-\mu)^2}{2\sigma^2}},$$

in which

Y = the frequency at a given value of X,
σ = the standard deviation of the distribution,
π = a constant equaling approximately 3.1416,
e = approximately 2.7183,
N = total frequency of the distribution,
μ = the mean of the distribution,
i = the width of the interval,
X = any score in the distribution.

It should be clear that there is a family of curves that may be called normal. By setting $Ni = 1$, a distribution is generated in which $\mu = 0$ and total area under the curve equals 1.

3. Finally, between the mean and 3 standard deviations above the mean are found 49.87% of all the cases. Similarly, 49.87% of the cases fall between the mean and −3 standard deviations. Thus we see that 99.74% of all cases fall between ±3 standard deviations. These relationships are shown in Fig. 7.1.

Now, by transforming the scores of a normally distributed variable to z-scores, we are, in effect, expressing these scores in units of the standard normal curve. For any given value of X with a certain proportion of area beyond it, there is a corresponding value of z with the same proportion of area beyond it. Thus, if we have a population in which $\mu = 30$ and $\sigma = 10$, the z of a score at the mean ($X = 30$) will equal zero, and the z of scores 1 standard deviation above and below the mean ($X = 40$ and $X = 20$) will be $+1.00$ and $−1.00$, respectively.

Finding Area between Given Scores

For expositional purposes, we confined our preceding discussion of area under the standard normal curve to selected points. As a matter of actual fact, however, it is possible to determine the percent of areas between *any* two points by making use of the tabled values of the area under the normal curve (see in by making use of the tabled values of the area under the normal curve (see Table A in the table section of this book.). The left-hand column headed by z represents the deviation from the mean expressed in standard deviation units. *By referring to the body of the table, we can determine the proportion of total area between a given score and the mean,* column (B), *and the area beyond a given score,* column (C). Thus, if an individual obtained a score of 24.65 on a normally distributed variable with $\mu = 16$ and $\sigma = 5$, her z-score would be

$$z = \frac{24.65 - 16}{5} = 1.73.$$

Figure 7.1
Areas between selected points under the normal curve.

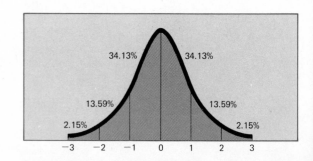

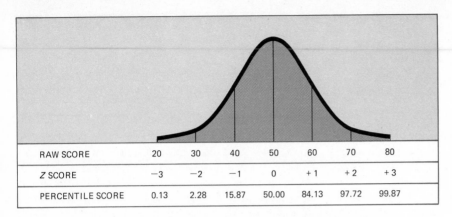

RAW SCORE	20	30	40	50	60	70	80
Z SCORE	−3	−2	−1	0	+1	+2	+3
PERCENTILE SCORE	0.13	2.28	15.87	50.00	84.13	97.72	99.87

Figure 7.2 Relationships among raw scores, z-scores, and percentile ranks of a normally distributed variable in which $\mu = 50$ and $\sigma = 10$.

Referring to column (B) in Table A we find that 0.4582 or 45.82%* of the area lies between his score and the mean. Since 50% of the area also falls below the mean in a symmetrical distribution, we may conclude that 95.82% of all the area falls below a score of 24.65. Note that we can now translate this score into a percentile rank of 95.82.

Let us suppose another individual obtained a score of 7.35 on the same normally distributed variable. His z-score would be

$$z = \frac{7.35 - 16}{5} = -1.73.$$

Since the normal curve is symmetrical, only the areas corresponding to the positive z-values are given in Table A. Negative z-values will have precisely the same proportions as their positive counterparts. Thus the area between the mean and a z of −1.73 is also 45.82%. The percentile rank of a score below the mean may be obtained either by subtracting 45.82% from 50%, or directly from column (C). In either case, the percentile rank of a score of 7.35 is 4.18.

You should carefully note that these relationships apply *only to scores from normally distributed populations.* Transforming the raw scores to standard scores does not in any way alter the form of the original distribution. The only change is to convert the mean to zero and the standard deviation to one. Thus, if the original distribution of scores is nonnormal, *the distribution of z-scores*

---

*The areas under the normal curve are expressed as proportions of area. To convert to percentage of area, multiply by 100 or merely move the decimal two places to the right.

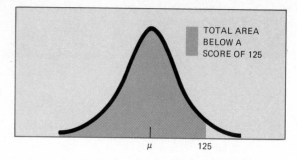

Figure 7.3
Proportions of area below a
score of 125 in a normal
distribution with $\mu = 100$
and $\sigma = 16$.

will be nonnormal. In other words, our transformation to z's will *not* convert a
nonnormal distribution to a normal distribution.*

Figure 7.2 further clarifies the relationships among raw scores, z-scores,
and percentile ranks of a normally distributed variable. It assumes that $\mu = 50$
and $\sigma = 10$.

7.4 Illustrative Problems

Let us take several sample problems in which we assume that the mean of the
general population, μ, is equal to 100 on a standard I.Q. test, and the standard
deviation, σ, is 16. It is assumed that the variable is normally distributed.

Problem 1.   John Doe obtains a score of 125 on an I.Q. test. What percent
of cases fall between his score and the mean? What is his percentile rank in
the general population?

At the outset, it is wise to construct a crude diagram representing the relationships in question. Thus, in the present example, the diagram would appear as shown in Fig. 7.3. To find the value of z corresponding to X = 125,
we subtract the population mean from 125 and divide by 16. Thus

$$z = \frac{125 - 100}{16} = 1.56.$$

Looking up 1.56 in column (B), Table A, we find that 44.06% of the area
falls between the mean and 1.56 standard deviations above the mean. John
Doe's percentile rank is therefore 50 + 44.06 or 94.06.

---

*Appendix B summarizes the procedures for transforming a nonnormal frequency distribution into a normal
distribution.

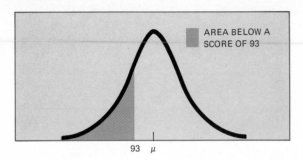

Figure 7.4
Proportion of area below a
score of 93 in a normal
distribution with $\mu = 100$
and $\sigma = 16$.

Problem 2. Mary Jones scores 93 on an I.Q. test. What is her percentile
rank in the general population (Fig. 7.4)?

$$z = \frac{93 - 100}{16} = -0.44.$$

The minus sign indicates that the score is below the mean. Looking up 0.44 in
column (C), we find that 33.00% of the cases fall below her score. Thus her
percentile rank is 33.00.

Problem 3. What percent of cases fall between a score of 120 and a score
of 88 (Fig. 7.5)?

Note that to answer this question we do *not* subtract 88 from 120 and
divide by σ. The areas in the normal probability curve are designated in relation to the mean as a fixed point of reference. We must therefore separately
calculate the area between the mean and a score of 120 and the area between
the mean and a score of 88. We then add the two areas to answer our
question.

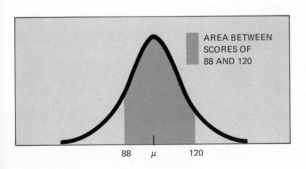

Figure 7.5
Proportion of area between
the scores 88 and 120 in a
normal distribution with
$\mu = 100$ and $\sigma = 16$.

Procedure:

Step 1. Find the z corresponding to $X = 120$:

$$z = \frac{120 - 100}{16} = 1.25.$$

Step 2. Find the z corresponding to $X = 88$:

$$z = \frac{88 - 100}{16} = -0.75.$$

Step 3. Find the required areas by referring to column (B), Table A:

Area between the mean and $z = 1.25$ is 39.44%;
Area between the mean and $z = -0.75$ is 27.34%.

Step 4. Add the two areas together.

Thus the area between 88 and 120 = 66.78%.

Problem 4. What percent of the area falls between a score of 123 and 135 (Fig. 7.6)?

Again, we cannot obtain the answer directly; we must find the area between the mean and a score of 123 and subtract this from the area between the mean and a score of 135.

Procedure:

Step 1. Find the z corresponding to $X = 135$:

$$z = \frac{135 - 100}{16} = 2.19.$$

Figure 7.6
Proportion of area between the scores 123 and 135 in a normal distribution with $\mu = 100$ and $\sigma = 16$.

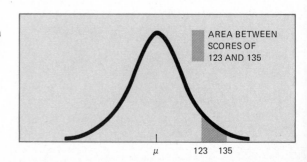

Step 2. Find the z corresponding to X = 123?

$$z = \frac{123 - 100}{16} = 1.44.$$

Step 3. Find the required areas by referring to column (B):

Area between the mean and z = 2.19 is 48.57%;
Area between the mean and z = 1.44 is 42.51%.

Step 4. Subtract to obtain the area between 123 and 135. The result is

$$48.57 - 42.51 = 6.06\%.$$

Problem 5. We stated earlier that our transformation to z-scores permits us to compare an individual's position on one variable with his or her position on another. Let us illustrate this important use of z-scores.

On a standard aptitude test, John G. obtained a score of 245 on the verbal scale and 175 on the mathematics scale. The means and the standard deviations of each of these normally distributed scales are as follows: Verbal, $\mu = 220$, $\sigma = 50$; Math, $\mu = 150$, $\sigma = 25$. On which scale did John score higher? All that we need to do is compare John's z-score on each variable. Thus

$$\text{Verbal } z = \frac{245 - 220}{50} \qquad \text{Math } z = \frac{175 - 150}{25}$$
$$= 0.50. \qquad\qquad = 1.00.$$

We conclude therefore that John scored higher on the math scale of the aptitude test. Of course, if we so desire, we may express these score as percentile ranks. Thus John's percentile rank is 84.13 on the math scale and only 69.15 on the verbal scale.

7.5 The Standard Deviation As an Estimate of Error and Precision

In the absence of any specific information, what is our best single basis for predicting a score that is obtained by any given individual? If the data are drawn from a normally distributed population, it turns out that the mean (or *any* measure of central tendency) is our best single predictor. The more compactly our scores are distributed about the mean, the smaller our errors will be in prediction, on the average. Conversely, the greater the spread or dispersion of scores about the mean, the greater will be our errors in prediction, on the average, when we use the mean to estimate or predict scores. Since the stan-

"I have some good news and some bad news, Captain. The bad news is that first we were 150 meters past the target; then 150 meters under; next 75 meters under and, then, 75 meters over. Not a single #*!#* shell on target. The good news is that, on the average, we were right on target!"

dard deviation reflects the dispersion of scores, it becomes, in a sense, an estimate of error. For the same reasons, the standard deviation is also a measure of precision. If two distributions have the same mean but different degrees of dispersion, the one with the smaller standard deviation provides more precise measures (i.e., measures closer to the mean), on the average.

To illustrate, imagine we compare two artillery units, Battery A and Battery B. A zero score means the shell was on target; a positive score means the shell

Table 7.1   Hypothetical scores made by two artillery batteries when firing at designated target.

Distance from Target (in meters)	Frequency Battery A	Frequency Battery B
200	2	0
150	4	1
100	5	5
50	7	10
0	9	13
−50	7	10
−100	5	5
−150	4	1
−200	2	0
$\overline{X} =$	0	0
$s =$	102.74	65.83*

*Note that, although the mean accuracy of both batteries was identical, the shelling of Battery B showed less dispersion or scattering.

went beyond the target, and a negative score indicates that it fell short of the target. Table 7.1 summarizes the results.

Although both batteries achieved the same mean, it is clear that more of the shells of Battery B landed close to the target than did the shells of Battery A. In other words, the firing of Battery B was more precise. This greater precision is reflected in the lower standard deviation of Battery B.

7.6 *The Transformation to Z-scores*

Many psychological and educational tests have been purposely constructed to yield a normal distribution of z-scores. Moreover, procedures are available for transforming nonnormal distributions into a standard normal distribution. These procedures are shown in Appendix B. Recall, however that z-scores include many negative values and are expressed in decimal form. Since it is often inconvenient and sometimes confusing to deal with negative numbers and decimals, the z-scores of normally distributed variables are frequently converted to Z-scores, employing the following transformation equation:

$$Z^* = 100 + 10z.$$

This transformation now yields a distribution with a mean of 100 and a standard deviation of 10. It eliminates all negative values. Thus a score with a z corresponding to -1.52 becomes:

$$Z = 100 + 10(-1.52)$$
$$= 100 - 15.2 = 84.8.$$

It is traditional to round to the nearest whole number, thereby eliminating the decimal.

We may readily convert Z-scores to units of the standard normal curve:

$$z = \frac{Z - \bar{Z}}{10}.$$

Thus a person obtaining a Z of 84.8 would have a corresponding z of

$$z = \frac{84.8 - 100}{10} = -\frac{15.2}{10} = -1.52.$$

---

*The transformation may involve the substitution of any desired constants into the equation. Thus, if a mean of 100 and a standard deviation of 20 is desired, the transformation equation becomes $100 + 20z$. There is a Z-score transformation that normalizes nonnormal distributions. The procedures are beyond the scope of this book. For reference see Helen M. Walker and Joseph Lev, *Elementary Statistical Methods*, 3rd ed. New York: Holt, Rinehart and Winston, 1969.

Employing the standard normal curve, this score is found to have a corresponding percentile rank of 6.43.

To eliminate the decimals entirely, we could use a transformation such as

$$Z = 500 + 100z.$$

A z of -1.52 would become

$$\begin{aligned} Z &= 500 + 100(-1.52) \\ &= 500 - 152 \\ &= 348. \end{aligned}$$

Chapter Summary

In this chapter, we demonstrated the value of the standard deviation for comparison of the dispersion of scores in different distributions of a variable, the interpretation of a score with respect to a single distribution, and the comparison of scores on two or more variables. We showed how to convert raw scores into units of the standard normal curve (transformation to z-scores), and explained the various characteristics of the standard normal curve. A series of problems demonstrated various ways to convert normally distributed variables to z-scores.

Finally, we discussed the standard deviation as an estimate of error and as an estimate of precision. We demonstrated the use of the Z-transformation as a convenient method for eliminating the negative values occurring when scores are expressed in terms of z.

Terms to Remember

standard normal distribution   **standard score** *(z)*

EXERCISES

1. Given a normal distribution with a mean of 45.2 and a standard deviation of 10.4, find the standard-score equivalents for the following scores.
    a. 55   b. 41   c. 45.2
    d. 31.5   e. 68.4   f. 18.9

2. Find the proportion of area under the normal curve between the mean and the following z-scores.
    a. -2.05 b. -1.90 c. -0.25

d. +0.40   **e.** +1.65   **f.** +1.96
g. +2.33   **h.** +2.58   **i.** +3.08

3. Assume normal distribution based on 1000 cases with a mean of 50 and a standard deviation of 10.
   a. Find the proportion of area and the number of cases between the mean and the following scores:

   60,   70,   45,   25.

   b. Find the proportion of area and the number of cases *above* the following scores:

   60,   70,   45,   25,   50.

   c. Find the proportion of area and the number of cases *between* the following scores:

   60–70,   25–60,   45–70,   25–45.

4. Below are student Spiegel's scores, the mean, and the standard deviation on each of three normally distributed tests.

Test	μ	σ	Spiegel's Score
Arithmetic	47.2	4.8	53
Verbal comprehension	64.6	8.3	71
Geography	75.4	11.7	72

   a. Convert each of Spiegel's test scores to standard scores.
   b. On which test did Spiegel stand highest? On which lowest?
   c. Spiegel's score in arithmetic was surpassed by what proportion of the population? Her score in verbal comprehension? In geography?

5. On a normally distributed mathematics aptitude test, for females,
$$\mu = 60, \qquad \sigma = 10,$$
and for males,
$$\mu = 64, \qquad \sigma = 8.$$
   a. Arthur obtained a score of 62. What is his percentile rank on both the male and the female norms?
   b. Helen's percentile rank is 73 on the female norms. What is her percentile rank on the male norms?

6. If frequency curves were constructed for each of the following, which would approximate a normal curve?
   a. Heights of a large representative sample of adult American males.
   b. Means of a large number of samples with a fixed N (say, $N = 100$) drawn from a normally distributed population of scores.
   c. Weights, in ounces, of ears of corn selected randomly from a cornfield.
   d. Annual income, in dollars, of a large number of American families selected at random.
   e. Weight, in ounces, of all fish caught in a popular fishing resort in a season.

7. In a normal distribution with $\mu = 72$ and $\sigma = 12$:
   a. What is the score at the 25th percentile?
   b. What is the score at the 75th percentile?
   c. What is the score at the 90th percentile?

     d. Find the percent of cases scoring above 80.

     e. Find the percent of cases scoring below 66.

     f. Between what scores do the middle 50 percent of the cases lie?

     g. Beyond what scores do the most extreme 10 percent lie?

     h. Beyond what scores do the most extreme 1 percent lie?

8. Answer the above questions (a) through (h) for

     a. $\mu = 72$ and $\sigma = 8$;

     b. $\mu = 72$ and $\sigma = 4$;

     c. $\mu = 72$ and $\sigma = 2$.

9. Using the following information, determine whether Larry did better on Test I or Test II. On which test did Mindy do better?

	Test I	Test II
μ	500	24
σ	40	1.4
Larry's scores	550	26
Mindy's scores	600	25

10. Are all sets of z-scores normally distributed? Why?

11. Is there more than one normal distribution?

12. Transform the following z-scores to Z-scores, using $Z = 50 + 10z$. Round to the nearest whole number.

     a. -2.43 **b.** 1.50 **c.** -0.50 **d.** 0.00

13. The transformation to Z-scores yields the following values when $Z = 500 + 100z$. Convert back to the original z-scores.

     a. 230 **b.** 500 **c.** 780 **d.** 640 **e.** 460

14. In what sense can the standard deviation be regarded as a measure of precision?

8

Correlation

139

8.1 *The Concept of Correlation*

Up to this point in the course, we have been interested in calculating various statistics that permit us to thoroughly describe the distribution of the values of a single variable and to relate these statistics to the interpretation of individual scores. However, as you are well aware, many of the problems in the behavioral sciences go beyond the description of a single variable in its various and sundry ramifications. We are frequently called upon to determine the relationships among two or more variables. For example, college administration officers are vitally concerned with the relationship between high-school grade averages or Scholastic Aptitude Test (SAT) scores and performance at college. Do students who do well in high school or who score high on the SAT also perform well in college? Conversely, do poor high-school students or those who score low on the SAT perform poorly at college? Do parents with high intelligence tend to have children of high intelligence? Is there a relationship between the declared dividend on stocks and their paper value in the exchange? Is there a relationship between socioeconomic class and recidivism in crime?

As soon as we raise questions concerning the relationships among variables, we are thrust into the fascinating area of **correlation.** In order to express quantitatively the extent to which two variables are related, it is necessary to calculate a **correlation coefficient.** There are many types of correlation coefficients. The decision to employ one of them with a specific set of data depends upon such factors as (1) the type of scale of measurement in which each variable is expressed, (2) the nature of the underlying distribution (continuous or discrete), and (3) the characteristics of the distribution of the scores (linear or nonlinear). Table 8.1 shows some of the correlation coefficients that are available for use with various types of scales. We present two correlation coefficients in this text: the *Pearson r,* or the *Pearson product-moment correlation coefficient,* employed with interval- or ratio-scaled variables, and r_s or the *Spearman rank-order correlation coefficient,* employed with ordered or ranked data.

No matter which correlational technique we use, all have certain characteristics in common.

1. Two sets of measurements are obtained on the same individuals (or events), or on pairs of individuals who are matched on some basis.
2. The values of the correlation coefficients vary between $+1.00$ and -1.00. Both extremes represent perfect relationships between the variables, and 0.00 represents the *absence* of a relationship.
3. A **positive relationship** means that individuals obtaining high scores on one variable tend to obtain high scores on a second variable. The con-

Correlation

Relationship between two variables.

Correlation Coefficient

A measure that expresses the extent to which two variables are related.

Positive Relationship

Variables are said to be positively related when a high score on one is accompanied by a high score on the other. Conversely, low scores on one variable are associated with low scores on the other.

140

GNP and life expectancy

BOX 8.1

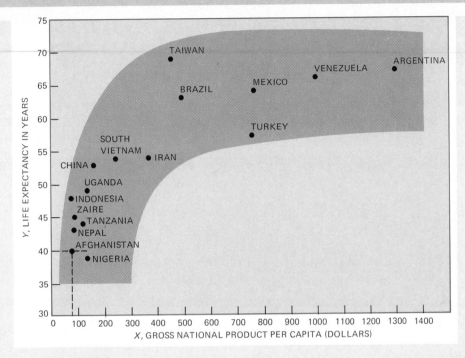

Y, LIFE EXPECTANCY IN YEARS

X, GROSS NATIONAL PRODUCT PER CAPITA (DOLLARS)

Is there a relationship between per-capita Gross National Product (GNP), expressed in dollars, and the life expectancy of children born at the present time in underdeveloped countries?

The table at left shows the mean per-capita income and the mean life expectancy in sixteen nations. We have called these variables *X* and *Y*, where *X* is the value in dollars of the GNP, and *Y* is the value (or score) on life expectancy. *Note:* each nation has two scores—one for the *X* and one for the *Y* variable.

Visualize these relationships on a scatter diagram. It is traditional to represent the values of the *X*-variable along the horizontal axis (also called *X*-axis) and the values of the *Y*-variable on the vertical axis (also called *Y*-axis). The points shown on the scatter diagram above represent the paired *X* and *Y* scores for each nation. Here is the procedure for constructing such a scatter diagram.

Note that the *X* value for Afghanistan is 75, and the corresponding *Y* value is 40. Follow the *X*-axis until a value of 75 is located. Draw a line at a right angle to the *X*-axis at this point. Now locate a value of 40 on the *Y*-axis. Draw a line perpendicular to the *Y*-axis. The point where the two lines meet represents the value of each variable, *X* and *Y*, for Afghanistan.

Scatter diagrams are useful for depicting the relationship between two variables. The diagram above shows a positive relationship between *X* and *Y* (i.e., low scores on *X* are generally associated with low scores on *Y*; high scores on *X* are associated with high scores on *Y*). Stated another way, citizens of underdeveloped nations with high per-capita GNPs have a long life expectancy. Citizens of nations with low GNPs have short life expectancies. It also appears that the relationship is not linear (straightline) but curvilinear.

Country	Per Capita GNP in Dollars, X	Life Expectancy, Years Y
Afghanistan	75	40
Nigeria	135	39
Nepal	87	43
Zaire	90	45
Tanzania	120	44
Indonesia	80	48
Uganda	140	49
China	170	53
South Vietnam	245	54
Iran	370	54
Turkey	760	57
Brazil	500	63
Taiwan	460	69
Mexico	770	64
Venezuela	1000	66
Argentina	1300	67

Table 8.1 **Several different types of correlation coefficients and the numerical scales with which they are used.**

Scale	Symbol	Used with
Nominal	r_{phi}* (phi coefficient)	Two dichotomous variables.
	r_b* (biserial r)	One dichotomous variable, with underlying continuity assumed; one variable that can take on more than two values.
	r_t* (tetrachoric r)	Two dichotomous variables in which underlying continuity can be assumed.
Ordinal	r_s (Spearman r)	Ranked data. If one variable is inherently ordinal and the second is interval/ratio, both must be expressed as ranks prior to calculating Spearman r.
	τ† (Kendall's tau, or rank correlation coefficient)	Ranked data.
Interval/Ratio	Pearson r	Both scales interval and/or ratio.
	Multiple R‡	Three or more interval- and/or ratio-level variables.

*See A. L. Edwards, *Statistical Methods,* 3rd ed. New York: Holt, Rinehart and Winston, 1973.
†See S. Siegel, *Nonparametric Statistics.* New York: McGraw-Hill, 1956.
‡See A. Haber and R. P. Runyon, *Business Statistics.* Homewood, Ill.: Irwin, 1982.

Negative Relationship

Variables are said to be negatively related when a high score on one is accompanied by a low score on the other. Conversely, low scores on one variable are associated with high scores on the other.

Scatter Diagram

Graphic device employed to represent the variation in two variables.

verse is also true; i.e., individuals scoring low on one variable tend to score low on a second variable.*

4. A **negative relationship** means that individuals scoring low on one variable tend to score high on a second variable. Conversely, individuals scoring high on one variable tend to score low on a second variable.*

Figure 8.1 shows a series of **scatter diagrams** illustrating various degrees of relationships between two variables, X and Y. In interpreting the figures it is important to remember that *every dot represents two values*: an individual's score on the X-variable and the same person's score on the Y-variable. As indicated earlier (Section 3.4), the X-variable is represented along the X-axis and the Y-variable along the Y-axis.

 *Pearson r- and z-scores*

A high positive Pearson r indicates that each individual obtains approximately the same z-score on both variables. In a *perfect* positive correlation ($r = 1.00$), each individual obtains *exactly* the same z-score on both variables.

*These characteristics are true for correlation coefficients that measure linear relationship, but not for all correlation coefficients.

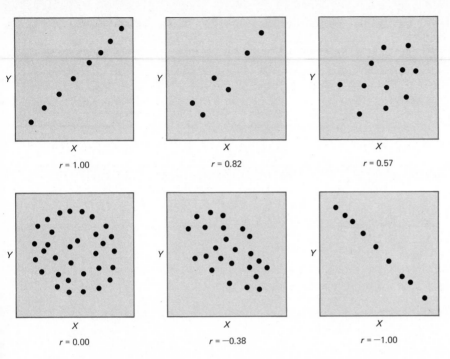

Figure 8.1 Scatter diagrams showing various degrees of relationship between two variables.

With a high negative r, each individual obtains approximately the same z-score on both variables, but opposite in sign.

Remembering that the z-score represents a measure of relative position on a given variable (i.e., a high positive z represents a high score relative to the remainder of the distribution, and a high negative z represents a low score relative to the remainder of the distribution), we may now generalize the meaning of the Pearson r.

> Pearson r represents the extent to which the same individuals or events occupy the same relative position on two variables.

In order to explore the fundamental characteristics of the Pearson r, let us examine a simplified example of a perfect positive correlation. In Table 8.2, we find the paired scores of 7 individuals on the two variables, X and Y.

Note that the scale values of X and Y do not need to be the same for the calculation of a Pearson r. In the example, we see that X ranges from 1 through 13, whereas Y ranges from 4 through 22. This independence of r from specific scale values permits us to investigate the relationships among an unlimited variety of variables. We can even correlate the length of the big toe with the I.Q. if we feel so inclined!

Table 8.2 Raw scores and corresponding z-scores made by 7 subjects on two variables (hypothetical data).

Subject	X	X − $\bar{X}$	$(X - \bar{X})^2$	z_x	Y	Y − $\bar{Y}$	$(Y - \bar{Y})^2$	z_y	$z_x z_y$
A	1	−6	36	−1.5	4	−9	81	−1.5	2.25
B	3	−4	16	−1.0	7	−6	36	−1.0	1.00
C	5	−2	4	−0.5	10	−3	9	−0.5	0.25
D	7	0	0	0	13	0	0	0	0
E	9	2	4	0.5	16	3	9	0.5	0.25
F	11	4	16	1.0	19	6	36	1.0	1.00
G	13	6	36	1.5	22	9	81	1.5	2.25

$$\sum X = 49 \qquad SS_x = 112 \qquad \sum Y = 91 \qquad SS_y = 252 \qquad \sum z_x z_y = 7.00$$

$$\bar{X} = 7.00 \qquad s_x = \sqrt{\frac{112}{7}} = 4.00 \qquad \bar{Y} = 13.00 \qquad s_y = \sqrt{\frac{252}{7}} = 6.00$$

Note also, as we have already pointed out, that the z-scores of each subject on each variable are identical in the event of a perfect positive correlation. Had we reversed the order of either variable, i.e., paired 1 with 22, paired 3 with 19, etc., the z-scores would still be identical, but would be opposite in sign. In this latter case, our correlation would be a maximum *negative* ($r = -1.00$).

If we multiply our paired z-scores and then sum the results, we obtain maximum values only when our correlation is 1.00. Indeed, as the correlation approaches zero, the sum of the products of the paired z-scores also approaches zero. Note that when the correlation is perfect, the sum of the products of the paired z-scores is equal to N, where N equals the number of pairs or the number of measurements of either the X- or Y-variables. These facts lead to one of the many different but algebraically equivalent formulas for r:

$$r = \frac{\sum (z_x z_y)}{N}. \tag{8.1}$$

In Section 7.2, we pointed out that $\sum z^2 = N$. You will note that, when the correlation is perfect, each z-score on the X-variable is identical to its corresponding z-score on the Y-variable. Thus $\sum z_x z_y = \sum z_x^2 = \sum z_y^2$, when $r = 1.00$. In other words, in a perfect correlation, $\sum z_x z_y = N$. The Pearson r then becomes N/N or 1.00.

Try taking the data in Table 8.1, rearranging them in a number of different ways, and calculating r, employing the Formula (8.1). You will arrive at a far more thorough understanding of r by working the problems than by reading the text (not that we are discouraging the latter).

It so happens that the formula is unwieldy in practice, since it requires the calculation of separate z's for each score of each individual. Imagine the Herculean task of calculating r when N exceeds 50 cases, as it often does in behavioral research!

For this reason, a number of different computational formulas are employed. In this text, we shall illustrate the use of two: (1) the mean-deviation formula, and (2) the raw-score formula.

8.3 *Calculation of Pearson r*

Mean-Deviation Method

The mean-deviation method for calculating a **Pearson r,** like the z-score formula above, is not often employed by behavioral scientists because it involves more time and effort than other computational techniques. It is being presented here primarily because it sheds further light on the characteristics of the Pearson r. However, with small N's, it is as convenient a computational formula as any, unless an automatic calculator is available. The computational formula for the Pearson r, employing the mean-deviation method, is

$$r = \frac{\sum(X - \bar{X})(Y - \bar{Y})}{\sqrt{SS_x \cdot SS_y}}. \tag{8.2}$$

Let us illustrate the mean-deviation method, employing the figures in Table 8.2 but arranging them in a different sequence (Table 8.3).

The computational procedures, employing the mean-deviation method, should be perfectly familiar to you. You have already encountered the SS_x and the SS_y when you studied the standard deviation. In fact, in calculating r only one step has been added, namely, the one to obtain the sum of the cross

Pearson r (Product-Moment Correlation Coefficient)

Correlation coefficient employed with interval- or ratio-scaled variables.

Table 8.3 Computational procedures for Pearson r employing mean-deviation method (hypothetical data)

Subject	X	$(X - \bar{X})$	$(X - \bar{X})^2$	Y	$(Y - \bar{Y})$	$(Y - \bar{Y})^2$	$(X - \bar{X})(Y - \bar{Y})$
A	1	−6	36	7	−6	36	36
B	3	−4	16	4	−9	81	36
C	5	−2	4	13	0	0	0
D	7	0	0	16	3	9	0
E	9	2	4	10	−3	9	−6
F	11	4	16	22	9	81	36
G	13	6	36	19	6	36	36

$$SS_x = 112 \qquad SS_y = 252 \qquad \sum(X - \bar{X})(Y - \bar{Y}) = 138$$

$$r = \frac{\sum(X - \bar{X})(Y - \bar{Y})}{\sqrt{SS_x \cdot SS_y}} = \frac{138}{\sqrt{(112)(252)}} = \frac{138}{168.00} = 0.82$$

products $\sum(X - \bar{X})(Y - \bar{Y})$. This is obtained easily enough by multiplying the deviation of each individual's score from the mean of the X-variable by its corresponding deviation on the Y-variable and then summing all of the cross products. Incidentally, you should notice the similarity of $\sum(X - \bar{X})(Y - \bar{Y})$ to $\sum(z_x z_y)$, which is discussed in Section 8.2. Everything that has been said with respect to the relationship between the variations in $\sum(z_x z_y)$ and r holds also for $\sum(X - \bar{X})(Y - \bar{Y})$ and r. Notice that, if maximum deviations in X had lined up with maximum deviations in Y, and so on down through the array, $\sum(X - \bar{X})(Y - \bar{Y})$ would have been equal to 168.00, which is the same as the value of the denominator, and would have produced a correlation of 1.00.

Raw-score Method

We have already seen that the raw-score formula for calculating the sum of squares is

$$SS_x = \sum X^2 - \frac{(\sum X)^2}{N}$$

and

$$SS_y = \sum Y^2 - \frac{(\sum Y)^2}{N}.$$

By analogy,* the raw-score formula for the sum of the cross products is

$$\sum(X - \bar{X})(Y - \bar{Y}) = \sum XY - \frac{(\sum X)(\sum Y)}{N}. \qquad (8.3)$$

In calculating the Pearson r by the raw-score method, you have the option of calculating all the above quantities separately and substituting them into formula (8.2), or defining r in terms of raw scores as in formula (8.4) as

---

*See Section 6.5 on variance and standard deviation for the proof of SS $= \sum X^2 - (\sum X)^2/N$. By analogy,

$$\sum(X - \bar{X})(Y - \bar{Y}) = \sum XY - \sum X\bar{Y} - \sum Y\bar{X} + \sum \bar{X}\bar{Y}.$$

Since

$$\sum X = N\bar{X}, \qquad \sum Y = N\bar{Y},$$

and

$$\sum \bar{X}\bar{Y} = N\bar{X}\bar{Y} \qquad \text{(Generalization 1, Chapter 2),}$$

it follows that

$$\sum(X - \bar{X})(Y - \bar{Y}) = \sum XY - N\bar{X}\bar{Y} - N\bar{Y}\bar{X} + N\bar{X}\bar{Y}$$

$$= \sum XY - N\bar{X}\bar{Y}$$

$$= \sum XY - N\left(\frac{\sum X}{N}\right)\left(\frac{\sum Y}{N}\right)$$

$$= \sum XY - \frac{(\sum X)(\sum Y)}{N}.$$

follows:

$$r = \frac{\sum XY - \frac{(\sum X)(\sum Y)}{N}}{\sqrt{\left[\sum X^2 - \frac{(\sum X)^2}{N}\right]\left[\sum Y^2 - \frac{(\sum Y)^2}{N}\right]}} \qquad (8.4)$$

Table 8.4 Computational procedures for Pearson *r* employing raw-score method (hypothetical data).

Subject	X	X²	Y	Y²	XY
A	1	1	7	49	7
B	3	9	4	16	12
C	5	25	13	169	65
D	7	49	16	256	112
E	9	81	10	100	90
F	11	121	22	484	242
G	13	169	19	361	247
	$\sum X = 49$	$\sum X^2 = 455$	$\sum Y = 91$	$\sum Y^2 = 1435$	$\sum XY = 775$

1. Using formula (8.2),

$$r = \frac{\sum(X - \bar{X})(Y - \bar{Y})}{\sqrt{SS_x \cdot SS_y}};$$

$$\sum(X - \bar{X})(Y - \bar{Y}) = \sum XY - \frac{(\sum X)(\sum Y)}{N}$$

$$= 775 - 637$$
$$= 138;$$

$$SS_x = \sum X^2 - \frac{(\sum X)^2}{N}$$

$$= 455 - \frac{(49)^2}{7}$$

$$= 112;$$

$$SS_y = \sum Y^2 - \frac{(\sum Y)^2}{N}$$

$$= 1435 - \frac{(91)^2}{7}$$

$$= 252;$$

$$r = \frac{\sum(X - \bar{X})(Y - \bar{Y})}{\sqrt{SS_x \cdot SS_y}}$$

$$= \frac{138}{\sqrt{112 \cdot 252}} = \frac{138}{168}$$

$$= 0.82.$$

2. Or, using formula (8.4),

$$r = \frac{\sum XY - \frac{(\sum X)(\sum Y)}{N}}{\sqrt{\left[\sum X^2 - \frac{(\sum X)^2}{N}\right]\left[\sum Y^2 - \frac{(\sum Y)^2}{N}\right]}}$$

$$= \frac{775 - \frac{(49)(91)}{7}}{\sqrt{\left(455 - \frac{(49)^2}{7}\right)\left(1435 - \frac{(91)^2}{7}\right)}}$$

$$= \frac{775 - 637}{\sqrt{(112)(252)}}$$

$$= \frac{138}{168}$$

$$= 0.82.$$

A useful alternative formula for calculating the Pearson r when the means and standard deviations have already been calculated for other purposes is

$$r = \frac{\dfrac{\sum XY}{N} - \overline{X}\,\overline{Y}}{s_x s_y}. \tag{8.5}$$

The procedures for calculating r by the raw-score method are summarized in Table 8.4. Here we find exactly the same coefficient as we did before. As with the mean deviation method, all the procedures, except those of obtaining the cross products, are familiar to you from our earlier use of the raw-score formula to obtain the standard deviation. The quantity $\sum XY$ is obtained very simply by multiplying each X-value by its corresponding Y and then summing these products.

8.4 A Word of Caution

When low correlations are found, one is strongly tempted to conclude that there is little or no relationship between the two variables under study. However, it must be remembered that the Pearson r reflects only the *linear* relationship between two variables. The failure to find evidence of a relationship may be due to one of two possibilities: (1) the variables are in fact unrelated, or (2) the variables are related in a *nonlinear* fashion. In the latter instance, the Pearson r would not be an appropriate measure of the degree of relationship between the variables. To illustrate, if we were plotting the relationship between age and strength of grip, we might obtain a picture somewhat like Fig. 8.2.

Figure 8.2
Scatter diagram of two variables that are related in a nonlinear fashion (hypothetical data).

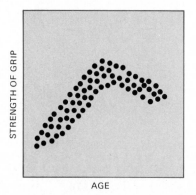

It is usually possible to determine whether there is a substantial departure from linearity by examining the scatter diagram. If the distribution of points in the scatter diagram is elliptical, without the decided bending of the ellipse that occurs in Fig. 8.2, it may safely be assumed that the relationship is linear. Any small departures from linearity will not greatly influence the size of the correlation coefficient.

On the other hand, where there is marked curvilinearity, as in Fig. 8.2, a curvilinear coefficient of correlation would better reflect the relationship between the two variables under investigation. Although it is beyond the scope of this text to investigate nonlinear coefficients of correlation, you should be aware of this possibility and, as a matter of course, you should construct a scatter diagram prior to your calculation of the Pearson r.

The assumption of linearity of relationship is the most important requirement to justify the use of the Pearson r as a measure of relationship between two variables. It is not necessary that r be calculated only with normally distributed variables. So long as the distributions are unimodal and relatively symmetrical, a Pearson r may legitimately be computed.

Another situation giving rise to spuriously low correlation coefficients results from restricting the range of values of one of the variables. For example, if we were interested in the relationship between age and height for children from 3 years to 16 years of age, we would undoubtedly obtain a rather high coefficient of correlation between these two variables. However, suppose that we were to restrict the range of one of our variables? What effect would this have on the size of the coefficient? That is, let us look at the same relationship between age and height but only for those children between the ages of 9 and 10. We would probably end up with a rather low coefficient. Let us look at this graphically.

You will note that the overall relationship illustrated in Fig. 8.3 is rather high. The inset illustrates what happens when we restrict our range. Note that the scatter diagram contained in the inset represents a very low correlation.

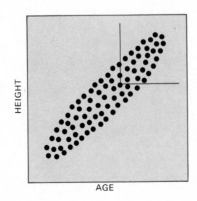

Figure 8.3
Scatter diagram illustrating high correlation over entire range of X- and Y-values, but low correlation when the range is truncated (hypothetical data).

Truncated Range

Restriction of the range of one or both variables, resulting in a deceptively low correlation between these variables.

This restriction of the range is frequently referred to as the **truncated range**. The problem of truncated range is not uncommon in behavioral research, since much of this research is conducted in the colleges and universities, where subjects have been preselected for intelligence and related variables. Thus they represent a fairly homogeneous group with respect to these variables. Consequently, when an attempt is made to demonstrate the relationship between variables like SAT scores and college grades, the resulting coefficient may be lowered because of the truncated range. Furthermore, the correlations would be expected to be lower for colleges that select their students from within a narrow range of SAT scores.

CASE EXAMPLE • 8.1
Craning and Gawking at Nothing

Bibb Lanane proposed a theory of social impact that specifies the effect of other persons on an individual. Basing these conclusions on many different avenues of social research, the author states ". . . when other people are the source of impact and the individual is the target, impact should be a multiplicative function of the strength, immediacy, and number of other people." He presents considerable evidence that the relationship between impact and number of people is not linear. In fact, the impact of each additional person added to the group is less than the impact of the preceding individual. This produces a curvilinear relationship between number of people and social impact.

Figure 8.4 Several studies showing curvilinear relationships among variables.

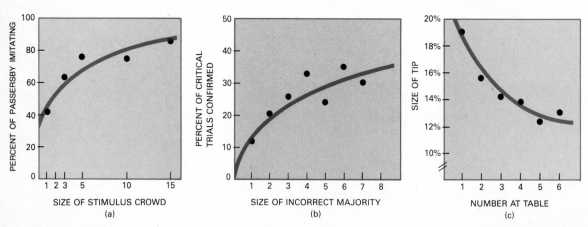

Have you ever been on a crowded city street and seen people craning and gawking at some nonexistent event? Figure 8.4(a)* shows that, as the size of the crowd increases, the percent of passersby who imitate craning and gawking behavior increases. Figure 8.4(b)† shows that, similarly, in an Asch type of study in which confederates gave incorrect answers to a length-of-line judging task, conformity increased with the size of the incorrect majority. Finally, in Fig. 8.4(c)‡ the size of the tip, in percent of total, decreases with the number of people seated at the table. Note that all describe curvilinear relationships between the independent variable (number of people involved) and the dependent measure.

---

*Data from S. Milgram, L. Bickman, and L. Berkowitz (1969), "Note on the Drawing Power of Crowds," *Journal of Personality and Social Psychology,* **13,** 79–82.

†Data from H. B. Gerard, R. A. Wilhelmy, and E. S. Conolley (1968), "Conformity and Group Size," *Journal of Personality and Social Psychology,* **8,** 79–82.

‡Data from S. Freeman, M. R. Walker, R. Borden, and B. Latané (1975), "Diffusion of Responsibility and Restaurant Tipping: Cheaper by the Bunch," *Personality and Social Psychology Bulletin,* **1,** 584–587.

Based on Bibb Latané (1981), "The Psychology of Social Impact," *American Psychologist,* **36**(4), 342–356.

 ## Ordinally Scaled Variables and r_s

Imagine that you are a grade-school teacher. After long years of observation in the classroom, you have developed a strong suspicion that intelligence and leadership are related variables. In an effort to test this hypothesis, you obtain I.Q. estimates on all the children in your class. However, you discover that no scales are available to measure classroom leadership and you can think of no satisfactory way to quantify this variable. Nevertheless, from numerous observations of the children in different leadership situations, you feel confident that you are able to *rank* the children from those highest in leadership to those lowest in this quality. The resulting measurements constitute, of course, an ordinal scale. Although we could obtain a Pearson r with ranked data, a variant of the product-moment correlation coefficient, which is referred to as the **Spearman r, r_s,** or the **rank correlation coefficient,** gives precisely the same answer but reduces the computational task involved in obtaining the correlation. The Spearman r is appropriate when one scale constitutes ordinal measurement and the remaining scale is either ordinal or interval/ratio. However, prior to applying the r_s formula, *both* scales must be expressed as ranks.

Realizing that your knowledge of the children's I.Q. scores might "contaminate" your estimates of their leadership qualities, you ask a fellow teacher to provide ranks for his or her children based on leadership qualities. You then

Spearman r (r_s or Rank Correlation Coefficient)

Correlation coefficient employed with ordered or ranked data.

Table 8.5 Computational procedures for calculating r_s from ranked variables (hypothetical data).

I.Q. Rank	Leadership Rank	D	D²	
1	4	−3	9	$r_s = 1 - \dfrac{6\sum D^2}{N(N^2 - 1)}$
2	2	0	0	
3	9	−6	36	
4	1	3	9	$= 1 - \dfrac{6 \cdot 204}{15(224)}$
5	7	−2	4	
6	10	−4	16	
7	8	−1	1	
8	13	−5	25	$= 1 - \dfrac{1224}{3360}$
9	5	4	16	
10	3	7	49	
11	11	0	0	$= 1 - 0.36$
12	6	6	36	
13	12	1	1	$= 0.64.$
14	15	−1	1	
15	14	1	1	
		$\sum D = 0$	$\sum D^2 = 204$	

obtain, independent of ranks, an estimate of their I.Q.'s. Following this, you rank the I.Q.'s from highest to lowest.

The rank correlation coefficient requires that you obtain the differences in the ranks, square and sum the squared differences, and substitute the resulting values into the formula

$$r_s = 1 - \frac{6\sum D^2}{N(N^2 - 1)}, \tag{8.6}$$

in which D = rank X − rank Y.

Table 8.5 shows the hypothetical data and the procedures involved in calculating r_s.

As a matter of course, $\sum D$ should be obtained even though it is not used in any of the calculations. It constitutes a useful check on the accuracy of your calculations up to this point since $\sum D$ must equal zero. If you obtain any value other than zero, you should recheck your original ranks and the subsequent subtractions.

Tied Ranks

Occasionally, when it is necessary to convert scores to ranks, you will find two or more tied scores.* In this event, assign the mean of the tied ranks to each

---

*When there are numerous tied ranks on either or both the X- and the Y-variables, the Spearman formula tends to yield a spuriously high coefficient of correlation. When there are many ties, it is preferable to apply the Pearson r formula to the *ranked* data.

of the tied scores. The next score in the array receives the rank normally assigned to it. Thus the ranks of the scores 128, 122, 115, 115, 115, 107, 103 would be 1, 2, 4, 4, 4, 6, 7, and the ranks of the scores 128, 122, 115, 115, 107, 103 would be 1, 2, 3.5, 3.5, 5, 6.

If you use a statistical calculator or a computer to obtain correlations and there is no program for r_s, you may use Pearson r to obtain the rank correlation. However, you enter the ranks rather than the values of the variable. If there are no ties, the Pearson formula will yield the same correlations as the Spearman formula. If there are many ties, the Pearson formula will be more accurate.

CASE EXAMPLE • 8.2
Help Is Where You Find It!

We previously examined some of the data in Cowen's report when we discussed ordinal scales of measurement (Case Example 2.1). Table 8.6 presents the rankings of four different occupational groups in terms of how frequently they use various help-giving strategies when engaged with clients. We want to learn the extent to which they agree or disagree in their use of the 11 different strategies.

We must now find all possible intercorrelations among the four occupational groups. All told, six different correlations must be calculated: hairdressers vs. bartenders, lawyers, and supervisors (three comparisons), bartenders vs. lawyers and supervisors (two comparisons), and lawyers vs. supervisors

Table 8.6 Ordinal position of response strategies of four different occupations when clients seek advice and counsel. A rank of 1 corresponds to the most frequently used strategy and 11 to the least frequently used strategy.

Strategy	Hairdressers	Bartenders	Lawyers	Supervisors
Offer support and sympathy	1	3	1	1.5
Try to be lighthearted	2	2	8	8
Just listen	3	1	5	1.5
Present alternatives	4	4	4	4
Tell person to count blessings	5	10	7	9
Share personal experiences	6	5	6	5
Try not to get involved	7	6	9.5	10
Give advice	8	7	3	7
Ask questions	9	9	2	3
Try to get person to talk to someone else	10	11	9.5	6
Try to change topic	11	8	11	11

Table 8.7 **Ordinal position of response strategies of two different occupations when clients seek advice and counsel. A rank of 1 corresponds to the most frequently used strategy and 11 to the least frequently used strategy.**

Strategy	Hairdressers	Bartenders	Difference	Difference Squared
Offer support and sympathy	1	3	−2	4
Try to be lighthearted	2	2	0	0
Just listen	3	1	2	4
Present alternatives	4	4	0	0
Tell person to count blessings	5	10	−5	25
Share personal experiences	6	5	1	1
Try not to get involved	7	6	1	1
Give advice	8	7	1	1
Ask questions	9	9	0	0
Try to get person to talk to someone else	10	11	−1	1
Try to change topic	11	8	3	9
				$\sum D^2 = 46$

(1 comparison). We'll show the calculation of r_s only for hairdressers vs. bartenders (Table 8.7) and will summarize all of their intercorrelations in Table 8.8. The Spearman rank correlation for these data is

$$r_s = 1 - \frac{6(46)}{1320}$$
$$= 0.79$$

Table 8.8 shows the intercorrelations among all four occupational groups in terms of their help-giving strategies.

Examination of Table 8.8 reveals that hairdressers and bartenders intercorrelate more than either does with lawyers and supervisors. The r_s of 0.79 is the highest of the 6 intercorrelations. Moreover, lawyers and supervisors inter-

Table 8.8 **Intercorrelations among four occupational groups on strategies for help-giving to clients.**

	Hairdressers	Bartenders	Lawyers	Supervisors
Hairdressers	—	0.79	0.43	0.46
Bartenders	—	—	0.30	0.43
Lawyers	—	—	—	0.78
Supervisors	—	—	—	—

correlated higher with each other than they do with hairdressers and bartenders.

Based on Emory L. Cowen's (1982), "Help Is Where You Find It," *American Psychologist,* **37**(4), 385–395.

Chapter Summary

In this chapter we discussed the concept of correlation and demonstrated the calculation of two correlation coefficients, i.e., the Pearson r employed with interval- or ratio-scaled data, and r_s used with ordinally scaled variables.

We saw that correlation is concerned with determining the extent to which two variables are related or tend to vary together. The quantitative expression of the extent of the relationship is given in terms of the magnitude of the correlation coefficient. Correlation coefficients vary between values of -1.00 and $+1.00$; both extremes represent perfect relationships. A coefficient of zero indicates the absence of a relationship between two variables.

We noted that the Pearson r is appropriate only for variables that are related in a linear fashion. With ranked data, the Spearman rank correlation coefficient is the exact counterpart of the Pearson r. The various computational formulas for the Pearson r may be employed in calculating r_s from ranked data. However, a computational formula for r_s was demonstrated that considerably simplifies the calculation of the rank correlation coefficient.

Terms to Remember

correlation

correlation coefficient

negative relationship

Pearson r (product-moment correlation coefficient)

positive relationship

scatter diagram

Spearman r (r_s or rank correlation coefficient)

truncated range

EXERCISES

1. The following data show the scores obtained by a group of 20 students on a college entrance examination and a verbal comprehension test. Prepare a scatter diagram and calculate a Pearson r for these data.

Student	College Entrance Exam (X)	Verbal Comprehension Test (Y)	Student	College Entrance Exam (X)	Verbal Comprehension Test (Y)
A	52	49	K	64	53
B	49	49	L	28	17
C	26	17	M	49	40
D	28	34	N	43	41
E	63	52	O	30	15
F	44	41	P	65	50
G	70	45	Q	35	28
H	32	32	R	60	55
I	49	29	S	49	37
J	51	49	T	66	50

2. The data in the table below represent scores obtained by 10 students on a statistics examination, and their final grade point average. Prepare a scatter diagram and calculate a Pearson r for these data.

Student	Score on Statistics Exam, X	Grade Point Average, Y	Student	Score on Statistics Exam, X	Grade Point Average, Y
A	90	2.50	F	70	1.00
B	85	2.00	G	70	1.00
C	80	2.50	H	60	0.50
D	75	2.00	I	60	0.50
E	70	1.50	J	50	0.50

3. A psychological study involved the rating of rats along a dominance–submissiveness continuum. In order to determine the reliability of the ratings, the ranks given by two different observers were tabulated. Are the ratings reliable? Explain your answer.

Animal	Rank by Observer A	Rank by Observer B	Animal	Rank by Observer A	Rank by Observer B
A	12	15	I	6	5
B	2	1	J	9	9
C	3	7	K	7	6
D	1	4	L	10	12
E	4	2	M	15	13
F	5	3	N	8	8
G	14	11	O	13	14
H	11	10	P	16	16

4. Explain in *your own words* the meaning of correlation.

5. In each of the examples presented below, identify a possible source of contamination in the collection and/or interpretation of the results of a correlational analysis.

    a. The relationship between age and reaction time for subjects from three months to 65 years of age.

b. The correlation between I.Q. and grades for honor students at a university.

c. The relationship between vocabulary and reading speed among children in an economically disadvantaged community.

6. For a group of 50 individuals $\sum z_x z_y$ is 41.3. What is the correlation between the two variables?

7. The following scores were made by five students on two tests. Calculate the Pearson r (using $r = \sum z_x z_y/N$). Convert to ranks and calculate r_s.

Student	Test X	Test Y
A	5	1
B	5	3
C	5	5
D	5	7
E	5	9

Generalize: What is the effect of tied ranks on r_s?

8. Show algebraically that

$$\sum (X - \bar{X})(Y - \bar{Y}) = \sum XY - \frac{\sum X \sum Y}{N}.$$

9. What effect does a departure from linearity have on the Pearson r?

10. How does the range of scores sampled affect the size of the correlation coefficient?

11. Following are the data showing scores on college-entrance examinations and college grade-point averages following the first semester. What is the relationship between these two variables?

Entrance Examinations	Grade Point Averages	Entrance Examinations	Grade Point Averages
440	1.57	528	2.08
448	1.83	550	2.15
455	2.05	582	3.44
460	1.14	569	3.05
473	2.73	585	3.19
485	1.65	593	3.42
489	2.02	620	3.87
500	2.98	650	3.00
512	1.79	690	3.12
518	2.63		

12. The data in the following table show the latitude of 35 cities in the northern hemisphere and the mean high and mean low annual temperatures.

a. What is the correlation between latitude and mean high temperature?

b. What is the correlation between latitude and mean low temperature?

c. What is the correlation between mean high and mean low temperature?

City	Latitude to Nearest Degree	Mean High Temperature	Mean Low Temperature
Acapulco	17	88	73
Accra	6	86	74
Algiers	37	76	71
Amsterdam	52	54	46
Belgrade	45	62	45
Berlin	53	55	40
Bogota	5	66	50
Bombay	19	87	74
Bucharest	44	62	42
Calcutta	22	89	70
Casablanca	34	72	55
Copenhagen	56	52	41
Dakar	15	84	70
Dublin	53	56	42
Helsinki	60	46	35
Hong Kong	22	77	68
Istanbul	41	64	50
Jerusalem	32	74	54
Karachi	25	87	70
Leningrad	60	46	33
Lisbon	39	67	55
London	52	58	44
Madrid	40	66	47
Manila	15	89	73
Monrovia	6	84	73
Montreal	46	50	35
Oslo	60	50	36
Ottawa	45	51	32
Paris	49	59	43
Phnom Penh	12	89	74
Prague	50	54	42
Rangoon	17	89	73
Rome	42	71	51
Saigon	11	90	74
Shanghai	31	69	53

13. In Exercises 17 and 18 of Chapter 5, we presented data on the systolic blood pressures of seven subjects during control and conditioning sessions.
   a. Find the Pearson r between these two measures.
   b. Transform both sets of scores to ranks and calculate r_s.

14. Throughout the blood-pressure study, the patients remained on drugs to control hypertension. Shown below are the rank order of amount of medication received by each subject (from lowest to highest) and the difference score (conditioning minus control) for each subject.

Subject	1	2	3	4	5	6	7
Rank of amount of drug	1	2	6	1	5	3	4
Difference score	−3.5	−33.8	−29.2	−16.5	−16.1	0.9	−17.3

Rank-order the difference scores from lowest (0.9) to highest (−33.8) reduction in systolic blood pressure, and find r_s.

---

15. Explain the difference between $r = 0.76$ and $r = -0.76$.

16. Suppose you wanted to study the relation between the efficiency of labor-saving machinery a manufacturer possesses and the mean price of the leather belts he produces. Because it is difficult to order the quality of machinery on a ratio scale, you rank the machines on an ordinal scale, with a rank of 15 indicating the most advanced machinery. You find the relation of price and type of the machines to be as follows:

15	$3.50	10	$4.25	5	$4.95
14	$3.75	9	$4.50	4	$5.50
13	$3.50	8	$4.45	3	$5.75
12	$4.00	7	$4.75	2	$5.45
11	$3.95	6	$5.00	1	$6.00

Determine the r_s between the quality of machinery and the price.

17. A store owner recorded the number of times consumers bought or asked for a given item. She called this amount the demand. Each month she had 15 of the items to sell. In addition, the owner recorded the price of the item each month.
   a. Determine the relation between demand and price, using Pearson r.
   b. Determine the relation between demand and price, using r_s.

Month	Demand	Price	Month	Demand	Price
Jan.	25	$0.50	July	13	$0.80
Feb.	10	.90	Aug.	19	.70
Mar.	12	.80	Sept.	18	.72
April	18	.75	Oct.	16	.74
May	11	.85	Nov.	15	.75
June	20	.70	Dec.	15	.75

18. Referring to Exercise 12 (this chapter), determine the correlation between latitude and mean high temperature for those areas with a latitude on or below 25 degrees. Compare this correlation with that obtained in Exercise 12(a). Why are the correlations different?

19. Again referring to Exercise 12, determine the correlation between latitude and mean high temperature for those areas with a latitude on or above 45 degrees. Compare this correlation with those obtained in Exercises 12(a) and 18. Why are they different?

20. Demonstrate that $\sum D^2 = 0$ for the following paired ranks:

1	1
2	2
3	3
4	4
5	5
6	6
7	7
8	8

21. Calculate r_s for Exercise 20.

22. Construct a scatter diagram for each of the following sets of data:

a. X	Y	b. X	Y	c. X	Y	d. X	Y
1.5	0.5	0.5	5.0	0.5	0.5	0.5	1.0
1.0	0.5	0.5	4.5	1.0	1.0	0.5	2.5
1.0	2.0	1.0	3.5	1.0	1.5	0.5	4.5
1.5	1.5	1.5	4.0	1.5	2.5	1.0	3.5
1.5	2.0	1.5	2.5	1.5	3.5	1.5	1.0
2.0	2.0	2.0	3.0	2.0	2.5	1.5	2.5
2.5	2.5	2.5	2.0	2.0	3.5	1.5	4.0
2.5	3.2	2.5	3.5	2.5	4.5	2.0	1.0
3.0	2.5	3.0	2.5	3.0	3.5	3.0	2.0
3.0	3.5	3.0	2.0	3.5	3.0	3.0	3.5
3.5	3.5	3.5	2.0	3.5	2.5	3.0	4.5
3.5	4.5	3.5	2.5	3.5	2.0	3.5	1.0
4.0	3.5	4.0	1.5	4.0	2.5	3.5	1.0
4.0	4.5	4.0	0.7	4.0	2.0	3.5	3.5
4.5	4.5	5.0	0.5	4.5	1.0	4.0	3.5
5.0	5.0			5.0	1.0	4.0	4.5
				5.0	0.5	4.5	2.5
						4.5	1.0

23. By inspecting the scatter diagrams for the data in Exercise 22, determine which one represents
   a. A curvilinear relation between X and Y.
   b. A positive correlation between X and Y.
   c. Little or no relation between X and Y.
   d. A negative correlation between X and Y.

24. In the study reported in Case Example 8.2, the investigator ascertained the frequency with which various feelings were experienced when people raised problems with them. The following are the rankings associated with 11 different feelings by members of the four occupations. Calculate the intercorrelations among all four occupational groups.

Feelings	Hairdressers	Lawyers	Supervisors	Bartenders
Gratified	1	4	4	4
Sympathetic	2	1	3	3
Encouraging	3	3	1	1
Supportive	4	2	2	2
Puzzled	5	7	5.5	7
Helpless	6	5	5.5	5.5
Uncomfortable	7	6	7	9
Bored	8	8	8	8
Trapped	9.5	11	9	5.5
Depressed	9.5	10	11	10
Angry	11	9	10	11

25. In the study reported in Case Example 8.2, the investigator ranked problems raised in order of their frequency of occurrence. The rankings are shown in the accompanying table:

Problem	Hair-dressers	Bar-tenders	Difference	Difference Squared
Difficulties with children	1	7		
Physical health	2	6		
Marital problems	3	2		
Depression	4	5		
Anxiety, nervousness	5	9		
Jobs	6	1		
Financial	7	3		
Sex	8	4		
Drugs	9	10		
Alcohol	10	9		

a. What is the correlation between the two occupational groups in terms of the problems raised?

b. How do you account for the low correlation when previous correlations have been so high?

26. Refer back to Case Example 6.1. Find the correlation between frequency separation of fundamental tones and percent of correct discriminations.

9

Regression
and Prediction

9.1 Introduction to Prediction

If we know a person's I.Q., what can we say about his prospects of satisfactorily completing a college curriculum? Knowing his prior voting record, can we make any informed guesses concerning his vote in the coming election? Knowing his mathematics aptitude score, can we estimate the quality of his performance in a course in statistics?

Let's look at an example. Suppose we are trying to predict student Jones's score on the final exam. If the only information available is that the class mean on the final was 75 ($\overline{Y} = 75$), the best guess we could make is that Jones scored 75 on the final.* However, far more information is usually available; e.g., Jones obtained a score of 62 on the midterm examination. How can we use this information to make a better prediction about performance on the final exam? If we know that the class mean on the midterm examination was 70 ($\overline{X} = 70$), we could reason that a score below the mean on the midterm would probably be followed by a score below the mean on the final. At this point, we appear to be closing in on a more accurate prediction of Jones's performance. How might we further improve the accuracy of our prediction? Simply knowing that this student scored below the mean on the midterm does not give us a clear picture of his or her relative standing on this exam. If, however, we know the standard deviation on the midterm, we could express this score in terms of its relative position, i.e., the z-score. Let us imagine that the standard deviation on the midterm was 4 ($s_x = 4$). Since Jones scored 2 standard deviations below the mean ($z_x = -2$), would we be justified in guessing that Jones will score 2 standard deviations below the mean on the final ($z_y = -2$)? That is, if $s_y = 8$, would you predict a score of 59 on final? No! You will note that an important piece of information is missing—the correlation between the midterm and the final. You may recall from our discussion of correlation† that the Pearson r represents the extent to which the same individuals or events occupy the same relative position on two variables. Thus we are justified in predicting a score of exactly 59 on the final only when the correlation is perfect (that is, when $r = +1.00$). Suppose that the correlation is equal to zero. Then it should certainly be obvious that we are not justified in predicting a score of 59; rather, we are once again back to our original prediction of 75 (that is, $\overline{Y}$).

In summary, when $r = 0$, our best prediction is 75 ($\overline{Y}$); when $r = +1.00$, our best prediction is 59 ($z_y = z_x$). It should be clear that predictions from intermediate values of r will fall somewhere between 59 and 75.‡

---

*See in Section 5.2, Properties of "the Arithmetic Mean," in which we demonstrated that the sum of the deviations from the mean is zero and that the sum of squares of deviations from the arithmetic mean is less than the sum of squares of deviations about any other score or potential score.

†See Section 8.2

‡We are assuming that the correlation is positive. If the correlation were -1.00, our best prediction would be a score of 91, that is, $z_y = -z_x$.

BOX 9.1

The heavyweight champions of gas-guzzling

One of the benefits of correlated data is that mathematicians have worked out ways of predicting values of one variable from knowledge of the values of a correlated variable. The method is *regression analysis*.

The following, adapted from *Winning with Statistics*, shows how correlated data may be used to guide decision making when you are purchasing the latest dream machine.

Living with Regression Analysis

The beauty of correlated data, particularly when the relationship is high, as in the case of weight of auto and miles per gallon, is that mathematicians have worked out ways of predicting values on one variable from knowledge of the values of a correlated variable. The method is known as *regression analysis*. Please don't let the term throw you. We can arrive at a pretty fair comprehension of regression without stumbling about in the arcane caverns of mathematics.

Take a look at the accompanying figure. It shows a scatter diagram of weight of automobile and miles per gallon. Note that I have drawn a line connecting the mean miles per gallon at each weight of car. The resulting line is a pretty good *approximation* to what mathematicians call the regression line for predicting *Y*-values (miles per gallon) from knowledge of *X*-values (auto weight). For purposes of discussion, we'll treat that line as if it were the regression line. In mathematical shorthand, it is called the line of regression of *Y* on *X*. But that is not important. What is important is that when the relationship between *X* and *Y* is high, we can use the regression line to predict *Y*-values from known *X*-values, achieving startling degrees of accuracy.

Let's see how this works. Let us say that you are considering buying one of two cars. Brand A is flaming red and weighs 3200 pounds when equipped. The second, brand B, is a metallic gold and weighs 2400 pounds. You can make your best guess about the overall performance of brand A by looking at [the figure] and drawing a vertical line at 3200 pounds until it intersects the regression line. Now look left to find the corresponding value for miles per gallon. Your best guess, then, is that the 3200-pound car will average somewhere around 15 miles per gallon. Repeat the same procedure for brand B, drawing a vertical line at 2400 pounds. That comes to about 20 miles per gallon, an improved fuel performance of about 33 percent, using 15 mpg as the base.

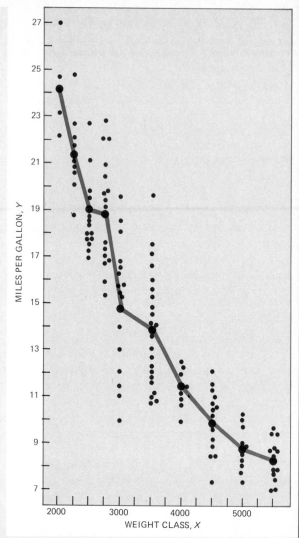

An approximation of the regression line for predicting miles per gallon from the weight class of automobile (regression of *Y* on *X*). The line is obtained by connecting the points showing the mean miles per gallon for each weight class.

So there it is. Regression analysis can be relevant to your daily living. Indeed, although you may not be aware of it, you have probably provided a numerical value in more than one regression equation in your lifetime, if you have ever applied for college admission, taken a series of tests for job placement, or filled out a life insurance application.

An outstanding advantage, then, of a correlational analysis stems from its application to problems involving predictions from one variable to another. Psychologists, educators, biologists, sociologists, and economists are constantly being called upon to perform this function. To provide an adequate explanation of r and to illustrate its specific applications, it is necessary to digress into an analysis of linear regression.

9.2 *Linear Regression*

To simplify our discussion, let us start with an example of two variables that are usually perfectly or almost perfectly related: monthly salary and yearly income. In Table 9.1 we have listed the monthly income of eight wage-earners in a small electronics firm. These data are shown graphically in Fig. 9.1. It is customary to refer to the horizontal axis as the X-axis and to the vertical axis as the Y-axis. If the variables are temporally related, the prior one is represented on the X-axis. It will be noted that all salaries are represented on a straight line extending diagonally from the lower left-hand corner to the upper right-hand corner.

Formula for Linear Relationships

The formula relating monthly salary to annual salary may be represented as

$$Y = 12X.$$

Table 9.1 **Monthly salaries and annual income of eight wage-earners in an electronics firm (hypothetical data).**

Employee	Monthly Salary	Annual Income
A	400	4800
B	450	5400
C	500	6000
D	575	6900
E	600	7200
F	625	7500
G	650	7800
H	675	8100

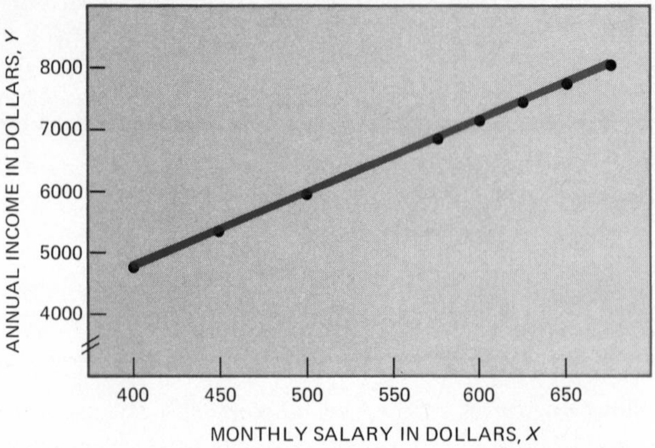

Figure 9.1
Relation of monthly salaries to annual income for eight employees in an electronic firm.

You may substitute any value of X into the formula and obtain the value of Y directly. For example, if another employee's monthly salary were $700, his annual income would be

$$Y = 12 \cdot 700 = 8400.$$

Let's add one more factor to this linear relationship. Suppose that the electronics firm had an exceptionally good year and that it decided to give each of its employees a Christmas bonus of $500. The equation would now read

$$Y = 500 + 12X.$$

Perhaps, thinking back to your high-school days of algebra, you will recognize the preceding formula as a special case of the general formula for a straight line; that is,

$$Y = a + b_y X, \tag{9.1}$$

in which Y and X represent variables that change from individual to individual, and a and b_y represent constants for a particular set of data. More specifically, b_y represents the slope of a line relating values of Y to values of X. This is referred to as the regression of Y on X. In the present example, the slope of the line is 12, which means that Y changes by a factor of 12 for each change in X. The letter a represents the value of Y when X = 0.

Note also that Formula (9.1) may be regarded as a method for predicting Y from known values of X. When the correlation is 1.00 (as in the present case), the predictions are perfect.

Predicting X and Y from Data on Two Variables

In behavioral research, however, the correlations we obtain are almost never perfect. Therefore we must find a straight line that best fits our data and we must make predictions from that line. But what do we mean by "best fit"? You will recall that, when discussing the mean and the standard deviation, we defined the mean as that point in a distribution that makes the sum of squares of deviations from it minimal (least sum squares). When applying the least-sum-square method to correlation and regression, the *best-fitting straight line* is defined as that line which makes the squared deviations around it minimal. This straight line is referred to as a **regression line.**

We might note at this time that the term "predict," as employed in statistics, does not carry with it any necessary implication of futurity, but simply refers to the fact that we are using information about one variable to obtain information about another. Thus, if we know students' college grade-point averages, we may use this information to "predict" their intelligence (which in our more generous moods we assume preceded their entrance into college).

At this point we shall introduce two new symbols: X' and Y'. These may be read as "X prime and Y prime," "X and Y predicted," or "estimated X and Y." We use these symbols whenever we employ the regression line or the regression equation to estimate or predict a score on one variable from a known score on another variable.

Returning to the formula for a straight line, we are faced with the problem of determining b and a for a particular set of data so that Y' may be obtained.

The formula for obtaining the slope of the line relating Y to X, which is known as the line of regression of Y on X, is

$$b_y = \frac{\sum(X - \bar{X})(Y - \bar{Y})}{SS_x}. \qquad (9.2)$$

From Formula (9.2) we may derive another useful formula for determining the slope of the line of Y on X: Since [Formula (8.2)]

$$r = \frac{\sum(X - \bar{X})(Y - \bar{Y})}{\sqrt{SS_x \cdot SS_y}}$$

it follows that

$$\sum(X - \bar{X})(Y - \bar{Y}) = r\sqrt{SS_x \cdot SS_y};$$

and from Formula (6.4), where $s^2 = SS/N$, it follows that

$$SS_x = Ns_x^2, \qquad SS_y = Ns_y^2.$$

Regression Line (Line of "Best Fit")

Straight line which makes the squared deviations around it minimal.

Thus

$$b_y = \frac{r\sqrt{N^2 s_x^2 \cdot s_y^2}}{N s_x^2}$$

$$= r\frac{N s_x s_y}{N s_x^2} \tag{9.3}$$

$$= r\frac{s_y}{s_x}.$$

The constant a is given by the formula

$$a = \overline{Y} + b_y \overline{X}. \tag{9.4}$$

In the computation of Y', it is unwieldy to obtain each of these values separately and substitute them into the formula for a straight line. However, by algebraically combining Formulas (9.3) and (9.4) and relating the result to Formula (9.1), we obtain a much more useful formula for Y':

$$Y' = \overline{Y} + r\frac{s_y}{s_x}(X - \overline{X}).* \tag{9.5}$$

Concentrating our attention upon the second term on the right of Formula (9.5), we can see that the larger the r, the greater the magnitude of the entire term. This term also represents the *predicted deviation from the sample mean resulting from the regression of Y on X*. Thus we may conclude that the greater the correlation, the greater the predicted deviation from the sample mean. In the event of a perfect correlation, the entire predicted deviation is maximal. On the other hand, when $r = 0$, the predicted deviation is also zero. Thus, when $r = 0$, we have $Y' = \overline{Y}$. All of this is another way of saying that, in the absence of a correlation between two variables, our best prediction of any given score on a specified variable is the mean of the distribution of that variable.

Thus far we have concentrated our attention on the regression of Y on X; that is, we have been predicting values of $Y(Y')$ from known values of X. There is also a separate regression formula for predicting scores on the X-variable from values of the Y-variable. Thus the slope of the regression line

---

*Since $Y' = a + b_y X$, $a = \overline{Y} - b_y \overline{X}$, and $b_y = r(s_y/s_x)$, then

$$Y' = \overline{Y} - r\left(\frac{s_y}{s_x}\right)\overline{X} + r\left(\frac{s_y}{s_x}\right)X = \overline{Y} + r\left(\frac{s_y}{s_x}\right)(X - \overline{X}).$$

X on Y may be expressed as

$$b_x = \frac{\sum(X - \bar{X})(Y - \bar{Y})}{SS_y} \qquad (9.6)$$

or

$$b_x = r\frac{s_x}{s_y}. \qquad (9.7)$$

Therefore the regression formula for predicting scores on the X-variable from values of the Y-variable is

$$X' = \bar{X} + r\frac{s_x}{s_y}(Y - \bar{Y}). \qquad (9.8)$$

The following raw-score formulas are often more convenient, especially because all the quantities shown are reaily obtained in the course of calculating Pearson r.

$$Y' = \bar{Y} + \frac{N\sum XY - (\sum X)(\sum Y)}{N\sum X^2 - (\sum X)^2}(X - \bar{X}). \qquad (9.9)$$

Similarly, the raw-score formula for predicting X is:

$$X' = \bar{X} + \frac{N\sum XY - (\sum X)(\sum Y)}{N\sum Y^2 - (\sum Y)^2}(Y - \bar{Y}). \qquad (9.10)$$

Illustrative Regression Problems

Here are two sample problems employing the data introduced in Section 9.1.

Problem 1. Jones, you will recall, scored 62 on the midterm examination. What is our prediction concerning Jones's score on the final examination? The relevant statistics are reproduced at the right.
    Employing Formula (9.5), we find

Midterm (X Variable)	Final (Y Variable)
$\bar{X} = 70$	$\bar{Y} = 75$
$s_x = 4$	$s_y = 8$
	$r = 0.60$

$$Y' = 75 + 0.60 \left(\frac{8}{4}\right)(62 - 70) = 75 - 9.60 = 65.40.$$

Problem 2. Smith, on the same midterm test, scored 76. What is our prediction concerning Smith's score on the final examination? Employing the tabular data of Problem 1, we obtain the following results:

$$Y' = 75 + 0.60 \left(\frac{8}{4}\right) (76 - 70) = 75 + 7.20 = 82.20.$$

Had our problem been to predict X-scores from known values of Y, the procedures would have been precisely the same as above, except that Formula (9.8) would have been employed.

A reasonable question at this point is, "Since we know $\bar{Y}$ and s_y in the two problems, we presumably have all the observed data at hand. Therefore why do we want to predict Y from X?" It should be pointed out that the purpose of these examples is to acquaint you with the prediction formulas. In actual practice, however, correlational techniques are most commonly employed in making predictions about future samples where Y is unknown.

For example, let us suppose that Ms. Holiday, the admissions officer of a college, has constructed an entrance examination that she has administered to all the applicants over a period of years. During this time she has accumulated much information concerning the relationship between entrance scores and subsequent quality point averages in school. She finds that it is now possible to use scores on the entrance examination (X-variable) to predict subsequent quality point averages (Y-variable), and then use this information to establish an entrance policy for future applicants.

Since we have repeatedly stressed the relationship between Pearson r and z-scores, it should be apparent that the prediction formulas may be expressed in terms of z-scores. Mathematically, it can be shown* that

$$z_{y'} = rz_x, \tag{9.11}$$

where $z_{y'} = Y'$ expressed in terms of a z-score.

Returning to Problem 1, we see that Jones's score of 62 on the midterm can be expressed as $z = -2.00$. Thus $z_{y'} = 0.60(-2.00) = -1.20$.

To assure yourself of the comparability of the two prediction formulas— Formulas (9.5) and (9.11)—you should translate the $z_{y'}$-score into a raw score, Y'.

Constructing Lines of Regression

Let us return to the problem of constructing regression lines for predicting scores on the variables X and Y. As we have already pointed out, the regres-

---

*$Y' = \bar{Y} + r(s_y/s_x)(X - \bar{X})$. By transposing terms:

$$\frac{Y' - \bar{Y}}{s_y} = r\frac{(X - \bar{X})}{s_x}, \quad \text{but} \quad \frac{X - \bar{X}}{s_x} = z_x \quad \text{and} \quad \frac{Y' - \bar{Y}}{s_y} = z_{y'}.$$

Therefore $z_{y'} = rz_x$.

sion line will not pass through all the paired scores. It will in fact pass among the paired scores in such a way as to minimize the squared deviations between the regression line (predicted scores) and the obtained scores. Earlier we pointed out that the mean is the point in a distribution that makes the squared deviations around it minimal. In discussing regression, we say the regression line is analogous to the mean, since the sum of deviations of scores around the regression line is zero and the sum of squares of these deviations is minimal, as we shall demonstrate.

Recall that all the values required to calculate predicted scores are readily found during the course of calculating r, that is, $\overline{X}$, $\overline{Y}$, s_x, s_y. Now to construct our regression line for predicting Y from X, all we need to do is take two extreme values of X, predict Y from each of these values, and then join these two points on the scatter diagram. The lines joining these points represents the regression lines for predicting Y from X, which is also referred to as the line of regression of Y on X. Similarly, to construct the regression line for predicting X from Y, we take two extreme values of Y, predict X for each of these values, and then join these two points on the scatter diagram. This is precisely what was done in Fig. 9.2 to construct the two regression lines from the data in Table 8.2.

Note that both regression lines intersect at the means of X and Y. In conceptualizing the relationship between the regression lines and the magnitude of r, it is helpful to think of the regression lines as rotating about the joint means

Figure 9.2 Scatter diagram representing paired scores on two variables and regression lines for predicting X from Y and Y from X. Note that the line predicting Y from X minimizes the vertical or Y-axis deviations of the data points (black lines). In contrast, the line predicting X from Y minimizes the horizontal or X-axis deviations (color lines).

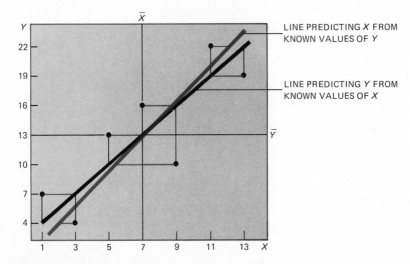

of X and Y. When $r = 1.00$, both regression lines will have identical slopes and will be superimposed upon one another, since they pass directly through all the paired scores. However, as r becomes smaller, the regression lines rotate away from each other, so that in the limiting case when $r = 0$, they are *perpendicular* to each other. At this point the regression line for predicting X from known values of Y is $\overline{X}$, and the regression line for predicting Y from known values of X is $\overline{Y}$.

9.3 *Residual Variance and Standard Error of Estimate*

Figure 9.3 shows a series of scatter diagrams, each reproduced from Fig. 9.2, showing only one regression line: the line for predicting Y from known values of X. Although our present discussion will be directed only to this regression line, all the conclusions we draw will be equally applicable to the line predicting X from known values of Y.

The regression line represents our best basis for predicting Y scores from known values of X. As we can see, not all the obtained scores fall on the regression line. However, if the correlation had been 1.00, all the scores *would* have fallen right on the regression line. The deviations $(Y - Y')$ in Fig. 9.3 represent our errors in prediction.

You will note the similarity of $Y - Y'$ (the deviation of scores from the regression line) to $Y - \overline{Y}$ (the deviation of scores from the mean). The algebraic sum of these deviations around the regression line is equal to zero. Earlier, we saw that the algebraic sum of the deviations around the mean is also equal to zero. In a sense, then, the regression line is a sort of "floating mean": one that takes on different values depending on the values of X that are employed in prediction.

You will also recall that in calculating the variance, s^2, we squared the deviations from the mean, summed, and divided by N. Finally, the square root of the variance provided our standard deviation. Now, if we were to square and sum the deviations of the scores from the regression line, $\sum(Y - Y')^2$, we would have a basis for calculating another variance and standard deviation. The variance around the regression line is known as the **residual variance** and is defined as follows:

Residual Variance

Variance around the regression line.

$$s^2_{\text{est } y} = \frac{\sum(Y - Y')^2}{N - 2}. \tag{9.12}$$

When the predictions are made from Y to X, the residual variance of X is

$$s^2_{\text{est } x} = \frac{\sum(X - X')^2}{N - 2}. \tag{9.13}$$

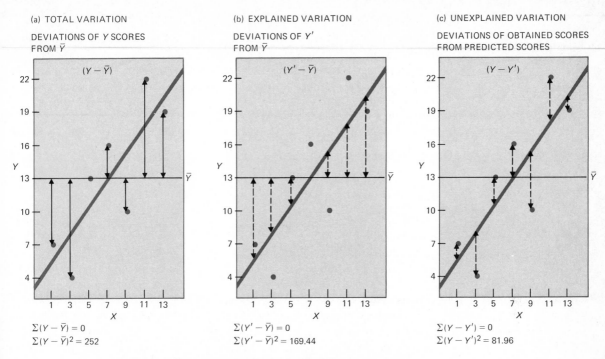

Figure 9.3 Scatter diagrams of paired scores on two variables, regression line for predicting Y-values from known values of X, and the mean of the distribution of Y-scores $\overline{Y}$: $r = 0.82$ (from data in Table 8.3).
(a) Deviations of scores $(Y - \overline{Y})$ from the mean of Y, total variation.
(b) Deviations of predicted scores $(Y' - \overline{Y})$ from the mean of Y, explained variation. (c) Deviations of scores $(Y - Y')$ from the regression line, unexplained variation.

The standard deviation around the regression line (referred to as the **standard error of estimate**) is, of course, the square root of the residual variance. Thus

$$s_{est\ y} = \sqrt{\frac{\sum(Y - Y')^2}{N - 2}}. \tag{9.14}$$

When predictions are made from Y to X, the standard error of estimate of X is

$$s_{est\ x} = \sqrt{\frac{\sum(X - X')^2}{N - 2}}. \tag{9.15}$$

You may be justifiably aghast at the amount of computation that is implied in the above formulas for calculating the standard error of estimate. However, as has been our practice throughout this text, we have shown the basic for-

Standard Error of Estimate

Standard deviation of scores around the regression line.

mulas so that you may have a conceptual grasp of the meaning of the standard error of estimate. It is, as we have seen, the standard deviation of scores around the regression line rather than around the mean of the distribution.

Fortunately, as in all previous illustrations in the text, there is a simplified method for calculating $s_{est\ y}$ and $s_{est\ x}$.

$$s_{est\ y} = s_y \sqrt{\frac{N(1 - r^2)}{N - 2}} \qquad (9.16)$$

and

$$s_{est\ x} = s_x \sqrt{\frac{N(1 - r^2)}{N - 2}}. \qquad (9.17)$$

You will note that when $r = \pm 1.00$, $s_{est\ y} = 0$, which means that there are no deviations from the regression line, and therefore no errors in prediction. On the other hand, when $r = 0$, the errors of prediction are maximal for that given distribution, that is, $s_{est\ y} = s_y$.

With the data in Exercise 1, Chapter 8, the following statistics were calculated:

College Entrance Exam (X Variable)	Verbal Comprehension Exam (Y Variable)
$\overline{X} = 47.65$	$\overline{Y} = 39.15$
$s_x = 13.82$	$s_y = 12.35$
$r = 0.8466$	

Thus

$$S_{est\ y} = 12.35 \sqrt{\frac{20(1 - 0.8466^2)}{18}}$$

$$= 12.35(0.5610) = 6.93.$$

As we have already indicated, the standard error of estimate has properties that are similar to those of the standard deviation. The smaller the standard error of estimate, the lesser the dispersion of scores around the regression line.

For each value of X, there is a distribution of scores on the Y-variable. The mean of each of these distributions is Y', and the standard deviation of each distribution is $s_{est\ y}$. When the distribution of Y-scores for each value of X has the same variability, we refer to this condition as **homoscedasticity.** In addition, if the distribution of Y-scores for each value of X is normally distributed, we may state relationships between the standard error of estimate and

Homoscedasticity

Homogeneous variability within the columns and the rows.

the normal curve (see Section 7.3). We can, for example, predict a value of Y from any given X, and then describe an interval within which it is likely that the true value of Y will be found. For normally distributed variables, approximately 68% of the time the value of Y (that is, Y_T) will be within the following interval:

$$\text{Interval including } Y_T = Y' \pm s_{\text{est } y} \sqrt{1 + \frac{1}{N} + \frac{(X - \overline{X})^2}{SS_x}}. \qquad (9.18)$$

Thus, if we predicted a Y-value of 39.15 from $X = 25$ and $s_{\text{est } y} = 6.51$, $Y' = 22.02$, $\overline{X} = 47.65$, $SS_x = 3822.53$, and $N = 20$:

$$\text{Interval including } Y_T = 22.02 \pm 6.93 \sqrt{1 + \frac{1}{20} + \frac{(25 - 47.65)^2}{3822.53}}$$

$$= 22.02 \pm (6.93)(1.088)$$

$$\pm 7.54$$

In other words, when $X = 25$, about 68 percent of the time the true Y will be found between scores of 14.48 and 29.56.

Using these data, we draw two lines, one above and one below the regression line for predicting Y from X (Fig. 9.4). For normally distributed variables, approximately 68 percent of the time the true values of Y will be found be-

Figure 9.4 Line of regression for predicting Y from X with parallel lines one $s_{\text{est } y}$ above and below the regression line (from data in Exercise 1, Chapter 8). Dots indicate individual scores on X and Y.

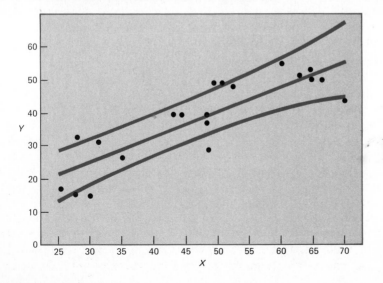

tween these lines when we use formula (9.18) to predict Y from various values of X. Note that the lines are more spread out when predicting Y from extreme values of X. The result is two slightly bowed lines, with minimum distance between them at the mean of X. (It should be noted that these relationships refer to the distributions of *both* X and Y.)

9.4 *Explained and Unexplained Variation**

If we look again at Fig. 9.3, we can see that there are three separate sum of squares that can be calculated from the data. These are

1. Variation of scores around the sample mean (Fig. 9.3a). This variation is given by $(Y - \overline{Y})^2$ and is, of course, basic to the determination of the variance and the standard deviation of the sample.

2. Variation of scores around the regression line (or predicted scores) (Fig. 9.3c). This variation is given by $(Y - Y')^2$ and is referred to as **unexplained variation.** It is the difference between the predicted score and the obtained score. The reason for this choice of terminology should be clear. If the correlation between two variables is ± 1.00, all the scores fall on the regression line. Consequently we have, in effect, explained *all* the variation in Y in terms of the variation in X and, conversely, all the variation of X in terms of the variation in Y. In other words, in the event of a perfect relationship, there is no unexplained variation. However, when the correlation is less than perfect, many of the scores will not fall right on the regression line, as we have seen. The deviations of these scores from the regression line represent variation that is not accounted for in terms of the correlation between two variables. Hence the term "unexplained variation" is employed.

Unexplained Variation

Variation of scores around the regression line.

Explained Variation

Variation of predicted scores about the mean of the distribution.

3. Variation of predicted scores about the mean of the distribution (Fig. 9.3b). This variation is given by $(Y' - \overline{Y})^2$ and is referred to as **explained variation.** It is the difference between the mean and the predicted score. The reason for this terminology should be clear from our discussion in the preceding paragraph and our prior reference to predicted deviation (Section 9.3). You will recall our previous observation that the greater the correlation, the greater the predicted deviation from the sample mean. It follows further that the greater the predicted deviation, the greater the explained variation. When the predicted deviation is

---

*Although analysis of variance is not covered until Chapter 15, much of the material in this section will serve as an introduction to some of the basic concepts of analysis of variance.

maximum, the correlation is perfect; and 100 percent of variation is explained.

It can be shown mathematically that the total sum of squares consists of two components, which may be added together. These two components represent explained variation and unexplained variation, respectively. Thus

$$\sum(Y - \overline{Y})^2 = \sum(Y - Y')^2 + \sum(Y' - \overline{Y})^2.$$

| Total | Unexplained | Explained | (9.19) |
| variation | variation | variation | |

The calculations are shown in Fig. 9.3. You will note that the sum of the explained variation (169.44) and the unexplained variation (81.96) is equal to the total variation. The slight discrepancy found in this example is due to rounding r to 0.82 prior to calculating the predicted scores.

Now, when $r = 0.00$, then $\sum(Y' - \overline{Y})^2 = 0.00$. (Why? See Section 9.2.) Consequently the total variation is equal to the unexplained variation. Stated another way, when $r = 0$, all the variation is unexplained. On the other hand, when $r = 1.00$, then $\sum(Y - Y')^2 = 0.00$, since all the scores are on the regression line. Under these circumstances, total variation is the same as explained variation. In other words, all the variation is explained when $r = 1.00$.

The ratio of the explained variation to the total variation is referred to as the **coefficient of determination** and is symbolized by r^2. The formula for the coefficient of determination is

Coefficient of Determination (r^2)

The ratio of the explained variation to the total variation.

$$r^2 = \frac{\text{Explained variation}}{\text{Total variation}} = \frac{\sum(Y' - \overline{Y})^2}{\sum(Y - \overline{Y})^2}.^* \qquad (9.20)$$

Referring to Fig. 9.3, we see that the proportion of explained variation to total variation is

$$r^2 = \frac{169.44}{252} = 0.67.$$

It can be seen that the coefficient of determination indicates the proportion of total variation that is explained in terms of the magnitude of the correlation coefficient. When $r = 0$, the coefficient of determination, r^2, equals 0. When $r = 0.5$, the coefficient of determination is 0.25. In other words, 25 percent of the total variation is accounted for. Finally, when $r = 1.00$, then $r^2 = 1.00$ and all variation is accounted for.

---

*Table H in the table section presents a number of functions of r for various values of r, including such useful functions as r^2, $1 - r^2$, and $\sqrt{1 - r^2}$. You should familiarize yourself with this table.

Figure 9.5 depicts graphically the proportion of variation in one variable that is accounted for by the variation in another variable when r takes on different values.

You have undoubtedly noted that the square root of the coefficient of determination provides another definition of r. Thus

$$r = \pm \sqrt{\frac{\text{Explained variation}}{\text{Total variation}}} = \pm \sqrt{\frac{\sum (Y' - \bar{Y})^2}{\sum (Y - \bar{Y})^2}}. \qquad (9.21)$$

We have previously shown that the coefficient of determination, r^2, is equal to 0.67 for the data summarized in Fig. 9.3. Note that the square root of this number (that is, $\sqrt{0.67}$) equals 0.82—which is r for these data.

Since r^2 represents the proportion of variation accounted for, $(1 - r^2)$ represents the proportion of variation that is *not* explained in terms of the correlation between X and Y. This concept is known as the **coefficient of nondetermination** and is symbolized by k^2. Thus k^2 represents the proportion of variation in Y that must be explained by variables other than X.

In summary, the relationship between k^2 and r^2 is

$$k^2 = 1 - r^2 \qquad (9.22)$$

or

$$k^2 + r^2 = 1. \qquad (9.23)$$

Coefficient of Nondetermination

Proportion of variation not explained in terms of the correlation between the two variables.

Figure 9.5 The proportion of the variation on one variable accounted for in terms of variations of a correlated variable at varying values of r.

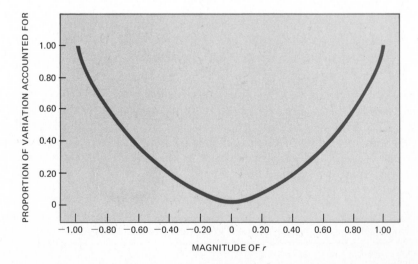

For the data in Fig. 9.3, k^2 may be obtained directly:

$$k^2 = \frac{\text{Unexplained variation}}{\text{Total variation}} = \frac{81.96}{252} = 0.33;$$

or, by use of Formula (9.22),

$$k^2 = 1 - r^2 = 1 - 0.67 = 0.33.$$

CASE EXAMPLE • 9.1
Why We Turn the Heat Down

With many of our key resources in jeopardy and the recently acknowledged risk of poisoning our food and water supplies with toxic substances, the field of environmental psychology is receiving increased attention. In one part of this study, the authors reviewed investigations that determined the effects of providing daily feedback on energy use. In an attempt to ascertain the role of economic factors in energy conservation practices, they related the percentage of reduction in overall energy use to (a) gross annual household income, (b) cost per month of targeted energy source, and (c) the budget share of gross monthly income expended for energy during the target month. The scatter diagrams for these data are shown in Fig. 9.6, with accompanying correlation coefficients (r) and coefficients of determination (r^2).

Figure 9.6 Percent change in overall targeted energy use in relation to the factors (a), (b), and (c).

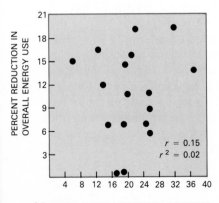
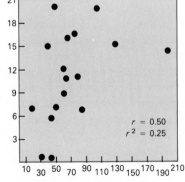
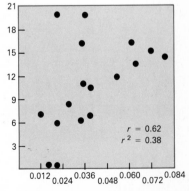
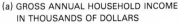

(a) GROSS ANNUAL HOUSEHOLD INCOME
IN THOUSANDS OF DOLLARS

(b) LOSS PER MONTH OF TARGETED
ENERGY SOURCE IN DOLLARS

(c) BUDGET SHARE OF GROSS MONTHLY
INCOME EXPENDED FOR ENERGY
DURING TARGET MONTH

It can be seen in Fig. 9.6(a) that there is only a small relationship between the reduction in energy use and the annual household income. If $r = 0.15$ can be considered an estimate of the population correlation, annual household income accounts for only 2% of the variance in the reduction of energy use. However, when the cost of the energy source is taken into account, as in Fig. 9.6(b), the correlation becomes 0.50 and 25% of the variance in the reduction of energy use is accounted for. Finally, when the proportion of the budget for energy is correlated with the reduction in energy use (Fig. 9.6c), the correlation is 0.62 and approximately 38% of the variance in energy reduction is accounted for. This study suggests that economic factors play a considerable role in obtaining compliance with energy conservation strategies.

Based on Robin C. Winkler and Richard A. Winett (1982), "Behavioral Interventions in Resource Conservation: A Systems Approach Based on Behavioral Economics," *American Psychologist,* **37**(4), 421–435.

9.5 *Correlation and Causation*

You have seen that when two variables are related it is possible to predict one from your knowledge of the other. This relationship between correlation and prediction often leads to a serious error in reasoning; that is, the relationship between two variables frequently carries with it the implication that one has caused the other. This is especially true when there is a temporal relationship between the variables in question, i.e., when one precedes the other in time. What is often overlooked is the fact that the variables may not be causally connected in any way, but that they may vary together by virtue of a common link with a third variable. Thus, if you are a bird watcher, you may note that as the number of birds increases in the spring the grass becomes progressively greener. However, recognizing that the extended number of hours and the increasing warmth of the sun is a third factor influencing both of these variables, you are not likely to conclude that the birds cause the grass to turn green, or vice versa. Unfortunately there are many occasions, particularly in the behavioral sciences, when it is not so easy to identify the third factor.

Suppose that you have demonstrated that there is a high positive correlation between the number of hours students spend studying for an exam and their subsequent grades on that exam. You may be tempted to conclude that the number of hours of study causes grades to vary. This seems to be a perfectly reasonable conclusion, and is probably in close agreement with what your parents and instructors have been telling you for years. Let's look more closely at the implications of a causal relationship. On the assumption that a greater number of hours of study causes grades to increase, we would be led to expect that *any* student who devotes more time to study is guaranteed a

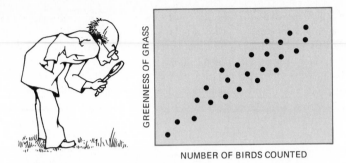

GREENNESS OF GRASS

NUMBER OF BIRDS COUNTED

Correlation is not causation.   Note that when the census count of birds is low, the grass is not very green. When there are many birds, the grass is very green. Therefore, the number of birds determines how green the grass will become. What is wrong with this conclusion?

high grade and that one who spends less time with his books is going to receive a low grade. This is not necessarily the case. We have overlooked the fact that it might be the better student (by virtue of higher intelligence, stronger motivation, better study habits, etc.) who devotes more time to study and performs better simply because he or she has a greater capacity to do so.

What we are saying is that correlational studies simply do not permit inferences of causation. Correlation is a *necessary* but not a *sufficient* condition to establish a causal relationship between two variables. In short, to establish a causal relationship, it is necessary to conduct an experiment in which an independent variable is manipulated by the experimenter, and the effects of these manipulations are reflected in the dependent, or criterion, variable. A correlational study lacks the requirement of independent manipulation.

Huff's book* includes an excellent chapter devoted to the confusion of correlation with causation. He refers to faulty causal inferences from correlational data as the *"post hoc"* fallacy. The following excerpt illustrates a common example of the **post hoc fallacy.**

"Post Hoc" Fallacy

Faulty causal inferences from correlational data.

Reams of pages of figures have been collected to show the value in dollars of a college education, and stacks of pamphlets have been published to bring these figures—and conclusions more or less based on them—to the attention of potential students. I am not quarreling with the intention. I am in favor of education myself, particularly if it includes a course in elementary statistics. Now these figures have pretty conclusively demonstrated that people who have gone to college make more money than people who have not. The exceptions are numerous, of course, but the tendency is strong and clear.

*How to Lie with Statistics.

The only thing wrong is that along with the figures and facts goes a totally unwarranted conclusion. This is the *post hoc* fallacy at its best. It says that these figures show that if *you* (your son, your daughter) attend college you will probably earn more money than if you decide to spend the next four years in some other manner. This unwarranted conclusion has for its basis the equally unwarranted assumption that since college-trained folks make more money, they make it because they went to college. Actually we don't know but that these are the people who would have made more money even if they had *not* gone to college. There are a couple of things that indicate rather strongly that this is so. Colleges get a disproportionate number of two groups of kids—the bright and the rich. The bright might show good earning power without college knowledge. And as for the rich ones—well money breeds money in several obvious ways. Few sons of rich men are found in low-income brackets whether they go to college or not.

Chapter Summary

Let's briefly review what we have discussed in this chapter. We saw that it is possible to "fit" two straight lines to a bivariate distribution of scores, one for predicting Y-scores from known X-values and one for predicting X-scores from known Y-values.

We saw that when the correlation is perfect all the scores fall upon the regression line. Therefore there is no error in prediction. The lower the degree of relationship, the greater the dispersion of scores around the regression line, and the greater the errors of prediction. Finally, when $r = 0$, the mean of the sample provides our "best" predictor for a given variable.

The regression line was shown to be analogous to the mean: The summed deviations around it are zero, and the sums of squares are minimal. The standard error of estimate was shown to be analogous to the standard deviation.

We saw that three separate sums of squares, reflecting variability, may be calculated from correlational data.

1. Variation about the mean of the distribution for each variable. This variation is referred to as the *total sum of squares.*
2. Variation of each score about the regression line. This variation is known as *unexplained variation.*
3. Variation of each predicted score about the mean of the distribution for each variable. This variation is known as *explained variation.*

We saw that the sum of the explained variation and the unexplained variation is equal to the total variation.

Finally, we saw that the ratio of the explained variation to the total variation provides us with the proportion of the toal variation that is explained. The term applied to this proportion is *coefficient of determination*. In addition, the converse concept of *coefficient of nondetermination* was discussed.

Terms to Remember

coefficient of determination (r^2)

coefficient of nondetermination

explained variation

homoscedasticity

"*post hoc*" fallacy

regression line (line of "*best fit*")

residual variance

standard error of estimate

unexplained variation

EXERCISES

1. Find the equation of the regression line for the following data.

X	1	2	3	4	5
Y	5	3	4	2	1

2. In a study concerned with the relationship between two variables, X and Y, the following was obtained:

$$\bar{X} = 119 \qquad \bar{Y} = 1.30$$
$$s_x = 10 \qquad s_y = 0.55$$
$$r = 0.70$$
$$N = 100$$

   a. Sally B. obtained a score of 130 on the X-variable. Predict her score on the Y-variable.
   b. A score of 1.28 on the Y-variable was predicted for Bill B. What was his score on the X-variable?
   c. Determine the standard error of estimate of Y.

3. A study was undertaken to find the relationship between "emotional stability" and performance in college. The following results were obtained:

   Emotional stability   College average
$$\bar{X} = 49 \qquad \bar{Y} = 1.35$$
$$s_x = 12 \qquad s_y = 0.50$$
$$r = 0.36$$
$$N = 60$$

a. Norma obtained a score of 65 on the X-variable. What is your prediction of her score on the Y-variable?

b. Determine the standard error of estimate of X and Y.

c. What proportion of total variation is accounted for by explained variation?

4. Assume that $\overline{X} = 30$, $s_x = 5$; $\overline{Y} = 45$, $s_y = 8$. Draw a separate graph for each pair of regression lines for the following values of r.

   a. 0.00   b. 0.20   c. 0.40   d. 0.60   e. 0.80   f. 1.00

Generalize: What is the relationship between the size of r and the angle formed by the regression lines? If the values of r given in (b) through (f) above were all negative, what is the relationship?

5. Given: The standard deviation of scores on a standardized vocabulary test is 15. The correlation of this test with I.Q. is 0.80. What would you expect the standard deviation on the vocabulary test to be for a large group of students with the same I.Q.? Explain.

6. A student obtains a score on test X that is 1.5 standard deviation above the mean. Predict the standard score for him or her on test Y, if r equals

   a. 0.00,   b. 0.40,   c. 0.80,   d. 1.00,   e. −0.50,   f. −0.80.

7. A personnel manager has made a study of employees involved in one aspect of a manufacturing process. He finds that after they have been on the job for a year he is able to obtain a performance measure that accurately reflects their proficiency. He designs a selection test aimed at predicting their eventual proficiency, and obtains a correlation of 0.65 with the proficiency measure (Y). The mean of the test is 50, $s_x = 6$; $\overline{Y} = 100$, $s_y = 10$, $N = 1000$. Answer the following questions based on these facts (assume that both the selection test and the proficiency measure are normally distributed):

   a. Herman J. obtained a score of 40 on the selection test. What is his predicted proficiency score?

   b. How likely is it that he will score as high as 110 on the proficiency scale?

   c. A score of 80 on the Y-variable is considered satisfactory for the job; below 80 is unsatisfactory. If the X-test is to be used as a selection device, which score should be used as a cut-off point? [*Hint:* Find the value of X that leads to a prediction of 80 on Y. Be sure to employ the appropriate prediction formula.]

   d. Sonya J. obtained a score of 30 on X. How likely is it that she will achieve an acceptable score on Y?

   e. Leon M. obtained a score of 60 on X. How likely is it that he will *fail* to achieve an acceptable score on Y?

   f. For a person to have prospects for a supervisory position, a score of 120 or higher on Y is deemed essential. What value of X should be employed for the selection of potential supervisory personnel?

   g. If 1000 persons achieve a score on X that predicts a $Y = 120$, approximately how many of them will obtain Y scores below 120? Above 130? Below 110? Above 110?

8. An owner of a mail-order house advertises that all orders are shipped within 24 hours of receipt. Since personnel in the shipping department are hired on a day-

to-day basis, it is important for her to be able to predict the number of orders
contained in each batch of daily mail so that she can hire sufficient personnel for
the following day. She hit on the idea of weighing each day's mail and correlating
the weight with the actual number of orders. Over a successive 30-day period, she
obtained the results shown in the table below:

Weight in Pounds	Number of Orders	Weight in Pounds	Number of Orders
20	5400	26	5400
15	4200	21	5000
23	5800	24	5400
17	5000	16	4300
12	3500	34	6700
35	6400	28	6100
29	6000	15	3600
21	5200	11	3200
10	4000	18	5300
13	3800	27	5800
25	5700	30	5900
14	4000	22	5500
18	4800	20	5200
30	6200	24	5000
33	6600	13	3700

a. Find the correlation between the weight of mail and the number of orders.
   [*Hint:* In calculating the correlation, consider dropping the final two digits on
   the Y-variable.]
b. If 10 persons are required to handle 1000 orders per day, how many should
   be hired to handle 22 pounds of mail? 15 pounds? 30? 38? [*Note:* Assume
   that employees are hired only in groups of 10.]

9. Peruse the magazine section of your Sunday newspaper, monthly magazines, television, and radio advertisements for examples of the *post hoc* fallacy.

10. Assume that students take two tests for entrance into the college of their choice.
    Both are normally distributed tests. The college-entrance examination has a mean
    of 47.63 and a standard deviation of 13.82. The verbal comprehension test has a
    mean equal to 39.15 and a standard deviation equal to 12.35. The correlation
    between the two tests equals 0.85.
    a. Estelle obtained a score of 40 on her college-entrance examination. Predict
       her score on the verbal comprehension test.
    b. How likely is it that she will score at least 40 on the verbal comprehension
       test?
    c. Howard obtained a score of 40 on the verbal comprehension test. Predict
       his score on the college-entrance examination.
    d. How likely is it that he will score at least 40 on the college-entrance exami-
       nation?

e. REC University finds that students who score at least 45 on the verbal comprehension test are most successful. What score on the college-entrance examination should be used as the cutoff point for selection?

f. Harris obtained a score of 55 on the college-entrance examination. Would he be selected by REC University? What are his chances of achieving an acceptable score on the verbal comprehension test?

11. On the basis of the obtained data (below), an experimenter asserts that the older a child is, the fewer irrelevant responses he or she makes in an experimental situation.

   a. Determine whether this conclusion is valid.
   b. Mindy, age 13, enters the experimental situation. What is the most probable number of irrelevant responses the experimenter would predict for Mindy?

Age	Number of Irrelevant Responses	Age	Number of Irrelevant Responses
2	11	7	12
3	12	9	8
4	10	9	7
4	13	10	3
5	11	11	6
5	9	11	5
6	10	12	5
7	7		

12. Why do we have two regression lines? Under what circumstances will the regression lines be identical?

13. The per-capita gross national product (GNP) is widely recognized as an estimate of the living standard of a nation. It has been claimed that per-capita energy consumption is, in turn, a good predictor of per capita GNP. Shown below are the GNP (expressed in dollars per capita) and the per-capita energy consumption (expressed in millions of BTU's per capita) of various nations.

   a. Construct a scatter diagram from the data at the top of p. 187.
   b. Determine the correlation between GNP and energy expenditures.
   c. Construct the regression line for predicting per-capita GNP from per-capita energy consumption.
   d. The following nations were not represented in the original sample. Their per-capita energy expenditures were: Chile, 21; Ireland, 49; Belgium, 88. Calculate the predicted per-capita GNP for each country. Compare the predicted values with the actual values, which are, respectively, 400; 630; 1400.

14. Show algebraically that

$$b_y = \frac{N\sum XY - (\sum X)(\sum Y)}{N\sum X^2 - (\sum X)^2}.$$

Country	Energy Consumption (in millions of BTUs)	GNP (dollars)
India	3.4	55
Ghana	3.0	270
Portugal	7.7	240
Colombia	12.0	290
Greece	12.0	390
Mexico	23.0	310
Japan	30.3	550
USSR	69.0	800
Netherlands	75.0	1100
France	58.0	1390
Norway	67.0	1330
West Germany	90.0	1410
Australia	88.0	1525
United Kingdom	113.0	1400
Canada	131.0	1900
United States	180.0	2900

15. Show algebraically that

$$Y' = \bar{Y} + \frac{N\sum XY - (\sum X)(\sum Y)}{N\sum X^2 - (\sum X)^2}(X - \bar{X}).$$

16.
$$\frac{X\ 3\ 4\ 5\ 6\ 7\ 8\ 9\ 10\ 11}{Y\ 4\ 3\ 5\ 6\ 8\ 7\ 9\ \ 9\ 11}$$

   a. Determine the correlation for the scores above.
   b. Given the correlations, and the computed mean for Y, predict the value of Y', for each X.
   c. Calculate $\sum(Y - \bar{Y})^2$.
   d. Calculate the unexplained variance.
   e. Calculate the explained variance.
   f. Calculate the coefficient of determination. Show that the square root of that value equals r.

17. A manager of a catering service found a correlation of 0.70 between the number of people at a party and the loaves of bread consumed.
   a. For a party of 60 people, calculate the predicted number of loaves needed.
   b. For a party of 35, calculate the predicted number of loaves needed.
   c. What is the $s_{est\ y}$?

Number of People	Number of Loaves
$\bar{X} = 50$	$\bar{Y} = 5$
$s_x = 15$	$s_y = 1.2$

18. In a recent study, Thornton (1977) explored the relationship of marital happiness to the frequency of sexual intercourse and to the frequency of arguments. Twenty-eight married couples volunteered to monitor their daily frequency of sexual intercourse and arguments for 35 consecutive days, and then they indicated their perceived marital happiness using a 7-point scale ranging from very unhappy (1) to perfectly happy (7). Some of Thornton's results are summarized here.

	Marital Happiness	Sexual Intercourse	Arguments
Mean	5.32	13.46	6.15
s	1.66	7.32	4.19

Correlation between happiness and arguments = $-.740$
Correlation between happiness and intercourse = $.705$

a. How happy would you predict a couple to be who reported having 10 arguments during the 35-day study period?

b. How happy would you predict a couple to be who reported having sexual intercourse one time each day during the 35-day study period?

c. A couple reporting that they are very unhappy (rating = 1.0) are most likely engaging in sexual intercourse how often?

d. What is the standard error of estimate for marital happiness when frequency of sexual intercourse is the predictor? What is the standard error of estimate when frequency of arguments is the predictor?

e. What proportion of the variability in ratings of marital happiness is accounted for by frequency of sexual intercourse? What proportion is accounted for by frequency of arguments?

f. What is the coefficient of nondetermination when marital happiness is predicted from frequency of sexual intercourse? What is the coefficient of nondetermination when marital happiness is predicted from frequency of arguments?

PART III

Inferential Statistics:
Parametric Tests of Significance

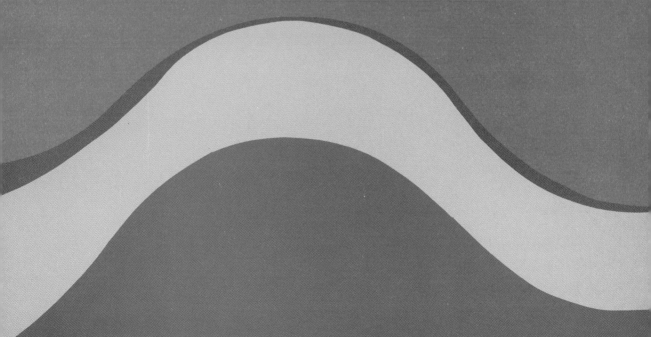

10

Probability

10.1 An Introduction to Probability Theory

In the past few chapters, we have been primarily concerned with the exposition of techniques employed by statisticians and scientists to describe and present data in the most economical and meaningful form. However, we pointed out in Chapter 1 that the interests of scientists go beyond the mere description of data. Fundamental to the strategy of science is the formulation of general statements about populations or the effects of experimental conditions on criterion variables. Thus, as we have already noted, scientists are not usually satisfied to report merely that the arithmetic mean of the drug group tested on variable X is higher or lower than the mean of the placebo group tested on this variable. They also want to make general statements such as, "The difference between the two groups is of such magnitude that we cannot reasonably ascribe it to chance variation. We may therefore conclude that the drug had an effect on the variable studied. More specifically, this effect was . . . etc., etc."

The problem of chance variation is an important one. We all know that the variability of our data in the behavioral sciences engenders the risk of drawing an incorrect conclusion. Take a look at the following example.

From casual observations, Experimenter A hypothesizes that first-grade girls have higher I.Q. scores than first-grade boys, and administers an I.Q. test to four boys and four girls in a first-grade class. The mean of the girls is found to be higher: 110 to 103. Is Experimenter A justified in concluding that his or her hypothesis has been confirmed? The answer is obviously negative. But why? After all, there is a difference between the sample means, isn't there? Intuitively, we might argue that the variability of intelligence among first-graders is so great, and the N in the study so small, that *some* differences in the means are inevitable as a result of our selection procedures. The critical questions that must be answered by inferential statistics then become: (1) Is the apparent difference in intelligence among first-graders reliable? (That is, will it appear regularly in repetitions of the study?) or (2) Is the difference the result of unsystematic factors that will vary from study to study, and thereby produce sets of differences without consistency?

A prime function of inferential statistics is to provide rigorous and logically sound procedures for answering these questions. As we shall see in this chapter and the next, *probability theory* provides the logical basis for deciding among all the various alternative interpretations of research data.

Probability theory is not as unfamiliar as many would think. Indeed, in everyday life we are constantly called upon to make probability judgments, although we may not recognize them as such. For example, let us suppose that, for various reasons, you are unprepared for today's class. You seriously consider not attending class. What are the factors that will influence your decision? Obviously, one consideration would be the likelihood that the instructor

192

BOX 10.1

The gambler's fallacy

Probability theory is the foundation stone of inferential statistics. Without it, our interpretation of data would progress little beyond sheer guesswork. Considering its importance, it is surprising that mistaken notions about probability pervade the thinking of many people. One is the "Gamber's Fallacy," illustrated in this excerpt from *Winning with Statistics*.

I'm Overdue for a Run of Luck

Famous last words! This one takes many forms and invades many fields. The gambler is tossing coins and loses four in a row. Reasoning that five losses in a row is exceedingly rare ($p = 0.031$, odds against = $31.25:1$), he decides to increase the ante. "I'm due for a win," he proclaims confidently. Your favorite baseball player has gone 4 for 0. When he comes to bat for the fifth time, you exude confidence: "he's due for a hit." The opposing quarterback has just completed six consecutive passes against your team. You breathe a sigh of relief: "The next is bound to be incomplete or intercepted."

Although these examples are not all exactly the same, they have one thing in common—the belief that events have memories. It is as if the gambler is reasoning, "The coin will remember that it came up heads four times in a row and will try to balance out the 'law of averages' by coming up tails on the next toss." This is sheer nonsense. So long as the coin is "honest," it is just as likely to come up heads as tails on the next toss or on any toss, for that matter. We speak of this condition as *independence*—the outcome of one trial has no effect on later trials. This is just another way of denying that coins or dice or cards or roulette wheels have memories.

It is somewhat different when dealing with activities involving behavior. Although a bat and ball have no memory, "turns at bat" are not always independent, particularly if they are against a pitcher of Tom Seaver's caliber. And your football team could have seven passes completed against it because of its porous defense. Nevertheless, it is incorrect to cite the "law of averages" as the reason for expecting something different on the next trial. The law of averages has no enforcement agency behind it, nor is there a Supreme Court to oversee the constitutionality of its "decisions." Indeed, the only thing it has in common with jurisprudence is its impartiality.

Excerpted from R. P. Runyon, *Winning with Statistics*. Reading, Mass.: Addison-Wesley, 1977.

will detect your lack of preparation. If the risk is high, you decide not to attend class; if low, then you will attend.

Let us look at this example in slightly different terms. There are two alternative possibilities:

Event A: Your lack of preparation *will* be detected.
Event B: Your lack of preparation *will not* be detected.

There is uncertainty in this situation because more than one alternative is possible. Your decision whether or not to attend class will depend upon the degree of assurance you associate with each of these alternatives. Thus, if you are fairly certain that the first alternative will prevail, you will decide not to attend class.

Suppose that your instructor frequently calls upon students to participate in class discussion. In fact, you have noted that most of the students are called upon in any given class session. This is an example of a situation in which a high degree of assurance is associated with the first alternative. Stated another way, the probability of Event A is higher than the probability of Event B. Thus you decide not to attend class.

Although you have not used any formal probability laws in this example, you have actually made a judgment based upon an *intuitive* use of probability.

You may have noted that many of the questions raised in the exercises began with, "What is the likelihood that . . .?" These questions were in preparation for the formal discussion of probability occurring in this and the following chapters. However, before learning the elements of probability theory, you should understand one of the most important concepts in inferential statistics, that of *randomness*.

10.2 *The Concept of Randomness*

You will recall that in discussing the role of inferential statistics we pointed out the fact that population parameters are rarely known or knowable. It is for this reason that we are usually forced to draw samples from a given population and estimate the parameters from the sample statistics. Obviously, we want to select these samples in such a way that they are representative of the populations from which they are drawn. One way to achieve representativeness is to employ simple **random sampling:** *selecting samples in such a way that each sample of a given size has precisely the same probability of being selected* or, alternatively, *selecting the events in the sample such that each event is equally likely to be selected in a sample of a given size.*

Consider selecting samples of $N = 2$ from a population of five numbers: 0, 1, 2, 3, 4. If, for any reason, any number is more likely to be drawn than any other number, each sample would *not* have an equal probability of being drawn. For example, if for any reason the number 3 were twice as likely to be drawn as any other number, there would be a preponderance of samples containing the value 3. Such sampling procedures are referred to as being **biased.** In the naturalistic type of study alluded to earlier, wherein our purpose is to describe certain characteristics of a population, the danger of bias is ever present. When we are interested in learning the characteristics of the general population on a given variable, we do not dare to select our sample from automobile registration lists or "at random" on a street corner in New York City. The dangers of generalizing to the general population from such biased samples should be obvious to you. Unless the condition of randomness is met, we may never know to what population we should generalize our results. Furthermore, with nonrandom samples we find that many of the rules of probability do not hold.

Random Sampling

Samples selected in such a way that each sample of a given size has precisely the same probability of being selected.

Bias

In sampling, when selections favor certain events or certain collections of events.

Moreover, the statistical tests presented in this text require *independent random sampling*. Two events are said to be independent if the selection of one has no effect upon the probability of selecting the other event. We can most readily grasp independence in terms of games of chance, assuming they are played honestly. Knowledge of the results of one toss of a coin, one throw of a die, one outcome of the roulette wheel, or one selection of a card from a well-shuffled deck (assuming replacement of the card after each selection) will not aid us one iota in our predictions of future outcomes.

When we are involved in conducting an experiment, we must concern ourselves with introducing randomness at two junctures of the study. We must *select* our subjects at random from the population of interest, and then we must *assign* these subjects at random to the experimental conditions.

It is beyond the scope of this text to delve deeply into sampling procedures, since that topic is a full course by itself. However, let us look at an illustration of the procedures by which we may achieve randomness in assigning subjects to experimental conditions.

Suppose you are interested in comparing three different methods of teaching reading readiness to preschool children. There are 87 subjects who are to be divided into 3 equal groups. The assignment of these subjects must be made in a random manner.

One method to achieve randomness would be to place each subject's name on a slip of paper. We shuffle these slips and then place them into three equal piles.

An alternative method would be to use the Table of Random Digits (Table Q in the table section of this book). Since the digits in this table have already been randomized, the effect of shuffling has been achieved. We assign to each of the 87 students a numeral from 01 to 87. We may start with any row or column of digits in Table Q.

After we have selected 29 numerals that correspond to 29 different subjects, we have formed our first group. We continue until we have 3 groups, each consisting of 29 different subjects. For example, if we start with the fifteenth row and choose consecutive pairs of digits, we obtain the following subjects: 65, 48, 11, 76, 74, 17, and so on. If any numeral over 87 or any repeated numeral appears, we disregard it.

Finally, most present-day computers have a wired-in function that generates random digits. If you have access to a computer, you will save much time by letting the computer do the selecting for you. This randomization function is at the heart of the many games that computer's play.

Here is a BASIC program that randomly generates 25 numbers between 0 and 99:

```
10 PRINT "THIS PROGRAM RANDOMLY SELECTS 25 NUMBERS
BETWEEN 0 AND 99"
20 PRINT "RANDOM NUMBERS"
```

```
30 FOR K=1 TO 25
40 LET X=INT (99*(RND(0)+1)
50 PRINT X
60 NEXT K
999 END
```

If you want to generate fewer or more random numbers, change the 25 in line 30 to the integer you desire.

The reason for the paramount importance of random procedures will become clear in this chapter and the next. Fundamentally, it is based on a fascinating fact of inferential statistics: *Each event may not be predictable when taken alone, but collections of random events can take on predictable forms.* The binomial distribution, which we shall discuss at greater length in Section 11.3, illustrates this fact. If we were to take, say, 20 unbiased coins and toss them into the air, we could not predict accurately the proportion that would land "heads." However, if we were to toss these 20 coins a great many times, record the number turning up heads on each trial, and construct a frequency distribution of outcomes in which the horizontal axis varies between no heads and all heads, the plot would take on a characteristic and predictable form known as the *binomial distribution.* By employing the binomial model, we would be able to predict with considerable accuracy over a large number of trials the percentage of the time various outcomes will occur. What is perhaps more fascinating is the fact that the distribution of outcomes of this two-category variable more and more closely approximates the normal curve as N (the number of tosses of a sample coin or the number of coins tossed at one time) becomes larger. Indeed, with large Ns we may use the normal curve to describe the probability of various outcomes of a binomial variable.

The same reasoning is true with respect to the normal curve model. In the absence of any specific information, we might not be able to predict a person's status with respect to a given trait (intelligence, height, weight, etc.). However, as we already know, frequency distributions of scores on these traits commonly take the form of the normal curve. Thus we may predict the proportion of individuals scoring between specified score limits.

Sampling Distribution
A theoretical probability distribution of a statistic that would result from drawing all possible samples of a given size from some population.

What is perhaps of more importance, from the point of view of inferential statistics, is the fact that distributions of sample statistics ($\overline{X}$, s, median, etc.), based on random sampling from a population, also take on highly predictable forms. Chapter 11 deals with the concept of **sampling distributions,** which are theoretical probability distributions of a statistic that would result from drawing all possible samples of a given size from some population.

With this brief introduction to the concept of randomness, you are prepared to look at probability theory.

10.3 *Approaches to Probability*

Probability may be regarded as a theory that is concerned with the possible outcomes of experiments. The experiments must be potentially repetitive; i.e., we must be able to repeat them under similar conditions. It must be possible to enumerate *every* outcome that can occur, and we must be able to state the expected relative frequencies of these outcomes.

It is the method of assigning relative frequencies to each of the possible outcomes that distinguishes the classical from the empirical approach to probability theory.

Classical Approach to Probability

The theory of probability has always been closely associated with games of chance. For example, suppose that we want to know the probability that a single card selected from a 52-card deck will be an ace of spades. There are 52 possible outcomes. We assume an ideal situation in which we expect that each outcome is equally likely to occur. Thus the probability of selecting an ace of spades is $\frac{1}{52}$. This kind of reasoning has led to the following classical definition or probability:

$$p(A) = \frac{\text{Number of outcomes favoring event } A}{\text{Total no. of outcomes (favoring } A + \text{ not favoring } A)}. \quad (10.1)$$

Note that probability is defined as a proportion (p). The most important point in the classical definition of probability is the assumption of an *ideal* situation in which the structure of the population is known; i.e., the total number of possible outcomes (N) is known. The expected relative frequency of each of these outcomes is arrived at by deductive reasoning. Thus the probability of an event is interpreted as a theoretical (or an idealized) relative frequency of the event. In the preceding example, the total number of possible outcomes was 52 (all cards in the deck), and each outcome was assumed to have an equal likelihood of occurrence. Thus p(ace of spades) = $\frac{1}{52}$; p(king of hearts) = $\frac{1}{52}$, and so on.

Empirical Approach to Probability

Although it is usually easy to assign expected relative frequencies to the possible outcomes of games of chance, we cannot do this for most real-life experiments. In actual situations, expected relative frequencies are assigned on the basis of empirical findings. Thus we may not know the exact proportion of students in a university who have blue eyes, but we may study a random sample of students and estimate the proportion who will have blue eyes. Once we have arrived at an estimate, we may employ classical probability theory to answer questions such as; What is the probability that in a sample of ten students, drawn at random from the student body, three or more will be blue-eyed? Or, what is the probability that student Jones, drawn at random from that student body, will have blue eyes?

If, in a random sample of 100 students, we found that 30 had blue eyes, we could estimate that the proportion of blue-eyed students in the university was 0.30 by employing formula (10.1):

$$p(\text{blue-eyed}) = \frac{30}{100} = 0.30.$$

Thus the probability is 0.30 that student Jones will have blue eyes. [*Note:* This represents an *empirical* probability; i.e., the expected relative frequency was assigned on the basis of empirical findings.]

Although it is easy to assign expected relative frequencies to the possible outcome of games of chance, we cannot do this for most real-life experiments. Take the gender of an about-to-be-born child. What is the probability that it will be a girl? On the surface, the answer would appear to be easy. Hypothetically, the birth of a boy or girl would appear to be equally likely, 0.50 in both cases. However, such is not the case. In the United States, the proportion of annual male birth has been exceptionally stable for many years—0.5041 for white and 0.5069 for black (See Table 10.1).

A gambler who made his livelihood on taking bets on the gender of chil-

Table 10.1 Proportion of male births, by race, in the United States between 1971–1977.

Year	White	Black
1970	0.5143	0.5076
1971	0.5136	0.5069
1972	0.5139	0.5059
1973	0.5138	0.5068
1974	0.5143	0.5074
1975	0.5143	0.5074
1976	0.5141	0.5067
1977	0.5141	0.5064
Mean	0.5141	0.5069

dren about to be born could do quite well, over the long run, by giving even odds that the child will be a girl. On every 10,000 bets, the gambler could expect to win, on the average, 5141 times and lose 4859 times.

The fundamental feature of empirical probabilities is that they are based on actual measurements rather than on theoretical proportions. As a matter of fact, there is usually little or no basis for assigning theoretical probabilities to most of the situations confronted by the student of behavior: for example, the probability that a person will require treatment for a disorder at some time in his/her life, the probability that a convicted felon will return to crime, or the probability that a child will be born with a congenital defect. Probabilities such as these must be obtained empirically and are always subject to revision in the light of additional data.

Subjective Approaches to Probability

There are many occasions when we lack the objective data for estimating probabilities. Nevertheless, we may have strong feelings that we term "a hunch," "common sense," or an intuition. The clinician may say, "I can't tell you precisely why I feel this way, but I believe that client A is at high risk for suicide." We should not dismiss these subjective probabilities out-of-hand. Even though subjective probabilities cannot, by their very nature, be documented and substantiated, they may nevertheless arise from a lifetime of observation and assessment of subtle cues. Indeed, it is likely that any important decision we have made in life includes subjective probabilities as a basic ingredient. For this reason, we accept the notion of subjective probabilities. Once made, we expect them to follow the same rules as probabilities obtained by either the classical or the empirical approach.

10.4 *Formal Properties of Probability*

Probabilities Vary between 0 and 1.00

From the classical definition of probability, p is always between 0 and 1, inclusively. If an event is certain to occur, its probability is 1; if it is certain not to occur, its probability is 0. For example, the probability of drawing the ace of spades from an ordinary deck of 52 playing cards is $\frac{1}{52}$. The probability of drawing a red ace of spades is zero, since there are no events favoring this result. If all events favor a result (for example, drawing a card with *some* marking on it), $p = 1$. Thus for any given event, say A, $0 \leq p(A) \leq 1.00$, in which the symbol $\leq$ means "less than or equal to."*

---

*The symbol $\geq$ means "greater than or equal to."

Expressing Probability

In addition to expressing probability as a proportion, several other ways are often employed. It is sometimes convenient to express probability as a *percentage* or as the *number of chances in* 100.

To illustrate: If the probability of an event is 0.05, we expect this event to occur 5% of the time, or *the chances that this event will occur* are 5 in 100. This same probability may be expressed by saying that the odds are 95 to 5 *against* the event occurring, or 19 to 1 against it.

Note that when expressing probability as the *odds against* the occurrence of an event we use the following formula:

Odds against event A =
(Total no. of outcomes − No. favoring A) *to* No. favoring A.   (10.2)

Thus, if $p(A)$ = 0.01, the *odds against* the occurrence of event A are 99 to 1.

Sample Space, Event, and Complex Experiments

So far in this chapter we have seen that probability plays an extremely important role in our personal and professional lives. Up to this point, we have restricted our outlook to simple statistical experiments, directing our attention to finding the probability of a single outcome like selecting the ace of spades from a deck of playing cards or giving birth to a female child. In real life, our inquiry typically extends into far more complex questions. For example, if ten patients are under psychotherapeutic treatment for an anxiety disorder, what are the probabilities that all ten, or 9, or 8 . . . show improvement within some specified period? Will a target person's physical attractiveness affect the probability that help will be offered by a bystander? Or, will knowledge of a person's mood alter our assessment of that person's recollection of pleasant versus unpleasant experiences?

Sample Space

All possible outcomes of an experiment.

In dealing with complex experiments, it is useful to introduce the concept of **sample space.** When dealing with simple experiments, we refer to the most elementary unit as an outcome. For example, in tossing a single die, the sample space consists of the outcomes: 1, 2, 3, 4, 5, 6. All possible outcomes constitute the sample space. If we classify the results of psychotherapy into two different categories—unimproved and improved—each of these categories constitute an outcome.

When these outcomes are combined into various subsets or collections, we have defined an event. Thus, with our patients under psychotherapy, an event might be "all patients improved," or "six improved, four unimproved," or "two improved, eight unimproved." With the die, an event may be an odd number (a collection of 3 outcomes), a six (a collection of one outcome), or a number greater than three (a collection of two outcomes). Suppose we call event A: an odd number. The complement of event A (symbolized by $\overline{A}$ and read not A) consists of all outcomes not included in A. When the two events, A and $\overline{A}$ exhaust all possible outcomes, $p(A) + p(\overline{A}) = 1.00$. The two events are said to be **exhaustive.** In addition, if two events cannot occur simultaneously, they are said to be **mutually exclusive.** In the example concerning a die, events A and $\overline{A}$ are mutually exclusive since the occurrence of A on a specific trial excludes the possibility of $\overline{A}$ on the same trial.

    Two useful techniques have been devised for diagramming various concepts of probability—the *Venn diagram* and the *tree diagram.* The Venn diagram is illustrated in Figure 10.1.

    The tree diagram is of greatest value when the events of interest occur in stages. To illustrate, suppose we want to diagram the possible results of assessing, at three different stages, the effects of treating a single patient for an anxiety disorder. At each stage, there are two mutually exclusive and exhaustive outcomes: unimproved versus improved. The tree diagram permits us to visually display all possible events from improvement shown at all stages to no improvement shown at any stage. We later illustrate the use of the tree diagram for calculating the probabilities of various events, but for the moment, note the simplicity and utility of using it to display events visually (Figure 10.2).

    Each fork in a tree diagram shows a specific outcome that can occur at each stage. For example, at stage one the patient can improve (upper branch) or be unimproved (lower branch). Each of these outcomes can serve as the fork for the next two possible outcomes. Thus a patient who improves at the first stage may either improve or show no improvement at the second stage. If the patient improves again, the event that describes this result is improve. With

Exhaustive

Two or more events are said to be exhaustive if they exhaust all possible outcomes. Symbolically, $p(A$ or B or . . .) $= 1.00$.

Mutually Exclusive

Events A and B are said to be mutually exclusive if they cannot occur simultaneously.

Figure 10.1 Various outcomes in the sample space of a single die to yield the events of (a), (b), and (c).

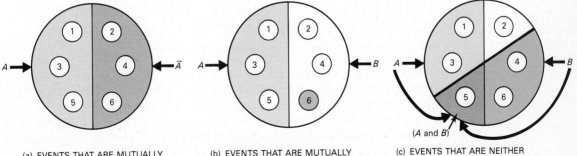

(a) EVENTS THAT ARE MUTUALLY EXCLUSIVE AND EXHAUSTIVE

EVENT A: ALL ODD NUMBERS

EVENT $\overline{A}$: ALL EVEN NUMBERS

(b) EVENTS THAT ARE MUTUALLY EXCLUSIVE BUT NOT EXHAUSTIVE

EVENT A: AN ODD NUMBER

EVENT B: THE NUMBER 6

(c) EVENTS THAT ARE NEITHER MUTUALLY EXCLUSIVE OR EXHAUSTIVE

EVENT A: AN ODD NUMBER

EVENT B: A NUMBER GREATER THAN 3

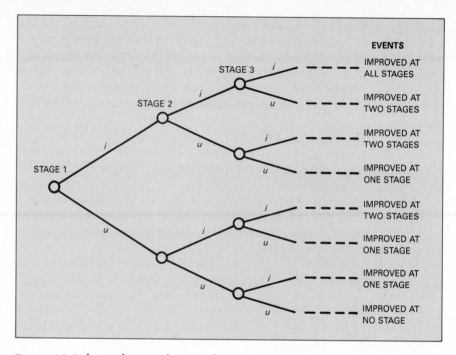

Figure 10.2 A tree diagram showing all possible consequences of treating a single patient, over three stages, for an anxiety disorder.

three different stages and two outcomes at each stage, a total of 8 different branches are produced. Each end branch represents an event. To see how this works, read from left to right. The top branch at the far right represents improvement at all stages. In contrast, the bottom branches *(u, u, u)* represent unimprovement at each stage in the treatment.

10.5 *Addition Rule*

When we know the sample space of an experiment, it is possible to identify any number of different events for purposes of probability analysis. To illustrate, we may raise such questions as

1. What is the probability of obtaining one event *or* another, e.g., drawing a queen *or* a club from a deck of playing cards?

2. What is the probability of obtaining two events simultaneously, e.g., selecting a queen *and* a club from a deck of playing cards?

To answer the first question, we must make use of the addition rule; and, for the second, we use the multiplication rule. We shall examine the addition rule in this section and the multiplication rule in Section 10.6.

When Events are Not Mutually Exclusive

Suppose that, in an effort to obtain data on current reasons for seeking professional help, a questionnaire was sent out to administrators at various mental health clinics throughout the country. One part of the questionnaire dealt with the abuse of drugs and alcohol among those receiving care at the clinics. The results of the questionnaires showed that out of 5900 patients, 354 abused alcohol and 236 abused drugs, of these, the abusers of alcohol and drugs 118 abused both. Let us define Event A as the abuse of alcohol and Event B as the abuse of drugs.

Based on the replies, we can estimate the probability of each event from the sample:

$$p(A) = \frac{354}{5900} = 0.06$$

$$p(B) = \frac{236}{5900} = 0.04$$

Now, if we wished to know the probability that a given patient was either an alcohol or drug abuser, we might be tempted to add together the number of patients abusing alcohol and the number abusing drugs, divide by n to obtain: $p(A \text{ or } B) = (354 + 236)/5900 = 0.10$. However, this probability does not take into account the 118 people who are counted twice—once as alcohol and once as drug abusers. In other words, the two categories are not mutually exclusive. This is shown as the overlapping area in the Venn diagram in Figure 10.3.

To determine the probability of event A or event B, we must subtract out the 118 cases that overlap both categories. This leads to the general case of the addition rule. It is called the general case because it applies equally to mutually exclusive and nonmutually exclusive categories:

$$p(A \text{ or } B) = p(A) + p(B) - p(A \text{ and } B), \qquad (10.3)$$

where $p(A \text{ and } B)$ represents the probability associated with the overlapping events.

In the present example, $p(A \text{ or } B) = 354/5900 + 236/5900 - 118/5900 = 0.08$. Thus, according to this survey, the probability is 0.08 that a given individual seeking help at a mental health clinic is either an alcohol or a drug abuser (or both).

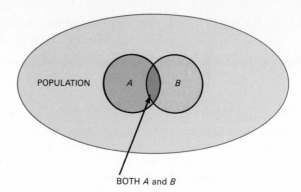

POPULATION   A   B

BOTH *A* and *B*

Figure 10.3   Venn diagram showing that the two categories, alcohol abuse and drug abuse, are not mutually exclusive. To obtain p(A or B), we must subtract out the area of overlap.

Overlapping categories is also characteristic of many games of chance, e.g., roulette or cards. To illustrate, if we want to know the probability of selecting either a heart (to fill a flush) or a jack (to fill a straight), we must take into account the fact that the jack of hearts overlaps both events. If we let event A equal the probability of a heart, $p(A)$ = 13/52. The probability of event B (a jack) is 4/52. However, the probability of both occurring (a jack of hearts) is 1/52. Therefore, $p(A$ or $B)$ = 13/52 + 4/52 − 1/52 = 0.31.

Mutually Exclusive Events

By definition, when events are mutually exclusive, there is no overlapping of the categories. Since both event A and event B cannot occur together, the probability of event A and event B is 0; that is, $p(A$ and $B)$ = 0.

Therefore, for mutually exclusive events, the last term in Formula 10.3 reduces to zero. Thus, the addition rule becomes

$$p(A \text{ or } B) = p(A) + p(B), \tag{10.4}$$

where the events are mutually exclusive.

To illustrate, in Exercise 26 of Chapter 4, we presented census figures on the size of U.S. families of Spanish origin. These figures are reproduced in Table 10.2.

What is the probability that a given family of Spanish origin has either 2 or 3 members? Using Formula 10.4, we find $p(2$ or $3)$ = $p(2)$ + $p(3)$ = 0.239 + 0.238 = 0.477.

What is the probability that such a family will number 6 or more? $p(6$ or 7 or more) = 0.079 + 0.078 = 0.157.

Table 10.2 **Size of U.S. families of Spanish origin in 1977.**

Size	Number (in thousands)	p
2	662	0.239
3	636	0.230
4	625	0.226
5	408	0.148
6	218	0.079
7 or more persons	216	0.078

Source: U.S. Bureau of Census. *Current Population Reports*, Series P-20, no. 339, U.S. Government Printing Office.

Formula (10.4) can be extended to include any number of mutually exclusive events. Thus

$$p(A \text{ or } B \text{ or} \ldots Z) = p(A) + p(B) + \ldots + p(Z).$$

In Chapters 11 and 17, we shall be dealing with problems based on *dichotomous, yes-no,* or *two-category* populations, in which the events in question are not only mutually exclusive, but are *exhaustive.* For example, in families of Spanish origin, what is the probability of drawing either a mean family size equal to or greater than 5, or a mean less than 5? Not only is it impossible to obtain both events simultaneously (i.e., they are mutually exclusive), but there is *no possible outcome other than a mean* equal to or greater than 5 or a mean less than 5. In the case of *mutually exclusive* and *exhaustive events,* we arrive at the very useful formulation:

$$p(A) + p(B) = 1.00. \qquad (10.5)$$

In treating dichotomous populations, it is common practice to employ the two symbols P and Q to represent, respectively, the probability of the occurrence of an event and the probability of the nonoccurrence of an event. Thus, if we are flipping a single coin, we can let P represent the probability of occurrence of a head and Q the probability of the nonoccurrence of a head (i.e., the occurrence of a tail). These considerations lead to three useful formulations:

$$P + Q = 1.00, \qquad (10.6)$$
$$P = 1.00 - Q, \qquad (10.7)$$
$$Q = 1.00 - P, \qquad (10.8)$$

when the events are *mutually exclusive and exhaustive.*

10.6 *The Multiplication Rule*

In the preceding section, we were concerned with determining the probability of obtaining one event or another based upon a *single* draw (or trial) from a set of 49 means. In statistical inference, we are often faced with the problem of ascertaining the probability of the joint or successive occurrence of two or more events when more than one draw or trial is involved. For example, what is the probability that we will draw a diamond and a heart on two successive draws from a deck of playing cards? Or, based on the results of the study by Benson et al. (Case Example 2.2), what is the probability that five out of five male subjects will engage in helping behavior (mailing the envelope containing the application or delivering it to an airport ticket counter)? Often our question will take on a somewhat modified form. If we assume an attractive female applicant, what is the probability that five out of five male subjects will engage in helping behavior? This last question is concerned with conditional probabilities. In this case, we are asking if the probability of obtaining helping behavior is conditional on the attractiveness of the applicant. In this section, we examine joint, marginal, and conditional probabilities as well as the multiplication rule for independent and nonindependent events.

Joint, Marginal, and Conditional Probabilities

To illustrate joint, marginal, and conditional probabilities, let's return to the data presented in Case Example 2.2.

If we divide each of the cell frequencies and the marginal (row and column) totals by *n*, we obtain a joint probability Table (10.4). Note that the table provides direct answers to such questions as "What is the probability that help was provided to an attractive applicant?" "For the total sample, what is the probability that help was not provided?" "What is the probability that help was not provided to an unattractive applicant?"

Table 10.3 **Number helping when the applicant is an attractive or unattractive female (whites and blacks combined) and the subject is a male.**

Helping Response	Characteristics of Target		Row Totals
	Attractive	**Unattractive**	
Helped	52	35	87
Did not help	62	71	133
Column totals	114	106	220

Table 10.4 **Joint probability table of helping behavior when the applicant was either attractive or unattractive.**

Helping Response	Attractive (A)	Unattractive (Ā)	Marginal Probability
Helped (B)	0.236	0.159	0.395
Did not help (B̄)	0.282	0.323	0.605
Marginal probability	0.518	0.482	1.000

Joint probabilities • Each cell in Table 10.4 shows the joint probability associated with the column and row variables. For example, the joint probability that the applicant was both attractive (Event A) and helped (Event B) is

$$p(A \text{ and } B) = \frac{52}{220} = 0.236.$$

However, the joint probability of an applicant being unattractive (Event A) and helped (Event B) is

$$p(\overline{A} \text{ and } B) = \frac{35}{220} = 0.159.$$

Also, the joint probability of an applicant being attractive (Event Ā) and not helped (Event B̄) is

$$p(A \text{ and } \overline{B}) = \frac{62}{220} = 0.282$$

Marginal probabilities • Note that each marginal probability represents a simple probability of an event and is *not* conditional on other events. For this reason, marginal probabilties are also referred to as unconditional probabilities. Thus, in Table 10.4, the right-hand or Row Marginals shows the simple probability of a person being helped or not helped without regard to whether or not she is attractive. Thus, the unconditional probability of being helped is 0.395, whereas the unconditional probability of not being helped is 0.605.

Similarly, the Column Marginals show the probability that the applicant was attractive (0.518) or unattractive (0.482) whether or not she was helped.

Conditional probabilities • When the information we have about events is limited to the marginal probabilities, our best predictions concerning the probability of a given event is similarly restricted to these marginal probabilities. Thus, if we know only that a male entered the phone booth that contained a "lost" job application, our best estimate of the probability that he will help is 0.395 and that he will not help is 0.605. But what if we are given some additional information, such as "The applicant was attractive." Will this information permit us to "fine tune" our assessment of the probability that the male entering the phone booth will engage in helping behavior? The answer is "Yes" if helping behavior is conditional on the attractiveness of the applicant.

To illustrate, Table 10.4 provides three probabilities for each helping response—the marginal probability that help will be provided, the joint probability that the applicant is attractive and helped, and the joint probability that the applicant is attractive and not helped. Now suppose we know in advance that the applicant is attractive. Will this additional information provide a basis for a better assessment of the probability that she will be helped? Let's see.

Conditional Probability

The probability of an event, given that another event has occurred. Represented symbolically as $p(A|B)$: the probability of A, given that B has occurred.

To find the **conditional probability** that the applicant will receive help, we divide the joint probability that she is attractive and helped $p(A$ and $B)$ by the marginal probability that she is attractive $p(A)$. Thus, in the present example,

$$p(B|A) = \frac{p(A \text{ and } B)}{p(A)} = \frac{0.236}{0.518,}$$
$$= 0.456,$$

where $p(B|A)$ is the conditional probability of event B given the probability that event A is known. Similarly,

$$p(A|B) = \frac{p(A \text{ and } B)}{p(B),}$$

where $p(A|B)$ is the conditional probability of event A given the probability that event B is known.

Note that, knowing only the marginal probability, we would have assessed the applicant's chance of being helped as 0.395. Knowing that she is attractive permitted us to raise our assessment of the probability to 0.456.

Let's look at one additional example. Knowing that an applicant is unattractive, what is our assessment of the probability of her not being helped, that is, of $p(\bar{B}|\bar{A})$?

$$p(\bar{B}|\bar{A}) = \frac{p(\bar{A} \text{ and } \bar{B})}{p(\bar{A})} = \frac{0.323}{0.482}$$
$$= 0.670$$

Using only the marginal probabilities, we would have estimated the probability of any applicant not being helped as 0.605. Taking into account our

Table 10.5 **Joint and conditional probability table of helping behavior when the applicant was either attractive or unattractive. The conditional probabilities are calculated by dividing the joint probabilities within each cell by its marginal probability.**

Helping Response	Attractive (A)	Unattractive ($\overline{A}$)	Marginal Probability	Conditional Probability
Helped (B)	0.236	0.159	0.395	$p(A\|B)$ $p(\overline{A}\|B)$ 0.597 0.403
Did not help ($\overline{B}$)	0.282	0.323	0.605	$p(A\|\overline{B})$ $p(\overline{A}\|\overline{B})$ 0.466 0.534
Marginal probability	0.518 $p(B\|A)$ 0.456 $p(\overline{B}\|A)$ 0.544	0.482 $p(\overline{B}\|\overline{A})$ 0.330 $p(\overline{B}\|\overline{A})$ 0.670	1.000	

knowledge of her unattractiveness, we were able to increase the probability assessment to 0.67.

Table 10.5 summarizes the conditional probabilities derived from Table 10.4.

Note that the conditional probabilities shown in the two columns at the right relate to the probability of the applicant being attractive (A) and unattractive ($\overline{A}$) when the status of helping is known. Thus, we see that the probability of not being attractive when help has not been received $p(\overline{A}|\overline{B})$ is 0.534.

Similarly, the two rows at the bottom of the table show the probabilities of the applicant receiving help (B) or not receiving help ($\overline{B}$) when the status of her attractiveness is known. Thus, the probability that an attractive person receives help $p(B|A)$ is 0.456.

The Multiplication Rule for Independent Events

Consider the following conceptual experiment. You toss a single coin into the air and a head appears. Assuming an ideal coin, the probability of a head is ½ and the probability of a tail is ½. Now toss the coin a second time. Does the outcome of the first toss in any way affect the outcome of the second toss? If it does not, the two outcomes are said to be **independent.** Since we have assumed an ideal coin (i.e., it is balanced, will not stand on end, is not motivated to change its behavior, etc.), we may assume that the two outcomes are independent so that the probability of obtaining a head remains ½ as does the probability of obtaining a tail. When outcomes or events are independent, the multiplication rule states:

Independence

The condition that exists when the occurrence of a given event will not affect the probability of the occurrence of another event.

> The probability of the simultaneous or successive occurrence of two events is the product of the separate probabilities of each event.

In symbolic form;

$$p(A \text{ and } B) = p(A)p(B). \qquad (10.9)$$

Suppose we toss a single coin on three successive occasions. What is the probability of obtaining the event "all heads"? To obtain this event, all three outcomes must be a head. Thus, $p(H,H, \text{ and } H) = p(H)p(H)p(H)$
$$= p(\tfrac{1}{2})\ (\tfrac{1}{2})(\tfrac{1}{2})$$
$$= \tfrac{1}{8} \text{ or } 0.125$$

Sampling with replacement is an example of independent events. Suppose we draw a single card from a deck of playing cards and obtain a king of hearts. The probability of this outcome is $\tfrac{1}{52} = 0.019$. If we return the card to the deck, shuffle the cards well and make a second selection, what is the probability of selecting the king of hearts again? It remains $\tfrac{1}{52}$. When sampling with replacement, what is the probability of selecting the king of hearts twice in succession? Using the multiplication rule for independent events, we obtain: $p(KH \text{ and } KH) = (\tfrac{1}{52})\ (\tfrac{1}{52}) = \tfrac{1}{2704} \text{ or } 0.00037$.

The Multiplication Rule for Nonindependent (Dependent) Events

The multiplication rule for dependent events can most readily be grasped by contrasting sampling with replacement with sampling without replacement. Imagine we were to make two successive draws from a deck of playing cards. What is the probability that we will obtain two kings?

If we use sampling with replacement, the two events are independent. Since the probability of selecting a king is $\tfrac{4}{52}$, the probability of drawing two consecutive kings $p(K \text{ and } K)$ is $(\tfrac{4}{52})(\tfrac{4}{52}) = 0.0059$.

However, if we use sampling without replacement, the events are not independent. If we select a king on the first draw, there will be only three kings left in a deck containing 51 cards. In other words, the results of the first draw influence the possible consequences of the second draw. In fact, the conditional probability of selecting a king on the second draw assuming that a king has been selected on the first draw $p(K|K)$ is $\tfrac{3}{51} = 0.059$.

For nonindependent or dependent events, the multiplication rule becomes

> Given two events A and B, the probability of obtaining both A and B jointly is the product of the probability of obtaining one of these events times the conditional probability of obtaining one event, given that the other event has occurred.

Stated symbolically,

$$p(A \text{ and } B) = p(A)p(B|A) = p(B)p(A|B). \qquad (10.10)$$

In the present example, the probability of selecting a king on the first draw $p(K)$ is equal to $\frac{4}{52}$. The probability of selecting a king on the second draw, given a king drawn on the first is $\frac{3}{51}$. Thus, when using sampling without replacement, the probability of selecting two consecutive kings is

$$
\begin{aligned}
p(K \text{ and } K) &= p(K)p(K|K) \\
&= (\tfrac{4}{52})\,(\tfrac{3}{51}) \\
&= 0.0045.
\end{aligned}
$$

Figure 10.4 is a tree diagram of this statistical experiment that illustrates the calculation of the probability of all possible events.

Note that we can calculate the probability of each event by successively multiplying the probability associated with each branch by the probability associated with connecting branches. Thus the probability of selecting two kings is found by multiplying the probabilities of the two top branches $(\frac{4}{52})(\frac{3}{51})$. Similarly, the two bottom branches provide the basis for calculating the selection of two non-kings on successive draws.

Figure 10.5 shows the tree diagram for calculating the conditional probabilities of study concerned with physical attractiveness of the target and the helping behavior by the subjects.

Figure 10.4   Tree diagram of the statistical experiment involving two draws, without replacement, from a deck of playing cards. The event of interest is the probability of selecting two consecutive kings.

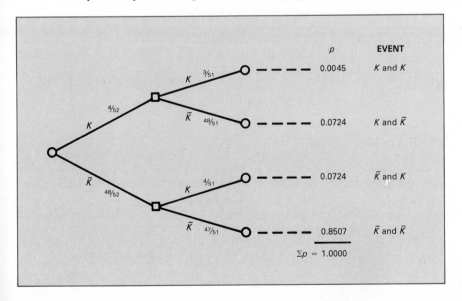

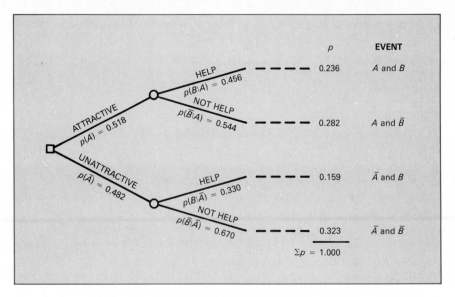

Figure 10.5   Tree diagram used to calculate the probability of various conditional events relating to physical attractiveness of the target and helping behavior by the subjects.

10.7 Probability and Continuous Variables

Up to this point we have considered probability in terms of the expected relative frequency of an event. In fact, as you will recall, probability was defined in terms of frequency and expressed as the following proportion [Formula (10.1)]:

$$P(A) = \frac{\text{No. outcomes favoring event } A}{\text{Total no. outcomes}}.$$

However, this definition presents a problem when we are dealing with continuous variables. As we pointed out in Section 3.7, it is generally advisable to represent frequency in terms of areas under a curve when we are dealing with continuous variables. Thus, for continuous variables, we may express probability as the following proportion:

$$p = \frac{\text{Area under portions of a curve}}{\text{Total area under the curve}}. \tag{10.11}$$

Since the total area in a probability distribution is equal to 1.00, we define p as the proportion of total area under portions of a curve.

Chapters 11 and 15 employ the standard normal curve as the probability model. Let's examine the probability-area relationship in terms of this model.

10.8   *Probability and the Normal-Curve Model*

In Section 7.3, we stated that the standard normal distribution has a μ of 0, a σ of 1, and a total area that is equal to 1.00. We saw that when scores on a normally distributed variable are transformed into z-scores, we are, in effect, expressing these scores in units of the standard normal curve. This permits us to express the difference between any two scores as proportions of total area under the curve. Thus we may establish probability values in terms of these proportions, as in Formula (10.11).

The following are several examples that illustrate the application of probability concepts to the normal-curve model.

Illustrative Problems*

For all problems, assume $\mu = 100$ and $\sigma = 16$.

Problem 1.   What is the probability of selecting at *random* from the general population a person with an I.Q. score of at least 132? The answer to this question is given by the proportion of area under the curve above a score of 132 (Fig. 10.6).

First, we must find the z-score corresponding to $X = 132$.

$$z = \frac{132 - 100}{16} = 2.00.$$

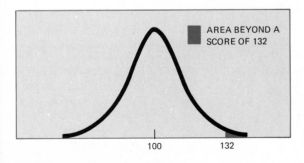

AREA BEYOND A
SCORE OF 132

100   132

Figure 10.6
Proportion of area above a score of 132 in a normal distribution with $\mu = 100$ and $\sigma = 16$.

*See Section 7.4.

In column (C) of Table A in the back of this book, we find that 0.0228 of the area lies at or beyond a z of 2.00. Therefore the probability of selecting at random a score of at least 132 is 0.0228.

Problem 2.   What is the probability of selecting at random an individual with an I.Q. score of at least 92?

We are dealing with two mutually exclusive and exhaustive areas under the curve. The area under the curve above a score of 92 is P; the area below a score of 92 is Q. In solving our problem we therefore employ Formula (10.7):

$$P = 1.00 - Q.$$

By expressing a score of 92 in terms of its corresponding z, we may obtain the proportion of area below $X = 92$ (that is Q) directly from column (C), Table A. The z-score corresponding to $X = 92$ is

$$z = \frac{92 - 100}{16} = -0.50.$$

The proportion of area below a z of -0.50 is 0.3085. Therefore the probability of selecting at random a score of at least 92 becomes

$$P = 1.00 - 0.3085 = 0.6915.$$

Figure 10.7 illustrates this relationship.

Problem 3.   Look at this example involving the multiplication law. Given that sampling with replacement is employed, what is the probability of drawing at random three individuals with I.Q.s equaling or exceeding 124? For this problem we will again assume that $\mu = 100$ and $\sigma = 16$.

$$z = \frac{124 - 100}{16} = 1.5.$$

In column (C), Table A, we find that 0.0668 of the area lies at or beyond $X = 124$. Therefore

$$p(A, B, C) = (0.0668)^3 = 0.0003.$$

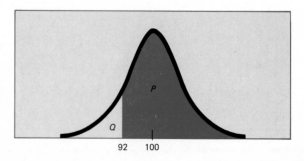

Figure 10.7
Proportion of area above (P) and below (Q) a score of 92 in a normal distribution with $\mu = 100$ and $\sigma = 16$.

10.9 *One- and Two-Tailed p-Values*

In Problem 1, we were seeking the probability of selecting at random a person with an I.Q. score as high as 132. We solved the problem by examining only one tail of the distribution, namely, scores as high as or higher than 132. For this reason we refer to the probability value that we obtained as being a **one-tailed *p*-value.**

In statistics and research, the following questions are more commonly asked: "What is the probability of obtaining a score (or statistic) this *deviant* from the mean? . . . or a score (or statistic) this *rare*? . . . or a result this *unusual*?" Clearly, when the frequency distribution of scores is symmetrical, a score of 68 or lower is every bit as deviant from a mean of 100 as is a score of 132. That is, both are two standard deviation units away from the mean. When we express the probability value, taking into account both tails of the distribution, we refer to the *p*-value as being *two-tailed*. In symmetrical distributions, **two-tailed *p*-values** may be obtained merely by doubling the one-tailed probability value. Thus, in the preceding problem, the probability of selecting a person with a score as *rare or unusual* as 132 is 2 × 0.0228 = 0.0456.

We may illustrate the distinction between one- and two-tailed *p*-values by referring to a sampling experiment we presented in the end-of-chapter exercised for Chapters 3, 4, 5, and 6. Figure 10.8 shows a probability histogram based upon a Table 10.6. This distribution was obtained by selecting with

One-Tailed *p*-Values

Probability values obtained by examining only one tail of the distribution.

Two-Tailed *p*-Values

Probability values that take into account both tails of the distribution.

Figure 10.8 Probability histogram of means based upon selecting, with replacement, samples of $N = 2$ from a population of seven numbers.

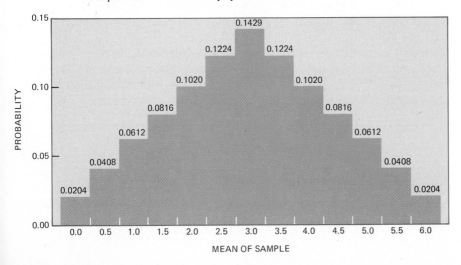

Table 10.6 Frequency and probability distribution of means of samples of size $N = 2$, drawn from a population of seven scores (0, 1, 2, 3, 4, 5, 6).

$\overline{X}$	f	$p(\overline{X})$
6.0	1	0.0204
5.5	2	0.0408
5.0	3	0.0612
4.5	4	0.0816
4.0	5	0.1020
3.5	6	0.1224
3.0	7	0.1429
2.5	6	0.1224
2.0	5	0.1020
1.5	4	0.0816
1.0	3	0.0612
0.5	2	0.0408
0.0	1	0.0204
	$N_{\overline{X}} = 49*$	$\sum p(\overline{X}) = 0.9997†$

*We use $N_{\overline{X}}$ to refer to the total number of means obtained in our sampling experiment and to distinguish it from N, which is the number of scores upon which each mean is based.
†$\sum p(\overline{X})$ should equal 1.000. The discrepancy of 0.0003 represents rounding error.

replacement of all possible samples of $N = 2$ from a population of seven scores.

If we ask, "What is the probability of obtaining a mean equal to zero?" we would need to refer only to the left tail of the probability histogram in order to find the answer of 0.0204. However, if we ask, "What is the probability of obtaining as deviant an outcome as a sample mean equal to zero?" we would have to look at both the left and the right tails. Since a mean of 6 is equally deviant from the mean of the distribution, we use the addition rule to obtain the two-tailed value:

$$p(\overline{X} = 0 \text{ or } \overline{X} = 6) = p(\overline{X} = 0) + p(\overline{X} = 6)$$
$$= 0.0204 + 0.0204 = 0.0408.$$

Let's look at two additional examples.

- *Example 1.*   What is the probability of obtaining a mean as low as 0.5 (i.e., a mean of 0.5 or lower)?

We find the probability of obtaining a mean of 0.5 and a mean of 0.0 (the only mean lower than 0.5), and add these probabilities together to obtain the one-tailed p-value:

$$p(\overline{X} \leq 0.5) = p(\overline{X} = 0.5) + p(\overline{X} = 0.0)$$
$$= 0.0408 + 0.0204 = 0.0612.$$

• **Example 2.** What is the probability of obtaining a mean as deviant from the distribution mean as a sample mean of 0.5?

The answer to this question calls for a two-tailed p-value obtained by applying the addition rule to

$$p(\overline{X} = 0.0) + p(\overline{X} = 0.5) + p(\overline{X} = 5.5) + p(\overline{X} = 6.0).$$

However, since the distribution is symmetrical, and means of 5.5 and 6.0 are equally as deviant as 0.5 and 0.0, respectively, we need only double the p-value obtained in Example 1:

$$p(0.5 \geq \overline{X} \geq 5.5) = 2(0.0612)$$
$$= 0.1224.$$

Incidentally, the left-hand member of the above expression is read: *The probability of a mean equal to or less than 0.5 or equal to or greater than 5.5.*

The distinction between one- and two-tailed probability values takes on added significance as we progress into inferential statistics.

Chapter Summary

In this chapter, we focused our discussion on five points:

1. *The importance of the concept of randomness in inferential statistics.* Randomness refers to selecting the events in the sample in such a way that each event is equally likely to be selected in a sample of a given size. Independent random sampling refers to the fact that the selection of one event has no effect upon the probability of selecting another event. Although the individual events are unpredictable, collections of random events take on characteristic and predictable forms. The binomial distribution and the normal curve were cited in this regard.

2. *The theory of probability, which is concerned with the outcomes of experiments.* We learned to distinguish between probabilities established by assuming *idealized* relative frequencies and those established empirically

by determining relative frequencies. Probability was defined as

$$p = \frac{\text{No. of outcomes favoring event}}{\text{Total no. of outcomes}}$$

3. *The formal properties of probability.*
   a. Probabilities vary between 0 and 1.00.
   b. The addition rule:
      If A and B are two events, the probability of obtaining either of them is equal to the probability of A plus the probability of B minus the probability of their joint occurrence. Thus

      $$p(A \text{ or } B) = p(A) + p(B) - p(A \text{ and } B).$$

      If events A and B are *mutually exclusive,* the addition rule becomes

      $$p(A \text{ or } B) = p(A) + p(B).$$

      Allowing P to represent the probability of occurrence and Q to represent the probability of nonoccurrence, we find that three additional useful formulations for mutually exclusive and exhaustive events are

      $$P + Q = 1.00, \qquad P = 1.00 - Q, \qquad Q = 1.00 - P.$$

   c. The multiplication rule:
      When events are independent. When sampling with replacement, the selection on one trial is independent of the selection on another trial. Given two events, A and B, the probability of obtaining both A and B in successive trials is the product of the probability of obtaining one of these events times the probability of obtaining the second of these events,

      $$p(A \text{ and } B) = p(A)p(B).$$

      When events are nonindependent. When sampling without replacement, the selection of one event affects the probability of selecting each remaining event. Thus, given two events (A and B), the probability of obtaining both A and B jointly or successively is the product of the probability of obtaining one of the events times the conditional probability of obtaining one event, given that the other event has occurred. Symbolically,

      $$p(A \text{ and } B) = p(A)p(B|A) = p(B)p(A|B).$$

4. *The application of probability theory to continuously distributed variables.* Probability is expressed in terms of the proportion of area under a curve. Hence

$$p = \frac{\text{Area under portions of a curve}}{\text{Total area under a curve}}.$$

We saw how we may employ z-scores and the standard normal curve to establish various probabilities for normally distributed variables.

5. *How to distinguish between one- and two-tailed probability values.*

Terms to Remember

bias	probability
conditional probability	random sampling
exhaustive	sample space
independence	sampling distribution
mutually exclusive	two-tailed *p*-values
one-tailed *p*-values	

EXERCISES

*1. Imagine that we have a population of the following four scores: 0, 3, 6, and 9.
   a. Construct a probability distribution and histogram of all possible means when sampling with replacement, $N = 2$.
   b. Construct a probability histogram of all possible means when sampling with replacement, $N = 3$. [*Hint:* The table for finding the means appears below. The values in the cells represent the means of the three draws.]

1st Draw		**0**				**3**				**6**				**9**		
2nd Draw		**0**	**3**	**6**	**9**	**0**	**3**	**6**	**9**	**0**	**3**	**6**	**9**	**0**	**3**	**6**	**9**
3rd Draw	0	0	1	2	3	1	2	3	4	2	3	4	5	3	4	5	6
	3	1	2	3	4	2	3	4	5	3	4	5	6	4	5	6	7
	6	2	3	4	5	3	4	5	6	4	5	6	7	5	6	7	8
	9	3	4	5	6	4	5	6	7	5	6	7	8	6	7	8	9

*2. The original population of the four scores in Exercise 1 was rectangular (they all had the same associated frequency of 1). Compare the probability distributions in 1(a) and 1(b) above and attempt to form a generalization about the form and the dispersion of the distribution of sample means as we increase the sample size.

*3. Answer the following questions based upon the probability histograms obtained in Exercise 1, above.

   a. Drawing a single sample of $N = 2$, what is the probability of obtaining a mean equal to zero? Contrast this result with the probability of randomly selecting a mean equal to zero when $N = 3$.

   b. For each distribution, determine the probability of selecting a sample with a mean as rare or as unusual as 9.

   c. From each probability histogram, determine the probability of selecting a sample with a mean as low as 3.

   d. From each probability histogram, determine the probability of selecting a sample mean as deviant from the population mean as a mean of 3.

*4. For the probability distribution of $N = 2$ [Exercise 1(a)] find
   a. $p(\overline{X} < 6)$,   b. $p(\overline{X} \geq 7.5)$,   c. $p(\overline{X} = 4.5)$.

*5. For the probability distribution of $N = 3$ [Exercise 1(b)] find
   a. $p(3 \leq \overline{X} \leq 6)$,   c. $p(4 \leq \overline{X} \leq 5)$,   b. $p(\overline{X} = 2 \text{ or } \overline{X} = 8)$.

*6. Let's now imagine a different type of sampling experiment. You have selected all possible samples of $N = 2$ from a population of scores and obtained the following means: 1, 2, 2, 3, 3, 3, 4, 4, 5. You now place paper tabs in a hat with these means written on them. You select one mean, record it, and replace it in the hat. You select a second mean, *subtract* it from the first and then replace it in the hat. The table for describing all possible *differences between means* of $N = 2$ is shown below.

| | | First Draw of Mean | | | | | | | | |
		1	2	2	3	3	3	4	4	5
Second Draw of Mean	1	0	1	1	2	2	2	3	3	4
	2	−1	0	0	1	1	1	2	2	3
	2	−1	0	0	1	1	1	2	2	3
	3	−2	−1	−1	0	0	0	1	1	2
	3	−2	−1	−1	0	0	0	1	1	2
	3	−2	−1	−1	0	0	0	1	1	2
	4	−3	−2	−2	−1	−1	−1	0	0	1
	4	−3	−2	−2	−1	−1	−1	0	0	1
	5	−4	−3	−3	−2	−2	−2	−1	−1	0

   a. Construct a frequency distribution of differences between means.
   b. Construct a probability distribution of differences between means.
   c. Find the mean and the standard deviation of the differences between means.

*7. Based upon the responses to Exercise 6 (above), answer the following questions. Drawing two samples at random and with replacement from the population of means, and subtracting the second mean from the first, what is the probability that you will select

    a. a difference between means equal to zero?

    b. a difference between means equal to or less than 1 *or* equal to or greater than -1? (Note: -2, -3, -4 are all less than -1).

    c. a difference between means equal to -4?

    d. a difference between means as rare or as deviant as -4.

    e. a difference between means equal to or greater than 3?

    f. a difference between means equal to or less than -3?

    g. a difference between means as rare or as unusual as -3?

    h. a difference between means equal to or less than 2 or equal to or greater than -2?

8. List all the possible outcomes of a coin that is tossed three times. Calculate the probability of

    a. 3 heads,   **b.** 3 tails,   **c.** 2 heads and 1 tail,   **d.** at least 2 heads.

9. A card is drawn at random from a deck of 52 playing cards. What is the probability that

    a. it will be the ace of spades?   **b.** it will be an ace?

    c. it will be an ace or a face card?   **d.** it will be a spade or a face card?

10. Express the probabilities in Exercises 8 and 9 in terms of *odds against.*

11. In a single throw of two dice, what is the probability that

    a. a 7 will appear?

    b. a doublet (two of the same number) will appear?

    c. a doublet or an 8 will appear?

    d. an even number will appear?

12. On a slot machine (commonly referred to as a "one-armed bandit"), there are three reels with five different fruits plus a star on each reel. After inserting a coin and pulling the handle, the player sees that the three reels revolve independently several times before stopping. What is the probability that

    a. three lemons will appear?

    b. any three of a kind will appear?

    c. two lemons and a star will appear?

    d. two lemons and any other fruit will appear?

    e. no star will appear?

13. Three cards are drawn at random (without replacement) from a deck of 52 cards. What is the probability that

    a. all three will be hearts?

    b. none of the three cards will be hearts?

    c. all three will be face cards?

14. Calculate the probabilities in Exercise 13 if each card is replaced after it is drawn.

15. A well-known test of intelligence is constructed so as to have normally distributed scores with a mean of 100 and a standard deviation of 16.

    a. What is the probability that someone picked at random will have an I.Q. of 122 or higher?

    b. There are I.Q.s so *high* that the probability is 0.05 that such I.Q.s would occur in a random sample of people. Those I.Q.s are beyond what value?

    c. There are I.Q.s so *extreme* that the probability is 0.05 that such I.Q.s would occur in a random sample of people. Those I.Q.s are beyond what values?

    d. The next time you shop you will undoubtedly see someone who is a complete stranger to you. What is the probability that his or her I.Q. will be between 90 and 110?

    e. What is the probability of selecting two people at random
      i. with I.Q.s of 122 or higher?
      ii. with I.Q.s between 90 and 110?
      iii. one with an I.Q. of 122 or higher, the other with an I.Q. between 90 and 110?

    f. What is the probability that on leaving your class, the first student you meet will have an I.Q. below 120? Can you answer this question on the basis of the information provided above? If not, why not?

16. Which of the following selection techniques will result in random samples? Explain your answers
    a. *Population:* Viewers of a given television program. *Sampling technique:* On a given night, interviewing every fifth person in the studio audience.
    b. *Population:* A home-made pie. *Sampling technique:* A wedge selected from any portion of the pie.
    c. *Population:* All the children in a suburban high school. *Sampling technique:* Selecting one child sent to you by each homeroom teacher.

17. In a study involving a test of visual acuity, four different hues varying slightly in brightness are presented to the subject. What is the probability that he or she will arrange them in order, from greatest brightness to least, by chance?

18. The proportion of people with type A blood in a particular city is 0.20. What is the probability that
    a. a given individual, selected at random, will have type A blood?
    b. two out of two individuals will have type A blood?
    c. a given individual will *not* have type A blood?
    d. two out of two individuals will *not* have type A blood?

19. In a manufacturing process, the proportion of items that are defective is 0.10. What is the probability that
    a. in a sample of four items, none will be defective?
    b. in a sample of four items, all will be defective?
    c. one or more but less than four will be defective?

20. In the manufacture of machine screws for the space industry, millions of screws measuring 0.010 cm are produced daily. The standard deviation is 0.001. A screw is considered defective if it deviates from 0.010 by as much as 0.002. Assuming normality, what is the probability that
    a. one screw selected at random will be defective?
    b. two out of two screws will be defective?
    c. one screw selected at random will *not* be defective?
    d. two out of two screws will *not* be defective?
    e. one screw selected at random will be too large?
    f. two out of two screws will be too small?

21. A bag contains 6 blue marbles, 4 red marbles, and 2 green marbles. If you select a single marble at random from the bag, what is the probability that it will be
    a. red?   b. blue?   c. green?   d. white?

22. Selecting *without* replacement from the bag described in Exercise 21, what is the probability that
    a. three out of three will be blue?   b. two out of two will be green?
    c. none out of four will be red?

23. Selecting *with* replacement from the bag described in Exercise 21, what is the probability that
    a. three out of three will be blue?   b. two out of two will be green?
    c. none out of four will be red?

24. Forty percent of the students at a given college major in business administration. Seventy percent of these are male and thirty percent female. Sixty percent of the students in the school are male. What is the probability that
    a. one student selected at random will be a BA major?
    b. one person selected at random will be a female BA major?
    c. two students selected at random will be BA majors?
    d. two persons selected at random will be BA majors, one male, one female?

25. What is the probability that a score chosen at random from a normally distributed population with a mean of 66 and a standard deviation of 8 will be
    a. greater than 70?
    b. less than 60?
    c. between 60 and 70?
    d. in the 70s?
    e. either equal to or less than 54 or equal to or greater than 72?
    f. either less than 52 or between 78 and 84?
    g. either between 56 and 64 or between 80 and 86?

26. What is meant by random sampling?

27. Refer back to Table 10.4. Construct a tree diagram of the conditional probabilities when the helping reponse of the subject is known.

28. In another facet of the study relating physical attractiveness to helping behavior, the target was either an attractive or unattractive male and the subjects were females. The results are shown in the following table.

Helping Response	Characteristics of Target		Row Totals
	Attractive	Unattractive	
Helped	19	13	32
Did not help	22	27	49
Column totals	41	40	81

    a. Prepare a joint probability table of the results.
    b. Calculate the conditional probabilities of events B and $\overline{B}$ when the attractiveness status of the subject is known.
    c. Construct a tree diagram of the conditional probabilities when the attractiveness status of the target person is known.
    d. Construct a tree diagram of the conditional probabilities when the helping status of the subject is known.

11

Introduction to Statistical Inference

11.1 Why Sample?

You are the leader of a religious denomination, and for the purpose of planning recruitment you want to know what proportion of the adults in the United States claim church membership. How would you go about getting this information?

You are a rat psychologist, and you are interested in the relationship between strength of drive and learning. Specifically, what are the effects of duration of hunger drive on the number of trials required for a rat to learn a T-maze?

You are a sociologist, and you want to study the differences in child-rearing practices among parents of delinquent and nondelinquent children.

You are a market researcher, and you want to know what proportion of individuals prefer certain car colors and their various combinations.

You are a park attendant, and you want to determine whether the ice is sufficiently thick to permit safe skating.

You are a gambler, and you want to determine whether a set of dice is "dishonest."

What do each of these problems have in common? You are asking questions about the parameter of a population to which you want to generalize your answers, but you have no hope of ever studying the *entire* population. Earlier (Section 1.2)* we defined a **population** as a *complete* or theoretical set of individuals, objects, or measurements having some common observable characteristic. It is frequently impossible to study *all* the members of a given population because the population is defined either has an infinite number of members, or is so large that it defies exhaustive study. Moreover, when we refer to "the population" we are often dealing with a hypothetical entity. In the typical experimental situation the actual population does not exist. We attempt to find out something about the characteristics of that population *if it did exist.* For example, when we administer a drug to a group of subjects (the **sample**), we wish to generalize our results to everyone who could potentially receive the drug. This *population* is, of course, hypothetical.

Since populations can rarely be studied exhaustively, we must depend on samples as a basis for arriving at a hypothesis concerning various characteris-

Population

A complete set of individuals, objects, or measurements having some common observable characteristic.

Sample

A subset of a population or universe.

---

*It is recommended that you reread Section 1.2 for purposes of reviewing several definitions of terms that will appear in this chapter.

225

BOX 11.1

Sampling: A matter of survival

We tend to think of sampling procedures as activities engaged in by only a handful of professionals—pollsters, laboratory scientists, demographers, to name a few. As the following excerpt from *Winning with Statistics* makes clear, sampling followed by decision making are among the most pervasive activities of living organisms.

We have three dogs on our ranch on the outskirts of Tucson, Arizona. The baby of the three, Millie Muffin, is an eight-month-old black and white springer spaniel. Although mischief should be her middle name, she is a sheer delight. She is constantly exploring the desert flora and fauna with the indefatigable curiosity of a three-year-old human child. When spying something that moves on its own (such as a giant spider, better known as a tarantula), she leaps about two feet off the ground—ears and feathers flapping—and retreats several feet away, all the while barking like a fierce Doberman. But I know better. In reality, she is the world's greatest coward. I'll tell you how I know.

While she is prancing mindlessly about the giant saguaro, the ocotillo, the cholla, and other assorted exotic plants of the desert, I will sneak downwind of her. Then I will raise myself on the balls of my toes, stretch my arms in front of me, and shuffle my feet as I ad-

vance toward her in my best Frankenstein-monster style. When she spies me, she lets out a startled "yip," springs into the air, and begins a barking retreat. But all the while, her nose is probing the air, sniffing constantly, desperately drawing in samples in an effort to make inferences about the nature of the intruder. While observing Millie's antics, it occurred to me that the actions involved in taking samples and drawing inferences from these samples are among the most pervasive of mammalian activities. The pet dog, the family feline, the lion in the jungle, the gorilla in the rain forest, and the wife, husband, daughter, son, businessperson, doctor, lawyer, and Indian chief have this characteristic in common. They are continuously probing aspects of their environment, assessing the risks against the benefits, making probability judgments concerning alternative avenues of behavior, and pursuing those lines of activity that appear most likely to lead to desired goals. By this I do not mean to imply that all this sampling and probability assessment is conscious or deliberate. The truth of the matter is that nature has designed us all to be exquisite probability-generating machines. Without the ability to sample and thereby judge peril, or the availability of food, or the receptivity of a sexual partner, all species presently inhabiting the earth would have come from a long line of unborn ancestors.

Excerpted from R. P. Runyon, *Winning with Statistics*. Reading Mass.: Addison-Wesley, 1977.

tics, or parameters, of the population. Note that our interest is not in descriptive statistics *per se,* but in making inferences from data. Thus, if we ask 100 people how they intend to vote in a forthcoming election, our primary interest is not in knowing how these 100 people will vote, but in estimating how the members of the entire voting population will cast their ballots.

Almost all research involves the observation and the measurement of a limited number of individuals or events. These measurements are presumed to tell us something about the population. In order to understand how we are able to make inferences about a population from a sample, it is necessary to introduce the concept of sampling distributions.

11.2 The Concept of Sampling Distributions

In actual practice, inferences about the parameters of a population are made from statistics that are calculated from a sample of N observations drawn at random from this population. If we continued to draw samples of size N from this population, we should not be surprised if we found some differences among the values of the sample statistics obtained. It would be extremely unlikely that we would draw exactly the same set of observations each time. On one occasion we might, by chance, select a set of observations in which most of the scores are high. On another, we might select mostly low scores. On still another, there might be a good mix of high and low observations. Indeed, it is this observation that has led to the concept of **sampling distributions.**

Sampling Distribution

A theoretical probability distribution of a statistic that would result from drawing all possible samples of a given size from some population.

> A sampling distribution is a theoretical probability distribution of the possible values of some sample statistic that would occur if we were to draw all possible samples of a fixed size from a given population.

There is a sampling distribution for every statistic—mean, standard deviation, variance, proportion, median, etc. It is one of the most important concepts in inferential statistics. You are already familiar with several sampling distributions, although we have not previously named them as such. Recall the various sampling problems we have introduced throughout the earlier chapters in the text. In one example, we started with a population of seven scores and selected with replacement samples of $N = 2$. We obtained all possible combinations of these scores, two at a time, and then found the mean of each of these samples. We then constructed a frequency distribution and probability distribution of means drawn from that population with a fixed sample size of $N = 2$.

Recall also that in Exercise 1, at the end of Chapter 10, we constructed sampling distributions based upon drawing with replacement all possible samples of $N = 2$ and $N = 3$ from a population of four scores (0, 3, 6, 9). Table 11.1 shows these two sampling distribution, plus the sampling distribution of the mean when $N = 4$.

Why is the concept of a sampling distribution so important? The answer is simple. Once you are able to describe the sampling distribution of *any statistic* (be it mean, standard deviation, proportion), you are in a position to entertain and test a wide variety of hypotheses. For example, you draw four numbers at random from some population. You obtain a mean equal to 6.00. You ask, "Is this mean an ordinary event or is it a rare event?" In the absence of a frame of reference, this question is meaningless. However, if we know the sampling distribution for this statistic, we would have the necessary frame of reference and the answer would be straightforward. If we were to tell you that

Table 11.1 Sampling distributions of means drawn from a population of four scores (0, 3, 6, 9; μ = 4.5 σ = 3.94) and sample sizes N = 2, N = 3, and N = 4.

N = 2		N = 3		N = 4	
$\overline{X}$	$p(\overline{X})$	$\overline{X}$	$p(\overline{X})$	$\overline{X}$	$p(\overline{X})$
9.0	0.0625	9.0	0.0156	9.0	0.0039
7.5	0.1250	8.0	0.0469	8.25	0.1056
6.0	0.1875	7.0	0.0938	7.50	0.0391
4.5	0.2500	6.0	0.1562	6.75	0.0781
3.0	0.1875	5.0	0.1875	6.00	0.1211
1.5	0.1250	4.0	0.1875	5.25	0.1562
0.0	0.0625	3.0	0.1562	4.50	0.1719
		2.0	0.0938	3,75	0.1562
		1.0	0.0469	3.00	0.1211
		0.0	0.0156	2.25	0.0781
				1.50	0.0391
				.75	0.0156
				0.00	0.0039
$\overline{X}$ = 4.5		$\overline{X}$ = 4.5		$\overline{X}$ = 4.5	
$s_{\overline{X}}$ = 2.37		$s_{\overline{X}}$ = 1.94		$s_{\overline{X}}$ = 1.68	

the appropriate sampling distribution is given in Table 11.1 when N = 4, you would have no trouble answering the question. A mean of 6.00 would be drawn about 12% of the time (p = 0.1211); and a mean of 6 or greater would occur almost 26% of the time (p = 0.1211 + 0.0781 + 0.0391 + 0.0156 + 0.0039 = 0.2578).

Whenever we estimate a population parameter from a sample, we ask such questions as: "How good an estimate do I have? Can I conclude that the population parameter is identical with the sample statistic? Or is there likely to be some error? If so, how much?" To answer each of these questions, we will compare our sample results with the "expected" results. The expected results are in turn given by the appropriate sampling distribution. But what does the sampling distribution of a particular statistic look like? How can we ever know the form of the distribution, and thus what the expected results are? Since the inferences we will be making imply knowledge of the *form* of the sampling distribution, it is necessary to set up certain idealized *models*. The normal curve and the **binomial distribution** are two models whose mathematical properties are known. Consequently these two distributions are frequently employed as models to describe particular sampling distributions. Thus, for example, if we know that the sampling distribution of a particular statistic takes the form

Binomial Distribution

A model with known mathematical properties used to describe sampling distribution dichotomous variables.

of a normal distribution, we may use the known properties of the normal distribution to make inferences and predictions about the statistic.

The following sections should serve to clarify these important points.

11.3 *Testing Statistical Hypotheses: Level of Significance*

Say you have a favorite coin that you use constantly in everyday life as a basis of "either-or" decision making. For example, you may ask, "Should I study tonight for the statistics quiz, or should I relax at the movies? Your solution: "Heads, I study; tails, I don't." Over a period of time, you have sensed that the decision has more often gone "against you" than "for you" (in other words, you have to study more often than relax!). You begin to question the accuracy and the adequacy of the coin. Does the coin come up heads more often than tails? How might you find out?

One thing is clear. The true proportion of heads and tails characteristic of this coin can never be known. You could start tossing the coin this very minute and continue for a million years (granting a long life and a remarkably durable coin) and you would not exhaust the population of possible outcomes. In this instance, the true proportion of heads and tails is unknowable because the universe, or population, is unlimited.

The fact that the *true* value is unknowable does not prevent us from trying to estimate what it is. We have already pointed out that since populations can rarely be studied exhaustively, we must depend on samples to estimate the parameters.

Returning to our problem with the coin, we clearly see that in order to determine whether or not the coin is biased, we will have to obtain a sample of the "behavior" of that coin and arrive at some generalization concerning its possible bias. For example, if we toss our coin 10 times and obtain 5 heads and 5 tails, would we begin to suspect our coin of being biased? Of course not, since this outcome is exactly a 50–50 split, and is in agreement with the hypothesis that the coin is not biased. What if we obtained 6 heads and 4 tails? Again, this is not an unusual outcome. In fact, we can answer the question of how often, given a theoretically perfect coin, we may expect an outcome at least this much different from a 50–50 split. Looking at Fig. 11.1, which represents the theoretical probability distribution of various numbers of heads when $N = 10$, reveals that departures from a 50–50 split are quite common. Indeed, whenever we obtain either 6 or more heads, or 4 or fewer heads, we are departing from a 50–50 split. Such departures will occur fully 75.4% of the time when we toss a perfect coin in a series of trials with 10 tosses per trial.

What if we obtained 9 heads and 1 tail? Clearly, we begin to suspect the honesty of the coin. Why? At what point do we change from attitudes accept-

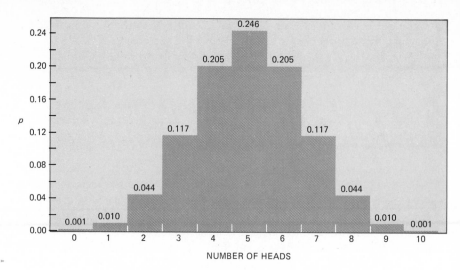

Figure 11.1 Bar graph of binomial sampling distribution of various numbers of heads obtained by tossing an unbiased coin ten times ($N = 10$), or by tossing ten coins one time.

ing the honesty of the coin to attitudes rejecting its honesty? This question takes us to the crux of the problem of inferential statistics. We have seen that the more unusual or rare the event, the more prone we are to look for non-chance explanations of the event. When we obtained 6 heads in 10 tosses of our coin, we felt no necessity to find an explanation for its departure from a 50–50 split, other than to state that such a departure would occur frequently "by chance." However, when we obtained 9 heads, we had an uncomfortable feeling concerning the honesty of the coin. Nine heads out of 10 tosses is such a rare occurrence that we begin to suspect that the explanation may be found in terms of the characteristics of the coin rather than in the so-called "laws of chance." The critical question is where do we draw the line that determines what inferences we make about the coin?

The answer to this question reveals the basic nature of science: its probabilistic rather than its absolutistic orientation. In the social sciences, most researchers have adopted one of the following two cutoff points as the basis for *inferring the operation of nonchance factors.*

Significance Level

A probability value that is considered so rare in the sampling distribution specified under the null hypothesis that one is willing to assert the operation of nonchance factors. Common significance levels are 0.05 and 0.01.

1. When the event or one more deviant would occur *five percent* of the time or less, *by chance,* some researchers are willing to assert that the results are due to nonchance factors. This cutoff point is known variously as the 0.05 **significance level,** or the 5.00% **significance level.**

2. When the event or one more deviant would occur *one percent* of the time or less, *by chance,* other researchers are willing to assert that the results are due to nonchance factors. This cutoff point is known as the 0.01 **significance level,** or the 1.00% **significance level.**

The level of significance set by the experimenter for inferring the operation of nonchance factors is known as the **alpha (α) level.** Thus, when employing the 0.05 level of significance, α = 0.05; when employing the 0.01 level of significance, α = 0.01.

Alpha (α) Level

The level of significance set by the experimenter for inferring the operation of nonchance factors.

In order to determine whether the results were due to nonchance factors in the present coin experiment, we need to calculate the probability of obtaining an event as *rare* as 9 heads out of 10 tosses. In determining the rarity of an event, we must consider the fact that the rare event can occur in both directions (e.g., 9 tails and 1 head) and that it includes more extreme events. In other words, the probability of an event as *rare* as 9 heads out of 10 tosses is equal to

$$p(9 \text{ heads}) + p(10 \text{ heads}) + p(1 \text{ head}) + p(0 \text{ heads}).$$

Since this distribution is symmetrical,

$$p(9 \text{ heads}) = p(1 \text{ head}) \quad \text{and} \quad p(10 \text{ heads}) = p(0 \text{ heads}).$$

Thus

$$p(9 \text{ heads}) + p(10 \text{ heads}) + p(1 \text{ head}) + p(0 \text{ heads})$$
$$= 2[p(9 \text{ heads}) + p(10 \text{ heads})].$$

These *p*-values may be obtained from Fig. 11.1 as follows:

$$p(9 \text{ heads}) = 0.010, \quad \text{and} \quad p(10 \text{ heads}) = 0.001.$$

Therefore the *two-tailed probability* of an event as rare as 9 heads out of 10 tosses is 2(0.010 + 0.001) = 0.022 or 2.2%

Employing the 0.05 significance level (α = 0.05), we would conclude that the coin was biased (i.e., the results were due to nonchance factors). However, if we employed the 0.01 significance level (α = 0.01), we would not be able to assert that these results were due to nonchance factors.

It should be noted and strongly emphasized that you do *not* run a study, analyze the results, arrive at a probability value, and then decide on an α-level. The α-level must be specified *prior* to the study as part of the overall strategy of designing the experiment.

11.4   Testing Statistical Hypotheses: Null Hypothesis and Alternative Hypothesis

Null Hypothesis (H_0)

A statement that specifies hypothesized values for one or more of the population parameters. Commonly, although not necessarily, involves the hypothesis of "no difference."

At this point, many students become disillusioned by the arbitrary nature of decision making in science. Let us examine the logic of statistical inference a bit further and see if we can resolve some of the doubts. Prior to the beginning of any experiment, the researcher sets up two mutually exclusive hypotheses:

1. The **null hypothesis (H_0)**, which specifies hypothesized values for one or more of the *population parameters*.

Alternative Hypothesis (H_1)

A statement specifying that the population parameter is some value other than the one specified under the null hypothesis.

2. The **alternative hypothesis (H_1)**, which asserts that the *population parameter* is some value other than the one hypothesized.

In the present coin experiment, these two hypotheses read as follows:

H_0: The coin is unbiased; that is,

$$P = Q = \frac{1}{2}.$$

H_1: The coin is biased; that is,

$$P \neq Q \neq \frac{1}{2}.$$

Nondirectional Hypothesis

An alternative hypothesis (H_1) that states only that the population parameter is *different* from the one specified under H_0.

The alternative hypothesis may be either **directional** or **nondirectional.** When H_1 asserts *only* that the population parameter is *different from* the one hypothesized, it is referred to as a *nondirectional* or *two-tailed* hypothesis; for example,

$$P \neq Q \neq \frac{1}{2}.$$

Directional Hypothesis

An alternative hypothesis that states the direction in which the population parameter differs from the one specified under H_0.

Two-Tailed Probability Value

Probability values that take into account both tails of the distribution.

Occasionally H_1 is **directional** or *one-tailed*. In this instance, in addition to asserting that the population parameter is different from the one hypothesized, we assert the *direction* of that difference; for example,

$$P > Q \quad \text{or} \quad P < Q.$$

One-Tailed Probability Value

Probability values obtained by examining only one tail of the distribution.

In evaluating the outcome of an experiment, **one-tailed probability values** should be employed whenever our alternative hypothesis is directional.

Moreover, when the alternative hypothesis is directional, so also is the null hypothesis. For example, if the alternative hypothesis is that $P > Q$, the null hypothesis is that $P \leq Q$. Conversely, if H_1 is $P < Q$, H_0 reads: $P \geq Q$.

The Notion of Indirect Proof

Careful analysis of the logic of statistical inference reveals that the null hypothesis can never be proved. For example, if we had obtained exactly 5 heads on 10 tosses of a coin, would this prove that the coin was unbiased? The answer is a categorical "No!" A bias, if it existed, might be of such a small magnitude that we failed to detect it in 10 trials. But what if we tossed the coin 100 times and obtained 50 heads? Wouldn't this prove something? Again, the same considerations apply. No matter how many times we toss the coin, we can never exhaust the population of possible outcomes. We can make the assertion, however, that *no basis exists for rejecting* the hypothesis that the coin is unbiased.

How, then, can we prove the alternative hypothesis that the coin is biased? Again, we cannot prove the alternative hypothesis directly. Think, for the moment, of the logic involved in the following problem.

Draw two lines on a paper and determine whether they are of different lengths. You compare them and say, "Well, certainly they are not equal. Therefore they must be of different lengths." By rejecting equality (in this case, the null hypothesis) you assert that there is a difference.

Statistical logic operates in exactly the same way. We cannot prove the null hypothesis, nor can we directly prove the alternative hypothesis. However, if we can *reject* the null hypothesis, we can assert its alternative—namely, that the population parameter is some value other than the one hypothesized. Applied to the coin problem, if we can reject the null hypothesis that $P = Q = \frac{1}{2}$. We can assert the alternative—namely, that $P \neq Q \neq \frac{1}{2}$. Note that the support of the alternative hypothesis is always *indirect*. We have supported it by rejecting the null hypothesis. On the other hand, since the alternative hypothesis can neither be proved nor disproved directly, we can *never prove the null hypothesis* by rejecting the alternative hypothesis. The strongest statement we are entitled to make in this respect is that we *failed to reject the null hypothesis*. In practice, many researchers use the expressions, "fail to reject the null hypothesis" and "accept the null hypothesis" interchangeably.

What, then, are the conditions for rejecting the null hypothesis? Simply this: When employing the 0.05 level of significance, you reject the null hypothesis when a given result occurs by chance 5% of the time or less. When employing the 0.01 level of significance, you reject the null hypothesis when a given result occurs by chance 1% of the time or less. Under these circumstances, of course, you *affirm* the alternative hypothesis.

In other words, one rejects the null hypothesis when the results occur by chance 5% of the time or less (or 1% of the time or less), *assuming that the null hypothesis is the true distribution*. That is, one assumes that the null hypothesis is true, calculates the probability on the basis of this assumption, and if the probability is small, one rejects the assumption.

For reasons stated above, the late R. A. Fisher, eminent British statistician, has affirmed:

> In relation to any experiment we may speak of this hypothesis as the "null hypothesis," and it should be noted that the null hypothesis is never proved or established, but is possibly disproved, in the course of experimentation. *Every experiment may be said to exist only in order to give the facts a chance of disproving the null hypothesis.*[*]

11.5 *Testing Statistical Hypotheses: The Two Types of Error*

You may now ask, "But aren't we taking a chance that we will be wrong in rejecting the null hypothesis? Isn't it possible that we have in fact obtained a statistically rare occurrence by chance?"

The answer to this question must be a simple and humble "Yes." This is precisely what we mean when we say that science is probabilistic. If there is any absolute statement that scientists are entitled to make, it is that we can never assert with complete confidence that our findings or propositions are true. There are countless examples in science in which an apparently firmly established conclusion has had to be modified in the light of further evidence.

In the coin experiment, even if all the tosses had resulted in heads, it is possible that the coin was not in fact biased. By chance, once in every 1024 experiments, "on the average," the coin will turn up heads 10 out of 10 times. When we employ the 0.05 level of significance, approximately 5% of the time we will be wrong when we reject the null hypothesis and assert its alternative.

These are some of the basic facts of the reality of inductive reasoning to which students must adjust. Students of behavior who insist on absolute certainty before they speak on issues are students who have been mute throughout all their years, and who will remain so the rest of their lives (probably).

These same considerations have led statisticians to formulate two types of errors that may be made in statistical inference.

Type I Error (Type α Error)

Type I Error (Type α Error)

The rejection of H_0 when it is actually true. The probability of a type I error is given by the α level.

In a **type I error,** we reject the null hypothesis when it is actually true. The probability of making a type I error is α. We have already pointed out that if we set our rejection point at the 0.05 level of significance, we will mistakenly reject H_0 approximately 5% of the time. It would seem, then, that in order to avoid this type of error we should set the rejection level as low as possible. For

---

[*](Italics supplied.) R. A. Fisher, *The Design of Experiments.* Edinburgh: Oliver & Boyd, 1935, p. 16.

example, if we were to set $\alpha = 0.001$, we would risk a type I error only about one time in every thousand. It should be noted that the 0.05 level is rather routinely used in the social and behavioral sciences unless there is a particular reason to be extremely conservative about making a type I error. For example, suppose we were comparing a totally new teaching method to the technique currently in use. Suppose also that the null hypothesis were really true; i.e., there were *no* difference between the two methods. If a type I error were made and the null hypothesis falsely rejected, this could conceivably lead to an extremely costly and time-consuming changeover to a method that was in fact no better than the one being used. In situations such as these we might want to set a more conservative level of significance (for example $\alpha = 0.01$). To familiarize you with the use of both α-levels, we have arbitrarily employed the $\alpha = 0.01$ and $\alpha = 0.05$ levels in examples presented throughout the text. However, the lower we set α, the greater is the likelihood that we will make a type II error.

Type II Error (Type β Error)

In a **type II error,** we fail to reject the null hypothesis when it is actually false. *Beta* (β) is the probability of making a type II error. This type of error is far more common than a type I error. For example, if we employ the 0.01 level of significance as the basis of rejecting the null hypothesis, and then conduct an experiment in which the result we obtained would have occurred by chance only 2% of the time, we cannot reject the null hypothesis. Consequently we cannot claim an experimental effect even though there very well may be one.

    It is clear, then, that the lower we set the rejection level, the less is the likelihood of a type I error, and the greater is the likelihood of a type II error. Conversely, the higher we set the rejection level, the greater the likelihood of a type I error, and the smaller the likelihood of a type II error.

    The fact that the rejection level is set as low as it is attests to the conservatism of scientists, i.e., the greater willingness on the part of the scientist to make an error in the direction of *failing* to claim a result than to make an error in the direction of *claiming* a result when he or she is wrong.

    Table 11.2 summarizes the type of error made as a function of the true status of the null hypothesis and the decision we have made. We should note that type I and type II errors are sampling errors and refer to samples drawn from hypothetical populations.

    Let's look at a few examples, in which for illustrative purposes we supply the following information about the underlying population: H_0, α-level, obtained p, statistical decision made, and the true status of H_0. Let's ascertain what type of error, if any, has been made.

1. $H_0 : \mu_1 = \mu_2$, $\alpha = 0.05$, two-tailed test. Obtained $p = 0.03$, two-tailed value. Statistical decision: H_0 is false. Actual status of H_0: True.

Type II Error (Type β Error)

The probability of accepting H_0 when it is actually false. The probability of a type II error is given by β.

Table 11.2 **The type of error made as a function of the true status of H_0 and the statistical decision we have made. To illustrate, if H_0 is true (column 1) and we have rejected H_0 (row 2), we have made a type I error. If H_0 is false (column 2) and we have rejected H_0, we have made a correct decision.**

		True status of H_0	
		H_0 True	H_0 False
Decision	Accept H_0	Correct $1 - \alpha$	Type II error β
	Reject H_0	Type I error α	Correct $1 - \beta$

Error: Type I—rejecting a true H_0.

2. $H_0 : \mu_1 = \mu_2$ $\alpha = 0.05$, two-tailed test. Obtained $p = 0.04$, two-tailed value. Statistical decision: H_0 is false. Actual status of H_0: False.

Error: No error has been made. A correct conclusion was drawn, since H_0 is false and the statistical decision was that H_0 is false.

3. $H_0 : \mu_1 = \mu_2$, $\alpha = 0.01$, two-tailed test. Obtained $p = 0.10$, two-tailed value. Statistical decision: fail to reject H_0. Actual status of H_0: False.

Error: Type II—failing to reject a false H_0.

4. $H_0 : \mu_1 = \mu_2$, $\alpha = 0.01$, two-tailed test. Obtained $p = 0.006$, two-tailed value. Statistical decision: Reject H_0. Actual status of H_0: False.

Error: No error has been made, since the statistical decision has been to reject H_0 when H_0 is actually false.

You may now ask, "In actual practice, how can we tell when we are making a type I or a type II error?" The answer is simple: We can't! If we examine once again the logic of statistical inference, we can see why. We have already stated that with rare exceptions we cannot or will not know the true parameters of a population. Without this knowledge, how can we know whether our sample statistics have approximated or have failed to approximate the true value? How can we know whether or not we have mistakenly rejected a null hypothesis? If we did know a population value, we could know whether or not we made an error. Under these circumstances, however, the need for sampling statistics is eliminated. We collect samples and draw inferences from samples only because our population values are unknowable for one reason or another. When they become known, the need for statistical inference is lost.

Is there no way, then, to know which experiments reporting significant results are accurate and which are not? The answer is a conditional "Yes." If we were to repeat the experiment and obtain similar results, we would have increased confidence that we were not making a type I error. For example, if we tossed our coin in a second series of 10 trials and obtained 9 heads, we would feel far more confident that our coin was biased. Parenthetically, repetition of experiments is one of the weaker areas in social-science research. The general attitude is that a study is not much good unless it is "different" and is therefore making a novel contribution. Replicating experiments, when they are performed, frequently go unpublished. In consequence we may feel assured that in studies employing the 0.05 significance level, approximately one out of every 20 that reject the null hypothesis is making a type I error.*

Chapter Summary

We have seen that one of the basic problems of inferential statistics involves estimating population parameters from sample statistics.

In inferential statistics we are frequently called upon to compare our *obtained* values with *expected* values. The expected values are given by the appropriate sampling distribution, which is a theoretical probability distribution of the possible values of a sample statistic.

We have seen how to use sampling distributions to interpret sample statistics.

We have seen that there are two mutually exclusive and exhaustive statistical hypotheses in every experiment: The null hypothesis (H_0) and the alternative hypothesis (H_1).

If the outcome of an experiment is rare (here "rare" is defined as some arbitrary but accepted probability value), we reject the null hypothesis and assert its alternative. If the event is not rare (i.e., the probability value is *greater* than what we have agreed upon as being significant), we fail to reject the null hypothesis. However, in no event are we permitted to claim that we have *proved* H_0.

The experimenter is faced with two types of errors in establishing a cutoff probability value that he or she will accept as significant:

Type I: Rejecting the null hypothesis when it is true.

Type II: Failing to reject ("accepting") the null hypothesis when it is false.

---

*The proportion is probably even higher, since our methods of accepting research reports for publication are heavily weighted in terms of the statistical significance of the results. Thus, if four identical studies were conducted independently, and only one obtained results that permitted rejection of the null hypothesis, *this* one would most likely be published. There is virtually no way for the general scientific public to know about the three studies that *failed* to reject the null hypothesis.

The basic conservatism of scientists causes them to establish a low level of significance, resulting in a greater incidence of type II errors than of type I errors.

Without replication of experiments we have no basis for knowing when a type I error has been made, and even with replication we cannot claim knowledge of absolute truth.

Finally, and perhaps most important, we have seen that scientific knowledge is probabilistic and not absolute.

Terms to Remember

alpha (α) level	population
alternative hypothesis (H_1)	sample
binomial distribution	sampling distribution
directional hypothesis	significance level
nondirectional hypothesis	two-tailed probability value
null hypothesis (H_0)	type I error (type α error)
one-tailed probability value	type II error (type β error)

EXERCISES

1. Explain in your own words the nature of drawing inferences in behavioral science. Be sure to specify the types of risks that are taken and the ways in which the researcher attempts to keep these risks within specifiable limits.

2. Give examples of experimental studies in which
   a. a type I error would be considered more serious than a type II error;
   b. a type II error would be considered more serious than a type I error.

3. After completing a study in experimental psychology, David S. concluded, "I have proved that no difference exists between the two experimental conditions." Criticize his conclusion according to the logic of drawing inferences in science.

4. Explain what is meant by the following statement: "It can be said that the purpose of any experiment is to provide the occasion for rejecting the null hypothesis."

5. An experimental psychologist hypothesizes that drive affects running speed. Assume that she has set up a study to investigate the problem employing two different drive levels. Formulate H_0 and H_1.

6. Identify H_0 and H_1 in the following:
   a. The population mean in intelligence is 100.

b. The proportion of Democrats in Watanabe County is not equal to 0.50.

c. The population mean in intelligence is not equal to 100.

d. The proportion of Democrats in Watanabe County is equal to 0.50.

7. Suppose that you are a personnel manager responsible for recommending the promotion of an employee to a high-level executive position. What type of error would you be making if
   a. the hypothesis that he is qualified (H_0) is erroneously accepted?
   b. the hypothesis that he is qualified is erroneously rejected?
   c. the hypothesis that he is qualified is correctly accepted?
   d. the hypothesis that he is qualified is correctly rejected?

8. A stock-market analyst recommends the purchase or sale of stock by her client on the basis of hypotheses she has formulated about the future behavior of these stocks. What type of error is she making if she makes the following claims under the given conditions?
   a. H_0: The stock will remain stable. *Fact:* It goes up precipitously.
   b. H_0: The stock will remain stable. *Fact:* It falls abruptly.
   c. H_0: The stock will remain stable. *Fact:* It shows only minor fluctuation about a central value.

9. An investigator sets $\alpha = 0.01$ for rejection of H_0. He conducts a study in which he obtains a *p*-value of 0.02 and fails to reject H_0. *Discuss:* Is it more likely that he is accepting a true or a false H_0?

10. *Comment:* A student of psychology has collected a mass of data to test 100 different null hypotheses. On completion of the analysis she finds that 5 of the 100 comparisons yield *p*-values ≤ 0.05. She concludes: "Using $\alpha = 0.05$, I have found a true difference in five of the comparisons."

11. *Comment:* As an investigator, you have tested 500 different individuals for evidence of extrasensory perception (ESP). Employing $\alpha = 0.01$, you conclude, "I have found 6 individuals who demonstrated ESP."

12. Does the null hypothesis in a one-tailed test differ from the null hypothesis in a two-tailed test?

13. Does the alternative hypothesis in a one-tailed test differ from the alternative hypothesis in a two-tailed test? Give an example.

14. In rejecting the null hypothesis for a one-tailed test, do all deviations count equally? Explain.

15. Suppose you want to test the hypothesis that there is not an equal number of male and female executives in a given large company. The appropriate null hypothesis would be as follows:
   a. There are more female than male executives.
   b. The numbers of male and female executives are equal.
   c. There are more male than female executive.

16. Suppose an efficiency expert finds a significant difference between the time it takes people to read a circular dial and the time it takes them to read a rectangular dial. Although $\alpha = 0.05$ or $\alpha = 0.01$ is traditionally applied as the level of significance, this choice is arbitrary. For each of the following levels of significance, state how many times in 1000 this difference would be expected to occur by chance.

a. 0.001	b. 0.01	c. 0.005	d. 0.06
e. 0.05	f. 0.095	g. 0.004	h. 0.10

17. With reference to Exercise 16, the adoption of which level of significance would be most likely to result in the following statements?
   a. There is a significant difference between the reading times of the two dials.
   b. It cannot be concluded that there is a significant difference between the reading times of the two dials.

18. Refer again to Exercise 16. The adoption of which level of significance would be most likely to result in the following errors? Identify the type of each error.
   a. There is a significant difference between the reading times of the two dials. *Fact:* There is no difference.
   b. It cannot be concluded that there is a significant difference between the reading times of the two dials. *Fact:* There is a difference.

19. If $\alpha = 0.05$, what is the probability of making a type I error?

20. Refer to Table 11.2. Suppose you are a clinician engaged in the diagnosis of individuals seeking help for emotional disorders. Assume that a person has a disorder or does not. Construct a table that describes the types of error that a clinician might make.

21. In view of the Table you constructed in Exercise 25, what are some circumstances in which a Type II error may have more serious consequences than a Type I error.

In Exercises 22 through 26, H_0, α, obtained p, and true status of H_0 are given. State whether or not an error in statistical decision has been made. If so, state the type of error.

22. $H_0: P = Q$, $\alpha = 0.01$, one-tailed test. Obtained $p = 0.008$, one-tailed value (in predicted direction). Actual status of H_0: True.

23. $H_0: P = Q$, $\alpha = 0.05$, two-tailed test. Obtained $p = 0.08$, two-tailed value. Actual status of H_0: True.

24. $H_0: P = Q$, $\alpha = 0.05$, two-tailed test. Obtained $p = 0.06$, two-tailed value. Actual status of H_0: False.

25. $H_0: P = Q$, $\alpha = 0.05$, two-tailed test. Obtained $p = 0.03$, two-tailed value. Actual status of H_0: False.

26. $H_0: P = Q$, $\alpha = 0.01$, two-tailed test. Obtained $p = 0.005$, two-tailed value. Actual status of H_0: False.

12

Statistical Inference and Continuous Variables

12.1 *Introduction*

In Chapter 11, we illustrated the use of a sampling distribution for a discrete two-category nominal variable (the binomial distribution) and for all possible means when drawing samples of a fixed N from a population of four scores. Table 11.1 showed the frequency and probability distributions of means when all possible samples of a given size were selected from the population of four scores. Figure 12.1 shows probability histograms, with superimposed curves obtained by connecting the midpoints of each bar.

Before proceeding with the discussion of sampling distributions for interval or ratio-scaled variables, examine Table 11.1 and Fig. 12.1 carefully. See if you can answer the following questions.

1. How does the mean of each sampling distribution of means compare with the mean of the population from which the samples were drawn?

2. How does the variability or dispersion of the sample means change as we increase the sample size upon which each sampling distribution is based?

Now compare your answers with ours:

1. The mean of the population of four scores is 4.5. The mean of each sampling distribution of means is 4.5. Thus the mean of a sampling distribution of means is the same as the population mean from which the sample means were drawn. This statement is true for all sizes of N. In other words, the mean of the sampling distribution does not vary with the sample size.

2. As you increase the sample size, the dispersion of sample means becomes less. A greater proportion of means are close to the population mean and extreme deviations are rarer as N becomes larger. To verify these statements, note the probability of obtaining a mean as rare as 0 or 9 at different sample sizes. Note also that the proportion of means in the middle of the distribution becomes greater as sample size is increased. For example, the proportion of means between and including 3 and 6 is 0.6250 when $N = 2$, 0.6874 when $N = 3$, and 0.7265 when $N = 4$.

Standard Error of the Mean

A theoretical standard deviation of sample means, of a given sample size, drawn from some specified population. When based upon a known population standard deviation, $\sigma_{\bar{x}} = \sigma/\sqrt{N}$; when estimated from a single sample, $s_{\bar{x}} = s/\sqrt{N-1}$.

Finally, the standard deviation of the sample means—which we'll call the **standard error of the mean** from this point forward—shows that the dispersion of sample means decreases as sample size is increased.

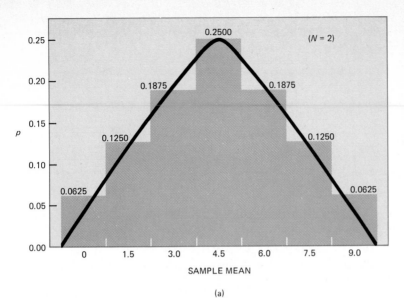

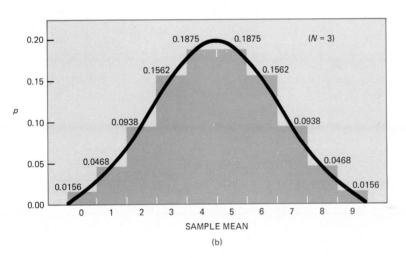

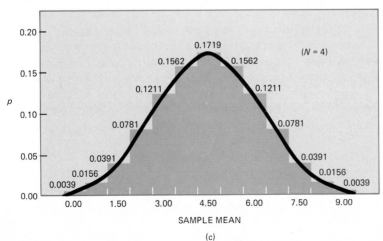

Figure 12.1
Probability histograms
based upon sampling
distributions of means
drawn, with replacement,
from a population of four
scores and sample sizes
$N = 2$, $N = 3$, and
$N = 4$.

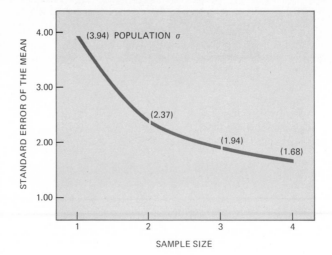

Figure 12.2
Magnitude of the standard error of the mean as a function of sample size.

Figure 12.2 is a line drawing showing the decreasing magnitude of s_x as the sample size increases. Shown are the population standard deviation of four scores and the standard error of the mean for the sampling distributions when $N = 2$, $N = 3$, and $N = 4$. Note that the decrease is not linear.

12.2 Sampling Distribution of the Mean

Imagine we are conducting a sampling experiment in which we randomly draw (with replacement)* a sample of two scores from a population in which $\mu = 5.00$ and $\sigma = 0.99$ (see Table 12.1). For example, we might draw scores of 3 and 6. We calculate the same mean and find $\overline{X} = 4.5$. Now suppose we continue to draw samples of $N = 2$ (e.g., we might draw scores of 2, 8; 3, 7; 4, 5; 5, 6; etc.) until we obtain an indefinitely large number of samples. If we calculate the sample mean for each sample drawn, and treat each of these sample means as a raw score, we may set up a frequency distribution of these sample means.

Let's repeat these procedures with increasingly larger sample sizes, for example, $N = 5$, $N = 15$. We now have three frequency distributions of sample means based on three different sample sizes.

Intuitively, what might we expect these distributions to look like? Since we are selecting at random from the population, we would expect the mean of the distribution of sample means to approximate the mean of the population.

---

*If the population is infinite or extremely large, the difference between sampling with or without replacement is negligible.

Table 12.1 **An approximately normally distributed population with $\mu = 5.00$ and $\sigma = 0.99$.**

X	f	p(X)
2	4	0.004
3	54	0.054
4	242	0.242
5	400	0.400
6	242	0.242
7	54	0.054
8	4	0.004
	$N = 1000$	$\sum p(X) = 1.000$

How might the dispersion of these sample means compare with the variability in the original distribution of scores? In the original distribution, when $N = 1$ the probability of obtaining a score as extreme as, say, 8 is 4/1000 or 0.004 (see Table 12.1). The probability of obtaining a sample *mean* equal to 8 when $N = 2$ (i.e., drawing scores of 8, 8) is equal to 0.004×0.004 or 0.000016 (Formula 10.9). In other words, the probability of selecting a sample with an *extreme mean* is less than the probability of selecting a single score that is equally extreme. What if we increased our sample size to $N = 4$? The probability of obtaining results this extreme ($\overline{X} = 8$) is exceedingly small $(0.004)^4 = .0000000003$. Generalizing, the probability of drawing extreme values of the sample mean is less as N increases. Since the standard deviation is a direct function of the number of extreme scores (see Chapter 6), it follows that a distribution containing proportionately fewer extreme scores will have a lower standard deviation. Therefore, if we treat each of the sample means as a raw score and then calculate the standard deviation ($\sigma_{\overline{X}}$, referred to as the *standard error of the mean**), it is clear that as the sample size increases the variability of the sample means decreases.

If these sampling experiments were actually conducted, the frequency curves of sample means would be obtained as in Fig. 12.3.

There are three important lessons which may be learned from a careful examination of Fig. 12.2.

1. The distribution of sample means, drawn from a normally distributed population, is bell-shaped or "normal." Indeed, it can be shown that even if the underlying distribution is skewed, the distribution of sample means will tend to be normal.

---

*This notation represents the standard deviation of a sampling distribution of means. This is purely a theoretical notation since, with an infinite number of sample means, it is not possible to assign a specific value to the number of sample means involved.

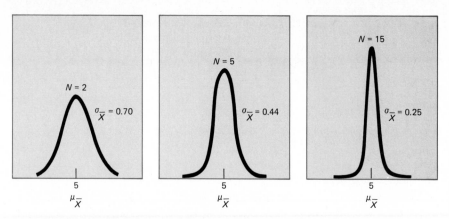

Figure 12.3 Frequency curves of sample means drawn from a population in which $\mu = 5.00$ and $\sigma = 0.99$

2. The mean of the sample means ($\mu_{\bar{X}}$) is equal to the mean of the population (μ) from which these samples were drawn.

3. The distribution of sample means becomes more and more compact as we increase the size of the sample. This is an extremely important point in statistical inference, about which we shall soon have a great deal more to say.

If we base our estimate of the population mean on a *single* sample drawn from the population, our approximation to the parameter is likely to be closer as we increase the size of the sample. In other words, if it is true that the dispersion of sample means decreases with increasing sample size, it also follows that the mean of any single sample is more likely to be closer to the mean of the population as the sample size increases.

Central-Limit Theorem

If random samples of a fixed N are drawn from *any* population (regardless of the form of the population distribution), as N becomes larger, the distribution of sample means approaches normality.

These three observations illustrate a rather startling theorem that is of fundamental importance in inferential statistics, i.e., the **central-limit theorem,** which states

If random samples of a fixed N are drawn from **any** population (regardless of the form of the population distribution), as N becomes larger, the distribution of sample means approaches normality, with the overall mean approaching μ, the variance of the sample means $\sigma_{\bar{X}}^2$ being equal to σ^2/N and a standard error $\sigma_{\bar{X}}$ of $\sigma/\sqrt{N}$.

Stated symbolically.

$$\sigma_{\bar{X}}^2 = \frac{\sigma^2}{N}, \tag{12.1}$$

and

$$\sigma_{\bar{X}} = \frac{\sigma}{\sqrt{N}}. \tag{12.2}$$

CASE EXAMPLE • 12.1
A Statistical Sampling Experiment

In this statistical experiment, the author had a computer select samples from a population and calculate the mean, variance, and standard deviation of each sample. The samples were selected from a population that was distributed in a completely uniform fashion—numbers from 1 to 85. The mean and standard deviation of the population were 42.5 and 24.68 respectively. Two sets of 22 samples were selected from this population—one with $N = 5$ and the other with $N = 15$. The results are shown in Table 12.2

Table 12.2 **Sample means obtained by randomly selecting 22 samples of $N = 5$ and 22 samples of $N = 15$ from a uniform population of 85 integers from 1 through 85.**

N = 5		N = 15	
25.4	45.6	25.07	42.27
29.2	46.0	31.07	42.40
34.2	47.0	31.40	43.00
35.4	48.8	33.00	43.60
35.6	48.8	36.67	43.60
36.2	49.0	37.40	44.07
38.6	49.2	37.67	45.07
38.8	50.6	40.00	45.73
42.6	51.6	40.80	50.07
42.8	57.8	41.50	54.13
43.6	61.8	41.60	55.93

$$\sum \bar{X} = 958.6 \qquad \sum \bar{X} = 906.05$$
$$N_s = 22 \qquad N_s = 22$$
$$\bar{X}_{\bar{X}} = 43.57 \qquad \bar{X}_{\bar{X}} = 41.18$$
$$s_{\bar{X}} = 8.85 \qquad s_{\bar{X}} = 7.24$$

where N_s is the number of sample means, $\bar{X}_{\bar{X}}$ is the mean of the sample means, and $s_{\bar{X}}$ is the standard deviation of the sample means.

Further inspection of Table 12.2 reveals a number of interesting findings:

1. Each sample mean is not equal to the population mean. However, the mean of the sample means is a pretty good approximation to the population mean. It can be shown that the means of randomly selected samples, averaged over all possible samples, will yield the population mean as the average value. The means are said to be **unbiased estimators** of the population mean.

Unbiased Estimator

An estimator that equals, on the average, the value of the corresponding parameter.

2. The variability among the sample means decreases as the sample size increases. The range and standard deviation of the population were 84 and 24.68 respectively. When $N = 5$, the range and standard deviations of the sample means were 36.4 and 8.85 respectively. Finally, with $N = 15$, the range fell to 30.86, and the standard deviation declined to 7.24.

3. The form of the distribution of sample means also changed with increased sample size. Figure 12.4 presents grouped frequency histograms of the sample means. It can be seen that they nicely illustrate the Central Limit Theorem.

Figure 12.4   Grouped frequency histograms of sample means based on Ns equal to 5 and 15 respectively. The samples were randomly and independently selected from a population in which the measurements are uniformly distributed.

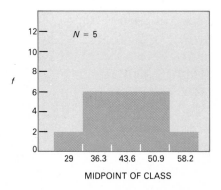
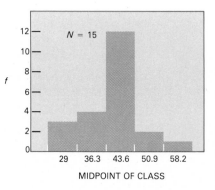

Based on Richard P. Runyon, "A Statistical Sampling Experiment," Chapter 7 of *Biostatistics*. Boston: Duxbury Press, 1984.

12.3 Testing Statistical Hypotheses: Population Mean and Standard Deviation Known

Finding the Probability That a Sample Mean Will Fall within a Certain Range

Let us briefly examine some of the implications of the relationships we have just discussed.

When μ and σ are *known* for a given population, it is possible to describe the form of the distribution of sample means when N is large (regardless of the form of the original distribution). It will be a normal distribution with a mean ($\mu_{\bar{X}}$) equal to μ and a standard error ($\sigma_{\bar{X}}$) equal to $\sigma/\sqrt{N}$. It now becomes possible to determine probability values in terms of areas under the normal curve. Thus we may use the known relationships of the normal probability curve to determine the probabilities associated with any sample mean (of a given N) randomly drawn from this population.

We have already seen (Section 7.3) that any normally distributed variable may be transformed into the normally distributed z-scale. We have also seen (Section 10.6) that we may establish probability values in terms of the relationships between z-scores and areas under the normal curve. That is, for any given raw-score value (X) with a certain proportion of area beyond it, there is a corresponding value of z with the same proportion of area beyond it. Similarly, for any given value of a sample mean ($\bar{X}$) with a certain proportion of area beyond it, there is a corresponding value of z with the same proportion of area beyond it. Thus assuming that the form of the distribution of sample means is normal, we may establish probability values in terms of the relationships between z-scores and areas under the normal curve.

To illustrate: Given a population with $\mu = 250$ and $\sigma = 50$, from which we randomly select 100 scores ($N = 100$), what is the probability that the sample mean ($\bar{X}$) will be equal to or greater than 255? Thus $H_0: \mu = \mu_0 = 250$.

The value of z corresponding to $\bar{X} = 255$ is obtained as follows:

$$z = \frac{\bar{X} - \mu_0}{\sigma_{\bar{X}}} \qquad (12.3)$$

where μ_0 = value of the population mean under H_0,

$$\sigma_{\bar{X}} = \frac{\sigma}{\sqrt{N}} = \frac{50}{\sqrt{100}} = 5.00, \quad \text{and} \quad z = \frac{255 - 250}{5.00} = 1.00.$$

Looking up a z of 1.00 in column (C) in Table A, at the back of this book, we find that 15.87% of the same means falls at or above $\overline{X}$ = 255. Therefore there are approximately 16 chances in 100 of obtaining a sample mean equal to or greater than 255 from this population when N = 100.

Testing Hypotheses about the Sample Mean

Now extend this logic to a situation in which we do not know from what population a sample is drawn. We suspect that it may have been selected from the above population with μ = 250 and σ = 50, but we are not certain. We want to test the hypothesis that our sample mean was indeed selected from this population. Imagine that we had obtained $\overline{X}$ = 263 for N = 100. Is it reasonable to assume that this sample was drawn from the suspected population?

Setting up this problem in formal statistical terms involves the following six steps that are common to all hypothesis testing situations:

1. *Null hypothesis* (H_0): The mean of the population (μ) from which the sample was drawn equals 250, that is, $\mu = \mu_0 = 250$.

2. *Alternative hypothesis* (H_1): The mean of the population from which the sample was drawn does *not* equal 250; $\mu \neq \mu_0$. Note that H_1 is nondirectional; consequently, a two-tailed test of significance will be employed.

3. *Statistical test*: The z statistic is used since σ is known.

4. *Significance level*: α = 0.01. If the difference between the sample mean and the specified population mean is so extreme that its associated probability of occurrence under H_0 is equal to or less than 0.01, we will reject H_0.

5. *Sampling distribution*: The normal probability curve.

6. *Critical region for rejection of H_0*: $|z| \geq |z_{0.01}| = 2.58$* A critical region is that portion of area under the curve that includes those values of a statistic that lead to rejection of the null hypothesis.

Critical Region

That portion of the area under curve which includes those values of a statistic that lead to rejection of the null hypothesis.

The critical region is chosen to correspond with the selected level of significance. Thus for α = 0.01, two-tailed test, the critical region is bounded by those values of $z_{0.01}$ that mark off a total of 1% of the area. Referring again to column (C), Table A, we find that the area beyond a z of 2.58 is approximately 0.005. We double 0.005 to account for both tails of the distribution. Figure 12.5 depicts the critical region for rejection of H_0 when α = 0.01, two-tailed test.

Therefore, in order to reject H_0 at the 0.01 level of significance, the ab-

---

*Since $z_{0.01} = \pm 2.58$, $|z| \geq |z_{0.01}|$ is equivalent to stating $z \geq 2.58$ or $z \leq -2.58$.

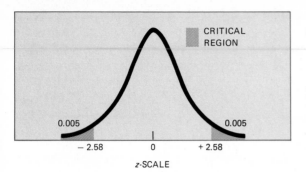

Figure 12.5
Critical region for rejection of H_0 when $\alpha = 0.01$, two-tailed test.

solute value of the obtained z must be equal to or greater than $|z_{0.01}|$ or 2.58. Similarly, if we are to be allowed to reject H_0 at the 0.05 level of significance, the absolute value of the obtained z must be equal to or greater than $|z_{0.05}|$ or 1.96.

In the present example, the value of z corresponding to $\overline{X} = 263$ is

$$z = \frac{\overline{X} - \mu_0}{\sigma_{\overline{X}}} = \frac{263 - 250}{5.00} = 2.60.$$

Decision: Since the obtained z falls within the critical region, (that is, $2.60 > z_{0.01}$), we may reject H_0 at the 0.01 level of significance.

12.4 *Estimation of Parameters: Point Estimation*

So far, we have been concerned with testing hypotheses when the population parameters are known. However, we have taken some pains in this book to point out that population values are rarely known, particularly when the population is extremely large. Every ten years, when the U.S. Federal Government undertakes that massive data collection effort called the census, we come close to knowing the parameters on the various response measures. But knowledge of parameters is not the usual case. However, the fact that we do not know the population values does not prevent us from using the logic developed in Section 12.3.

Whenever we make inferences about population parameters from sample data, we compare our sample results with the expected results given by the appropriate sampling distribution. A hypothetical sampling distribution of sample means is associated with any sample mean. This distribution has a mean, $\mu_{\overline{X}}$, and a standard deviation, $\sigma_{\overline{X}}$. So far, in order to obtain the values of $\mu_{\overline{X}}$ and $\sigma_{\overline{X}}$, we have required a knowledge of μ and σ. In the absence of

knowledge concerning the exact values of the parameters, we are forced to
estimate μ and σ from the statistics calculated from sample data. Since in actual practice we rarely select more than one sample, our estimates are generally based on the statistics calculated from a single sample. All such estimates
involving the use of single sample values are known as **point estimates.**

Estimating $\sigma_{\bar{X}}$ From Sample Data

You will recall that we previously defined the variance of a sample as

$$s^2 = \frac{\sum(X - \bar{X})^2}{N}$$

in Formula (6.2). We obtained the standard deviation, s, by finding the square
root of this value. These definitions are perfectly appropriate so long as we are
interested only in *describing* the variability of a sample. However, when our
interest shifts to *estimating* the population variance from a sample value, we
find the preceding definition inadequate, since $\sum(X - \bar{X})^2/N$ tends on the
average to *underestimate* the population variance. In other words, it provides
a **biased estimate** of the population variance, whereas an unbiased estimate
is required.

We define an *unbiased estimate* as an estimate that equals, on the average, the value of the parameter. That is, when we make the statement that
a statistic is an unbiased estimate of a parameter, we are saying that the mean
of the distribution of an extremely large number of sample statistics, drawn
from a given population, tends to center on the corresponding value of the
parameter. We demonstrated in Box 12.1 that an unbiased estimate of the
population variance may be obtained by dividing the sum of squares by
$N - 1$. We now employ the symbol $\hat{s}^2$ to represent a sample variance providing an *unbiased estimate of the population variance,* and $\hat{s}$ to represent a sample standard deviation based on the unbiased variance estimate. Thus

$$\text{Unbiased estimate of } \sigma^2 = \hat{s}^2 = \frac{\sum(X - \bar{X})^2}{N - 1} \tag{12.4}$$

and

$$\text{Estimated } \sigma = \hat{s} = \sqrt{\hat{s}^2}. \tag{12.5}$$

We are now able to estimate $\sigma_{\bar{X}}^2$ and $\sigma_{\bar{X}}$ from sample data. We shall employ the symbols $s_{\bar{X}}^2$ and $s_{\bar{X}}$ to refer to the estimated variance and standard
error of the mean, respectively. Since we do not know σ^2, we accept the unbiased variance estimate ($\hat{s}^2$) as the best estimate we have of the population

BOX 12.1

Unbiased estimate of the population variance

Throughout this book, we have turned to a sampling experiment whenever we wanted to illustrate a concept of fundamental importance in statistical analysis. Let's take a look at the denominator of the variance formula, and show that $N - 1$ in the denominator provides an unbiased estimate of the population variance, whereas N in the denominator underestimates the population variance.

Imagine the following sampling experiment. You place the following population of four scores in a hat: 1, 2, 3, 4. The mean of this population is 2.5 and the variance is 1.25. You select, with replacement, all possible samples of $N = 2$ and calculate the variance of each sample, using N and $N - 1$ in the denominator. Just as we previously placed the mean of each sample in the cell corresponding to both draws, we now place the *variance* of each sample in the appropriate cell.

First, let's do this using N in the denominator when calculating each sample variance.

Let us now construct a frequency distribution of these variances, and calculate the mean variance.

The mean variance is found to be $10/16 = 0.625$. Recall that the variance of the population is 1.25. In this sampling experiment, employing N in the denominator of the variance formula, the mean variance of all possible samples of $N = 2$ underestimates the population variance. Generalizing, sample variances that employ N in the denominator provide a biased estimate of the population variance.

Now let us repeat the same procedures, using $N - 1$ to calculate the variance of each sample.

The frequency distribution and mean of the sample variances are shown in the fourth table.

Now the mean variance is $20/16 = 1.25$. Note that this is identical to the original variance of the population. Thus using $N - 1$ in the denominator provides an unbiased estimate of the population variance.

Variance of each sample when using N in the denominator ($N = 2$).

| | | First Draw | | | |
		1	2	3	4
Second Draw	1	0.00	0.25	1.00	2.25
	2	0.25	0.00	0.25	1.00
	3	1.00	0.25	0.00	0.25
	4	2.25	1.00	0.25	0.00

s^2	f	fs^2
2.25	2	4.50
1.00	4	4.00
0.25	6	1.50
0.00	4	0.00
	$\sum f = 16$	$\sum fs^2 = 10.00$

Variance of each sample when using $N - 1$ in the denominator ($N = 2$).

| | | First Draw | | | |
		1	2	3	4
Second Draw	1	0.00	0.50	2.00	4.50
	2	0.50	0.00	0.50	2.00
	3	2.00	0.50	0.00	0.50
	4	4.50	2.00	0.50	0.00

s^2	f	fs^2
4.50	2	9.00
2.00	4	8.00
0.50	6	3.00
0.00	4	0.00
	$\sum f = 16$	$\sum fs^2 = 20.00$

variance. Thus the formula for determining the variance of the sampling distribution of the mean from sample data is

$$\text{Estimated } \sigma_{\bar{X}}^2 = s_{\bar{X}}^2 = \frac{\hat{s}^2}{N}. \tag{12.6}$$

We estimate the standard error of the mean by finding the square root of this value:

$$\text{Estimated } \sigma_{\bar{X}} = s_{\bar{X}} = \sqrt{\frac{\hat{s}^2}{N}} = \frac{\hat{s}}{\sqrt{N}}. \tag{12.7}$$

If the sample variance (not the unbiased estimate) is used, we may estimate $\sigma_{\bar{X}}$ as:

$$\text{Estimated } \sigma_{\bar{X}} = s_{\bar{X}} = \frac{s}{\sqrt{N-1}} = \sqrt{\frac{\sum(X - \bar{X})^2}{N(N-1)}} = \sqrt{\frac{SS}{N(N-1)}}. \tag{12.8}*$$

Formula (12.8) is the one most frequently employed in the behavioral sciences to estimate the standard error of the mean. We shall follow this practice.

Before proceeding further, let us review some of the symbols we have been discussing. Table 12.3 shows the various symbols for means, variances, and standard deviations depending upon whether we are dealing with population parameters, unbiased population estimators, or sample statistics.

---

*The following algebraic proof demonstrates how we arrive at this estimate of $\sigma_{\bar{X}}$:

$$s^2 = \frac{\sum(X - \bar{X})^2}{N},$$

multiplying both sides of the equation by $N/(N-1)$ we get:

$$\frac{N}{N-1}s^2 = \frac{N\sum(X - \bar{X})^2}{N(N-1)} = \hat{s}^2 \quad \text{(see Formula 12.4)}.$$

Thus, from formula (12.7),

$$s_{\bar{X}} = \sqrt{\frac{\hat{s}^2}{N}}.$$

Substituting

$$\hat{s}^2 = \frac{N}{N-1}s^2,$$

we find

$$s_{\bar{X}} = \sqrt{\frac{Ns^2}{N(N-1)}} = \frac{s}{\sqrt{N-1}}.$$

Table 12.3 Review of symbols

	Population Parameters (theoretical)	Parameters of Sampling Distribution of Mean (theoretical)	Unbiased Population Estimators for Sampling Distribution of Mean (empirical)	Sample Statistics (empirical)
Means	μ, μ_0	$\mu_{\overline{X}}$	$\overline{X}$	$\overline{X}$
Variances	σ^2	$\sigma_{\overline{X}}^2$	$\hat{s}^2$, $s_{\overline{X}}^2$	s^2
Standard Deviations	σ	$\sigma_{\overline{X}}$	$\hat{s}$, $s_{\overline{X}}$	s

12.5 Testing Statistical Hypotheses with Unknown Parameters: Student's t

We previously pointed out that when the parameters of a population are known, it is possible to describe the form of the sampling distribution of sample means. It will be a normal distribution with $\sigma_{\overline{X}}$ equal to $\sigma/\sqrt{N}$. By employing the relationship between the *z*-scale and the normal distribution, we are able to test hypotheses using

$$z = \frac{(\overline{X} - \mu_0)}{\sigma_{\overline{X}}}$$

as a test statistic. When σ is not known, we are forced to estimate its value from sample data. Consequently, estimated $\sigma_{\overline{X}}$ (that is, $s_{\overline{X}}$) must be based on the estimated σ (that is, $\hat{s}$), as

$$s_{\overline{X}} = \frac{\hat{s}}{\sqrt{N}}.$$

Now, if substituting $\hat{s}$ for σ provided a reasonably good approximation to the sampling distribution of means, we could continue to use *z* as our test statistic, and the normal curve as the model for our sampling distribution. As a matter of fact, however, this is not the case. At the turn of the century a statistician by the name of William Gosset, who published under the pseudonym of Student, noted that the approximation of $\hat{s}$ to σ is poor, particularly for small samples. This failure of approximation is due to the fact that, with small samples, $\hat{s}$ will tend to underestimate σ more than one-half the time. Consequently, the statistic

$$\frac{\overline{X} - \mu_0}{\hat{s}/\sqrt{N}}$$

will tend to be spread out more than the normal distribution.

Gosset's major contribution to statistics consisted of his description of a family of distributions that permits the testing of hypotheses with samples drawn from normally distributed populations when σ is not known. These distributions are referred to variously as the **t-distributions** or *Student's t*. The ratio employed in the testing of hypotheses is known as the **t-ratio:**

t-Distributions

Theoretical symmetrical sampling distributions with a mean of zero and a standard deviation that becomes smaller as degrees of freedom (df) increase. Employed in relation to the Student *t*-ratio.

$$t = \frac{\overline{X} - \mu_0}{s_{\overline{X}}}, \tag{12.9}$$

where μ_0 is the value of the population mean under H_0.

t-Ratio

A test statistic for determining the significance of a difference between means (two-sample case) or for testing the hypothesis that a given sample mean was drawn from a population with the mean specified under the null hypothesis (one-sample case). Employed when population standard deviation (or standard deviations) is not known.

The *t*-statistic is similar in many respects to the previously discussed *z*-statistic. Both statistics are expressed as the deviation of a sample mean from a population mean (known or hypothesized) in terms of the standard error of the mean. By reference to the appropriate sampling distribution, we may express this deviation in terms of probability. When the *z*-statistic is used, the standard normal curve is the appropriate sampling distribution. For the *t*-statistic there is a family of distributions which vary as a function of **degrees of freedom (df).**

The term "degrees of freedom" refers to the number of values that are free to vary after we have placed certain restrictions on our data. To illustrate, let us imagine that we have four numbers: 18, 23, 27, 32. The sum is 100 and the mean is $\overline{X} = 100/4 = 25$. Recall that if we subtract the mean from each score, we should obtain a set of four deviations that add up to zero. Thus

Degrees of Freedom (df)

The number of values that are free to vary after we have placed certain restrictions upon our data.

$$(18 - 25) + (23 - 25) + (27 - 25) + (32 - 25)$$
$$= (-7) + (-2) + 2 + 7 = 0.$$

Note also that the four deviations are not independent. Once we have imposed the restriction that the deviations are taken from the mean, the values of only three deviations are free to vary. As soon as three deviations are known, the fourth is completely determined. Stated another way, the values of only three deviations are free to vary. For example, if we know three deviations to be -7, -2, and 7, we may calculate the unknown deviation by use of the equality:

$$(X_1 - \overline{X}) + (X_2 - \overline{X}) + (X_3 - \overline{X}) + (X_4 - \overline{X}) = 0.$$

Therefore

$$(X_4 - \overline{X}) = 0 - [(X_1 - \overline{X}) + (X_2 - \overline{X}) + (X_3 - \overline{X})].$$

In the present example,

$$\begin{aligned}(X_4 - \overline{X}) &= 0 - (-7) + (-2) + 2 \\ &= 0 + 7 - 2 + 2 = 7.\end{aligned}$$

To generalize: For any given sample on which we have placed a single restriction, the number of degrees of freedom is $N - 1$. In the above example, $N = 4$; therefore degrees of freedom are $4 - 1 = 3$.

Note that when $s/\sqrt{N - 1}$ (Formula 12.8) is employed to obtain $s_{\overline{X}}$, the quantity under the square root sign $(N - 1)$ is the degrees of freedom.

We noted above that the use of Student's t depends on the assumption that the underlying population is normally distributed. This requirement stems from a unique property of normal distributions. *Given that observations are independent and random, the sample means and sample variances are independent only when the population is normally distributed.* As we previously pointed out, two scores or statistics are independent only when the values of one do not depend on the values of the other and vice versa. Tests of significance of means demand that the means and variances be independent of one another. They cannot vary together in some systematic way—for example, with the variances becoming larger as the means become larger. If they do vary in a systematic way, the underlying population cannot be normal and tests of significance based on the assumption of normality may be invalid. It is for this reason that the assumption of normality underlies the use of Student's t-ratio.

One final note: Student's t-ratio is referred to as a *robust test*, meaning that statistical inferences are likely to be valid even when there are fairly large departures from normality in the population distribution. This robustness is another consequence of the central limit theorem. If we have serious doubts concerning the normality of the population distribution, it is wise to increase the N in each sample.

Characteristics of t-Distributions

Let us compare the characteristics of the t-distributions with the already familiar standard normal curve. First, both distributions are symmetrical about a mean of zero. Therefore the proportion of area beyond a particular positive t-value is equal to the proportion of area below the corresponding negative t.

Second, the t-distributions are more spread out than the normal curve. Consequently the proportion of area beyond a specific value of t is *greater* than the proportion of area beyond the corresponding value of z. However, the greater the df, the more the t-distributions resemble the standard normal curve. In order that you may see the contrast between the t-distributions and the normal curve we have reproduced three curves in Fig. 12.6: the sampling distributions of t when df $= 3$, df $= 10$, and the normal curve.

Inspection of Fig. 12.6 permits several interesting observations. We have already seen that with the standard normal curve, $|z| \geq 1.96$ defines the region of rejection at the 0.05 level of significance. However, when df $= 3$, a $|t| \geq 1.96$ includes approximately 15% of the total area. Consequently, if we were to employ the normal curve for testing hypotheses when N is small (therefore df is small) and σ is unknown, we would be in serious danger of making a type I error, i.e., rejecting H_0 when it is true. Obviously, a much larger value of t is required to mark off the bounds of the critical region of rejection. Indeed, when df $= 3$, the absolute value of the obtained t must be equal to or greater than 3.18 to reject H_0 at the 0.05 level of significance (two-tailed test). However, as df increases, the differences in the proportions of area under the normal curve and Student's t-distributions become negligible.

Critical Values of t

Those values that bound the critical rejection regions corresponding to varying levels of significance.

In contrast to our use of the normal curve, the tabled values for t (see table C, in Tables) are *critical values*, i.e., *those values which bound the critical rejection regions corresponding to varying levels of significance*. Thus, in using the table for the distribution of t, we locate the appropriate number of degrees

Figure 12.6   Sampling distributions of $t = (\overline{X} = \mu_0)/s_{\overline{X}}$ when df $= 3$, and 10, compared to the standard normal curve.

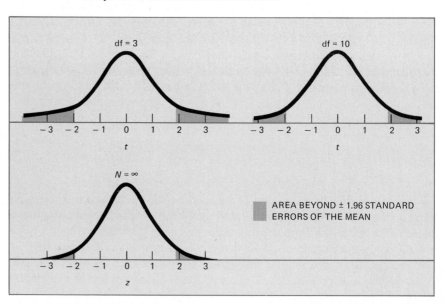

of freedom in the left-hand column, and then find the column corresponding to the chosen α. The tabled values represent the t-ratio required for significance. If the absolute value of our obtained t-ratio equals or exceeds this tabled value, we may reject H_0.

Illustrative Problem: Student's t

Let us now examine a hypothetical case involving a small sample.

A group of 17 ninth-grade students selected on the basis of an expressed "interest" in science were given a test measuring their knowledge of basic scientific concepts. The test was constructed to yield a normal distribution with a mean for ninth graders equal to 78. The results of the study were

$$\overline{X} = 84, \quad s = 16, \quad N = 17.$$

It is reasonable to assume that these ninth graders are representative of a population in which $\mu = 78$?

Let us set up this problem in more formal statistical terms.

1. *Null hypothesis* (H_0): The mean of the population from which the sample was drawn equals 78 ($\mu = \mu_0 = 78$).
2. *Alternative hypothesis* (H_1): The mean of the population from which the sample was drawn does *not* equal 78 ($\mu \neq \mu_0$). [*Note:* This is a nondirectional alternative.]
3. *Statistical test*: The Student t-ratio is chosen because we are dealing with a normally distributed variable in which σ is unknown.
4. *Significance level*: $\alpha = 0.05$.
5. *Sampling distribution*: The sampling distribution is the Student t-distribution with df $= 16$. [*Note:* df $= N - 1$.]
6. *Critical region*: $|t_{0.05}| \geq 2.12$. Since H_1 is nondirectional, the critical region consists of all values of $t \geq 2.12$ and $t \leq -2.12$.

In the present example, the value of t corresponding to $\overline{X} = 84$ is

$$t = \frac{\overline{X} - \mu_0}{s_{\overline{X}}} = \frac{84 - 78}{16/\sqrt{16}} = 1.50.$$

Decision: Since the obtained t does not fall within the critical region (that is, $1.50 < t_{0.05}$), we fail to reject H_0. In other words, we do not have statistical justification to believe that this sample was drawn from a population in which the true mean was a value other than 78.

$$12.6$$ ***Estimation of Parameters:***
Interval Estimation

We have repeatedly pointed out that one of the basic problems in inferential statistics is the estimation of the parameters of a population from statistics calculated from a sample. This problem in turn involves two subproblems: (1) **point estimation,** and (2) **interval estimation.**

Point Estimation

An estimate of a population parameter that involves a single value, selected by the criterion of "best estimate." (Contrast *interval estimation.*)

Interval Estimation

The determination of an interval within which the population parameter is presumed to fall. (Contrast *point estimation.*)

When we estimate parameters employing single sample values, these estimates are known as *point estimates.* A single sample value drawn from a population provides an estimate of the population parameter. But how good an estimate is it? If a population mean were known to be 100, would a sample mean of 60 constitute a good estimate? How about a sample mean of 130, 105, 98, or 99.4? Under what conditions do we consider an estimate good? Since we know that the population parameters are virtually never known and that we generally employ samples to estimate these parameters, is there any way to determine the size of error we are likely to make? The answer to this question is a negative one. However, it is possible not only to estimate the population parameter (*point estimation*), but also to state a range of values within which we are confident that the parameter falls (*interval estimation*). Moreover, we may express our confidence in terms of probabilities.

Imagine that we are to estimate the weight of a man, basing our estimate on physical inspection. Let's assume that we are unable to place him on a scale, and that we cannot ask him his weight. This problem is similar to many we have faced throughout this text. We cannot know the population value (the man's true weight), and hence we are forced to estimate it. Let us say that we have the impression that he weighs about 200 pounds. If we are asked, "How confident are you that he weighs *exactly* 200 pounds?" we would probably reply, "I doubt that he weighs exactly 200 pounds. If he does, you can credit me with a fantastically lucky guess. However, I feel reasonably confident that he weighs between 190 and 210 pounds." In doing this, we have stated the interval within which we feel confident that his true weight falls. After a moment's reflection, we might hedge slightly, "Well, he is almost certainly between 180 and 220 pounds. In any event, I feel perfectly confident that his true weight falls somewhere between 170 and 230 pounds." Note that the greater the size of the interval, the greater is our feeling of certitude that the true value is encompassed between these limits. Note also that in stating these confidence limits, we are in effect making two statements: (1) We are stating the limits between which we feel our subject's true weight falls, and (2) we are rejecting the possibility that his true weight falls outside of these limits. Thus, if someone asks, "Is it conceivable that our subject weighs as much as 240 pounds or as little as 160 pounds?" our reply would be a negative one.

12.7 Confidence Intervals and Confidence Limits

In the preceding example, we were in a sense concerning ourselves with the problem of estimating *confidence limits*. In effect we were attempting to determine the interval within which any hypotheses concerning the weight of the man might be considered tenable and outside which any hypotheses would be considered untenable. The interval within which we consider hypotheses tenable is known as the **confidence interval,** and the limits defining the interval are referred to as **confidence limits.**

Let's look at a sample problem and apply our statistical concepts to the estimation of confidence intervals.

A school district is trying to decide on the feasibility of setting up a vocational training program in its public high-school curriculum. In part the decision will depend on estimates of the average I.Q. of high-school students within the district. With only one school psychologist in the district, it is impossible to administer an individual test to each student. Consequently we must content ourselves with testing a random sample of students and basing our estimates on this sample. We administer an I.Q. test to a random sample of 26 students and obtain the following results:

$$\overline{X} = 108, \quad s = 15, \quad N = 26.$$

Our best estimate of the population mean (i.e., the mean I.Q. of children within the school district) is 108. However, even though our sample statistics provides our best estimates of population values, we recognize that such estimates are subject to error. As with the weight problem, we would be fantastically lucky if the mean I.Q. of the high-school population were actually 108. On the other hand, if we have employed truly random selection procedures, we have a right to believe that our sample value is fairly close to the population mean. The critical question becomes, Between what limits will we entertain, as tenable, hypotheses concerning the value of the population mean (μ) in intelligence?

We have seen that the mean of the sampling distribution of sample means ($\mu_{\overline{X}}$) is equal to the mean of the population. We have also seen that since, for any given N, we may determine how far sample means are likely to deviate from any given or hypothesized value of μ, we may determine the likelihood that a particular $\overline{X}$ could have been drawn from a population with a mean of μ_0, where μ_0 represents the value of the population mean under H_0. Now, since we do not know the value of the population mean, we are free to hypothesize *any* value we desire.

It should be clear that we could entertain any unlimited number of hypotheses concerning the population mean and subsequently reject them, or fail

Confidence Interval

Interval within which we consider hypotheses about the population parameter tenable. Common confidence intervals are 95% and 99%.

Confidence Limits

Limits defining the confidence interval.

to reject them, on the basis of the size of the t-ratios. For example, in the present problem, let us select a number of hypothetical population means. We may employ the 0.05 level of significance (two-tailed test), and test the hypothesis that $\mu_0 = 98$. The value of t corresponding to $\overline{X} = 108$ is

$$t = \frac{108 - 98}{15/\sqrt{25}} = 3.333.$$

In Table C, we find that $t_{0.05}$ for 25 df is 2.060. Since our obtained t is greater than this critical value, we reject the hypothesis that $\mu_0 = 98$. In other words, it is unlikely that $\overline{X} = 108$ was drawn from a population with a mean of 98.

Our next hypothesis is that $\mu_0 = 100$, which gives a t of

$$t = \frac{108 - 100}{3} = 2.667.$$

Since $2.667 > t_{0.05}$ (or 2.060), we may reject the hypothesis that the population mean is 100.

If we hypothesize $\mu_0 = 102$, the resulting t-ratio of 2.000 is less than $t_{0.05}$. Consequently we may consider the hypothesis that $\mu_0 = 102$ tenable. Similarly, if we obtained the appropriate t-ratios, we would find that the hypothesis $\mu_0 = 114$ is tenable, where as hypotheses of values greater than 114 are untenable. Thus $\overline{X} = 108$ was probably drawn from a population whose mean falls in the interval $102 - 114$ (note that these limits, 102 and 114, represent approximate limits, i.e., the closest integers). The hypothesis that $\overline{X} = 108$ was drawn from a population with $\mu < 102$ or $\mu > 114$ may be rejected at the 0.05 level of significance. The interval within which the population mean probably lies is called the *confidence interval*. We refer to the limits of this interval as the *confidence limits*. Since we have been employing $\alpha = 0.05$, we call it the *95-percent confidence interval*. Similarly, if we employed $\alpha = 0.01$, we could obtain the *99-percent confidence interval*.

It was not necessary to perform all these calculations to establish the confidence limits. We may calculate the exact limits of the 95-percent confidence interval directly.

To determine the upper limit for the 95-percent confidence interval:

$$\text{Upper limit } \mu_0 = \overline{X} + t_{0.05} (s_{\overline{X}}). \tag{12.10}$$

Similarly, for the lower limit,

$$\text{Lower limit } \mu_0 = \overline{X} - t_{0.05}(s_{\overline{X}}). \tag{12.11}$$

For the 99-percent confidence interval, merely substitute $t_{0.01}$ in the above formulas.

You will note that these formulas are derived algebraically from Formula (12.9):

$$t_{0.05} = \frac{\overline{X} - \mu_0}{s_{\overline{X}}};$$

therefore $\mu_0 = \overline{X} - t_{0.05}(s_{\overline{X}})$.

Employing Formula (12.10), we find that the upper 95-percent confidence limit in the above problem is

$$\text{Upper limit } \mu_0 = 108 + (2.060)(3.0)$$
$$= 108 + 6.18 = 114.18.$$

Similarly, employing Formula (12.11), we find that the lower confidence limit is

$$\text{Lower limit } \mu_0 = 108 - (2.060)(3.0)$$
$$= 108 - 6.18 = 101.82.$$

Having established the lower and the upper limits as 101.82 and 114.18, respectively, we may now draw this conclusion: On the basis of our obtained mean and standard deviation, which were computed from scores drawn from a population in which the true mean is unknown, we assert that the population mean is likely to fall within the interval that we have established.

Some words of caution in interpreting the confidence interval. In establishing the interval within which we believe the population mean falls, we have *not* established any probability that our obtained mean is correct. In other words, we cannot claim that the chances are 95 in 100 that the population mean is 108. Our statements are valid only with respect to the interval and not with respect to any particular value of the sample mean. In addition, since the population is a fixed value and does not have a distribution, our probability statements never refer to μ. The probability we assert is about the interval— i.e., about the probability that the interval contains μ.

Finally, we have established the confidence interval of the mean, we are not stating that the probability is 0.95 that the particular interval we have calculated contains the population mean. It should be clear that if we were to select repeated samples from a population, both the sample means and the standard deviations would differ from sample to sample. Consequently, our estimates of the confidence interval would also vary from sample to sample. When we have established the 95-percent confidence interval of the mean, then we are stating that if repeated samples of a given size are drawn from the population, 95% of the interval estimates will include the population mean.

12.8 Test of Significance for Pearson r: One-Sample Case

In Chapter 8, we discussed the calculation of two statistics—the Pearson r and r_s—commonly employed to describe the extent of the relationship between two variables. It will be recalled that the coefficient of correlation varies between ± 1.00, with $r = 0.00$ indicating the absence of a relationship. It is easy to overlook the fact that correlation coefficients based on sample data are only estimates of the corresponding population parameter and, as such, will distribute themselves about the population value. Thus it is quite possible that a sample drawn from a population in which the true correlation is zero may yield a high positive or negative correlation by *chance*. The null hypothesis most often investigated in the one-sample case is that the *population correlation coefficient* (ρ) is zero.

It is clear that a test of significance is called for. However, the test is complicated by the fact that the sampling distribution of ρ is usually nonnormal, particularly as ρ approaches the limiting values of ± 1.00. Consider the case in which ρ equals $+0.80$. It is clear that sample correlation coefficients drawn from this population will distribute themselves around $+0.80$ and can take on any value from -1.00 to $+1.00$. It is equally clear, however, that there is a definite restriction in the range of values that sample statistics greater than $+0.80$ can assume, whereas there is no similar restriction for values less than $+0.80$. The result is a negatively skewed sampling distribution. The departure from normality will usually be less as the number of paired scores in the sample increases. When the population correlation from which the sample is drawn is

Figure 12.7 Illustrative sampling distributions of correlation coefficients when $\rho = -0.80$ and when $\rho = +0.80$.

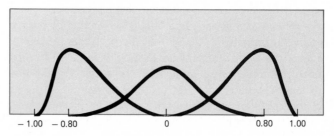

-1.00	-0.80	0	0.80	1.00

equal to zero, the sampling distribution is more likely to be normal. These relationships are demonstrated in Fig. 12.7, which illustrates the sampling distribution of the correlation coefficient what $\rho = -0.80$, 0, and $+0.80$.

Testing H_0: $\rho = 0$

When testing the null hypothesis that the population correlation coeffient is zero, the following *t*-test should be used:

$$t = \frac{r\sqrt{N-2}}{\sqrt{1-r^2}} \qquad\qquad (12.12)$$

The number of degrees of freedom is equal to $N - 2$.

   Let us look at an illustrative example: A team of social psychologists has developed a scale that purports to measure the degree of submission to authority. The scores made on the scale by 15 subjects are correlated with their scores on an inventory which reveals the degree of prejudice felt toward minority groups. They obtain a Pearson *r* of 0.60. May they conclude that the obtained correlation is not likely to have been drawn from a population in which the true correlation is zero?

   Let us set up this problem in formal statistical terms.

1. *Null hypothesis (H_0)*: The population correlation coefficient from which this sample was drawn equals 0.00 ($\rho = 0.00$).
2. *Alternative hypothesis (H_1)*: The population correlation coefficient from which the sample was drawn does *not* equal 0.00 ($\rho \neq 0.00$).
3. *Statistical test*: The *t*-test, with $N - 2$ degrees of freedom.
4. *Significance level*: $\alpha = 0.05$, two-tailed test.
5. *Sampling distribution*: The Student *t*-distribution with df $= 13$.
6. *Critical region*: $|t_{0.05}| \geq 2.160$. Since H_1 is nondirectional, the critical region consists of all values of $t \geq 2.160$ and $t \leq -2.160$.

In the present example,

$$t = \frac{0.60\sqrt{13}}{0.80} = 2.70.$$

Decision: Since the obtained $t > t_{0.05}$, it falls within the critical region for rejecting H_0. Thus it may be concluded that the sample was drawn from a population in which $\rho > 0.00$.

Testing Other Null Hypotheses Concerning ρ

The t-test should not be used for testing hypothesis other than $\rho = 0.00$ since, as we pointed out earlier, the sampling distribution is not normal for values of ρ that are different from zero.

Fisher has described a procedure for transforming sample r's to a statistic z_r, which yields a sampling distribution more closely approximating the normal curve, even for samples employing small N's.

The test statistic is the normal deviate, z, in which

$$z = \frac{z_r - Z_r}{\sqrt{1/(N - 3)}} \tag{12.13}$$

where

z_r = the transformed value of the sample r, and
Z_r = the transformed value of the population correlation coefficient specified under H_0.

Using the same example as above, let us test H_0 that the population ρ from which the sample was drawn is 0.25. Recall that $r = 0.60$ and $N = 15$.

Obtaining z_r is greatly simplified by Table F, in Tables, which shows the value of z_r, corresponding to each value of r, in steps of 0.01, between 0.00 and 0.99. Thus, referring to Table F, we see that an r of 0.60, for example, has a corresponding z_r of 0.693.

Similarly, ρ of 0.25 has a corresponding Z_r of 0.256. Substituting these values in the formula for z, we find

$$z = \frac{0.693 - 0.256}{\sqrt{1/(15 - 3)}} = \frac{0.437}{0.289} = 1.51.$$

Decision: At the 0.05 level, two-failed test, $|z_{0.05}| \geq 1.96$ is required for significance. Since $z = 1.51$ is less than the critical values, we cannot reject H_0. It is quite possible that the sample was drawn from a population in which the true correlation is 0.25.

Test of Significance of r_s: One-Sample Case

Table G, in the Table section, presents the critical values of r_s, one- and two-tailed tests, for selected values of N from 5 to 30.

In Section 8.5, we demonstrated the calculation of r_s from data consisting of 15 pairs of ranked scores and found a correlation of 0.64.

Since $N = 15$ is not listed in Table G, it is necessary to interpolate, employing the critical values for $N = 14$ and 16. The critical value at the 0.05 level, two-tailed test, for $N = 14$ is 0.544; at $N = 16$ it is 0.506. By employing linear interpolation, we may roughly approximate the critical value corresponding to $N = 15$.

With Table G, linear interpolation merely involves adding together the boundary values of r_s and dividing by 2. Thus

$$r_{s(0.05)} = \frac{0.544 + 0.506}{2} = 0.525.$$

Since our obtained r_s of 0.64 exceeds the critical value at the 0.05 level, we may conclude that the population value of the Spearman correlation coefficient from which the sample was drawn is greater than 0.00.

Chapter Summary

We have seen that if we take a number of samples from a given population, then:

1. The distribution of sample means tends to be normal.
2. The mean of these sample means ($\mu_{\bar{X}}$) is equal to the mean of the population (μ).
3. The standard error of the mean ($\sigma_{\bar{X}}$) is equal to $\sigma\sqrt{N}$. As N increases, the variability decreases.

We used these relationships in the testing of hypotheses (for example, $\mu = \mu_0$) when the standard deviation of a population was known, employing the familiar z-statistic and the standard normal curve.

For testing when σ is not known, we demonstrated the use of sample statistics to estimate these parameters. We used these estimates of the parameters to test hypotheses, employing the Student t-ratio and the corresponding sampling distributions. We compared these t-distributions, which vary as a function of degrees of freedom (df), with the standard normal curve.

We employed the t-ratio as a basis for establishing confidence intervals.

Finally, we demonstrated the test of significance for the Pearson r and the Spearman r_s, one-sample case.

Terms to Remember

biased estimate of a parameter	**interval estimation**
central-limit theorem	**point estimation**
confidence interval	**standard error of the mean**
confidence limits	**t-distributions**
critical region	**t-ratio**
critical values of *t*	**unbiased estimator**
degrees of freedom	

EXERCISES

1. Describe what happens to the distribution of sample means when you
   a. increase the size of each sample,   b. increase the number of samples.

2. Explain why the standard deviation of a sample will usually underestimate the standard deviation of a population. Give an example.

3. Given that $\overline{X} = 24$ and $s = 4$ for $N = 15$, use the *t*-distribution to find
   a. the 95% confidence limits for μ,   b. the 99% confidence limits for μ.

4. Given that $\overline{X} = 24$ and $s = 4$ for $N = 121$, use the *t*-distribution to find
   a. the 95% confidence limits for μ,   b. the 99% confidence limits for μ.

   Compare the results with Exercise 3.

5. An instructor gives his class an examination that, as he knows from years of experience, yields $\mu = 78$ and $\sigma = 7$. His present class of 22 obtains a mean of 82. Is he correct in assuming that this is a superior class? Employ $\alpha = 0.01$, two-tailed test.

6. An instructor gives his class an examination that, as he knows from years of experience, yields $\mu = 78$. His present class of 22 obtains $\overline{X} = 82$ and $s = 7$. Is he correct in assuming that this is a superior class? Employ $\alpha = 0.01$, two-tailed test.

7. Explain the difference between Exercises 5 and 6. What test statistic is employed in each case, and why? Why is the decision different?

Generalize: What is the effect of knowing σ upon the likelihood of a type II error?

8. The superintendent of Zody school district claims that the children in her district are brighter, on the average, than the general population of students. In order to determine the I.Q. of school children in the district, a study was conducted. The results were as shown in the accompanying table. The mean of the general population of school children is 106. Set this up in formal statistical terms (that is, H_0,

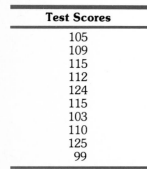

Test Scores
105
109
115
112
124
115
103
110
125
99

H_1, etc.) and draw the appropriate conclusions. Employ a one-tailed test, $\alpha = 0.05$.

9. For a particular population with $\mu = 28.5$ and $\sigma = 5.5$, what is the probability that, in a sample of 100, the $\overline{X}$ will be
   a. equal to or less than 30.0?   **b.** equal to or less than 28.0?
   c. equal to or more than 29.5?   **d.** between 28.0 and 29.0?

10. Given that $\overline{X} = 40$ for $N = 24$ from a population in which $\sigma = 8$, find
    a. the 95% confidence limits for μ,
    b. the 99% confidence limits for μ.

11. It is axiomatic that when pairs of individuals are selected at random and the intelligence tests scores of the first members of the pairs are correlated with the second members, $\rho = 0.00$
    a. Thirty-nine pairs of siblings are randomly selected and an $r = +0.27$ is obtained between members of the pairs for intelligence. Are siblings more alike in intelligence than unrelated individuals?
    b. A study of 28 pairs of identical twins yields $r = +0.91$ on intelligence test scores. What do you conclude?

12. Overton University claims that, because of its superior facilities and close faculty supervision, its students complete the Ph.D. program earlier than is usual. They base this assertion on the fact that the national mean age for completion is 32.11. whereas the mean age of their 26 Ph.D.s is 29.61 with $s = 6.00$. Test the validity of their assumption.

13. Employing the data in the above Exercise, find the interval within which you are confident that the true population mean (average age for Ph.D.s at Overton University) probably falls, using the 95% confidence interval.

14. A sociologist asserts that the average length of courtship is longer before a second marriage than before a first. She bases this assertion on the fact that the average for first marriages is 265 days, whereas the average for second marriages (e.g., of her 626 subjects) is 268.5 days, with $s = 50$. Test the validity of her assumption.

15. Employing the data in Exercise 14, find the interval within which you are 99% confident that the true population mean (average courtship days for a second marriage) probably falls.

16. Random samples of size 2 are selected from the following finite population of scores: 1, 3, 5, 7, 9, and 11.
    a. Calculate the mean and standard deviation of the population.
    b. Construct a histogram showing the sampling distribution of means when $N = 2$. Employ sampling *without* replacement.
    c. Construct a histogram showing the means of all possible samples that can be drawn employing sampling *with* replacement.

17. Employing (b) in Exercise 16, answer the following: Selecting a sample with $N = 2$, what is the probability that
    a. a mean as high as 10 will be obtained?
    b. a mean as low as 2 will be obtained?

    c. a mean as deviant as 8 will be obtained?

    d. a mean as low as 1 will be obtained?

18. Employing (c) in Exercise 16, answer the following: Selecting a sample with $N = 2$, what is the probability that

    a. a mean as high as 10 will be obtained?

    b. a mean as low as 2 will be obtained?

    c. a mean as deviant as 8 will be obtained?

    d. a mean as low as 1 will be obtained?

19. A stock analyst claims that he has an unusually accurate method for forecasting price gains of listed common stock. During a given period, stocks he advocated showed the following price gains: $1.25, $2.50, $1.75, $2.25, $3.25, $3.00, $2.00, $2.00. During the same period, the market as a whole showed a mean price gain of $1.83. Set up and test the H_0 that the stocks he selected have been randomly selected from the population of stock gains during the specified period.

20. In a test of a gasoline additive, ten carefully engineered automobiles were run at a testing site under rigorously supervised conditions. The numbers of miles obtained from a single gallon of gasoline were, 25, 22, 23, 26, 27, 21, 24, 25, 23, 24. Thousands of prior trials with the same gasoline minus the additive had yielded the expectation of 22.63 miles per gallon. Using $\alpha = 0.05$, can it be concluded that the additive improved gasoline mileage?

21. A restaurant owner ranked her 17 waiters in terms of their speed and efficiency on the job. She correlated these ranks with the total amount of tips each of these waiters received for a one-week period, and obtained $r_s = 0.438$. What do you conclude?

22. The owner of a car-leasing company ranked 25 of his customers on their neatness and general care of their rented cars during a three-month period. He correlated these ranks with the number of miles each customer drove during this same period. The obtained $r_s = -0.397$. Employing $\alpha = 0.05$, two-tailed test, what do you conclude?

23. As a requirement for admission to Blue Chip University, a candidate must take a standardized entrance examination. The correlation between performance on this examination and college grades is 0.43.

    a. The director of admissions claims that a better way to predict college success is by using high-school grade averages. To test her claim, she randomly selects 52 students and correlates their college grades with their high-school averages. She obtains $r = 0.54$. What do you conclude?

    b. The director's assistant constructs a test that he claims is better for predicting college success than the one currently used. He randomly selects 67 students and correlates their grade-point averages with performance on his test. The obtained $r = 0.61$. What do you conclude?

24. What are the statistics used to describe the distribution of a sample? The distribution of a sample statistic?

25. Is s^2 an unbiased estimate of σ^2? Explain.

26. Is $\hat{s}^2$ an unbiased estimate of σ^2? Explain.

27. What is a confidence interval?

28. Give an example to show the effect of the α-level on the precision of a confidence interval.

29. How do the t-distributions differ from the normal distribution? Are they ever the same?

*30. Imagine the following sampling experiment. You have two populations of means consisting of the following values:

Population 1: 3, 4, 5, 5, 6, 6, 6, 7, 7, 8, 9
Population 2: 0, 1, 2, 2, 3, 3, 3, 4, 4, 5, 6,

You place tabs with these means into two separate hats—one for each population. You select a mean from population 1, replace it in the hat, and then select a mean from population 2 and replace it in the hat. You subtract mean 2 from mean 1 to obtain a difference between means. The cell entries in the table below show all possible differences between means that you could obtain.

		Selection from Means in Population 1									
		3	4	5	5	6	6	6	7	7	8	9
Selection from Means in Population 2	0	3	4	5	5	6	6	6	7	7	8	9
	1	2	3	4	4	5	5	5	6	6	7	8
	2	1	2	3	3	4	4	4	5	5	6	7
	2	1	2	3	3	4	4	4	5	5	6	7
	3	0	1	2	2	3	3	3	4	4	5	6
	3	0	1	2	2	3	3	3	4	4	5	6
	3	0	1	2	2	3	3	3	4	4	5	6
	4	-1	0	1	1	2	2	2	3	3	4	5
	4	-1	0	1	1	2	2	2	3	3	4	5
	5	-2	-1	0	0	1	1	1	2	2	3	4
	6	-3	-2	-1	-1	0	0	0	1	1	2	3

Note that the mean of the means of population 1 is 6; the corresponding mean of population 2 is 3.

a. Construct a frequency and probability distribution of differences between means ($\overline{X}_1 - \overline{X}_2$).

b. Intuitively, estimate what the mean of these differences should be. Now calculate the mean of the differences. How accurate was your estimate?

Generalize: What is the mean of the sampling distributions of differences between means?

*31. Vary the above sampling experiment slightly. Imagine that you know that hat 1 contains the population of means identified as population 1. However, the population of means in the second hat is a complete mystery. You select a sample mean from hat 1 and a sample mean from hat 2. By subtracting the second mean from the first mean, obtain a difference between sample means.

a. What statistical hypothesis are you most likely to test?

b. What is the sampling distribution against which you should test $H_0: \mu_1 = \mu_2$?

c. Construct a frequency and probability distribution of differences between means under the hypothesis $H_0: \mu_1 = \mu_2$. [Hint: Assume that population 2 is identical to population 1, and find all possible differences between means.] This probability distribution is known as the sampling distribution of differences between means, in which the null hypothesis is that you are sampling from identical populations.

*32. Employing the sampling distribution under $H_0: \mu_1 = \mu_2$ (Exercise 31 above), find the probability of obtaining a difference in sample means:

a. $5 \leq \overline{X}_1 - \overline{X}_2 \leq -5$ b. $\overline{X}_1 - \overline{X}_2 \geq 6$ c. $\overline{X}_1 - \overline{X}_2 \leq -3$
d. $6 \leq X_1 - \overline{X}_2 \leq -6$ e. $\overline{X}_1 - \overline{X}_2 = -6$

*33. Imagine that the *true* situation is the sampling distribution of differences between means found in response to Exercise 30 above. Find the probability of obtaining a difference in sample means:

a. $5 \leq \overline{X}_1 - \overline{X}_2 \leq -5$ b. $\overline{X}_1 - \overline{X}_2 \geq 6$ c. $\overline{X}_1 - \overline{X}_2 \leq -3$
d. $6 \leq \overline{X}_1 - \overline{X}_2 \leq -6$ e. $\overline{X}_1 - \overline{X}_2 = -6$

*34. Compare the probability values obtained in response to Exercises 32 and 33. See if you can formulate any broad observations about the different answers you obtained.

35. Assume that the mean number of words typed per minute by secretaries is 50. A group of people who attended a certain secretarial school show the following typing speeds (words per minute):

$$55 \quad 50 \quad 45 \quad 75 \quad 80 \quad 75 \quad 80 \quad 80$$
$$85 \quad 60 \quad 50 \quad 65 \quad 60 \quad 50 \quad 80 \quad 50$$

Calculate the value of t. Can you conclude that the school produced secretaries with superior typing abilities?

36. A sports fan found a r_s of 0.15 between batting averages of 20 baseball players and the amount of vitamins in their breakfast cereals. Can she conclude that this correlation is significant?

37. Mr. Smith stated that his training program for selling life insurance enables a compny to sell more insurance than the "average" company. The mean amount of life insurance sold by all salesmen per month is $100,000. A sample of ten people who have been through the training program show monthly selling rates (in thousands) of

$$\$100 \quad \$120 \quad \$130 \quad \$120 \quad \$125$$
$$\$ 90 \quad \$130 \quad \$135 \quad \$140 \quad \$110$$

If you were a supervisor of insurance salesmen, would you adopt Mr. Smith's training program? Calculate the value of t.

38. In a study of marital success and failure, Bentler and Newcomb (1978) gave a personality questionnaire to 162 newly married couples. Four years later 77 couples from the original sample were located; of these, 53 were still married, whereas 24 had separated or divorced. Among the still-married group it was found that the correlation between the husband's and wife's score on an attractiveness scale was 0.59, and that the correlation between their scores on a generosity scale was 0.23. Among the divorced group the correlation between the ex-husband's and ex-wife's score on the attractiveness scale was 0.07, and the correlation between their scores on the generosity scale was 0.13.

a. Using $\alpha = 0.05$, set up and test the null hypothesis that the correlation between the married couples' scores on attractiveness is equal to zero. Also set up and test the null hypothesis that the correlation between the divorced couples' scores on attractiveness is equal to zero.

b. Using $\alpha = 0.05$, set up and test the null hypothesis that the correlation between the married couples' scores on generosity is equal to zero. Also set up and test the null hypothesis that the correlation between the divorced couples' scores on generosity is equal to zero.

13

Statistical Inference: Two Independent Samples

13.1 Sampling Distribution of the Difference Between Means

What is the effect of drug versus no drug on maze learning?

Does the recidivism rate of juvenile offenders who are provided with "father figures" differ from those without "father figures"?

Do students in the ungraded classroom differ in performance on standardized achievement tests from students in the age-classroom setting?

Each of the answers to these questions involves the comparison of at least two samples. Thus far, for heuristic purposes, we have restricted our examination of hypothesis-testing to the one-sample case. However, most behavioral research involves the comparison of two or more samples to determine whether or not these samples might have reasonably been drawn from the same population. If the means of two samples differ, must we conclude that these samples were drawn from two different populations?

Recall our previous discussion on the sampling distribution of sample means (Section 12.2). We saw that some variability in the sample statistics is to be expected, even when these samples are drawn from the same population. We were able to describe this variability in terms of the sampling distribution of sample means. To conceptualize this distribution, we imagined drawing from a population an extremely large number of samples, of a fixed N, to obtain the distribution of sample means. In the two-sample case we should imagine drawing pairs of samples, finding the difference between the means of each pair, and obtaining a distribution of these differences. The resulting distribution would be the *sampling distribution of the difference between means*.

To illustrate, imagine that from the population described in Table 12.1, in which $\mu = 5.00$ and $\sigma = 0.99$, we randomly draw (with replacement) two samples at a time. For illustrative purposes, let us draw two cases for the first sample (that is, $N_1 = 2$), and three cases for the second sample (that is, $N_2 = 3$). For example, we might draw scores of 5, 6 for our first sample and scores of 4, 4, 7 for our second sample. Thus, since $\overline{X}_1 = 5.5$ and $\overline{X}_2 = 5.0$, $\overline{X}_1 - \overline{X}_2 = 0.5$. Now suppose we continue to draw samples of $N_1 = 2$ and $N_2 = 3$ until we obtain an indefinitely large number of pairs of samples. If we calculate the differences between these pairs of sample means and treat each of these differences as a raw score, we may set up a frequency distribution of these differences.

Intuitively, what might we expect this distribution to look like? Since we are selecting pairs of samples at random from the *same* population, we would expect a normal distribution with a mean of zero.

Going one step further, we may describe the distribution of the difference between pairs of sample means, even when these samples are *not* drawn from

BOX 13.1

The Eyes: Windows of the Soul

The eyes have been referred to as the "windows of the soul." Research has demonstrated that changes in the size of the pupils may be taken as an indication of "what turns people on." The pupils of male subjects become larger when viewing pictures of women; and, conversely, the pupils of females become larger when viewing pictures of males.

Questions raised in one study were: "Do male homosexuals show a greater pupillary response to pictures of males than to pictures of females? How do their pupillary responses compare to those of heterosexual males?"

The accompanying graph* shows a line drawing of the mean changes in pupil reponse obtained by two groups of subjects—homosexual males and heterosexual males—when viewing pictures of males and females.

A number of interesting questions involving inferential statistics may be raised. Consider these:

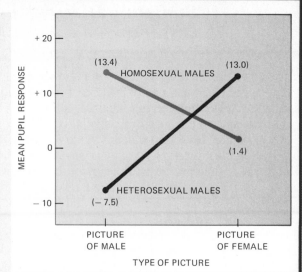

1. Is there a statisically significant difference between the mean pupil response of heterosexual vs. homosexual males when viewing the pictures of males?
2. Is there a statistically significant difference between the mean pupil response of heterosexual vs. homosexual males when viewing the pictures of women?

Additional questions are taken up in the end-of-chapter exercises for Chapter 13 (Exercises 31 and 32) and Chapter 14 (Exercises 23 and 24.)

*Source: E. H. Hess, A. L. Seltzer, and J. M. Shlien (1965), "Pupil response of hetero- and homosexual males to pictures of men and women: A pilot study," J. Abn. Psych., **70**, 165–168. Copyright 1965 by The American Psychological Association. Reprinted with permission.

Standard Error of the Difference between Means

Standard deviation of the sampling distribution of the difference between means.

the same population. It will be a normal distribution with a mean ($\mu_{\bar{X}_1 - \bar{X}_2}$) equal to $\mu_1 - \mu_2$ and a standard deviation ($\sigma_{\bar{X}_1 - \bar{X}_2}$, referred to as the **standard error of the difference between means**) equal to $\sqrt{\sigma_{\bar{X}_1}^2 + \sigma_{\bar{X}_2}^2}$.

Thus the sampling distribution of the statistic

$$z = \frac{(\bar{X}_1 - \bar{X}_2) - (\mu_1 - \mu_2)}{\sigma_{\bar{X}_1 - \bar{X}_2}}$$

is normal, and therefore permits us to employ the standard normal curve in the testing of hypotheses.

13.2 Estimation of $\sigma_{\bar{X}_1 - \bar{X}_2}$ from sample data

The statistic z is employed only when the population standard deviations are known. Since it is rare that these parameters are known, we are once again forced to estimate the standard error in which we are interested, that is, estimated $\sigma_{\bar{X}_1 - \bar{X}_2}$.

Historically, the estimated standard error of the difference between means was defined as follows:

$$S_{\bar{X}_1 - \bar{X}_2} = \sqrt{s_{\bar{X}_1}^2 + s_{\bar{X}_2}^2}.$$

However, this formula provides a biased estimate whenever N_1 is not equal to N_2.

If we randomly select a sample of N_1 observations from a population with unknown variance and a second random sample of N_2 observations also from a population with unknown variance, the following is an unbiased estimate of the standard error of the difference. This estimate, which assumes that the two samples are drawn from a population with the same variance, pools the sum of squares and degrees of freedom of the two samples to obtain a pooled estimate of the standard error of the difference. Hence

$$s_{\bar{X}_1 - \bar{X}_2} = \sqrt{\left(\frac{SS_1 + SS_2}{N_1 + N_2 - 2}\right)\left(\frac{1}{N_1} + \frac{1}{N_2}\right)}. \qquad (13.1)*$$

However, if $N_1 = N_2 = N$, Formula (13.1) simplifies to

$$s_{\bar{X}_1 - \bar{X}_2} = \sqrt{\frac{SS_1 + SS_2}{N(N - 1)}}. \qquad (13.2)*$$

In order to obtain the sum of squares for our two groups, we apply Formula (6.6) to each sample and obtain

$$SS_1 = \sum X_1^2 - \frac{(\sum X_1)^2}{N_1}, \quad \text{and} \quad SS_2 = \sum X_2^2 - \frac{(\sum X_2)^2}{N_2}.$$

---

*This formula can be presented in terms of raw scores. Refer to the endpapers of this book.

13.3 *Testing Statistical Hypotheses: Student's t*

The statistic employed in the testing of hypotheses, when population standard deviations are not known, is the familiar t-ratio

$$t = \frac{(\bar{X}_1 - \bar{X}_2) - (\mu_1 - \mu_2)}{s_{\bar{X}_1 - \bar{X}_2}},\qquad (13.3)$$

in which $(\mu_1 - \mu_2)$ is the expected value as stated in the null hypothesis.

The most common null hypothesis tested is that both samples come from the same population of means, that is, $(\mu_1 - \mu_2) = 0$. However, there are times when the null hypothesis may specify a difference between population means. As an example, let us imagine that we know (or have a reasonable estimate of) the difference in heights of male and female adults. Imagine we have reason to believe that in a specific locality this difference may be affected by environmental factors such as smog or diet. In this case the null hypothesis would specify the known difference in heights. Thus, if the heights of males are known to be 5 in. greater than the heights of females on the average, the null hypothesis would read:

$$H_0: \mu_M - \mu_F = 5 \text{ in.}$$

You will recall that Table C, in the Table section, provides the critical values of t required for significance at various levels of α. Since the degrees of freedom for each sample is $N_1 - 1$ and $N_2 - 1$, the total df in the two-sample case is $N_1 + N_2 - 2$.

Illustrative Problem: Student's *t*

In Case Example 5.1 we presented the results of research related to near-SIDS (Suddent Infant Death Syndrome). Many parents react to this tragedy with feelings of guilt mingled with accusations toward the spouse of carelessness and blame. Many researchers, however, are convinced that the fault lies in biological mechanisms within the infant. Orlowski (1982) has suggested one possible mechanism—higher than normal levels of the bodies own narcotic-like substances, the endorphins and enkaphalins. Recall that the β-endorphin levels in the cerebrospinal fluid of 8 infants who had experienced near-SIDS were compared to the levels in two control infants. The results are reproduced in Table 13.1.

Table 13.1 β-endorphin levels in 8 infants who had experienced near-SIDS compared to the levels in two control infants.

Group 1 Experimental		Group 2 Control	
X_1	X_1^2	X_2	X_2^2
52	2,704	1	1
52	2,704	10	100
66	4,356		
54	2,916		
47	2,209		
66	4,356		
90	8,100		
50	2,500		
$\sum$ = 477	29,845	11	101

Let's set up the test of significance in formal statistical terms.

1. *Null Hypothesis (H_0)*: The mean difference in β-endorphin levels between the infants experiencing near-SIDS is equal to or less than zero; i.e., $\mu_1 \leq \mu_2$.
2. *Alternative Hypothesis (H_1)*: The mean difference in endorphin-levels between the near-SIDS infants and control infants is greater than zero; i.e. $\mu_1 > \mu_2$.
3. *Statistical Test*: The t-ratio is used since the N in each group < 30. The assumptions of normality and equal variances are made.
4. *Significance level*: $\mu = 0.05$, one-tailed test. If the difference between the two sample means is so large that its associated probability of occurrence under the sampling distribution is equal to or less than 0.05, we shall reject H_0.
5. *Sampling distribution*: The student t distribution at df = 8.
6. *Critical Region for Rejection of H_0*: $t_{0.05}$ (one-tailed) = 1.860.

The sum of squares for each condition is

$$SS_1 = 29,445 - \frac{477^2}{8} \qquad SS_2 = 101 - \frac{11^2}{2}$$
$$= 1,403.875 \qquad\qquad\quad = 40.5$$

Since $N_1 \neq N_2$ and the population variances are assumed to be equal, we use Formula (13.1) to estimate the standard error of the difference between means.

$$s_{\bar{X}_1 - \bar{X}_2} = \sqrt{\left(\frac{1403.875 + 40.5}{8}\right)\left(\frac{10}{16}\right)}$$

$$s_{\bar{X}_1 - \bar{X}_2} = \sqrt{112.1418} = 10.62.$$

The value of t in the present problem is

$$t = \frac{(\bar{X}_1 - \bar{X}_2) - (\mu_1 - \mu_2)}{s_{\bar{X}_1 - \bar{X}_2}}$$

$$= \frac{59.625 - 5.5}{10.62}$$

$$= 5.097.$$

Decision: Since the obtained t falls within the critical region (i.e., $t \geq 1.860$) we reject H_0. From this we can conclude that the two groups differ significantly in their endorphin levels. Note that this is not a true experiment. Therefore, a strong conclusion of causality cannot be drawn. It is possible that the endorphin levels are merely correlated with a variable that causes the near-SIDS or that the high levels of endorphins represent a consequence of the cessation of breathing during sleep.

Student t-ratio when sample means and standard deviations are known

When we read research reports in the literature of the behavioral sciences, we find that summary statements are usually given in terms of means and standard deviations rather than in terms of SS. Moreover, some statistical programs on the computer and on statistical calculators provide only means and standard deviations. When we do not know the sum of squares, Formula 13.4 should be used.

$$s_{\bar{X}_1 - \bar{X}_2} = \sqrt{\left[\frac{(N_1 - 1)s_1^2 + (N_2 - 1)s_2^2}{N_1 + N_2 - 2}\right]\left[\frac{N_1 + N_2}{N_1 N_2}\right]}. \qquad (13.4)$$

Note that Formula 13.4 assumes that we are using standard deviations based on the unbiased estimators of the population variance; i.e., $N - 1$ is used in the denominator when we calculate the sample standard deviation. If the sample standard deviations were calculated with N in the denominator, we should substitute N_1 for $N_1 - 1$ and N_2 for $N_2 - 1$ in Formula 13.4.

13.4 Estimating the Degree of Association between the Experimental and Dependent Variables

The finding of a statistically significant t-ratio means that some degree of association exists between the experimental and dependent variables. However, the fact of statistical significance does not automatically confer "importance" to a finding. Given a sufficiently large N, even a trivial difference may be found to be statistically significant.

One way of clarifying the "significance" of a statistically significant difference is to ascertain the extent to which variations in the experimental variable (the treatment administered) account for variations in the dependent measure. In general, the higher the degree of relationship, the greater the importance of the finding. A measure of association is ω^2 **(omega squared),** which is estimated by

Omega Squared (ω^2)

An estimate of the variance in the dependent variable accounted for by variations in the independent or experimental variable.

$$\text{est } \omega^{2*} = \frac{t^2 - 1}{t^2 + N_1 + N_2 - 1}. \tag{13.5}$$

• **Example.**   In the near-SIDS study, we found $t = 5.097$ with $N_1 = 8$ and $N_2 = 2$. Therefore,

$$\text{est } \omega^2 = \frac{25.98 - 1}{25.98 + 8 + 2 - 1}$$
$$= \frac{24.98}{34.98} = 0.714.$$

This may be interpreted in very much the same way as the coefficient of determination (r^2), which was discussed in Chapter 9 (see Section 9.4). Recall that a coefficient of determination of 0.714 would mean that we estimate 71.4% of the variance of Y to be accounted for by variations in X. Similarly, $\omega^2 = 0.714$ may be interpreted to mean that approximately 71.4% of the variance in the dependent measure is accounted for in terms of variations in the treatment variable. When we consider the multitude of variables that usually influence the dependent measures, finding a single variable that accounts for 71.4% of the variance would appear to describe a real and important effect.

Note that we cannot judge the magnitude of the association by merely looking at the value of the t-ratio. For example, imagine we had found the

---

*If $|t|$ is less than 1.00, ω^2 will be negative. Since a negative ω^2 is meaningless, we arbitrarily set $\omega^2 = 0$ when $|t| \le 1.00$.

same t-ratio of 5,097 with $N_1 = N_2 = 75$. The difference is clearly statistically significant. However, does it also account for a high degree of association between the experimental and dependent variables? Let's see.

When $t = 5.097$ and $N_1 = N_2 = 75$,

$$\text{est } \omega^2 = \frac{25.98 - 1}{25.98 + 75 + 75 - 1}$$
$$= \frac{24.98}{174.98}$$
$$= 0.143.$$

In spite of the high t-ratio, we estimate the experimental variable to account for only about 14% of the variance in the dependent variable. These examples illustrate the fact that a significant t-ratio with small N may well be describing a more *important* relationship between the independent and the dependent variables than a significant t-ratio with a large N.

13.5 The t-Ratio and Homogeneity of Variance

The assumptions underlying the use of the t-distributions are as follows:

1. The sampling distribution of the difference between means if normally distributed.

2. Estimated $\sigma_{\bar{X}_1 - \bar{X}_2}$ (that is, $s_{\bar{X}_1 - \bar{X}_2}$) is based on the unbiased estimate of the population variance.

3. Both samples are drawn from populations whose variances are equal. This assumption is referred to as **homogeneity of variance.**

Homogeneity of Variance

The condition that exists when two or more sample variances have been drawn from populations with equal variances.

Occasionally, for reasons that may not be very clear, the scores of one group may be far more widely distributed than the scores of another group. Such scores may indicate that we are sampling two different distributions, but the critical question is this: Two different distributions of what? Means or variances?

To determine whether or not two variances differ significantly from one another, we must refer to yet another distribution: the F-distribution. Named after R. A. Fisher, the statistician who first described it, the F-distribution is unlike any other we have encountered so far; it is *tridimensional* in nature. To employ the F Table (Table D_1, Table section), we must begin at the entry stating the number of degrees of freedom of the group with the larger variance, and move down the column until we find the entry for the number of degrees of freedom of the group with the smaller variance. At that point we will find the critical value of F required for rejecting the null hypothesis of no difference in variances. The **F-ratio** is defined as follows:

F-ratio

A ratio between sample variances.

$$F = \frac{\hat{s}^2 \text{ (larger variance)}}{\hat{s}^2 \text{ (smaller variance)}}. \qquad (13.6)$$

The test is two-tailed, as we are interested in determining if either variance differs significantly from the other. It would be one-tailed *only* if we were interested in determining whether a specific variance is significantly greater than another. This is an unlikely comparison. Since Table D_1 is one-tailed, the use of the 0.025 critical value yields the 0.05 two-tailed significance level. In the preceding sample problem, the variance for group 1 is 135.56/8 or 16.94; and for group 2, 164.9/9 or 18.32. The F-ratio becomes

$$F = \frac{18.32}{16.94} = 1.08, \qquad df = \frac{9}{8}.$$

Referring to Table D_1 under 9 and 8 df, we find that an $F \geq 4.36$ is significant at the 0.05 level. We may therefore conclude that it is reasonable to assume that both samples were drawn from a population with the same variances.

What if we found a significant difference in variances? Would it have increased our likelihood of rejecting the null hypothesis of no difference between means? Very little, in all probability; as we have already pointed out, the t-ratio is a robust test. Our conclusions are not likely to be altered by any but extremely large departures from such assumptions as homogeneity of variances and normality.

Why, then, do we concern ourselves with an analysis of the variances? Frequently a significant difference in variances (particularly when the variance of the experimental group is significantly greater than that of the control group) is indicative of a *dual* effect of the experimental conditions. A larger variance indicates more extreme scores *at both ends* of a distribution. The alert researcher will seize upon these facts as a basis for probing into the possibility of dual effects.

For example, years ago the experimental question, "Does anxiety improve or hinder performance on complex psychological tasks?" was thoroughly studied, with rather ambiguous results. More recently we have come to recognize that anxiety-induced conditions have dual effects, depending on a host of factors, e.g., personality variables. An increase in anxiety causes some individuals to become better oriented to the task at hand, while others "come apart at the seams," so to speak. A study of the variances of our experimental groups may facilitate the uncovering of such interesting and theoretically important dual effects.

Chapter Summary

We have seen that if we take a number of pairs of samples either from the same population or from two different populations, then

1. The distribution of differences between pairs of sample means tends to be normal.

2. The mean of these differences between means ($\mu_{\bar{X}_1 - \bar{X}_2}$) is equal to the difference between the population means, that is, $\mu_1 - \mu_2$.

3. The standard error of the difference between means ($\sigma_{\bar{X}_1 - \bar{X}_2}$) is equal to $\sqrt{\sigma_{\bar{X}_1}^2 + \sigma_{\bar{X}_2}^2}$.

We presented formulas for estimating $\sigma_{\bar{X}_1 - \bar{X}_2}$ from sample data. Employing estimated $\sigma_{\bar{X}_1 - \bar{X}_2}$ (that is, $s_{\bar{X}_1 - \bar{X}_2}$), we demonstrated the use of Student's t to test hypotheses in the two-sample case.

Also presented was a method for estimating the degree of association between an experimental variable and the dependent measure. Omega squared (ω^2) provides an estimate of the variance in the dependent variable accounted for by variations in the experimental variable.

An important assumption underlying the use of the t-distribution is that both samples are drawn from populations with equal variances. Although failure to find homogeneity of variance will probably not seriously affect our interpretations, the fact of heterogeneity of variance may have important theoretical implications.

Terms to Remember

F-ratio

omega squared (ω^2)

homogeneity of variance

standard error of the difference between means

EXERCISES

1. Two statistics classes of 25 students each obtained the following results on the final examination: $\bar{X}_1 = 82$, $SS_1 = 384.16$; $\bar{X}_2 = 77$, $SS_2 = 1536.64$. Test the hypothesis that the two classes are equal in ability, employing $\alpha = 0.01$.

2. In an experiment on the effects of a particular drug on the number of errors in the maze-learning behavior of rats, the following results were obtained:

Drug Group	Placebo Group
$\sum X_1 = 324$	$\sum X_2 = 256$
$\sum X_1^2 = 6516$	$\sum X_2^2 = 4352$
$N_1 = 18$	$N_2 = 16$

Set up this experiment in formal statistical terms, employing $\alpha = 0.05$, and draw the appropriate conclusions concerning the effect of the drug on the number of errors.

3. On a psychomotor task involving two target sizes, the following results were obtained:

Group 1	Group 2
9	6
6	7
8	7
8	9
9	8

Set up this experiment in formal statistical terms, employing $\alpha = 0.05$, and draw the appropriate conclusions.

4. A study was undertaken to determine whether or not the acquisition of a response is influenced by a drug. The criterion variable was the number of trials required to master the task (X_1 is the experimental group and X_2 is the control group).

X_1	6	8	14	9	10	4	7
X_2	4	5	3	7	4	2	1	3

    a. Set up this study in formal statistical terms, and state the appropriate conclusions, employing $\alpha = 0.01$.

    b. Is there evidence of heterogeneity of variance?

5. Given two normal populations,

$$\mu_1 = 80, \ \sigma_1 = 6; \qquad \mu_2 = 77, \qquad \sigma_2 = 6.$$

If a sample of 36 cases is drawn from population 1 and a sample of 36 cases from population 2, what is the probability that

    a. $\bar{X}_1 - \bar{X}_2 \geq 5$?   **b.** $\bar{X}_1 - \bar{X}_2 \geq 0$?

    c. $\bar{X}_1 - \bar{X}_2 \leq 0$?   **d.** $\bar{X}_1 - \bar{X}_2 \leq -5$?

6. Assuming the same two populations as in Exercise 5, calculate the probability that $\bar{X}_1 - \bar{X}_2 \geq 0$, when

    a. $N_1 = N_2 = 4$,   **b.** $N_1 = N_2 = 9$,

    c. $N_1 = N_2 = 16$,   **d.** $N_1 = N_2 = 25$.

7. Graph the above probabilities as a function of N. Can you formulate any generalization about the probability of finding a difference in the correct direction between sample means (that is, $\bar{X}_1 - \bar{X}_2 \geq 0$, when $\mu_1 > \mu_2$) as a function of N?

8. A gasoline manufacturer runs tests to determine the relative performance of automobiles employing two different additives. The results are as follows (expressed in terms of miles per gallon of gasoline:

Additive 1:   12, 17, 15, 13, 11, 10, 14, 12,
Additive 2:   16, 14, 18, 19, 17, 13, 11, 18

Set up and test the appropriate null hypothesis.

9. Each of two market analysts claim that her ability to forecast price gains in common stock is better than her rival's. Over a specified period, each analyst selected ten common stocks that she predicted would show a gain. When increases in the prices of the stocks were later compiled, the results were as follows:

Analyst 1: $1.25, $2.50, $1.75, $2.25, $2.00, $1.75, $2.25, $1.00, $1.75, $2.00
Analyst 2: $1.25, $0.75, $1.00, $1.50, $2.00, $1.75, $0.50, $1.50, $0.25, $1.25

Set up and test the appropriate null hypothesis.

10. A toothpaste manufacturer claims that children brushing their teeth daily with his company's product (Brand A) will have fewer cavities than children using Brand X. In a carefully supervised study, the number of cavities in a sample of children using Brand A toothpaste was compared with the number of cavities among children using Brand X. The results were as follows:

Brand A: 1, 2, 0, 3, 0, 2, 1, 4, 2, 3, 1, 2, 1, 1
Brand X: 3, 1, 2, 4, 1, 5, 2, 0, 5, 6, 3, 2, 4, 3

Test the manufacturer's claim.

11. In a longitudinal study of adolescent development, 582 male and 1052 female students in junior high school completed a questionnaire that included measures of personality and measures of drug use (Wingard, Huba, and Bentler: 1979). On the personality scale of "generosity," the following data were obtained:

Males	Females
$\sum X_1 = 10{,}371$	$\sum X_2 = 20{,}609$
$\sum X_1^2 = 198{,}503$	$\sum X_2^2 = 427{,}764$
$N_1 = 582$	$N_2 = 1{,}052$

a. Using $\alpha = 0.05$, set up and test the null hypothesis that males and females do not differ on the generosity scale. Find ω^2.

A five-point response scale that ranged from "never used the drug" (1) to "use the drug regularly" (5) yielded following data:

Males	Females
$\sum X_1 = 10{,}371$	$\sum X_2 = 20{,}609$
$\sum X_1^2 = 198{,}503$	$\sum X_2^2 = 427{,}764$
$N_1 = 582$	$N_2 = 1{,}052$

b. Using $\alpha = 0.05$, set up and test the null hypothesis that males and females do not differ in their frequency of marijuana use. Find ω^2.

12. In a study of the television viewing habits of preschool children, Friedrich and Stein (1973) asked 52 boys and 45 girls to name their favorite television programs. The authors then tabulated the number of programs that were considered violent and aggressive and obtained the following data:

Boys	Girls
$\sum X_1 = 71$	$\sum X_2 = 49$
$\sum X_1^2 = 185$	$\sum X_2^2 = 147$
$N_1 = 52$	$N_2 = 45$

Set up and test the null hypothesis that boys and girls do not differ in the number of violent programs they name as their favorites. Use $\alpha = 0.05$.

13. A training director in a large industrial firm claims that employees taking her training course perform better on the job than those not receiving training. Of 30 recently hired employees, 15 are randomly selected to receive training. The remaining 15 are employed as controls. Six months later, on-the-job test evaluations yield the following statistics for the training group: $\overline{X}_1 = 24.63$, $s_1 = 3.53$. The controls obtain $\overline{X}_2 = 21.45$ and $s_2 = 4.02$. Set up and test the appropriate null hypothesis, employing $\alpha = 0.05$.

14. A publisher claims that students who receive instruction in mathematics based on his newly developed textbook will score at least five points higher on end-of-term grades than those instructed using the old textbook. Thirty-six students are randomly assigned to two classes: The experimental group employs the new textbook for instruction, and the control group uses the old textbook. Students in the experimental group achieve $\overline{X}_1 = 83.05$ and $s_1 = 6.04$ as final grades, wherease the controls obtain $\overline{X}_2 = 76.85$ and $s_2 = 5.95$. Set up and test the appropriate null hypothesis employing $\alpha = 0.01$, one-tailed test. [*Note:* Remember that the numerator in the test statistic is: $(\overline{X}_1 - \overline{X}_2) - (\mu_1 - \mu_2)$.]

15. In a study of memory development, Wingard, Buchanan, and Burnell (1978) selected a set of pictures that could be classified into five semantic categories (food, clothes, toys, furniture, animals). The pictures were randomly presented to 64 four-year-olds and 64 five-year-olds, and the children were asked to recall as many of them as possible. The authors measured the children's tendency to cluster together pictures from the same semantic categories as they recalled them. Four-year-olds showed $\overline{X} = .192$ and $s = .302$ in semantic clustering, whereas five-year olds showed $\overline{X} = .291$ and $s = .359$. Set up and test the null hypothesis that the five-year-olds showed no more semantic clustering than the four-year-olds. Since the alternative hypothesis was directional (five-year-olds were expected to show more clustering as a consequence of greater cognitive development), use $\alpha = .05$, one-tailed test. Calculate ω^2.

16. If we found a significant difference between means at the 5% level of significance, it would follow that (true or false):
    a. This difference is significant at the 1% level of significance.
    b. This difference is significant at the 10% level of significance.
    c. The difference observed between means is the true difference.

For Exercises 17 through 21, the following two finite populations of scores are given:

Population 1:   2, 4, 6, 8
Population 2:   1, 3, 5, 7

*17. Random samples of size 2 are selected (*without replacement*) from each population. Construct a histogram showing the sampling distribution of differences between the sample means.

*18. What is the probability that
   a. $\overline{X}_1 - \overline{X}_2 \geq 0$?
   b. $\overline{X}_1 - \overline{X}_2 \geq 1$?
   c. $\overline{X}_1 - \overline{X}_2 \leq 0$?
   d. $\overline{X}_1 - \overline{X}_2 \leq -1$?
   e. $\overline{X}_1 - \overline{X}_2 \geq 4$?
   f. $\overline{X}_1 - \overline{X}_2 \leq -4$?
   g. $\overline{X}_1 - \overline{X}_2 \geq 2$ or $\overline{X}_1 - \overline{X}_2 \leq -2$?

*19. Calculate the mean and standard deviation of each population.

*20. If a sample of 25 cases is drawn from population 1 and a sample of 25 cases from population 2, what is the probability that
   a. $\overline{X}_1 - \overline{X}_2 \geq 0$?
   b. $\overline{X}_1 - \overline{X}_2 \geq 1$?
   c. $\overline{X}_1 - \overline{X}_2 \leq 0$?
   d. $\overline{X}_1 - \overline{X}_2 \leq 1$?
   e. $\overline{X}_1 - \overline{X}_2 \geq 4$?
   f. $\overline{X}_1 - \overline{X}_2 \geq 1$ or $\overline{X}_1 - \overline{X}_2 \leq -1$?
   g. $\overline{X}_1 - \overline{X}_2 \geq 2$ or $\overline{X}_1 - \overline{X}_2 \leq -2$?

*21. Calculate the probability that $\overline{X}_1 - \overline{X}_2 \leq 0$, when
   a. $N_1 = N_2 = 4$,
   b. $N_1 = N_2 = 9$,
   c. $N_1 = N_2 = 16$,
   d. $N_1 = N_2 = 36$.

22. A manufacturer sampled the number of dresses produced per day for 10 days by a group of 26 workers (Group A) who were operating on a fixed-wage plan. She then introduced a wage incentive plan to 26 other employees (Group B) and recorded their output for 10 days. The number of dresses produced per day were as follows:

Group A: 75   72   73   76   78   72   80   74   76   75
Group B: 80   83   84   78   79   81   84   85   78   86

The wages paid to each group are equal. Can the manufacturer conclude that the wage incentive plan is more efficient? Calculate the value of t.

23. Company A finds that the mean number of burning hours of its lightbulbs is 1200, with $\sigma_{\overline{X}_1}^2 = 100$; Company B shows a mean of 1250 burning hours, with $\sigma_{\overline{X}_2}^2 = 125$. It is probable that the lightbulbs at the two companies are from the same population of lightbulbs? What is the value of z?

24. From records of past employees, two large companies sampled the number of years that secretaries stayed with the company. Using a sample of 25 employees each, Company A found that $SS_1 = 42$ and $\overline{X}_1 = 40$, and Company B found that $SS_2 = 58$ and $\overline{X}_2 = 50$. Is this difference significant at the 0.05 level? What is the value of t?

25. A manager finds that the number of employee errors increases as the day progresses, reaching a peak between 3:00 and 5:00. He divides a sample of 20 empoyees into two groups. One group proceeds on the same work schedule as before, but the other group gets a 15-minute coffee break from 2:45 to 3:00. The

subsequent number of errors made between 3:00 and 5:00 are:

No break group: 5 6 7 4 8 9 6 5 7 6
Break group: 2 3 4 3 4 4 3 1 5 4

Does the break significantly reduce the number of errors? Calculate the value of t.

26. Determine whether the variances are homogeneous in Exercise 25. Calculate the value of F.

27. Banks A and B use two different forms for recording checks written. The banks found that the following number of checks had bounced for 15 customers during the last 10 years:

Bank A: 4 8 3 0 3 5 3 4 0 5 2 4 6 2 0
Bank B: 2 0 1 2 1 1 3 3 4 3 1 4 0 5 0

Determine whether there is a significant difference between the number of checks bounced at each bank. Employ $\alpha = 0.05$.

28. State A finds that the mean number of cigarettes smoked per week by smokers of that state is 120, with a $\sigma_{\bar{X}_1}^2$ of 10. State B's cigarette tax is $0.05 greater per pack. The mean number smoked per week is 110, with a $\sigma_{\bar{X}_2}^2$ of 9. Is there a significant difference in the number of cigarettes smoked between the two states? What is the value of z?

29. Two grocery-store managers find that they have an overstock of spaghetti sauce. The price and usual amount sold in the two stores are identical. Manager A keeps the sauce in its regular place, while manager B piles the cans close to the checkout counters for a month. The managers record the number of cans sold during 10 days, with the following results:

A: 19 20 20 21 18 20 19 21 23 17
B: 26 24 25 23 25 24 22 26 27 25

Is there a significant difference in the number of cans sold? What is the value of t?

30. Determine whether the variances are homogeneous in Exercise 29. Calculate F.

31. In the displayed material at the start of this chapter, we showed a graph based on research into the pupil responses of heterosexual and homosexual males when viewing pictures of men and women. The table below shows the change in pupil size of five heterosexual and five homosexual males when viewing pictures of a male.

Subject	Heterosexuals	Subject	Homosexuals
1	−00.4	6	+18.8
2	−54.5	7	−04.6
3	+12.5	8	+18.9
4	+06.3	9	+18.2
5	−01.5	10	+15.8

Formulate H_0 and H_1, two-tailed test. Using the Student t-ratio for independent samples, determine whether H_0 may be rejected at $\alpha = 0.05$. [*Hint:* To facilitate calculations when negative numbers are involved, algebraically add 55 to each score. This procedure eliminates all the negative values and makes use of the generalization shown in Section 2.3.]

To calculate the mean for each group.

$$\frac{\sum\limits_{i=1}^{5} X_i}{N} = \frac{\sum\limits_{i=1}^{5} X_i - 5(55)}{N}.$$

[*Note:* Adding 55 to all scores will not change the difference between means and the standard error of the difference, since the relative differences among scores are maintained. However, the mean for each group will increase by 55.]

32. The table shows the change in pupil size of five heterosexual and five homosexual males when viewing pictures of a female.

Subject	Heterosexuals	Subject	Homosexuals
1	+05.9	6	+11.2
2	−22.4	7	−38.0
3	+19.2	8	+18.1
4	+39.0	9	−05.6
5	+23.1	10	+21.5

Formulate H_0 and H_1, two-tailed test. Using the Student t-ratio for independent samples, determine whether H_0 may be rejected at $\alpha = 0.05$. [*Hint:* To facilitate calculations when negative numbers are involved, algebraically add 39 to each score.]

33. In a study on the long-range effects of concentration-camp internment on Nazi victims, Dor-Shav (1978) compared 43 survivors of the camps to 21 control subjects who were of similar age, background, and education but who had escaped imprisonment during World War II. Both groups were given a series of psychological tests including the Rorschach Inkblot Test and the Sixteen Personality Factor Questionnaire. On the Rorschach Inkblot Test the following data were obtained:

Survivors	Controls
$\sum X_1 = 17$	$\sum X_2 = 39$
$\sum X_1^2 = 81$	$\sum X_2^2 = 357$
$N_1 = 43$	$N_2 = 21$

a. Using $\alpha = 0.05$, set up and test the null hypothesis that the survivors do not differ from the control subjects in the number of abstract responses given on the Rorschach Inkblot test. Find ω^2.

On the Personality Factor Questionnaire, 14 young survivors aged 50 and below and 5 young control subjects also aged 50 and below showed the following results on the Shrewdness scale.

Survivor	Controls
$\sum X_1 = 182$	$\sum X_2 = 52$
$\sum X_1^2 = 2396$	$\sum X_2^2 = 552$
$N_1 = 14$	$N_2 = 5$

b. Using $\alpha = 0.05$, set up and test the null hypothesis that the young survivors do not differ from the young control subjects on the Shrewdness scale of the Personality Factor Questionnaire. Find ω^2.

34. Using the data in Table 13.1, calculate the standard deviations for each sample. Then calculate the student t-ratio using Formula (13.4). Confirm that the same value of t is obtained.

14

Statistical Inference with Correlated Samples

14.1 Introduction

One of the fundamental problems confronting behavioral scientists is the extreme variability of their data. Indeed, it is *because* of this variability that they are so concerned with the field of inferential statistics.

When an experiment is conducted, data comparing two or more groups are obtained, a difference in some measure of central tendency is found, and then we raise the question: Is the difference of such magnitude that it is unlikely to be due to chance factors? As we have seen, a visual inspection of the data is not usually sufficient to answer this question because there is so much overlapping of the experimental groups. The overlapping, in turn, is due to the fact that the experimental subjects themselves manifest widely varying aptitudes and proficiencies relative to the criterion measure. In an experiment the score of any subject on the criterion variable may be thought to reflect at least three factors: (1) the subject's ability and/or proficiency on the criterion task; (2) the effects of the experimental variable; and (3) random error due to a wide variety of different causes, e.g., minor variations from time to time in experimental procedures or conditions, or momentary fluctuations in such things as attention span and motivation of the experimental subjects. There is little we can do about *random error* except to maintain as close control over experimental conditions as possible. The *effects of the experimental variable* are, of course, what we are interested in assessing. In the majority of studies the *individual differences among subjects* is by and large the most significant factor contributing to the scores and the variability of scores on the criterion variable. Anything we can do to take this factor into account or "statistically remove" its effects will improve our ability to estimate the effects of the experimental variable on the criterion scores. This chapter is concerned with a technique that is commonly employed to accomplish this very objective: the employment of *correlated samples*.

14.2 Standard Error of the Difference between Means for Correlated Groups

In our earlier discussion of Student's *t*-ratio, we presented the formula for the unpooled estimate of the standard error of the difference between means as

$$s_{\bar{X}_1 - \bar{X}_2} = \sqrt{s_{\bar{X}_1}^2 + s_{\bar{X}_2}^2}.$$

BOX 14.1

Automatic transmission: guzzle, guzzle

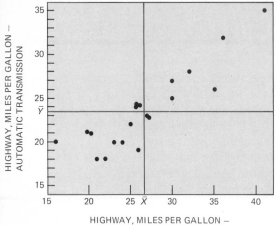

HIGHWAY, MILES PER GALLON — AUTOMATIC TRANSMISSION

HIGHWAY, MILES PER GALLON — MANUAL TRANSMISSION

used as the basis for calculating the error term. If the correlation is low, these differences are large. So also is the error term based on these differences. When r is high, the differences are small. The higher the correlation, the smaller the differences between the paired scores. The error term is similarly reduced.

The accompanying scatter diagram suggests that the correlation between the paired observations is very high. As a matter of actual fact, $r = 0.89$. The resulting error term, referred to as the standard error of the mean difference ($s_{\bar{D}}$), is much lower than the error term ($s_{\bar{X}_1 - \bar{X}_2}$) that we would have used in the absence of correlated samples.

In Chapter 13 we saw that $s_{\bar{X}_1 - \bar{X}_2}$ is a sort of benchmark against which we evaluate the difference between means. If $s_{\bar{X}_1 - \bar{X}_2}$ is large relative to the mean difference, we are less likely to reject H_0 than if $s_{\bar{X}_1 - \bar{X}_2}$ is small relative to the same difference between means.

If there were some way to legitimately reduce the size of the error term ($s_{\bar{X}_1 - \bar{X}_2}$), our benchmark would be more sensitive. Just such an opportunity is provided by correlational analysis. Recall from Chapter 9 that the higher the correlation between two variables, the greater is the *explained variation* and the less the *unexplained* or random variation. Since the unexplained variation represents error, correlational analysis provides a legitimate way to lessen unexplained variation and thereby reduce error.

The table shows the highway miles-per-gallon scores achieved by twenty cars with manual transmission and twenty cars with automatic transmission. Each pair represents the same model car. In other words, both members of each pair are identical except for the type of transmission. When correlated samples are employed, the *difference* between the paired scores is

Car Model	Type of Transmission		Difference
	Manual	Automatic	
Gremlin	26	19	7
Hornet	16	20	−4
Audi Fox	36	32	4
Skyhawk	26	24	2
Vega	30	27	3
Datsun 210	41	35	6
Datsun 280	25	22	3
Fiat 131	30	25	5
Mustang II	24	20	4
Granada	20	21	−1
Capri II	27	23	4
Monarch	20	21	−1
Starfire	26	24	2
Valiant/Duster	23	20	3
Sunbird	26	24	2
Lemans	21	18	3
Corolla	35	26	9
Corona MK. II	22	18	4
Volvo	27	23	4
LUV pickup	32	28	4

Highway mileage of twenty pairs of 1976 automobiles. Each pair consists of one car with manual transmission and the same model car with automatic transmission.

A more general formula for the standard error of the difference is

$$s_{\bar{X}_1 - \bar{X}_2} = \sqrt{s_{\bar{X}_1}^2 + s_{\bar{X}_2}^2 - 2rs_{\bar{X}_1}s_{\bar{X}_2}}. \qquad (14.1)$$

We drop the last term whenever our sample subjects are assigned to experimental conditions at *random*, for the simple reason that when scores are paired at random, the correlation between the two samples will average zero. Any observed correlation will be spurious, since it will represent a chance association. Consequently, when subjects are assigned to experimental conditions at random, the last term reduces to zero (since $r = 0$).

However, there are many experimental situations in which we do not randomly assign our subjects to each experimental condition. Most of these situations can be placed in one of two classes.

1. Before-after design • A reading on the *same* subjects is taken both before and after the introduction of the experimental variable. It is presumed that each individual will remain relatively consistent. Thus there will be a correlation between the **before** sample and the **after** sample. Note that each subject may have been *selected* at random from a subject pool but, since he or she participates in both conditions, we cannot say that the subjects have been *assigned* randomly to experimental conditions.

Before-After Design

A correlated-samples design in which each individual is measured on the criterion task both before and after the introduction of the experimental conditions.

2. Matched-group design • The subjects available for participation in the study are matched on some variable known to be correlated with the criterion or dependent variable. The result is a set of paired subjects in which each member of a given pair obtains approximately the same score on the matching variable. Then one member of each pair is randomly assigned to the experimental condition and the other is assigned to the control group. Thus, if we wanted to determine the effect of some drug on the ease of learning the solution to a mathematical problem, we might match individuals on the basis of I.Q. estimates, the amount of mathematical training, grades in statistics, or performance on other mathematics problems. Such a design has two advantages:

Matched-Group Design

A correlated-samples design in which pairs of subjects are matched on a variable correlated with the criterion measure. Each member of a pair receives different experimental conditions.

   a. It ensures that the experimental groups are "equivalent" in initial ability.
   b. It permits us to take advantage of the correlation based on initial ability and allows us in effect to remove one source of error from our measurements.

To understand the advantage of employing correlated samples, let us look at a sample problem and calculate the standard error of the difference between means using $\sqrt{s_{\bar{X}_1}^2 + s_{\bar{X}_2}^2}$, based upon unmatched groups, and Formula (14.1), which takes the correlation into account. Table 14.1 presents data for two groups of subjects matched on a variable known to be correlated with the criterion variable. The members comprising each pair are assigned at random to the experimental conditions.

Table 14.1 **Scores of two groups of subjects in an experiment employing matched-group design (hypothetical data).**

Matched Pairs	X_1	X_1^2	X_2	X_2^2	$X_1 X_2$
A	2	4	4	16	8
B	3	9	3	9	9
C	4	16	5	25	20
D	5	25	6	36	30
Σ	14	54	18	86	67

The following steps are employed in the calculation of the standard error of the difference between means for *unmatched* groups.

Step 1.   The sum of squares for group 1 is

$$SS_1 = 54 - \frac{(14)^2}{4} = 5.$$

Step 2.   The standard deviation for group 1 is

$$s_1 = \sqrt{\frac{5}{4}} = 1.1180.$$

Step 3.   The standard error of the mean for group 1 is

$$s_{\bar{X}_1} = \frac{s_1}{\sqrt{N_1 - 1}} = \frac{1.1180}{\sqrt{3}} = 0.6455. *$$

Step 4.   Similarly, the standard error of the mean for group 2 is

$$s_{\bar{X}_1} = 0.6455.$$

Step 5.   The standard error of the difference between means for independent groups is

$$s_{\bar{X}_1 - \bar{X}_2} = \sqrt{s_{\bar{X}_1}^2 + s_{\bar{X}_2}^2} = 0.91.$$

---

*The standard error of the mean may be obtained directly by employing Formula (12.8), that is,

$$s_{\bar{X}_1} = \sqrt{\frac{SS}{N_1(N_1 - 1)}} = \sqrt{\frac{5}{4(3)}} = 0.6455.$$

To calculate the standard error of the difference between means for *matched* groups, the following steps are employed.

Step 1.   Employing formula (8.2),* we find that the correlation between the two groups is

$$r = \frac{\sum(X_1 - \bar{X}_1)(X_2 - \bar{X}_2)}{\sqrt{(SS_1)(SS_2)}} - \frac{4}{\sqrt{(5)(5)}} = 0.80.$$

Step 2.   The standard error of the difference between means for matched groups is

$$s_{\bar{X}_1 - \bar{X}_2} = \sqrt{s_{\bar{X}_1}^2 + s_{\bar{X}_2}^2 - 2rs_{\bar{X}_1}s_{\bar{X}_2}}$$
$$= \sqrt{0.4167 + 0.4167 - 2(0.80)(0.6455)(0.6455)} = 0.41.$$

You will note that Formula (14.1), which takes correlation into account, provides a markedly reduced error term for assessing the significance of the difference between means. In other words, it provides a more sensitive test of this difference and is more likely to lead to the rejection of the null hypothesis when it is false. In the language of inferential statistics, it is a more *powerful* test. We discuss the concept of power more fully in Chapter 16. Of course, the greater power or sensitivity of Formula (14.1) is directly related to our success in matching subjects on a variable that is correlated with the criterion variable. When *r* is large, $s_{\bar{X}_1 - \bar{X}_2}$ will be correspondingly small. As *r* approaches zero, the advantage of employing correlated samples becomes progressively smaller.

Balanced against the increased sensitivity of the standard error of the difference between means when *r* is large, is the *loss* of degrees of freedom. Whereas the number of degrees of freedom for unmatched samples is $N_1 + N_2 - 2$, when correlated samples are employed the number of degrees of freedom is the number of pairs minus one $(N - 1)$. This difference can be critical when the number of degrees of freedom is small, since, as we saw in Section 12.5, larger *t*-ratios are required for significance when the degrees of freedom are small.

14.3   The Direct-Difference Method: Student's *t*-Ratio

Fortunately, it is not necessary to actually determine the correlation between samples in order to find $s_{\bar{X}_1 - \bar{X}_2}$. Another method is available that permits the direct calculation of the standard error of the difference. We refer to this

---

*Note that $(X_2 - \bar{X}_2)$ replaces $(Y - \bar{Y})$ in Formula (8.2).

method as the *direct-difference method* and represent the standard error of the difference as $s_{\bar{D}}$.

In brief, the direct-difference method consists of finding the differences between the criterion scores obtained by each pair of matched subjects, and treating these differences as if they were raw scores. In effect, the direct-difference method transforms a two-sample into a one-sample case. We find one sample mean and a standard error based on one standard deviation. The null hypothesis is that the obtained mean of the difference scores ($\sum D/N$, symbolized as $\mu_{\bar{D}}$) comes from a sampling distribution of mean differences (the population) in which the mean difference (μ_D) is some specified value. The *t*-ratio employed to test $H_0 : \mu_{\bar{D}} = 0$ is

$$ t = \frac{\bar{D} - \mu_{\bar{D}}}{s_{\bar{D}}} = \frac{\bar{D}}{s_{\bar{D}}} \qquad (14.2) $$

The raw-score formula for calculating the sum of squares of the difference score is

$$ SS_D = \sum D^2 - \frac{(\sum D)^2}{N}, \qquad (14.3) $$

where D is the difference between paired scores. It follows then that the standard deviation of the difference scores is

$$ \hat{s}_D = \sqrt{\frac{SS_D}{(N-1)}}. \qquad (14.4) $$

Standard Error of the Mean Difference

Standard error based upon a correlated-samples design. Employed in the Student *t*-ratio for correlated samples.

Furthermore, the **standard error of the mean difference** $s_{\bar{D}}$ may be obtained by dividing Formula (14.4) by $\sqrt{N}$. Thus

$$ s_{\bar{D}} = \sqrt{\frac{SS_D}{N(N-1)}} \qquad (14.5) $$

$$ s_D = \frac{\hat{s}_D}{\sqrt{N}} \qquad (14.6)^* $$

Sample Problem

The directors of a small private college find it necessary to increase the size of classes. A special film, utilizing the most advanced propaganda techniques, presents the advantages of larger-size classes. The attitude of a group of ten stu-

---

*An alternative formula for obtaining $s_{\bar{D}}$ is $s_{\bar{D}} = s_D/\sqrt{N-1}$, where $s_D = \sqrt{SS_D/N}$.

dents is assessed before and after the presentation of this film. It is anticipated that more favorable attitudes (i.e., higher scores) will result from exposure to the film. Let's set up this problem in formal statistical terms.

1. *Null hypothesis* (H_0): The difference in the attitudes of students before and after viewing the film is equal to or greater than zero, that is $\mu_{\overline{D}} \geq 0$.

2. *Alternative hypothesis* (H_1): The attitudes of the students will be more favorable after viewing the film, that is $\mu_D < 0$. Note that our alternative hypothesis is directional; consequently a one-tailed test of significance will be employed.

3. *Statistical test*: Since we are employing a before-after design, the Student *t*-ratio for correlated samples is appropriate.

4. *Significance level*: $\alpha = 0.01$.

5. *Sampling distribution*: The sampling distribution is Student's *t*-distribution with df = $N - 1$, or $10 - 1 = 9$.

6. *Critical region*: $t_{0.01} \leq -2.821$. Since H_1 predicts that the scores in the *after* condition will be higher than those in the *before* condition, we expect the difference scores to be *negative*. Therefore the critical region consists of all values of $t \leq -2.821$.

Table 14.2 presents the results of this experiment. The following steps are employed in the direct-difference method.

Table 14.2 Scores of ten subjects in an experiment employing before-after design (hypothetical data).

Subject	Before X_1	After X_2	Difference D	D^2
1	25	28	−3	9
2	23	19	4	16
3	30	34	−4	16
4	7	10	−3	9
5	3	6	−3	9
6	22	26	−4	16
7	12	13	−1	1
8	30	47	−17	289
9	5	16	−11	121
10	14	9	5	25
Σ	171	208	−37	511

Step 1. The sum of squares of the difference scores is

$$SS_D = 511 - \frac{(-37)^2}{10} = 374.10.$$

Step 2. The standard error of the mean difference is

$$s_{\overline{D}} = \sqrt{374.10/10(9)} = 2.04.$$

Step 3. The value of $\overline{D}$ is $\overline{D} = -37/10 = -3.70$. (To check the accuracy of $\sum D$ we subtract $\sum X_2$ from $\sum X_1$, that is, $\sum X_1 - \sum X_2 = \sum D$, $171 - 208 = -37$.)

Step 4. The value of t in the present problem is

$$t = \frac{\overline{D}}{s_{\overline{D}}} = \frac{3.70}{2.04} = -1.81.$$

Decision: Since the obtained t does not fall within the critical region (that is, $-1.81 > t_{0.01}$), we fail to reject H_0. We are not justified in concluding that the film produced a statistically significant change in attitudes.

14.4 Sandler's A-Statistic

Sandler's A-Statistic

A statistic, rigorously derived from Student's t-ratio, for testing significant differences between correlated samples.

Some years ago, a psychologist, Joseph Sandler, demonstrated an extremely simple procedure for arriving at probability values in all situations involving $H_0: \mu_1 - \mu_2 = 0$ for which the Student t-ratio for correlated samples is appropriate. Indeed, since **Sandler's statistic, A**, is rigorously derived from Student's t-ratio,* the probability values are identical with Student's p-values.

The statistic, A, is defined as follows:

$$A = \frac{\text{The sum of the squares of the differences}}{\text{The square of the sum of the differences}} = \frac{\sum D^2}{(\sum D)^2}. \quad (14.7)$$

By referring to the table of A (Table E, Table section) under $(N - 1)$ degrees

---

*The following formulas show the conversion of t to A:

$$A = \frac{N-1}{Nt^2} + \frac{1}{N}$$

and A to t:

$$t = \sqrt{\frac{N-1}{AN-1}}.$$

of freedom, we can determine whether our obtained A is *equal to* or *less than* the tabled values at various levels of significance.

Let us illustrate the calculation of A from our previous example. It will be recalled that $\sum D^2 = 511$ and $\sum D = -37$. The value of A becomes

$$A = \frac{511}{-37^2} = 0.373.$$

Referring to Table E under 9 degrees of freedom, we find that an A *equal to or less than* 0.213 is required for significance at the 0.01 level (one-tailed test). Since 0.373 is greater than the tabled value, we fail to reject the null hypothesis. It will be noted that our conclusion is precisely the same as the one we arrived at by employing Student's t-ratio. This is correct, of course, since the two are mathematically equivalent. Since the calculation of A requires far less time and labor than the determination of t, Sandler's A-distribution can replace Student's t whenever correlated samples are employed.

Chapter Summary

A general formula for the standard error of the difference is

$$s_{\bar{X}_1 - \bar{X}_2} = \sqrt{s_{\bar{X}_1}^2 + s_{\bar{X}_2}^2 - 2rs_{\bar{X}_1}s_{\bar{X}_2}}.$$

It is obvious that by matching samples on a variable correlated with the criterion variable, we may reduce the magnitude of the standard error of the difference and thereby provide a more sensitive test of the difference between means. The higher the correlation, of course, the greater the reduction in the standard error of the difference.

We demonstrated the use of the direct-difference method for determining the significance of the difference between the means of correlated samples.

Finally, we demonstrated the use of a mathematically equivalent test, the Sandler's A-statistic. Due to its computational ease, the Sandler test will unquestionably replace the Student's t-ratio when correlated samples are employed.

Terms to Remember

before-after design

matched-group design

Sandler's A-statistic

standard error of the mean difference

EXERCISES

1. An investigator employs an experimental procedure wherein each subject (S) performs a task that requires the cooperation of a partner. By prearrangement the partner plays the role of a complaining, rejecting teammate. When the task is completed, S is asked to recall any remarks made by the partner. Prior to the experiment, each S has been tested and classified as either *secure* or *insecure* in interpersonal relations and then matched on the basis of intelligence.

   The statistics at left were derived from data indicating the number of remarks recalled; $r = 0.55$ between number of remarks recalled and intelligence.

   Set up this task in formal statistical terms, employing $\alpha = 0.01$ (two-tailed test), and state the appropriate conclusions.

Secure S	Insecure S
$\bar{X}_1 = 14.2$	$\bar{X}_1 = 12.9$
$s_1 = 2.0$	$s_2 = 1.5$
$N_1 = 17$	$N_2 = 17$

2. Had we not employed a matched-group design (that is, $r = 0.00$), would our conclusion have been any different? Explain. *Hint:* In calculating $s_{\bar{X}_1 - \bar{X}_2}$, employ

$$s_{\bar{X}_1 - \bar{X}_2} = \sqrt{s_{\bar{X}_1}^2 + s_{\bar{X}_2}^2}.$$

3. Carmen C., manager of a Little League team in the American League, has said that the American League is more powerful than the National League. Determine the validity of this statement from the home-run (*HR*) figures given below. Employ Student's *t*-ratio for correlated samples *and* Sandler's *A*, $\alpha = 0.05$.

Final Standing in Respective League	American League	Number of HR	National League	Number of HR
1	Minnesota	16	Los Angeles	18
2	Chicago	17	San Francisco	11
3	Baltimore	15	Pittsburgh	14
4	Detroit	12	Cincinnati	10
5	Cleveland	11	Milwaukee	12
6	New York	9	Philadelphia	13
7	California	13	St. Louis	8
8	Washington	16	Chicago	10
9	Boston	18	Houston	9
10	Kansas City	14	New York	15

4. In Exercise 3, the teams were paired on the basis of final standings in their respective leagues. The matching technique assumes a correlation between final standing and number of home runs. Is this assumption valid?

5. Calculate a Student's *t*-ratio for independent samples from the data in Exercise 3. Why is the obtained *t*-ratio closer to the rejection region than the answer to Exercise 3 was?

6. Experimenter Laurie designs a study in which she matches subjects on a variable that she believes to be correlated with the criterion variable. Assuming H_0 to be false, what is the likelihood of a type II error (compare to the use of Student's *t*-ratio for uncorrelated samples) in the following situations?
   a. The matching variable is uncorrelated with the criterion variable.
   b. The matching variable is highly correlated with the criterion variable.

7. It has often been stated that women have a higher life expectancy than men. Using the data in the accompanying table and employing $\alpha = 0.05$, determine the validity of this statement for
   a. white Americans,   b. nonwhite Americans,
   c. white males compared to nonwhite females.

Expectation of life in the United States*

Age	White Male	White Female	Nonwhite (chiefly black) Male	Nonwhite (chiefly black) Female	Age	White Male	White Female	Nonwhite (chiefly black) Male	Nonwhite (chiefly black) Female
0	67.5	74.4	60.9	66.5	11	58.6	65.2	53.5	58.7
1	68.2	74.8	62.9	68.0	12	57.6	64.2	52.6	57.7
2	67.3	73.9	62.1	67.2	13	56.7	63.2	51.6	56.7
3	66.4	73.0	61.2	66.3	14	55.7	62.2	50.7	55.7
4	65.4	72.0	60.3	65.4	15	54.7	61.3	49.7	54.8
5	64.4	71.0	59.3	64.5	16	53.8	60.3	48.8	53.8
6	63.5	70.1	58.4	63.5	17	52.8	59.3	47.8	52.8
7	62.5	69.1	57.4	62.5	18	51.9	58.3	46.9	51.9
8	61.6	68.1	56.5	61.6	19	51.0	57.4	46.0	50.9
9	60.6	67.1	55.5	60.6	20	50.1	56.4	45.1	50.0
10	59.6	66.2	54.5	59.6					

*Source: Reader's Digest 1966 Almanac, p. 492. New York: Reader's Digest Association, with permission.

8. Numerous consumer organizations have criticized the automobile industry for employing odometers that show large variations in efficiency from one instrument to another and from one manufacturer to another. To test whether or not odometers from two competing manufacturers may be considered to have been drawn from a common population, eleven different cars were equipped with two odometers each, one from each manufacturer. All automobiles were driven over a measured course of 100 mi. and their odometer readings were tabulated. Apply the appropriate test for the significance of the difference between the odometer readings of each manufacturer, employing $\alpha = 0.01$.

Automobile	Manufacturer A	Manufacturer B	Automobile	Manufacturer A	Manufacturer B
1	104	102	7	97	99
2	112	106	8	107	102
3	103	107	9	100	98
4	115	110	10	104	101
5	99	93	11	108	102
6	104	101			

9. Another complaint by consumer organizations is that the odometers are purposely constructed to *overestimate* the distance traveled in order to inflate the motorist's estimates of gasoline mileage. As a review of Chapter 12, conduct a one-sample test of $H_0: \mu_0 = 100$ miles for the product of *each* manufacturer.

10. Runyon (1968) showed that a simple extension of Sandler's A-test may be em-

ployed as an algebraically equivalent substitute for Student's t-ratio, one-sample case. The technique consists of subtracting the value of the mean hypothesized under H_0 from each score, summing the differences and squaring $[(\sum D)^2]$, squaring the differences and summing $[\sum D^2]$, and substituting these values in the formula for the A-statistic, that is, $A = \sum D^2 / (\sum D)^2$. Degrees of freedom equal $N - 1$. Conduct a one-sample test of $H_0: \mu_0 = 100$ miles for the odometers of each manufacturer. Compare the results of this analysis with the results of the foregoing analysis.

11. In a study aimed at determining the effectiveness of a new diet, an insurance company selects a sample of 12 overweight men between age 40 and 50, and obtains their weight measurements both before initiating the diet and sixty days later. Set up and test the appropriate null hypothesis, employing $\alpha = 0.05$.

	Weight			Weight	
Subject	Before	After	Subject	Before	After
1	203	207	7	209	215
2	235	231	8	192	215
3	175	172	9	201	184
4	159	164	10	187	196
5	183	187	11	178	184
6	210	204	12	185	173

12. A difficulty with interpreting the results of Exercise 11 is that a control group is lacking. It is possible that a random selection of overweight men who are *not* on a diet will reveal weight losses over a two-month period. A control group, matched in weight with the experiment subjects in Exercise 11, demonstrated the following before-after changes. Set up and test the appropriate null hypothesis for the control subjects. Employ $\alpha = 0.05$.

	Weight			Weight	
Subject	Before	After	Subject	Before	After
1	202	180	7	209	205
2	237	221	8	191	196
3	173	175	9	200	185
4	161	158	10	189	187
5	185	180	11	177	172
6	210	197	12	184	186

13. Employing only the "after" weight for the matched subjects in Exercises 11 and 12, test for the significance of the difference between the two conditions, employing $\alpha = 0.05$.

14. Obtain the before-after difference score for each subject in Exercises 11 and 12. Conduct a "matched-pairs" analysis of the difference scores, employing $\alpha = 0.05$. Compare the results of this analysis with the foregoing analysis.

15. A large discount house advertises that its prices are lower than its largest competitor's. To test the validity of this claim, the prices of 15 randomly selected items are compared. If the results are as shown in the accompanying table, what do you conclude?

Discount House	Competitor
$3.77	$3.95
7.50	7.75
4.95	4.99
3.18	3.25
5.77	5.98
2.49	2.39
8.77	9.49
6.99	6.49
2.99	2.95
1.98	2.49
0.49	0.52
5.50	5.62
0.99	0.98
6.49	6.66
5.49	5.55

16. A company has just switched to a four-day workweek. It measured the number of units produced per week for 10 employees before and after the change. Using the Sandler A-test, test the null hypothesis at $\alpha = 0.05$ level of significance.

Employee	No. of Units Before	After
A	25	23
B	26	24
C	27	26
D	22	23
E	29	30
F	25	24
G	29	26
H	30	32
I	25	25
J	28	29

17. Referring to Exercise 25, Chapter 13, assume that the two groups had been matched on their abilities before the coffee break was instituted. Assume that the pairs are in identical order for the two groups. Determine the standard error of the difference between means and the t-scores. Compare the obtained value with that of Exercise 25, Chapter 13.

18. A store owner wants to increase the number of people walking into his store. For a week, he records the number coming in per day. He then hires a designer to set

up the window display and records the number the following week. The records show the following:

Day	Before	After
Monday	150	200
Tuesday	175	180
Wednesday	140	180
Thursday	180	175
Friday	170	190
Saturday	160	175

Did the new display help the owner? What is the value of A?

19. In an attempt to increase record sales, a manager advertises that five records are on sale. For a sample of 10 albums not on sale, she finds the following amounts were sold a day before the sale and on a day during the sale:

Record	Before	After	Record	Before	After
A	25	30	F	5	5
B	15	17	G	0	1
C	10	13	H	40	45
D	25	30	I	50	45
E	30	25	J	35	40

Did the sale significantly increase the number of other records sold? What is the value of A?

20. A merchant recorded the number of packs of cigarettes sold for five brands on three different occasions: one day just one month before a $0.04-per-pack tax increase, the day after the increase, and one day a month after the increase,

	Before Tax	One Day After	One Month After
Brand A	50	45	49
Brand B	40	35	42
Brand C	60	57	59
Brand D	65	67	67
Brand E	50	40	47

Is there a significant difference between the number of packs sold before the tax and one day after? What is the value of A?

21. Referring to Exercise 20, determine if there was a significant difference between the number sold one month before and one month after the tax was increased? What is the value of A?

22. Again referring to Exercise 20, determine if there was a significant difference between the number sold one day and one month after the tax was increased? Calculate the value of A.

23. Shown below are the results of a preliminary study to determine whether the pupil response of hetero- and homosexual males differ when shown pictures of men and women. The crucial values are given in the fourth and eighth columns. A

positive score means greater pupillary response to the picture of a female; a negative score means greater pupillary response to a picture of a male.

| | Heterosexuals | | | | Homosexuals | | |
| | Total Response | | Relative M vs. F Response Score | | Total Response | | Relative M vs. F Response Score |
Subject	To Male Pictures	To Female Pictures		Subject	To Male Pictures	To Female Pictures	
1	− 0.4	+ 5.9	+ 6.3	6	+18.8	+11.2	− 7.6
2	−54.5	−22.4	+32.1	7	− 4.6	−38.0	−33.4
3	+12.5	+19.2	+ 6.7	8	+18.9	+18.1	− 0.8
4	+ 6.3	+39.0	+32.7	9	+18.2	− 5.6	−23.8
5	− 1.5	+23.1	+24.6	10	+15.8	+21.5	+ 5.7

a. Conduct a Sandler's A on the difference scores (last column) of the heterosexual sample. Employ $\alpha = 0.05$, two-tailed test. Is there support for the
   view that heterosexual males give a diffferent pupillary response to pictures
   of females than to pictures of males?
b. Conduct a Sandler's A on the difference scores of the homosexual sample.
   Employ $\alpha = 0.05$, two-tailed test. Is there support for the view that homosexual males give a different pupillary response to the pictures of males than
   to pictures of females?
c. Conduct an independent-samples t-test, using the difference scores of heterosexual vs. homosexual males. Employing $\alpha = 0.05$, two-tailed test, determine if there is is a basis for claiming a differential response of male heterosexuals and homosexuals to pictures of males and females, respectively.
   [*Hint:* To facilitate calculations when negative numbers are involved, algebraically add 34 to each score. This procedure eliminates all the negative
   values and makes use of the generalization shown in Section 2.3.]

To calculate the mean for each group, use the formula

$$\frac{\sum_{i=1}^{5} X_i}{N} = \frac{\sum_{i=1}^{5} X_i - 5(34)}{N}.$$

Note: Adding 34 to all scores will not change the difference between means and
the standard error of the difference, since the relative differences among scores are
maintained. However, the mean for each group will increase by 34.

24. In the preceding exercise, you rejected the null hypothesis in two out of three
   comparisons. As a statistician, would you feel more confident in rejecting H_0 if you
   had obtained the same A- and t-statistics with a larger N? (Hess, 1965).

25. The effects of the hallucinogenic drug mescaline on aggressive behavior were investigated by Sbordone, Wingard, Elliott, and Jervey (1978). Each of 45 experimental rats was injected with a placebo and then placed in a cage with another
   rat. The amount of "pathological aggression" (boxing, biting, and shoving) initiated
   by the experimental rats during this baseline period was measured. Next the experimental animals were injected with a dose of mescaline, again placed in cages

with other rats, and again the amount of pathological aggression was measured. During the baseline period the experimental rats initiated $\overline{X} = 1.31$ and $s = 0.92$ pathological aggression, whereas after being injected with mescaline they initiated $\overline{X} = 2.13$ and $s = 1.78$ pathological aggression. The correlation between pathological aggression during the baseline period and pathological aggression after injection of mescaline was $r = 0.56$.

   a. Using $\alpha = 0.05$, set up and test the null hypothesis that the correlation between pathological aggression during baseline and pathological aggression after injection of mescaline is equal to zero.

   b. Using $\alpha = 0.05$, set up and test the null hypothesis that there is no difference in the amount of aggression initiated before or after injection of mescaline.

   c. Determine the 95-percent confidence intervals for the mean pathological aggression initiated during the baseline period and after injection of mescaline.

15

An Introduction to the Analysis of Variance

15.1 *Multigroup Comparisons*

We have reviewed the classic design of experiments on several different occasions in this text. The classic study consists of two groups, an experimental and a control. The purpose of statistical inference is to test specific hypotheses, e.g., whether or not both groups could reasonably have been drawn from the same population (see Chapter 13).

Although this classical research design is still employed in many studies, its limitations should be apparent to you. To restrict our observations to two groups on all occasions is to overlook the wonderful complexity of the phenomena that the scientist investigates. Rarely do events in nature conveniently order themselves into two groups, an experimental and a control. More commonly the questions we pose to nature are of this variety: Which of several alternative schedules of reinforcement leads to the greatest resistance to experimental extinction? Which of five different methods of teaching the concept of fractions to the primary grades leads to the greatest learning gains? Which form of psychotherapy leads to the greatest incidence of patient recovery?

Obviously the research design necessary to provide experimental answers to the above questions would require comparison of more than two groups. You may wonder: But why should multigroup comparisons provide any obstacles? Can we not simply compare the mean of each group with the mean of every other group and obtain a Student's *t*-ratio for each comparison? For example, if we had four experimental groups, A, B, C, D, could we not calculate Student's *t*-ratios comparing A with B, C, and D; B with C and D; and C with D?

If you will think for a moment of the errors in inference that we have so frequently discussed, you will recall that our greatest concern has been to avoid type-I errors. When we establish the region of rejection at the 0.05 level, we are in effect acknowledging our willingness to take the risk of being wrong as often as 5% of the time in our rejection of the null hypothesis. Now what happens when we have numerous comparisons to make? For an extreme example, let us imagine that we have conducted a study involving the calculation of 1000 separate Student *t*-ratios. Would we be terribly impressed if, say, 50 of the *t*'s proved to be significant at the 0.05 level? Of course not. Indeed, we would probably murmur something such as "With 1000 comparisons, we would be surprised if we didn't obtain approximately 50 comparisons that are significant *by chance* (i.e., due to predictable sampling error)."

The *analysis of variance* (sometimes abbreviated ANOVA) is a technique of statistical analysis that permits us to overcome the ambiguity involved in assessing significant differences when more than one comparison is made. It allows us to answer this question: Is there an overall indication that the experimental treatments are producing differences among the means of the various groups? Although the analysis of variance may be used in the two-sample case

Interactions: The spice of research

BOX 15.1

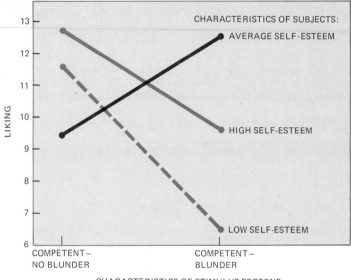

CHARACTERISTICS OF SUBJECTS:

AVERAGE SELF-ESTEEM

HIGH SELF-ESTEEM

LOW SELF-ESTEEM

LIKING

COMPETENT— NO BLUNDER

COMPETENT— BLUNDER

CHARACTERISTICS OF STIMULUS PERSONS

One of the charms of the analysis-of-variance technique is that it frees the researcher from the constraints of the traditional two-group experimental design. Not only does it provide a method for analyzing the effects of an unlimited number of treatment levels of a single experimental variable, but it also provides a statistical basis for analyzing marvelously complex designs consisting of two or more independent variables. The research interest in such experiments often goes beyond the question, "What are the effects of each experimental variable?" More often than not, the investigator is interested in knowing whether or not two or more independent variables *interact*. Two variables are said to interact if the effects of one variable are dependent on the level of a second variable. When trying to conceptualize interaction, it often helps to graph the experimental results.

The accompanying figure summarizes a set of experimental results in one part of a study concerned with the effects of seeing a stimulus person commit a blunder. The subjects were divided into three conditions—those of low, average, and high self-esteem. Some subjects in each esteem group saw a competent person make a blunder (spilling a cup of coffee). For the remaining subjects, the competent stimulus person did not commit any blunder. The dependent measure was a "liking" score of the stimulus person.

The figure shows a clear interaction. For subjects of low and high self-esteem, witnessing the stimulus person commit a blunder caused them to like that person less. In contrast, subjects of average self-esteem had a greater liking for the stimulus person who committed a blunder. Interactions such as these add a bit of spice to the bland diet of many research efforts.

Attraction toward the competent stimulus person, with higher scores indicating greater attraction. (R. Helmreich, E. Aronson, and J. LeFan (1970), "To err is human—sometimes: Effects of self-esteem, competence, and a pratfall on interpersonal attraction," *Journal of Personality and Social Psychology* **16**, 262. Copyright 1970 by the American Psychological Association. Reprinted by permission.)

(in which event it yields precisely the same probability values as the Student's *t*-ratio), it has its greatest usefulness when two or more *independent* variables are studied. For purposes of exposing the fundamental characteristics of the analysis of variance, our initial illustrative material will involve the two-sample case with independent groups. The procedures shown below may be generalized to any number of independent groups.

15.2 *The Concept of Sums of Squares*

Variance Estimate

Sum of the squared deviations from the mean divided by degrees of freedom.

You will recall that we previously defined the unbiased **variance estimate** as

$$s^2 = \frac{\sum(X - \bar{X})^2}{N - 1} = \frac{SS}{N - 1}.$$

Also recall that when the deviation of scores from the mean $(X - \bar{X})$ is large, the variance, and therefore the variability of scores, is also large. When the deviations are small, the variance is correspondingly small.

Now if we think back to the Student's t-ratio for a moment, we note that both the numerator and denominator give us some estimate of variability:

$$t = \frac{\bar{X}_1 - \bar{X}_2}{s_{\bar{X}_1 - \bar{X}_2}}.$$

The denominator, which we referred to as the standard error of the difference between means, is based on the pooled estimate of the variability within each experimental group; that is,

$$s_{\bar{X}_1 - \bar{X}_2} = \sqrt{\frac{SS_1 + SS_2}{N_1 + N_2 - 2}\left(\frac{1}{N_1} + \frac{1}{N_2}\right)}.$$

However, the numerator is also a measure of variability, i.e., the variability between means. When the difference between means is large relative to $s_{\bar{X} - \bar{X}_2}$, Student's t-ratio is large. When the difference between means is small relative to $s_{\bar{X}_1 - \bar{X}_2}$, the t-ratio is also small.

Between-Group Variance

Estimate of variance based upon variability between groups.

Within-Group Variance

Estimate of variance based upon the variability within groups.

The analysis of variance consists of obtaining two independent estimates of variance, one based upon variability between groups **between-group variance)** and the other based upon the variability within groups **(within-group variance).** The significance of the difference between these two variance estimates is provided by Fisher's F-distributions. (We are already familiar with F-distributions from our prior discussion of homogeneity of variance, Section 13.5). If the *between-group variance* estimate is large (i.e., the difference between means is large) relative to the *within-group variance* estimate, the F-ratio is large. Conversely, if the *between-group variance* estimate is small relative to the *within-group variance* estimate, the F-ratio will be small.

A basic concept in the analysis of variance is the **sum of squares.** We have already encountered the sum of squares in calculating the standard deviation, the variance, and the standard error of the difference between means. It is simply the numerator in the formula for variance, that is, SS. As you will recall, the raw-score formula for calculating the sum of squares is

$$SS = \sum X^2 - \frac{(\sum X)^2}{N}.$$

Sum of Squares

Deviations from the mean squared and summed.

The advantage of the analysis of variance technique is that we can partition the total sum of squares (SS_{tot}) into two components, the *within-group sum of squares* (SS_w) and the *between-group sum of squares* (SS_{bet}). Before proceeding any further, let us clarify each of these concepts with a simple example.

Imagine that we have completed a study comparing two experimental treatments, and obtained the scores listed in Table 15.1.

The mean for group 1 is 4; the mean for group 2 is 8. The overall mean, $\bar{X}_{tot}$, is 48/8 or 6. Now, if we were to subtract the overall mean from each score and square, we would obtain the total sum of squares:

$$SS_{tot} = \sum (X - \bar{X}_{tot})^2. \tag{15.1}$$

The alternative raw-score formula is

$$SS_{tot} = \sum X_{tot}^2 - \frac{(\sum X_{tot})^2}{N} \tag{15.2}$$

Table 15.1 **Scores of two groups of subjects in a hypothetical experiment.**

Group 1		Group 2	
X_1	X_1^2	X_2	X_2^2
1	1	6	36
2	4	7	49
5	25	9	81
8	64	10	100
$\sum 16$	94	32	266

$N_1 = 4,\quad \bar{X}_1 = 4\quad N_2 = 4,\quad \bar{X}_2 = 8$
$\sum X_{tot} = 48,\quad N = 8,\quad \bar{X}_{tot} = 6.$

For the data in Table 15.1, the total sum of squares is

$$SS_{tot} = 360 - \frac{(48)^2}{8}$$
$$= 360 - 288 = 72.$$

The within-group sum of squares is merely the sum of the sum of squares obtained within each group, that is,

$$SS_w = SS_1 + SS_2$$
$$SS_1 = \sum X_1^2 - \frac{(\sum X_1)^2}{N_1}$$
$$= 94 - \frac{(16)^2}{4} = 94 - 64 = 30, \quad (15.3)$$
$$SS_2 = \sum X_2^2 - \frac{(\sum X_2)^2}{N_2}$$
$$= 266 - \frac{(32)^2}{4} = 266 - 256 = 10,$$
$$SS_w = 30 + 10 = 40.$$

Finally, the between-group sum of squares (SS_{bet}) may be obtained by subtracting the overall mean from each group mean, squaring the result, multiplying by the N in each group, and summing across all the groups. Thus

$$SS_{bet} = \sum N_i(\bar{X}_i - \bar{X}_{tot})^2, \quad (15.4)$$

where N_i is the number in the ith group, and $\bar{X}_i$ is the mean of the ith group.

$$SS_{bet} = 4(4 - 6)^2 + 4(8 - 6)^2 = 32.$$

The raw-score formula for calculating the between-group sum of squares is

$$SS_{bet} = \sum \frac{(\sum X_i)^2}{N_i} - \frac{(\sum X_{tot})^2}{N}, \quad (15.5)$$

and

$$SS_{bet} = \frac{(16)^2}{4} + \frac{(32)^2}{4} - \frac{(48)^2}{8}$$
$$= 64 + 256 - 288$$
$$= 320 - 288 = 32.$$

Note that the total sum of squares is equal to the sum of the between-group sum of squares and the within-group sum of squares. In other words,

$$SS_{tot} = SS_w + SS_{bet}. \qquad (15.6)$$

In our experimental example of two groups, $SS_{tot} = 72$, $SS_w = 40$, and $SS_{bet} = 32$. Thus $72 = 40 + 32$.

15.3 *Obtaining Variance Estimates*

Now, to arrive at variance estimates from between- and within-group sum of squares, all we need to do is divide each by the appropriate number of degrees of freedom.* The degrees of freedom of the between-group is simply the number of cells (k) minus 1.

$$df_{bet} = k - 1. \qquad (15.7)$$

With two groups, $k = 2$. Therefore $df = 2 - 1 = 1$. Thus our between-group variance estimate for the problem at hand is

$$\hat{s}_{bet}^2 = \frac{SS_{bet}}{df_{bet}} = \frac{32}{1} = 32, \qquad df = 1. \qquad (15.8)$$

The number of degrees of freedom of the within-groups is the total N minus the number of cells. Thus

$$df_w = N - k. \qquad (15.9)$$

In the present problem, $df_w = 8 - 2 = 6$ and our within-group variance estimate becomes

$$\hat{s}_w^2 = \frac{SS_w}{df_w} = \frac{40}{6} = 6.67, \qquad df = 6. \qquad (15.10)$$

Now, all that is left is to calculate the F-ratio and determine whether or not our two variance estimates could have reasonably been drawn from the same population. If not, we shall conclude that the significantly larger between-group variance is due to the operation of the experimental conditions. In other

---

*The rationale for the degrees of freedom concept was presented in Section 12.5. The same rationale applies here. Degrees of freedom represent the number of values that are free to vary once we have placed certain restrictions on our data.

F-Ratio

The between-group variance estimate divided by the within-group variance estimate.

words, we shall conclude that the experimental treatments produced a significant difference in means. The **F-ratio,** in analysis of variance, is the between-group variance estimate divided by the within-group variance estimate. Symbolically,

$$F = \frac{\hat{s}_{bet}^2}{\hat{s}_w^2}.$$ (15.11)

For the above problem our F-ratio is

$$F = \frac{32}{6.67} = 4.80, \qquad df = \frac{1}{6}.$$

Looking up the F-ratio under 1 and 6 degrees of freedom in Table D, in the Table section, we find that an F-ratio of 5.99 or larger is required for significance at the 0.05 level. For the present problem, then, we cannot reject the null hypothesis. Note that Table D provides two-tailed values. The analysis of variance test for significance is automatically two-tailed since *any* difference among the sample means will enlarge the entire value of F, not just the difference in which the researcher is interested.

15.4 Fundamental Concepts of Analysis of Variance

Analysis of Variance (ANOVA)

A method, described initially by R. A. Fisher, partitioning the sum of squares for experimental data into known components of variation.

In these few pages, we have examined all the basic concepts necessary to understand simple **analysis of variance.** Before proceeding with an example involving three groups, let's briefly review these fundamental concepts.

1. We have seen that in an experiment involving two or more groups it is possible to identify two different bases for estimating the population variance: the between-group and the within-group.
   a. The between-group variance estimate reflects the magnitude of the difference between and/or among the group means. The larger the difference between means, the larger the between-group variance.
   b. The within-group variance estimate reflects the dispersion of scores within each treatment group. The within-group variance is analogous to $s_{\bar{X}_1 - \bar{X}_2}$ in the Student's t-ratio. It is often referred to as the *error term*.

2. The null hypothesis is that the samples were drawn from the same population, or that $\mu_1 = \mu_2 = \cdots = \mu_k$.

3. The alternative hypothesis is that the samples were not drawn from the same population, i.e., $\mu_1 \neq \mu_2 \cdots \neq \mu_k$.

4. The F-ratio consists of the between-group variance estimate divided by the within-group variance estimate. By consulting Table D of the distri-

bution of F, we can determine whether the null hypothesis of equal population means can reasonably be entertained. In the event of a significant F-ratio, we may conclude that the group means are not all estimates of a common population mean.

5. In the two-sample case, the F-ratio yields probability values identical to those of Student's t-ratio. Indeed, in the one-degree-of-freedom situation (that is, $k = 2$), $t = \sqrt{F}$ or $t^2 = F$. You may check this statement by calculating the t-ratio for the sample problem we have just completed.

15.5 An Example Involving Three Groups

Imagine that you have just completed a study concerned with the determination of the effectiveness of varying motivational levels on the acquisition of arithmetic skills. Twenty-seven primary-grade children were randomly assigned to three equal groups, employing one of the methods for achieving randomness described in Section 10.2. Group 1, the control condition, received a low amount of classroom motivation. Subjects in group 2 were exposed to motivational levels that independent persons judged to be medium. Finally, group-3 subjects were exposed to high motivational levels.

Following the completion of their instruction, all children were tested on an "Inventory of Basic Arithmetic." The results of this hypothetical study are presented in Table 15.2.

The following steps are employed in a three-group analysis of variance.

Step 1.   Employing Formula (15.2), the total sum of squares is

$$SS_{tot} = 1216 - \frac{158^2}{27} = 291.41.$$

Step 2.   Employing Formula (15.5) for three groups, the between-group sum of squares is

$$SS_{bet} = \frac{46^2}{9} + \frac{78^2}{9} + \frac{34^2}{9} - \frac{158^2}{27} = 114.96.$$

Step 3.   The within-group sum of squares may be obtained by employing Formula (15.3) for three groups:

$$SS_w = \left(292 - \frac{46^2}{9}\right) + \left(756 - \frac{78^2}{9}\right) + \left(168 - \frac{34^2}{9}\right) = 176.45.$$

Note that SS_w may also be obtained by subtraction. Thus

$$SS_w = SS_{tot} - SS_{bet} = 291.41 - 114.96 = 176.45.$$

Table 15.2 Scores of three groups of subjects in a hypothetical experiment.

Group 1		Group 2		Group 3	
X_1	X_1^2	X_2	X_2^2	X_3	X_3^2
4	16	12	144	1	1
5	25	8	64	3	9
4	16	10	100	4	16
3	9	5	25	6	36
6	36	7	49	8	64
10	100	9	81	5	25
1	1	14	196	3	9
8	64	9	81	2	4
5	25	4	16	2	4
$\sum$ 46	292	78	756	34	168

$N_1 = 9, \quad \overline{X}_1 = 5.11 \quad N_2 = 9, \quad \overline{X}_2 = 8.67 \quad N_3 = 9, \quad \overline{X}_3 = 3.78$

$$\sum X_{tot} = 46 + 78 + 34 = 158,$$
$$\sum X_{tot}^2 = 292 + 756 + 168 = 1216,$$
$$N = 27.$$

Step 4.   The between-group variance estimate is

$$df_{bet} = k - 1 = 2, \qquad \hat{s}_{bet}^2 = \frac{114.96}{2} = 57.48.$$

Step 5.   The within-group variance estimate is

$$df_w = N - k = 24, \qquad \hat{s}_w^2 = \frac{176.45}{24} = 7.35.$$

Step 6.   Employing Formula (15.11) we find that the value of F is

$$F = \frac{57.48}{7.35} = 7.82, \qquad df = 2/24.$$

To summarize these steps, we employ the format shown in Table 15.3.

By employing the format recommended in Table 15.3, you have a final check upon your calculation of sum of squares and your assignment of degrees of freedom. Thus $SS_{bet} + SS_w$ must equal SS_{tot}. The degrees of freedom of

Table 15.3 **Summary table for representing the relevant statistics in analysis-of-variance problems.**

Source of Variation	Sum of Squares	Degrees of Freedom	Variance Estimate*	
Between-groups	114.96	2	57.48	7.82
Within-groups	176.45	24	7.35	
Total	291.41	26		

*In many texts, the term "mean square" appears in this box. However, the authors prefer the term "variance estimate" since this term accurately describes the nature of the entries in the column.

the total are found by

$$\text{df}_{\text{tot}} = N - 1. \qquad (15.12)$$

In the present example, the number of degrees of freedom for the total is

$$\text{df}_{\text{tot}} = 27 - 1 = 26.$$

15.6 *The Interpretation of F*

When we look up the F required for significance with 2 and 24 degrees of freedom, we find that an F of 3.40 or larger is significant at the 0.05 level.

Since our F of 7.86 exceeds this value, we may conclude that the three-group means are not all estimates of a common population mean. Now do we stop at this point? After all, are we not interested in determining whether or not one of the three methods of instructing the fundamentals of arithmetic is superior to the other two? The answer to the first question is negative and the answer to the second is affirmative.

The truth of the matter is that our finding an overall significant F-ratio now permits us to investigate specific hypotheses. In the absence of a significant F-ratio, any significant differences between specific comparisons would have to be regarded as suspicious—very possibly representing a chance difference.

Over the past several years behavioral scientists have developed a large number of tests that permit the researcher to investigate specific hypotheses concerning population parameters. Two broad classes of such tests exist:

1. ***A priori* or planned comparisons:** When comparisons are planned in advance of the investigation, an *a priori* test is appropriate. For *a priori* tests, it is not necessary that the overall F-ratio be significant.

A Priori or Planned Comparisons

Comparisons planned in advance to investigate specific hypotheses concerning population parameters.

A Posteriori Comparisons

Comparisons not planned in advance to investigate specific hypotheses concerning population parameters.

2. ***A posteriori* comparisons:** When the comparisons are not planned in advance, an *a posteriori* test is appropriate.

In the present example we illustrate the use of an *a posteriori* test for making comparisons among pairs of means, also known as pairwise comparisons.

Tukey (1953) has developed such a test, which he named the HSD (honestly significant difference) test. To employ this test, the overall *F*-ratio must be significant.

A difference between two means is significant as a given α-level if it equals or exceeds HSD, which is

$$\text{HSD} = q_\alpha \sqrt{\frac{\hat{s}_w^2}{N,}} \qquad (15.13)$$

in which

$\hat{s}_w^2$ = the within-group variance estimate,

N = number of subjects in each condition,

q_α = tabled value for a given α-level found in Table O for df_w and k (number of means).

A Worked Example

Let us employ the data from Section 15.5 to illustrate the application of the HSD test. We shall employ $\alpha = 0.05$ for testing the significance of the difference between each pair of means.

Step 1.   Prepare a matrix showing the mean of each condition and the differences between pairs of means. This is shown in Table 15.4.

Step 2.   Referring to Table O under error df = 24, $k = 3$ at $\alpha = 0.05$, we find $q_{0.05} = 3.53$.

Step 3.   Find HSD by multiplying $q_{0.05}$ by $\sqrt{\hat{s}_w^2/N}$. The quantity $\hat{s}_w^2$ is found in Table 15.3 under within-group variance estimate. The N per condition is 9. Thus

$$\text{HSD} = 3.53 \sqrt{\frac{7.35}{9}} = 3.53(0.90) = 3.18.$$

Step 4.   Referring to Table 15.4, we find that the differences between X_1 versus X_2 and X_2 vs. X_3 both exceed HSD = 3.18. We may therefore conclude that these differences are statistically

Table 15.4 Differences among means.

	$\bar{X}_1$	$\bar{X}_2$	$\bar{X}_3$
	$\bar{X}_1 = 5.11$	$\bar{X}_2 = 8.87$	$\bar{X}_3 = 3.78$
$\bar{X}_1 = 5.11$	. . .	3.56	1.33
$\bar{X}_2 = 8.67$	. . .	. . .	4.89
$\bar{X}_3 = 3.78$	. . .	. . .	. . .

significant at $\alpha = 0.05$. Since the group-2 mean is significantly higher than the mean of the other two conditions, we may conclude that this condition produced significantly higher performance on the dependent measure (Inventory of Basic Arithmetic). It would appear that medium motivational levels produced superior learning gains in this hypothetical experiment.

15.7 Estimating the Degree of Association between the Experimental and Dependent Variables

In Section 13.4, we saw the use of omega squared (ω^2) to estimate the proportion of variance in the dependent measure that may be attributed to variations in the treatment variable. A similar estimate is available in the one-way analysis of variance:

$$\text{est } \omega^2 = \frac{SS_{bet} - (k-1)\hat{s}_w^2}{SS_{tot} + \hat{s}_w^2}. \tag{15.14}$$

In Table 15.3, we saw the $SS_{bet} = 114.96$, $k - 1 = 2$, $\hat{s}_w^2 = 7.35$, and $SS_{tot} = 291.41$. Substituting in Formula (15.14), we find:

$$\text{est } \omega^2 = \frac{114.96 - (2)(7.35)}{291.41 - 7.35}$$
$$= \frac{100.26}{298.76} = 0.35.$$

Considering all the factors that influence scholastic performance, finding a variable that accounts for 35% of the variance must be regarded as important.

Of course, this conclusion is based on hypothetical data. One does not often find values of ω^2 this high in behavioral research.

15.8 Two-Way Analysis of Variance: Factorial Design

One-Way Analysis of Variance

Statistical analysis of various categories or levels of a *single* treatment variable.

We have just been looking at a **one-way analysis of variance,** which derives its name from the fact that the various treatment groups represent different levels or different categories of a *single* treatment variable. By making possible the simultaneous assessment of several levels or categories of an experimental variable, it frees us from the limitations of the traditional two-group, experimental versus control-group design.

Advanced analysis-of-variance techniques introduce still more profound advantages: They (1) permit the evaluation of more than one variable at a time; (2) allow the assessment of possible interactive effects between and among variables; and (3) represent an efficient means of using research time and effort, since in many analysis-of-variance designs every observation provides information about each variable, interaction of variables, and error.

Interaction

The joint effect of two or more factors on the dependent variable, independent of the separate effects of either factor.

Let's pause a moment and look at the concept of **interaction.** Two variables (or factors) are said to interact when the effect of one variable on some measure of behavior depends upon either the presence or the amount of a second variable. For example, suppose a particular teaching method improved test scores for high-intelligence subjects but *not* for low-intelligence subjects. If the *effects* of the different teaching methods were the same across all intelligence levels, there would be no interaction. Let's look at another example. Refer back to the data presented in Box 13.1. Notice that the mean pupil response (dependent variable) to pictures of males and females (independent variable *A*) depended on the sexual orientation (independent variable *B*) of the male subjects. Thus the variability in the dependent variable (pupil response) can best be understood by looking at the *joint* effect of the two independent variables, i.e., the *interaction* between these factors. For still another example of interaction, look again at Case Example 3.1 (Bower, 1981) on the effects of hypnotically induced mood and the emotional quality of past incidents on the recall of these experiences. The better recall of pleasant experiences when the mood is pleasant versus the superior recall of unpleasant experiences when the mood is unpleasant nicely describes interacting variables. Both the induced mood of the subject *and* the emotional quality of past experiences influenced the recall of the experiences.

Two-Way Analysis of Variance

Statistical analysis of various categories or levels of two-treatment variables.

Thus, when we are looking at one-way analyses of variance, we see that the variability in the dependent measure is due either to the variability *between* the groups (treatment effects) or to the variability *within* the groups (differences due to "chance"). In the **two-way analysis of variance,** the variability *between* the groups may be further partitioned:

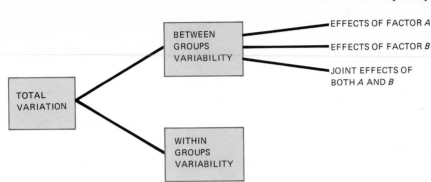

In a two-way analysis of variance, there are two different experimental or treatment variables. One or both of these variables may be either qualitative or quantitative. **Qualitative variables** differ in kind rather than "how much"; examples might be different methods of teaching or different types of psycho-therapy. **Quantitative variables** differ in quantity, as in the amount of drug or amount of positive reinforcement administered to experimental subjects.

While there are only two experimental variables in a two-way analysis of variance, there may be any number of subclasses or levels of treatment of each variable. A given study might involve two levels of one variable and four levels of a second variable, or three levels of two (each) variables, etc. The traditional way of designating a two-way analysis of variance is by citing the number of levels (or subclasses) of each variable. To illustrate, a study with two levels of one variable and four levels of a second variable is referred to as having a 2×4 design. A study with three levels of each variable is referred to as having a 3×3 design. A study with three levels of one variable and four levels of a second variable is referred to as having a 3×4 design.

Qualitative Variables

Variables that differ in kind, such as gender.

Quantitative Variables

Variables that differ in "how much," such as level of intelligence.

The Concept of a Treatment Combination

In a **factorial design,** some level of each treatment variable is administered to each experimental subject. The particular combination of experimental conditions is referred to as a treatment combination. For example, if in a 3×4 factorial design a given subject is administered the second level of variable A and the third level of variable B, the subject's treatment combination is A_2B_3.

Factorial Design

A research design in which some level of each treatment variable is administered to each subject.

- *Example:*
  a.   Treatment combinations in a 2×2 factorial design.

	A_1		A_2	
	B_1	B_2	B_1	B_2
Treatment combination	A_1B_1	A_1B_2	A_2B_1	A_2B_2

b. Treatment combinations in a 2×3 factorial design.

	A_1			A_2		
	B_1	B_2	B_3	B_1	B_2	B_3
Treatment combination	A_1B_1	A_1B_2	A_1B_3	A_2B_1	A_2B_2	A_2B_3

The total number of treatment combinations or cells in any factorial design is equal to the product of the treatment levels of all factors or variables.

- *Examples.* In a 2×2 factorial design, there are four treatment combinations or cells.

    In a 2×3 factorial design, there are six treatment combinations or cells.

    In more complex factorial designs, the same principle applies. In a $2 \times 3 \times 4$ factorial design, there are 24 treatment combinations or cells.

Partitioning the Sum of Squares

Let us now look at the analysis of a 3×3 factorial design. However, the analysis may be readily generalized to any number of levels or subclasses of each of the two variables.

In a two-way analysis of variance, the total sum of squares is partitioned into two broad components—within-group sum of squares and between-group sum of squares:

$$SS_{tot} = SS_w + SS_{bet}.$$

The between-group sum of squares is itself partitioned into three components—sum of squares for the A variable (SS_A), sum of squares for the B variable (SS_B), and sum of squares for the interaction of the A and B variables ($SS_{A \times B}$):

$$SS_{bet} = SS_A + SS_B + SS_{A \times B}.$$

When divided by the appropriate number of degrees of freedom, each of the treatment effects provides an independent estimate of the population variances:

$$\hat{s}_A^2 = \frac{SS_A}{df_A}, \qquad df_A = A - 1,$$

in which A is the number of levels of A;

$$\hat{s}_B^2 = \frac{SS_B}{df_B}, \qquad df_B = B - 1,$$

in which B is the number of levels of B;

$$\hat{s}_{A \times B}^2 = \frac{SS_{A \times B}}{df_{A \times B}}, \qquad df_{A \times B} = df_A \times df_B.$$

When divided by the appropriate degrees of freedom, the within-group sum of squares provides an independent estimate of the population variance:

$$\hat{s}_w^2(\text{error}) = \frac{SS_w}{df_w}, \qquad df_w = N - k,$$

in which k is the number of cells or treatment combinations.

A Worked Example Using a 3 × 3 Factorial Design

	A_1			A_2			A_3		
	B_1	B_2	B_3	B_1	B_2	B_3	B_1	B_2	B_3
	2	3	6	1	2	5	4	5	6
	4	5	7	3	5	8	5	8	10
	5	8	9	6	7	6	3	7	12
	7	11	12	7	9	11	7	9	11
Treatment combination	A_1B_1	A_1B_2	A_1B_3	A_2B_1	A_2B_2	A_2B_3	A_3B_1	A_3B_2	A_3B_3
Σ	18	27	34	17	23	30	19	29	39

$$\Sigma X = 236$$

Let's determine if there is a significant effect of the A variable, the B variable, or an interaction between the two variables. We use $\alpha = 0.01$.

Step 1.   Find SS_{tot}. Square each score, sum all of the squared values, and subtract $(\Sigma X)^2/N$:

$$SS_{tot} = \sum X^2 - \frac{(\sum X)^2}{N}.$$

In the present example,

$$SS_{tot} = 2^2 + 4^2 + 5^2 + \cdots + 11^2 - \frac{236^2}{36}$$

$$= 1842 - 1547.11$$

$$= 294.89.$$

Step 2.   Find df_{tot}:

$$df_{tot} = N - 1$$
$$= 36 - 1$$
$$= 35.$$

Step 3.   Enter SS_{tot} and df_{tot} into the summary table (Table 15.5).

Step 4.   Find the between-group sum of squares. In the present problem,

$$SS_{bet} = \frac{(\sum A_1B_1)^2}{N_{A_1B_1}} + \frac{(\sum A_1B_2)^2}{N_{A_1B_2}} + \cdots$$

$$+ \frac{(\sum A_3B_3)^2}{N_{A_3B_3}} - \frac{(\sum X)^2}{N}$$

$$= \frac{(18)^2}{4} + \frac{(27)^2}{4} + \cdots + \frac{(39)^2}{4} - 1547.11.$$

Since N is the same for each treatment combination, there will be less rounding error if the squares of the treatment combinations are summed and then divided by the N in each group (N_k):

$$SS_{bet} = \frac{(\sum A_1B_1)^2 + (\sum A_1B_2)^2 + \cdots + (\sum A_3B_3)^2}{N_k} - \frac{(\sum X)^2}{N}$$

$$= \frac{(18)^2 + (27)^2 + (34)^2 + (17)^2 + (23)^2 + (30)^2 + (19)^2 + (29)^2 + (39)^2}{4}$$

$$- 1547.11$$

$$= \frac{6650}{4} - 1547.11$$

$$= 1662.50 - 1547.11 = 115.39$$

Step 5.   Find the number of degrees of freedom for the between-group sum of squares:

$$df_{bet} = k - 1,$$

Table 15.5 Summary table for two-way analysis of variance.

Source of Variation	Sum of Squares	Degrees of Freedom	Variance Estimate	F
Between-group	115.39	8		
A variable	12.06	2	6.03	0.91
B variable	100.06	2	50.03	7.52
A × B	3.27	4	0.82	0.12
Within-group (error)	179.50	27	6.65	
Total	294.89	35		

in which k is the number of cells or treatment combinations. In the present example,

$$\text{df}_{\text{bet}} = 9 - 1 = 8.$$

Step 6. Enter the between-group sum of squares and the corresponding degrees of freedom in Table 15.5.

Step 7. Begin the partitioning of the between-group sum of squares by finding the sum of squares for the A variable:

$$SS_A = \frac{(\sum X_{A1})^2}{N_{A1}} + \frac{(\sum X_{A2})^2}{N_{A2}} + \frac{(\sum X_{A3})^2}{N_{A3}} - \frac{(\sum X)^2}{N}$$

$$= \frac{(79)^2}{12} + \frac{(70)^2}{12} + \frac{(87)^2}{12} - 1547.11.$$

Since N is the same for each A condition, there will be less rounding error if the squares of each level of A are summed and then divided by the N in each A condition:

$$SS_A = \frac{(\sum X_{A_1})^2 + (\sum X_{A_2})^2 + (\sum X_{A_3})^2}{N_A} - \frac{(\sum X)^2}{N}$$

$$= \frac{(79)^2 + (70)^2 + (87)^2}{N_A} - 1547.11$$

$$= \frac{18,710}{12} - 1547.11$$

$$= 1559.17 - 1547.11 = 12.06.$$

Step 8. Find the number of degrees of freedom for the A condition:

$$df_A = A - 1,$$

in which A is the number of levels of A. In the present example,

$$df_A = 3 - 1 = 2.$$

Step 9. Enter the sum of squares for the A variable and the corresponding degrees of freedom in Table 15.5

Step 10. Find the sum of squares of the B variable:

$$SS_B = \frac{(\sum X_{B1})^2}{N_{B1}} + \frac{(\sum X_{B2})^2}{N_{B2}} + \frac{(\sum X_{B3})^2}{N_{B3}} - \frac{(\sum X)^2}{N}$$

$$= \frac{(54)^2}{12} + \frac{(79)^2}{12} + \frac{(103)^2}{12} - 1547.11.$$

Since N is the same for each B condition, there will be less rounding error if the squares of each level of B are summed and then divided by the N in each condition:

$$SS_B = \frac{(54)^2 + (79)^2 + (103)^2}{12} - 1547.11$$

$$= \frac{19,766}{12} - 1547.11$$

$$= 1647.17 - 1547.11 = 100.06.$$

Step 11. Find the number of degrees of freedom for the B condition,

$$df_B = B - 1,$$

in which B is the number of levels of B. In the present example,

$$df_B = 3 - 1 = 2.$$

Step 12. Enter the sum of squares for the B variable and the corresponding degrees of freedom in Table 15.5.

Step 13. Find the interaction sum of squares by subtraction:

$$SS_{A \times B} = SS_{bet} - (SS_A + SS_B)$$

$$= 115.39 - (12.06 + 100.06)$$

$$= 3.27.$$

Step 14. Find the number of degrees of freedom for the interaction sum of squares:

$$df_{A \times B} = (A - 1)(B - 1)$$
$$= (2)(2) = 4.$$

Step 15. Enter the interaction sum of squares and the corresponding degrees of freedom in Table 15.5.

Step 16. Find the within-group sum of squares. The within-group sum of squares may be obtained by subtraction:

$$SS_w = SS_{tot} - SS_{bet}$$
$$= 294.89 - 115.39 = 179.5.$$

Step 17. Find the within-group degrees of freedom:

$$df_w = N - k$$
$$= 36 - 9$$
$$= 27.$$

Step 18. Enter the within-group sum of squares and degrees of freedom in Table 15.5.

Step 19. Check to ascertain that

$$SS_{bet} + SS_w = SS_{tot}$$

and

$$SS_A + SS_B + SS_{A \times B} = SS_{bet}.$$

Step 20. Find the $A \times B$ interaction variance estimate by dividing the interaction sum of squares by $df_{A \times B}$:

$$s_{A \times B}^2 = \frac{SS_{A \times B}}{df_{A \times B}} = \frac{3.27}{4} = 0.82.$$

Place in Table 15.5.

Step 21. Find the B-variance estimate by dividing the B-variable sum of squares by df_B:

$$s_B^2 = \frac{SS_B}{df_B} = \frac{100.06}{2} = 50.03.$$

Step 22.   Find the A-variable variance estimate by dividing the A-variable sum of squares by df_A:

$$\hat{s}_A^2 = \frac{SS_A}{df_A} = \frac{12.06}{2} = 6.03.$$

Step 23.   Find the within-group variance estimate (error) by dividing the within-group sum of squares by df_w:

$$\hat{s}_w^2 = \frac{SS_w}{df_w} = \frac{179.50}{27} = 6.65.$$

Step 24.   Find the interaction F-ratio by dividing the interaction estimated variance by the within-group estimated variance:

$$F = \frac{\hat{s}_{A \times B}^2}{\hat{s}_w^2} = \frac{0.82}{6.65} = 0.12, \qquad df = \frac{4}{27}.$$

Step 25.   Consult Table D under 4 and 27 df to find the critical value of F required to reject H_0 at the $\alpha = 0.01$ level. Since $F_{0.01} \geq 4.11$, we fail to reject H_0.

Step 26.   Find the B-variable F-ratio by dividing the estimated B-variance by the within-group estimated variance:

$$F = \frac{\hat{s}_B^2}{\hat{s}_w^2} = \frac{50.03}{6.65} = 7.52, \qquad df = \frac{2}{27}.$$

Step 27.   Consult Table D under 2 and 27 df to find the critical value of F required to reject H_0 at the $\alpha = 0.01$ level. Since $F_{0.01} \geq 5.49$, the obtained ratio of 7.52 is in the critical region for rejecting H_0. There is a significant effect of the B-variable.

Step 28.   Find the A-variable F-ratio by dividing the estimated A-variance by the within-group estimated variance:

$$F = \frac{\hat{s}_A^2}{s\hat{s}_w^2} = \frac{6.03}{6.65} = 0.91, \qquad df = \frac{2}{27}.$$

Step 29.   Consult Table D under 2 and 27 df to find the critical value required to reject H_0 at the $\alpha = 0.01$ level. Since $F_{0.01} \geq 5.49$, the obtained F of 0.91 is not within the critical region. We fail to reject H_0.

Conclusion: Of the three effects evaluated—A-variable, B-variable, and the interaction of A and B—only the B-variable was found to be statistically significant. It is now appropriate to employ a multicomparison test in order to test pairwise differences among means. The Tukey HSD test shown in Section 15.6 may be used to make these comparisons.

Chapter Summary

We began this chapter with the observation that the scientist is frequently interested in conducting studies that are more extensive than the classical two-group design. However, when more than two groups are involved in a study, we increase the risk of making a type-I error if we accept as significant *any* comparison that falls within the rejection region. In multigroup studies it is desirable to know whether or not there is an indication of any overall effect of the experimental treatments before we investigate specific hypotheses. The analysis-of-variance technique provides such a test.

In this chapter, we presented a mere introduction to the complexities of analysis of variance. We showed that total sums of squares can be partitioned into two component sums of squares: the within-group and the between-group. These two component sums of squares provide us in turn with independent estimates of the population variance. A between-group variance estimate that is large, relative to the within-group variance, suggests that the experimental treatments are responsible for the large differences among the group means. The significance of the difference in variance estimates is obtained by reference to the F-table (Table D.)

When the overall F-ratio is found to be statistically significant, we are free to investigate specific hypotheses, employing a multiple-comparison test.

Finally, we saw that the analysis of variance can be applied to complex designs in which more than one independent variable is used. We saw the use of a two-way analysis of variance to evaluate the effects of two independent variables and the interaction between these variables.

Terms to Remember

analysis of variance (ANOVA)

a posteriori comparisons

a priori or planned comparisons

between-group variance

factorial design

F-ratio

interaction

one-way analysis of variance

qualitative variables

quantitative variables

sum of squares

two-way analysis of variance

variance estimate

within-group variance

EXERCISES

1. Using the following data derived from the 10-year period 1955–1964, determine whether there is a significant difference at the 0.01 level in death rate among the various seasons. (*Note:* Assume death rates for any given year to be independent.)

Winter	Spring	Summer	Fall
9.8	9.0	8.8	9.4
9.9	9.3	8.7	9.4
9.8	9.3	8.8	10.3
10.6	9.2	8.6	9.8
9.9	9.4	8.7	9.4
10.7	9.1	8.3	9.6
9.7	9.2	8.8	9.5
10.2	8.9	8.8	9.6
10.9	9.3	8.7	9.5
10.0	9.3	8.9	9.4

2. Conduct an HSD test, comparing the death rates of each season with every other season. Employ the 0.01 level, two-tailed test for each comparison.

3. Conduct an analysis of variance on the data in Chapter 13, Exercise 3. Verify that in the two-group condition $F = t^2$.

4. Manufacturer Pass negotiates contracts with 10 different independent research organizations to compare the effectiveness of his product with that of his leading competitor. A significant difference (0.05 level) in favor of Mr. Pass's product is found in one of the 10 studies. He subsequently advertises that independent research has demonstrated the superiority of his product over the leading competitor. Criticize this conclusion.

5. Various drug companies make the claim that they manufacture an analgesic that releases its active ingredient "faster." A random selection of the products of each manufacturer revealed the following times, in seconds, required for the release of 50% of the analgesic agent. Test the null hypothesis that all the analgesics are drawn from a common population of means.

Brand A	Brand B	Brand C	Brand D
28	34	29	22
19	23	24	31
30	20	33	18
25	16	21	24

6. A consumer organization randomly selected several gas clothes dryers of three leading manufacturers for study. The time required for each machine to dry a standard load of clothes was tabulated. Set up and test the appropriate null hypothesis. Conduct an HSD test comparing each brand with every other brand, employing $\alpha = 0.05$.

Brand A	Brand B	Brand C
42	52	38
36	48	44
47	43	33
43	49	35
38	51	32

7. Automobile tires, selected at random from six different brands, required the following braking distances, in feet, when moving at 25 mi/hr.* Set up and test the appropriate null hypothesis. Conduct an HSD test comparing each brand with every other brand, employing $\alpha = 0.01$.

Brand A	Brand B	Brand C	Brand D	Brand E	Brand F
22	25	17	21	27	20
20	23	19	24	29	14
24	26	15	25	24	17
18	22	18	23	25	15

8. If the F-ratio is less than 1.00, what should you conclude?

9. Determine whether there is a significant difference in state gasoline taxes among the three geographical areas given.

New England		Mideast		Far West	
Maine	8	New York	7	Wash.	9
N.H.	7	New Jersey	7	Oregon	7
Vermont	8	Penn.	8	Nevada	6
Mass.	6.5	Delaware	7	Calif.	7
R.I.	8	Maryland	7	Alaska	8
Conn.	8	D.C.	7	Hawaii	5

10. Perform an analysis of variance, using the data given in Exercise 27, Chapter 13.

11. Suppose typing speeds (words per minute) are compared for a sample of 24 people who attended four different secretarial schools. The following data are obtained:

School A	School B	School C	School D
50	55	50	70
50	60	65	80
55	65	75	65
60	55	55	70
45	70	60	75
55	65	65	60

Is there a significant difference in the typing speeds among the four groups?

---

*Source: Federal Highway Administration. *The 1962 World Almanac and Book of Facts.* L. H. Long (ed.). New York: Newspaper Enterprise Association, Inc., 1971, p. 122.

12. A nutritional expert divides a sample of bicyclers into three groups. Group B is given a vitamin supplement and group C is given a diet of health foods. Group A is instructed to eat as they normally do. The expert subsequently records the number of minutes it takes each person to ride six miles. See table below.

A	B	C
15	14	13
16	13	12
14	15	11
17	16	14
15	14	11

Set up the appropriate hypothesis and conduct an analysis of variance.

13. For Exercise 12, determine which diet or diets are superior.

14. In 1971 three baseball clubs showed the following numbers of home runs made by their players

Chicago Cubs:	2	16	28	2	21	2	2	19	0	4	8	6
Houston Astros:	9	2	1	10	13	1	12	0	1	2	7	7
Cincinnati Reds:	13	39	25	9	3	0	13	27	5	1	2	

Test the hypothesis that all three clubs were drawn from the same population with respect to hitting home runs. (See *The 1972 World Almanac*, p. 910–911.)

15. Assume that there are only four manufacturers of house paint, and manufacturer A states that his paint is superior to all the other paints. To test this claim, an investigator samples the number of years between the time a house is painted and the time it needs repainting, with the results shown in the accompanying table. Is manufacturer A's claim supported by the data? Compare the records of A and B.

A	B	C	D
4.5	4.0	2.5	3.5
5.5	4.5	3.0	3.0
5.0	4.0	3.0	4.0
5.5	3.5	3.5	3.0
6.0	3.0	4.0	4.5
5.0	4.5	2.5	3.0

16. Following are scores made by subjects in a 3×3 factorial experiment. Conduct the appropriate analysis of variance and show conclusions warranted by the analysis. Use $\alpha = 0.05$.

	A_1			A_2			A_3	
B_1	B_2	B_3	B_1	B_2	B_3	B_1	B_2	B_3
8	10	12	5	9	16	6	10	17
1	7	9	3	10	11	5	7	9
7	9	11	8	10	12	4	11	12
9	7	5	8	6	4	10	8	6
4	8	15	6	8	10	8	10	12
12	14	15	10	12	13	13	14	14

17. Following are scores made by subjects in a 2×3 factorial experiment. Conduct the appropriate analysis of variance and show conclusions warranted by the analysis. Use $\alpha = 0.05$.

	A_3			A_2	
B_1	B_2	B_3	B_1	B_2	B_3
4	5	4	8	6	11
6	8	6	7	9	9
7	3	2	9	12	13
9	7	5	11	8	7

PART IV

Inferential Statistics
Nonparametric
Tests of Significance

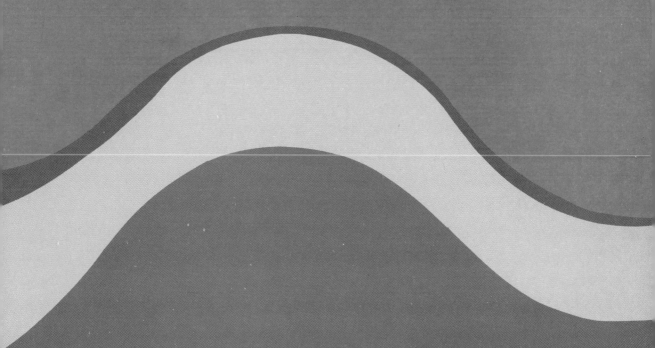

16

Power
and Power
Efficiency of a
Statistical Test

16.1 *The Concept of Power*

Throughout the first two parts of this book, only fleeting references were made to the power and the power efficiency of a statistical test (although they were not identified as such). Before proceeding into nonparametric tests of significance, we need to examine these concepts in more detail.

While discussing type I and type II errors in Section 11.5, we pointed out that the basic conservatism of scientists causes them to set up a rejection level sufficiently low to make type I errors less frequent than type II errors. In other words, the scientist would rather make the mistake of accepting a false null hypothesis than the mistake of rejecting a true one. However, this conservatism should not be construed to mean that the scientist is happy about the prospect of making type II errors. To the contrary, it is quite likely that many promising research projects have been abandoned because of the failure of the experimenter to reject the null hypothesis when it was actually false.

Now up to this point in the book, our concern has been to establish a level of significance that will reduce the likelihood of falsely rejecting the null hypothesis. In other words, we have been primarily concerned with avoiding type I rather than type II errors. However, the ideal statistical test is one which effects some sort of balance between these two types of error. Ideally, we should specify in advance of our study the probability of making both a type I and a type II error. In practice, however, most researchers content themselves with stating only the *p*-value, which they will employ to reject the null hypothesis. As we have seen, this *p*-value represents the probability of a type I error (that is, α).

When we begin to concern ourselves with effecting a balance between type I and type II errors, we are dealing with the concept of the **power of a test.** The power of a test is defined simply as the probability of rejecting the null hypothesis when it is in fact false. Symbolically, power is defined as follows:

Power of a Test

The probability of rejecting the null hypothesis when it is in fact false.

$$\text{Power} = 1 - \text{Probability of a type II error.}$$

If we let β represent the probability of a type II error, the definition of power becomes:

$$\text{Power} = 1 - \beta. \tag{16.1}$$

We can calculate the power of a test only when H_0 is false and we are given the true value of the population mean under H_1.

Before proceeding with a formal discussion of power, let us review a series of problems that appeared in the end-of-chapter exercises for Chapter 12 (Exercises 30 through 33). You will recall that we imagined drawing all possible pairs of samples from two populations of means.

Population 1 means: 3, 4, 5, 5, 6, 6, 6, 7, 7, 8, 9; $\mu_1 = 6$;
Population 2 means: 0, 1, 2, 2, 3, 3, 3, 4, 4, 5, 6; $\mu_2 = 3$.

We obtained the sampling distribution of differences between means shown in Table 16.1.

Then we pretended not to know the characteristics of the second population. We formulated the null hypothesis that the first and second populations are the same ($\mu_1 = \mu_2$). This sampling distribution of differences between means is shown in Table 16.2.

Note that, under the null hypotheses of no difference between population means, a difference equal to or greater than 5 or equal to or less than -5 would lead to the rejection of H_0 at $\alpha = 0.05$ ($0.0248 + 0.0248 = 0.0496$), two-tailed test.

Table 16.1 **Frequency and sampling distributions of differences between means when all possible sample means are selected, with replacement, from two populations of means in which $\mu_1 = 6$ and $\mu_2 = 3$. This represents the true sampling distribution of differences between means for the indicated populations of means.**

$\overline{X}_1 - \overline{X}_2$	f	$p(\overline{X}_1 - \overline{X}_2)$
9	1	0.0083
8	2	0.0165
7	5	0.0413
6	10	0.0826
5	14	0.1157
4	18	0.1488
3	21	0.1736
2	18	0.1488
1	14	0.1157
0	10	0.0826
-1	5	0.0413
-2	2	0.0165
-3	1	0.0083
$N_{\overline{X}_1 - \overline{x}_2} = 121$		$\sum p(\overline{X}_1 - \overline{X}_2) = 1.000$

Table 16.2 **Sampling distribution of the differences between means under $H_0 : \mu_1 = \mu_2$. (*Note:* We have assumed that population 2 is identical to population 1, that is, $\mu_1 = \mu_2$, and found all possible differences between means.)**

$\overline{X}_1 - \overline{X}_2$	f	$p(\overline{X}_1 - \overline{X}_2)$
6	1	0.0083 } 0.0248
5	2	0.0165
4	5	0.0413
3	10	0.0826
2	14	0.1157
1	18	0.1488
0	21	0.1736
−1	18	0.1488
−2	14	0.1157
−3	10	0.0826
−4	5	0.0413
−5	2	0.0165 } 0.0248
−6	1	0.0083
$N_{\overline{X}_1 - \overline{X}_2} = 121$		$\sum p(\overline{X}_1 - \overline{X}_2) = 1.0000$

Now we return to the *true* sampling distribution of differences between sample means (Table 16.1) and ask, "Under $H_0 : \mu_1 = \mu_2$, how often would we have rejected this false null hypothesis when $\alpha = 0.05$, two-tailed test? How often would we have *failed* to reject this false H_0?" Stated another way, how often would we have made a type II error?

Let's look at each of these questions in turn. Under $H_0 : \mu_1 = \mu_2$, we would reject the null hypothesis at $\alpha = 0.05$, two-tailed test, whenever we obtained a difference in sample means equal to or greater than 5 or equal to or less than −5. Looking at Table 16.1, we see that, under the *true* sampling distribution of differences, we would obtain a difference in means equal to or greater than 5 about 26% of the time (0.1157 + 0.0826 + 0.0413 + 0.0165 + 0.0083 = 0.2644). Under the *true* distribution, we would never obtain a difference in means equal to or less than −5. Thus the probability of correctly rejecting H_0 is 0.2644.

How often would we fail to reject H_0? Any difference in means less than 5 would not cause us to reject the null hypothesis. Since we know H_0 to be false, this entire region would represent a type II error. The probability of a type II error is therefore $1.000 - 0.2644 = 0.7356$. In other words, we would *fail* to reject a false null hypothesis almost 74 percent of the time. The power of the test is 0.2644, which means that we would correctly reject a false null hypothesis only about 26 percent of the time.

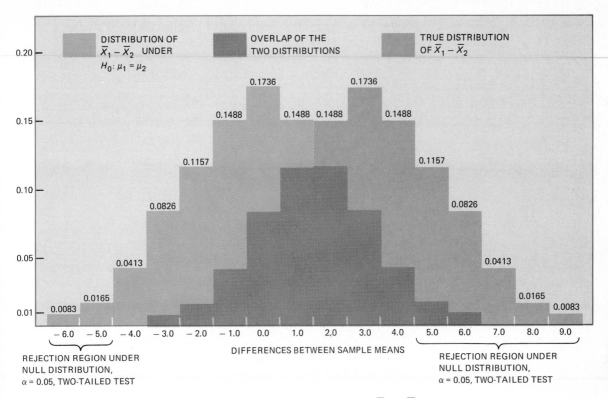

Figure 16.1 Probability histograms for the null and true distributions of $\overline{X}_1 - \overline{X}_2$ for the sampling example given in the text.

Figure 16.1 graphically presents probability histograms for both the null and the *true* distributions of $\overline{X}_1 - \overline{X}_2$ for the sampling problem we have been discussing.

We might note that failure to reject H_0 when it is false is not only a statistical and research problem; it is also an economic one. Research costs both time and money. One must question the advisability of undertaking a project when the probability of making a type II error is high. In this chapter, we discuss several strategies for reducing the risk of a type II error.

The following section illustrates the calculation of power.

16.2 *Calculation of Power: One-Sample Case*

A psychologist working for a large industrial firm has constructed two aptitude scales, which he administers interchangeably to incoming groups of trainees. He knows that the mean performance on scale A is 70, and on scale B is 72.

Both scales have a standard deviation of 5. He is chagrined to discover that his assistant failed to record which scale was administered to a group of 16 trainees. Scanning the data and noticing a number of low scores, he believes that this sample came from a population in which $\mu = 70$ (i.e., the scale A test was administered to this group), or $H_0: \mu = \mu_0 = 70$.

As a matter of fact, however, scale B had been administered. Thus, since we know that H_0 is false and we know that true value of μ under H_1 ($\mu = \mu_1 = 72$), we may calculate the power of the test (that is, the probability that he will correctly reject the false null hypothesis).

Let's set up this problem in formal statistical terms.

1. *Null hypothesis* (H_0): The mean of the population from which this sample was drawn equals 70; that is, $\mu = \mu_0 = 70$.

2. *Alternative hypothesis* (H_1): The mean of the population from which this sample was drawn equals 72, that is $\mu = \mu_1 = 72$.

3. *Statistical test:* Since σ is known, $z = (\overline{X} - \mu_0)/\sigma_{\overline{X}}$ is the appropriate test statistic.

4. *Significance level:* $\alpha = 0.01$ (one-tailed test).

5. *Sampling distribution:* The sampling distribution of the mean is known to be a normal distribution.

6. *Critical region:* $z_{0.01} = +2.33$. Since we are employing a one-tailed test, the critical region consists of all values of $z = (\overline{X} - \mu_0)/\sigma_{\overline{X}} \geq 2.33$.

Therefore the critical value of the sample statistic (the minimum value of $\overline{X}$ leading to rejection of H_0) is

$$\overline{X} = (2.33)\sigma_{\overline{X}} + \mu_0.$$

Thus the power equals the probability of obtaining this critical value in the distribution under H_1. The following steps are employed.

Step 1. Calculate the value of $\sigma_{\overline{X}}$:

$$\sigma_{\overline{X}} = \frac{\sigma}{\sqrt{N}} = \frac{5}{\sqrt{16}} = 1.25.$$

Step 2. Determine the critical value of $\overline{X}$ ($\alpha = 0.01$, one-tailed test):

$$\overline{X} = (2.33)(1.25) + 70 = 72.91.$$

Step 3. Determine the probability of obtaining this critical value in the *true* sampling distribution under H_1. The critical value of $\overline{X}$ has a z-score, in the distribution under H_1, of

$$z = \frac{72.91 - \mu_1}{\sigma_{\overline{X}}} = \frac{72.91 - 72.00}{1.25} = 0.73.$$

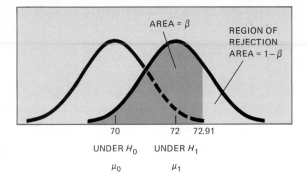

Figure 16.2
Region of rejection for H_0 in the distribution under H_1.

Referring to column C, Table A, in the Table section, we see that the probability of correctly rejecting H_0 is 23.27%. This probability is $1 - \beta$, or the power of the test. Incidentally, the probability of making a type II error (β) is 76.73%.

Figure 16.2 clarifies these relationships by indicating the region of rejection for H_0 in the *true* distribution under H_1, $1 - \beta$ or power. The shaded area indicates β, which is the probability of falsely accepting H_0.

16.3   *The Effect of Sample Size on Power*

Power varies as a function of several different factors. Let us examine the effect of varying the size of the sample on the power of the test. For example, let us employ $N = 25$ in the problem described in the previous section, and see what effect this has on the power of the test.

Employing the same procedures as described above, we shall test the hypothesis:

$$H_0 : \mu = \mu_0 = 70,$$

given that the true hypothesis is

$$H_1 : \mu = \mu_1 = 72.$$

Since, with $\alpha = 0.01$ (one-tailed test), the critical region consists of all values of $z = (\overline{X} - \mu_0)/\sigma_{\overline{X}} \geq 2.33$, the critical value of $\overline{X} = (2.33)\sigma_{\overline{X}} + \mu_0$. Thus

Step 1.   The value of $\sigma_{\overline{X}}$ is

$$\sigma_{\overline{X}} = \frac{\sigma}{\sqrt{N}} = \frac{5}{\sqrt{25}} = 1.00.$$

Step 2.   The critical value of $\overline{X}$ is

$$\overline{X} = (2.33)(1.00) + 70 = 72.33.$$

Step 3.   The critical value of $\overline{X}$ has a z-score in the distribution under H_1 of

$$z = \frac{72.33 - 72.00}{1.00} = 0.33.$$

Referring to column C, Table A, we see that the power of the test is 37.07%.

We have seen in our illustrative problem that when $N = 16$, then the power is 23.27%. When we increased our N to 25, power increased to 37.07%. Had we determined power for $N = 100$ for the above example, we would find that the power = 95.15%. Thus we may conclude that the power of a test is a function of N.

16.4 *The Effect of α-Level on Power*

In our previous discussion of type I and type II errors (Section 11.6), we indicated that the lower we set α, the less the likelihood of a type I error and the more the likelihood of a type II error. Since β is the probability that a type II error will occur, and power $= 1 - \beta$, the higher the α-level chosen, the greater the power of the test. One can readily demonstrate this relationship between α and power by substituting a different α-level in the preceding problems and observing the change in power.

For example, employing $\alpha = 0.05$ (one-tailed test) with $N = 16$, we find that the critical region consists of all values of

$$z = \frac{\overline{X} - \mu_0}{\sigma_{\overline{X}}} \geq 1.65.^*$$

Therefore the critical value of $\overline{X} = (1.65)\sigma_{\overline{X}} + \mu_0 = 72.06$. Thus power = 48.01% when $\alpha = 0.05$, as compared to 23.27% when $\alpha = 0.01$ in the example from Section 16.2.

---

*When $\alpha = 0.05$ (one-tailed test), the critical value of z is exactly halfway between 1.64 and 1.65. We shall employ $z = 1.65$ as the critical value so that $p < 0.05$ rather than $z = 1.64$, which results in $p > 0.05$.

Table 16.3   **Critical values of z required to reject H_0 at various α-levels as a function of the nature of H_1.**

Nature of H_1	
Directional (one-tailed test)	**Nondirectional (two-tailed test)**
$\alpha = 0.005$ $z = 2.58$	$z = \pm 2.81$
$\alpha = 0.01$ $z = 2.33$	$z = \pm 2.58$
$\alpha = 0.025$ $z = 1.96$	$z = \pm 2.24$
$\alpha = 0.05$ $z = 1.65$	$z = \pm 1.96$

16.5 The Effect of the Nature of H_1 on Power

The power of a test is also a function of the nature of the alternative hypothesis. In the event that H_0 is actually false, the directional or one-tailed H_1 is more powerful than the two-tailed test so long as the parameter is in the predicted direction.

Inspection of Table 16.3 reveals that the higher the α-level, the lower the absolute value of z required to reject H_0. We have already seen that power increases with increasing α. If follows that power increases as the critical value of z decreases. Table 16.3 shows that for any given α-level, the critical value of z is lower for a one-tailed test than for a two-tailed test. Therefore an obtained z that is not significant for a two-tailed test may be significant for a one-tailed test. Thus the one-tailed test is more powerful than its two-tailed alternative, unless the parameter happens to lie in a direction opposite to the one predicted. In this case, the one-tailed test will be less powerful.

16.6 Parametric versus Nonparametric Tests: Power

Another factor determining the power of a statistical test is the nature of the test itself. We can state as a general rule that for any given N, the parametric tests are more powerful than their nonparametric counterparts. It is primarily for this reason that we have deferred the discussion of statistical power until the present section of the text. For any given N, the parametric tests of significance (those assuming normally distributed populations with the same variance) entail less risk of a type II error. They are more likely to reject H_0 when H_0 is false. Thus given the choice between a nonparametric and a parametric test of significance, the parametric test should be employed so long as its underlying assumptions are fulfilled. However, as we shall see in the following chapters, there are numerous situations in which the very nature of our data excludes the possibility of a parametric test of significance. We shall therefore be forced to employ less powerful nonparametric tests.*

Why do nonparametric tests have less power? Succinctly stated, the answer is that parametric statistical tests (as opposed to nonparametric tests) make maximum use of all the information that is inherent in the data when the populations are normally distributed. Let's look at a simple illustration. Imagine that we have obtained the following scores in the course of conducting a study: 50, 34, 21, 12, 10. Now, if we were to convert these scores into ranks (an operation basic to nonparametric statistics involving ordinal scales), we would obtain 1, 2, 3, 4, 5. Note that all the information concerning the *magnitudes* of the scores is lost when we convert to ranks. The difference between the scores of 50 and 34 becomes "equivalent" when expressed as ranks to the difference between, say, 12 and 10. This greater sensitivity of the parametric tests to the magnitudes of scores makes them a more accurate basis for arriving at probability values when the basic assumptions of cardinality are met.

16.7   Calculation of Power: Two-Sample Case

So far, we have examined the effect of various factors on power, employing the one-sample case. All of the conclusions drawn apply equally to the two-sample case.

At this point, we should like to illustrate a sample problem in which we calculate the power of a test for the two-sample case.

Let us suppose that we have two populations with the following parameters:

$$\mu_1 = 80, \qquad \mu_2 = 75,$$
$$\sigma_1 = 6, \qquad \sigma_2 = 6.$$

If we draw a sample of nine cases from each of the two populations ($N_1 = 9$, $N_2 = 9$), we may test for the significance of the difference between the two

---

*It must be reiterated that the parametric tests are more powerful only when the assumptions underlying their use are valid. When the assumptions are not met, a nonparametric treatment may be as powerful as the parametric.

sample means obtained. First, let us set up this problem in formal statistical terms.

1. *Null hypothesis (H_0):* The two samples were drawn from populations with equal means, that is, $\mu_1 = \mu_2$.

2. *Alternative hypothesis (H_1):* The two samples were drawn from populations with different means, that is, $\mu_1 \neq \mu_2$.

3. *Statistical test:* Since we are comparing two sample means drawn from normally distributed populations with known variances, z is the appropriate test statistic.

4. *Significance level:* $\alpha = 0.01$.

5. *Sampling distribution:* The sampling distribution of the statistic $(\bar{X}_1 - \bar{X}_2)$ is known to be a normal distribution.

6. *Critical region:* $|z_{0.01}| \geq 2.58$ and $z \leq -2.58$.

In other words, when

$$|z| = \left| \frac{(\bar{X}_1 - \bar{X}_2) - (\mu_1 - \mu_2)}{\sigma_{\bar{X}_1 - \bar{X}_2}} \right| \geq 2.58,$$

we will reject H_0. Since H_0 means that $\mu_1 - \mu_2 = 0$, the lower critical value of $(\bar{X}_1 - \bar{X}_2) = (-2.58)\sigma_{\bar{X}_1 - \bar{X}_2}$, and the upper critical value of $(\bar{X}_1 - \bar{X}_2) = (+2.58)\sigma_{\bar{X}_1 - \bar{X}_2}$.

Now, since we know H_0 to be false (that is, $\mu_1 - \mu_2 \neq 0$), the power of the test is equal to the probability of obtaining these critical values. Any obtained sample difference which is less than these critical values will lead to a type II error (i.e., acceptance of a false H_0).

We employ the following steps to calculate power:

Step 1.   Calculate the value of $\sigma_{\bar{X}_1 - \bar{X}_2}$:

$$\sigma_{\bar{X}_1} = \frac{\sigma_1}{\sqrt{N_1}} = 2, \qquad \sigma_{\bar{X}_2} = \frac{\sigma_2}{\sqrt{N_2}} = 2,$$

$$\sigma_{\bar{X}_1 - \bar{X}_2} = \sqrt{\sigma_{\bar{X}_1}^2 + \sigma_{\bar{X}_2}^2} = 2.828.$$

Step 2.   Determine the critical values of $(\bar{X}_1 - \bar{X}_2)$, $\alpha = 0.01$, two-tailed test. The lower critical value is $(\bar{X}_1 - \bar{X}_2) = (-2.58)(2.828) = -7.296$. The upper critical value is $(\bar{X}_1 - \bar{X}_2) = 7.296$.

Step 3.   Determine the probability of obtaining these critical values in the *true* sampling distribution under H_1. The upper critical value of $(\bar{X}_1 - \bar{X}_2)$ has a z-score, in the distribution under H_1, of

$$z = \frac{7.296 - \mu_{\bar{X}_1 - \bar{X}_2}}{\sigma_{\bar{X}_1 - \bar{X}_2}} = \frac{7.296 - 5.0}{2.828} = 0.81.$$

Referring to column C, Table A, we see that the area beyond a z of 0.81 is 20.90%. The lower critical value of $(\bar{X}_1 - \bar{X}_2)$ has a z-score of

$$z = \frac{-7.296 - 5.0}{2.828} = -4.35.$$

A z of -4.35 is so large that only a negligible proportion of area falls beyond it ($<0.003\%$). Thus the power $= 20.90\%$.

16.8 The Effect of Correlated Measures on Power

In Section 14.2, we indicated that when subjects have been successfully matched on a variable correlated with the criterion variable, a statistical test that takes this correlation into account provides a more powerful test than one that does not. This may be readily demonstrated.

Employing the data in the preceding problem, let us assume that the nine subjects drawn from population 1 are matched on a related variable with the nine subjects drawn from population 2 and that the correlation between these two variables is 0.80

Since, with $\alpha = 0.01$ (two-tailed test), the critical region consists of all values of

$$|z| = \left| \frac{(\bar{X}_1 - \bar{X}_2) - (\mu_1 - \mu_2)}{\sigma_{\bar{X}_1 - \bar{X}_2}} \right| \geq 2.58,$$

the critical values of $(\bar{X}_1 - \bar{X}_2) = (\pm 2.58)\sigma_{\bar{X}_1 - \bar{X}_2}$.

Step 1. The value of $\sigma_{\bar{X}_1 - \bar{X}_2}$ is

$$\sigma_{\bar{X}_1 - \bar{X}_2} = \sqrt{\sigma_{\bar{X}_1}^2 + \sigma_{\bar{X}_2}^2 - 2r\sigma_{\bar{X}_1}\sigma_{\bar{X}_2}} = 1.26.$$

Step 2. The critical values of $(\bar{X}_1 - \bar{X}_2)$ are

$$(\bar{X}_1 - \bar{X}_2) = (\pm 2.58)(1.26) = \pm 3.25.$$

Step 3.   The lower critical value of $(\overline{X}_1 - \overline{X}_2)$ *has a z-score, in the distribution under* H_1, of

$$z = \frac{(-3.25 - 5.00)}{1.26} = -6.55.$$

Referring to Table A, we find that the area beyond a z of -6.55 is negligible. Therefore power will be determined according to the upper critical value.

The upper critical value of $(\overline{X}_1 - \overline{X}_2)$ has a z of

$$z = \frac{3.25 - 5.00}{1.26} = -1.39.$$

To find the probability of obtaining $(\overline{X}_1 - \overline{X}_2) \geq 3.25$, we refer to Table A to find the area *above* a z of -1.39. Thus power $= 100.00\% - 8.23\% = 91.77\%$. Since power $= 1 - \beta$, the probability of a type II error (β) is 8.23%.

16.9 *Power, Type I and Type II Errors*

Let us take a moment to tie together some of our observations about power and type I and type II errors. To begin, we must emphasize the fact that there are only two possibilities with respect to the null hypothesis; i.e., either it is true (for example, $\mu_1 = \mu_2$) or it is not true (for example, $\mu_1 \neq \mu_2$). These are two mutually exclusive situations. Now, since a type I error is defined as the probability of rejecting H_0 when it is true, two points should immediately be obvious.

1. If H_0 is *false,* the probability of a type I error is zero.
2. It is only when we *reject* H_0 that any possibility exists for a type I error. Such an error will be made only when H_0 is true, in which case the probability of a type I error is α.

Further, since a type II error is defined as the probability of accepting H_0 when it is false, we arrive at the following conclusions.

1. If H_0 is *true,* the probability of a type II error is zero.
2. It is only when we *accept* H_0 that any possibility exists for a type II error. Such an error will be made only when H_0 is false, in which case the probability of a type II error is β. It should be clear, then, that the concept of power, which is defined in terms of a type II error $(1 - \beta)$, applies only when H_0 is not true.

Table 16.4   **The type of error made as a function of the true status of H_0 and the statistical decision we have made. To illustrate, if H_0 is true (column 1) and we have rejected H_0 (row 2), we have made a type I error. If H_0 is false (column 2) and we have rejected H_0, we have made a correct decision.**

		True Status of H_0	
		H_0 True	H_0 False
Decision	Accept H_0	Correct $1 - \alpha$	Type II error β
	Reject H_0	Type I error α	Correct $1 - \beta$

Table 16.4 summarizes the probabilities associated with acceptance or rejection of H_0 depending on the true state of affairs. (Recall that this table was presented in Section 11.5.)

16.10 *Power Efficiency of a Statistical Test*

In Section 16.6, we pointed out that, when the underlying assumptions can be considered valid, parametric tests are more powerful than nonparametric tests for any given N. However, it is also true that when nonparametric tests are to be utilized, we can make any specific nonparametric test as powerful as a parametric test by employing a larger sample size. Thus test A may be more powerful than test B when the N's are equal, but B may be as powerful as A when an N of, say, 40 is used compared to an N of 30 with test A.

Power Efficiency

The increase in sample size required to make one test as powerful as a competing test.

The concept of **power efficiency** is concerned with the increase in sample size required to make one test as powerful as a competing test. Let us assume that test A is the most powerful for the type of data that we are analyzing. Let us also assume that test B is equal in power to test A when their Ns are 40 and 30 respectively. We let N_b represent the N required to make it as powerful as test A when N_a is used. The power efficiency of test B may now be stated:

$$\text{Power efficiency of test } B = 100 \frac{N_a}{N_b} \text{ percent.} \qquad (16.2)$$

Thus, the power efficiency of test B relative to test A is $100(^{30}/_{40})$ or 75%. Therefore, given that all the assumptions for employing test A are met, we shall have to use four cases of test B for every three cases of test A to achieve equal power. Of course, if the assumptions underlying test A are not met, the concept of power efficiency has no meaning, since test A should not be employed.

Chapter Summary

In this chapter, we discussed two important concepts: power and power efficiency. Power is defined as the probability of rejecting H_0 when it is actually false; i.e., *power* $= 1 - \beta$.

We demonstrated the calculation of power for the one-sample and the two-sample cases when H_0 is known to be false and the true value of the parameter under H_1 is known.

The calculation of power requires that we compute:

1. the standard error of the sampling distribution under both H_0 and H_1,
2. the critical value of the sample statistic—$\overline{X}$ in the one-sample case, $\overline{X}_1 - \overline{X}_1$ in the two-sample case,
3. the probability of obtaining this critical value in the sampling distribution under H_1. This probability is the power of the test.

We showed that power varies as a function of

1. sample size,
2. α level,
3. the nature of H_1,
4. the nature of the statistical test,
5. the use of correlated measures.

Power efficiency is concerned with the increase in sample size of a given test necessary to make it as powerful as another test employing a smaller N. Symbolically, the power efficiency of test B relative to test A may be represented as

$$\text{Power efficiency of test } B = (100)\frac{N_a}{N_b} \text{ percent.}$$

Terms to Remember

power of a test   power efficiency

EXERCISES

1. Test A has a power efficiency of 80% relative to test B. If in test B we employed a total of 24 subjects, what is the N required to achieve equal power with test A?

2. Employing the sample problem in Section 16.3, calculate power when $N = 100$.

3. Employing the sample problem in Section 16.7, demonstrate the effect of the nature of H_1 on power by calculating the power when $\alpha = 0.01$, *one*-tailed test— that is, $H_1 : \mu_1 > \mu_2$.

4. Employ $\alpha = 0.01$, two-tailed test, with the following two normal populations:

$$\mu_1 = 100, \qquad \mu_2 = 90,$$
$$\sigma_1 = 10, \qquad \sigma_2 = 10.$$

   a. If a sample of 25 cases is drawn from each population, find
      i. the probability of a type I error,
      ii. the probability of a type II error,
      iii. the power of the test.
   b. If two samples of 25 cases each are drawn from population 1, find
      i. the probability of a type I error,
      ii. the probability of a type II error,
      iii. the power of the test.

5. For Problem 6, Chapter 13, calculate the power for each of the four examples, employing $\alpha = 0.01$, one-tailed test. Which of the factors influencing power do these examples illustrate?

6. In Chapter 14, Problems 3 through 5, we saw that the use of correlated samples produced a t-ratio further removed from the region of rejection than the t-ratio based on independent samples. This would appear to contradict Section 16.8. Reconcile this disparity.

7. Explain why power is an economic as well as a research and statistical problem.

8. Why doesn't the concept of power apply when the null hypothesis is true?

9. Explain why a type I error cannot be made when the null hypothesis is false.

10. Assume that test A is the most powerful test for the data we are analyzing. What is the power efficiency of test B when $N_a = 20$ and the following values of N_b are required to make test B equally powerful?
    a. 25   b. 30   c. 35   d. 40   e. 50

11. Summarize the various factors affecting the power of a test. Enumerate the various ways that power may be increased.

17

Statistical Inference: Categorical Variables

17.1 *Introduction*

In recent years there has been a broadening in both the scope and the penetration of research in the behavioral and social sciences. Much provocative and stimulating research has been initiated in such diverse areas as personality, psychotherapy, group processes, economic forecasts, etc. New variables have been added to the arsenal of the researcher, many of which do not lend themselves to traditional parametric statistical treatment, either because of the scales of measurement employed or because of flagrant violations of the assumptions of these parametric tests. For these reasons, many new statistical techniques have been developed. In this chapter and the following one, we present a few choice dishes in the extensive nonparametric menu. See the following table.

Table of nonparametric tests appearing in chapters 17 and 18.

Scale of Measurement	One-Sample Case	Two-Sample Case	
		Related Samples	Independent Samples

Nominal	Binomial test
	  Section 17.2–17.3
	χ^2 test
	  Section 17.4
			χ^2 test
			  Section 17.5–17.6

Ordinal		Sign test
		  Section 18.4
		
		Wilcoxon matched-pairs
		signed-rank test
		  Section 18.5
			Mann-Whitney U
			  Section 18.2

A nonparametric test of significance is defined as one which makes no assumptions concerning the shape of the parent distribution or population, and accordingly is commonly referred to as a distribution-free test of significance.

Parametric techniques are usually preferable because of their greater sensitivity. This generalization is not true, however, when the underlying assumptions are seriously violated. Indeed, under certain circumstances (e.g., badly skewed distributions, particularly with small sample sizes) a nonparametric test may well be as powerful as its parametric counterpart.* Consequently the re-

---

*Numerous investigators have demonstrated the robustness of the *t* and *F* tests; i.e., even substantial departures from the assumptions underlying parametric tests do not seriously affect the validity of statistical inferences. For articles dealing with this topic, see Haber, Runyon, and Badia, *Readings in Statistics*. Reading, Mass.: Addison-Wesley Publishing Co., Inc. 1970.

Dogs: The best friend of a coronary patient?

BOX 17.1

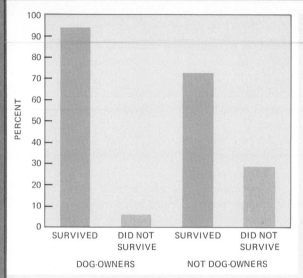

The cliché "Dog is man's best friend" is celebrated in both song and legend. Recent evidence suggests that the presence of a dog may also be therapeutic (Friedman, 1979)* A group of coronary patients were studied for one year following their release from the hospital. Fifty-three of these patients owned dogs and 39 did not. One year later, 11 of the patients who did not own dogs had died whereas only three of the dog owners succumbed.

In this study there are two nominal variables—status with respect to ownership of a pet dog and survival record after suffering a coronary heart disease. There are two values of each variable: owning vs. not owning a dog, and surviving vs. not surviving a heart condition. At the descriptive level, we could determine the percent of pet owners versus the percent of non-pet-owners who survived and failed to survive at least one year following hospitalization. These results are summarized in the bar graph at the left.

At the inferential level, the data can be cast in the form of a 2 × 2 contingency table. Reading downward, we see that fifty of fifty-three dog-owners survived at least one year. In contrast, only twenty-eight of thirty-nine non-dog-owners enjoyed a similar survival record. The appropriate test of significance—the chi square test—permits us to ascertain whether or not dog ownership and survival are related.

Survival Status	Status of Dog Ownership		
	Owners	Not Owners	Totals
Survived one year	50	28	78
Did not survive	3	11	14
Totals	53	39	92

2 × 2 contingency table showing the number of dog-owners and the number of non-dog-owners who survived at least one year following the onset of a coronary disease.

*Cited in a syndicated column by Dr. Neil Solomon in The Los Angeles Times, Jan. 25, 1979.

searcher is frequently faced with the difficult choice of a statistical test appropriate for his or her data.

At this point let us interject a word of caution with respect to the choice of statistical tests of inference. For heuristic purposes, we will take a few sample problems and subject them to statistical analyses employing several different tests of significance. This procedure will serve to clarify points of differences among the various tests. However, you may inadvertently draw an erroneous conclusion, namely, that researchers first collect their data, and then "shop around" for a statistical test that will be the most sensitive to any differences that exist. Actually, nothing could be further from the truth. The null hypothesis, alternative hypothesis, statistical test, sampling distribution, and level of significance should all be specified in *advance* of the collection of data. If we "shop around," so to speak, after the collection of the data, we tend to maximize the effects of any chance differences that favor one test over another. As a result, the possibility of a type I error (rejecting the null hypothesis when it is is true) is substantially increased.

Usually, we do not have the problem of choosing statistical tests in relation to categorical variables because nonparametric tests alone are suitable for enumerative data.

The problem of choosing a statistical treatment usually arises when we employ small samples* and/or when there is doubt concerning the normality of the underlying population distribution. In Chapter 18, we demonstrate several nonparametric statistical tests employed when such doubts arise.

17.2 *The Binomial Test*

Two-Category (Dichotomous) Population

Simplest form of nominal scale, containing two classes or categories.

In Section 2.4, when discussing various scales of measurement, we pointed out that the observation of unordered variables constitutes the lowest level of measurement. In turn, the simplest form of nominal scale is one that contains only two classes or categories, and is referred to variously as a **two-category** or **dichotomous population.** Examples of two-category populations are numerous: male and female, right and wrong on a test item, married and single, juvenile delinquent and nondelinquent, literate and illiterate. Some of these populations may be thought of as inherently dichotomous (e.g., male vs. female) and therefore not subject to measurement on a higher-level numerical scale, whereas others (e.g., literate and illiterate) may be thought of as continuous, varying from the absence of the quality under observation to different degrees of its manifestation. Obviously, whenever possible, the data we collect should be at the highest level of measurement that we can achieve. However, for a variety of reasons we cannot always scale a variable at the ordinal level or higher. Nevertheless, we are often called upon to collect nominally scaled data and to draw inferences from these data.

In a two-category population we define P as the proportion of cases in one class and $Q = 1 - P$ as the proportion of the other class.

Use of the binomial sampling distribution to test hypotheses concerning the value of P under H_0 was demonstrated in Chapter 11. For illustrative purposes we restricted our discussion to $H_0: P = Q = \frac{1}{2}$. However, it is possible to test hypotheses concerning *any* value of P.

---

*When large samples are employed, the parametric tests are almost always appropriate because of the *central-limit theorem* (Section 12.2).

The probabilities associated with specific outcomes may be obtained by employing Formula (17.1):

$$p(x) = \frac{N!}{x!(N-x)!} P^x Q^{N-x}, \qquad (17.1)$$

where

x = the number of objects in one category or the number of successes,

$N - x$ = the number of objects in the remaining category or the number of failures.

N = the total number of objects or total number of trials,

$p(x)$ = the probability of x objects in one category,

$!$ = the factorial sign directs us to multiply the indicated value by all integers less than it but greater than zero, e.g., if $N = 5$, $N!* = 5 \cdot 4 \cdot 3 \cdot 2 \cdot 1 = 120$.

A sample problem should serve to illustrate the use of Formula (17.1) in the testing of hypotheses.

Sample Problem

The dean of students in a large university claims that ever since the sale of cigarettes was prohibited on campus, the proportion of students who smoke has dropped to 0.30. However, previous observations at other institutions where the sale of cigarettes had been banned found little effect on smoking behavior; i.e., far greater than 0.30 of the students continue to smoke.

Nine students, selected at random, are asked to indicate whether or not they smoke. Six of these students respond in the affirmative.

To test the validity of the dean's claim, we will let P represent the proportion of students in the population who smoke, and Q, the proportion of students. who do not smoke.

1. *Null hypothesis* (H_0): $P \leq 0.30$, $Q \geq 0.70$.
2. *Alternative hypothesis* (H_1): $P > 0.30$, $Q < 0.70$. Note that H_1 is directional.
3. *Statistical test:* Since we are dealing with a two-category population, the binomial test is appropriate.
4. *Significance level:* $\alpha = 0.05$.
5. *Sampling distribution:* The sampling distribution is given by the binomial expansion, Formula (17.1).

---

*In obtaining the binomial probabilities, it is important to remember that $0! = 1$ and any value other than zero raised to the zero power equals 1, i.e., $X^0 = 1$.

6. *Critical region:* The critical region consists of all values of x that are so large that the probability of their occurrence under H_0 is less than or equal to 0.05. Since H_1 is directional, the critical region is one-tailed.

In order to determine whether the obtained x lies in the critical region, we must obtain the sum of the probabilities associated with $x = 9$, $x = 8$, $x = 7$, and $x = 6$.

To illustrate, employing Formula (17.1) we find that the probability of $x = 9$, that is, if $P = 0.3$ (under H_0) the probability that all of the 9 students smoke, is

$$p9 = \frac{9!}{9!(9-9)!}(0.3)^9(0.7)^{9-9}$$
$$= 0.3^9 = 0.000019683.$$

The probability of $x = 8$ is

$$p8 = 9(0.3)^8(0.7)^1 = 0.000413343.$$

The probability of $x = 7$ is

$$p7 = 36(0.3)^7(0.7)^2 = 0.003857868.$$

Finally, the probability of $x = 6$ is

$$p6 = 84(0.3)^6(0.7)^3 = 0.021003948.$$

Thus the probability that at least 6 out of 9 students smoke when $P = 0.30$ is the sum of the above probabilities, that is, $p(x \geq 6) = 0.025$.

Decision • Since the obtained probability is less than 0.05, we may reject H_0. In other words, the dean's claim would appear to be in error.

The preceding example was offered to illustrate the application of Formula (17.1) when $P \neq Q \neq \frac{1}{2}$. However, when $N \leq 49$, and $P \neq Q \neq \frac{1}{2}$, Table N, in the Table section, may be employed to obtain the critical values of x directly for selected values of P and Q. Referring to Table N, for $N = 9$ and $P = 0.30$, we find that x must be equal to or greater than 6 to reject H_0 at $\alpha = 0.05$.

Incidentally, when $P = Q = \frac{1}{2}$ and $N \leq 50$, Table M provides both one- and two-tailed critical values of x, at $\alpha = 0.01$ and $\alpha = 0.05$, when x is defined as the larger of the observed frequencies. For example, if we toss a coin ten times ($N = 10$), we find that a critical value of $x = 9$ is required for rejection of H_0 ($P = Q = \frac{1}{2}$) at $\alpha = 0.05$, two-tailed test.

17.3 Normal-Curve Approximation to Binomial Values

As N increases, the binomial distribution approaches the normal distribution. The approximation is more rapid as P and Q approach $\frac{1}{2}$. On the other hand, as P or Q approaches 0, the approximation to the normal curve becomes poorer for any given N. A good rule of thumb to follow, when considering the normal-curve approximation to the binomial, is that the product NPQ should equal at least 9 when P approaches 0 or 1, and N should equal 25 or greater when $P = Q = \frac{1}{2}$. Even with somewhat smaller Ns, however, the approximation is excellent. Accepting these restrictions, we see that the sampling distribution of x, defined as the number of objects in one category, is normal, with a mean equal to NP and a standard deviation equal to $\sqrt{NPQ}$.

To test the null hypothesis, we put x into standardized form:

$$z = \frac{x - NP}{\sqrt{NPQ}}. \qquad (17.2)$$

The distribution of the z-scores is approximately normal, with a mean equal to zero and a standard deviation equal to one. Thus the probability of any given x equals the probability of its corresponding z-score.

Let us look at an example in which $x = 5$, $N = 20$, $P = Q = \frac{1}{2}$, and $\alpha = 0.05$, two-tailed test. To obtain the probability of $x \leq 5$, we put x into standardized form and we have

$$z = \frac{5 - 10}{\sqrt{(20)(0.5)(0.5)}}$$
$$= \frac{-5.00}{\sqrt{5.00}} = \frac{-5.00}{2.24} = -2.23.$$

Recall that $z \geq |1.96|$ is required for significance at $\alpha = 0.05$, two-tailed test. Since our obtained z of -2.23 exceeds the critical value, we may reject H_0.

Note that, if we look up the result in Table M under $N = 20$ and $\alpha = 0.05$, two-tailed test, we find that $N - x \geq 15$ is required to reject H_0. In the present problem, $N - x = 15$, so we reject the null hypothesis and assert H_1. This is precisely the same decision we make when using the normal approximation to binomial values. Since Table M presents critical values through $N = 50$, we recommend using the normal approximation to the binomial only when N exceeds 50.

17.4 *The χ^2 One-Variable Case*

Suppose you are a market researcher hired by a soap manufacturer to conduct research on the packaging of its product. Realizing that color may be an important determinant of consumer selection, you conduct the following study. Six hundred homemakers, selected by an accepted sampling technique, are each given three differently packaged cakes of the same brand of soap. They are told that the three soaps are made according to different formulas and that the distinctive coloring of the packages is merely to aid their identification of each soap. One month later, you inform the homemakers that they are each to receive a free case of soap of their own choosing. Their selections are listed below.

	Color of Wrapper			Marginal Total
	Red	White	Brown	
Number of homemakers selecting	200	300	100	600

One-Variable Test ("Goodness-of-Fit" Technique)

Test of whether or not a significant difference exists between the *observed* number of cases falling into each category, and the *expected* number of cases, based on the null hypothesis.

This is the type of problem for which the χ^{2}* **one-variable test** is ideally suited. In single-variable applications, the χ^2 test has been described as a **"goodness-of-fit" technique:** It permits us to determine whether or not a significant difference exists between the *observed* number of cases falling into each category, and the *expected* number of cases, based on the null hypothesis. In other words, it permits us to answer the question, "How well does our observed distribution fit the theoretical distribution?"

What we require, then, is a null hypothesis that allows us to specify the expected frequencies in each category and, subsequently, a test of this null hypothesis. The null hypothesis may be tested by

$$\chi^2 = \sum_{i=1}^{k} \frac{(f_o - f_e)^2}{f_e},\qquad(17.3)$$

where

f_o = the observed number in a given category,
f_e = the expected number in that category,

$$\sum_{i=1}^{k} = \text{directs us to sum this ratio over all } k \text{ categories.}$$

---

*The symbol χ^2 will be used to denote the test of significance as well as the quantity obtained from applying the test to observed frequencies, whereas the word "chi-square" will refer to the theoretical chi-square distribution.

As is readily apparent, if there is close agreement between the observed frequencies and the expected frequencies, the resulting χ^2 will be small, leading to a failure to reject the null hypothesis. As the discrepancy $(f_o - f_e)$ increases, the value of χ^2 increases. The larger the χ^2, the more likely we are to reject the null hypothesis.

In our example, the null hypothesis would be that there is an equal preference for each color, i.e., 200 is the expected frequency in each category. Thus

$$\chi^2 = \frac{(200 - 200)^2}{200} + \frac{(300 - 200)^2}{200} + \frac{(100 - 200)^2}{200}$$
$$= 0 + 50.00 + 50.00$$
$$= 100.00.$$

In studying Student's t-ratio (Section 12.5), we saw that the sampling distributions of t varied as a function of degrees of freedom. The same is true for χ^2. However, assignments of degrees of freedom with the t-ratio are based on N, whereas for χ^2 the degrees of freedom are a function of the number of categories (k). In the one-variable case, df $= k - 1$.* Table B lists the critical values of χ^2 for various α-levels. If the obtained χ^2 value exceeds the critical value at a given probability level, the null hypothesis may be rejected at that level of significance.

In this example, $k = 3$. Therefore df $= 2$. Employing $\alpha = 0.01$, we find that Table B indicates that a χ^2 value of 9.21 or greater is required for significance. Since our obtained value of 100.00 is greater than 9.21, we may reject the null hypothesis and assert instead that color of packaging is a significant determinant for soap preference among homemakers.

17.5   The χ^2 Test of the Independence of Categorical Variables†

So far in this chapter, we have been concerned with the one-variable case. In practice, we do not encounter the one-variable case too frequently when employing categorical variables. More often we ask questions concerning the interrelationships between and among variables. For example, we may ask:

---

*Since the marginal total is fixed, only $k - 1$ categories are free to vary. Given that the total is 600, as soon as two cells or categories are filled, the third is completely determined. Thus, there are only two degrees of freedom: once red is 200 and white is 300, brown *must* be 100.

†Most textbooks recommend the Yates correction for continuity and that expected cell frequencies equal or exceed 5 when df $= 1$. Based on convincing evidence (Dunlap, 1974; Camilli and Hopkins, 1978), we have dropped these recommendations in this edition.

1. Is there a difference in the crime rate of children coming from different socioeconomic backgrounds? (In other words, is crime rate independent of socioeconomic background, or does it depend in part on this background?)

2. If we are conducting an opinion poll, can we determine whether there is a difference between males and females in their opinions about a given issue? (Stated another way, does the opinion on a given issue depend to any extent on the gender of the respondent?)

These are but two examples of problems for which the χ^2 technique has an application. You could undoubtedly extend this list to include many campus activities, such as attitudes of fraternity brothers versus nonfraternity students toward certain basic issues (e.g., cheating on exams), or differences in grading practices among professors in various departments of study. All these problems have some things in common: (1) They deal with two or more nominal categories in which (2) the data consist of a frequency count that is tabulated and placed in the appropriate cells.

These examples also share an additional and more important characteristic: (3) There is no immediately obvious way to assign expected frequency values to each category. However, as we shall point out shortly, what we must do is base our expected frequencies on the obtained frequencies themselves.

Let's take a look at an actual example. Visitors in developing nations frequently experience an acute intestinal affliction that is variously referred to as Montezuma's Revenge, Delhi Belly, Galloping Gollies, or, mundanely, Traveler's Diarrhea. Indeed, the anticipation of traveling to distant lands is often dimmed by the relatively high risk of spending much of the vacation sightseeing in the toilet. A team of medical researchers recently evaluated the effectiveness of a drug called doxycycline in curbing the incidence of this disorder. A total of 39 Peace-Corps volunteers in Kenya participated in the study. Over a three-week period, 18 received the actual drug, while the remaining 21 volunteers were given a placebo—an inert substance that resembled the drug. The results of this study are summarized in Table 17.1. We must now apply a test of significance. In formal statistical terms,

1. *Null hypothesis (H_0):* There is no difference in the incidence of Traveler's Diarrhea among those receiving the drug and those receiving the placebo.

2. *Alternative hypothesis (H_1):* There is a difference in the incidence of the disorder among drug and placebo subjects.

3. *Statistical test:* Since the two groups (drug and placebo) are independent and the data are in terms of frequencies in discrete categories, the χ^2 test of independence is the appropriate statistical test.

4. *Significance level:* $\alpha = 0.05$.

Table 17.1 **2 × 2 contingency table, showing the number of volunteers in the drug and placebo groups contracting Traveler's Diarrhea over a three-week period.**

Experimental Condition	Outcome of Study		Totals
	Contracted Disorder	**Failed to Contract Disorder**	
Drug group	a) 1	b) 17	18
Placebo group	c) 9	d) 12	21
Totals	10	29	39

5. *Sampling distribution:* The sampling distribution is the chi-square distribution with df $= (r - 1)(c - 1)$.

   Since marginal totals are fixed, the frequency of only one cell is free to vary. Therefore we have a one-degree-of-freedom situation. The general rule for finding df in the two-variable case is $(r - 1)(c - 1)$, in which r = number of rows and c = number of columns. Thus in the present example, df $= (2 - 1)(2 - 1) = 1$.

6. *Critical region:* Table B shows that for df $= 1$, $\alpha = 0.05$, the critical region consists of all values of $\chi^2 \geq 3.84$. χ^2 is calculated from the formula

$$\chi^2 = \sum_{r=1}^{r} \sum_{c=1}^{c} \frac{(f_o - f_e)^2}{f_e},$$
(17.4)

where

$$\sum_{r=1}^{r} \sum_{c=1}^{c}$$

directs us to sum this ratio over both rows and columns.

The *main problem* now is to decide on a basis for determining the expected cell frequencies. Let us concentrate for a moment on cell (a). The two marginal totals common to cell (a) are row 1 marginal and column 1 marginal. If the null hypothesis is correct, and the incidence of the disorder is independent of condition, we would expect the same proportion of subjects in the drug group to contract the disorder as subjects in the placebo group. Since 18 of the total sample of 39 are in the drug condition, we would expect that $(18/39) \times 10$ would be found in cell (a). This figure comes to 4.62.

Since we have a one-degree-of-freedom situation, the expected frequencies in all the remaining cells are determined as soon as we have calculated one expected cell frequency. Consequently we obtain all the remaining expected cell frequencies by subtracting from the appropriate marginal totals. Thus cell (b) is $18 - 4.62$ or 13.38, cell (c) is $10 - 4.62$ or 5.38, and cell (d) is $29 - 13.38$ or 15.62. To make certain that no error was made in our original calculation of the expected frequency for cell (a), it is wise to independently calculate the expected frequency for *any* of the remaining cells. If this figure agrees with the result we obtained by subtraction, we may feel confident that we made no error. Thus the expected frequency for cell (d), obtained through direct calculation, is

$$\frac{21}{39} \times 29 = 15.62.$$

Since this figure does agree with the result obtained by subtraction, we may proceed with our calculation of the χ^2 value.

Incidentally, you may have noted that there is a simple rule that may be followed in determining expected frequency of a given cell: You multiply the marginal frequencies common to that cell and divide by N.

Table 17.2 presents the obtained data, with the expected cell frequencies in the lower right-hand corner of each cell.

Now, all that remains is to calculate the χ^2 value.

It can be seen that a total of ten subjects became ill. Of these, only one was in the drug condition. The remaining nine were in the control or placebo group. Is this difference sufficiently large to justify the conclusion that the drug was effective?

$$\chi^2 = \frac{(1 - 4.62)^2}{4.62} + \frac{(17 - 13.38)^2}{13.38} + \frac{(9 - 5.38)^2}{5.38} + \frac{(12 - 15.62)^2}{15.62}$$

Table 17.2   Number of volunteers in the drug and placebo groups contracting Traveler's Diarrhea over a three-week period (expected frequencies within parentheses).

Experimental Condition	Outcome of Study		Totals
	Contracted Disorder	Failed to Contract Disorder	
Drug group	1 (4.62)	17 (13.38)	18
Placebo group	9 (5.38)	12 (15.62)	21
Totals	10	29	

Since the χ^2 value of 7.09 is greater than 3.84 required for significance at the 0.05 level, we may reject H_0. In other words, we may conclude that the drug is effective in curbing the incidence of Traveler's Diarrhea.

In research we often find that we have more than two subgroups within a nominal class. For example, we might have three categories in one scale and four in another, resulting in a 3×4 contingency table. The procedure for obtaining the expected frequencies is the same as the one for the 2×2 contingency table. Of course, the degrees of freedom will be greater than 1 (e.g., 3×4 contingency table, df = 6).

CASE EXAMPLE • 17.1
The Successful Women

With the relatively recent changes in the traditional female sex roles, much attention has been directed to the possible impact of these changes on various aspects of the behavior and emotions of contemporary women. In this study, 33 women completed Horner's scale of fear of success (FOS), as well as other questionnaires aimed at tapping attitudes about sex-role traditionalism, political beliefs, and educational levels.

In one facet of the study, the women were subdivided into two groups—those with fear of success (FOS) and those without fear of success (no-FOS). They were further subdivided in terms of educational level. The results are summarized in Table 17.3.

Let's test the null hypothesis that there is no difference in fear of success by educational level against the alternative hypothesis that there is a difference. We shall use $\alpha = 0.01$.

Table 17.3   Relationship between FOS and educational level.

Educational level	FOS	No-FOS	Total
Less than BA	6	8	14
BA degree	6	1	7
Some graduate school	10	1	11
Column totals	22	10	33

The expected cell frequencies are shown in Table 17.4

The critical value at $\alpha = 0.01$ with df = 2 is 9.210. Since obtained χ^2 exceeds this value, we may reject H_0 and assert H_1. Examination of the data

Table 17.4 **Expected cell frequencies in the study of the relationship between FOS and educational level.**

Educational Level	FOS	No-FOS	Total
Less than BA	7.21	6.79	14
BA degree	3.60	3.39	7
Some graduate school	5.67	5.33	11
Column totals	17	16	33

$$X^2 = \frac{(6 - 7.21)^2}{7.21} + \frac{(9 - 6.79)}{6.79} + \cdots + \frac{(1 - 5.33)^2}{5.33}$$
$$= 11.634$$
$$df = (r - 1)(c - 1) = 2$$

reveals a clear-cut tendency for fear of success to increase with increasing educational level. Note that this study is not a true experiment, but is more in the nature of a correlational investigation. Although we can conclude that there is a statistically significant increase in FOS with educational level, we cannot make a strong statement of causality. Several possibilities present themselves one of which is that the more educated women are employed at levels that put them into competition with men, the more they may demand of themselves.

Based on Carmen M. Caballero, Patricia Giles, and Phillip Shaver (1975), "Sex-Role Traditionalism and Fear of Success", *Sex Roles,* **1** *(4),* 319–326.

17.6 *Limitations in the Use of* χ^2

A fundamental assumption in the use of χ^2 is that each observation or frequency is independent of all other observations. Consequently one may not make several observations of the same individual and treat each as though it were independent of all the other observations. Such an error produces what is referred to as an **inflated N,** that is, you are treating the data as though you had a greater number of independent observations than you actually have. This error is extremely serious and may easily lead to the rejection of the null hypothesis when it is in fact true.

Consider the following hypothetical example. Imagine that you are a student in a sociology course and as a class project you decide to poll the student body to determine whether male and female students differ in their opinions on some issue of contemporary significance. Each of 15 members of the class is asked to obtain replies from 10 respondents, 5 male and 5 female. The results are listed in Table 17.5

Inflated N

An error produced whenever several observations are made on the same individual and treated as though they were independent observations.

Table 17.5

Sex	Response to Question		
	Approve	Disapprove	
Male	30 (40)	45 (35)	75
Female	50 (40)	25 (35)	75
	80	70	150

$$\chi^2 = 10.71$$

Employing $\alpha = 0.05$, we find that the critical region consists of all the values of $\chi^2 \geq 3.84$. Since the obtained χ^2 of 10.71 > 3.84, you reject the null hypothesis of no difference in the opinions of male and female students on the issue in question. You conclude instead that approval of the issue is dependent on the sex of the respondent.

Subsequent to the study, you discover that a number of students were inadvertently polled as many as two or three times by different members of the class. Consequently the frequencies within the cells are not independent since some individuals had contributed as many as two or three responses. In a reanalysis of the data, in which only one frequency per respondent was permitted, you obtain the results shown in Table 17.6

Note that now the obtained χ^2 of 2.72 < 3.84; thus you must accept H_0. The failure to achieve independence of responses resulted in a serious error in the original conclusion. Incidentally, you should note that the requirement of independence within a cell or condition is basic to *all* statistical tests. We have mentioned this specifically in connection with the χ^2 test because violations may be very subtle and not easily recognized.

Table 17.6

Sex	Response to Question		
	Approve	Disapprove	
Male	28 (32.5)	37 (32.5)	65
Female	32 (27.5)	23 (27.5)	55
	60	60	120

$$\chi^2 = 2.72$$

Chapter Summary

In this chapter, we have discussed four tests of significance employed with categorical variables, i.e., the binomial test, the normal approximation to the binomial, the χ^2 one-variable test, and the χ^2 two-variable test.

1. We saw that the binomial may be employed to test null hypotheses when frequency counts are distributed between two categories or cells. When $P = Q = \frac{1}{2}$ and when $N \leq 50$, Table M provides both one- and two-tailed critical values $\alpha = 0.05$ and $\alpha = 0.01$. When $P \neq Q$, probabilities may be obtained by employing Formula (17.1), which is based on the binomial expansion. When $N \leq 49$, Table N provides the critical values for the selected values of P and Q. A rule of thumb is that NPQ must equal or exceed 9 as P approaches 0 or 1, to permit the use of the normal approximation to the binomial.

2. The χ^2 one-variable test has been described as a "goodness-of-fit" technique, permitting us to determine whether or not a significant difference exists between the *observed* number of cases appearing in each category and the *expected* number of cases specified under the null hypothesis.

3. The χ^2 two-variable case may be employed to determine whether two variables are related or independent. If the χ^2 value is significant, we may conclude that the variables are dependent, or related. In this chapter, we restricted our discussion to the 2×2 contingency table. However, the procedures are easily extended to include more than two categories within each variable.

4. Finally, we discussed an important limitation on the use of the χ^2 test: the frequency counts must be independent of one another. Failure to meet this requirement results in an error known as the *inflated N* and may well lead to the rejection of the null hypothesis when it is true (type I error).

Terms to Remember

two-category (dichotomous) population   **inflated N**

one-variable test ("goodness-of-fit" technique)

EXERCISES

1. In 9 tosses of a single coin,
    a. what is the probability of obtaining exactly 7 heads?
    b. what is the probability of obtaining as many as 8 heads?
    c. what is the probability of obtaining a result as rare as 8 heads?

2. A revelation to many students is the surprisingly low probability of obtaining a passing grade on multiple-choice examinations when the selection of alternatives is made purely on a chance basis (i.e., without any knowledge of the material covered on the exam). If 60% is considered a passing grade on a 40-item multiple-choice test, determine the probability of passing when there are
    a. four alternatives,   b. three alternatives,   c. two alternatives.

3. In reference to Exercise 4, Chapter 15, show how Table N might be employed to determine the critical values of various numbers of successes (i.e., rejection of H_0 at $\alpha = 0.05$) out of ten attempts.

4. A study was conducted in which three groups of rats (5 per group) were reinforced under three different schedules of reinforcement (100% reinforcement, 50% reinforcement, 25% reinforcement). The number of bar-pressing responses obtained during extinction are shown below.

100%	50%	25%
615	843	545

Criticize the use of chi-square as the appropriate statistical technique.

5. The World Series may last from four to seven games. During the period 1922–1979, the distribution of the number of games played per series was as follows:

Number of games	4	5	6	7
Frequency of occurrence	11	11	11	25

For these data, test the hypothesis that each number of games is equally likely to occur.

6. In a large Eastern university, a study of the composition of the student council reveals that 6 of its 8 members are political-science majors. In the entire student body of 1200 students, 400 are political-science majors. Set up this study in formal statistical terms and draw the appropriate conclusions.

7. A study was conducted to determine if there is a relationship between socioeconomic class and attitudes toward a new urban-renewal program. The results are listed below.

Socioeconomic Class	Disapprove	Approve
Middle	90	60
Lower	200	100

Set up this study in formal statistical terms and draw the appropriate conclusion.

8. Construct the sampling distribution of the binomial when $P = 0.20$, $Q = 0.80$, and $N = 6$.

9. Out of 300 castings on a given mold, 27 were found to be defective. Another mold produced 31 defective castings in 500. Determine whether there is a significant different in the proportion of defective castings produced by the two molds.

10. Employ the χ^2 test, one-variable case for the example shown in Section 17.3 of the text. Verify that $\chi^2 = z^2$ in the one-degree-of-freedom situation.

11. In a study concerned with preferences of packaging for potato chips, 100 people in a high-income group and 200 people in a lower-income group were interviewed. The results of their choices follow:

Preference Stated	Upper-Income Group	Lower-Income Group
Prefer metallic package	36	84
Prefer waxed-paper package	39	51
Prefer cellophane package	16	44
Have no preference	9	21

What conclusions would you draw from these data?

12. Suppose that 100 random drawings with replacement from a deck of cards produced 28 hearts, 19 clubs, 31 diamonds, and 22 spades. Would you consider these results unusual?

13. In polling 46 interviewees drawn at random from a specified population, we find that 28 favor and 18 oppose a certain routing of a highway. Test the hypothesis that the sample was drawn from a population in which $P = Q = \frac{1}{2}$. Use $\alpha = 0.05$, two-tailed test.

14. Suppose a study was conducted that compared the types of investments made by 115 persons who were considered conservative and 125 individuals who were judged as likely to take risks. What can you conclude from the following results:

Type of Investment	Type of Investor	
	Conservative	Risk-Taker
Government bonds	75	45
Stocks	40	80

15. Suppose a company manufactured an equal number of three different file cabinets. The capacity of each cabinet was equal, but the designs were different. The first 300 buyers ordered 125 of type A, 100 of type B, 75 of type C. Should the company continue to produce an equal number of each design?

16. In Exercise 15, if the first 300 buyers ordered 115 cabinets of type A, 95 of type B, and 90 of type C, should the company continue its present production policy?

17. Assume you are testing a die to determine if it is biased. With 90 tosses, you obtain 13 ones, 18 twos, 13 threes, 23 fours, 9 fives, and 14 sixes. What would you conclude?

18. In Exercise 17, suppose you wanted to compare the number of times a toss shows an odd number with the number of times it is even. Using the z-score, can you conclude that the die is unbiased?

19. Use the χ^2 test to determine the answers for Exercise 18.

20. Suppose that a recording company is interested in the type of cover to put on an album. It sends the same record with three different covers to a store. At the end of a month, it is found that the following number of albums have been sold:

Type A Cover	Type B Cover	Type C Cover
41	50	20

Is the company in a position to determine which type of cover it should use?

21. In Chapter 1, Exercise 4, we reported a study by Professor Yetman showing the number of white and black athletes who had an opportunity to appear in commercials. The following 2×2 table summarizes the results:

Racial Background of Athletes	Appearance in Commercials	
	No Opportunity	Opportunity
White	3	8
Nonwhite	11	2

Test the null hypothesis that opportunity to appear in commercials is independent of racial background (i.e., whites and nonwhites have an equal opportunity to appear).

22. Using the data presented at the beginning of this chapter, test the null hypothesis that ownership of a dog is unrelated to survival.

23. In the exercise above, we found a significant relationship between dog ownership and survival following coronary heart disease. Critique the conclusion, "Dog ownership leads to better survival rates of coronary victims," in the light of what we know about correlation and causation.

24. In the study reported in Case Example 17.1 (Caballero, et al., 1975), the political beliefs of FOS subjects were compared with those of no-FOS subjects.* The results are summarized below:

Political Categories	FOS	No-FOS
Radical or liberal	14	4
Moderate or conservative	2	8

*Five subjects failed to provide political information.

Set up and test H_0 that political beliefs and FOS are independent, using $\alpha = 0.01$.

25. A field study tested the hypothesis that "complex social behavior that appears to be enacted mindfully instead may be performed without conscious attention to

relevant semantics." (Ellen Langer, Arthur Blank, and Benzoin Chanowitz (1978), "The Mindlessness of Ostensibly Thoughtful Action: The Role of Placebic Information in Interpersonal Interaction," *J. Pers. and Soc. Psych.*, **36** *(6)* 635–642, the quotation from 635). The experimenter requested that another person step aside to allow the experimenter to use the machine. In the no-information condition, the experimenter gave no reason for the request. In the placebic condition, the experimenter said, "Excuse me, I have 5 (20) pages. May I use the Xerox machine, because I have to make copies?" In the information condition, the reason given for the request was that the experimenter was in a rush. A small favor was a request to make five copies of a single page as compared to a big favor to make 20 copies. For instructional purposes, we have divided the analyses into three separate comparisons shown in the table below.

Set up and test three separate null hypotheses, using $\alpha = 0.05$.

| Response of Subjects | Conditions | | | | | |
| | (a) No Information | | (b) Placebic Information | | (c) Information | |
	Small Request	Large Request	Small Request	Large Request	Small Request	Large Request
Complied	9	6	14	6	15	5
Did not comply	6	9	1	9	9	1

Refer to Exercise 24, and graph the proportions complying in each condition. Is there evidence of an interaction between compliance and size of the request?

18

Statistical Inference: Ordinally Scaled Variables

18.1 Introduction

In the previous chapter, we pointed out that the researcher is frequently faced with a choice as to which statistical test is appropriate for the data. You will recall that this was not really a problem in relation to categorical variables because nonparametric tests alone are suitable for nominally-scaled data.

In this chapter, we discuss several statistical techniques that are frequently employed as alternatives to parametric tests.

18.2 Mann-Whitney U-Test

Mann-Whitney U-Test

Powerful nonparametric statistical test commonly employed as an alternative to the Student t-ratio when the measurements fail to achieve interval scaling.

The **Mann-Whitney U-test** is one of the most powerful nonparametric statistical tests, since it utilizes most of the quantitative information that is inherent in the data. It is most commonly employed as an alternative to the Student's t-ratio when the measurements fail to achieve interval scaling or when the researcher wishes to avoid the assumptions of the parametric counterpart.

Imagine that we have drawn two independent samples of N_1 and N_2 observations. The null hypothesis is that both samples are drawn from populations with the same distributions. The two-tailed alternative hypothesis, against which we test the null hypothesis, is that the parent populations from which the samples were drawn are different. Imagine further that we combine the $N_1 + N_2$ observations and assign a rank of 1 to the smallest value, a rank of 2 to the next smallest value, and continue until we have assigned ranks to all the observations. Let us refer to our two groups as E and C respectively. If we were to count the number of times each C precedes each E in the ranks, we would expect under the null hypothesis that it would equal the number of times each E precedes a C. In other words, if there is no difference between the two groups, the order of Es preceding Cs, and vice cersa, should be random. However, if the null hypothesis is not true, we would expect a bulk of the E-scores or the C-scores to precede their opposite number.

For example, suppose you have the hypothesis that leadership is a trainable quality. You set up two groups, one to receive special training in leadership (E) and the other to receive no special instruction (C). Following the training, independent estimates of the leadership qualities of all the subjects are obtained. The results are:

$$
\begin{array}{lccccc}
E\text{-scores} & 12 & 18 & 31 & 45 & 47 \\
C\text{-scores} & 2 & 8 & 15 & 19 & 38 \\
\end{array}
$$

In employing the Mann-Whitney test, we are concerned with the sampling distribution of the statistic "U". To find U, we must first rank all the scores

Table 18.1

Rank	1	2	3	4	5	6	7	8	9	10
Score	2	8	12	15	18	19	31	38	45	47
Condition	*C*	*C*	*E*	*C*	*E*	*C*	*E*	*C*	*E*	*E*

from the lowest to the highest, retaining the identity of each score as *E* or *C* (Table 18.1).

You note that the number of *E*s preceding *C*s is less than the number of *C*s preceding *E*s. The next step is to count the number of times each *E* precedes a *C*. Note that the first *E* (score of 12) precedes three *C*s (scores of 15, 19, and 38 respectively). The second *E* (score of 18) precedes two *C*s (scores of 19 and 38). The third *E* (score of 31) precedes one *C* (score of 38). Finally, the last two *E*s precede no *C*s. *U* is the sum of the number of times each *E* precedes a *C*. Thus in our hypothetical problem, $U = 3 + 2 + 1 + 0 + 0 = 6$. Had we concentrated on the number of times *C*s precede *E*s we would have obtained a sum of $5 + 5 + 4 + 3 + 2 = 19$. We shall refer to this greater sum as U'. Under the null hypotheses, U and U' should be equal. The question is whether the magnitude of the observed difference is sufficient to warrant the rejection of the null hypothesis.

The sampling distribution of U under the null hypothesis is known. Tables I_1 through I_4 show the values of U and U' which are significant at various α-levels. To be significant at a given α-level, the obtained U must be equal to or *less* than the tabled value, or the obtained U' must be equal to or *greater* than its corresponding critical value. Employing $\alpha = 0.05$, two-tailed test, we find (Table I_3) that for $N_1 = 5$ and $N_2 = 5$, either $U \leq 2$ or $U' \geq 23$ is required to reject H_0. Since our obtained U of $6 > 2$, we may not reject the null hypothesis.

Formula (18.1) may be employed as a check on the calculation of U and U':

$$U = N_1 N_2 - U'. \tag{18.1}$$

The counting technique for arriving at U can become tedious, particularly with large *N*'s, and frequently leads to error. An alternative procedure, which provides identical results, is to *assign ranks* to the combined groups as we did before, and then to employ either of the following formulas to arrive at U and/or U':

$$U = N_1 N_2 + \frac{N_1(N_1 + 1)}{2} - R_1, \tag{18.2}$$

or

$$U' = N_1 N_2 + \frac{N_2(N_2 + 1)}{2} - R_2, \tag{18.3}$$

where

$$R_1 = \text{the sum of ranks assigned to the group with a sample size of } N_1,$$
$$R_2 = \text{the sum of ranks assigned to the group with a sample size of } N_2.$$

Suppose we conducted a study to determine the effects of a drug on the reaction time to a visual stimulus. Since reaction time and related measures (such as latency, time to traverse a runway, etc.) are commonly skewed to the right because of a restriction on the left of the distribution (i.e., no score can be less than zero) and no restrictions on the right (i.e., the score can take on *any* value greater than zero), the Mann-Whitney U-test was selected in preference to the Student's t-ratio. The results of the hypothetical study and the computational procedures are shown in Table 18.2.

To check the calculations below, we should first obtain the value of U', employing Formula (18.3):

$$U' = N_1N_2 + \frac{N_2(N_2 + 1)}{2} - 39 = 45.$$

We employ Formula (18.1) as a check of our calculations:

$$U = N_1N_2 - U'$$
$$= 56 - 45 = 11.$$

Table 18.2 The calculation of the Mann-Whitney U employing Formula (18.2) (hypothetical data).

Experimental		Control		Computation
Time (milliseconds)	Rank	Time (milliseconds)	Rank	
140	4	130	1	$U = N_1N_2 + \dfrac{N_1(N_1 + 1)}{2} - 81$
147	6	135	2	
153	8	138	3	$= 56 + \dfrac{8(9)}{2} - 81$
160	10	144	5	
165	11	148	7	$= 56 + 36 - 81$
170	13	155	9	$= 11.$
171	14	168	12	
193	15			
	$R_1 = 81$		$R_2 = 39$	
	$N_1 = 8$		$N_2 = 7$	

Employing $\alpha = 0.01$, two-tailed test, for $N_1 = 8$ and $N_2 = 7$, we find (in Table I_1) that a $U \leq 6$ is required to reject H_0. Since the obtained U of 11 is greater than this value, we accept H_0. We do not have a valid statistical basis for asserting that the drug affected reaction time.

Tables I_1 through I_4 have been constructed so that it is not necessary to calculate both U and U'. Indeed, it is not even necessary to identify which of these statistics has been calculated. For any given N_1 and N_2, at a specific α-level, the tabled values represent the upper and the lower limits of the critical region. The obtained statistic, whether it is actually U or U', must fall *outside* these limits to be significant. Thus you need not be concerned about labeling which of the statistics you have calculated.

Mann-Whitney U-test with Tied Ranks

A problem that often arises with data is that several scores may be exactly the same. Although the underlying dimension on which we base our measures may be continuous, our measures are, for the most part, quite crude. Even though, theoretically, there should be no ties (if we had sufficiently sensitive measuring instruments), we do in fact obtain ties quite often. Although ties within a group do not constitute a problem (U is unaffected), we do face some difficulty when ties occur between two or more observations that involve both groups. There is a formula available that corrects for the effects of ties. Unfortunately, the use of this formula is rather involved and is beyond the scope of this introductory textbook.* However, the failure to correct for ties results in a test that is more "conservative," i.e., decreases the probability of a type I error (rejecting the null hypothesis when it should not be rejected). Correcting for ties is recommended only when their proportion is high and when the uncorrected U approaches our previously set level of significance.

In the event that several ties occur, we recommend that you calculate the Mann-Whitney without correcting for ties. If the uncorrected U approaches but does not achieve the α-level we have set for rejecting the null hypothesis, consult the source shown in the footnote and recalculate the Mann-Whitney U, correcting for ties.

Mann-Whitney U-Test when N_1 and/or N_2 Exceed 20

Tables I_1 through I_4 provide critical values of U for sample sizes up to and including $N_1 = 20$ and $N_2 = 20$. What test of significance should be used when either N_1 or N_2 exceeds 20? As with many other statistics, the sampling distribution approaches the normal curve as the sample size becomes larger.

---

*See Siegel (1956), pp. 123–125, for corrections when a large number of ties occur.

As long as both Ns are approximately equal in number and one exceeds 20, the normal curve and the z-statistic may be used to evaluate the significance of the difference between ranks. The z-statistic takes the following form:

$$z = \frac{U_1 - U_E}{s_U},$$

in which U_1 is the sum of ranks of group 1, U_E is the sum expected under H_0, and s_U is the standard error of the U-statistic.

In turn,

$$U_E = \frac{N_1(N_1 + N_2 + 1)}{2},$$

and

$$s_U = \sqrt{\frac{N_1 N_2 (N_1 + N_2 + 1)}{12}}.$$

Imagine that an investigator has completed a study in which $N_1 = 22$ and $N_2 = 22$. The sum of the ranks is 630. At $\alpha = 0.05$, test the null hypothesis that both groups were drawn from populations with the same mean rank. The critical value of z is ± 1.96.

The standard error of the ranks is

$$s_U = \sqrt{\frac{(22)(22)(22 + 22 + 1)}{12}}$$

$$= \sqrt{\frac{21780}{12}} = 42.60.$$

The expected rank under H_0 is

$$U_E = \frac{22(22 + 22 + 1)}{2} = \frac{990}{2} = 495.$$

The test statistic z becomes

$$z = \frac{630 - 495}{42.60} = 3.17.$$

Since our obtained z of 3.17 exceeds the critical value of 1.96, we may reject the null hypothesis and assert that the experimental treatment produced a significant difference between conditions.

18.3 Nonparametric Tests Involving Correlated Samples

In Chapter 14, when discussing the Student's *t*-ratio for correlated samples and the algebraically equivalent Sandler *A*-statistic, we noted the advantages of employing correlated samples wherever feasible. The same advantages accrue to nonparametric tests involving matched or correlated samples. In the following sections, we discuss two such tests for ordinally scaled variables—the *sign test* and the *Wilcoxon signed-rank test*.

18.4 The Sign Test

Suppose that we are repeating the leadership experiment with which we introduced the chapter, employing larger samples. On the expectation that intelligence and leadership ability are correlated variables, we set up two groups, an experimental and a control, that are matched on the basis of intelligence. On completion of the leadership training course, independent observers are asked to rate the leadership qualities of each subject on a 50-point scale. The results are listed in Table 18.3.

The rating scales seem to be extremely crude and we are unwilling to affirm that the scores have any precise quantitative properties. The only assumption we feel justified in making is that any existing difference between two paired scores is a valid indicator of the direction and not the magnitude of the difference.

There are 13 pairs of observations in Table 18.3. Since pair *M* is tied and there is consequently no indication of a difference one way or another, we drop these paired observations. Of the remaining 12 pairs, we would expect, on the basis of the null hypothesis, half of the changes to be in the positive direction and half of the changes to be in the negative direction. In other words, under H_0, the probability of any difference being positive is equal to the probability that it will be negative. Since we are dealing with a two-category population (positive differences and negative differences), H_0 may be expressed in precisely the same fashion as in the binomial test when $P = Q = \frac{1}{2}$. That is, in the present problem, $H_0: P = Q = \frac{1}{2}$. Indeed, the **sign test** is merely a variation of the binomial test introduced in Section 17.2.

Out of 12 comparisons showing a difference ($N = 12$) in the present example, 9 are positive, and 3 are negative. Since $P = Q = \frac{1}{2}$, we refer to

Sign Test

Nonparametric statistical test for ordinally-scaled variables, used with matched or correlated samples. The sign test simply utilizes information concerning the *direction* of the differences between pairs of scores.

Table 18.3 Ratings of two groups of matched subjects on qualities of leadership (hypothetical data).

Matched Pair	Leadership Score Experimental	Control	Sign of Difference $(E - C)$
A	47	40	+
B	43	38	+
C	36	42	−
D	38	25	+
E	30	29	+
F	22	26	−
G	25	16	+
H	21	18	+
I	14	8	+
J	12	4	+
K	5	7	−
L	9	3	+
M	5	5	(0)

Table M, under $x = 9$, $N = 12$, and find that the critical value at $\alpha = 0.05$, two-tailed test, is 10. Since x is less than the critical value, we fail to reject H_0.

The assumptions underlying the use of the sign test are that the pairs of measurements must be independent of each other and that these measurements must represent, at least, ordinal scaling.

One of the disadvantages of the sign test is that it completely eliminates any quantitative information that may be inherent in the data (for example, $-8 = -7 = -6$, etc.). The sign test treats all plus-differences as if they were the same and all minus-differences as if they were the same.

If this is the only assumption warranted by the scale of measurement employed, we have little choice but to employ the sign test. If, on the other hand, the data *do* permit us to make such quantitative statements as "a difference of $8 > 7 > 6 > \cdots$," we lose power when we employ the sign test.

Wilcoxon Matched-Pairs Signed-Rank Test

Nonparametric statistical test for ordinally scaled variables used with matched or correlated samples; more powerful than the sign test since it utilizes information concerning the *magnitude* of the differences between pairs of scores.

18.5 *Wilcoxon Matched-Pairs Signed-Rank Test*

We have seen that the sign test simply utilizes information concerning the direction of the differences between pairs. If the *magnitude* as well as the *direction* of these differences may be considered, a more powerful test may be employed. The **Wilcoxon matched-pairs signed-rank test** achieves greater power by utilizing the quantitative information inherent in the ranking of the differences.

For heuristic purposes, let us return to the data in Table 18.3 and make a different assumption about the scale of measurement employed. Suppose that the rating scale is not as crude as we had imagined; i.e., not only do the measurements achieve ordinal scaling, but also the differences between measures achieve ordinality. Table 18.4 reproduces these data, with an additional entry indicating the magnitude of the differences.

Note that the difference column represents differences in scores rather than in ranks. The following column represents the ranking of these differences from smallest to largest without regard to the algebraic sign. We have placed the negative sign in parentheses so that we can keep track of the differences bearing positive and negative signs. Now, if the null hypothesis were correct, we would expect the sum of the positive and that of the negative ranks to more or less balance each other. The more the sums of the ranks are preponderantly positive or negative, the more likely we are to reject the null hypothesis.

The statistic T is the sum of the ranks with the smaller sum. In this problem, T is equal to -13. Table J presents the critical values of T for sample sizes up to 50 pairs. All entries are for the absolute value of T. In the present example, we find that a T of 13 or less is required for significance at the 0.05

Table 18.4 **Ratings of two groups of matched subjects on qualities of leadership (hypothetical data).**

Matched Pair	Leadership Score Experimental	Control	Difference	Rank of Difference	Ranks with Smaller Sum
A	47	40	+7	9	
B	43	38	+5	5	
C	36	42	−6	(−)7	−7
D	38	25	+13	12	
E	30	29	+1	1	
F	22	26	−4	(−)4	−4
G	25	16	+9	11	
H	21	18	+3	3	
I	14	8	+6	7	
J	12	4	+8	10	
K	5	7	−2	(−)2	−2
L	9	3	+6	7	
M	5	5	(0)		
					$T = -13$

level (two-tailed test) when $N = 12$. Note that we dropped the M-pair from our calculations since, as with the sign test, a zero difference in scores cannot be considered as either a negative or a positive change. Since our obtained T was 13, we may reject the null hypothesis. We may conclude that the leadership training produced higher ratings for the experimental subjects.

You will recall that the sign test applied to these same data did not lead to the rejection of the null hypothesis. The reason should be apparent; i.e., we were not taking advantage of all the information inherent in our data when we employed the sign test.

Assumptions Underlying Wilcoxon's Matched-Pairs Signed-Rank Test

An assumption involved in the use of the Wilcoxon signed-rank test is that the scale of measurement is at least ordinal in nature. In other words, the assumption is that the scores permit the ordering of the data into relationships of greater-than and less-than. However, the signed-rank test makes one additional assumption, which may rule it out of some potential applications; namely, it assumes that the differences in scores also constitute an ordinal scale. It is not always clear whether or not this assumption is valid for a given set of data. Take, for example, a personality scale purported to measure "manifest anxiety" in a testing situation. Can we validly claim that a difference between matched pairs of, say, 5 points on one part of the scale is greater than a difference of 4 points on another part of the scale? If we cannot validly make this assumption, we must employ another form of statistical analysis, even if it requires that we move to a less sensitive test of significance. Once again, our basic conservatism as scientists makes us more willing to risk a type II than a type I error.

Chapter Summary

In this chapter, we have pointed out that the behavioral scientist does not first collect data and then "shop around" for a statistical test to determine the significance of differences between experimental conditions. *The researcher must specify in advance of the experiment* the null hypothesis, alternative hypothesis, test of significance, and the probability value that is acceptable as the basis for rejecting the null hypothesis.

We demonstrated the use of the Mann-Whitney U-test as an alternative to the Student's t-ratio when the measurements fail to achieve interval scaling or when the researcher wishes to avoid the assumptions of the parametric counterpart. It is one of the most powerful of the nonparametric tests, since it utilizes most of the quantitative information inherent in the data.

We have seen that by taking into account correlations between subjects on a variable correlated with the criterion measure, we can increase the sensitivity of our statistical test.

The sign test accomplishes this objective by employing before-after measures on the same individuals.

We have also seen that the sign test, although taking advantage of the *direction* of differences involved in ordinal measurement, fails to make use of information concerning *magnitudes* of difference.

The Wilcoxon matched-pairs signed-rank test takes advantage of both *direction* and *magnitude* implicit in ordinal measurement with correlated samples. When the assumptions underlying the test are met, the Wilcoxon paired-replicates technique is an extremely sensitive basis for obtaining probability values.

Terms to Remember

Mann-Whitney *U*-test

sign test

Wilcoxon matched-pairs signed-rank test

EXERCISES

1. From the data presented in the accompanying table, determine whether there is a significant difference in the number of stolen bases obtained by two leagues, employing
   a. the sign test,
   b. the Wilcoxon matched-pairs test,
   c. the Mann-Whitney *U*-test.

   Which is the best statistical test for these data? Why?

Team Standing	Number of Stolen Bases	
	League 1	League 2
1	91	81
2	46	51
3	108	63
4	99	51
5	110	46
6	105	45
7	191	66
8	57	64
9	34	90
10	81	28

2. In a study to determine the effect of a drug on aggressiveness, group A received a drug and group B received a placebo. A test of aggressiveness was applied following the drug administration. The scores obtained were as follows (the higher the score, the greater the aggressiveness):

Group A	10	8	12	16	5	9	7	11	6
Group B	12	15	20	18	13	14	9	16	

Set up this study in formal statistical terms and state the conclusion that is warranted by the statistical evidence.

3. The personnel director at a large insurance office claims that insurance agents who are trained in personal-social relations make more favorable impressions on prospective clients. To test this hypothesis, 22 individuals are randomly selected from those most recently hired and half are assigned to the personal-social-relations course. The remaining 11 individuals constitute the control group. Following the training period, all 22 individuals are observed in a simulated interview with a client, and they are rated on a ten-point scale (0–9) for their ease in establishing relationships. The higher the score, the better the rating. Set up and test H_0, employing the appropriate test statistic. Use $\alpha = 0.01$.

Experimentals: 8 7 9 4 7 9 3 7 8 9 3
Controls: 5 6 2 6 0 2 6 5 1 0 5

4. Assume that the subjects in Exercise 3 were matched on a variable known to be correlated with the criterion variable. Employ the appropriate test statistic to test H_0: $\alpha = 0.01$.

5. Fifteen husbands and their wives were administered an opinion scale to assess their attitudes about a particular political issue. The results were as follows (the higher the score, the more favorable the attitude):

Husband	Wife	Husband	Wife
37	33	32	46
46	44	35	32
59	48	39	29
17	30	37	45
41	56	36	29
36	30	45	48
29	35	40	35
38	38		

What do you conclude?

6. Suppose that during last track season, there was no difference in the mean running speeds of the runners from two schools. Assume that the same people are on the teams this year.

School A trains as usual for this season. However, the coach at school B introduces bicycle riding in the training classes. During a meet, the following times (in minutes) were recorded for the runners of the two schools:

A	10.2	11.1	10.5	10.0	9.7	12.0	10.7	10.9	11.5	10.4
B	9.9	10.3	11.0	10.1	9.8	9.5	10.8	10.6	9.6	9.4

Test the hypothesis that bicycle riding does not affect running speed.

7. Suppose that in Exercise 6 the people on each team had been previously matched on running speed for the 50-yard dash. The matches are as listed above. Using the sign test and the Wilcoxon matched-pairs signed-rank test, set up and test the null hypothesis.

8. An investigator wants to measure the effectiveness of an advertisement that promotes his brand of toothpaste. He matched subjects (all of whom had never bought his brand of toothpaste) according to the number of tubes of toothpaste they usually buy in six months. He then divided the sample into two groups and showed one group the advertisement. After six months, he found that the number of tubes of his brand of toothpaste the people bought during that time was:

Advertisement group	4	4	3	1	2	0	1	0
No advertisement group	1	2	0	2	0	1	0	1

Was the advertisement effective?

9. Suppose a supervisor is interested in increasing the efficiency of her employees. She divides 20 employees into two groups and gives a special training program to one group. Because the job is diversified, there is no scale available to measure efficiency. Therefore, she elicits the help of an efficiency expert who observes all 20 employees and ranks them on job efficiency, with the following results (a rank of "one" is most efficient).

Training group	1	2	4	5	6	7	8	10	11	12
Control			3	9	13	14	15	16	17	18	19	20

What can the supervisor conclude about the effectiveness of the training program?

References

Auble, D. (1953), "Extended Tables for the Mann–Whitney Statistic," *Bulletin of the Institute of Educational Research at Indiana University,* **1** (2).

Barkley, R. A., and C. E. Cunningham (1979), "The Effects of Methylphenidate on the Mother-Child Interactions of Hyperactive Children," *Arch. Gen. Psychiatry,* **36**, 201–208.

Benson, H., D. Shapiro, B. Tursky, and G. E. Schwartz (1971), "Decreased Systolic Blood Pressure through Operant Conditioning Techniques in Patients with Essential Hypertension, *Science,* **173**, 740–742.

Benson, P. L., S. A. Karabenick, and R. M. Lerner (1976), "Pretty Pleases: The Effects of Physical Attractiveness, Race, and Sex on Receiving Help," *J. Exper. Soc. Psych.,* **12**, 409–415.

Bentler, P. M., and M. D. Newcomb, (1978), "Longitudinal Study of Marital Success and Failure," *J. Consulting and Clinical Psychology,* **46**, 1053–1070.

Bingham, W. V., *Aptitudes and Aptitude Testing.* New York: Harper and Bros., 1937.

Bower, G. H. (1981), "Mood and Memory," *American Psychologist,* **36** (2), 129–148.

Cowen's, E. L. (1982), "Help Is Where You Find It," *American Psychologist,* **37** (4), 385–395.

Dingle, J. H. (1973), "The Ills of Man," *Scientific American,* **229** (3), 77–84.

Dor–Shav, N. K. (1978), "On the Long-range Effects of Concentration Camp Internment on Nazi Victims: 25 Years Later," *J. Consulting and Clinical Psychology,* **46**, 1–11.

Dunlap, J. W., and A. K. Kurtz, *Handbook of Statistical Nomographs, Tables, and Formulas.* New York: World Book Company, 1932.

Edwards, A. L., *Statistical Analysis,* 3rd ed. New York: Holt, Rinehart and Winston, 1969.

———, *Experimental Design in Psychological Research,* 3rd ed. New York: Rinehart, 1950.

Fisher, R. A., *Statistical Methods for Research Workers.* Edinburgh: Oliver and Boyd, Ltd., 1935.

———, *The Design of Experiments.* Edinburgh: Oliver and Boyd, Ltd., 1935.

Fisher, R. A., and F. Yates, *Statistical Tables for Biological, Agricultural, and Medical Research.* Edinburgh: Oliver and Boyd, Ltd., 1948.

Friedrich, L. K., and A. H. Stein (1973), "Aggressive and Prosocial Television Programs and the Natural Behavior of Preschool Children," *Monographs of the Society for Research in Child Development,* Serial no. 151, 38.

Grinspoon, L. (1969), "Marihuana," *Scientific American,* **21** (6), 17–25.

Haber, A., R. P. Runyon, and P. Badia, *Readings in Statistics.* Reading, Mass.: Addison-Wesley, 1970.

Hess, E. H., A. L. Seltzer, and J. J. Shlien, (1965), "Pupil Response of Hetero- and Homosexual males to Pictures of Men and Women: A Pilot Study," *J. Abn. Soc. Psych.,* **70**, 165–168.

Huff, D., *How to Lie with Statistics.* New York: W. W. Norton, 1954.

Kanin, E. J. (1967), "An Examination of Sexual Aggression as a Response to Sexual Frustration," *J. Marriage Family,* **29**, 428–433.

Kirk, R. E., *Experimental Design: Procedures for the Behavioral Sciences.* California: Brooks/Cole., 1968.

Klein, A. (1981), "Adolescent Hypertention," *Therapaeia,* Sept., 37–41.

Latané, B. (1981), "The Psychology of Social Impact," *American Psychologist,* **36** (4), 342–356.

Lipson, G., and D. Wolman (1972), "Polling Americans on Birth Control and Population," *Family Planning Perspectives,* **4** (1), 39–42.

Mann, H. B., and D. R. Whitney (1947), "On a Test of Whether One of Two Random Variables Is Stochastically Larger than the Other," *Ann. Math. Statist.,* **18**, 52–54.

McFadden, D., and E. G. Pasanen (1975), "Binaural Beats at High Frequencies," *Science,* **190**, 394–396.

McNemar, Q., *Psychological Statistics.* New York: John Wiley, 1962.

Merrington, M., and C. M. Thompson (1943), "Tables of Percentage Points of the Inverted Beta Distribution," *Biometrika,* **33** (1), 73.

Olds, E. G. (1949), "The 5 Percent Significance Levels of Sums of Squares of Rank Differences and a Correction," *Ann. Math. Statist.,* **20**, 117–118.

Orlowski, J. P. (1982), "Endorphins in Infant Apnea," *New England J. Medicine,* **307** (3), 186–187.

Pearson, E. S., and H. O. Hartley, *Biometrika Tables for Statisticians,* vol. 1, 2nd ed. New York: Cambridge, 1958.

Rand Corporation, *A Million Random Digits.* Glencoe, Ill.: Free Press of Glencoe, 1955.

Rocks, L., and R. P. Runyon, *The Energy Crisis.* New York: Crown Publishers, 1972.

Runyon, R. P., *Winning with Statistics.* Reading, Mass.: Addison-Wesley, 1977.

———, *Non-Parametric Statistics.* Reading, Mass.: Addison-Wesley, 1977.

——— (1968), "Note on Use of the A-statistic as a Substitute for t in the One-Sample Case," *Psychological Reports,* **22**, 361–362.

Runyon, R. P., and M. Kosacoff, "Olfactory Stimuli as Reinforcers of Bar Pressing Behavior." Paper presented at meeting of Eastern Psych. Assn., Philadelphia, 1965.

Runyon, R. P., and W. J. Turner, *A Study of the Effects of Drugs on the Social Behavior of White Rats.* New York: Long Island University, 1964.

Russo, N. F., E. L. Olmedo, J. Stapp, and R. Fulcher (1981), "Women and Minorities in Psychology," *American Psychologist,* **36** (11), 1315–1363.

Salk, L. (1973), "The Role of the Heartbeat in the Relations between Mother and Infant," *Scientific American,* **228** (5), 26–29.

Sandler, J. (1955), "A Test of the Significance of the Difference between the Means of Correlated Measures, Based on a Simplification of Student's *t*," *Brit. J. Psychol.,* **46**, 225–226.

Sbordone, R. J., J. A. Wingard, M. L. Elliott, and J. Jervey (1978), "Mescaline Produces Pathological Aggression in Rats Regardless of Age or Strain," *Pharmacology, Biochemistry and Behavior,* **8**, 543–546.

Seiden, R. H. (1966), "Campus Tragedy: A Story of Student Suicide," *J. Abn. Soc. Psych.,* **71**, 1966, 389–399.

Siegel, S., *Non-Parametric Statistics.* New York: McGraw-Hill, 1956.

Snedecor, G. W., and W. G. Cochran, *Statistical Methods,* 6th ed. Ames, Iowa: Iowa State University Press, 1956.

Thornton, B. (1977), "Toward a Linear Prediction Model of Marital Happiness," *Personality and Social Psychology Bulletin,* **3**, 674–676.

Tukey, J. W. (1953), "The Problem of Multiple Comparisons." Princeton University. Ditto, 396 pp.

Walker, H., and J. Lev, *Statistical Inference.* New York: Henry Holt, 1953.

Wilcoxon, F., and R. A. Wilcox, *Some Rapid Approximate Statistical Procedures.* New York: Lederle Laboratories, 1964.

——, *Critical Values and Probability Levels for the Wilcoxon Rank-Sum Test and the Wilcoxon Signed-Rank Test.* New York: American Cyanamid Co., 1963.

Wingard, J. A., J. P. Buchanan, and A. Burnell (1978), "Organizational Changes in the Memory of Young Children," *Perceptual and Motor Skills,* **46**, 735–742.

Wingard, J. A., G. J. Huba, and P. M. Bentler (1979), "The Relationship of Personality Structure to Patterns of Adolescent Substance Use," *J. Multivariate Behavioral Research,* **14**, 131–143.

Winkler, R. C., and R. A. Winett (1982), "Behavioral Interventions in Resource Conservation: A Systems Approach Based on Behavioral Economics," *American Psychologist,* **37** (4), 421–435.

Zelson, C., E. Rubio, and E. Wasserman (1971), "Neonatal Narcotic Addiction: 10-Year Observation," *Pediatrics,* **48** (2), 178–188.

Review of Basic Mathematics

Arithmetic Operations

You already know that addition is indicated by the sign "+," subtraction by the sign "−," multiplication in one of three ways—2×4, $2(4)$, or $2 \cdot 4$—and division by a slash, "/," an overbar, "−," or the symbol "÷." However, it is not unusual to forget the rules concerning addition, subtraction, multiplication, and division, particularly when these operations occur in a single problem.

Addition and Subtraction

When numbers are added together, the order of adding the numbers has no influence on the sum. Thus we may add $2 + 5 + 3$ in any of the following ways:

$$2 + 5 + 3, \quad 5 + 2 + 3, \quad 2 + 3 + 5,$$
$$5 + 3 + 2, \quad 3 + 2 + 5, \quad 3 + 5 + 2.$$

When a series of numbers containing both positive and negative signs are added, the order of adding the numbers has no influence on the sum. However, it is often desirable to group together the numbers preceded by positive signs, group together the numbers preceded by negative signs, add each group separately, and subtract the latter sum from the former. Thus

$$-2 + 3 + 5 - 4 + 2 + 1 - 8$$

may best be added by grouping in the following ways:

$$
\begin{array}{ll}
\begin{array}{r}
+3 \\
+5 \\
+2 \\
\underline{+1} \\
+11
\end{array}
&
\begin{array}{r}
-2 \\
-4 \\
\underline{-8} \\
-14 = -3.
\end{array}
\end{array}
$$

Incidentally, to subtract a larger numerical value from a smaller numerical value, as in the above example $(11 - 14)$, we ignore the signs, subtract the small number from the larger, and affix the sign of the larger to the sum. Thus $-14 + 11 = -3$.

Multiplication

The order in which numbers are multiplied has no effect on the product. In other words,

$$2 \times 3 \times 4 = 2 \times 4 \times 3 = 3 \times 2 \times 4$$
$$= 3 \times 4 \times 2 = 4 \times 2 \times 3 = 4 \times 3 \times 2 = 24.$$

When addition, subtraction, and multiplication occur in the same expression, we must develop certain procedures governing *which* operations are to be performed first.

In the expression

$$2 \times 4 + 7 \times 3 - 5,$$

multiplication is performed first. Thus the above expression is equal to

$$
\begin{array}{ll}
\text{a. } \begin{array}{rl}
2 \times 4 &= 8, \\
7 \times 3 &= 21, \\
-5 &= -5,
\end{array}
& \text{b. } 8 + 21 - 5 = 24.
\end{array}
$$

We may *not* add first and then multiply. Thus $2 \times 4 + 7$ is *not* equal to $2(4 + 7)$ or 22.

If a problem involves finding the product of one term multiplied by a second expression that includes two or more terms either added or subtracted, we may multiply first and then add, or add first and then multiply. Thus the solution to the following problem becomes

$$8(6 - 4) = 8 \times 6 - 8 \times 4$$
$$= 48 - 32$$
$$= 16,$$

or

$$8(6 - 4) = 8(2)$$
$$= 16.$$

In most cases, however, it is more convenient to reduce the expression within the parentheses first. Thus, generally speaking, the second of these solutions will be more frequently employed.

Finally, if numbers having like signs are multiplied, the product is always positive; e.g., $(+2) \times (+4) = +8$ and $(-2) \times (-4) = +8$. If numbers bearing unlike signs are multiplied, the product is always negative; for example,

$$(+2) \times (-4) = -8 \qquad (-2) \times (+4) = -8.$$

The same rule applies also to division: When we obtain the quotient of two numbers of like signs, it is always positive; when the numbers differ in sign, the quotient is always negative.

Multiplication as successive addition ● Many students tend to forget that multiplication is a special form of successive addition. Thus

$$15 + 15 + 15 + 15 + 15 = 5(15)$$

and

$$(15 + 15 + 15 + 15 + 15) + (16 + 16 + 16 + 16) = 5(15) + 4(16).$$

This formulation is useful in understanding the advantages of "grouping" scores into what is called a frequency distribution. In obtaining the sum of an array of scores, some of which occur a number of times, it is desirable to multiply each score by the frequency with which it occurs, and then add the products. Thus, if we were to obtain the following distribution of scores.

12, 13, 13, 13, 14, 14, 14, 14, 15, 15, 15, 15,
15, 15, 15, 16, 16, 16, 17, 17, 17, 17, 18,

and wanted the sum of these scores, it would be advantageous to form the following frequency distribution:

x	f	fx
12	1	12
13	3	39
14	4	56
15	7	105
16	3	48
17	4	68
18	1	18

$$N = 23 \quad \sum fX = 346$$

Algebraic Operations

Transposing

To transpose a term from one side of an equation to another, you merely have to *change the sign* of the transposed term. All the following are equivalent statements:

$$a + b = c,$$
$$a = c - b,$$
$$b = c - a,$$
$$0 = c - a - b,$$
$$0 = c - (a + b).$$

Solving equations involving fractions • Much of the difficulty encountered in solving equations that involve fractions can be avoided by remembering one important mathematical principle:

Equals multiplied by equals are equal.

Let's look at a few sample problems.

1. Solve the following equation for x:

$$b = \frac{a}{x}.$$

In solving for x, we want to express the value of x in terms of a and b. In other words, we want our final equation to read, $x = $ _____.

Note that we may multiply both sides of the equation by x/b and obtain the following:

Similarly,

$$b \cdot \frac{x}{b} = \frac{a}{x} \cdot \frac{x}{b}.$$

This reduces to

$$x = \frac{a}{b}.$$

2. Solve the equation above for a.

Similarly, if we wanted to solve the equation in terms of a, we could multiply both sides of the equation by x. Thus

$$b \cdot x = \frac{a}{x} \cdot x$$

becomes $bx = a$, or $a = bx$.

In each of the above solutions, you will note that the net effect of multiplying by a constant has been to rearrange the terms in the numerator and the denominator of the equations. In fact we may state two general rules which will permit us to solve these problems without having to employ multiplication by equals (although multiplication by equals is implicit in the arithmetic operations):

a. A term in the denominator on one side of the equation may be moved to the other side of the equation by multiplying it by the numerator on the other side. Thus

$$\frac{x}{a} = b \qquad \text{becomes} \qquad x = ab.$$

b. A term in the numerator on one side of an equation may be moved to the other side of the equation by dividing the numerator on the other side by it. Thus

$$ab = x \qquad \text{may become} \qquad a = \frac{x}{b} \quad \text{or} \quad b = \frac{x}{a}.$$

Thus we have seen that all of the following are equivalent statements:

$$b = \frac{a}{x}, \qquad a = bx, \qquad x = \frac{a}{b}.$$

Similarly,

$$\frac{\sum X}{N} = \overline{X}, \qquad \sum X = N\overline{X}, \qquad \frac{\sum X}{\overline{X}} = N.$$

Dividing by a sum or a difference • It is true that

$$\frac{x + y}{z} = \frac{x}{z} + \frac{y}{z} \qquad \frac{x - y}{z} = \frac{x}{z} - \frac{y}{z}.$$

We cannot, however, smplify the following expressions as easily:

$$\frac{x}{y + z} \qquad \text{or} \qquad \frac{x}{y - z}.$$

Thus

$$\frac{x}{y + z} \neq \frac{x}{y} + \frac{x}{z},$$

in which $\neq$ means "not equal to."

Reducing Fractions to Simplest Expressions

This is corollary to the rule that equals multiplied by equals are equal:

Unequals multiplied by equals remain proportional.

Thus, if we were to multiply $\frac{1}{4}$ by $\frac{8}{8}$, the product, $\frac{8}{32}$, is in the same proportion as $\frac{1}{4}$. This corollary is useful in reducing the complex fractions to their simplest expression. Let us look at an example.

• *Example.* Reduce

$$\frac{a/b}{c/d} \quad \text{or} \quad \frac{a}{b} \div \frac{c}{d}$$

to its simplest expression.

Note that if we multiply both the numerator and the denominator by

$$\frac{bd/1}{bd/1},$$

we obtain

$$\frac{(a/b) \cdot (bd/1)}{(c/d) \cdot (bd/1)},$$

which becomes *ad/bc*.

However, we could obtain the same result if we were to *invert the divisor and multiply.* Thus

$$\frac{a/b}{c/d} = \frac{a}{b} \cdot \frac{d}{c} = \frac{ad}{bc}.$$

We may now formulate a general rule for dividing one fraction into another fraction. In dividing fractions, we *invert the divisor and multiply.* Thus

$$\frac{x/y}{a^2/b} \quad \text{becomes} \quad \frac{x}{y} \cdot \frac{b}{a^2}, \quad \text{which equals} \quad \frac{bx}{a^2 y}.$$

To illustrate: If $a = 5$, $b = 2$, $x = 3$, and $y = 4$, the preceding expressions become

$$\frac{3/4}{5^2/2} = \frac{3}{4} \cdot \frac{2}{5^2} = \frac{2 \cdot 3}{4 \cdot 5^2} = \frac{6}{100}.$$

A general practice you should follow when substituting numerical values into fractional expressions is to reduce the expression to its simplest form *prior* to substitution.

Multiplication and Division of Terms Having Exponents

An exponent indicates how many times a number is to be multiplied by itself. For example, X^5 means that X is to be multiplied by itself 5 times, or

$$X^5 = X \cdot X \cdot X \cdot X \cdot X.$$

If $X = 3$,

$$X^5 = 3 \cdot 3 \cdot 3 \cdot 3 \cdot 3 = 243 \quad \text{and} \quad \left(\frac{1}{X}\right)^5 = \frac{1^5}{X^5} = \frac{1 \cdot 1 \cdot 1 \cdot 1 \cdot 1}{3 \cdot 3 \cdot 3 \cdot 3 \cdot 3} = \frac{1}{243}.$$

To multiply X raised to the ath power (X^a) times X raised to the bth power, you simply *add the exponents*, thus raising X to the $(a + b)$th power. The reason for the addition of exponents may be seen from the following illustration.

If $a = 3$ and $b = 5$, then

$$X^a \cdot X^b = X^3 X^5 = (X \cdot X \cdot X)(X \cdot X \cdot X \cdot X \cdot X),$$

which equals X^8.

Now, if $X = 5$, $a = 3$, and $b = 5$, then

$$X^a \cdot X^b = X^{a+b} = X^{3+5} = X^8 = 5^8 = 390,625.$$

If $X = \frac{1}{6}$, $a = 2$, and $b = 3$,

$$x^a \cdot X^b = X^{a+b} = \left(\frac{1}{6}\right)^{2+3} = \left(\frac{1}{6}\right)^5 = \frac{1^5}{6^5} = \frac{1}{7776}.$$

To divide X raised to the ath power by X raised to the bth power, you simply *subtract* the exponent in the denominator from the exponent in the numerator.* The reason for the subtraction is made clear in the following illus-

---

*This leads to an interesting exception to the rule that an exponent indicates the number of times a number is multiplied by itself; that is,

$$\frac{X^N}{X^N} = X^{N-N} = X^0;$$

however,

$$\frac{X^N}{X^N} = 1; \quad \text{therefore} \quad X^0 = 1.$$

Any number raised to the zero power is equal to 1.

tration.

$$\frac{X^a}{X^b} = \frac{X^5}{X^2} = \frac{X \cdot X \cdot X \cdot X \cdot X}{X \cdot X} = X^3 = 3^3 = 27.$$

If $X = \frac{5}{6}$, $a = 4$, $b = 2$, then

$$\frac{X^a}{X^b} = X^{a-b} = X^{4-2} = X^2.$$

Substituting $\frac{5}{6}$ for X, we have

$$X^2 = \left(\frac{5}{6}\right)^2 = \frac{5^2}{6^2} = \frac{25}{36}.$$

Extracting Square Roots

The square root of a number is the value that, when multiplied by itself, equals that number. Table P contains square roots.

The usual difficulty encountered in calculating square roots is the decision as to how many digits precede the decimal, for example $\sqrt{25,000,000} = 5000$, not 500 or 50,000; that is, there are four digits before the decimal. In order to calculate the number of digits preceding the decimal, simply count the number of *pairs* to the left of the decimal:

Number of pairs = Number of digits.

However, if there is an odd number of digits, then the number of digits preceding the decimal equals the number of pairs + 1. The following examples illustrate this point:

a. $\quad \overset{50.0}{\sqrt{2500.00}}$, $\quad \overset{5.0}{\sqrt{25.00}}$;

b. $\quad \overset{15.8}{\sqrt{250.00}}$, $\quad \overset{1.58}{\sqrt{2.5000}}$.

APPENDIX B

Handling Nonnormal Distributions

Transforming Nonnormal Frequency Distributions into Areas of the Standard Normal Curve

There are several techniques for normalizing a frequency distribution of scores. All yield more or less the same results. The method shown here is the one preferred by the authors.

To illustrate the procedures for normalizing frequency distributions, we employ a grouped frequency distribution ($i = 2$) of miles-per-gallon ratings of sixty 1976 cars. These are reproduced below. Note the extreme positive skew.

Real Limits of Class Interval	f	Cum f
27.5–29.5	1	60
25.5–27.5	1	59
23.5–25.5	2	58
21.5–23.5	3	56
19.5–21.5	7	53
17.5–19.5	6	46
15.5–17.5	10	40
13.5–15.5	6	30
11.5–13.5	10	24
9.5–11.5	14	14

Step A. List all the integers from the highest in the upper class ($X = 29$) to the lowest in the bottom class ($X = 10$). See column (A) of Table 1 in this appendix.

Step B. Select a value near the upper real limit of the highest class (29.4) and to the lower real limit of the lowest class (9.6). This is done to provide "anchor" points for drawing the graph.

Step C. Find the score with a corresponding percentile rank of 50. In the present example:
   a. $50 \times 60 \div 100 = 30$
   b. 30th score is found at the upper real limit of the interval 13.5–15.5. Thus the score at the 50th percentile is 15.5. This score will correspond to the mean, median, and mode in the normalized distribution. It should be placed between 15 and 16 in Table 1.

Step D. Use the procedure learned in Chapter 4 to find the percentile rank of each of the scores.

Table 1

(A) Score	(B) Percentile Rank	(C) Corresponding z under Standard Normal Curve	(D) Height of Ordinate
29.4	99.92	3.14	0.0029
29	99.58	2.64	0.0122
28	98.75	2.24	0.0325
27	97.92	2.04	0.0498
26	97.08	1.89	0.0669
25	95.83	1.73	0.0893
24	94.17	1.57	0.1163
23	92.08	1.41	0.1476
22	89.58	1.26	0.1804
21	85.42	1.05	0.2299
20	79.58	0.83	0.2827
19	74.17	0.65	0.3230
18	69.17	0.50	0.3521
17	62.50	0.32	0.3790
16	54.17	0.10	0.3970
15.5	50.00	0.00	0.3989
15	47.50	−0.06	0.3988
14	42.50	−0.19	0.3918
13	35.83	−0.36	0.3739
12	27.50	−0.60	0.3332
11	17.50	−0.93	0.2589
10	05.83	−1.57	0.1163
9.6	01.17	−2.27	0.0303

- **Examples.**   Percentile rank of score of 29.4 is

$$\frac{(1.9/2)1 + 59}{60} \times 100 = \frac{59.95}{60} \times 100$$
$$= 99.92$$

Percentile rank of score of 19 is

$$\frac{(1.5/2)6 + 40}{60} \times 100 = \frac{44.5}{60} \times 100$$
$$= 74.17$$

Step E.   Turn to Table A, Table Section. Find in the body of the table the percentile rank that most closely approximates the percentile ranks listed in column (B) of Table 1. For example, the score of 12 has a percentile rank of 27.50. The closest value to this is 27.43. The z corresponding to 27.32 is −0.60. Record each z in column (C).

- **Examples**

    1. A score of 28 is at the 98.75th percentile. The z corresponding to this percentile rank is 2.24.
    2. A score of 15 is at the 47.50th percentile. The value closest to this in the body of the table is 47.61. This corresponds to a z of −0.06.

Transforming to T-scores

We have now transformed the nonnormal frequency distribution into a normal distribution with a mean of 0 and a standard deviation of 1. However, most scores involve decimal values and all scores below the mean are negative. It is usually desirable to express values for a normally distributed variable in terms of a positive number. This can be accomplished by a simple transformation:

$$T = a + bz.$$

The selection of the constants a and b depends upon which mean and standard deviation you want in the final transformed distribution. For example, if you want the mean of the transformed distribution to be 500, you set a equal to 500. If you want the scores of the transformed distribution to be a whole number, you set b equal to 100 or more.

• *Examples.* Show the *T*-transformation necessary to produce a mean equal to 50 and a standard deviation equal to 5.

$$T = a + bz$$
$$= 50 + 5z$$

Show the transformation necessary to produce a mean of 500 and a standard deviation of 100:

$$T = a + bz$$
$$= 500 + 100z$$

Let us now transform the miles-per-gallon scores into a *T*-score so that we obtain a mean equal to 50 and a standard deviation equal to 10.

Step A. Take the *z* corresponding to each score and multiply by *b* = 10.

• *Examples.* The *z* of a score of 29.4 is 3.14:

$$b \times 3.14 = 10 \times 3.14$$
$$= 31.4.$$

The *z* of the mean score, 15.5, is 0:

$$b \times 0 = 10 \times 0$$
$$= 0.$$

Step B. Add the constant *a* = 50 to each *bz* to yield the transformed score, *T*. The score of 29.4 becomes

$$T = a + bz$$
$$= 50 + 31.4$$
$$= 81.4.$$

(*Note:* In many practical applications of the *T*-score transformation, the number is rounded to the nearest integer so that the *T* is expressed as a positive *whole* number.)

• *Examples.* The *T* of the mean becomes

$$T = a + bz$$
$$= 50 + 0$$
$$= 50.$$

The T of a score of 11 becomes

$$T = a + bz$$
$$= 50 + 10(-0.93)$$
$$= 40.7.$$

Shown below are the T-score transformations of all the normalized values of the miles-per-gallon data.

Score	Corresponding z under Standard Normal Curve	T-Transformation $(T = 50 + 10z)$	Rounded to Nearest Whole Number
29.4	3.14	81.4	81
29	2.64	76.4	76
28	2.24	72.4	72
27	2.04	70.4	70
26	1.89	68.9	69
25	1.73	67.3	67
24	1.57	65.7	66
23	1.41	64.1	64
22	1.26	62.6	63
21	1.05	60.5	60
20	0.83	58.3	58
19	0.65	56.5	56
18	0.50	55.0	55
17	0.32	53.2	53
16	0.10	51.0	51
15.5	0.00	50.0	50
15	-0.06	49.7	50
14	-0.10	48.1	48
13	-0.36	46.4	46
12	-0.60	44.0	44
11	-0.93	40.7	41
10	-1.57	34.3	34
9.6	-2.27	27.3	27

Any transformed score can be readily interpreted by converting to units of the standard normal curve.

● *Examples*

1. A score of 81.9 yields the following:

$$z = \frac{81.9 - 50}{10} = \frac{31.9}{10} = 3.19.$$

Table A reveals that the corresponding percentile rank is 99.93.

2. A score of 37.8 yields the following:

$$z = \frac{37.8 - 50}{10} = \frac{-12.2}{10} = -1.22.$$

Table A reveals that the corresponding percentile rank is 11.12.

Plotting a Graph of a Normalized Distribution

To illustrate the procedures for constructing a graph of a normalized distribution of z-scores, we shall use the previously calculated transformed miles-per-gallon scores. These are reproduced below.

(A) Score	(B) Corresponding z under Standard Normal Curve	(C) Height of Y-axis
29.4	3.14	
29	2.64	
28	2.24	
27	2.04	
26	1.89	
25	1.73	
24	1.57	
23	1.41	
22	1.26	
21	1.05	
20	0.83	
19	0.65	
18	0.50	
17	0.32	
16	0.10	
15.5	0.00	
15	-0.06	
14	-0.19	
13	-0.36	
12	-0.60	
11	-0.93	
10	-1.57	
9.6	-2.27	

Step A.   Refer to column (D) of Table 1. This shows the height of ordinate corresponding to each z-score. Find the height of the ordinate corresponding to each z in the preceding table and place in column (C).

• *Examples*

1. The height of the ordinate corresponding to $z = 3.14$ is 0.0029.
2. The height of the ordinate corresponding to $z = 0$ is 0.3989.
3. The height of the ordinate corresponding to $z = -1.57$ is 0.1163.

Step B.   On a piece of graph paper, drawn the horizontal or X-axis so that values between -3.4 through 3.4 are equally spaced.

Step C.   Draw the vertical or Y-axis so that two-placed decimal values from 0.00 to 0.40 are represented.

Step D.   Locate each z-score along the horizontal axis and move vertically until you find the corresponding value representing the height of the ordinate. Place a dot at this point.

Step E.   When you have completed all the values and joined the dots, you will have a normal distribution of your transformed scores. You may also add the corresponding original scores and their transformed T-scores to the legend along the X-axis (See Fig. 1 below).

Figure 1 Graph showing a normalized distribution of miles-per-gallon figures of sixty 1976 cars.

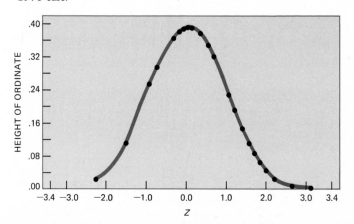

Symbol Glossary

The following are symbols and their definitions as used in this textbook, followed by the page number.

English letters and Greek letters are listed separately in their approximate alphabetical order. Mathematical operators are also listed separately.

SYMBOL	DEFINITION	PAGE

Mathematical Operators

SYMBOL	DEFINITION	PAGE
$\neq$	Not equal to	29
$a < b$	a is less than b	29
$a > b$	a is greater than b	29
$\leq$	Less than or equal to	201
$\geq$	Greater than or equal to	201
$\sqrt{}$	Square root	23
X^a	X raised to the ath power	23
$N!$	Factorial: multiply N by all integers less than it but greater than zero: $$(N)(N-1)(N-2 \cdots (2)(1)$$	359
$\lvert X \rvert$	Absolute value of X	110
$\sum$	Sum all quantities or scores that follow	23
$\displaystyle\sum_{i=1}^{N} X_i$	Sum all quantities X_1 through X_N: $$X_1 + X_2 + \cdots + X_N$$	23

Greek Letters

SYMBOL	DEFINITION	PAGE
α	Probability of a Type I error; probability of rejecting H_0 when it is true	231

SYMBOL	DEFINITION	PAGE
β	Probability of a type II error; probability of accepting H_0 when it is false	235
χ^2	Chi square	362
μ	Population mean	91
μ_0	Value of the population mean under H_0	249
μ_1	Value of the population mean under H_1	344
$\mu_{\bar{X}}$	Mean of the distribution of sample means	246
$\mu_{\bar{X}_1 - \bar{X}_2}$	Mean of the distribution of the difference between pairs of sample means	276
$\mu_{\bar{D}}$	Mean of the difference between paired scores	298
σ^2	Population variance	111
σ	Population standard deviation	111
$\sigma_{\bar{X}}^2 = \dfrac{\sigma^2}{N}$	Variance of the sampling distribution of the mean	246
$\sigma_{\bar{X}} = \dfrac{\sigma}{\sqrt{N}}$	True standard error of the mean given random samples of a fixed N	246
$\sigma_{\bar{X}_1 - \bar{X}_2}$	True standard error of the difference between means	276
ω^2	Omega squared; degree of association between the dependent and the independent variables	281

English Letters

$A = \dfrac{\sum D^2}{(\sum D)^2}$	Statistic employed to test hypotheses for correlated samples	300
a	Constant term in a regression equation	166
b_y	Slope of a line relating values of Y to values of X	166
c	Number of columns in a contingency table	365
cum f	Cumulative frequency	52
cum f_{ll}	Cumulative frequency at the lower real limit of the interval containing X	77
cum %	Cumulative percent	53
D	1. Rank on X-variable − rank on Y-variable (r_s formula)	152
	2. Score on X-variable − Score on Y-variable ($X - Y$)	298
$\bar{D}$	Mean of the differences between the paired scores	298
df	Degrees of freedom: Number of values free to vary after certain restrictions have been placed on the data	256

SYMBOL	DEFINITION	PAGE
F	A ratio of two variances	283
f	Frequency	48
f_i	Number of cases within the interval containing X	77
f_e	Expected number in a given category	362
f_o	Observed number in a given category	362
fX	A score multiplied by its corresponding frequency	91
H_0	The null hypothesis; hypothesis actually tested	232
H_1	The alternative hypothesis; hypothesis entertained if H_0 is rejected	232
i	Width of the class interval	51
k	Number of groups or categories or cells	315
k^2	Coefficient of nondetermination	178
M.D.	Mean deviation	109
N	1. Number of pairs	145
	2. Number in either sample	277
	3. Total number of scores or quantities	22
$N_{\bar{X}}$	Total number of means obtained in a sampling experiment	196
p	Probability	197
$p(A)$	Probability of event A	203
$p(B\vert A)$	Probability of B given that A has occurred	208
P	1. Probability of the occurrence of an event	205
	2. Proportion of cases in one class in a two-category population	358
Q	1. Probability of the nonoccurrence of an event	205
	2. Proportion of cases in the other class of a two-category population	358
Q_1	First quartile, 25th percentile	108
Q_3	Third quartile, 75th percentile	108
r	1. Pearson product-moment correlation coefficient	140
	2. Number of rows in a contingency table	365
r^2	Coefficient of determination	177
r_s	Spearman rank-order correlation coefficient	140
R_1	Sum of ranks assigned to the group with a sample size of N_1 (Mann-Whitney U-formula)	378
R_2	Sum of ranks assigned to the group with a sample size of N_2 (Mann-Whitney U-formula)	378
$s^2 = \dfrac{SS}{N}$	Variance of a sample	112

SYMBOL	DEFINITION	PAGE
$s = \sqrt{\dfrac{SS}{N}}$	Standard deviation of a sample	112
$\hat{s}^2 = \dfrac{\sum(X - \bar{X})^2}{N-1} = \dfrac{SS}{N-1}$	Unbiased estimate of the population variance	112
$\hat{s} = \sqrt{\dfrac{SS}{N-1}}$	Sample standard deviation based on unbiased variance estimate	312
$s_{\bar{X}}^2$	Estimated variance of the sampling distribution of the mean	296
$s_{\bar{X}} = \dfrac{\hat{s}}{\sqrt{N}} = \dfrac{s}{\sqrt{N-1}}$	Estimated standard error of the mean	242
$s_{\bar{X}_1 - \bar{X}_2}$	Estimated standard error of the difference between means	277
$\hat{s}_D$	Standard deviation of the difference scores	298
$s_{\bar{D}}$	Estimated standard error of the difference between means, direct-difference method	298
$\hat{s}_{bet}^2$	Between-group variance estimate	314
$\hat{s}_w^2$	Within-group variance estimate	316
$\hat{s}_{A \times B}$	Interaction variance estimate	324
$s_{est\ y}$	Standard error of estimate when predictions are made from X to Y	173
$s_{est\ x}$	Standard error of estimate when predictions are made from Y to X	173
$SS = \sum(X - \bar{X})^2$	Sum of squares, sum of the squared deviations from the mean	112
$SS_{A \times B}$	Interaction sum of squares	324
SS_{tot}	Total sum of squares, sum of the squared deviations of each score (X) from the overall mean $(\bar{X}_{tot})$	313
SS_w	Within-group sum of squares; sum of the squared deviations of each score (X) from the mean of its own group $(\bar{X}_i)$	313
SS_{bet}	Between-group sum of squares, sum of the squared deviations of each group mean $(\bar{X}_i)$ from the overall mean $(\bar{X}_{tot})$, multiplied by the N in each group	313
T	Sum of the ranks with the least frequent sign	313
t	Statistic employed to test hypotheses when σ is unknown	256
U, U'	Statistics in the Mann-Whitney test	376
X, Y	Variables; quantities or scores of variables	21

SYMBOL	DEFINITION	PAGE
X_i, Y_i	Specific quantities indicated by the subscript i	23
$\overline{X}, \overline{Y}$	Arithmetic means	90
$\overline{X}_i$	Mean of the ith group	314
$\overline{X}_{tot} = \dfrac{\sum X_{tot}}{N}$	Overall mean	313
$(X - \overline{X})$	Deviation of a score from its mean	92
x	Number of objects in one category or the number of successes	359
$\sum X^2$	Sum of the squares of the raw scores	113
$(\sum X)^2$	Sum of the raw scores, the quantity squared	113
X_{ll}	Score at lower real limit of interval containing X	77
X', Y'	Scores predicted by regression equations	167
Y_T	Interval around the regression line within which the true value occurs	175
z	1. Deviation of a specific score from the mean, expressed in standard deviation units	124
	2. Statistic employed to test hypotheses when σ is known	250
$z_{0.01} = \pm 2.58$	Critical value of z, minimum z required to reject H_0 at the 0.01 level of significance, two-tailed test	250
$z_{0.05} = \pm 1.96$	Minimum value of z required to reject H_0 at the 0.05 level of significance, two-tailed test	251
z_y	Y' expressed in terms of a z-score	170

Tables

414

Table A
Proportions of area under the normal curve

The Use of Table A

The use of Table A requires that the raw score be transformed into a z-score and that the variable be normally distributed.

The values in Table A represent the proportion of area in the standard normal curve, which has a mean of 0, a standard deviation of 1.00, and a total area also equal to 1.00.

Since the normal curve is symmetrical, it is sufficient to indicate only the areas corresponding to positive z-values. Negative z-values will have precisely the same proportions of area as their positive counterparts.

Column B represents the proportion of area between the mean and a given z. Column C represents the proportion of area beyond a given z.

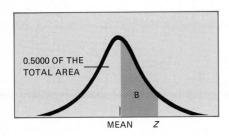
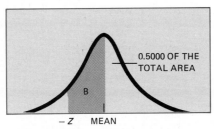
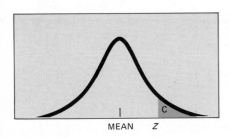
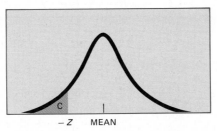

Table A

(A) z	(B) area between mean and z	(C) area beyond z	(A) z	(B) area between mean and z	(C) area beyond z	(A) z	(B) area between mean and z	(C) area beyond z
0.00	.0000	.5000	0.55	.2088	.2912	1.10	.3643	.1357
0.01	.0040	.4960	0.56	.2123	.2877	1.11	.3665	.1335
0.02	.0080	.4920	0.57	.2157	.2843	1.12	.3686	.1314
0.03	.0120	.4880	0.58	.2190	.2810	1.13	.3708	.1292
0.04	.0160	.4840	0.59	.2224	.2776	1.14	.3729	.1271
0.05	.0199	.4801	0.60	.2257	.2743	1.15	.3749	.1251
0.06	.0239	.4761	0.61	.2291	.2709	1.16	.3770	.1230
0.07	.0279	.4721	0.62	.2324	.2676	1.17	.3790	.1210
0.08	.0319	.4681	0.63	.2357	.2643	1.18	.3810	.1190
0.09	.0359	.4641	0.64	.2389	.2611	1.19	.3830	.1170
0.10	.0398	.4602	0.65	.2422	.2578	1.20	.3849	.1151
0.11	.0438	.4562	0.66	.2454	.2546	1.21	.3869	.1131
0.12	.0478	.4522	0.67	.2486	.2514	1.22	.3888	.1112
0.13	.0517	.4483	0.68	.2517	.2483	1.23	.3907	.1093
0.14	.0557	.4443	0.69	.2549	.2451	1.24	.3925	.1075
0.15	.0596	.4404	0.70	.2580	.2420	1.25	.3944	.1056
0.16	.0636	.4364	0.71	.2611	.2389	1.26	.3962	.1038
0.17	.0675	.4325	0.72	.2642	.2358	1.27	.3980	.1020
0.18	.0714	.4286	0.73	.2673	.2327	1.28	.3997	.1003
0.19	.0753	.4247	0.74	.2704	.2296	1.29	.4015	.0985
0.20	.0793	.4207	0.75	.2734	.2266	1.30	.4032	.0968
0.21	.0832	.4168	0.76	.2764	.2236	1.31	.4049	.0951
0.22	.0871	.4129	0.77	.2794	.2206	1.32	.4066	.0934
0.23	.0910	.4090	0.78	.2823	.2177	1.33	.4082	.0918
0.24	.0948	.4052	0.79	.2852	.2148	1.34	.4099	.0901
0.25	.0987	.4013	0.80	.2881	.2119	1.35	.4115	.0885
0.26	.1026	.3974	0.81	.2910	.2090	1.36	.4131	.0869
0.27	.1064	.3936	0.82	.2939	.2061	1.37	.4147	.0853
0.28	.1103	.3897	0.83	.2967	.2033	1.38	.4162	.0838
0.29	.1141	.3859	0.84	.2995	.2005	1.39	.4177	.0823
0.30	.1179	.3821	0.85	.3023	.1977	1.40	.4192	.0808
0.31	.1217	.3783	0.86	.3051	.1949	1.41	.4207	.0793
0.32	.1255	.3745	0.87	.3078	.1922	1.42	.4222	.0778
0.33	.1293	.3707	0.88	.3106	.1894	1.43	.4236	.0764
0.34	.1331	.3669	0.89	.3133	.1867	1.44	.4251	.0749
0.35	.1368	.3632	0.90	.3159	.1841	1.45	.4265	.0735
0.36	.1406	.3594	0.91	.3186	.1814	1.46	.4279	.0721
0.37	.1443	.3557	0.92	.3212	.1788	1.47	.4292	.0708
0.38	.1480	.3520	0.93	.3238	.1762	1.48	.4306	.0694
0.39	.1517	.3483	0.94	.3264	.1736	1.49	.4319	.0681
0.40	.1554	.3446	0.95	.3289	.1711	1.50	.4332	.0668
0.41	.1591	.3409	0.96	.3315	.1685	1.51	.4345	.0655
0.42	.1628	.3372	0.97	.3340	.1660	1.52	.4357	.0643
0.43	.1664	.3336	0.98	.3365	.1635	1.53	.4370	.0630
0.44	.1700	.3300	0.99	.3389	.1611	1.54	.4382	.0618
0.45	.1736	.3264	1.00	.3413	.1587	1.55	.4394	.0606
0.46	.1772	.3228	1.01	.3438	.1562	1.56	.4406	.0594
0.47	.1808	.3192	1.02	.3461	.1539	1.57	.4418	.0582
0.48	.1844	.3156	1.03	.3485	.1515	1.58	.4429	.0571
0.49	.1879	.3121	1.04	.3508	.1492	1.59	.4441	.0559
0.50	.1915	.3085	1.05	.3531	.1469	1.60	.4452	.0548
0.51	.1950	.3050	1.06	.3554	.1446	1.61	.4463	.0537
0.52	.1985	.3015	1.07	.3577	.1423	1.62	.4474	.0526
0.53	.2019	.2981	1.08	.3599	.1401	1.63	.4484	.0516
0.54	.2054	.2946	1.09	.3621	.1379	1.64	.4495	.0505

Table A (*Cont.*)

(A) z	(B) area between mean and z	(C) area beyond z	(A) z	(B) area between mean and z	(C) area beyond z	(A) z	(B) area between mean and z	(C) area beyond z
1.65	.4505	.0495	2.22	.4868	.0132	2.79	.4974	.0026
1.66	.4515	.0485	2.23	.4871	.0129	2.80	.4974	.0026
1.67	.4525	.0475	2.24	.4875	.0125	2.81	.4975	.0025
1.68	.4535	.0465	2.25	.4878	.0122	2.82	.4976	.0024
1.69	.4545	.0455	2.26	.4881	.0119	2.83	.4977	.0023
1.70	.4554	.0446	2.27	.4884	.0116	2.84	.4977	.0023
1.71	.4564	.0436	2.28	.4887	.0113	2.85	.4978	.0022
1.72	.4573	.0427	2.29	.4890	.0110	2.86	.4979	.0021
1.73	.4582	.0418	2.30	.4893	.0107	2.87	.4979	.0021
1.74	.4591	.0409	2.31	.4896	.0104	2.88	.4980	.0020
1.75	.4599	.0401	2.32	.4898	.0102	2.89	.4981	.0019
1.76	.4608	.0392	2.33	.4901	.0099	2.90	.4981	.0019
1.77	.4616	.0384	2.34	.4904	.0096	2.91	.4982	.0018
1.78	.4625	.0375	2.35	.4906	.0094	2.92	.4982	.0018
1.79	.4633	.0367	2.36	.4909	.0091	2.93	.4983	.0017
1.80	.4641	.0359	2.37	.4911	.0089	2.94	.4984	.0016
1.81	.4649	.0351	2.38	.4913	.0087	2.95	.4984	.0016
1.82	.4656	.0344	2.39	.4916	.0084	2.96	.4985	.0015
1.83	.4664	.0336	2.40	.4918	.0082	2.97	.4985	.0015
1.84	.4671	.0329	2.41	.4920	.0080	2.98	.4986	.0014
1.85	.4678	.0322	2.42	.4922	.0078	2.99	.4986	.0014
1.86	.4686	.0314	2.43	.4925	.0075	3.00	.4987	.0013
1.87	.4693	.0307	2.44	.4927	.0073	3.01	.4987	.0013
1.88	.4699	.0301	2.45	.4929	.0071	3.02	.4987	.0013
1.89	.4706	.0294	2.46	.4931	.0069	3.03	.4988	.0012
1.90	.4713	.0287	2.47	.4932	.0068	3.04	.4988	.0012
1.91	.4719	.0281	2.48	.4934	.0066	3.05	.4989	.0011
1.92	.4726	.0274	2.49	.4936	.0064	3.06	.4989	.0011
1.93	.4732	.0268	2.50	.4938	.0062	3.07	.4989	.0011
1.94	.4738	.0262	2.51	.4940	.0060	3.08	.4990	.0010
1 95	.4744	.0256	2.52	.4941	.0059	3.09	.4990	.0010
1 96	.4750	.0250	2.53	.4943	.0057	3.10	.4990	.0010
1.97	.4756	.0244	2.54	.4945	.0055	3.11	.4991	.0009
1.98	.4761	.0239	2.55	.4946	.0054	3.12	.4991	.0009
1.99	.4767	.0233	2.56	.4948	.0052	3.13	.4991	.0009
2.00	.4772	.0228	2.57	.4949	.0051	3.14	.4992	.0008
2.01	.4778	.0222	2.58	.4951	.0049	3.15	.4992	.0008
2.02	.4783	.0217	2.59	.4952	.0048	3.16	.4992	.0008
2.03	.4788	.0212	2.60	.4953	.0047	3.17	.4992	.0008
2.04	.4793	.0207	2.61	.4955	.0045	3.18	.4993	.0007
2.05	.4798	.0202	2.62	.4956	.0044	3.19	.4993	.0007
2.06	.4803	.0197	2.63	.4957	.0043	3.20	.4993	.0007
2.07	.4808	.0192	2.64	.4959	.0041	3.21	.4993	.0007
2.08	.4812	.0188	2.65	.4960	.0040	3.22	.4994	.0006
2.09	.4817	.0183	2.66	.4961	.0039	3.23	.4994	.0006
2.10	.4821	.0179	2.67	.4962	.0038	3.24	.4994	.0006
2.11	.4826	.0174	2.68	.4963	.0037	3.25	.4994	.0006
2.12	.4830	.0170	2.69	.4964	.0036	3.30	.4995	.0005
2.13	.4834	.0166	2.70	.4965	.0035	3.35	.4996	.0004
2.14	.4838	.0162	2.71	.4966	.0034	3.40	.4997	.0003
2.15	.4842	.0158	2.72	.4967	.0033	3.45	.4997	.0003
2.16	.4846	.0154	2.73	.4968	.0032	3.50	.4998	.0002
2.17	.4850	.0150	2.74	.4969	.0031	3.60	.4998	.0002
2.18	.4854	.0146	2.75	.4970	.0030	3.70	.4999	.0001
2.19	.4857	.0143	2.76	.4971	.0029	3.80	.4999	.0001
2.20	.4861	.0139	2.77	.4972	.0028	3.90	.49995	.00005
2.21	.4864	.0136	2.78	.4973	.0027	4.00	.49997	.00003

Table B
Two-tailed critical ratios of χ^2.

Degrees of freedom df	.10	.05	.02	.01
1	2.706	3.841	5.412	6.635
2	4.605	5.991	7.824	9.210
3	6.251	7.815	9.837	11.341
4	7.779	9.488	11.668	13.277
5	9.236	11.070	13.388	15.086
6	10.645	12.592	15.033	16.812
7	12.017	14.067	16.622	18.475
8	13.362	15.507	18.168	20.090
9	14.684	16.919	19.679	21.666
10	15.987	18.307	21.161	23.209
11	17.275	19.675	22.618	24.725
12	18.549	21.026	24.054	26.217
13	19.812	22.362	25.472	27.688
14	21.064	23.685	26.873	29.141
15	22.307	24.996	28.259	30.578
16	23.542	26.296	29.633	32.000
17	24.769	27.587	30.995	33.409
18	25.989	28.869	32.346	34.805
19	27.204	30.144	33.687	36.191
20	28.412	31.410	35.020	37.566
21	29.615	32.671	36.343	38.932
22	30.813	33.924	37.659	40.289
23	32.007	35.172	38.968	41.638
24	33.196	36.415	40.270	42.980
25	34.382	37.652	41.566	44.314
26	35.563	38.885	42.856	45.642
27	36.741	40.113	44.140	46.963
28	37.916	41.337	45.419	48.278
29	39.087	42.557	46.693	49.588
30	40.256	43.773	47.962	50.892

Table C
Critical values of *t*.

For any given df, the table shows the values of *t* corresponding to various levels of probability. Obtained *t* is significant at a given level if it is equal to or *greater than* the value shown in the table.

df	Level of significance for one-tailed test					
	.10	.05	.025	.01	.005	.0005
	Level of significance for two-tailed test					
	.20	.10	.05	.02	.01	.001
1	3.078	6.314	12.706	31.821	63.657	636.619
2	1.886	2.920	4.303	6.965	9.925	31.598
3	1.638	2.353	3.182	4.541	5.841	12.941
4	1.533	2.132	2.776	3.747	4.604	8.610
5	1.476	2.015	2.571	3.365	4.032	6.859
6	1.440	1.943	2.447	3.143	3.707	5.959
7	1.415	1.895	2.365	2.998	3.499	5.405
8	1.397	1.860	2.306	2.896	3.355	5.041
9	1.383	1.833	2.262	2.821	3.250	4.781
10	1.372	1.812	2.228	2.764	3.169	4.587
11	1.363	1.796	2.201	2.718	3.106	4.437
12	1.356	1.782	2.179	2.681	3.055	4.318
13	1.350	1.771	2.160	2.650	3.012	4.221
14	1.345	1.761	2.145	2.624	2.977	4.140
15	1.341	1.753	2.131	2.602	2.947	4.073
16	1.337	1.746	2.120	2.583	2.921	4.015
17	1.333	1.740	2.110	2.567	2.898	3.965
18	1.330	1.734	2.101	2.552	2.878	3.922
19	1.328	1.729	2.093	2.539	2.861	3.883
20	1.325	1.725	2.086	2.528	2.845	3.850
21	1.323	1.721	2.080	2.518	2.831	3.819
22	1.321	1.717	2.074	2.508	2.819	3.792
23	1.319	1.714	2.069	2.500	2.807	3.767
24	1.318	1.711	2.064	2.492	2.797	3.745
25	1.316	1.708	2.060	2.485	2.787	3.725
26	1.315	1.706	2.056	2.479	2.779	3.707
27	1.314	1.703	2.052	2.473	2.771	3.690
28	1.313	1.701	2.048	2.467	2.763	3.674
29	1.311	1.699	2.045	2.462	2.756	3.659
30	1.310	1.697	2.042	2.457	2.750	3.646
40	1.303	1.684	2.021	2.423	2.704	3.551
60	1.296	1.671	2.000	2.390	2.660	3.460
120	1.289	1.658	1.980	2.358	2.617	3.373
∞	1.282	1.645	1.960	2.326	2.576	3.291

Table C is taken from Table III (page 46) of Fisher and Yates *Statistical Tables for Biological, Agricultural, and Medical Research,* 6th ed., published by Longman Group Ltd., 1974, London (previously published by Oliver and Boyd, Edinburgh), and by permission of the authors and publishers.

Table D
Critical values of *F*.

The obtained *F* is significant at a given level if it is equal to or *greater than* the value shown in the table. 0.05 (light row) and 0.01 (dark row) points for the distribution of *F*.

The values shown are the right tail of the distribution obtained by dividing the larger variance estimate by the smaller variance estimate. To find the complementary left or lower tail for a given df and α level, reverse the degrees of freedom and find the reciprocal of that value in the *F*-table. For example, the value cutting off the top 5% of the area for df 7 and 12 is 2.85. To find the cutoff point of the bottom 5% of the area, find the tabled value of the α = 0.05 level for 12 and 7 df. This is found to be 3.57. The reciprocal is 1/3.57 = 0.28. Thus 5% of the area falls *at or below an F* = 0.28.

Each cell shows the 0.05 value (light) over the 0.01 value (dark).

Denom df \ Num df	1	2	3	4	5	6	7	8	9	10	11	12	14	16	20	24	30	40	50	75	100	200	500	∞
1	161 / 4052	200 / 4999	216 / 5403	225 / 5625	230 / 5764	234 / 5859	237 / 5928	239 / 5981	241 / 6022	242 / 6056	243 / 6082	244 / 6106	245 / 6142	246 / 6169	248 / 6208	249 / 6234	250 / 6258	251 / 6286	252 / 6302	253 / 6323	253 / 6334	254 / 6352	254 / 6361	254 / 6366
2	18.51 / 98.49	19.00 / 99.01	19.16 / 99.17	19.25 / 99.25	19.30 / 99.30	19.33 / 99.33	19.36 / 99.34	19.37 / 99.36	19.38 / 99.38	19.39 / 99.40	19.40 / 99.41	19.41 / 99.42	19.42 / 99.43	19.43 / 99.44	19.44 / 99.45	19.45 / 99.46	19.46 / 99.47	19.47 / 99.48	19.47 / 99.48	19.48 / 99.49	19.49 / 99.49	19.49 / 99.49	19.50 / 99.50	19.50 / 99.50
3	10.13 / 34.12	9.55 / 30.81	9.28 / 29.46	9.12 / 28.71	9.01 / 28.24	8.94 / 27.91	8.88 / 27.67	8.84 / 27.49	8.81 / 27.34	8.78 / 27.23	8.76 / 27.13	8.74 / 27.05	8.71 / 26.92	8.69 / 26.83	8.66 / 26.69	8.64 / 26.60	8.62 / 26.50	8.60 / 26.41	8.58 / 26.30	8.57 / 26.27	8.56 / 26.23	8.54 / 26.18	8.54 / 26.14	8.53 / 26.12
4	7.71 / 21.20	6.94 / 18.00	6.59 / 16.69	6.39 / 15.98	6.26 / 15.52	6.16 / 15.21	6.09 / 14.98	6.04 / 14.80	6.00 / 14.66	5.96 / 14.54	5.93 / 14.45	5.91 / 14.37	5.87 / 14.24	5.84 / 14.15	5.80 / 14.02	5.77 / 13.93	5.74 / 13.83	5.71 / 13.74	5.70 / 13.69	5.68 / 13.61	5.66 / 13.57	5.65 / 13.52	5.64 / 13.48	5.63 / 13.46
5	6.61 / 16.26	5.79 / 13.27	5.41 / 12.06	5.19 / 11.39	5.05 / 10.97	4.95 / 10.67	4.88 / 10.45	4.82 / 10.27	4.78 / 10.15	4.74 / 10.05	4.70 / 9.96	4.68 / 9.89	4.64 / 9.77	4.60 / 9.68	4.56 / 9.55	4.53 / 9.47	4.50 / 9.38	4.46 / 9.29	4.44 / 9.24	4.42 / 9.17	4.40 / 9.13	4.38 / 9.07	4.37 / 9.04	4.36 / 9.02
6	5.99 / 13.74	5.14 / 10.92	4.76 / 9.78	4.53 / 9.15	4.39 / 8.75	4.28 / 8.47	4.21 / 8.26	4.15 / 8.10	4.10 / 7.98	4.06 / 7.87	4.03 / 7.79	4.00 / 7.72	3.96 / 7.60	3.92 / 7.52	3.87 / 7.39	3.84 / 7.31	3.81 / 7.23	3.77 / 7.14	3.75 / 7.09	3.72 / 7.02	3.71 / 6.99	3.69 / 6.94	3.68 / 6.90	3.67 / 6.88
7	5.59 / 12.25	4.74 / 9.55	4.35 / 8.45	4.12 / 7.85	3.97 / 7.46	3.87 / 7.19	3.79 / 7.00	3.73 / 6.84	3.68 / 6.71	3.63 / 6.62	3.60 / 6.54	3.57 / 6.47	3.52 / 6.35	3.49 / 6.27	3.44 / 6.15	3.41 / 6.07	3.38 / 5.98	3.34 / 5.90	3.32 / 5.85	3.29 / 5.78	3.28 / 5.75	3.25 / 5.70	3.24 / 5.67	3.23 / 5.65
8	5.32 / 11.26	4.46 / 8.65	4.07 / 7.59	3.84 / 7.01	3.69 / 6.63	3.58 / 6.37	3.50 / 6.19	3.44 / 6.03	3.39 / 5.91	3.34 / 5.82	3.31 / 5.74	3.28 / 5.67	3.23 / 5.56	3.20 / 5.48	3.15 / 5.36	3.12 / 5.28	3.08 / 5.20	3.05 / 5.11	3.03 / 5.06	3.00 / 5.00	2.98 / 4.96	2.96 / 4.91	2.94 / 4.88	2.93 / 4.86
9	5.12 / 10.56	4.26 / 8.02	3.86 / 6.99	3.63 / 6.42	3.48 / 6.06	3.37 / 5.80	3.29 / 5.62	3.23 / 5.47	3.18 / 5.35	3.13 / 5.26	3.10 / 5.18	3.07 / 5.11	3.02 / 5.00	2.98 / 4.92	2.93 / 4.80	2.90 / 4.73	2.86 / 4.64	2.82 / 4.56	2.80 / 4.51	2.77 / 4.45	2.76 / 4.41	2.73 / 4.36	2.72 / 4.33	2.71 / 4.31
10	4.96 / 10.04	4.10 / 7.56	3.71 / 6.55	3.48 / 5.99	3.33 / 5.64	3.22 / 5.39	3.14 / 5.21	3.07 / 5.06	3.02 / 4.95	2.97 / 4.85	2.94 / 4.78	2.91 / 4.71	2.86 / 4.60	2.82 / 4.52	2.77 / 4.41	2.74 / 4.33	2.70 / 4.25	2.67 / 4.17	2.64 / 4.12	2.61 / 4.05	2.59 / 4.01	2.56 / 3.96	2.55 / 3.93	2.54 / 3.91
11	4.84 / 9.65	3.98 / 7.20	3.59 / 6.22	3.36 / 5.67	3.20 / 5.32	3.09 / 5.07	3.01 / 4.88	2.95 / 4.74	2.90 / 4.63	2.86 / 4.54	2.82 / 4.46	2.79 / 4.40	2.74 / 4.29	2.70 / 4.21	2.65 / 4.10	2.61 / 4.02	2.57 / 3.94	2.53 / 3.86	2.50 / 3.80	2.47 / 3.74	2.45 / 3.70	2.42 / 3.66	2.41 / 3.62	2.40 / 3.60
12	4.75 / 9.33	3.88 / 6.93	3.49 / 5.95	3.26 / 5.41	3.11 / 5.06	3.00 / 4.82	2.92 / 4.65	2.85 / 4.50	2.80 / 4.39	2.76 / 4.30	2.72 / 4.22	2.69 / 4.16	2.64 / 4.05	2.60 / 3.98	2.54 / 3.86	2.50 / 3.78	2.46 / 3.70	2.42 / 3.61	2.40 / 3.56	2.36 / 3.49	2.35 / 3.46	2.32 / 3.41	2.31 / 3.38	2.30 / 3.36
13	4.67 / 9.07	3.80 / 6.70	3.41 / 5.74	3.18 / 5.20	3.02 / 4.86	2.92 / 4.62	2.84 / 4.44	2.77 / 4.30	2.72 / 4.19	2.67 / 4.10	2.63 / 4.02	2.60 / 3.96	2.55 / 3.85	2.51 / 3.78	2.46 / 3.67	2.42 / 3.59	2.38 / 3.51	2.34 / 3.42	2.32 / 3.37	2.28 / 3.30	2.26 / 3.27	2.24 / 3.21	2.22 / 3.18	2.21 / 3.16
14	4.60 / 8.86	3.74 / 6.51	3.34 / 5.56	3.11 / 5.03	2.96 / 4.69	2.85 / 4.46	2.77 / 4.28	2.70 / 4.14	2.65 / 4.03	2.60 / 3.94	2.56 / 3.86	2.53 / 3.80	2.48 / 3.70	2.44 / 3.62	2.39 / 3.51	2.35 / 3.43	2.31 / 3.34	2.27 / 3.26	2.24 / 3.21	2.21 / 3.14	2.19 / 3.11	2.16 / 3.06	2.14 / 3.02	2.13 / 3.00
15	4.54 / 8.68	3.68 / 6.36	3.29 / 5.42	3.06 / 4.89	2.90 / 4.56	2.79 / 4.32	2.70 / 4.14	2.64 / 4.00	2.59 / 3.89	2.55 / 3.80	2.51 / 3.73	2.48 / 3.67	2.43 / 3.56	2.39 / 3.48	2.33 / 3.36	2.29 / 3.29	2.25 / 3.20	2.21 / 3.12	2.18 / 3.07	2.15 / 3.00	2.12 / 2.97	2.10 / 2.92	2.08 / 2.89	2.07 / 2.87

Degrees of freedom for numerator (columns); Degrees of freedom for denominator (rows).

Each cell shows two critical values (upper / lower).

df																								
16	2.01 / 2.75	2.02 / 2.77	2.04 / 2.80	2.07 / 2.86	2.09 / 2.89	2.13 / 2.96	2.16 / 3.01	2.20 / 3.10	2.24 / 3.18	2.28 / 3.25	2.33 / 3.37	2.37 / 3.45	2.42 / 3.55	2.45 / 3.61	2.49 / 3.69	2.54 / 3.78	2.59 / 3.89	2.66 / 4.03	2.74 / 4.20	2.85 / 4.44	3.01 / 4.77	3.24 / 5.29	3.63 / 6.23	4.49 / 8.53
17	1.96 / 2.65	1.97 / 2.67	1.99 / 2.70	2.02 / 2.76	2.04 / 2.79	2.08 / 2.86	2.11 / 2.92	2.15 / 3.00	2.19 / 3.08	2.23 / 3.16	2.29 / 3.27	2.33 / 3.35	2.38 / 3.45	2.41 / 3.52	2.45 / 3.59	2.50 / 3.68	2.55 / 3.79	2.62 / 3.93	2.70 / 4.10	2.81 / 4.34	2.96 / 4.67	3.20 / 5.18	3.59 / 6.11	4.45 / 8.40
18	1.92 / 2.57	1.93 / 2.59	1.95 / 2.62	1.98 / 2.68	2.00 / 2.71	2.04 / 2.78	2.07 / 2.83	2.11 / 2.91	2.15 / 3.00	2.19 / 3.07	2.25 / 3.19	2.29 / 3.27	2.34 / 3.37	2.37 / 3.44	2.41 / 3.51	2.46 / 3.60	2.51 / 3.71	2.58 / 3.85	2.66 / 4.01	2.77 / 4.25	2.93 / 4.58	3.16 / 5.09	3.55 / 6.01	4.41 / 8.28
19	1.88 / 2.49	1.90 / 2.51	1.91 / 2.54	1.94 / 2.60	1.96 / 2.63	2.00 / 2.70	2.02 / 2.76	2.07 / 2.84	2.11 / 2.92	2.15 / 3.00	2.21 / 3.12	2.26 / 3.19	2.31 / 3.30	2.34 / 3.36	2.38 / 3.43	2.43 / 3.52	2.48 / 3.63	2.55 / 3.77	2.63 / 3.94	2.74 / 4.17	2.90 / 4.50	3.13 / 5.01	3.52 / 5.93	4.38 / 8.18
20	1.84 / 2.42	1.85 / 2.44	1.87 / 2.47	1.90 / 2.53	1.92 / 2.56	1.96 / 2.63	1.99 / 2.69	2.04 / 2.77	2.08 / 2.86	2.12 / 2.94	2.18 / 3.05	2.23 / 3.13	2.28 / 3.23	2.31 / 3.30	2.35 / 3.37	2.40 / 3.45	2.45 / 3.56	2.52 / 3.71	2.60 / 3.87	2.71 / 4.10	2.87 / 4.43	3.10 / 4.94	3.49 / 5.85	4.35 / 8.10
21	1.81 / 2.36	1.82 / 2.38	1.84 / 2.42	1.87 / 2.47	1.88 / 2.51	1.93 / 2.58	1.96 / 2.63	2.00 / 2.72	2.05 / 2.80	2.09 / 2.88	2.15 / 2.99	2.20 / 3.07	2.25 / 3.17	2.28 / 3.24	2.32 / 3.31	2.37 / 3.40	2.42 / 3.51	2.49 / 3.65	2.57 / 3.81	2.68 / 4.04	2.84 / 4.37	3.07 / 4.87	3.47 / 5.78	4.32 / 8.02
22	1.78 / 2.31	1.80 / 2.33	1.81 / 2.37	1.84 / 2.42	1.87 / 2.46	1.91 / 2.53	1.93 / 2.58	1.98 / 2.67	2.03 / 2.75	2.07 / 2.83	2.13 / 2.94	2.18 / 3.02	2.23 / 3.12	2.26 / 3.18	2.30 / 3.26	2.35 / 3.35	2.40 / 3.45	2.47 / 3.59	2.55 / 3.76	2.66 / 3.99	2.82 / 4.31	3.05 / 4.82	3.44 / 5.72	4.30 / 7.94
23	1.76 / 2.26	1.77 / 2.28	1.79 / 2.32	1.82 / 2.37	1.84 / 2.41	1.88 / 2.48	1.91 / 2.53	1.96 / 2.62	2.00 / 2.70	2.04 / 2.78	2.10 / 2.89	2.14 / 2.97	2.20 / 3.07	2.24 / 3.14	2.28 / 3.21	2.32 / 3.30	2.38 / 3.41	2.45 / 3.54	2.53 / 3.71	2.64 / 3.94	2.80 / 4.26	3.03 / 4.76	3.42 / 5.66	4.28 / 7.88
24	1.73 / 2.21	1.74 / 2.23	1.76 / 2.27	1.80 / 2.33	1.82 / 2.36	1.86 / 2.44	1.89 / 2.49	1.94 / 2.58	1.98 / 2.66	2.02 / 2.74	2.09 / 2.85	2.13 / 2.93	2.18 / 3.03	2.22 / 3.09	2.26 / 3.17	2.32 / 3.25	2.36 / 3.36	2.43 / 3.50	2.51 / 3.67	2.62 / 3.90	2.78 / 4.22	3.01 / 4.72	3.40 / 5.61	4.26 / 7.82
25	1.71 / 2.17	1.72 / 2.19	1.74 / 2.23	1.77 / 2.29	1.80 / 2.32	1.84 / 2.40	1.87 / 2.45	1.92 / 2.54	1.96 / 2.62	2.00 / 2.70	2.06 / 2.81	2.11 / 2.89	2.16 / 2.99	2.20 / 3.05	2.24 / 3.13	2.30 / 3.21	2.34 / 3.32	2.41 / 3.46	2.49 / 3.63	2.60 / 3.86	2.76 / 4.18	2.99 / 4.68	3.38 / 5.57	4.24 / 7.77
26	1.69 / 2.13	1.70 / 2.15	1.72 / 2.19	1.76 / 2.25	1.78 / 2.28	1.82 / 2.36	1.85 / 2.41	1.90 / 2.50	1.95 / 2.58	1.99 / 2.66	2.05 / 2.77	2.10 / 2.86	2.15 / 2.96	2.18 / 3.02	2.22 / 3.09	2.28 / 3.17	2.32 / 3.29	2.39 / 3.42	2.47 / 3.59	2.59 / 3.82	2.74 / 4.14	2.98 / 4.64	3.37 / 5.53	4.22 / 7.72
27	1.67 / 2.10	1.68 / 2.12	1.71 / 2.16	1.74 / 2.21	1.76 / 2.25	1.80 / 2.33	1.84 / 2.38	1.88 / 2.47	1.93 / 2.55	1.97 / 2.63	2.03 / 2.74	2.08 / 2.83	2.13 / 2.93	2.16 / 2.98	2.20 / 3.06	2.25 / 3.14	2.30 / 3.26	2.37 / 3.39	2.46 / 3.56	2.57 / 3.79	2.73 / 4.11	2.96 / 4.60	3.35 / 5.49	4.21 / 7.68
28	1.65 / 2.06	1.67 / 2.09	1.69 / 2.13	1.72 / 2.18	1.75 / 2.22	1.78 / 2.30	1.81 / 2.35	1.87 / 2.44	1.91 / 2.52	1.96 / 2.60	2.02 / 2.71	2.06 / 2.80	2.12 / 2.90	2.15 / 2.95	2.19 / 3.03	2.24 / 3.11	2.29 / 3.23	2.36 / 3.36	2.44 / 3.53	2.56 / 3.76	2.71 / 4.07	2.95 / 4.57	3.34 / 5.45	4.20 / 7.64
29	1.64 / 2.03	1.65 / 2.06	1.68 / 2.10	1.71 / 2.15	1.73 / 2.19	1.77 / 2.27	1.80 / 2.32	1.85 / 2.41	1.90 / 2.49	1.94 / 2.57	2.00 / 2.68	2.05 / 2.77	2.10 / 2.87	2.14 / 2.92	2.18 / 3.00	2.22 / 3.08	2.28 / 3.20	2.35 / 3.33	2.43 / 3.50	2.54 / 3.73	2.70 / 4.04	2.93 / 4.54	3.33 / 5.42	4.18 / 7.60
30	1.62 / 2.01	1.64 / 2.03	1.66 / 2.07	1.69 / 2.13	1.72 / 2.16	1.76 / 2.24	1.79 / 2.29	1.84 / 2.38	1.89 / 2.47	1.93 / 2.55	1.99 / 2.66	2.04 / 2.74	2.09 / 2.84	2.12 / 2.90	2.16 / 2.98	2.21 / 3.06	2.27 / 3.17	2.34 / 3.30	2.42 / 3.47	2.53 / 3.70	2.69 / 4.02	2.92 / 4.51	3.32 / 5.39	4.17 / 7.56

Degrees of freedom for denominator

Table D (Cont.)

Degrees of freedom for numerator

Denominator df	1	2	3	4	5	6	7	8	9	10	11	12	14	16	20	24	30	40	50	75	100	200	500	∞
32	4.15 / 7.50	3.30 / 5.34	2.90 / 4.46	2.67 / 3.97	2.51 / 3.66	2.40 / 3.42	2.32 / 3.25	2.25 / 3.12	2.19 / 3.01	2.14 / 2.94	2.10 / 2.86	2.07 / 2.80	2.02 / 2.70	1.97 / 2.62	1.91 / 2.51	1.86 / 2.42	1.82 / 2.34	1.76 / 2.25	1.74 / 2.20	1.69 / 2.12	1.67 / 2.08	1.64 / 2.02	1.61 / 1.98	1.59 / 1.96
34	4.13 / 7.44	3.28 / 5.29	2.88 / 4.42	2.65 / 3.93	2.49 / 3.61	2.38 / 3.38	2.30 / 3.21	2.23 / 3.08	2.17 / 2.97	2.12 / 2.89	2.08 / 2.82	2.05 / 2.76	2.00 / 2.66	1.95 / 2.58	1.89 / 2.47	1.84 / 2.38	1.80 / 2.30	1.74 / 2.21	1.71 / 2.15	1.67 / 2.08	1.64 / 2.04	1.61 / 1.98	1.59 / 1.94	1.57 / 1.91
36	4.11 / 7.39	3.26 / 5.25	2.86 / 4.38	2.63 / 3.89	2.48 / 3.58	2.36 / 3.35	2.28 / 3.18	2.21 / 3.04	2.15 / 2.94	2.10 / 2.86	2.06 / 2.78	2.03 / 2.72	1.98 / 2.62	1.93 / 2.54	1.87 / 2.43	1.82 / 2.35	1.78 / 2.26	1.72 / 2.17	1.69 / 2.12	1.65 / 2.04	1.62 / 2.00	1.59 / 1.94	1.56 / 1.90	1.55 / 1.87
38	4.10 / 7.35	3.25 / 5.21	2.85 / 4.34	2.62 / 3.86	2.46 / 3.54	2.35 / 3.32	2.26 / 3.15	2.19 / 3.02	2.14 / 2.91	2.09 / 2.82	2.05 / 2.75	2.02 / 2.69	1.96 / 2.59	1.92 / 2.51	1.85 / 2.40	1.80 / 2.32	1.76 / 2.22	1.71 / 2.14	1.67 / 2.08	1.63 / 2.00	1.60 / 1.97	1.57 / 1.90	1.54 / 1.86	1.53 / 1.84
40	4.08 / 7.31	3.23 / 5.18	2.84 / 4.31	2.61 / 3.83	2.45 / 3.51	2.34 / 3.29	2.25 / 3.12	2.18 / 2.99	2.12 / 2.88	2.07 / 2.80	2.04 / 2.73	2.00 / 2.66	1.95 / 2.56	1.90 / 2.49	1.84 / 2.37	1.79 / 2.29	1.74 / 2.20	1.69 / 2.11	1.66 / 2.05	1.61 / 1.97	1.59 / 1.94	1.55 / 1.88	1.53 / 1.84	1.51 / 1.81
42	4.07 / 7.27	3.22 / 5.15	2.83 / 4.29	2.59 / 3.80	2.44 / 3.49	2.32 / 3.26	2.24 / 3.10	2.17 / 2.96	2.11 / 2.86	2.06 / 2.77	2.02 / 2.70	1.99 / 2.64	1.94 / 2.54	1.89 / 2.46	1.82 / 2.35	1.78 / 2.26	1.73 / 2.17	1.68 / 2.08	1.64 / 2.02	1.60 / 1.94	1.57 / 1.91	1.54 / 1.85	1.51 / 1.80	1.49 / 1.78
44	4.06 / 7.24	3.21 / 5.12	2.82 / 4.26	2.58 / 3.78	2.43 / 3.46	2.31 / 3.24	2.23 / 3.07	2.16 / 2.94	2.10 / 2.84	2.05 / 2.75	2.01 / 2.68	1.98 / 2.62	1.92 / 2.52	1.88 / 2.44	1.81 / 2.32	1.76 / 2.24	1.72 / 2.15	1.66 / 2.06	1.63 / 2.00	1.58 / 1.92	1.56 / 1.88	1.52 / 1.82	1.50 / 1.78	1.48 / 1.75
46	4.05 / 7.21	3.20 / 5.10	2.81 / 4.24	2.57 / 3.76	2.42 / 3.44	2.30 / 3.22	2.22 / 3.05	2.14 / 2.92	2.09 / 2.82	2.04 / 2.73	2.00 / 2.66	1.97 / 2.60	1.91 / 2.50	1.87 / 2.42	1.80 / 2.30	1.75 / 2.22	1.71 / 2.13	1.65 / 2.04	1.62 / 1.98	1.57 / 1.90	1.54 / 1.86	1.51 / 1.80	1.48 / 1.76	1.46 / 1.72
48	4.04 / 7.19	3.19 / 5.08	2.80 / 4.22	2.56 / 3.74	2.41 / 3.42	2.30 / 3.20	2.21 / 3.04	2.14 / 2.90	2.08 / 2.80	2.03 / 2.71	1.99 / 2.64	1.96 / 2.58	1.90 / 2.48	1.86 / 2.40	1.79 / 2.28	1.74 / 2.20	1.70 / 2.11	1.64 / 2.02	1.61 / 1.96	1.56 / 1.88	1.53 / 1.84	1.50 / 1.78	1.47 / 1.73	1.45 / 1.70
50	4.03 / 7.17	3.18 / 5.06	2.79 / 4.20	2.56 / 3.72	2.40 / 3.41	2.29 / 3.18	2.20 / 3.02	2.13 / 2.88	2.07 / 2.78	2.02 / 2.70	1.98 / 2.62	1.95 / 2.56	1.90 / 2.46	1.85 / 2.39	1.78 / 2.26	1.74 / 2.18	1.69 / 2.10	1.63 / 2.00	1.60 / 1.94	1.55 / 1.86	1.52 / 1.82	1.48 / 1.76	1.46 / 1.71	1.44 / 1.68
55	4.02 / 7.12	3.17 / 5.01	2.78 / 4.16	2.54 / 3.68	2.38 / 3.37	2.27 / 3.15	2.18 / 2.98	2.11 / 2.85	2.05 / 2.75	2.00 / 2.66	1.97 / 2.59	1.93 / 2.53	1.88 / 2.43	1.83 / 2.35	1.76 / 2.23	1.72 / 2.15	1.67 / 2.06	1.61 / 1.96	1.58 / 1.90	1.52 / 1.82	1.50 / 1.78	1.46 / 1.71	1.43 / 1.66	1.41 / 1.64
60	4.00 / 7.08	3.15 / 4.98	2.76 / 4.13	2.52 / 3.65	2.37 / 3.34	2.25 / 3.12	2.17 / 2.95	2.10 / 2.82	2.04 / 2.72	1.99 / 2.63	1.95 / 2.56	1.92 / 2.50	1.86 / 2.40	1.81 / 2.32	1.75 / 2.20	1.70 / 2.12	1.65 / 2.03	1.59 / 1.93	1.56 / 1.87	1.50 / 1.79	1.48 / 1.74	1.44 / 1.68	1.41 / 1.63	1.39 / 1.60
65	3.99 / 7.04	3.14 / 4.95	2.75 / 4.10	2.51 / 3.62	2.36 / 3.31	2.24 / 3.09	2.15 / 2.93	2.08 / 2.79	2.02 / 2.70	1.98 / 2.61	1.94 / 2.54	1.90 / 2.47	1.85 / 2.37	1.80 / 2.30	1.73 / 2.18	1.68 / 2.09	1.63 / 2.00	1.57 / 1.90	1.54 / 1.84	1.49 / 1.76	1.46 / 1.71	1.42 / 1.64	1.39 / 1.60	1.37 / 1.56
70	3.98 / 7.01	3.13 / 4.92	2.74 / 4.08	2.50 / 3.60	2.35 / 3.29	2.23 / 3.07	2.14 / 2.91	2.07 / 2.77	2.01 / 2.67	1.97 / 2.59	1.93 / 2.51	1.89 / 2.45	1.84 / 2.35	1.79 / 2.28	1.72 / 2.15	1.67 / 2.07	1.62 / 1.98	1.56 / 1.88	1.53 / 1.82	1.47 / 1.74	1.45 / 1.69	1.40 / 1.62	1.37 / 1.56	1.35 / 1.53
80	3.96 / 6.96	3.11 / 4.88	2.72 / 4.04	2.48 / 3.56	2.33 / 3.25	2.21 / 3.04	2.12 / 2.87	2.05 / 2.74	1.99 / 2.64	1.95 / 2.55	1.91 / 2.48	1.88 / 2.41	1.82 / 2.32	1.77 / 2.24	1.70 / 2.11	1.65 / 2.03	1.60 / 1.94	1.54 / 1.84	1.51 / 1.78	1.45 / 1.70	1.42 / 1.65	1.38 / 1.57	1.35 / 1.52	1.32 / 1.49

Degrees of freedom for denominator

Degrees of freedom for denominator

df																								
100	1.28 / 1.43	1.30 / 1.46	1.34 / 1.51	1.39 / 1.59	1.42 / 1.64	1.48 / 1.73	1.51 / 1.79	1.57 / 1.89	1.63 / 1.98	1.68 / 2.06	1.75 / 2.19	1.79 / 2.26	1.85 / 2.36	1.88 / 2.43	1.92 / 2.51	1.97 / 2.59	2.03 / 2.69	2.10 / 2.82	2.19 / 2.99	2.30 / 3.20	2.46 / 3.51	2.70 / 3.98	3.09 / 4.82	3.94 / 6.90
125	1.25 / 1.37	1.27 / 1.40	1.31 / 1.46	1.36 / 1.54	1.39 / 1.59	1.45 / 1.68	1.49 / 1.75	1.55 / 1.85	1.60 / 1.94	1.65 / 2.03	1.72 / 2.15	1.77 / 2.23	1.83 / 2.33	1.86 / 2.40	1.90 / 2.47	1.95 / 2.56	2.01 / 2.65	2.08 / 2.79	2.17 / 2.95	2.29 / 3.17	2.44 / 3.47	2.68 / 3.94	3.07 / 4.78	3.92 / 6.84
150	1.22 / 1.33	1.25 / 1.37	1.29 / 1.43	1.34 / 1.51	1.37 / 1.56	1.44 / 1.66	1.47 / 1.72	1.54 / 1.83	1.59 / 1.91	1.64 / 2.00	1.71 / 2.12	1.76 / 2.20	1.82 / 2.30	1.85 / 2.37	1.89 / 2.44	1.94 / 2.53	2.00 / 2.62	2.07 / 2.76	2.16 / 2.92	2.27 / 3.13	2.43 / 3.44	2.67 / 3.91	3.06 / 4.75	3.91 / 6.81
200	1.19 / 1.28	1.22 / 1.33	1.26 / 1.39	1.32 / 1.48	1.35 / 1.53	1.42 / 1.62	1.45 / 1.69	1.52 / 1.79	1.57 / 1.88	1.62 / 1.97	1.69 / 2.09	1.74 / 2.17	1.80 / 2.28	1.83 / 2.34	1.87 / 2.41	1.92 / 2.50	1.98 / 2.60	2.05 / 2.73	2.14 / 2.90	2.26 / 3.11	2.41 / 3.41	2.65 / 3.88	3.04 / 4.71	3.89 / 6.76
400	1.13 / 1.19	1.16 / 1.24	1.22 / 1.32	1.28 / 1.42	1.30 / 1.44	1.38 / 1.57	1.42 / 1.64	1.49 / 1.74	1.54 / 1.84	1.60 / 1.92	1.67 / 2.04	1.72 / 2.12	1.78 / 2.23	1.81 / 2.29	1.85 / 2.37	1.90 / 2.46	1.96 / 2.55	2.03 / 2.69	2.12 / 2.85	2.23 / 3.06	2.39 / 3.36	2.62 / 3.83	3.02 / 4.66	3.86 / 6.70
1000	1.08 / 1.11	1.13 / 1.19	1.19 / 1.28	1.26 / 1.38	1.28 / 1.41	1.36 / 1.54	1.41 / 1.61	1.47 / 1.71	1.53 / 1.81	1.58 / 1.89	1.65 / 2.01	1.70 / 2.09	1.76 / 2.20	1.80 / 2.26	1.84 / 2.34	1.89 / 2.43	1.95 / 2.53	2.02 / 2.66	2.10 / 2.82	2.22 / 3.04	2.38 / 3.34	2.61 / 3.80	3.00 / 4.62	3.85 / 6.66
∞	1.00 / 1.00	1.11 / 1.15	1.17 / 1.25	1.24 / 1.36	1.28 / 1.41	1.35 / 1.52	1.40 / 1.59	1.46 / 1.69	1.52 / 1.79	1.57 / 1.87	1.64 / 1.99	1.69 / 2.07	1.75 / 2.18	1.79 / 2.24	1.83 / 2.32	1.88 / 2.41	1.94 / 2.51	2.01 / 2.64	2.09 / 2.80	2.21 / 3.02	2.37 / 3.32	2.60 / 3.78	2.99 / 4.60	3.84 / 6.64

Table D₁
Critical values of F that cut off the upper and lower 2.5% of the F-distributions.

A difference in variances is significant at $\alpha = 0.05$ with df₁ and df₂ if it equals or exceeds the upper value in each cell or is *less than or equal to* the lower value in that cell, e.g., if $s_1^2 = 8.69$, df = 12 and $s_2^2 = 2.63$, df = 9, F = 3.30. The critical values at df₁₂ and df₉ are .291 and 3.87. Since obtained F is between these values, we fail to reject the hypothesis of homogeneity of variances. *Note:* Had we calculated F with s_1^2 in the denominator, the critical lower and upper values at 9 and 12 df would have been .259 and 3.44.

df	1	2	3	4	5	6	7	8	9	10	11	12	15	20	24	30	40	50	60	100	200	500
1	.002 / 648	.026 / 800	.057 / 864	.082 / 900	.100 / 922	.113 / 937	.124 / 948	.132 / 957	.139 / 963	.144 / 969	.149 / 973	.153 / 977	.161 / 985	.170 / 993	.175 / 997	.180 / 1000	.184 / 1010	.187 / 1010	.189 / 1010	.193 / 1010	.196 / 1020	.198 / 1020
2	.001 / 38.5	.026 / 39.0	.062 / 39.2	.094 / 39.2	.119 / 39.3	.138 / 39.3	.153 / 39.4	.165 / 39.4	.175 / 39.4	.183 / 39.4	.190 / 39.4	.196 / 39.4	.210 / 39.4	.224 / 39.4	.232 / 39.5	.239 / 39.5	.247 / 39.5	.251 / 39.5	.255 / 39.5	.261 / 39.5	.266 / 39.5	.269 / 39.5
3	.001 / 17.4	.026 / 16.0	.065 / 15.4	.100 / 15.1	.129 / 14.9	.152 / 14.7	.170 / 14.6	.185 / 14.5	.197 / 14.5	.207 / 14.4	.216 / 14.4	.224 / 14.3	.241 / 14.3	.259 / 14.2	.269 / 14.1	.279 / 14.1	.289 / 14.0	.295 / 14.0	.299 / 14.0	.308 / 14.0	.314 / 13.9	.318 / 13.9
4	.001 / 12.2	.026 / 10.6	.066 / 9.98	.104 / 9.60	.135 / 9.36	.161 / 9.20	.181 / 9.07	.198 / 8.98	.212 / 8.90	.224 / 8.84	.234 / 8.79	.243 / 8.75	.263 / 8.66	.284 / 8.56	.296 / 8.51	.308 / 8.46	.320 / 8.41	.327 / 8.38	.332 / 8.36	.342 / 8.32	.351 / 8.29	.356 / 8.27
5	.001 / 10.0	.025 / 8.43	.067 / 7.76	.107 / 7.39	.140 / 7.15	.167 / 6.98	.189 / 6.85	.208 / 6.76	.223 / 6.68	.236 / 6.62	.248 / 6.57	.257 / 6.52	.280 / 6.43	.304 / 6.33	.317 / 6.28	.330 / 6.23	.344 / 6.18	.353 / 6.14	.359 / 6.12	.370 / 6.08	.380 / 6.05	.386 / 6.03
6	.001 / 8.81	.025 / 7.26	.068 / 6.60	.109 / 6.23	.143 / 5.99	.172 / 5.82	.195 / 5.70	.215 / 5.60	.231 / 5.52	.246 / 5.46	.258 / 5.41	.268 / 5.37	.293 / 5.27	.320 / 5.17	.334 / 5.12	.349 / 5.07	.364 / 5.01	.375 / 4.98	.381 / 4.96	.394 / 4.92	.405 / 4.88	.415 / 4.86
7	.001 / 8.07	.025 / 6.54	.068 / 5.89	.110 / 5.52	.146 / 5.29	.176 / 5.12	.200 / 4.99	.221 / 4.90	.238 / 4.82	.253 / 4.76	.266 / 4.71	.277 / 4.67	.304 / 4.57	.333 / 4.47	.348 / 4.42	.364 / 4.36	.381 / 4.31	.392 / 4.28	.399 / 4.25	.413 / 4.21	.426 / 4.18	.433 / 4.16
8	.001 / 7.57	.025 / 6.06	.069 / 5.42	.111 / 5.05	.148 / 4.82	.179 / 4.65	.204 / 4.53	.226 / 4.43	.244 / 4.36	.259 / 4.30	.273 / 4.24	.285 / 4.20	.313 / 4.10	.343 / 4.00	.360 / 3.95	.377 / 3.89	.395 / 3.84	.407 / 3.81	.415 / 3.78	.431 / 3.74	.442 / 3.70	.450 / 3.68
9	.001 / 7.21	.025 / 5.71	.069 / 5.08	.112 / 4.72	.150 / 4.48	.181 / 4.32	.207 / 4.20	.230 / 4.10	.248 / 4.03	.265 / 3.96	.279 / 3.91	.291 / 3.87	.320 / 3.77	.352 / 3.67	.370 / 3.61	.388 / 3.56	.408 / 3.51	.420 / 3.47	.428 / 3.45	.446 / 3.40	.459 / 3.37	.467 / 3.35
10	.001 / 6.94	.025 / 5.46	.069 / 4.83	.113 / 4.47	.151 / 4.24	.183 / 4.07	.210 / 3.95	.233 / 3.85	.252 / 3.78	.269 / 3.72	.283 / 3.66	.296 / 3.62	.327 / 3.52	.360 / 3.42	.379 / 3.37	.398 / 3.31	.419 / 3.26	.431 / 3.22	.441 / 3.20	.459 / 3.15	.474 / 3.12	.483 / 3.09

df																						
11	.495	.485	.472	.450	.442	.429	.407	.386	.368	.332	.301	.288	.273	.256	.236	.212	.185	.152	.114	.069	.025	.001
	2.90	2.92	2.96	3.00	3.03	3.06	3.12	3.17	3.23	3.33	3.43	3.47	3.53	3.59	3.66	3.76	3.88	4.04	4.28	4.63	5.26	6.72
12	.508	.498	.481	.461	.450	.437	.416	.394	.374	.337	.305	.292	.276	.259	.238	.214	.186	.153	.114	.070	.025	.001
	2.74	2.76	2.80	2.85	2.87	2.91	2.96	3.02	3.07	3.18	3.28	3.32	3.37	3.44	3.51	3.61	3.73	3.89	4.12	4.47	5.10	6.55
15	.538	.526	.508	.485	.474	.458	.433	.410	.389	.349	.315	.300	.284	.265	.244	.219	.190	.156	.116	.070	.025	.001
	2.41	2.44	2.47	2.52	2.55	2.59	2.64	2.70	2.76	2.86	2.96	3.01	3.06	3.12	3.20	3.29	3.41	3.58	3.80	4.15	4.76	6.20
20	.575	.562	.541	.514	.503	.484	.456	.430	.406	.363	.325	.310	.292	.273	.250	.224	.193	.158	.117	.071	.025	.001
	2.10	2.13	2.17	2.22	2.25	2.29	2.35	2.41	2.46	2.57	2.68	2.72	2.77	2.84	2.91	3.01	3.13	3.29	3.51	3.86	4.46	5.87
24	.599	.585	.562	.531	.518	.498	.468	.441	.415	.370	.331	.315	.297	.277	.253	.227	.195	.159	.117	.071	.025	.001
	1.95	1.98	2.02	2.08	2.11	2.15	2.21	2.27	2.33	2.44	2.54	2.59	2.64	2.70	2.78	2.87	2.99	3.15	3.38	3.72	4.32	5.72
30	.625	.610	.585	.551	.535	.515	.482	.453	.426	.378	.337	.321	.302	.281	.257	.229	.197	.161	.118	.071	.025	.001
	1.81	1.84	1.88	1.94	1.97	2.01	2.07	2.14	2.20	2.31	2.41	2.46	2.51	2.57	2.65	2.75	2.87	3.03	3.25	3.59	4.18	5.57
40	.662	.641	.610	.573	.556	.533	.498	.466	.437	.387	.344	.327	.307	.285	.260	.232	.199	.162	.119	.071	.025	.001
	1.66	1.69	1.74	1.80	1.83	1.88	1.94	2.01	2.07	2.18	2.29	2.33	2.39	2.45	2.53	2.62	2.74	2.90	3.13	3.46	4.05	5.42
60	.704	.680	.641	.600	.581	.555	.515	.481	.450	.396	.351	.333	.313	.290	.264	.235	.202	.163	.120	.071	.025	.001
	1.51	1.54	1.60	1.67	1.70	1.74	1.82	1.88	1.94	2.06	2.17	2.22	2.27	2.33	2.41	2.51	2.63	2.79	3.01	3.34	3.93	5.29
120	.762	.729	.684	.633	.611	.580	.536	.498	.464	.406	.359	.340	.318	.295	.268	.238	.204	.165	.120	.072	.025	.001
	1.34	1.39	1.45	1.53	1.56	1.61	1.69	1.76	1.82	1.95	2.05	2.10	2.16	2.22	2.30	2.39	2.52	2.67	2.89	3.23	3.80	5.15

Table E
Critical values of A.

For any given value of $N - 1$, the table shows the values of A corresponding to various levels of probability. A is significant at a given level if it is equal to or *less than* the value shown in the table. *Example:* If $\sum D^2 = 60$, $(\sum D)^2 = 200$, $\alpha = 0.05$, two-tailed test, and $N - 1 = 28$, $A = 0.300$. Since this is not equal to or less than 0.265 required to reject H_0, we fail to reject the null hypothesis.

	Level of significance for one-tailed test					
	.05	.025	.01	.005	.0005	
	Level of significance for two-tailed test					
$N - 1$*	.10	.05	.02	.01	.001	$N - 1$*
1	0.5125	0.5031	0.50049	0.50012	0.5000012	1
2	0.412	0.369	0.347	0.340	0.334	2
3	0.385	0.324	0.286	0.272	0.254	3
4	0.376	0.304	0.257	0.238	0.211	4
5	0.372	0.293	0.240	0.218	0.184	5
6	0.370	0.286	0.230	0.205	0.167	6
7	0.369	0.281	0.222	0.196	0.155	7
8	0.368	0.278	0.217	0.190	0.146	8
9	0.368	0.276	0.213	0.185	0.139	9
10	0.368	0.274	0.210	0.181	0.134	10
11	0.368	0.273	0.207	0.178	0.130	11
12	0.368	0.271	0.205	0.176	0.126	12
13	0.368	0.270	0.204	0.174	0.124	13
14	0.368	0.270	0.202	0.172	0.121	14
15	0.368	0.269	0.201	0.170	0.119	15
16	0.368	0.268	0.200	0.169	0.117	16
17	0.368	0.268	0.199	0.168	0.116	17
18	0.368	0.267	0.198	0.167	0.114	18
19	0.368	0.267	0.197	0.166	0.113	19
20	0.368	0.266	0.197	0.165	0.112	20
21	0.368	0.266	0.196	0.165	0.111	21
22	0.368	0.266	0.196	0.164	0.110	22
23	0.368	0.266	0.195	0.163	0.109	23
24	0.368	0.265	0.195	0.163	0.108	24
25	0.368	0.265	0.194	0.162	0.108	25
26	0.368	0.265	0.194	0.162	0.107	26
27	0.368	0.265	0.193	0.161	0.107	27
28	0.368	0.265	0.193	0.161	0.106	28
29	0.368	0.264	0.193	0.161	0.106	29
30	0.368	0.264	0.193	0.160	0.105	30
40	0.368	0.263	0.191	0.158	0.102	40
60	0.369	0.262	0.189	0.155	0.099	60
120	0.369	0.261	0.187	0.153	0.095	120
∞	0.370	0.260	0.185	0.151	0.092	∞

*N = number of pairs

Table F
Transformation of r to z_r

r	z_r	r	z_r	r	z_r
.01	.010	.34	.354	.67	.811
.02	.020	.35	.366	.68	.829
.03	.030	.36	.377	.69	.848
.04	.040	.37	.389	.70	.867
.05	.050	.38	.400	.71	.887
.06	.060	.39	.412	.72	.908
.07	.070	.40	.424	.73	.929
.08	.080	.41	.436	.74	.950
.09	.090	.42	.448	.75	.973
.10	.100	.43	.460	.76	.996
.11	.110	.44	.472	.77	1.020
.12	.121	.45	.485	.78	1.045
.13	.131	.46	.497	.79	1.071
.14	.141	.47	.510	.80	1.099
.15	.151	.48	.523	.81	1.127
.16	.161	.49	.536	.82	1.157
.17	.172	.50	.549	.83	1.188
.18	.181	.51	.563	.84	1.221
.19	.192	.52	.577	.85	1.256
.20	.203	.53	.590	.86	1.293
.21	.214	.54	.604	.87	1.333
.22	.224	.55	.618	.88	1.376
.23	.234	.56	.633	.89	1.422
.24	.245	.57	.648	.90	1.472
.25	.256	.58	.663	.91	1.528
.26	.266	.59	.678	.92	1.589
.27	.277	.60	.693	.93	1.658
.28	.288	.61	.709	.94	1.738
.29	.299	.62	.725	.95	1.832
.30	.309	.63	.741	.96	1.946
.31	.321	.64	.758	.97	2.092
.32	.332	.65	.775	.98	2.298
.33	.343	.66	.793	.99	2.647

Table G
Critical values of r_s.

A given value of r_s is statistically significant if it equals or exceeds the tabled value at the designated α level at a given N. To interpolate, sum the critical values above and below the N of interest and divide by 2. Thus the critical value at $\alpha = 0.05$, two-tailed test, when $N = 21$, is $(0.450 + 0.428)/2 = 0.439$.

	Level of significance for one-tailed test			
	.05	.025	.01	.005
	Level of significance for two-tailed test			
N^*	.10	.05	.02	.01
5	.900	1.000	1.000	--
6	.829	.886	.943	1.000
7	.714	.786	.893	.929
8	.643	.738	.833	.881
9	.600	.683	.783	.833
10	.564	.648	.746	.794
12	.506	.591	.712	.777
14	.456	.544	.645	.715
16	.425	.506	.601	.665
18	.399	.475	.564	.625
20	.377	.450	.534	.591
22	.359	.428	.508	.562
24	.343	.409	.485	.537
26	.329	.392	.465	.515
28	.317	.377	.448	.496
30	.306	.364	.432	.478

$^*N$ = number of pairs

Table H
Functions of *r*.

r	$\sqrt{r}$	r^2	$\sqrt{r-r^2}$	$\sqrt{1-r}$	$1-r^2$	$\sqrt{1-r^2}$	$100(1-k)$	r
						k	% Eff.	
1.00	1.0000	1.0000	0.0000	0.0000	0.0000	0.0000	100.00	1.00
.99	.9950	.9801	.0995	.1000	.0199	.1411	85.89	.99
.98	.9899	.9604	.1400	.1414	.0396	.1990	80.10	.98
.97	.9849	.9409	.1706	.1732	.0591	.2431	75.69	.97
.96	.9798	.9216	.1960	.2000	.0784	.2800	72.00	.96
.95	.9747	.9025	.2179	.2236	.0975	.3122	68.78	.95
.94	.9695	.8836	.2375	.2449	.1164	.3412	65.88	.94
.93	.9644	.8649	.2551	.2646	.1351	.3676	63.24	.93
.92	.9592	.8464	.2713	.2828	.1536	.3919	60.81	.92
.91	.9539	.8281	.2862	.3000	.1719	.4146	58.54	.91
.90	.9487	.8100	.3000	.3162	.1900	.4359	56.41	.90
.89	.9434	.7921	.3129	.3317	.2079	.4560	54.40	.89
.88	.9381	.7744	.3250	.3464	.2256	.4750	52.50	.88
.87	.9327	.7569	.3363	.3606	.2431	.4931	50.69	.87
.86	.9274	.7396	.3470	.3742	.2604	.5103	48.97	.86
.85	.9220	.7225	.3571	.3873	.2775	.5268	47.32	.85
.84	.9165	.7056	.3666	.4000	.2944	.5426	45.74	.84
.83	.9110	.6889	.3756	.4123	.3111	.5578	44.22	.83
.82	.9055	.6724	.3842	.4243	.3276	.5724	42.76	.82
.81	.9000	.6561	.3923	.4359	.3439	.5864	41.36	.81
.80	.8944	.6400	.4000	.4472	.3600	.6000	40.00	.80
.79	.8888	.6241	.4073	.4583	.3759	.6131	38.69	.79
.78	.8832	.6084	.4142	.4690	.3916	.6258	37.42	.78
.77	.8775	.5929	.4208	.4796	.4071	.6380	36.20	.77
.76	.8718	.5776	.4271	.4899	.4224	.6499	35.01	.76
.75	.8660	.5625	.4330	.5000	.4375	.6614	33.86	.75
.74	.8602	.5476	.4386	.5099	.4524	.6726	32.74	.74
.73	.8544	.5329	.4440	.5196	.4671	.6834	31.66	.73
.72	.8485	.5184	.4490	.5292	.4816	.6940	30.60	.72
.71	.8426	.5041	.4538	.5385	.4959	.7042	29.58	.71
.70	.8367	.4900	.4583	.5477	.5100	.7141	28.59	.70
.69	.8307	.4761	.4625	.5568	.5239	.7238	27.62	.69
.68	.8246	.4624	.4665	.5657	.5376	.7332	26.68	.68
.67	.8185	.4489	.4702	.5745	.5511	.7424	25.76	.67
.66	.8124	.4356	.4737	.5831	.5644	.7513	24.87	.66
.65	.8062	.4225	.4770	.5916	.5775	.7599	24.01	.65
.64	.8000	.4096	.4800	.6000	.5904	.7684	23.16	.64
.63	.7937	.3969	.4828	.6083	.6031	.7766	22.34	.63
.62	.7874	.3844	.4854	.6164	.6156	.7846	21.54	.62
.61	.7810	.3721	.4877	.6245	.6279	.7924	20.76	.61
.60	.7746	.3600	.4899	.6325	.6400	.8000	20.00	.60
.59	.7681	.3481	.4918	.6403	.6519	.8074	19.26	.59
.58	.7616	.3364	.4936	.6481	.6636	.8146	18.54	.58
.57	.7550	.3249	.4951	.6557	.6751	.8216	17.84	.57
.56	.7483	.3136	.4964	.6633	.6864	.8285	17.15	.56
.55	.7416	.3025	.4975	.6708	.6975	.8352	16.48	.55
.54	.7348	.2916	.4984	.6782	.7084	.8417	15.83	.54
.53	.7280	.2809	.4991	.6856	.7191	.8480	15.20	.53
.52	.7211	.2704	.4996	.6928	.7296	.8542	14.58	.52
.51	.7141	.2601	.4999	.7000	.7399	.8602	13.98	.51
.50	.7071	.2500	.5000	.7071	.7500	.8660	13.40	.50

Table H (*Cont.*)

r	$\sqrt{r}$	r^2	$\sqrt{r - r^2}$	$\sqrt{1 - r}$	$1 - r^2$	$\sqrt{1 - r^2}$	$100(1 - k)$	r
						k	% Eff.	
.50	.7071	.2500	.5000	.7071	.7500	.8660	13.40	.50
.49	.7000	.2401	.4999	.7141	.7599	.8717	12.83	.49
.48	.6928	.2304	.4996	.7211	.7696	.8773	12.27	.48
.47	.6856	.2209	.4991	.7280	.7791	.8827	11.73	.47
.46	.6782	.2116	.4984	.7348	.7884	.8879	11.21	.46
.45	.6708	.2025	.4975	.7416	.7975	.8930	10.70	.45
.44	.6633	.1936	.4964	.7483	.8064	.8980	10.20	.44
.43	.6557	.1849	.4951	.7550	.8151	.9028	9.72	.43
.42	.6481	.1764	.4936	.7616	.8236	.9075	9.25	.42
.41	.6403	.1681	.4918	.7681	.8319	.9121	8.79	.41
.40	.6325	.1600	.4899	.7746	.8400	.9165	8.35	.40
.39	.6245	.1521	.4877	.7810	.8479	.9208	7.92	.39
.38	.6164	.1444	.4854	.7874	.8556	.9250	7.50	.38
.37	.6083	.1369	.4828	.7937	.8631	.9290	7.10	.37
.36	.6000	.1296	.4800	.8000	.8704	.9330	6.70	.36
.35	.5916	.1225	.4770	.8062	.8775	.9367	6.33	.35
.34	.5831	.1156	.4737	.8124	.8844	.9404	5.96	.34
.33	.5745	.1089	.4702	.8185	.8911	.9440	5.60	.33
.32	.5657	.1024	.4665	.8246	.8976	.9474	5.25	.32
.31	.5568	.0961	.4625	.8307	.9039	.9507	4.93	.31
.30	.5477	.0900	.4583	.8367	.9100	.9539	4.61	.30
.29	.5385	.0841	.4538	.8426	.9159	.9570	4.30	.29
.28	.5292	.0784	.4490	.8485	.9216	.9600	4.00	.28
.27	.5196	.0729	.4440	.8544	.9271	.9629	3.71	.27
.26	.5099	.0676	.4386	.8602	.9324	.9656	3.44	.26
.25	.5000	.0625	.4330	.8660	.9375	.9682	3.18	.25
.24	.4899	.0576	.4271	.8718	.9424	.9708	2.92	.24
.23	.4796	.0529	.4208	.8775	.9471	.9732	2.68	.23
.22	.4690	.0484	.4142	.8832	.9516	.9755	2.45	.22
.21	.4583	.0441	.4073	.8888	.9559	.9777	2.23	.21
.20	.4472	.0400	.4000	.8944	.9600	.9798	2.02	.20
.19	.4359	.0361	.3923	.9000	.9639	.9818	1.82	.19
.18	.4243	.0324	.3842	.9055	.9676	.9837	1.63	.18
.17	.4123	.0289	.3756	.9110	.9711	.9854	1.46	.17
.16	.4000	.0256	.3666	.9165	.9744	.9871	1.29	.16
.15	.3873	.0225	.3571	.9220	.9775	.9887	1.13	.15
.14	.3742	.0196	.3470	.9274	.9804	.9902	.98	.14
.13	.3606	.0169	.3363	.9327	.9831	.9915	.85	.13
.12	.3464	.0144	.3250	.9381	.9856	.9928	.72	.12
.11	.3317	.0121	.3129	.9434	.9879	.9939	.61	.11
.10	.3162	.0100	.3000	.9487	.9900	.9950	.50	.10
.09	.3000	.0081	.2862	.9539	.9919	.9959	.41	.09
.08	.2828	.0064	.2713	.9592	.9936	.9968	.32	.08
.07	.2646	.0049	.2551	.9644	.9951	.9975	.25	.07
.06	.2449	.0036	.2375	.9695	.9964	.9982	.18	.06
.05	.2236	.0025	.2179	.9747	.9975	.9987	.13	.05
.04	.2000	.0016	.1960	.9798	.9984	.9992	.08	.04
.03	.1732	.0009	.1706	.9849	.9991	.9995	.05	.03
.02	.1414	.0004	.1400	.9899	.9996	.9998	.02	.02
.01	.1000	.0001	.0995	.9950	.9999	.9999	.01	.01
.00	.0000	.0000	.0000	1.0000	1.0000	1.0000	.00	.00

Table I_1

Critical values of U and U' for a one-tailed test at $\alpha = 0.005$ or a two-tailed test at $\alpha = 0.01$.

To be significant for any given N_1 and N_2: Obtained U must be equal to or *less than* the value shown in the table. Obtained U' must be equal to or *greater than* the value shown in the table. *Example:* If $\alpha = 0.01$, two-tailed test, $N_1 = 13$, $N_2 = 15$, and obtained $U = 150$, we cannot reject H_0 since obtained U is within the upper (153) and lower (42) critical values.

N_2 \ N_1	1	2	3	4	5	6	7	8	9	10	11	12	13	14	15	16	17	18	19	20
1	--	--	--	--	--	--	--	--	--	--	--	--	--	--	--	--	--	--	--	--
2	--	--	--	--	--	--	--	--	--	--	--	--	--	--	--	--	--	--	0 38	0 40
3	--	--	--	--	--	--	--	--	0 27	0 30	0 33	1 35	1 38	1 41	2 43	2 46	2 49	2 52	3 54	3 57
4	--	--	--	--	--	0 24	0 28	1 31	1 35	2 38	2 42	3 45	3 49	4 52	5 55	5 59	6 62	6 66	7 69	8 72
5	--	--	--	--	0 25	1 29	1 34	2 38	3 42	4 46	5 50	6 54	7 58	7 63	8 67	9 71	10 75	11 79	12 83	13 87
6	--	--	--	0 24	1 29	2 34	3 39	4 44	5 49	6 54	7 59	9 63	10 68	11 73	12 78	13 83	15 87	16 92	17 97	18 102
7	--	--	--	0 28	1 34	3 39	4 45	6 50	7 56	9 61	10 67	12 72	13 78	15 83	16 89	18 94	19 100	21 105	22 111	24 116
8	--	--	--	1 31	2 38	4 44	6 50	7 57	9 63	11 69	13 75	15 81	17 87	18 94	20 100	22 106	24 112	26 118	28 124	30 130
9	--	--	0 27	1 35	3 42	5 49	7 56	9 63	11 70	13 77	16 83	18 90	20 97	22 104	24 111	27 117	29 124	31 131	33 138	36 144
10	--	--	0 30	2 38	4 46	6 54	9 61	11 69	13 77	16 84	18 92	21 99	24 106	26 114	29 121	31 129	34 136	37 143	39 151	42 158
11	--	--	0 33	2 42	5 50	7 59	10 67	13 75	16 83	18 92	21 100	24 108	27 116	30 124	33 132	36 140	39 148	42 156	45 164	48 172
12	--	--	1 35	3 45	6 54	9 63	12 72	15 81	18 90	21 99	24 108	27 117	31 125	34 134	37 143	41 151	44 160	47 169	51 177	54 186
13	--	--	1 38	3 49	7 58	10 68	13 78	17 87	20 97	24 106	27 116	31 125	34 125	38 144	42 153	45 163	49 172	53 181	56 191	60 200
14	--	--	1 41	4 52	7 63	11 73	15 83	18 94	22 104	26 114	30 124	34 134	38 144	42 154	46 164	50 174	54 184	58 194	63 203	67 213
15	--	--	2 43	5 55	8 67	12 78	16 89	20 100	24 111	29 121	33 132	37 143	42 153	46 164	51 174	55 185	60 195	64 206	69 216	73 227
16	--	--	2 46	5 59	9 71	13 83	18 94	22 106	27 117	31 129	36 140	41 151	45 163	50 174	55 185	60 196	65 207	70 218	74 230	79 241
17	--	--	2 49	6 62	10 75	15 87	19 100	24 112	29 124	34 148	39 148	44 160	49 172	54 184	60 195	65 207	70 219	75 231	81 242	86 254
18	--	--	2 52	6 66	11 79	16 92	21 105	26 118	31 131	37 143	42 156	47 169	53 181	58 194	64 206	70 218	75 231	81 243	87 255	92 268
19	--	0 38	3 54	7 69	12 83	17 97	22 111	28 124	33 138	39 151	45 164	51 177	56 191	63 203	69 216	74 230	81 242	87 255	93 268	99 281
20	--	0 40	3 57	8 72	13 87	18 102	24 116	30 130	36 144	42 158	48 172	54 186	60 200	67 213	73 227	79 241	86 254	92 268	99 281	105 295

(Dashes in the body of the table indicate that no decision is possible at the stated level of significance.)

Table I$_2$
Critical values of U and U' for a one-tailed test at $\alpha = 0.01$ or a two-tailed test at $\alpha = 0.02$

To be significant for any given N_1 and N_2: Obtained U must be equal to or *less than* the value shown in the table. Obtained U' must be equal to or *greater than* the value shown in the table.

N_2 \\ N_1	1	2	3	4	5	6	7	8	9	10	11	12	13	14	15	16	17	18	19	20
1	--	--	--	--	--	--	--	--	--	--	--	--	--	--	--	--	--	--	--	--
2	--	--	--	--	--	--	--	--	--	--	--	--	0 / 26	0 / 28	0 / 30	0 / 32	0 / 34	0 / 36	1 / 37	1 / 39
3	--	--	--	--	--	--	0 / 21	0 / 24	1 / 26	1 / 29	1 / 32	2 / 34	2 / 37	2 / 40	3 / 42	3 / 45	4 / 47	4 / 50	4 / 52	5 / 55
4	--	--	--	--	0 / 20	1 / 23	1 / 27	2 / 30	3 / 33	3 / 37	4 / 40	5 / 43	5 / 47	6 / 50	7 / 53	7 / 57	8 / 60	9 / 63	9 / 67	10 / 70
5	--	--	--	0 / 20	1 / 24	2 / 28	3 / 32	4 / 36	5 / 40	6 / 44	7 / 48	8 / 52	9 / 56	10 / 60	11 / 64	12 / 68	13 / 72	14 / 76	15 / 80	16 / 84
6	--	--	--	1 / 23	2 / 28	3 / 33	4 / 38	6 / 42	7 / 47	8 / 52	9 / 57	11 / 61	12 / 66	13 / 71	15 / 75	16 / 80	18 / 84	19 / 89	20 / 94	22 / 98
7	--	--	0 / 21	1 / 27	3 / 32	4 / 38	6 / 43	7 / 49	9 / 54	11 / 59	12 / 65	14 / 70	16 / 75	17 / 81	19 / 86	21 / 91	23 / 96	24 / 102	26 / 107	28 / 112
8	--	--	0 / 24	2 / 30	4 / 36	6 / 42	7 / 49	9 / 55	11 / 61	13 / 67	15 / 73	17 / 79	20 / 84	22 / 90	24 / 96	26 / 102	28 / 108	30 / 114	32 / 120	34 / 126
9	--	--	1 / 26	3 / 33	5 / 40	7 / 47	9 / 54	11 / 61	14 / 67	16 / 74	18 / 81	21 / 87	23 / 94	26 / 100	28 / 107	31 / 113	33 / 120	36 / 126	38 / 133	40 / 140
10	--	--	1 / 29	3 / 37	6 / 44	8 / 52	11 / 59	13 / 67	16 / 74	19 / 81	22 / 88	24 / 96	27 / 103	30 / 110	33 / 117	36 / 124	38 / 132	41 / 139	44 / 146	47 / 153
11	--	--	1 / 32	4 / 40	7 / 48	9 / 57	12 / 65	15 / 73	18 / 81	22 / 88	25 / 96	28 / 104	31 / 112	34 / 120	37 / 128	41 / 135	44 / 143	47 / 151	50 / 159	53 / 167
12	--	--	2 / 34	5 / 43	8 / 52	11 / 61	14 / 70	17 / 79	21 / 87	24 / 96	28 / 104	31 / 113	35 / 121	38 / 130	42 / 138	46 / 146	49 / 155	53 / 163	56 / 172	60 / 180
13	--	0 / 26	2 / 37	5 / 47	9 / 56	12 / 66	16 / 75	20 / 84	23 / 94	27 / 103	31 / 112	35 / 121	39 / 130	43 / 139	47 / 148	51 / 157	55 / 166	59 / 175	63 / 184	67 / 193
14	--	0 / 28	2 / 40	6 / 50	10 / 60	13 / 71	17 / 81	22 / 90	26 / 100	30 / 110	34 / 120	38 / 130	43 / 139	47 / 149	51 / 159	56 / 168	60 / 178	65 / 187	69 / 197	73 / 207
15	--	0 / 30	3 / 42	7 / 53	11 / 64	15 / 75	19 / 86	24 / 96	28 / 107	33 / 117	37 / 128	42 / 138	47 / 148	51 / 159	56 / 169	61 / 179	66 / 189	70 / 200	75 / 210	80 / 220
16	--	0 / 32	3 / 45	7 / 57	12 / 68	16 / 80	21 / 91	26 / 102	31 / 113	36 / 124	41 / 135	46 / 146	51 / 157	56 / 168	61 / 179	66 / 190	71 / 201	76 / 212	82 / 222	87 / 233
17	--	0 / 34	4 / 47	8 / 60	13 / 72	18 / 84	23 / 96	28 / 108	33 / 120	38 / 132	44 / 143	49 / 155	55 / 166	60 / 178	66 / 189	71 / 201	77 / 212	82 / 224	88 / 234	93 / 247
18	--	0 / 36	4 / 50	9 / 63	14 / 76	19 / 89	24 / 102	30 / 114	36 / 126	41 / 139	47 / 151	53 / 163	59 / 175	65 / 187	70 / 200	76 / 212	82 / 224	88 / 236	94 / 248	100 / 260
19	--	1 / 37	4 / 53	9 / 67	15 / 80	20 / 94	26 / 107	32 / 120	38 / 133	44 / 146	50 / 159	56 / 172	63 / 184	69 / 197	75 / 210	82 / 222	88 / 235	94 / 248	101 / 260	107 / 273
20	--	1 / 39	5 / 55	10 / 70	16 / 84	22 / 98	28 / 112	34 / 126	40 / 140	47 / 153	53 / 167	60 / 180	67 / 193	73 / 207	80 / 220	87 / 233	93 / 247	100 / 260	107 / 273	114 / 286

(Dashes in the body of the table indicate that no decision is possible at the stated level of significance.)

Table I₃

Critical values of U and U' for a one-tailed test at $\alpha = 0.025$ or a two-tailed test at $\alpha = 0.05$.

To be significant for any given N_1 and N_2: Obtained U must be equal to or *less than* the value shown in the table. Obtained U' must be equal to or *or greater than* the value shown in the table.

N_2 \ N_1	1	2	3	4	5	6	7	8	9	10	11	12	13	14	15	16	17	18	19	20
1	--	--	--	--	--	--	--	--	--	--	--	--	--	--	--	--	--	--	--	--
2	--	--	--	--	--	--	--	0/16	0/18	0/20	0/22	1/23	1/25	1/27	1/29	1/31	2/32	2/34	2/36	2/38
3	--	--	--	--	0/15	1/17	1/20	2/22	2/25	3/27	3/30	4/32	4/35	5/37	5/40	6/42	6/45	7/47	7/50	8/52
4	--	--	--	0/16	1/19	2/22	3/25	4/28	4/32	5/35	6/38	7/41	8/44	9/47	10/50	11/53	11/57	12/60	13/63	13/67
5	--	--	0/15	1/19	2/23	3/27	5/30	6/34	7/38	8/42	9/46	11/49	12/53	13/57	14/61	15/65	17/68	18/72	19/76	20/80
6	--	--	1/17	2/22	3/27	5/31	6/36	8/40	10/44	11/49	13/53	14/58	16/62	17/67	19/71	21/75	22/80	24/84	25/89	27/93
7	--	--	1/20	3/25	5/30	6/36	8/41	10/46	12/51	14/56	16/61	18/66	20/71	22/76	24/81	26/86	28/91	30/96	32/101	34/106
8	--	0/16	2/22	4/28	6/34	8/40	10/46	13/51	15/57	17/63	19/69	22/74	24/80	26/86	29/91	31/97	34/102	36/108	38/111	41/119
9	--	0/18	2/25	4/32	7/38	10/44	12/51	15/57	17/64	20/70	23/76	26/82	28/89	31/95	34/101	37/107	39/114	42/120	45/126	48/132
10	--	0/20	3/27	5/35	8/42	11/49	14/56	17/63	20/70	23/77	26/84	29/91	33/97	36/104	39/111	42/118	45/125	48/132	52/138	55/145
11	--	0/22	3/30	6/38	9/46	13/53	16/61	19/69	23/76	26/84	30/91	33/99	37/106	40/114	44/121	47/129	51/136	55/143	58/151	62/158
12	--	1/23	4/32	7/41	11/49	14/58	18/66	22/74	26/82	29/91	33/99	37/107	41/115	45/123	49/131	53/139	57/147	61/155	65/163	69/171
13	--	1/25	4/35	8/44	12/53	16/62	20/71	24/80	28/89	33/97	37/106	41/115	45/124	50/132	54/141	59/149	63/158	67/167	72/175	76/184
14	--	1/27	5/37	9/47	13/57	17/67	22/76	26/86	31/95	36/104	40/114	45/123	50/132	55/141	59/151	64/160	67/171	74/178	78/188	83/197
15	--	1/29	5/40	10/50	14/61	19/71	24/81	29/91	34/101	39/111	44/121	49/131	54/141	59/151	64/161	70/170	75/180	80/190	85/200	90/210
16	--	1/31	6/42	11/53	15/65	21/75	26/86	31/97	37/107	42/118	47/129	53/139	59/149	64/160	70/170	75/181	81/191	86/202	92/212	98/222
17	--	2/32	6/45	11/57	17/68	22/80	28/91	34/102	39/114	45/125	51/136	57/147	63/158	67/171	75/180	81/191	87/202	93/213	99/224	105/235
18	--	2/34	7/47	12/60	18/72	24/84	30/96	36/108	42/120	48/132	55/143	61/155	67/167	74/178	80/190	86/202	93/213	99/225	106/236	112/248
19	--	2/36	7/50	13/63	19/76	25/89	32/101	38/114	45/126	52/138	58/151	65/163	72/175	78/188	85/200	92/212	99/224	106/236	113/248	119/261
20	--	2/38	8/52	13/67	20/80	27/93	34/106	41/119	48/132	55/145	62/158	69/171	76/184	83/197	90/210	98/222	105/235	112/248	119/261	127/273

(Dashes in the body of the table indicate that no decision is possible at the stated level of significance.)

Table I$_4$
Critical values of U and U' for a one-tailed test at $\alpha = 0.05$ or a two-tailed test at $\alpha = 0.10$.

To be significant for any given N_1 and N_2: Obtained U must be equal to or *less than* the value shown in the table. Obtained U' must be equal to or *greater than* the value shown in the table.

Each cell shows U (top) / U' (bottom).

N_2 \ N_1	1	2	3	4	5	6	7	8	9	10	11	12	13	14	15	16	17	18	19	20
1	--	--	--	--	--	--	--	--	--	--	--	--	--	--	--	--	--	--	0/19	0/20
2	--	--	--	--	0/10	0/12	0/14	1/15	1/17	1/19	1/21	2/22	2/24	2/26	3/27	3/29	3/31	4/32	4/34	4/36
3	--	--	0/9	0/12	1/14	2/16	2/19	3/21	3/24	4/26	5/28	5/31	6/33	7/35	7/38	8/40	9/42	9/45	10/47	11/49
4	--	--	0/12	1/15	2/18	3/21	4/24	5/27	6/30	7/33	8/36	9/39	10/42	11/45	12/48	14/50	15/53	16/56	17/59	18/62
5	--	0/10	1/14	2/18	4/21	5/25	6/29	8/32	9/36	11/39	12/43	13/47	15/50	16/54	18/57	19/61	20/65	22/68	23/72	25/75
6	--	0/12	2/16	3/21	5/25	7/29	8/34	10/38	12/42	14/46	16/50	17/55	19/59	21/63	23/67	25/71	26/76	28/80	30/84	32/88
7	--	0/14	2/19	4/24	6/29	8/34	11/38	13/43	15/48	17/53	19/58	21/63	24/67	26/72	28/77	30/82	33/86	35/91	37/96	39/101
8	--	1/15	3/21	5/27	8/32	10/38	13/43	15/49	18/54	20/60	23/65	26/70	28/76	31/81	33/87	36/92	39/97	41/103	44/108	47/113
9	--	1/17	3/24	6/30	9/36	12/42	15/48	18/54	21/60	24/66	27/72	30/78	33/84	36/90	39/96	42/102	45/108	48/114	51/120	54/126
10	--	1/19	4/26	7/33	11/39	14/46	17/53	20/60	24/66	27/73	31/79	34/86	37/93	41/99	44/106	48/112	51/119	55/125	58/132	62/138
11	--	1/21	5/28	8/36	12/43	16/50	19/58	23/65	27/72	31/79	34/87	38/94	42/101	46/108	50/115	54/122	57/130	61/137	65/144	69/151
12	--	2/22	5/31	9/39	13/47	17/55	21/63	26/70	30/78	34/86	38/94	42/102	47/109	51/117	55/125	60/132	64/140	68/148	72/156	77/163
13	--	2/24	6/33	10/42	15/50	19/59	24/67	28/76	33/84	37/93	42/101	47/109	51/118	56/126	61/134	65/143	70/151	75/159	80/167	84/176
14	--	2/26	7/35	11/45	16/54	21/63	26/72	31/81	36/90	41/99	46/108	51/117	56/126	61/135	66/144	71/153	77/161	82/170	87/179	92/188
15	--	3/27	7/38	12/48	18/57	23/67	28/77	33/87	39/96	44/106	50/115	55/125	61/134	66/144	72/153	77/163	83/172	88/182	94/191	100/200
16	--	3/29	8/40	14/50	19/61	25/71	30/82	36/92	42/102	48/112	54/122	60/132	65/143	71/153	77/163	83/173	89/183	95/193	101/203	107/213
17	--	3/31	9/42	15/53	20/65	26/76	33/86	39/97	45/108	51/119	57/130	64/140	70/151	77/161	83/172	89/183	96/193	102/204	109/214	115/225
18	--	4/32	9/45	16/56	22/68	28/80	35/91	41/103	48/114	55/123	61/137	68/148	75/159	82/170	88/182	95/193	102/204	109/215	116/226	123/237
19	0/19	4/34	10/47	17/59	23/72	30/84	37/96	44/108	51/120	58/132	65/144	72/156	80/167	87/179	94/191	101/203	109/214	116/226	123/238	130/250
20	0/20	4/36	11/49	18/62	25/75	32/88	39/101	47/113	54/126	62/138	69/151	77/163	84/176	92/188	100/200	107/213	115/225	123/237	130/250	138/262

(Dashes in the body of the table indicate that no decision is possible at the stated level of significance.)

Table J
Critical values of *T*.

The symbol *T* denotes the smaller sum of ranks associated with differences that are all of the same sign. For any given *N* (number of ranked differences), the obtained *T* is significant at a given level if it is equal to or *less than* the value shown in the table. All entries are for the *absolute* value of *T*.

	Level of significance for one-tailed test					Level of significance for one-tailed test			
	.05	.025	.01	.005		.05	.025	.01	.005
	Level of significance for two-tailed test					Level of significance for two-tailed test			
N	.10	.05	.02	.01	*N*	.10	.05	.02	.01
5	0	--	--	--	28	130	116	101	91
6	2	0	--	--	29	140	126	110	100
7	3	2	0	--	30	151	137	120	109
8	5	3	1	0	31	163	147	130	118
9	8	5	3	1	32	175	159	140	128
10	10	8	5	3	33	187	170	151	138
11	13	10	7	5	34	200	182	162	148
12	17	13	9	7	35	213	195	173	159
13	21	17	12	9	36	227	208	185	171
14	25	21	15	12	37	241	221	198	182
15	30	25	19	15	38	256	235	211	194
16	35	29	23	19	39	271	249	224	207
17	41	34	27	23	40	286	264	238	220
18	47	40	32	27	41	302	279	252	233
19	53	46	37	32	42	319	294	266	247
20	60	52	43	37	43	336	310	281	261
21	67	58	49	42	44	353	327	296	276
22	75	65	55	48	45	371	343	312	291
23	83	73	62	54	46	389	361	328	307
24	91	81	69	61	47	407	378	345	322
25	100	89	76	68	48	426	396	362	339
26	110	98	84	75	49	446	415	379	355
27	119	107	92	83	50	466	434	397	373

Slight discrepancies will be found between the critical values appearing in the table above and in Table 2 of the 1964 revision of F. Wilcoxon and R. A. Wilcox, *Some Rapid Approximate Statistical Procedures*, New York: Lederle Laboratories. The disparity reflects the latter's policy of selecting the critical value nearest a given significance level, occasionally overstepping that level. For example, for *N* = 8,

the probability of a *T* of 3 = 0.0390 (two-tail),

and

the probability of a *T* of 4 = 0.0546 (two-tail).

Wilcoxon and Wilcox selects a *T* of 4 as the critical value at the 0.05 level of significance (two-tail), whereas Table J reflects a more conservative policy by setting a *T* of 3 as the critical value at this level.

Table K
Factorials of
numbers 1 to 20.

N	N!
0	1
1	1
2	2
3	6
4	24
5	120
6	720
7	5040
8	40320
9	362880
10	3628800
11	39916800
12	479001600
13	6227020800
14	87178291200
15	1307674368000
16	20922789888000
17	355687428096000
18	6402373705728000
19	121645100408832000
20	2432902008176640000

Table L
Binomial coefficients.

N	$\binom{N}{0}$	$\binom{N}{1}$	$\binom{N}{2}$	$\binom{N}{3}$	$\binom{N}{4}$	$\binom{N}{5}$	$\binom{N}{6}$	$\binom{N}{7}$	$\binom{N}{8}$	$\binom{N}{9}$	$\binom{N}{10}$
0	1										
1	1	1									
2	1	2	1								
3	1	3	3	1							
4	1	4	6	4	1						
5	1	5	10	10	5	1					
6	1	6	15	20	15	6	1				
7	1	7	21	35	35	21	7	1			
8	1	8	28	56	70	56	28	8	1		
9	1	9	36	84	126	126	84	36	9	1	
10	1	10	45	120	210	252	210	120	45	10	1
11	1	11	55	165	330	462	462	330	165	55	11
12	1	12	66	220	495	792	924	792	495	220	66
13	1	13	78	286	715	1287	1716	1716	1287	715	286
14	1	14	91	364	1001	2002	3003	3432	3003	2002	1001
15	1	15	105	455	1365	3003	5005	6435	6435	5005	3003
16	1	16	120	560	1820	4368	8008	11440	12870	11440	8008
17	1	17	136	680	2380	6188	12376	19448	24310	24310	19448
18	1	18	153	816	3060	8568	18564	31824	43758	48620	43758
19	1	19	171	969	3876	11628	27132	50388	75582	92378	92378
20	1	20	190	1140	4845	15504	38760	77520	125970	167960	184756

Table M
Critical values of x or $N - x$ (whichever is larger) at 0.05 and 0.01 levels when $P = Q = 1/2$.

x is the frequency in the P category, and $N - x$ is the frequency in the Q category. The obtained x or $N - x$ must be *equal to or greater than* the value shown for significance at the chosen level. Dashes indicate that no decision is possible for N at the given α-level.

N	ONE-TAILED TEST		TWO-TAILED TEST	
	0.05	0.01	0.05	0.01
5	5	—	—	—
6	6	—	6	—
7	7	7	7	—
8	7	8	8	—
9	8	9	8	9
10	9	10	9	10
11	9	10	10	11
12	10	11	10	11
13	10	12	11	12
14	11	12	12	13
15	12	13	12	13
16	12	14	13	14
17	13	14	13	15
18	13	15	14	15
19	14	15	15	16
20	15	16	15	17
21	15	17	16	17
22	16	17	17	18
23	16	18	17	19
24	17	19	18	19
25	18	19	18	20
26	18	20	19	20
27	19	20	20	21
28	19	21	20	22
29	20	22	21	22
30	20	22	21	23
31	21	23	22	24
32	22	24	23	24
33	22	24	23	25
34	23	25	24	25
35	23	25	24	26
36	24	26	25	27
37	24	27	25	27
38	25	27	26	28
39	26	28	27	28
40	26	28	27	29
41	27	29	28	30
42	27	29	28	30
43	28	30	29	31
44	28	31	29	31
45	29	31	30	32
46	30	32	31	33
47	30	32	31	33
48	31	33	32	34
49	31	34	32	35
50	32	34	33	35

Table N
Critical values of x at $\alpha = 0.05$ (lightface) and $\alpha = 0.01$ (boldface) at varying values of P and Q for N's equal to 2 through 49.

The Use of Table N

This table was prepared to expedite decision-making when dealing with binomial populations in which $P \neq Q$. *Example:* A researcher has conducted twelve independent repetitions of the same study, using $\alpha = 0.01$. Four of these studies achieved statistical significance. Is this result (four out of twelve statistically significant outcomes) itself statistically significant, or is it within chance expectations? Looking in the column headed .01 opposite $N = 12$, we find that two or more differences significant at $\alpha = .01$ is in itself significant at $\alpha = .01$. Thus the researcher may conclude that the overall results of his or her investigations justify rejecting H_0.

A given value of x is significant at a given α-level if it equals or exceeds the critical value shown in table. All values shown are one-tailed. Since the binomial is not symmetrical when $P \neq Q \neq 1/2$, there is no straightforward way to obtain two-tailed values.

Table N

N	P: .01 / Q: .99	.02 / .98	.03 / .97	.04 / .96	.05 / .95	.06 / .94	.07 / .93	.08 / .92	.09 / .91	.10 / .90	.11 / .89	.12 / .88	.13 / .87	.14 / .86	.15 / .85	.16 / .84	.17 / .83	.18 / .82	.19 / .81	.20 / .80	.21 / .79	.22 / .78	.23 / .77	.24 / .76	.25 / .75
2	1	1	2	2	2	2	2	2	2	2	2	2	2	2	2	2	2	2	2	2	2	2	—	—	—
2	**1**	**2**	**2**	**2**	**2**	**2**	**2**	**2**	**2**	**2**	**—**	**—**	**—**	**—**	**—**	**—**	**—**	**—**	**—**	**—**	**—**	**—**	**—**	**—**	**—**
3	1	2	2	2	2	2	2	2	2	2	2	2	2	3	3	3	3	3	3	3	3	3	3	3	3
3	**2**	**2**	**2**	**2**	**2**	**3**	**3**	**3**	**3**	**3**	**3**	**3**	**3**	**3**	**3**	**3**	**3**	**3**	**3**	**3**	**3**	**—**	**—**	**—**	**—**
4	1	2	2	2	2	2	2	2	2	3	3	3	3	3	3	3	3	3	3	3	3	3	3	3	4
4	**2**	**2**	**2**	**2**	**3**	**3**	**3**	**3**	**3**	**3**	**3**	**3**	**3**	**3**	**4**	**4**	**4**	**4**	**4**	**4**	**4**	**4**	**4**	**4**	**4**
5	1	2	2	2	2	2	2	3	3	3	3	3	3	3	3	3	3	3	4	4	4	4	4	4	4
5	**2**	**2**	**2**	**3**	**3**	**3**	**3**	**3**	**3**	**3**	**4**	**4**	**4**	**4**	**4**	**4**	**4**	**4**	**4**	**4**	**4**	**4**	**5**	**5**	**5**
6	2	2	2	2	2	2	3	3	3	3	3	3	3	3	3	4	4	4	4	4	4	4	4	5	5
6	**2**	**2**	**3**	**3**	**3**	**3**	**3**	**3**	**4**	**4**	**4**	**4**	**4**	**4**	**4**	**4**	**4**	**5**	**5**	**5**	**5**	**5**	**5**	**5**	**5**
7	2	2	2	2	2	3	3	3	3	3	3	3	4	4	4	4	4	4	4	4	4	4	5	5	5
7	**2**	**2**	**3**	**3**	**3**	**3**	**3**	**4**	**4**	**4**	**4**	**4**	**4**	**4**	**5**	**5**	**5**	**5**	**5**	**5**	**5**	**6**	**6**	**6**	**6**
8	2	2	2	2	3	3	3	3	3	3	3	4	4	4	4	4	4	4	5	5	5	5	5	5	5
8	**2**	**3**	**3**	**3**	**3**	**3**	**4**	**4**	**4**	**4**	**4**	**4**	**5**	**5**	**5**	**5**	**5**	**5**	**5**	**6**	**6**	**6**	**6**	**6**	**6**
9	2	2	2	2	3	3	3	3	3	4	4	4	4	4	4	4	5	5	5	5	5	5	5	5	5
9	**2**	**3**	**3**	**3**	**3**	**4**	**4**	**4**	**4**	**4**	**5**	**5**	**5**	**5**	**5**	**5**	**5**	**6**	**6**	**6**	**6**	**6**	**6**	**6**	**6**
10	2	2	2	3	3	3	3	3	4	4	4	4	4	4	4	4	5	5	5	5	5	5	6	6	6
10	**2**	**3**	**3**	**3**	**4**	**4**	**4**	**4**	**4**	**5**	**5**	**5**	**5**	**5**	**5**	**6**	**6**	**6**	**6**	**6**	**6**	**7**	**7**	**7**	**7**
11	2	2	2	3	3	3	3	4	4	4	4	4	4	5	5	5	5	5	5	6	6	6	6	6	6
11	**2**	**3**	**3**	**3**	**4**	**4**	**4**	**4**	**5**	**5**	**5**	**5**	**5**	**6**	**6**	**6**	**6**	**6**	**6**	**7**	**7**	**7**	**7**	**7**	**7**
12	2	2	2	3	3	3	3	4	4	4	4	4	5	5	5	5	5	5	6	6	6	6	6	6	7
12	**2**	**3**	**3**	**4**	**4**	**4**	**4**	**5**	**5**	**5**	**5**	**5**	**6**	**6**	**6**	**6**	**6**	**7**	**7**	**7**	**7**	**7**	**7**	**8**	**8**
13	2	2	3	3	3	3	4	4	4	4	4	5	5	5	5	5	6	6	6	6	6	6	7	7	7
13	**2**	**3**	**3**	**4**	**4**	**4**	**5**	**5**	**5**	**5**	**5**	**6**	**6**	**6**	**6**	**6**	**7**	**7**	**7**	**7**	**7**	**8**	**8**	**8**	**8**
14	2	2	3	3	3	3	4	4	4	4	5	5	5	5	5	6	6	6	6	6	7	7	7	7	7
14	**2**	**3**	**3**	**4**	**4**	**4**	**5**	**5**	**5**	**5**	**6**	**6**	**6**	**6**	**7**	**7**	**7**	**7**	**7**	**8**	**8**	**8**	**8**	**8**	**9**
15	2	2	3	3	3	4	4	4	4	5	5	5	5	5	6	6	6	6	6	7	7	7	7	7	8
15	**2**	**3**	**3**	**4**	**4**	**5**	**5**	**5**	**5**	**6**	**6**	**6**	**6**	**7**	**7**	**7**	**7**	**7**	**8**	**8**	**8**	**8**	**9**	**9**	**9**

Table N *(Cont.)*

.26	.27	.28	.29	.30	.31	.32	.33	.34	.35	.36	.37	.38	.39	.40	.41	.42	.43	.44	.45	.46	.47	.48	.49	.50
.74	.73	.72	.71	.70	.69	.68	.67	.66	.65	.64	.63	.62	.61	.60	.59	.58	.57	.56	.55	.54	.53	.52	.51	.50
—	—	—	—	—	—	—	—	—	—	—	—	—	—	—	—	—	—	—	—	—	—	—	—	—
—	—	—	—	—	—	—	—	—	—	—	—	—	—	—	—	—	—	—	—	—	—	—	—	—
3	3	3	3	3	3	3	3	3	3	3	3	—	—	—	—	—	—	—	—	—	—	—	—	—
4	4	4	4	4	4	4	4	4	4	4	4	4	4	4	4	4	4	4	4	4	—	—	—	—
4	4	4	4	4	4	—	—	—	—	—	—	—	—	—	—	—	—	—	—	—	—	—	—	—
4	4	4	4	4	4	4	4	4	5	5	5	5	5	5	5	5	5	5	5	5	5	5	5	5
5	5	5	5	5	5	5	5	5	5	5	5	5	5	5	—	—	—	—	—	—	—	—	—	—
5	5	5	5	5	5	5	5	5	5	5	5	5	5	5	6	6	6	6	6	6	6	6	6	6
5	5	5	5	6	6	6	6	6	6	6	6	6	6	6	6	6	6	6	6	6	—	—	—	—
5	5	5	5	5	5	5	5	5	6	6	6	6	6	6	6	6	6	6	6	6	7	7	7	7
6	6	6	6	6	6	6	6	6	6	7	7	7	7	7	7	7	7	7	7	7	7	7	7	7
5	5	5	6	6	6	6	6	6	6	6	6	6	6	6	7	7	7	7	7	7	7	7	7	7
6	6	6	6	7	7	7	7	7	7	7	7	7	7	7	8	8	8	8	8	8	8	8	8	8
6	6	6	6	6	6	6	6	6	7	7	7	7	7	7	7	7	7	7	8	8	8	8	8	8
7	7	7	7	7	7	7	7	7	8	8	8	8	8	8	8	8	8	8	9	9	9	9	9	9
6	6	6	6	6	7	7	7	7	7	7	7	7	7	8	8	8	8	8	8	8	8	8	8	9
7	7	7	7	8	8	8	8	8	8	8	8	9	9	9	9	9	9	9	9	9	9	9	9	10
6	6	7	7	7	7	7	7	7	8	8	8	8	8	8	8	8	9	9	9	9	9	9	9	9
7	8	8	8	8	8	8	8	9	9	9	9	9	9	9	9	9	10	10	10	10	10	10	10	10
7	7	7	7	7	7	8	8	8	8	8	8	8	9	9	9	9	9	9	9	9	9	10	10	10
8	8	8	8	8	9	9	9	9	9	9	9	10	10	10	10	10	10	10	10	11	11	11	11	11
7	7	7	8	8	8	8	8	8	9	9	9	9	9	9	9	9	10	10	10	10	10	10	10	10
8	8	9	9	9	9	9	9	10	10	10	10	10	10	10	10	11	11	11	11	11	11	11	11	12
7	8	8	8	8	8	9	9	9	9	9	9	9	9	10	10	10	10	10	10	11	11	11	11	11
9	9	9	9	9	10	10	10	10	10	10	10	11	11	11	11	11	11	11	12	12	12	12	12	12
8	8	8	8	9	9	9	9	9	9	10	10	10	10	10	10	10	11	11	11	11	11	11	12	12
9	9	9	10	10	10	10	10	10	11	11	11	11	11	11	12	12	12	12	12	12	12	13	13	13

Table N (*Cont.*)

N	P .01 / Q .99	.02 / .98	.03 / .97	.04 / .96	.05 / .95	.06 / .94	.07 / .93	.08 / .92	.09 / .91	.10 / .90	.11 / .89	.12 / .88	.13 / .87	.14 / .86	.15 / .85	.16 / .84	.17 / .83	.18 / .82	.19 / .81	.20 / .80	.21 / .79	.22 / .78	.23 / .77	.24 / .76	.25 / .75
16	2	2	3	3	3	4	4	4	4	5	5	5	5	6	6	6	6	7	7	7	7	7	8	8	8
	3	3	4	4	4	5	5	5	6	6	6	6	7	7	7	7	8	8	8	8	8	9	9	9	9
17	2	2	3	3	4	4	4	4	5	5	5	5	6	6	6	6	7	7	7	7	7	8	8	8	8
	3	3	4	4	4	5	5	5	6	6	6	7	7	7	7	7	8	8	8	9	9	9	9	9	10
18	2	2	3	3	4	4	4	4	5	5	5	6	6	6	6	7	7	7	7	8	8	8	8	8	9
	3	3	4	4	5	5	5	6	6	6	7	7	7	7	7	8	8	8	9	9	9	9	10	10	10
19	2	3	3	3	4	4	4	5	5	5	6	6	6	6	7	7	7	7	8	8	8	9	9	9	9
	3	3	4	4	5	5	5	6	6	6	7	7	7	8	8	8	9	9	9	9	10	10	10	10	10
20	2	3	3	3	4	4	5	5	5	6	6	6	7	7	7	7	8	8	8	8	9	9	9	9	9
	3	3	4	4	5	5	6	6	7	7	7	8	8	8	9	9	9	9	9	10	10	10	10	10	11
21	2	3	3	3	4	4	5	5	5	6	6	6	6	7	7	7	8	8	8	8	9	9	9	9	10
	3	3	4	4	5	5	6	6	6	7	7	7	8	8	8	9	9	9	10	10	10	10	11	11	11
22	2	3	3	4	4	4	5	5	5	6	6	7	7	7	8	8	8	9	9	9	9	9	10	10	10
	3	3	4	5	5	5	6	6	7	7	7	8	8	9	9	9	10	10	10	10	11	11	11	11	11
23	2	3	3	4	4	4	5	5	6	6	6	6	7	7	7	8	8	8	9	9	9	9	10	10	10
	3	4	4	5	5	6	6	6	7	7	7	8	8	9	9	9	9	10	10	10	11	11	11	12	12
24	2	3	3	4	4	5	5	5	6	6	6	7	7	7	8	8	8	9	9	9	9	10	10	10	11
	3	4	4	5	5	6	6	7	7	7	8	8	8	9	9	9	10	10	10	11	11	11	12	12	12
25	2	3	3	4	4	5	5	5	6	6	6	7	7	8	8	8	9	9	9	9	10	10	10	11	11
	3	4	4	5	5	6	6	7	7	7	8	8	9	9	9	10	10	10	11	11	11	12	12	12	13
26	2	3	3	4	4	5	5	6	6	6	7	7	7	8	8	8	9	9	9	10	10	10	11	11	11
	3	4	4	5	5	6	6	7	7	8	8	8	9	9	10	10	10	11	11	11	12	12	12	13	13
27	2	3	3	4	4	5	5	6	6	6	7	7	8	8	8	9	9	9	10	10	10	11	11	11	12
	3	4	4	5	6	6	6	7	7	8	8	9	9	9	10	10	11	11	11	12	12	12	13	13	13
28	2	3	4	4	4	5	5	6	6	7	7	7	8	8	8	9	9	10	10	10	11	11	11	12	12
	3	4	4	5	6	6	7	7	8	8	8	9	9	10	10	10	11	11	12	12	12	13	13	13	14
29	2	3	4	4	5	5	5	6	6	7	7	8	8	8	9	9	9	10	10	10	11	11	12	12	12
	3	4	5	5	6	6	7	7	8	8	9	9	9	10	10	11	11	11	12	12	13	13	13	14	14
30	2	3	4	4	5	5	6	6	6	7	7	8	8	8	9	9	10	10	10	11	11	11	12	12	13
	3	4	5	5	6	6	7	7	8	8	9	9	10	10	10	11	11	12	12	12	13	13	14	14	14
31	2	3	4	4	5	5	6	6	7	7	7	8	8	9	9	9	10	10	11	11	11	12	12	12	13
	3	4	5	5	6	6	7	7	8	8	9	9	10	10	11	11	12	12	12	13	13	14	14	14	15
32	2	3	4	4	5	5	6	6	7	7	8	8	8	9	9	10	10	10	11	11	12	12	12	13	13
	3	4	5	5	6	7	7	8	8	9	9	10	10	10	11	11	12	12	13	13	13	14	14	15	15
33	2	3	4	4	5	5	6	6	7	7	8	8	9	9	9	10	10	11	11	12	12	13	13	13	13
	3	4	5	5	6	7	7	8	8	9	9	10	10	11	11	12	12	12	13	13	14	14	15	15	15
34	2	3	4	4	5	6	6	7	7	7	8	8	9	9	10	10	11	11	11	12	12	13	13	13	14
	3	4	5	6	6	7	7	8	8	9	9	10	10	11	11	12	12	13	13	14	14	14	15	15	16
35	2	3	4	5	6	6	6	7	7	8	8	9	9	9	10	10	11	11	12	12	12	13	13	14	14
	3	4	5	6	6	7	7	8	9	9	10	10	11	11	12	12	13	13	13	14	14	15	15	16	16
36	3	3	4	5	5	6	6	7	7	8	8	9	9	10	10	11	11	11	12	12	13	13	14	14	14
	3	4	5	6	6	7	8	8	9	9	10	10	11	11	12	12	13	13	14	14	15	15	15	16	16
37	3	3	4	5	5	6	6	7	7	8	8	9	9	10	10	11	11	12	12	13	13	13	14	14	15
	3	4	5	6	6	7	8	8	9	9	10	11	11	12	12	13	13	13	14	14	15	15	16	16	17

Table N (Cont.)

| .26 | .27 | .28 | .29 | .30 | .31 | .32 | .33 | .34 | .35 | .36 | .37 | .38 | .39 | .40 | .41 | .42 | .43 | .44 | .45 | .46 | .47 | .48 | .49 | .50 |
.74	.73	.72	.71	.70	.69	.68	.67	.66	.65	.64	.63	.62	.61	.60	.59	.58	.57	.56	.55	.54	.53	.52	.51	.50
8	8	9	9	9	9	9	9	10	10	10	10	10	10	11	11	11	11	11	11	12	12	12	12	12
9	**10**	**10**	**10**	**10**	**10**	**11**	**11**	**11**	**11**	**11**	**11**	**12**	**12**	**12**	**12**	**12**	**12**	**13**	**13**	**13**	**14**	**14**	**14**	**14**
8	9	9	9	9	9	10	10	10	10	10	11	11	11	11	11	12	12	12	12	12	12	13	13	13
10	**10**	**10**	**10**	**11**	**11**	**11**	**11**	**11**	**12**	**12**	**12**	**12**	**12**	**13**	**13**	**13**	**13**	**13**	**13**	**14**	**14**	**14**	**14**	**14**
9	9	9	9	9	10	10	10	10	10	11	11	11	11	11	12	12	12	12	13	13	13	13	13	13
10	**10**	**11**	**11**	**11**	**11**	**12**	**12**	**12**	**12**	**12**	**13**	**13**	**13**	**13**	**13**	**13**	**14**	**14**	**14**	**14**	**14**	**14**	**15**	**15**
9	9	10	10	10	10	10	11	11	11	11	12	12	12	12	12	13	13	13	13	13	13	14	14	14
11	**11**	**11**	**11**	**12**	**12**	**12**	**12**	**12**	**13**	**13**	**13**	**13**	**13**	**14**	**14**	**14**	**14**	**14**	**15**	**15**	**15**	**15**	**15**	**15**
10	10	10	10	10	11	11	11	11	12	12	12	12	12	13	13	13	13	13	14	14	14	14	14	15
11	**11**	**11**	**12**	**12**	**12**	**12**	**13**	**13**	**13**	**13**	**14**	**14**	**14**	**14**	**14**	**15**	**15**	**15**	**15**	**15**	**16**	**16**	**16**	**16**
10	10	10	11	11	11	11	12	12	12	12	12	13	13	13	13	14	14	14	14	14	15	15	15	15
11	**12**	**12**	**12**	**12**	**13**	**13**	**13**	**13**	**14**	**14**	**14**	**14**	**14**	**15**	**15**	**15**	**15**	**16**	**16**	**16**	**16**	**16**	**17**	**17**
10	10	11	11	11	11	12	12	12	12	13	13	13	13	14	14	14	14	15	15	15	15	15	16	16
12	**12**	**12**	**13**	**13**	**13**	**13**	**14**	**14**	**14**	**14**	**15**	**15**	**15**	**15**	**15**	**16**	**16**	**16**	**16**	**17**	**17**	**17**	**17**	**17**
11	11	11	11	12	12	12	12	13	13	13	13	14	14	14	14	15	15	15	15	16	16	16	16	16
12	**12**	**13**	**13**	**13**	**13**	**14**	**14**	**14**	**15**	**15**	**15**	**15**	**16**	**16**	**16**	**16**	**17**	**17**	**17**	**17**	**17**	**18**	**18**	**18**
11	11	11	12	12	12	13	13	13	13	14	14	14	14	15	15	15	15	16	16	16	16	17	17	17
13	**13**	**13**	**13**	**14**	**14**	**14**	**14**	**15**	**15**	**15**	**15**	**16**	**16**	**16**	**16**	**17**	**17**	**17**	**17**	**18**	**18**	**18**	**18**	**19**
11	12	12	12	12	13	13	13	13	14	14	14	15	15	15	15	16	16	16	16	17	17	17	17	18
13	**13**	**13**	**14**	**14**	**14**	**15**	**15**	**15**	**15**	**16**	**16**	**16**	**17**	**17**	**17**	**17**	**18**	**18**	**18**	**18**	**19**	**19**	**19**	**19**
12	12	12	12	13	13	13	14	14	14	14	15	15	15	16	16	16	16	17	17	17	17	18	18	18
13	**14**	**14**	**14**	**14**	**15**	**15**	**15**	**16**	**16**	**16**	**16**	**17**	**17**	**17**	**18**	**18**	**18**	**18**	**19**	**19**	**19**	**19**	**20**	**20**
12	12	12	13	13	13	14	14	14	15	15	15	15	16	16	16	17	17	17	17	18	18	18	18	19
14	**14**	**14**	**15**	**15**	**15**	**15**	**16**	**16**	**16**	**17**	**17**	**17**	**18**	**18**	**18**	**18**	**19**	**19**	**19**	**19**	**20**	**20**	**20**	**20**
12	13	13	13	13	14	14	14	15	15	15	16	16	16	16	17	17	17	18	18	18	18	19	19	19
14	**14**	**15**	**15**	**15**	**16**	**16**	**16**	**17**	**17**	**17**	**17**	**18**	**18**	**18**	**19**	**19**	**19**	**19**	**20**	**20**	**20**	**21**	**21**	**21**
13	13	13	14	14	14	15	15	15	16	16	16	17	17	17	17	18	18	18	18	19	19	19	20	20
14	**15**	**15**	**15**	**16**	**16**	**17**	**17**	**17**	**18**	**18**	**18**	**19**	**19**	**19**	**19**	**20**	**20**	**20**	**21**	**21**	**21**	**21**	**21**	**22**
13	13	14	14	14	15	15	15	16	16	16	17	17	17	17	18	18	18	19	19	19	20	20	20	20
15	**15**	**15**	**16**	**16**	**16**	**17**	**17**	**17**	**18**	**18**	**18**	**19**	**19**	**19**	**20**	**20**	**20**	**21**	**21**	**21**	**21**	**22**	**22**	**22**
13	14	14	14	15	15	15	16	16	16	17	17	17	18	18	18	19	19	19	20	20	20	20	21	21
15	**15**	**16**	**16**	**16**	**17**	**17**	**17**	**18**	**18**	**19**	**19**	**19**	**19**	**20**	**20**	**20**	**21**	**21**	**21**	**22**	**22**	**22**	**23**	**23**
14	14	14	15	15	15	16	16	16	17	17	17	18	18	18	19	19	19	20	20	20	21	21	21	22
15	**16**	**16**	**16**	**17**	**17**	**18**	**18**	**18**	**19**	**19**	**19**	**20**	**20**	**20**	**21**	**21**	**21**	**22**	**22**	**22**	**22**	**23**	**23**	**24**
14	14	15	15	15	16	16	16	17	17	17	18	18	19	19	19	20	20	20	21	21	21	22	22	22
16	**16**	**16**	**17**	**17**	**18**	**18**	**18**	**19**	**19**	**19**	**20**	**20**	**20**	**21**	**21**	**21**	**22**	**22**	**22**	**23**	**23**	**23**	**24**	**24**
14	15	15	15	16	16	16	17	17	18	18	18	19	19	19	20	20	21	21	21	22	22	22	23	23
16	**16**	**17**	**17**	**17**	**18**	**18**	**19**	**19**	**20**	**20**	**20**	**21**	**21**	**21**	**22**	**22**	**22**	**23**	**23**	**23**	**24**	**24**	**24**	**25**
14	15	15	16	16	16	17	17	18	18	18	19	19	19	20	20	21	21	21	22	22	22	23	23	23
16	**17**	**17**	**18**	**18**	**18**	**19**	**19**	**20**	**20**	**20**	**21**	**21**	**21**	**22**	**22**	**23**	**23**	**23**	**24**	**24**	**24**	**25**	**25**	**25**
15	15	16	16	16	17	17	18	18	18	19	19	20	20	20	21	21	21	22	22	22	23	23	24	24
17	**17**	**18**	**18**	**18**	**19**	**19**	**20**	**20**	**20**	**21**	**21**	**22**	**22**	**22**	**23**	**23**	**23**	**24**	**24**	**25**	**25**	**25**	**26**	**26**
15	16	16	16	17	17	18	18	18	19	19	20	20	20	21	21	22	22	22	23	23	23	24	24	24
17	**18**	**18**	**18**	**19**	**19**	**20**	**20**	**20**	**21**	**21**	**22**	**22**	**22**	**23**	**23**	**24**	**24**	**24**	**25**	**25**	**25**	**26**	**26**	**27**

Table N (*Cont.*)

N	P / Q	.01 / .99	.02 / .98	.03 / .97	.04 / .96	.05 / .95	.06 / .94	.07 / .93	.08 / .92	.09 / .91	.10 / .90	.11 / .89	.12 / .88	.13 / .87	.14 / .86	.15 / .85	.16 / .84	.17 / .83	.18 / .82	.19 / .81	.20 / .80	.21 / .79	.22 / .78	.23 / .77	.24 / .76	.25 / .75
38	P	3	3	4	5	5	6	6	7	8	8	9	9	10	10	10	11	11	12	12	13	13	14	14	15	15
	Q	3	4	5	6	7	7	8	8	9	10	10	11	11	12	12	13	13	14	14	15	15	16	16	17	17
39	P	3	3	4	5	5	6	6	7	8	8	9	9	10	10	11	11	12	12	13	13	14	14	14	15	15
	Q	3	4	5	6	7	7	8	9	9	10	10	11	11	12	12	13	13	14	14	15	15	16	16	17	17
40	P	3	3	4	5	5	6	7	7	8	8	9	9	10	10	11	11	12	12	13	13	14	14	15	15	16
	Q	3	4	5	6	7	7	8	9	9	10	10	11	12	12	13	13	14	14	15	15	16	16	17	17	18
41	P	3	3	4	5	6	6	7	7	8	8	9	10	10	11	11	12	12	13	13	14	14	15	15	15	16
	Q	3	4	5	6	7	8	8	9	9	10	11	11	12	12	13	13	14	14	15	16	16	17	17	18	18
42	P	3	4	4	5	6	6	7	7	8	9	9	10	10	11	11	12	12	13	13	14	14	15	15	16	16
	Q	3	4	5	6	7	8	8	9	10	10	11	11	12	12	13	14	14	15	15	16	16	17	17	18	18
43	P	3	4	4	5	6	6	7	8	8	9	9	10	10	11	11	12	13	13	14	14	15	15	16	16	17
	Q	3	5	5	6	7	8	8	9	10	10	11	12	12	13	13	14	14	15	16	16	17	17	18	18	19
44	P	3	4	4	5	6	6	7	8	8	9	9	10	11	11	12	12	13	13	14	14	15	15	16	16	17
	Q	3	5	5	6	7	8	9	9	10	11	11	12	12	13	14	14	15	15	16	16	17	17	18	18	19
45	P	3	4	4	5	6	7	7	8	8	9	10	10	11	11	12	12	13	13	14	15	15	16	16	17	17
	Q	4	5	6	6	7	8	9	9	10	11	11	12	13	13	14	14	15	15	16	17	17	18	18	19	19
46	P	3	4	4	5	6	7	7	8	9	9	10	10	11	11	12	13	13	14	14	15	15	16	16	17	17
	Q	4	5	6	6	7	8	9	9	10	11	11	12	13	13	14	15	15	16	16	17	17	18	19	19	20
47	P	3	4	5	5	6	7	7	8	9	9	10	10	11	12	12	13	13	14	15	15	16	16	17	17	18
	Q	4	5	6	7	7	8	9	10	10	11	12	12	13	14	14	15	15	16	17	17	18	18	19	19	20
48	P	3	4	5	5	6	7	7	8	9	9	10	11	11	12	12	13	14	14	15	15	16	16	17	18	18
	Q	4	5	6	7	7	8	9	10	10	11	12	12	13	14	14	15	16	16	17	17	18	19	19	20	20
49	P	3	4	5	5	6	7	8	8	9	10	10	11	11	12	13	13	14	14	15	16	16	17	17	18	18
	Q	4	5	6	7	8	8	9	10	11	11	12	13	13	14	15	15	16	16	17	18	18	19	19	20	21

Table N *(Cont.)*

| .26 | .27 | .28 | .29 | .30 | .31 | .32 | .33 | .34 | .35 | .36 | .37 | .38 | .39 | .40 | .41 | .42 | .43 | .44 | .45 | .46 | .47 | .48 | .49 | .50 |
.74	.73	.72	.71	.70	.69	.68	.67	.66	.65	.64	.63	.62	.61	.60	.59	.58	.57	.56	.55	.54	.53	.52	.51	.50
15	16	16	17	17	18	18	18	19	19	20	20	20	21	21	22	22	22	23	23	24	24	24	25	25
17	**18**	**18**	**19**	**19**	**20**	**20**	**20**	**21**	**21**	**22**	**22**	**23**	**23**	**23**	**24**	**24**	**24**	**25**	**25**	**26**	**26**	**26**	**27**	**27**
16	16	17	17	17	18	18	19	19	20	20	20	21	21	22	22	22	23	23	24	24	24	25	25	26
18	**18**	**19**	**19**	**20**	**20**	**20**	**21**	**21**	**22**	**22**	**23**	**23**	**23**	**24**	**24**	**25**	**25**	**25**	**26**	**26**	**27**	**27**	**27**	**28**
16	17	17	17	18	18	19	19	20	20	20	21	21	22	22	23	23	23	24	24	25	25	25	26	26
18	**19**	**19**	**20**	**20**	**20**	**21**	**21**	**22**	**22**	**23**	**23**	**23**	**24**	**24**	**25**	**25**	**26**	**26**	**26**	**27**	**27**	**28**	**28**	**28**
16	17	17	18	18	19	19	20	20	20	21	21	22	22	23	23	23	24	24	25	25	26	26	26	27
18	**19**	**19**	**20**	**20**	**21**	**21**	**22**	**22**	**23**	**23**	**23**	**24**	**24**	**25**	**25**	**26**	**26**	**26**	**27**	**27**	**28**	**28**	**28**	**29**
17	17	18	18	19	19	19	20	20	21	21	22	22	23	23	23	24	24	25	25	26	26	26	27	27
19	**19**	**20**	**20**	**21**	**21**	**22**	**22**	**23**	**23**	**23**	**24**	**24**	**25**	**25**	**26**	**26**	**27**	**27**	**27**	**28**	**28**	**29**	**29**	**29**
17	18	18	18	19	19	20	20	21	21	22	22	23	23	24	24	24	25	25	26	26	27	27	27	28
19	**20**	**20**	**21**	**21**	**22**	**22**	**23**	**23**	**23**	**24**	**24**	**25**	**25**	**26**	**26**	**27**	**27**	**28**	**28**	**28**	**29**	**29**	**30**	**30**
17	18	18	19	19	20	20	21	21	22	22	23	23	24	24	24	25	25	26	26	27	27	28	28	28
19	**20**	**21**	**21**	**21**	**22**	**22**	**23**	**23**	**24**	**24**	**25**	**25**	**26**	**26**	**27**	**27**	**28**	**28**	**28**	**29**	**29**	**30**	**30**	**31**
18	18	19	19	20	20	21	21	22	22	23	23	24	24	24	25	25	26	26	27	27	28	28	29	29
20	**20**	**21**	**21**	**22**	**22**	**23**	**23**	**24**	**24**	**25**	**25**	**26**	**26**	**27**	**27**	**28**	**28**	**29**	**29**	**29**	**30**	**30**	**31**	**31**
18	18	19	20	20	21	21	22	22	22	23	23	24	24	25	25	26	26	27	27	28	28	29	29	30
20	**21**	**21**	**22**	**22**	**23**	**23**	**24**	**24**	**25**	**25**	**26**	**26**	**27**	**27**	**28**	**28**	**29**	**29**	**30**	**30**	**30**	**31**	**31**	**32**
18	19	19	20	20	21	21	22	22	23	23	24	24	25	25	26	26	27	27	28	28	29	29	30	30
21	**21**	**22**	**22**	**23**	**23**	**24**	**24**	**25**	**25**	**26**	**26**	**27**	**27**	**28**	**28**	**29**	**29**	**30**	**30**	**31**	**31**	**31**	**32**	**32**
19	19	20	20	21	21	22	22	23	23	24	24	25	25	26	26	27	27	28	28	29	29	30	30	31
21	**21**	**22**	**22**	**23**	**24**	**24**	**25**	**25**	**26**	**26**	**27**	**27**	**28**	**28**	**29**	**29**	**30**	**30**	**31**	**31**	**32**	**32**	**33**	**33**
19	19	20	21	21	22	22	23	23	24	24	25	25	26	26	27	27	28	28	29	29	30	30	31	31
21	**22**	**22**	**23**	**23**	**24**	**24**	**25**	**26**	**26**	**27**	**27**	**28**	**28**	**29**	**29**	**30**	**30**	**31**	**31**	**32**	**32**	**33**	**33**	**34**

Table O
Percentage points of the Studentized range.

Error df	α	\(k\) = number of means or number of steps between ordered means									
		2	3	4	5	6	7	8	9	10	11
5	.05	3.64	4.60	5.22	5.67	6.03	6.33	6.58	6.80	6.99	7.17
	.01	5.70	6.98	7.80	8.42	8.91	9.32	9.67	9.97	10.24	10.48
6	.05	3.46	4.34	4.90	5.30	5.63	5.90	6.12	6.32	6.49	6.65
	.01	5.24	6.33	7.03	7.56	7.97	8.32	8.61	8.87	9.10	9.30
7	.05	3.34	4.16	4.68	5.06	5.36	5.61	5.82	6.00	6.16	6.30
	.01	4.95	5.92	6.54	7.01	7.37	7.68	7.94	8.17	8.37	8.55
8	.05	3.26	4.04	4.53	4.89	5.17	5.40	5.60	5.77	5.92	6.05
	.01	4.75	5.64	6.20	6.62	6.96	7.24	7.47	7.68	7.86	8.03
9	.05	3.20	3.95	4.41	4.76	5.02	5.24	5.43	5.59	5.74	5.87
	.01	4.60	5.43	5.96	6.35	6.66	6.91	7.13	7.33	7.49	7.65
10	.05	3.15	3.88	4.33	4.65	4.91	5.12	5.30	5.46	5.60	5.72
	.01	4.48	5.27	5.77	6.14	6.43	6.67	6.87	7.05	7.21	7.36
11	.05	3.11	3.82	4.26	4.57	4.82	5.03	5.20	5.35	5.49	5.61
	.01	4.39	5.15	5.62	5.97	6.25	6.48	6.67	6.84	6.99	7.13
12	.05	3.08	3.77	4.20	4.51	4.75	4.95	5.12	5.27	5.39	5.51
	.01	4.32	5.05	5.50	5.84	6.10	6.32	6.51	6.67	6.81	6.94
13	.05	3.06	3.73	4.15	4.45	4.69	4.88	5.05	5.19	5.32	5.43
	.01	4.26	4.96	5.40	5.73	5.98	6.19	6.37	6.53	6.67	6.79
14	.05	3.03	3.70	4.11	4.41	4.64	4.83	4.99	5.13	5.25	5.36
	.01	4.21	4.89	5.32	5.63	5.88	6.08	6.26	6.41	6.54	6.66
15	.05	3.01	3.67	4.08	4.37	4.59	4.78	4.94	5.08	5.20	5.31
	.01	4.17	4.84	5.25	5.56	5.80	5.99	6.16	6.31	6.44	6.55
16	.05	3.00	3.65	4.05	4.33	4.56	4.74	4.90	5.03	5.15	5.26
	.01	4.13	4.79	5.19	5.49	5.72	5.92	6.08	6.22	6.35	6.46
17	.05	2.98	3.63	4.02	4.30	4.52	4.70	4.86	4.99	5.11	5.21
	.01	4.10	4.74	5.14	5.43	5.66	5.85	6.01	6.15	6.27	6.38
18	.05	2.97	3.61	4.00	4.28	4.49	4.67	4.82	4.96	5.07	5.17
	.01	4.07	4.70	5.09	5.38	5.60	5.79	5.94	6.08	6.20	6.31
19	.05	2.96	3.59	3.98	4.25	4.47	4.65	4.79	4.92	5.04	5.14
	.01	4.05	4.67	5.05	5.33	5.55	5.73	5.89	6.02	6.14	6.25
20	.05	2.95	3.58	3.96	4.23	4.45	4.62	4.77	4.90	5.01	5.11
	.01	4.02	4.64	5.02	5.29	5.51	5.69	5.84	5.97	6.09	6.19
24	.05	2.92	3.53	3.90	4.17	4.37	4.54	4.68	4.81	4.92	5.01
	.01	3.96	4.55	4.91	5.17	5.37	5.54	5.69	5.81	5.92	6.02
30	.05	2.89	3.49	3.85	4.10	4.30	4.46	4.60	4.72	4.82	4.92
	.01	3.89	4.45	4.80	5.05	5.24	5.40	5.54	5.65	5.76	5.85
40	.05	2.86	3.44	3.79	4.04	4.23	4.39	4.52	4.63	4.73	4.82
	.01	3.82	4.37	4.70	4.93	5.11	5.26	5.39	5.50	5.60	5.69
60	.05	2.83	3.40	3.74	3.98	4.16	4.31	4.44	4.55	4.65	4.73
	.01	3.76	4.28	4.59	4.82	4.99	5.13	5.25	5.36	5.45	5.53
120	.05	2.80	3.36	3.68	3.92	4.10	4.24	4.36	4.47	4.56	4.64
	.01	3.70	4.20	4.50	4.71	4.87	5.01	5.12	5.21	5.30	5.37
∞	.05	2.77	3.31	3.63	3.86	4.03	4.17	4.29	4.39	4.47	4.55
	.01	3.64	4.12	4.40	4.60	4.76	4.88	4.99	5.08	5.16	5.23

Table P
Squares, square roots, and reciprocals of numbers from 1 to 1,000.

N	N²	√N	1/N	N	N²	√N	1/N	N	N²	√N	1/N
1	1	1.0000	1.000000	61	3721	7.8102	.016393	121	14641	11.0000	.00826446
2	4	1.4142	.500000	62	3844	7.8740	.016129	122	14884	11.0454	.00819672
3	9	1.7321	.333333	63	3969	7.9373	.015873	123	15129	11.0905	.00813008
4	16	2.0000	.250000	64	4096	8.0000	.015625	124	15376	11.1355	.00800452
5	25	2.2361	.200000	65	4225	8.0623	.015385	125	15625	11.1803	.00800000
6	36	2.4495	.166667	66	4356	8.1240	.015152	126	15876	11.2250	.00793651
7	49	2.6458	.142857	67	4489	8.1854	.014925	127	16129	11.2694	.00787402
8	64	2.8284	.125000	68	4624	8.2462	.014706	128	16384	11.3137	.00781250
9	81	3.0000	.111111	69	4761	8.3066	.014493	129	16641	11.3578	.00775194
10	100	3.1623	.100000	70	4900	8.3666	.014286	130	16900	11.4018	.00769231
11	121	3.3166	.090909	71	5041	8.4261	.014085	131	17161	11.4455	.00763359
12	144	3.4641	.083333	72	5184	8.4853	.013889	132	17424	11.4891	.00757576
13	169	3.6056	.076923	73	5329	8.5440	.013699	133	17689	11.5326	.00751880
14	196	3.7417	.071429	74	5476	8.6023	.013514	134	17956	11.5758	.00746269
15	225	3.8730	.066667	75	5625	8.6603	.013333	135	18225	11.6190	.00740741
16	256	4.0000	.062500	76	5776	8.7178	.013158	136	18496	11.6619	.00735294
17	289	4.1231	.058824	77	5929	8.7750	.012987	137	18769	11.7047	.00729927
18	324	4.2426	.055556	78	6084	8.8318	.012821	138	19044	11.7473	.00724638
19	361	4.3589	.052632	79	6241	8.8882	.012658	139	19321	11.7898	.00719424
20	400	4.4721	.050000	80	6400	8.9443	.012500	140	19600	11.8322	.00714286
21	441	4.5826	.047619	81	6561	9.0000	.012346	141	19881	11.8743	.00709220
22	484	4.6904	.045455	82	6724	9.0554	.012195	142	20164	11.9164	.00704225
23	529	4.7958	.043478	83	6889	9.1104	.012048	143	20449	11.9583	.00699301
24	576	4.8990	.041667	84	7056	9.1652	.011905	144	20736	12.0000	.00694444
25	625	5.0000	.040000	85	7225	9.2195	.011765	145	21025	12.0416	.00689655
26	676	5.0990	.038462	86	7396	9.2736	.011628	146	21316	12.0830	.00684932
27	729	5.1962	.037037	87	7569	9.3274	.011494	147	21609	12.1244	.00680272
28	784	5.2915	.035714	88	7744	9.3808	.011364	148	21904	12.1655	.00675676
29	841	5.3852	.034483	89	7921	9.4340	.011236	149	22201	12.2066	.00671141
30	900	5.4772	.033333	90	8100	9.4868	.011111	150	22500	12.2474	.00666667
31	961	5.5678	.032258	91	8281	9.5394	.010989	151	22801	12.2882	.00662252
32	1024	5.6569	.031250	92	8464	9.5917	.010870	152	23104	12.3288	.00657895
33	1089	5.7446	.030303	93	8649	9.6437	.010753	153	23409	12.3693	.00653595
34	1156	5.8310	.029412	94	8836	9.6954	.010638	154	23716	12.4097	.00649351
35	1225	5.9161	.028571	95	9025	9.7468	.010526	155	24025	12.4499	.00645161
36	1296	6.0000	.027778	96	9216	9.7980	.010417	156	24336	12.4900	.00641026
37	1369	6.0828	.027027	97	9409	9.8489	.010309	157	24649	12.5300	.00636943
38	1444	6.1644	.026316	98	9604	9.8995	.010204	158	24964	12.5698	.00632911
39	1521	6.2450	.025641	99	9801	9.9499	.010101	159	25281	12.6095	.00628931
40	1600	6.3246	.025000	100	10000	10.0000	.010000	160	25600	12.6491	.00625000
41	1681	6.4031	.024390	101	10201	10.0499	.00990099	161	25921	12.6886	.00621118
42	1764	6.4807	.023810	102	10404	10.0995	.00980392	162	26244	12.7279	.00617284
43	1849	6.5574	.023256	103	10609	10.1489	.00970874	163	26569	12.7671	.00613497
44	1936	6.6332	.022727	104	10816	10.1980	.00961538	164	26896	12.8062	.00609756
45	2025	6.7082	.022222	105	11025	10.2470	.00952381	165	27225	12.8452	.00606061
46	2116	6.7823	.021739	106	11236	10.2956	.00943396	166	27556	12.8841	.00602410
47	2209	6.8557	.021277	107	11449	10.3441	.00934579	167	27889	12.9228	.00598802
48	2304	6.9282	.020833	108	11664	10.3923	.00925926	168	28224	12.9615	.00595238
49	2401	7.0000	.020408	109	11881	10.4403	.00917431	169	28561	13.0000	.00591716
50	2500	7.0711	.020000	110	12100	10.4881	.00909091	170	28900	13.0384	.00588235
51	2601	7.1414	.019608	111	12321	10.5357	.00900901	171	29241	13.0767	.00584795
52	2704	7.2111	.019231	112	12544	10.5830	.00892857	172	29584	13.1149	.00581395
53	2809	7.2801	.018868	113	12769	10.6301	.00884956	173	29929	13.1529	.00578035
54	2916	7.3485	.018519	114	12996	10.6771	.00877193	174	30276	13.1909	.00574713
55	3025	7.4162	.018182	115	13225	10.7238	.00869565	175	30625	13.2288	.00571429
56	3136	7.4833	.017857	116	13456	10.7703	.00862069	176	30976	13.2665	.00568182
57	3249	7.5498	.017544	117	13689	10.8167	.00854701	177	31329	13.3041	.00564972
58	3364	7.6158	.017241	118	13924	10.8628	.00847458	178	31684	13.3417	.00561798
59	3481	7.6811	.016949	119	14161	10.9087	.00840336	179	32041	13.3791	.00558659
60	3600	7.7460	.016667	120	14400	10.9545	.00833333	180	32400	13.4164	.00555556

Table P (*Cont.*)

N	N²	√N	1/N	N	N²	√N	1/N	N	N²	√N	1/N
181	32761	13.4536	.00552486	241	58081	15.5242	.00414938	301	90601	17.3494	.00332226
182	33124	13.4907	.00549451	242	58564	15.5563	.00413223	302	91204	17.3781	.00331126
183	33489	13.5277	.00546448	243	59049	15.5885	.00411523	303	91809	17.4069	.00330033
184	33856	13.5647	.00543478	244	59536	15.6205	.00409836	304	92416	17.4356	.00328047
185	34225	13.6015	.00540541	245	60025	15.6525	.00408163	305	93025	17.4642	.00328947
186	34596	13.6382	.00537634	246	60516	15.6844	.00406504	306	93636	17.4929	.00326797
187	34969	13.6748	.00534759	247	61009	15.7162	.00404858	307	94249	17.5214	.00325733
188	35344	13.7113	.00531915	248	61504	15.7480	.00403226	308	94864	17.5499	.00321675
189	35721	13.7477	.00529101	249	62001	15.7797	.00401606	309	95481	17.5784	.00323625
190	36100	13.7840	.00526316	250	62500	15.8114	.00400000	310	96100	17.6068	.00322581
191	36481	13.8203	.00523560	251	63001	15.8430	.00398406	311	96721	17.6352	.00321543
192	36864	13.8564	.00520833	252	63504	15.8745	.00396825	312	97344	17.6635	.00320513
193	37249	13.8924	.00518135	253	64009	15.9060	.00395257	313	97969	17.6918	.00319489
194	37636	13.9284	.00515464	254	64516	15.9374	.00393701	314	98596	17.7200	.00318471
195	38025	13.9642	.00512821	255	65025	15.9687	.00392157	315	99225	17.7482	.00317460
196	38416	14.0000	.00510204	256	65536	16.0000	.00390625	316	99856	17.7764	.00316456
197	38809	14.0357	.00507614	257	66049	16.0312	.00389105	317	100489	17.8045	.00315457
198	39204	14.0712	.00505051	258	66564	16.0624	.00387597	318	101124	17.8326	.00314465
199	39601	14.1067	.00502513	259	67081	16.0935	.00386100	319	101761	17.8606	.00313480
200	40000	14.1421	.00500000	260	67600	16.1245	.00384615	320	102400	17.8885	.00312500
201	40401	14.1774	.00497512	261	68121	16.1555	.00383142	321	103041	17.9165	.00311526
202	40804	14.2127	.00495050	262	68644	16.1864	.00381679	322	103684	17.9444	.00310559
203	41209	14.2478	.00492611	263	69169	16.2173	.00380228	323	104329	17.9722	.00309598
204	41616	14.2829	.00490196	264	69696	16.2481	.00378788	324	104976	18.0000	.00308642
205	42025	14.3178	.00487805	265	70225	16.2788	.00377358	325	105625	18.0278	.00307692
206	42436	14.3527	.00485437	266	70756	16.3095	.00375940	326	106276	18.0555	.00306748
207	42849	14.3875	.00483092	267	71289	16.3401	.00374532	327	106929	18.0831	.00305810
208	43264	14.4222	.00480769	268	71824	16.3707	.00373134	328	107584	18.1108	.00304878
209	43681	14.4568	.00478469	269	72361	16.4012	.00371747	329	108241	18.1384	.00303951
210	44100	14.4914	.00476190	270	72900	16.4317	.00370370	330	108900	18.1659	.00303030
211	44521	14.5258	.00473934	271	73441	16.4621	.00369004	331	109561	18.1934	.00302115
212	44944	14.5602	.00471698	272	73984	16.4924	.00367647	332	110224	18.2209	.00301205
213	45369	14.5945	.00469484	273	74529	16.5227	.00366300	333	110889	18.2483	.00300300
214	45796	14.6287	.00467290	274	75076	16.5529	.00364964	334	111556	18.2757	.00299401
215	46225	14.6629	.00465116	275	75625	16.5831	.00363636	335	112225	18.3030	.00298507
216	46656	14.6969	.00462963	276	76176	16.6132	.00362319	336	112896	18.3303	.00297619
217	47089	14.7309	.00460829	277	76729	16.6433	.00361011	337	113569	18.3576	.00296736
218	47524	14.7648	.00458716	278	77284	16.6733	.00359712	338	114244	18.3848	.00295858
219	47961	14.7986	.00456621	279	77841	16.7033	.00358423	339	114921	18.4120	.00294985
220	48400	14.8324	.00454545	280	78400	16.7332	.00357143	340	115600	18.4391	.00294118
221	48841	14.8661	.00452489	281	78961	16.7631	.00355872	341	116281	18.4662	.00293255
222	49284	14.8997	.00450450	282	79524	16.7929	.00354610	342	116964	18.4932	.00292398
223	49729	14.9332	.00448430	283	80089	16.8226	.00353357	343	117649	18.5203	.00291545
224	50176	14.9666	.00446429	284	80656	16.8523	.00352113	344	118336	18.5472	.00290698
225	50625	15.0000	.00444444	285	81225	16.8819	.00350877	345	119025	18.5742	.00289855
226	51076	15.0333	.00442478	286	81796	16.9115	.00349650	346	119716	18.6011	.00289017
227	51529	15.0665	.00440529	287	82369	16.9411	.00348432	347	120409	18.6279	.00288184
228	51984	15.0997	.00438596	288	82944	16.9706	.00347222	348	121104	18.6548	.00287356
229	52441	15.1327	.00436681	289	83521	17.0000	.00346021	349	121801	18.6815	.00286533
230	52900	15.1658	.00434783	290	84100	17.0294	.00344828	350	122500	18.7083	.00285714
231	53361	15.1987	.00432900	291	84681	17.0587	.00343643	351	123201	18.7350	.00284900
232	53824	15.2315	.00431034	292	85264	17.0880	.00342466	352	123904	18.7617	.00284091
233	54289	15.2643	.00429185	293	85849	17.1172	.00341297	353	124609	18.7883	.00283286
234	54756	15.2971	.00427350	294	86436	17.1464	.00340136	354	125316	18.8149	.00282486
235	55225	15.3297	.00425532	295	87025	17.1756	.00338983	355	126025	18.8414	.00281690
236	55696	15.3623	.00423729	296	87616	17.2047	.00337838	356	126736	18.8680	.00280899
237	56169	15.3948	.00421941	297	88209	17.2337	.00336700	357	127449	18.8944	.00280112
238	56644	15.4272	.00420168	298	88804	17.2627	.00335570	358	128164	18.9209	.00279330
239	57121	15.4596	.00418410	299	89401	17.2916	.00334448	359	128881	18.9473	.00278552
240	57600	15.4919	.00416667	300	90000	17.3205	.00333333	360	129600	18.9737	.00277778

Table P (*Cont.*)

N	N²	√N	1/N	N	N²	√N	1/N	N	N²	√N	1/N
361	130321	19.0000	.00277008	421	177241	20.5183	.00237530	481	231361	21.9317	.00207900
362	131044	19.0263	.00276243	422	178084	20.5426	.00236967	482	232324	21.9545	.00207469
363	131769	19.0526	.00275482	423	178929	20.5670	.00236407	483	233289	21.9773	.00207039
364	132496	19.0788	.00274725	424	179776	20.5913	.00235849	484	234256	22.0000	.00206612
365	133225	19.1050	.00273973	425	180625	20.6155	.00235294	485	235225	22.0227	.00206186
366	133956	19.1311	.00273224	426	181476	20.6398	.00234742	486	236196	22.0454	.00205761
367	134689	19.1572	.00272480	427	182329	20.6640	.00234192	487	237169	22.0681	.00205339
368	135424	19.1833	.00271739	428	183184	20.6882	.00233645	488	238144	22.0907	.00204918
369	136161	19.2094	.00271003	429	184041	20.7123	.00233100	489	239121	22.1133	.00204499
370	136900	19.2354	.00270270	430	184900	20.7364	.00232558	490	240100	22.1359	.00204082
371	137641	19.2614	.00269542	431	185761	20.7605	.00232019	491	241081	22.1585	.00203666
372	138384	19.2873	.00268817	432	186624	20.7846	.00231481	492	242064	22.1811	.00203252
373	139129	19.3132	.00268097	433	187489	20.8087	.00230947	493	243049	22.2036	.00202840
374	139876	19.3391	.00267380	434	188356	20.8327	.00230415	494	244036	22.2261	.00202429
375	140625	19.3649	.00266667	435	189225	20.8567	.00229885	495	245025	22.2486	.00202020
376	141376	19.3907	.00265957	436	190096	20.8806	.00229358	496	246016	22.2711	.00201613
377	142129	19.4165	.00265252	437	190969	20.9045	.00228833	497	247009	22.2935	.00201207
378	142884	19.4422	.00264550	438	191844	20.9284	.00228311	498	248004	22.3159	.00200803
379	143641	19.4679	.00263852	439	192721	20.9523	.00227790	499	249001	22.3383	.00200401
380	144400	19.4936	.00263158	440	193600	20.9762	.00227273	500	250000	22.3607	.00200000
381	145161	19.5192	.00262467	441	194481	21.0000	.00226757	501	251001	22.3830	.00199601
382	145924	19.5448	.00261780	442	195364	21.0238	.00226244	502	252004	22.4054	.00199203
383	146689	19.5704	.00261097	443	196249	21.0476	.00225734	503	253009	22.4277	.00198807
384	147456	19.5959	.00260417	444	197136	21.0713	.00225225	504	254016	22.4499	.00198413
385	148225	19.6214	.00259740	445	198025	21.0950	.00224719	505	255025	22.4722	.00198020
386	148996	19.6469	.00259067	446	198916	21.1187	.00224215	506	256036	22.4944	.00197628
387	149769	19.6723	.00258398	447	199809	21.1424	.00223714	507	257049	22.5167	.00197239
388	150544	19.6977	.00257732	448	200704	21.1660	.00223214	508	258064	22.5389	.00196850
389	151321	19.7231	.00257069	449	201601	21.1896	.00222717	509	259081	22.5610	.00196464
390	152100	19.7484	.00256410	450	202500	21.2132	.00222222	510	260100	22.5832	.00196078
391	152881	19.7737	.00255754	451	203401	21.2368	.00221729	511	261121	22.6053	.00195695
392	153664	19.7990	.00255102	452	204304	21.2603	.00221239	512	262144	22.6274	.00195312
393	154449	19.8242	.00254453	453	205209	21.2838	.00220751	513	263169	22.6495	.00194932
394	155236	19.8494	.00253807	454	206116	21.3073	.00220264	514	264196	22.6716	.00194553
395	156025	19.8746	.00253165	455	207025	21.3307	.00219870	515	265225	22.6936	.00194175
396	156816	19.8997	.00252525	456	207936	21.3542	.00219298	516	266256	22.7156	.00193798
397	157609	19.9249	.00251889	457	208849	21.3776	.00218818	517	267289	22.7376	.00193424
398	158404	19.9499	.00251256	458	209764	21.4009	.00218341	518	268324	22.7596	.00193050
399	159201	19.9750	.00250627	459	210681	21.4243	.00217865	519	269361	22.7816	.00192678
400	160000	20.0000	.00250000	460	211600	21.4476	.00217391	520	270400	22.8035	.00192308
401	160801	20.0250	.00249377	461	212521	21.4709	.00216920	521	271441	22.8254	.00191939
402	161604	20.0499	.00248756	462	213444	21.4942	.00216450	522	272484	22.8473	.00191571
403	162409	20.0749	.00248139	463	214369	21.5174	.00215983	523	273529	22.8692	.00191205
404	163216	20.0998	.00247525	464	215296	21.5407	.00215517	524	274576	22.8910	.00190840
405	164025	20.1246	.00246914	465	216225	21.5639	.00215054	525	275625	22.9129	.00190476
406	164836	20.1494	.00246305	466	217156	21.5870	.00214592	526	276676	22.9347	.00190114
407	165649	20.1742	.00245700	467	218089	21.6102	.00214133	527	277729	22.9565	.00189753
408	166464	20.1990	.00245098	468	219024	21.6333	.00213675	528	278784	22.9783	.00189394
409	167281	20.2237	.00244499	469	219961	21.6564	.00213220	529	279841	23.0000	.00189036
410	168100	20.2485	.00243902	470	220900	21.6795	.00212766	530	280900	23.0217	.00188679
411	168921	20.2731	.00243309	471	221841	21.7025	.00212314	531	281961	23.0434	.00188324
412	169744	20.2978	.00242718	472	222784	21.7256	.00211864	532	283024	23.0651	.00187970
413	170569	20.3224	.00242131	473	223729	21.7486	.00211416	533	284089	23.0868	.00187617
414	171396	20.3470	.00241546	474	224676	21.7715	.00210970	534	285156	23.1084	.00187266
415	172225	20.3715	.00240964	475	225625	21.7945	.00210526	535	286225	23.1301	.00186916
416	173056	20.3961	.00240385	476	226576	21.8174	.00210084	536	287296	23.1517	.00186567
417	173889	20.4206	.00239808	477	227529	21.8403	.00209644	537	288369	23.1733	.00186220
418	174724	20.4450	.00239234	478	228484	21.8632	.00209205	538	289444	23.1948	.00185874
419	175561	20.4695	.00238663	479	229441	21.8861	.00208768	539	290521	23.2164	.00185529
420	176400	20.4939	.00238095	480	230400	21.9089	.00208333	540	291600	23.2379	.00185185

Table P (*Cont.*)

N	N²	√N	1/N	N	N²	√N	1/N	N	N²	√N	1/N
541	292681	23.2594	.00184843	601	361201	24.5153	.00166389	661	436921	25.7099	.00151286
542	293764	23.2809	.00184502	602	302404	24.5357	.00166113	662	438244	25.7294	.00151057
543	294849	23.3024	.00184162	603	363609	24.5561	.00165837	663	439569	25.7488	.00150830
544	295936	23.3238	.00183824	604	364816	24.5764	.00165563	664	440896	25.7682	.00150602
545	297025	23.3452	.00183486	605	366025	24.5967	.00165289	665	442225	25.7876	.00150376
546	298116	23.3666	.00183150	606	367236	24.6171	.00165017	666	443556	25.8070	.00150150
547	299209	23.3880	.00182815	607	368449	24.6374	.00164745	667	444889	25.8263	.00149925
548	300304	23.4094	.00182482	608	369664	24.6577	.00164474	668	446224	25.8457	.00149701
549	301401	23.4307	.00182149	609	370881	24.6779	.00164204	669	447561	25.8650	.00149477
550	302500	23.4521	.00181818	610	372100	24.6982	.00163934	670	448900	25.8844	.00149254
551	303601	23.4734	.00181488	611	373321	24.7184	.00163666	671	450241	25.9037	.00149031
552	304704	23.4947	.00181159	612	374544	24.7386	.00163399	672	451584	25.9230	.00148810
553	305809	23.5160	.00180832	613	375769	24.7588	.00163132	673	452929	25.9422	.00148588
554	306916	23.5372	.00180505	614	376996	24.7790	.00162866	674	454276	25.9615	.00148368
555	308025	23.5584	.00180180	615	378225	24.7992	.00162602	675	455625	25.9808	.00148148
556	309136	23.5797	.00179856	616	379456	24.8193	.00162338	676	456976	26.0000	.00147929
557	310249	23.6008	.00179533	617	380689	24.8395	.00162075	677	458329	26.0192	.00147710
558	311364	23.6220	.00179211	618	381924	24.8596	.00161812	678	459684	26.0384	.00147493
559	312481	23.6432	.00178891	619	383161	24.8797	.00161551	679	461041	26.0576	.00147275
560	313600	23.6643	.00178571	620	384400	24.8998	.00161290	680	462400	26.0768	.00147059
561	314721	23.6854	.00178253	621	385641	24.9199	.00161031	681	463761	26.0960	.00146843
562	315844	23.7065	.00177936	622	386884	24.9399	.00160772	682	465124	26.1151	.00146628
563	316969	23.7276	.00177620	623	388129	24.9600	.00160514	683	466489	26.1343	.00146413
564	318096	23.7487	.00177305	624	389376	24.9800	.00160256	684	467856	26.1534	.00146199
565	319225	23.7697	.00176991	625	390625	25.0000	.00160000	685	469225	26.1725	.00145985
566	320356	23.7908	.00176678	626	391876	25.0200	.00159744	686	470596	26.1916	.00145773
567	321489	23.8118	.00176367	627	393129	25.0400	.00159490	687	471969	26.2107	.00145560
568	322624	23.8328	.00176056	628	394384	25.0599	.00159236	688	473344	26.2298	.00145349
569	323761	23.8537	.00175747	629	395641	25.0799	.00158983	689	474721	26.2488	.00145138
570	324900	23.8747	.00175439	630	396900	25.0998	.00158730	690	476100	26.2679	.00144928
571	326041	23.8956	.00175131	631	398161	25.1197	.00158479	691	477481	26.2869	.00144718
572	327184	23.9165	.00164825	632	399424	25.1396	.00158228	692	478864	26.3059	.00144509
573	328329	23.9374	.00174520	633	400689	25.1595	.00157978	693	480249	26.3249	.00144300
574	329476	23.9583	.00174216	634	401956	25.1794	.00157729	694	481636	26.3439	.00144092
575	330625	23.9792	.00173913	635	403225	25.1992	.00157480	695	483025	26.3629	.00143885
576	331776	24.0000	.00173611	636	404496	25.2190	.00157233	696	484416	26.3818	.00143678
577	332929	24.0208	.00173310	637	405769	25.2389	.00156986	697	485809	26.4008	.00143472
578	334084	24.0416	.00173010	638	407044	25.2587	.00156740	698	487204	26.4197	.00143266
579	335241	24.0624	.00172712	639	408321	25.2784	.00156495	699	488601	26.4386	.00143062
580	336400	24.0832	.00172414	640	409600	25.2982	.00156250	700	490000	26.4575	.00142857
581	337561	24.1039	.00172117	641	410881	25.3180	.00156006	701	491401	26.4764	.00142653
582	338724	24.1247	.00171821	642	412164	25.3377	.00155763	702	492804	26.4953	.00142450
583	339889	24.1454	.00171527	643	413449	25.3574	.00155521	703	494209	26.5141	.00142248
584	341056	24.1661	.00171233	644	414736	25.3772	.00155280	704	495616	26.5330	.00142045
585	342225	24.1868	.00170940	645	416025	25.3969	.00155039	705	497025	26.5518	.00141844
586	343396	24.2074	.00170648	646	417316	25.4165	.00154799	706	498436	26.5707	.00141643
587	344569	24.2281	.00170358	647	418609	25.4362	.00154560	707	499849	26.5895	.00141443
588	345744	24.2487	.00170068	648	419904	25.4558	.00154321	708	501264	26.6083	.00141243
589	346921	24.2693	.00169779	649	421201	25.4755	.00154083	709	502681	26.6271	.00141044
590	348100	24.2899	.00169492	650	422500	25.4951	.00153846	710	504100	26.6458	.00140845
591	349281	24.3105	.00169205	651	423801	25.5147	.00153610	711	505521	26.6646	.00140647
592	350464	24.3311	.00168919	652	425104	25.5343	.00153374	712	506944	26.6833	.00140449
593	351649	24.3516	.00168634	653	426409	25.5539	.00153139	713	508369	26.7021	.00140252
594	352836	24.3721	.00168350	654	427716	25.5734	.00152905	714	509796	26.7208	.00140056
595	354025	24.3926	.00168067	655	429025	25.5930	.00152672	715	511225	26.7395	.00139860
596	355216	24.4131	.00167785	656	430336	25.6125	.00152439	716	512656	26.7582	.00139665
597	356409	24.4336	.00167504	657	431649	25.6320	.00152207	717	514089	26.7769	.00139470
598	357604	24.4540	.00167224	658	432964	25.6515	.00151976	718	515524	26.7955	.00139276
599	358801	24.4745	.00166945	659	434281	25.6710	.00151745	719	516961	26.8142	.00139082
600	360000	24.4949	.00166667	660	435600	25.6905	.00151515	720	518400	26.8328	.00138889

Table P (*Cont.*)

N	N²	√N	1/N	N	N²	√N	1/N	N	N²	√N	1/N
721	519841	26.8514	.00138696	781	609961	27.9464	.00128041	841	707281	29.0000	.00118906
722	521284	26.8701	.00138504	782	611524	27.9643	.00127877	842	708964	29.0172	.00118765
723	522729	26.8887	.00138313	783	613089	27.9821	.00127714	843	710649	29.0345	.00118624
724	524176	26.9072	.00138122	784	614656	28.0000	.00127551	844	712336	29.0517	.00118483
725	525625	26.9258	.00137931	785	616225	28.0179	.00127389	845	714025	29.0689	.00118343
726	527076	26.9444	.00137741	786	617796	28.0357	.00127226	846	715716	29.0861	.00118203
727	528529	26.9629	.00137552	787	619369	28.0535	.00127065	847	717409	29.1033	.00118064
728	529984	26.9815	.00137363	788	620944	28.0713	.00126904	848	719104	29.1204	.00117925
729	531441	27.0000	.00137174	789	622521	28.0891	.00126743	849	720801	29.1376	.00117786
730	532900	27.0185	.00136986	790	624100	28.1069	.00126582	850	722500	29.1548	.00117647
731	534361	27.0370	.00136799	791	625681	28.1247	.00126422	851	724201	29.1719	.00117509
732	535824	27.0555	.00136612	792	627264	28.1425	.00126263	852	725904	29.1890	.00117371
733	537289	27.0740	.00136426	793	628849	28.1603	.00126103	853	727609	29.2062	.00117233
734	538756	27.0924	.00136240	794	630436	28.1780	.00125945	854	729316	29.2233	.00117096
735	540225	27.1109	.00136054	795	632025	28.1957	.00125786	855	731025	29.2404	.00116959
736	541696	27.1293	.00135870	796	633616	28.2135	.00125628	856	732736	29.2575	.00116822
737	543169	27.1477	.00135685	797	635209	28.2312	.00125471	857	734449	29.2746	.00116686
738	544644	27.1662	.00135501	798	636804	28.2489	.00125313	858	736164	29.2916	.00116550
739	546121	27.1846	.00135318	799	638401	28.2666	.00125156	859	737881	29.3087	.00116414
740	547600	27.2029	.00135135	800	640000	28.2843	.00125000	860	739600	29.3258	.00116279
741	549081	27.2213	.00134953	801	641601	28.3019	.00124844	861	741321	29.3428	.00116144
742	550564	27.2397	.00134771	802	643204	28.3196	.00124688	862	743044	29.3598	.00116009
743	552049	27.2580	.00134590	803	644809	28.3373	.00124533	863	744769	29.3769	.00115875
744	553536	27.2764	.00134409	804	646416	28.3549	.00124378	864	746496	29.3939	.00115741
745	555025	27.2947	.00134228	805	648025	28.3725	.00124224	865	748225	29.4109	.00115607
746	556516	27.3130	.00134048	806	649636	28.3901	.00124069	866	749956	29.4279	.00115473
747	558009	27.3313	.00133869	807	651249	28.4077	.00123916	867	751689	29.4449	.00115340
748	559504	27.3496	.00133690	808	652864	28.4253	.00123762	868	753424	29.4618	.00115207
749	561001	27.3679	.00133511	809	654481	28.4429	.00123609	869	755161	29.4788	.00115075
750	562500	27.3861	.00133333	810	656100	28.4605	.00123457	870	756900	29.4958	.00114943
751	564001	27.4044	.00133156	811	657721	28.4781	.00123305	871	758641	29.5127	.00114811
752	565504	27.4226	.00132979	812	659344	28.4956	.00123153	872	760384	29.5296	.00114679
753	567009	27.4408	.00132802	813	660969	28.5132	.00123001	873	762129	29.5466	.00114548
754	568516	27.4591	.00132626	814	662596	28.5307	.00122850	874	763876	29.5635	.00114416
755	570025	27.4773	.00132450	815	664225	28.5482	.00122699	875	765625	29.5804	.00114286
756	571536	27.4955	.00132275	816	665856	28.5657	.00122549	876	767376	29.5973	.00114155
757	573049	27.5136	.00132100	817	667489	28.5832	.00122399	877	769129	29.6142	.00114025
758	574564	27.5318	.00131926	818	669124	28.6007	.00122249	878	770884	29.6311	.00113895
759	576081	27.5500	.00131752	819	670761	28.6182	.00122100	879	772641	29.6479	.00113766
760	577600	27.5681	.00131579	820	672400	28.6356	.00121951	880	774400	29.6648	.00113636
761	579121	27.5862	.00131406	821	674041	28.6531	.00121803	881	776161	29.6816	.00113507
762	580644	27.6043	.00131234	822	675684	28.6705	.00121655	882	777924	29.6985	.00113379
763	582169	27.6225	.00131062	823	677329	28.6880	.00121507	883	779689	29.7153	.00113250
764	583696	27.6405	.00130890	824	678976	28.7054	.00121359	884	781456	29.7321	.00113122
765	585225	27.6586	.00130719	825	680625	28.7228	.00121212	885	783225	29.7489	.00112994
766	586756	27.6767	.00130548	826	682276	28.7402	.00121065	886	784996	29.7658	.00112867
767	588289	27.6948	.00130378	827	683929	28.7576	.00120919	887	786769	29.7825	.00112740
768	589824	27.7128	.00130208	828	685584	28.7750	.00120773	888	788544	29.7993	.00112613
769	591361	27.7308	.00130039	829	687241	28.7924	.00120627	889	790321	29.8161	.00112486
770	592900	27.7489	.00129870	830	688900	28.8097	.00120482	890	792100	29.8329	.00112360
771	594441	27.7669	.00129702	831	690561	28.8271	.00120337	891	793881	29.8496	.00112233
772	595984	27.7849	.00129534	832	692224	28.8444	.00120192	892	795664	29.8664	.00112108
773	597529	27.8029	.00129366	833	693889	28.8617	.00120048	893	797449	29.8831	.00111982
774	599076	27.8209	.00129199	834	695556	28.8791	.00119904	894	799236	29.8998	.00111857
775	600625	27.8388	.00129032	835	697225	28.8964	.00119760	895	801025	29.9166	.00111732
776	602176	27.8568	.00128866	836	698896	28.9137	.00119617	896	802816	29.9333	.00111607
777	603729	27.8747	.00128700	837	700569	28.9310	.00119474	897	804609	29.9500	.00111483
778	605284	27.8927	.00128535	838	702244	28.9482	.00119332	898	806404	29.9666	.00111359
779	606841	27.9106	.00128370	839	703921	28.9655	.00119190	899	808201	29.9833	.00111235
780	608400	27.9285	.00128205	840	705600	28.9828	.00119048	900	810000	30.0000	.00111111

Table P (*Cont.*)

N	N²	√N	1/N	N	N²	√N	1/N	N	N²	√N	1/N
901	811801	30.0167	.00110988	936	876096	30.5941	.00106838	971	942841	31.1609	.00102987
902	813604	30.0333	.00110865	937	877969	30.6105	.00106724	972	944784	31.1769	.00102881
903	815409	30.0500	.00110742	938	879844	30.6268	.00106610	973	946729	31.1929	.00102775
904	817216	30.0666	.00110619	939	881721	30.6431	.00106496	974	948676	31.2090	.00102669
905	819025	30.0832	.00110497	940	883600	30.6594	.00106383	975	950625	31.2250	.00102564
906	820836	30.0998	.00110375	941	885481	30.6757	.00106270	976	952576	31.2410	.00102459
907	822649	30.1164	.00110254	942	887364	30.6920	.00106157	977	954529	31.2570	.00102354
908	824464	30.1330	.00110132	943	889249	30.7083	.00106045	978	956484	31.2730	.00102249
909	826281	30.1496	.00110011	944	891136	30.7246	.00105932	979	958441	31.2890	.00102145
910	828100	30.1662	.00109890	945	893025	30.7409	.00105820	980	960400	31.3050	.00102041
911	829921	30.1828	.00109769	946	894916	30.7571	.00105708	981	962361	31.3209	.00101937
912	831744	30.1993	.00109649	947	896809	30.7734	.00105597	982	964324	31.3369	.00101833
913	833569	30.2159	.00109529	948	898704	30.7896	.00105485	983	966289	31.3528	.00101729
914	835396	30.2324	.00109409	949	900601	30.8058	.00105374	984	968256	31.3688	.00101626
915	837225	30.2490	.00109290	950	902500	30.8221	.00105263	985	970225	31.3847	.00101523
916	839056	30.2655	.00109170	951	904401	30.8383	.00105152	986	972196	31.4006	.00101420
917	840889	30.2820	.00109051	952	906304	30.8545	.00105042	987	974169	31.4166	.00101317
918	842724	30.2985	.00108932	953	908209	30.8707	.00104932	988	976144	31.4325	.00101215
919	844561	30.3150	.00108814	954	910116	30.8869	.00104822	989	978121	31.4484	.00101112
920	846400	30.3315	.00108696	955	912025	30.9031	.00104712	990	980100	31.4643	.00101010
921	848241	30.3480	.00108578	956	913936	30.9192	.00104603	991	982081	31.4802	.00100908
922	850084	30.3645	.00108460	957	915849	30.9354	.00104493	992	984064	31.4960	.00100806
923	851929	30.3809	.00108342	958	917764	30.9516	.00104384	993	986049	31.5119	.00100705
924	853776	30.3974	.00108225	959	919681	30.9677	.00104275	994	988036	31.5278	.00100604
925	855625	30.4138	.00108108	960	921600	30.9839	.00104167	995	990025	31.5436	.00100503
926	857476	30.4302	.00107991	961	923521	31.0000	.00104058	996	992016	31.5595	.00100402
927	859329	30.4467	.00107875	962	925444	31.0161	.00103950	997	994009	31.5753	.00103842
928	861184	30.4631	.00107759	963	927369	31.0322	.00103842	998	996004	31.5911	.00100200
929	863041	30.4795	.00107643	964	929296	31.0483	.00103734	999	998001	31.6070	.00100100
930	864900	30.4959	.00107527	965	931225	31.0644	.00103627	1000	1000000	31.6228	.00100000
931	866761	30.5123	.00107411	966	933156	31.0805	.00103520				
932	868624	30.5287	.00107296	967	935089	31.0966	.00103413				
933	870489	30.5450	.00107181	968	937024	31.1127	.00103306				
934	872356	30.5614	.00107066	969	938961	31.1288	.00103199				
935	874225	30.5778	.00106952	970	940900	31.1448	.00103093				

Table Q
Random digits.

Row number													
00000	10097	32533		76520	13586		34673	54876		80959	09117		39292	74945
00001	37542	04805		64894	74296		24805	24037		20636	10402		00822	91665
00002	08422	68953		19645	09303		23209	02560		15953	34764		35080	33606
00003	99019	02529		09376	70715		38311	31165		88676	74397		04436	27659
00004	12807	99970		80157	36147		64032	36653		98951	16877		12171	76833
00005	66065	74717		34072	76850		36697	36170		65813	39885		11199	29170
00006	31060	10805		45571	82406		35303	42614		86799	07439		23403	09732
00007	85269	77602		02051	65692		68665	74818		73053	85247		18623	88579
00008	63573	32135		05325	47048		90553	57548		28468	28709		83491	25624
00009	73796	45753		03529	64778		35808	34282		60935	20344		35273	88435
00010	98520	17767		14905	68607		22109	40558		60970	93433		50500	73998
00011	11805	05431		39808	27732		50725	68248		29405	24201		52775	67851
00012	83452	99634		06288	98033		13746	70078		18475	40610		68711	77817
00013	88685	40200		86507	58401		36766	67951		90364	76493		29609	11062
00014	99594	67348		87517	64969		91826	08928		93785	61368		23478	34113
00015	65481	17674		17468	50950		58047	76974		73039	57186		40218	16544
00016	80124	35635		17727	08015		45318	22374		21115	78253		14385	53763
00017	74350	99817		77402	77214		43236	00210		45521	64237		96286	02655
00018	69916	26803		66252	29148		36936	87203		76621	13990		94400	56418
00019	09893	20505		14225	68514		46427	56788		96297	78822		54382	14598
00020	91499	14523		68479	27686		46162	83554		94750	89923		37089	20048
00021	80336	94598		26940	36858		70297	34135		53140	33340		42050	82341
00022	44104	81949		85157	47954		32979	26575		57600	40881		22222	06413
00023	12550	73742		11100	02040		12860	74697		96644	89439		28707	25815
00024	63606	49329		16505	34484		40219	52563		43651	77082		07207	31790
00025	61196	90446		26457	47774		51924	33729		65394	59593		42582	60527
00026	15474	45266		95270	79953		59367	83848		82396	10118		33211	59466
00027	94557	28573		67897	54387		54622	44431		91190	42592		92927	45973
00028	42481	16213		97344	08721		16868	48767		03071	12059		25701	46670
00029	23523	78317		73208	89837		68935	91416		26252	29663		05522	82562
00030	04493	52494		75246	33824		45862	51025		61962	79335		65337	12472
00031	00549	97654		64051	88159		96119	63896		54692	82391		23287	29529
00032	35963	15307		26898	09354		33351	35462		77974	50024		90103	39333
00033	59808	08391		45427	26842		83609	49700		13021	24892		78565	20106
00034	46058	85236		01390	92286		77281	44077		93910	83647		70617	42941
00035	32179	00597		87379	25241		05567	07007		86743	17157		85394	11838
00036	69234	61406		20117	45204		15956	60000		18743	92423		97118	96338
00037	19565	41430		01758	75379		40419	21585		66674	36806		84962	85207
00038	45155	14938		19476	07246		43667	94543		59047	90033		20826	69541
00039	94864	31994		36168	10851		34888	81553		01540	35456		05014	51176
00040	98086	24826		45240	28404		44999	08896		39094	73407		35441	31880
00041	33185	16232		41941	50949		89435	48581		88695	41994		37548	73043
00042	80951	00406		96382	70774		20151	23387		25016	25298		94624	61171
00043	79752	49140		71961	28296		69861	02591		74852	20539		00387	59579
00044	18633	32537		98145	06571		31010	24674		05455	61427		77938	91936
00045	74029	43902		77557	32270		97790	17119		52527	58021		80814	51748
00046	54178	45611		80993	37143		05335	12969		56127	19255		36040	90324
00047	11664	49883		52079	84827		59381	71539		09973	33440		88461	23356
00048	48324	77928		31249	64710		02295	36870		32307	57546		15020	09994
00049	69074	94138		87637	91976		35584	04401		10518	21615		01848	76938
00050	09188	20097		32825	39527		04220	86304		83389	87374		64278	58044
00051	90045	85497		51981	50654		94938	81997		91870	76150		68476	64659
00052	73189	50207		47677	26269		62290	64464		27124	67018		41361	82760
00053	75768	76490		20971	87749		90429	12272		95375	05871		93823	43178
00054	54016	44056		66281	31003		00682	27398		20714	53295		07706	17813
00055	08358	69910		78542	42785		13661	58873		04618	97553		31223	08420
00056	28306	03264		81333	10591		40510	07893		32604	60475		94119	01840
00057	53840	86233		81594	13628		51215	90290		28466	68795		77762	20791
00058	91757	53741		61613	62669		50263	90212		55781	76514		83483	47055
00059	89415	92694		00397	58391		12607	17646		48949	72306		94541	37408

Table Q *(Cont.)*

Row number									
00060	77513	03820	86864	29901	68414	82774	51908	13980	72893	55507
00061	19502	37174	69979	20288	55210	29773	74287	75251	65344	67415
00062	21818	59313	93278	81757	05686	73156	07082	85046	31853	38452
00063	51474	66499	68107	23621	94049	91345	42836	09191	08007	45449
00064	99559	68331	62535	24170	69777	12830	74819	78142	43860	72834
00065	33713	48007	93584	72869	51926	64721	58303	29822	93174	93972
00066	85274	86893	11303	22970	28834	34137	73515	90400	71148	43643
00067	84133	89640	44035	52166	73852	70091	61222	60561	62327	18423
00068	56732	16234	17395	96131	10123	91622	85496	57560	81604	18880
00069	65138	56806	87648	85261	34313	65861	45875	21069	85644	47277
00070	38001	02176	81719	11711	71602	92937	74219	64049	65584	49698
00071	37402	96397	01304	77586	56271	10086	47324	62605	40030	37438
00072	97125	40348	87083	31417	21815	39250	75237	62047	15501	29578
00073	21826	41134	47143	34072	64638	85902	49139	06441	03856	54552
00074	73135	42742	95719	09035	85794	74296	08789	88156	64691	19202
00075	07638	77929	03061	18072	96207	44156	23821	99538	04713	66994
00076	60528	83441	07954	19814	59175	20695	05533	52139	61212	06455
00077	83596	35655	06958	92983	05128	09719	77433	53783	92301	50498
00078	10850	62746	99599	10507	13499	06319	53075	71839	06410	19362
00079	39820	98952	43622	63147	64421	80814	43800	09351	31024	73167
00080	59580	06478	75569	78800	88835	54486	23768	06156	04111	08408
00081	38508	07341	23793	48763	90822	97022	17719	04207	95954	49953
00082	30692	70668	94688	16127	56196	80091	82067	63400	05462	69200
00083	65443	95659	18238	27437	49632	24041	08337	65676	96299	90836
00084	27267	50264	13192	72294	07477	44606	17985	48911	97341	30358
00085	91307	06991	19072	24210	36699	53728	28825	35793	28976	66252
00086	68434	94688	84473	13622	62126	98408	12843	82590	09815	93146
00087	48908	15877	54745	24591	35700	04754	83824	52692	54130	55160
00088	06913	45197	42672	78601	11883	09528	63011	98901	14974	40344
00089	10455	16019	14210	33712	91342	37821	88325	80851	43667	70883
00090	12883	97343	65027	61184	04285	01392	17974	15077	90712	26769
00091	21778	30976	38807	36961	31649	42096	63281	02023	08816	47449
00092	19523	59515	65122	59659	86283	68258	69572	13798	16435	91529
00093	67245	52670	35583	16563	79246	86686	76463	34222	26655	90802
00094	60584	47377	07500	37992	45134	26529	26760	83637	41326	44344
00095	53853	41377	36066	94850	58838	73859	49364	73331	96240	43642
00096	24637	38736	74384	89342	52623	07992	12369	18601	03742	83873
00097	83080	12451	38992	22815	07759	51777	97377	27585	51972	37867
00098	16444	24334	36151	99073	27493	70939	85130	32552	54846	54759
00099	60790	18157	57178	65762	11161	78576	45819	52979	65130	04860
00100	03991	10461	93716	16894	66083	24653	84609	58232	88618	19161
00101	38555	95554	32886	59780	08355	60860	29735	47762	71299	23853
00102	17546	73704	92052	46215	55121	29281	59076	07936	27954	58909
00103	32643	52861	95819	06831	00911	98936	76355	93779	80863	00514
00104	69572	68777	39510	35905	14060	40619	29549	69616	33564	60780
00105	24122	66591	27699	06494	14845	46672	61958	77100	90899	75754
00106	61196	30231	92962	61773	41839	55382	17267	70943	78038	70267
00107	30532	21704	10274	12202	39685	23309	10061	68829	55986	66485
00108	03788	97599	75867	20717	74416	53166	35208	33374	87539	08823
00109	48228	63379	85783	47619	53152	67433	35663	52972	16818	60311
00110	60365	94653	35075	33949	42614	29297	01918	28316	98953	73231
00111	83799	42402	56623	34442	34994	41374	70071	14736	09958	18065
00112	32960	07405	36409	83232	99385	41600	11133	07586	15917	06253
00113	19322	53845	57620	52606	66497	68646	78138	66559	19640	99413
00114	11220	94747	07399	37408	48509	23929	27482	45476	85244	35159
00115	31751	57260	68980	05339	15470	48355	88651	22596	03152	19121
00116	88492	99382	14454	04504	20094	98977	74843	93413	22109	78508
00117	30934	47744	07481	83828	73788	06533	28597	20405	94205	20380
00118	22888	48893	27499	98748	60530	45128	74022	84617	82037	10268
00119	78212	16993	35902	91386	44372	15486	65741	14014	87481	37220

Table Q (Cont.)

Row number										
00120	41849	84547	46850	52326	34677	58300	74910	64345	19325	81549
00121	46352	33049	69248	93460	45305	07521	61318	31855	14413	70951
00122	11087	96294	14013	31792	59747	67277	76503	34513	39663	77544
00123	52701	08337	56303	87315	16520	69676	11654	99893	02181	68161
00124	57275	36898	81304	48585	68652	27376	92852	55866	88448	03584
00125	20857	73156	70284	24326	79375	95220	01159	63267	10622	48391
00126	15633	84924	90415	93614	33521	26665	55823	47641	86225	31704
00127	92694	48297	39904	02115	59589	49067	66821	41575	49767	04037
00128	77613	19019	88152	00080	20554	91409	96277	48257	50816	97616
00129	38688	32486	45134	63545	59404	72059	43947	51680	43852	59693
00130	25163	01889	70014	15021	41290	67312	71857	15957	68971	11403
00131	65251	07629	37239	33295	05870	01119	92784	26340	18477	65622
00132	36815	43625	18637	37509	82444	99005	04921	73701	14707	93997
00133	64397	11692	05327	82162	20247	81759	45197	25332	83745	22567
00134	04515	25624	95096	67946	48460	85558	15191	18782	16930	33361
00135	83761	60873	43253	84145	60833	25983	01291	41349	20368	07126
00136	14387	06345	80854	09279	43529	06318	38384	74761	41196	37480
00137	51321	92246	80088	77074	88722	56736	66164	49431	66919	31678
00138	72472	00008	80890	18002	94813	31900	54155	83436	35352	54131
00139	05466	55306	93128	18464	74457	90561	72848	11834	79982	68416
00140	39528	72484	82474	25593	48545	35247	18619	13674	18611	19241
00141	81616	18711	53342	44276	75122	11724	74627	73707	58319	15997
00142	07586	16120	82641	22820	92904	13141	32392	19763	61199	67940
00143	90767	04235	13574	17200	69902	63742	78464	22501	18627	90872
00144	40188	28193	29593	88627	94972	11598	62095	36787	00441	58997
00145	34414	82157	86887	55087	19152	00023	12302	80783	32624	68691
00146	63439	75363	44989	16822	36024	00867	76378	41605	65961	73488
00147	67049	09070	93399	45547	94458	74284	05041	49807	20288	34060
00148	79495	04146	52162	90286	54158	34243	46978	35482	59362	95938
00149	91704	30552	04737	21031	75051	93029	47665	64382	99782	93478
00150	94015	46874	32444	48277	59820	96163	64654	25843	41145	42820
00151	74108	88222	88570	74015	25704	91035	01755	14750	48968	38603
00152	62880	87873	95160	59221	22304	90314	72877	17334	39283	04149
00153	11748	12102	80580	41867	17710	59621	06554	07850	73950	79552
00154	17944	05600	60478	03343	25852	58905	57216	39618	49856	99326
00155	66067	42792	95043	52680	46780	56487	09971	59481	37006	22186
00156	54244	91030	45547	70818	59849	96169	61459	21647	87417	17198
00157	30945	57589	31732	57260	47670	07654	46376	25366	94746	49580
00158	69170	37403	86995	90307	94304	71803	26825	05511	12459	91314
00159	08345	88975	35841	85771	08105	59987	87112	21476	14713	71181
00160	27767	43584	85301	88977	29490	69714	73035	41207	74699	09310
00161	13025	14338	54066	15243	47724	66733	47431	43905	31048	56699
00162	80217	36292	98525	24335	24432	24896	43277	58874	11466	16082
00163	10875	62004	90391	61105	57411	06368	53856	30743	08670	84741
00164	54127	57326	26629	19087	24472	88779	30540	27886	61732	75454
00165	60311	42824	37301	42678	45990	43242	17374	52003	70707	70214
00166	49739	71484	92003	98086	76668	73209	59202	11973	02902	33250
00167	78626	51594	16453	94614	39014	97066	83012	09832	25571	77628
00168	66692	13986	99837	00582	81232	44987	09504	96412	90193	79568
00169	44071	28091	07362	97703	76447	42537	98524	97831	65704	09514
00170	41468	85149	49554	17994	14924	39650	95294	00556	70481	06905
00171	94559	37559	49678	53119	70312	05682	66986	34099	74474	20740
00172	41615	70360	64114	58660	90850	64618	80620	51790	11436	38072
00173	50273	93113	41794	86861	24781	89683	55411	85667	77535	99892
00174	41396	80504	90670	08289	40902	05069	95083	06783	28102	57816
00175	25807	24260	71529	78920	72682	07385	90726	57166	98884	08583
00176	06170	97965	88302	98041	21443	41808	68984	83620	89747	98882
00177	60808	54444	74412	81105	01176	28838	36421	16489	18059	51061
00178	80940	44893	10408	36222	80582	71944	92638	40333	67054	16067
00179	19516	90120	46759	71643	13177	55292	21036	82808	77501	97427

Table Q *(Cont.)*

Row number										
00180	49386	54480	23604	23554	21785	41101	91178	10174	29420	90438
00181	06312	88940	15995	69321	47458	64809	98189	81851	29651	84215
00182	60942	00307	11897	92674	40405	68032	96717	54244	10701	41393
00183	92329	98932	78284	46347	71209	92061	39448	93136	25722	08564
00184	77936	63574	31384	51924	85561	29671	58137	17820	22751	36518
00185	38101	77756	11657	13897	95889	57067	47648	13885	70669	93406
00186	39641	69457	91339	22502	92613	89719	11947	56203	19324	20504
00187	84054	40455	99396	63680	67667	60631	69181	96845	38525	11600
00188	47468	03577	57649	63266	24700	71594	14004	23153	69249	05747
00189	43321	31370	28977	23896	76479	68562	62342	07589	08899	05985
00190	64281	61826	18555	64937	13173	33365	78851	16499	87064	13075
00191	66847	70495	32350	02985	86716	38746	26313	77463	55387	72681
00192	72461	33230	21529	53424	92581	02262	78438	66276	18396	73538
00193	21032	91050	13058	16218	12470	56500	15292	76139	59526	52113
00194	95362	67011	06651	16136	01016	00857	55018	56374	35824	71708
00195	49712	97380	10404	55452	34030	60726	75211	10271	36633	68424
00196	58275	61764	97586	54716	50259	46345	87195	46092	26787	60939
00197	89514	11788	68224	23417	73959	76145	30342	40277	11049	72049
00198	15472	50669	48139	36732	46874	37088	63465	09819	58869	35220
00199	12120	86124	51247	44302	60883	52109	21437	36786	49226	77837

Acknowledgments

The authors are grateful to the authors and publishers listed below for permission to adapt from the following tables.

Table B   R. A. Fisher, *Statistical Methods for Research Workers* (14th ed.). Reprinted with permission of Macmillan Publishing Company, Inc. Copyright © 1970, University of Adelaide.

Table C   Table III of R. A. Fisher and F. Yates, *Statistical Tables for Biological, Agricultural, and Medical Research,* 6th ed. London: Longman Group Ltd., 1974. (Previously published by Oliver and Boyd, Ltd., Edinburgh.)

Table D   G. W. Snedecor and William G. Cochran, *Statistical Methods,* 7th ed. Ames, Iowa: Iowa State University Press, copyright © 1980.

Table E   J. Sandler (1955), "A Test of the Significance of the Difference between the Means of Correlated Measures, Based on a Simplification of Student's *t*," *Brit. J. Psychol.,* **46**, 225–226.

Table F   Q. McNemar, Table B of *Psychological Statistics.* New York: John Wiley, 1962.

Table G   E. G. Olds (1949), "The 5 Percent Significance Levels of Sums of Squares of Rank Differences and a Correction," *Ann. Math. Statist.,* **20**, 117–118.
E. G. Olds, (1938), "Distribution of Sums of Squares of Rank Differences for Small Numbers of Individuals," *Ann. Math. Statist.,* **9**, 133–148.

Table H   W. V. Bingham, Table XVII of *Aptitudes and Aptitude Testing.* New York: Harper and Bros., 1937.

Table I   H. B. Mann and D. R. Whitney (1947), "On a Test of Whether One of Two Random Variables is Stochastically Larger than the Other," *Ann. Math. Statist.,* **18**, 52–54.
D. Auble (1953), "Extended Tables for the Mann-Whitney Statistic," *Bulletin of the Institute of Educational Research at Indiana University,* **1** (2).

Table J   F. Wilcoxon, S. Katti, and R. A. Wilcox, *Critical Values and Probability Levels for the Wilcoxon Rank Sum Test and the Wilcoxon Signed Rank Test.* New York: American Cyanamid Co., 1963.
F. Wilcoxon and R. A. Wilcox, *Some Rapid Approximate Statistical Procedures.* New York: Lederle Laboratories, 1964.

Table L   S. Siegel, *Nonparametric Statistics.* New York: McGraw-Hill, 1956.

Table M   R. P. Runyon, Table A of *Nonparametric Statistics,* Reading, Mass: Addison-Wesley, 1977.

Table N   R. P. Runyon, Table B of *Nonparametric Statistics.* Reading, Mass: Addison-Wesley, 1977.

Table O   E. S. Pearson and H. O. Hartley, *Biometrika Tables for Statisticians,* vol. 1, 2nd ed. New York: Cambridge, 1958.

Table P   A. L. Edwards, *Statistical Analysis,* 3rd ed. New York: Holt, Rinehart and Winston, 1969.

J. W. Dunlap and A. K. Kurtz, *Handbook of Statistical Nomographs, Tables, and Formulas.* New York: World Book Company, 1932.

Table Q   RAND Corporation, *A Million Random Digits.* New York: Free Press of Glencoe, 1955.

Answers to Selected Exercises

In problems involving many steps, you may occasionally find a discrepancy between the answers you obtained and those shown here. Where the discrepancies are small, they are probably due to rounding errors. These disparities are more common today because of the wide differences in methods employed; i.e., varying degrees of sophistication among calculators, adding machines, and hand calculations.

Chapter 1

1. **a.** statistic **b.** inference from statistics **c.** data
   d. data **e.** inference from statistics

3. **a.** constant **b.** variable **c.** variable **d.** variable
   e. constant **f.** variable **g.** constant **h.** variable

4. **a.** data **b.** data

5. These are not statistics; they are data. Statistics that may be calculated from these data include proportion or percentage of passes completed by each team, proportion or percentage of yards gained on the ground or in the air, proportion or percentage of time of possession. (See Chapter 2 for a discussion of proportions and percentages.)

6. (d)   7. (b)   8. (a)   9. (b)   10. (d)   11. (a)

Chapter 2

1. **a.**

	Proportion	Percentage
Too little	0.77	77
About right	0.21	21
Too much	0.02	2
No opinion	0.01	1

b.

	Proportion*	Percentage*
Too little	0.71	71
About right	0.24	24
Too much	0.03	3
No opinion	0.02	2

*The slight disparity from 1.00 and 100 is due to rounding error.

457

c.

	Proportion	Percentage
Too little	0.83	83
About right	0.13	13
Too much	0.02	2
No opinion	0.02	2

d.

	Proportion*	Percentage*
Too little	0.25	25
About right	0.28	28
Too much	0.43	43
No opinion	0.03	3

*The slight disparity from 1.00 and 100 is due to rounding error.

The majority of the respondents appear to want more information about earthquakes and how to prepare for them. Thus, the results appear to contradict the view that Californians would prefer not thinking about earthquakes.

2. $a = 5$ 3. $y = 22$ 4. $\sum X = 1200$ 5. $\overline{X} = 4$ 6. $N = 40$ 7. $s^2 = 20$

8. a. 100.00   b. 46.41   c. 2.96   d. 0.01   e. 16.46   f. 1.05   g. 86.21   h. 10.00

9. male $= 0.77$; female $= 0.23$ 10. Guns $= 0.66$; cutting or stabbing $= 0.17$; strangulations or beatings $= 0.08$; blunt object $= 0.05$; arson $= 0.01$; other $= 0.02$.   11. suicides $= 0.5445$; homicides $= 0.4555$

12.

	(a)	(b)
Year	Percentage of Male* Homicide Victims	Percentage of Female* Homicide Victims
1968	13.85	13.85
1969	14.14	14.67
1970	15.91	15.79
1971	17.51	17.16
1972	18.50	17.56
1973	20.10	20.98

*The slight disparity from 100.00 is due to rounding error.

13. a. 25   b. 60   c. 37   d. 31   e. 60   f. 44

14. a. $\sum_{i=1}^{3} X_i$ b. $\sum_{i=1}^{N} X_i$ c. $\sum_{i=3}^{6} X_i^2$ d. $\sum_{i=4}^{N} X_i^2$

15. a. ratio   b. ratio   c. nominal   d. ordinal

16. a. ratio; continuous
    b. If time of the day is regarded in the narrow sense (midnight to midnight), ratio statements may be made with respect to the 24-hour period. If time of the day is conceptualized as but a brief interval in cosmic time, the scale is interval; continuous.   c. nominal; discontinuous

17. a. 12.65   b. 4.00   c. 1.26   d. 0.40   e. 0.13

18. a. -0.5 to $+0.5$ b. 0.45 to 0.55   c. 0.95 to 1.05
    d. 0.485 to 0.495   e. -4.5 to -5.5 f. -4.45 to -4.55

19. $\sum_{i=1}^{N} X_i^2 = 4^2 + 5^2 + 7^2 + 9^2 + 10^2 + 11^2 + 14^2 = 588$

$$\left(\sum_{i=1}^{N} X_i \right)^2 = (4 + 5 + 7 + 9 + 10 + 11 + 14)^2$$

$$= 60^2 = 3600,$$

$588 \neq 3600$

20. **a.** discrete **b.** discrete **c.** continuous **d.** continuous **e.** continuous **f.** discrete

21. **a.**

		b. 38.10	**c.** 13.33	**d.** 58.33 Males
Business administration	20.00%	4.76	20.00	41.67% Females
Education	75.00%	14.29	26.67	
Humanities	57.14%	23.81	13.33	
Science	28.57%	19.05	26.67	
Social science	50.00%			

22. **a.** continuous **b.** discrete **c.** continuous **d.** discrete **e.** discrete

23.

Year	% Males	% Females
1950	51.31	48.69
1955	51.24	48.76
1960	51.20	48.80
1965	51.25	48.75
1970	51.33	48.67

24. **a.**

	Aggressive Males (Percent)	Nonaggressive Males (Percent)
Attempted to get girl intoxicated	37.9	9.1
Falsely promised marriage	8.0	7.5
Falsely professed love	44.8	14.6
Threatened to terminate relationship	9.2	3.5

b. The results do not support the hypothesis. In fact they are in a direction opposite to the hypothesis.

25.

	Berkeley	Yale
Firearms	35	40
Poisoning	26	12
Asphyxiation	17	20
Hanging	9	24
Jumping from high places	9	4
Cutting instruments	4	0

26. **a.** 0.57% (*Note:* This is not 57%. It is fifty seven hundredths of one percent)
b. 72.7%, 15.4%.

27. **a.** 37.0% **b.** 41.5 and 58.5 **c.** 32.5 and 67.5

28. Although it is not possible to precisely specify the population, it involves airline passengers at a large metropolitan airport who use the telephone. Many of these passengers are relatively affluent and are business people. There are probably relatively few blue-collar workers and the working poor represented in the sample. It is unlikely that the sample is representative of the general population.

Chapter 3

1.

	True Limits	Midpoint	Width
a.	7.5–12.5	10	5
b.	5.5–7.5	6.5	2
c.	(−0.5)–(+2.5)	1	3
d.	4.5–14.5	9.5	10
e.	(−8.5)–(−1.5)	−5	7
f.	2.45–3.55	3	1.1
g.	1.495–1.755	1.625	0.26
h.	(−3.5)–(+3.5)	0	7

2.

	Width	Apparent Limits	True Limits	Midpoint
i.	7	0–6	−0.5–6.5	3
ii.	1	29	28.5–29.5	29
iii.	2	18–19	17.5–19.5	18.5
iv.	4	(−30)–(−27)	(−30.5)–(−26.5)	−28.5
v.	0.01	0.30	0.295–0.305	0.30
vi.	0.006	0.206–0.211	0.2055–0.2115	0.2085

3.

Classes	True Limits	Midpoint	f	Cum. f	Cum. %
95–99	94.5–99.5	97	1	40	100.0%
90–94	89.5–94.5	92	3	39	97.5
85–89	84.5–89.5	87	4	36	90.0
80–84	79.5–84.5	82	8	32	80.0
75–79	74.5–79.5	77	11	24	60.0
70–74	69.5–74.5	72	4	13	32.5
65–69	64.5–69.5	67	3	9	22.5
60–64	59.5–64.5	62	3	6	15.0
55–59	54.5–59.5	57	0	3	7.5
50–54	49.5–54.5	52	1	3	7.5
45–49	44.5–49.5	47	1	2	5.0
40–44	39.5–44.5	42	1	1	2.5

4. b. $i = 3$

Classes	f	Classes	f
97–99	1	67–69	2
94–96	1	64–66	1
91–93	2	61–63	2
88–90	1	58–60	1
85–87	3	55–57	0
82–84	4	52–54	1
79–81	6	49–51	0
76–78	8	46–48	1
73–75	2	43–45	0
70–72	3	40–42	1

c. $i = 10$ **d.** $i = 20$

Classes	f
90–99	4
80–89	12
70–79	15
60–69	6
50–59	1
40–49	2

Classes	f
80–99	16
60–79	21
40–59	3

5.

Classes	True Limits	Midpoint	f
9.6–9.9	9.55–9.95	9.75	1
9.2–9.5	9.15–9.55	9.35	3
8.8–9.1	8.75–9.15	8.95	1
8.4–8.7	8.35–8.75	8.55	4
8.0–8.3	7.95–8.35	8.15	7
7.6–7.9	7.55–7.95	7.75	10
7.2–7.5	7.15–7.55	7.35	2
6.8–7.1	6.75–7.15	6.95	4
6.4–6.7	6.35–6.75	6.55	2
6.0–6.3	5.95–6.35	6.15	3
5.6–5.9	5.55–5.95	5.75	0
5.2–5.5	5.15–5.55	5.35	1
4.8–5.1	4.75–5.15	4.95	0
4.4–4.7	4.35–4.75	4.55	1
4.0–4.3	3.95–4.35	4.15	1

Width = 0.4

6. a. $i = 7$ b. 14.5–21.5   c. 18
            7.5–14.5   11
            0.5–7.5   4

7.

Classes	f
65–69	1
60–64	2
55–59	3
50–54	4
45–49	5
40–44	6
35–39	8
30–34	6
25–29	5
20–24	4
15–19	3
10–14	2
5–9	1

8.

Classes	f
63–67	3
58–62	0
53–57	7
48–52	0
43–47	11
38–42	0
33–37	14
28–32	0
23–27	9
18–22	0
13–17	5
8–12	0
3–7	1

9.

Classes	f
66–67	1
64–65	1
62–63	1
60–61	0
58–59	0
56–57	2
54–55	3
52–53	2
50–51	0
48–49	0
46–47	2
44–45	7
42–43	2
40–41	0
38–39	0
36–37	7
34–35	4
32–33	3
30–31	0
28–29	0
26–27	4
24–25	3
22–23	2
20–21	0
18–19	0
16–17	2
14–15	2
12–13	1
10–11	0
8–9	0
6–7	0
4–5	1

10.

Classes	f
60–69	3
50–59	7
40–49	11
30–39	14
20–29	9
10–19	5
0–9	1

12.

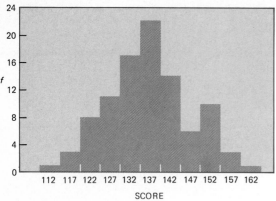

16.

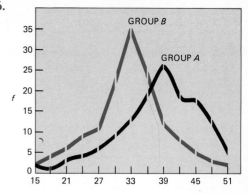

17. **a.** positively skewed   **b.** normal   **c.** normal   **d.** bimodal

18.

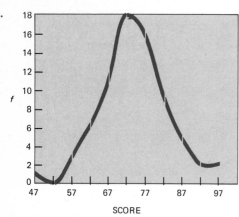

19.

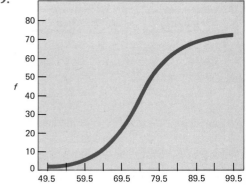

20.

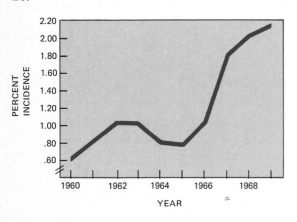

21.

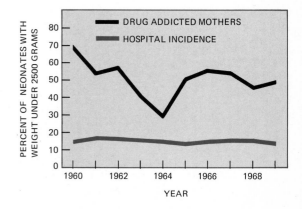

22. a. 34.62%

b.

Classes	f	cf
92–94	1	52
89–91	0	51
86–88	2	51
83–85	0	49
80–82	0	49
77–79	3	49
74–76	5	46
71–73	7	41
68–70	5	34
65–67	10	29
62–64	11	19
59–61	4	8
56–58	4	4

c.

d.

Classes	f	cf
90–94	1	52
85–89	2	51
80–84	0	49
75–79	7	49
70–74	9	42
65–69	14	33
60–64	15	19
55–59	4	4

23.

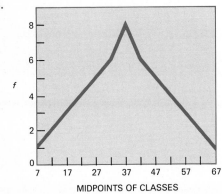

MIDPOINTS OF CLASSES

24.

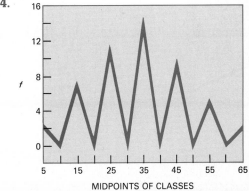

MIDPOINTS OF CLASSES

25.

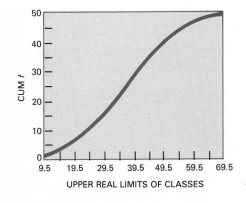

UPPER REAL LIMITS OF CLASSES

26.

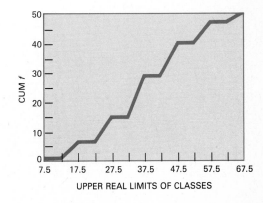

UPPER REAL LIMITS OF CLASSES

27. **a.**

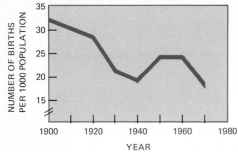

b. There does appear to be a generally declining trend.

*28. **a.**

Sum of Two Scores	f
12	1
11	2
10	3
9	4
8	5
7	6
6	7
5	6
4	5
3	4
2	3
1	2
0	1
	$N = 49$

b.

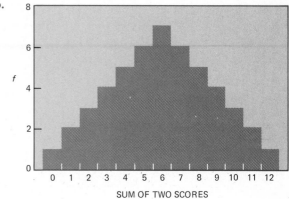

29.

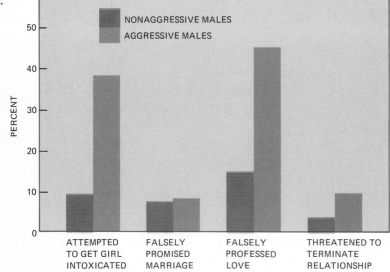

30.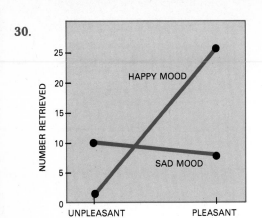

31.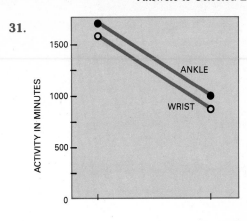

Chapter 4

2. a. 26.36   **b.** 46.82   **c.** 88.45   **4. a.** 103.88   **b.** 113.03   **c.** 124.78

6. a. 81.02   **b.** 94.76   **c.** 88.04

7. a. $\dfrac{16.9}{110} = 15.36\%$ **b.** $\dfrac{93.1}{110} = 84.64\%$ **c.** 2.45%   **d.** 0.18%   **e.** 26.73%   **f.** 3.73%

8. b. 57, 76   **c.** Law-school freshmen, 60

9. 89.58   **10.** 54.17   **11.** 94.17   **12.** 74.17   **13.** 17.50   **14.** 79.58   **15.** 10.36

16. 19.17   **17.** 11.70   **18.** 11.04   **19.** 20.76   **20.** 10.87

21. and **22.**

A. 88.8	F. 42.0	K. 77.2	P. 42.0	U. 42.0
B. 77.2	G. 96.4	L. 61.6	Q. 25.6	V. 13.2
C. 25.6	H. 61.6	M. 4.8	R. 4.8	W. 61.6
D. 61.6	I. 77.2	N. 25.6	S. 0.4	X. 25.6
E. 42.0	J. 13.2	O. 88.8	T. 13.2	Y. 42.0

*23.

Sum	f	Cum. f	Cum. %
12	1	49	100
11	2	48	98
10	3	46	94
9	4	43	88
8	5	39	80
7	6	34	69
6	7	28	57
5	6	21	43
4	5	15	31
3	4	10	20
2	3	6	12
1	2	3	6
0	1	1	2

$N = 49$

*24. a. 98%   **b.** 45%   **c.** 12%   **d.** 12%   **e.** 24%

25. b. Maria   **c.** Matthew   **e.** Alicia

26. a. 24 %ile   **b.** 70th %ile   **c.** Cannot be calculated since the class is open-ended.

27. All of the following are obtained by visual inspection and are subject to error. Thus, all values shown are approximate.   **a.** 25th %ile   **b.** 25th %ile   **c.** 50th %ile   **d.** 75th %ile   **e.** 90th %ile   **f.** 60th %ile.

Chapter 5

1. a. $\overline{X} = 5.0$ median $= 5.5$ mode $= 8$ **2.** (c)   **4.** All measures of central tendency will be
   b. $\overline{X} = 5.0$ median $= 5.0$ mode $= 5.0$ reduced by 5.
   c. $\overline{X} = 17.5$ median $= 3.83$ mode $= 4$

5. All measures of central tendency will be divided by 16.

6. Chapter 3, Problem 13:   median $= 136.32$; mode $= 137$
   Chapter 3, Problem 20:   median $= 73.81$; mode $= 72$

7. $\overline{X} = 5.0$; median unchanged, mode unchanged

8. a. negative skew   **b.** positive skew   **c.** no evidence of skew   **d.** no evidence of skew

9. 8 (c) symmetrical   8 (d) bimodal

10. $\overline{X} = 5.0$:   **a.** $\overline{X} = 7.0$ **b.** $\overline{X} = 3.0$ **c.** No change   **d.** $\overline{X} = 10.0$ **e.** $\overline{X} = 2.5$

11. group A: median; group B: mean

12. b.

	Means f	Medians f
6	1	3
5	6	5
4	11	9
3	7	6
2	4	3
1	1	4

d. Drawing from means: **i.** $\frac{1}{30}$ **ii.** $\frac{1}{30}$ **iii.** $\frac{2}{30}$
   Drawing from medians: **i.** $\frac{3}{30}$ **ii.** $\frac{4}{30}$ **iii.** $\frac{7}{30}$

13. The distribution is symmetrical.

15. a. 0.89   **b.** -5.11 **16.** 0.25   **17.** $\overline{X} = 164.94$ **18.** $\overline{X} = 148.44$

19. a. $\overline{X} = -16.50$ **b.** The difference between means is the same as the mean difference.

20. raise median: (c)   **23.** 1.83%   **24.** 2.08   **25. a.** mean $= 30$ median $= 30$ mode $= 30$
   raise mean: (b)   **b.** mean $= 30$ median $= 30$ mode $= 25$; 30; 35
                                                           c. mean $= 26.0$ median $= 27.5$ mode $= 25$; 30

26. a.

X	$(X - \overline{X})$
10	-16
25	-1
30	4
36	10
25	-1
30	4
$\sum(X - \overline{X}) = 0$	

b.

X	Median $(X - 27.5)$	Mode $(X - 25)$	Mode $(X - 30)$
10	-17.5	-15	-20
25	-2.5	0	-5
30	2.5	5	0
36	8.5	11	6
25	-2.5	0	-5
30	2.5	5	0
$\sum -9.0$	6	-24

27. mean = 6; median = 6.5; mode = 7
28. $4.90   **29.** manufacturer A: either mean, median or mode; manufacturer B: mode
30. a. 820.56   **b.** 109,135.1
***31.**

	First Draw						
	0	**1**	**2**	**3**	**4**	**5**	**6**
0	0	0.5	1.0	1.5	2.0	2.5	3.0
1	0.5	1.0	1.5	2.0	2.5	3.0	3.5
2	1.0	1.5	2.0	2.5	3.0	3.5	4.0
3	1.5	2.0	2.5	3.0	3.5	4.0	4.5
4	2.0	2.5	3.0	3.5	4.0	4.5	5.0
5	2.5	3.0	3.5	4.0	4.5	5.0	5.5
6	3.0	3.5	4.0	4.5	5.0	5.5	6.0

(Second Draw labels rows)

***32.**

	f
6.0	1
5.5	2
5.0	3
4.5	4
4.0	5
3.5	6
3.0	7
2.5	6
2.0	5
1.5	4
1.0	3
.5	2
0	1
	$N = 49$

***33. a.** 2%   **b.** 6%   **c.** 43%   **d.** 12%
***34.** The two means are identical.

Chapter 6

1. $s^2 = 1.66$, $s = 1.29$
  a. no change   **b.** no change   **c.** increase   **d.** increase   **e.** decrease
3. Only the standard deviation satisfies these conditions. However, if the properties included *powers* of the constant, the variance would qualify as a measure of dispersion.
4. Exercise 5.4: no change   **5.** All scores have the same value.
  Exercise 5.5: standard deviation will be divided by 16.
6. a. 3.52   **b.** 2.31   **c.** 5.89   **d.** 0
7. The distribution is extremely skewed to the right. Extreme deviations increase the size of the standard deviation.
8. a. 10   **b.** 8   **c.** 20   **d.** 0
9. a. $s^2 = 16.77$, $s = 4.10$ **b.** $s^2 = 34.77$, $s = 5.90$
  c. $s^2 = 26.44$, $s = 5.14$
10. $\overline{X} = 7.59$, $s = 3.01$
11. a. $\overline{X} = 63.10$ **b.** range = 35, semi-interquartile range = 4.00, M.D. = 5.61
  c. $s = 7.89$, $s^2 = 62.25$
12. The standard deviation is expressed in the original units of measurement whereas the variance is based on the square of these units.
13. $\overline{X} = 68.25$, $s = 7.61$

16.

		January, 1965	January, 1966	May, 1965	May, 1966
a.	$\overline{X}$	35.58	38.65	76.90	70.42
b.	range	39	43	42	33
	M.D.	7.78	7.40	7.47	7.81
c.	s	9.72	9.39	9.53	9.23
	s^2	94.48	88.17	90.82	85.19

17. $0.40; $0.40   **18. a.** crude range $= 4$, $s^2 = 1.59$; $s = 1.26$
        b. crude range $= 18$, $s^2 = 28.09$; $s = 5.3$

19. Barrow: $s = 0.07$; $s = 0.27$ ***20.** $s = 1.41$ **21. a.** $s^2 = 471.04$, $s = 21.70$
    Burlington $s^2 = 0.42$; $s = 0.65$ **b.** $s^2 = 287.37$, $s = 16.95$
    Honolulu: $s^2 = 1.30$; $s = 1.14$ **c.** $s^2 = 133.31$, $s = 11.55$
    Seattle-Tacoma: $s^2 = 3.31$; $s = 1.82$

22. a. 13.247   **b.** 4.5

23. Median $= 52$, $\overline{X} = 59.62$, skew $= 22.86/13.2471 = 1.73$. The skew is positive and too large to consider the distribution symmetrical.

Chapter 7

1. a. 0.94   **b.** -0.40 **c.** 0.00   **d.** -1.32 **e.** 2.23   **f.** -2.53

2. a. 0.4798   **b.** 0.4713   **c.** 0.0987   **d.** 0.1554   **e.** 0.4505
   f. 0.4750   **g.** 0.4901   **h.** 0.4951   **i.** 0.4990

3. a. i. 0.3413; 341   **ii.** 0.4772; 477   **iii.** 0.1915; 192   **iv.** 0.4938; 494
   b. i. 0.1587; 159   **ii.** 0.0228; 23   **iii.** 0.6915; 692   **iv.** 0.9938; 994   **v.** 0.5000; 500
   c. i. 0.1359; 136   **ii.** 0.8351; 835   **iii.** 0.6687; 669   **iv.** 0.3023; 302

4. a. arithmetic: $z = 1.21$; verbal comprehension: $z = 0.77$; geography: $z = -0.29$
   b. arithmetic; geography   **c.** 0.1131, 0.2206, 0.6141

5. a. 40.13; 57.93   **b.** 60.26   **6.** (a), (b), (c)

7. a. $z = -0.67$ **b.** $z = 0.67$
       $X = 63.96$ $X = 80.04$
   c. $z = 1.28$ **d.** $z = 0.67$
       $X = 87.36$ 25.14% score above
   e. $z = -0.5$ **f.** $z = -0.67$ and $z = 0.67$
       30.85% score below $63.96 - 80.04$
   g. $z = \pm1.64$ **h.** $z = \pm2.58$
       below 52.32,   below 41.04,
       above 91.68   above 102.96

8. $\mu = 72$, $\sigma = 8$:   **8.** $\mu = 72$, $\sigma = 4$:
   a. 66.64   **b.** 77.36   **a.** 69.32   **b.** 74.68
   c. 82.24   **d.** $z = 1.00$ **c.** 77.12   **d.** $z = 2.00$
   e. $z = -0.75$ 15.87% score above   **e.** $z = -1.5$ 2.28% score above
       22.66% score below   **f.** $66.64 - 77.36$ 6.68% score below   **f.** $69.32 - 74.68$
   g. below 58.88,   **h.** below 51.36,   **g.** below 65.44,   **h.** below 61.68
       above 85.12   above 92.64   above 78.56   above 82.32

8. $\mu = 72$, $\sigma = 2$:
   - **a.** 70.66
   - **b.** 73.34
   - **c.** 74.56
   - **d.** $z = 4.00$
   - **e.** $z = -3.00$
     - 0.13% score below
     - 0.003% score above
   - **f.** 70.66 – 73.34
   - **g.** below 68.72, above 75.28
   - **h.** below 66.84, above 77.16

9. test 2, test 1

10. No, z-scores merely reflect the form of the distributions from which they were derived. Normally distributed variables will yield normally distributed z-scores.

11. The normal distribution includes a family of bell-shaped curves of which the standard normal distribution ($\mu = 0$, $\sigma = 1.0$) is one.

12. **a.** 26   **b.** 65   **c.** 45   **d.** 50   13. **a.** -2.7 **b.** 0.0   **c.** 2.8   **d.** 1.4   **e.** -0.4

14. The smaller the standard deviation, the smaller the deviations of scores about the mean. When using the mean to predict a given score, the error will be, on the average, small when the standard deviation is small. In the limiting case, when $s = 0.00$, all of the scores are identical. There is no error in prediction.

Chapter 8

1. $r = 0.8466$ 2. $r = 0.9107$ 3. $r_s = 0.906$

5. **a.** nonlinear relationship   **b.** truncated range   **c.** truncated range

6. $r = 0.8260$ 7. $r = 0$; $r_s = 0.50$

8. $\sum (X - \bar{X})(Y - \bar{Y}) = \sum (XY - X\bar{Y} - Y\bar{X} + \bar{X}\bar{Y}) = \sum XY - \sum X\bar{Y} - \sum Y\bar{X} + N\bar{X}\bar{Y}$

Since $\sum X = N\bar{X}$ and $\sum Y - N\bar{Y}$, therefore:

$$\sum (X - \bar{X})(Y - \bar{Y}) = \sum XY - N\bar{X}\bar{Y} - N\bar{X}\bar{Y} + N\bar{X}\bar{Y} = \sum XY - N\bar{X}\bar{Y}$$

$$= \sum XY - N\left(\frac{\sum X}{N}\right)\left(\frac{\sum Y}{N}\right) = \sum XY - \frac{(\sum X)(\sum Y)}{N}$$

9. Nonlinear relationships give rise to spuriously low Pearson r correlation coefficients.

10. If the range if markedly restricted (truncated range), the Pearson r will be spuriously low.

11. $r = 0.7614$ 12. **a.** $r = -0.8924$ **b.** $r = -0.8720$ **c.** $r = 0.9729$

13. $r = 0.85$; $r_s = 0.81$. There appears to be a high positive correlation between the blood pressures of subjects during control and conditioning sessions.

14. $r_s = -0.21$. There appears to be a slight negative relationship between the amount of drug and the change in systolic blood pressure resulting from the conditioning procedures.

15. The degree of relationship is the same in both cases. In the first, however, the relationship is positive; it is negative in the second.

16. $r_s = -0.9705$ 17. **a.** $r = -0.9536$ **b.** $r_s = -0.9406$ 18. $r = 0.330$; truncated range

19. $r = -0.598$; truncated range   21. 1

22. a. 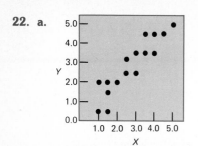 **b.** 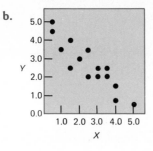 **c.**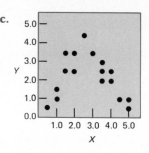

d. 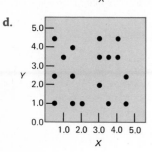 **23. a.** (c) **b.** (a) **c.** (d) **d.** (b)

24.

	Hairdressers	Bartenders	Lawyers	Supervisors
Hairdressers	———	0.88	0.90	0.81
Bartenders	———	———	0.92	0.77
Lawyers	———	———	———	0.91
Supervisors	———	———	———	———

25. a. 0.22 **b.** The clientel of most hairdressers consist of women, whereas, for bartenders, it is men. The low correlation probably reflects different focuses of daily activities.

26. $r = 0.875$

Chapter 9

1. $Y' = 3 - 0.9(X - 3)$

2. a. 1.72 **b.** 118.48 **c.** $s_{est\ y} = 0.3967$ **3. a.** 1.59 **b.** $s_{est\ y} = 0.4502; s_{est\ x} = 10.80$
c. 0.1296

4. As r increases, the angle formed by the regression lines decreases. In the limiting cases ($r = \pm 1.00$), the regression lines are superimposed upon each other. When $r = 0$, the regression lines are at right angles to each other.

5. 9.0. The standard deviation for a group with the same I.Q. is the standard error of estimate:
$s_{est\ y} = s_y \sqrt{1 - r^2} = 9$.

6. a. 0 **b.** 0.60 **c.** 1.20 **d.** 1.5 **e.** −0.75 **f.** −1.20

7. a. $Y' = 89.17$ **b.** The proportion (p) of area corresponding to a score of 110 or higher is 0.0031.
c. $X = 31.54$ **d.** $p = 0.4129$ **e.** $p < 0.00003$ **f.** $X = 68.64$ **g.** 500, 93, 93, 907

8. a. $r = 0.9398$ **b.** 50, 40, 60, 70

10. a. 33.35 **b.** $p = 0.1539$ **c.** 46.82 **e.** 53.19 **f.** yes, $p = 0.4840$ **g.** yes, $p = 0.2912$

11. a. $r = -0.8450$ **b.** 3.78 **12.** The regression lines will be identical when $r = \pm 1.00$.

13. b. $r = 0.9658$ **d.** Chile: 429.858   Ireland: 831.364   Belgium: 1390.606

14. Formula (9.2) $b_y = \dfrac{\sum(X - \bar{X})(Y - \bar{Y})}{SS_x}$

From Formula (8.3), where

$$\sum(X - \bar{X})(Y - \bar{Y}) = \sum XY - \frac{(\sum X)(\sum Y)}{N}.$$

Since $N/N = 1$, we may multiply $\sum XY$ by N/N without changing its value. Thus

$$\sum(X - \bar{X})(Y - \bar{Y}) = \frac{N\sum XY - (\sum X)(\sum Y)}{N}$$

and

$$SS_x = \sum X^2 - \frac{(\sum X)^2}{N} = \frac{N\sum X^2 - (\sum X)^2}{N}. \quad \left(\text{multiply } \sum X^2 \text{ by } \frac{N}{N}\right)$$

Thus

$$b_y = \frac{N\sum XY - (\sum X)(\sum Y)}{N} \div \frac{N\sum X^2 - (\sum X)^2}{N} = \frac{N\sum XY - (\sum X)(\sum Y)}{N\sum X^2 - (\sum X)^2}.$$

15. Since $Y = a + b_y X$ and $a = \bar{Y} - b_y\bar{X}$, therefore

$$Y' = \bar{Y} - b_y\bar{X} + b_y X \quad \text{or} \quad Y' = \bar{Y} + b_y(X - \bar{X}).$$

Since

$$b_y = \frac{N\sum XY - (\sum X)(\sum Y)}{N\sum X^2 - (\sum X)^2}$$

by substitution:

$$Y' = \bar{Y} + \left(\frac{N\sum XY - (\sum X)(\sum Y)}{N\sum X^2 - (\sum X)^2}\right)(X - \bar{X}).$$

16. a. $r = 0.9584$
   b. Y' for 3 = 3.222 Y' for 4 = 4.139
       Y' for 5 = 5.055 Y' for 6 = 5.972
       Y' for 7 = 6.889 Y' for 8 = 7.806
       Y' for 9 = 8.722 Y' for 10 = 9.639
       Y' for 11 = 10.556
   c. 54.889   **d.** 4.473   **e.** 50.424   **f.** 0.919

17. a. 5.56   **b.** 4.16   **c.** 0.857

18. a. 4.19, or moderately happy.
   b. 8.76, or perfectly happy since the predicted score is beyond the upper limit of the rating scale!
   c. 0.03, or less than once in the 35-day study period.

d. 1.18 with sexual intercourse as the predictor, and 1.12 with arguments as the predictor.

e. 49.7% is accounted for by frequency of sexual intercourse, and 54.7% is accounted for by frequency of arguments.

f. 0.50 with frequency of sexual intercourse as the predictor, and 0.45 with frequency of arguments as the predictor.

Chapter 10

1. a.

b.

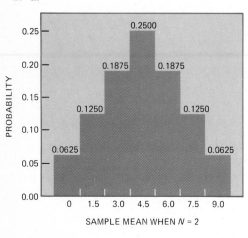

(a)

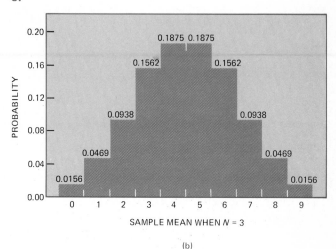

(b)

2. An extreme deviation is rarer as sample size increases.

3. a. 0.0625; 0.0156   **b.** 0.1250; 0.0312   **c.** 0.3750; 0.3125   **d.** 0.7500; 0.6250

4. a. 0.6250   **b.** 0.1875   **c.** 0.2500

5. a. 0.6874   **b.** 0.3750   **c.** 0.1407

6. a. and b.

c. Mean = 0.00;
Standard deviation = 1.63

X	f	$p(\overline{X})$
4	1	0.0123
3	4	0.0494
2	10	0.1235
1	16	0.1975
0	19	0.2346
−1	16	0.1975
−2	10	0.1235
−3	4	0.0494
−4	1	0.0123
$N_{\overline{X}}$ = 81	$\Sigma p(\overline{X})$ = 1.000	

7. a. 0.2346 **b.** 0.6296 **c.** 0.0123 **d.** 0.0246
e. 0.0617 **f.** 0.0617 **g.** 0.1234 **h.** 0.8766

8. a. 0.1250 **b.** 0.1250 **c.** 0.3750 **d.** 0.5000

9. a. 0.0192 **b.** 0.0769 **c.** 0.3077 **d.** 0.4231

10. Problem 1: **a.** 7 to 1 against, **b.** 7 to 1 against
Problem 2: **a.** 51 to 1 against, **b.** 12 to 1 against

11. a. 0.1667 **b.** 0.1667 **c.** 0.2778 **d.** 0.5000

12. a. 0.0046 **b.** 0.0278 **c.** 0.0139 **d.** 0.0556 **e.** 0.5787

13. a. 0.0129 **b.** 0.4135 **c.** 0.0100 **14. a.** 0.0156 **b.** 0.4219 **c.** 0.0123

15. a. 0.0838 **b.** 126.40 **c.** < 68.64 and > 131.36 **d.** 0.4648
e. i. 0.0070 **ii.** 0.2160 **iii.** 2(0.3895) = 0.0779

16. (b) **17.** $p = \frac{1}{24}$ **18. a.** $p = 0.20$ **b.** $p = 0.04$ **c.** $p = 0.80$ **d.** $p = 0.64$

19. a. 0.6561 **b.** 0.0001 **c.** 0.3438

20. a. $p = 0.0456$ **b.** $p = 0.0021$ **c.** $p = 0.9544$
d. $p = 0.9109$ **e.** $p = 0.0228$ **f.** $p = 0.000520$

21. a. $\frac{1}{3}$ **b.** $\frac{1}{2}$ **c.** $\frac{1}{6}$ **d.** 0 **22. a.** $\frac{1}{11}$ **b.** $\frac{1}{66}$ **c.** $\frac{14}{99}$

23. a. $\frac{1}{8}$ **b.** $\frac{1}{36}$ **c.** $\frac{16}{81}$ **24. a.** 0.40 **b.** 0.12 **c.** 0.16 **d.** 2(0.0336) = 0.0672

25. a. $p = 0.3085$ **b.** $p = 0.2266$ **c.** $p = 0.4649$
d. $p = 0.2564$ **e.** $p = 0.2934$ **f.** $p = 0.0947$ **g.** $p = 0.3296$

27.

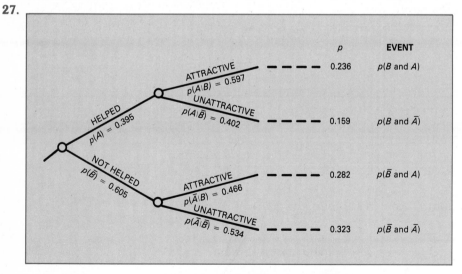

28. a.

Helping Response	Attractive (A)	Unattractive (Ā)	Marginal Probability
Helped (B)	0.235	0.160	0.395
Did not help (B̄)	0.271	0.333	0.605
Marginal Probability	0.506	0.494	1.000

b. $p(B|A) = 0.464$, $p(B|\bar{A}) = 0.324$, $p(\bar{B}|A) = 0.536$, $p(\bar{B}|\bar{A}) = 0.674$.

Chapter 11

2. a. In the event a critical theoretical issue is involved, the commission of a type I error might lead to false conclusion concerning the validity of the theory.

   b. In many studies in which the toxic effects of new drugs are being studied, the null hypothesis is that the drug has no adverse effects. In the event of a type II error, a toxic drug might be mistakenly introduced into the market.

3. The null hypothesis cannot be proved. Failure to reject the null hypothesis does not constitute proof that the null hypothesis is correct.

4. All experiments involve two statistical hypotheses: the null hypothesis and the alternative hypothesis. One designs the experiment so that the rejection of the null hypothesis leads to affirmation of the alternative hypothesis.

5. H_0: There is no difference in running speed of organisms operating under different drive levels.

    H_1: There is a difference in running speed of organisms operating under different drive levels.

6. a. H_0 **b.** H_1 **c.** H_1 **d.** H_0

7. a type II   **b.** type I   **c.** no error   **d.** no error

8. a. type II   **b.** type II   **c.** no error

9. It is more likely that he is accepting a false H_0, since the probability that the observed event occurred by chance is still quite low ($p = 0.02$).

10. By chance, one would expect five differences to be statistically significant at the 0.05 level.

11. By chance, one would expect five (give or take a few) statistically significant differences when $\alpha = 0.01$.

12. Yes.

13. Yes. Two-tailed H_1: There is a difference in running speed of organisms operating under different drive levels. One-tailed H_1: The running speed is greater for organisms operating under stronger drive levels.

14. No. The only deviations that count are those in the direction specified under H_1.

15. (b)   **16. a.** 1   **b.** 10   **c.** 5   **d.** 60   **e.** 50   **f.** 95   **g.** 4   **h.** 100

17. a. (h)   **b.** (a)   **18. a.** (h), type I   **b.** (a), type II

19. The probability of making a type I error is equal to α. In the present case, $\alpha = 0.05$.

20.

		True Status of Individual's Emotional Health	
		Does Not have a Specific Emotional Disorder	**Has a Specific Emotional Disorder**
Reported Status	Person does not have condition	**Correct**	**Type II error** False safe report.
	Person does have condition	**Type I errors** False danger report.	**Correct**

21. Failure to detect a potentially serious condition in a client (e.g., suicidal tendency) may lead to the false conclusion that nothing need be done to intervene in the client's behalf. Similarly, failure to detect possible unfavorable reactions to a treatment (e.g., thalidomide) may lead to the certification of the treatment as safe.

22. On the basis of the data, we would reject H_0. However, since H_0 is true, we have made a type I or type α error.

23. On the basis of the data, we would fail to reject H_0. Since H_0 is true, we have made the correct decision.

24. We fail to reject H_0. Since H_0 is false, we have failed to reject a false H_0. Therefore, we have made a type II or type β error.

25. We reject H_0. Since H_0 is false, we have made a correct decision.

26. We reject H_0. Since H_0 is false, we have made a correct decision.

Chapter 12

1. **a.** As sample size increases, the dispersion of sample means decreases.

   b. As you increase the number of samples, you are more likely to obtain extreme values of the sample mean. For example, suppose the probability of obtaining a sample mean of a given value is 0.01. If the number of samples drawn is 10, you probably will not obtain any sample means with that value. However, if you draw as many as 1,000 samples, you would expect to obtain approximately 10 sample means with values so extreme that the probability of their occurrence is 0.01.

2. Suppose we have a population in which the mean = 100 and the standard deviation = 10. The probability of obtaining scores as extreme as 80 or less or 120 or more (± 2 standard deviations) is 0.0456, or less than five in a hundred. The probability of obtaining scores even more extreme (for example, 50, 60, 70, or 130, 140, 150) is even lower. Thus, we would expect very few (if any) of these extreme scores to occur in a given sample. Since the value of the standard deviation is a direct function of the number of extreme scores, the standard deviation of a sample will usually underestimate the standard deviation of the population.

3. **a.** $21.71 - 26.29$ **b.** $20.82 - 27.18$ 4. **a.** $23.28 - 24.72$
   b. $23.05 - 24.95$

5. Reject H_0; $z = 2.68$ in which $z_{0.01} = \pm 2.58$

6. Accept H_0; $t = 2.618$ in which $t_{0.01} = \pm 2.831$, df $= 21$

7. In Problem 5 the value of the population standard deviation is known; thus, we may employ the z-statistic and determine probability values in terms of areas under the normal curve. In Problem 6 the value of the population standard deviation is not known and must be estimated from the sample data. Thus, the test statistic is the t-ratio.

   Since the t-distributions are more spread out than the normal curve, the proportion of area beyond a specific value of t is greater than the proportion of area beyond the corresponding value of z. Thus, a larger value of t is required to mark off the bounds of the critical region of rejection. In Problem 5, the absolute value of the obtained z must equal or exceed 2.58. In Problem 6, the absolute value of the obtained t must equal or exceed 2.83.

To generalize: the probability of making a type II error is less when we know the population standard deviation.

8. Reject H_0; $t = 2.134$ in which $t_{0.05} = 1.833$ (one-tailed test), df $= 9$

9. a. $z = 2.73$, $p = 0.9968$ **b.** $z = -0.91$, $p = 0.1814$
   c. $z = 1.82$, $p = 0.0344$ **d.** $p = 0.6372$

10. a. $36.80 - 43.20$ **b.** $35.79 - 44.21$ **11. a.** $t = 1.706$ **b.** $t = 11.19$

12. $t = 2.083$, df $= 25$ **13.** $27.14 - 32.08$

14. $t = 1.75$, df $= 625$ **15.** $263.34 - 273.66$ **16. a.** $\mu = 6.0$, $\sigma = 3.42$

17. a. $p = \frac{1}{15}$ **b.** $p = \frac{1}{15}$ **c.** $p = \frac{8}{15}$ **d.** $p = 0$

18. a. $p = \frac{1}{12}$ **b.** $p = \frac{1}{12}$ **c.** $p = \frac{5}{9}$ **d.** $p = \frac{1}{36}$

19. $\overline{X} - \mu_0 = 0.42$, $s_{\overline{X}} = 0.2315$, $t = 1.814$, df $= 7$

20. $\overline{X} - \mu_0 = 1.38$, $s_{\overline{X}} = 0.58$, $t = 2.379$, df $= 9$

21. The conclusion we draw depends upon the nature of the alternative hypothesis. If H_1 is directional and we employ $\alpha = 0.05$, we reject H_0, since the obtained r_s of 0.438 exceeds the value required (interpolating for $N = 17$, the critical value of r_s for $\alpha = 0.05$, one-tailed test, is 0.412). However, if we employ a two-tailed test, we must accept H_0.

22. The critical value of r_s for $N = 25$ ($\alpha = 0.05$, two-tailed test) may be obtained by interpolating as follows: 0.409 for $N = 24$, 0.392 for $N = 26$; thus the critical value for $N = 25$ is 0.400. Since the absolute value of the obtained r_s is less than the critical value, we accept H_0.

23. a. $z = 1.01$ **b.** $z = 1.99$

24. The statistics used to describe the distribution of a sample are $\overline{X}$ (the mean) and s (the standard deviation). The statistics used to describe the distribution of a sample statistic are the mean ($\mu_{\overline{X}}$) and the standard error of the mean ($\sigma_{\overline{X}}$).

25. s^2 is not an unbiased estimate of σ^2. When we use N in the denominator of the variance formula, we underestimate the population variance ($s^2 = SS/N$).

26. $\hat{s}^2$ is an unbiased estimate of σ^2 since $N - 1$ is used in the denominator of the formula $\hat{s}^2 = SS/(N - 1)$).

27. The interval within which the population mean probably lies is called the confidence interval.

28. Using the example in Section 12.7 of the test, we find the 99% confidence interval:

$$\text{Upper limit } \mu_0 = 108 + (2.787)(3.0) = 116.36,$$
$$\text{Lower limit } \mu_0 = 108 - (2787)(3.0) = 99.64.$$

Thus, the 99% confidence limits are $99.64 - 116.36$ as compared to the 95% confidence limits: $101.82 - 114.18$.

29. The t-distributions are more spread out than the normal curve. Thus, the proportion of area beyond a specific value of t is greater than the proportion of area beyond the corresponding value of z. As df increases, the t-distributions more closely resemble the normal curve.

30. a.

$X_1 - X_2$	f	$p(X_1 - X_2)$
9	1	0.0083
8	2	0.0165
7	5	0.0413
6	10	0.0826
5	14	0.1157
4	18	0.1488
3	21	0.1736
2	18	0.1488
1	14	0.1157
0	10	0.0826
-1	5	0.0413
-2	2	0.0165
-3	1	0.0083

$N_{\bar{X}_1-\bar{X}_2} = 121 \quad \sum p(\bar{X}_1-\bar{X}_2; = 1.0000$

b. The mean of the differences = 3. The mean of the sampling distribution of differences between means is equal to the difference between the means of the population from which these samples were drawn.

31. a. H_0: $\mu_1 = \mu_2$; i.e., the two populations of means from which we are drawing samples are the same.

b. The sampling distribution of differences between means under the null hypothesis.

c.

$X_1 - X_2$	f	$p(\bar{X}_1 - X_2)$
6	1	0.0083
5	2	0.0165
4	5	0.0413
3	10	0.0826
2	14	0.1157
1	18	0.1488
0	21	0.1736
-1	18	0.1488
-2	14	0.1157
-3	10	0.0826
-4	5	0.0413
-5	2	0.0165
-6	1	0.0083

32. a. 0.0496   **b.** 0.0083   **c.** 0.1487   **d.** 0.0166   **e.** 0.0083
33. a. 0.2644   **b.** 0.1487   **c.** 0.0083   **d.** 0.1487   **e.** 0.0000
35. $t = 4.28$ **36.** $r_{s(0.05)} = 0.450$ **37.** $t = 4$
38. a. Married couples: $t = 5.219$, df $= 51$, $p < 0.05$
     Divorced couples: $t = 0.329$, df $= 22$, not significant
b. Married couples: $t = 1.688$, df $= 51$, not significant
     Divorced couples: $t = 0.615$, df $= 22$, not significant

Chapter 13

1. $t = 2.795$, reject H_0 **2.** $t = 1.074$, accept H_0 **3.** $t = 0.802$, accept H_0
4. a. $t = 3.522$, reject H_0 **b.** $F = 3.00$, accept H_0

5. a. $z = 1.41, p = 0.0793$ **b.** $z = -2.12, p = 0.9830$ **c.** $z = -2.12, p = 0.0170$
   d. $z = -5.66, p < 0.00003$

6. a. $z = -0.71, p = 0.7611$ **b.** $z = -1.06, p = 0.8554$ **c.** $z = -1.41, p = 0.9207$
   d. $z = -1.77, p = 0.9616$

7.

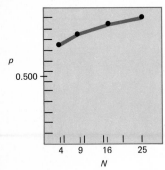

The probability of finding a difference in the correct direction between sample means increases as N increases.

8. $t = 2.148$, df $= 14$ **9.** $t = 2.913$, df $= 18$ **10.** $t = 2.304$, df $= 26$

11. a. $SS_1 = 13696.06$, $SS_2 = 24027.66$ **b.** $SS_1 = 910.32$ $SS_2 = 1590.21$
   $\overline{X}_1 = 17.82$, $\overline{X}_2 = 19.59$ $\overline{X}_1 = 1.75$, $\overline{X}_2 = 1.61$
   $t = 7.080$,   df $= 1632$ $t = 2.333$,   df $= 1632$
         $\omega^2 = 0.029$ $\omega^2 = 0.003$

12. $SS_1 = 88.06$, $SS_2 = 93.64$
   $\overline{X}_1 = 1.37$, $\overline{X}_2 = 1.09$
   $t = 0.994$,   df $= 95$

13. $t = 2.224$, df $= 28$ **14.** $t = 0.583$, df $= 34$

15. $t = 1.864$, df $= 126, p < .05$, one-tailed test, $\omega^2 = 0.019$ **16. a.** false   **b.** true   **c.** false

17.

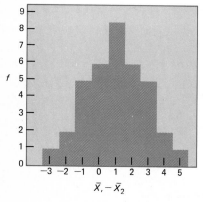

$\overline{X}_1 - \overline{X}_2$	f
5	1
4	2
3	5
2	6
1	8
0	6
-1	5
-2	2
-3	1

18. a. $p = 0.7778$ **b.** $p = 0.6111$ **c.** $p = 0.3889$ **d.** $p = 0.2222$
   e. $p = 0.0833$ **f.** $p = 0$ **g.** $p = 0.4722$

19. $\mu_1 = 5.0, \sigma_1 = 2.24; \mu_2 = 4.0, \sigma_2 = 2.24$

20. a. $z = -1.59, p = 0.9441$ **b.** $z = 0.00, p = 0.5000$ **c.** $z = -1.59, p = 0.0559$

d. $z = -3.18$, $p = 0.0007$ e. $z = 4.76$, $p = 0.00003$ f. $p = 0.5007$
g. $p = 0.0559$

21. a. $z = -0.63$, $p = 0.2643$ b. $z = -0.94$, $p = 0.1736$ c. $z = -1.27$, $p = 0.1020$
d. $z = -1.92$, $p = 0.0274$

22. $t = -5.399$ 23. $z = 3.33$ 24. $t = 24.50$ 25. $t = 5.02$ 26. $F = 1.66$ 27. $t = 1.76$

28. $z = 2.29$ 29. $t = -6.88$ 30. $F = 1.27$

31. $t = 1.63$, df $= 8$; accept H_0.   32. $t = 0.77$, df $= 8$; accept H_0.

33. a. $SS_1 = 74.28$, $SS_2 = 284.57$ b. $SS_1 = 30.00$, $SS_2 = 11.2$
$\overline{X}_1 = 0.40$ $\overline{X}_2 = 1.86$ $\overline{X}_1 = 13.00$, $\overline{X}_2 = 10.40$
$t = 2.281$,   df $= 62$ $t = 3.206$,   df $= 17$
$\omega^2 = 0.062$ $\omega^2 = 0.328$

34. $s_1 = 14.16$, $s_2 = 6.36$ (using $n - 1$ in the denominator)

Chapter 14

1. $t = 3.027$, df $= 16$; reject H_0.   2. $t = 2.08$, df $= 32$; accept H_0.
3. $t = 1.571$, $A = 0.465$, df $= 9$; accept H_0.
4. r_s between final standing and home runs in American League is 0.04; for National League it is 0.36. Both correlations are too low to justify use of correlated samples.
5. $t = 1.590$, df $= 18$, accept H_0. The obtained t-ratio is closer to the rejection region because the number of degrees of freedom is larger (18 as compared to 9) when we employ independent samples.
6. a. Greater risk of a type II error because of the loss of degrees of freedom.
   b. Less risk of a type II error because of the greater sensitivity of the standard error of the difference.
7. a. $A = 0.048$ b. $A = 0.048$ c. $A = 0.778$ 8. $A = 0.199$
9. Manufacturer A: $t = \dfrac{104.82 - 100}{1.63} = 2.96$, df $= 10$;

Manufacturer B: $t = \dfrac{101.91 - 100}{1.39} = 1.37$, df $= 10$.

Employing $\alpha = 0.05$ (two-tailed test), we accept H_0 for B and reject H_0 for A.

10. Manufacturer A: $A = 0.195$; Manufacturer B: $A = 0.573$ 11. $A = 0.216$
12. $A = 5.480$ 13. $A = 0.226$ 14. $A = 0.230$ 15. $A = 0.422$ 16. $A = 1.625$
17. $t = 8.22$
18. $A = 0.3056$ 19. $A = 0.6406$ 20. $A = 0.3696$ 21. $A = 19$ 22. $A = 0.295$
23. a. $A = 0.266$, df $= 4$. Since this is less than the critical value of 0.304, we reject H_0. Male heterosexuals show a greater pupillary response to pictures of females than to pictures of males.
   b. $A = 0.494$, df $= 4$. Since this is greater than the critical value of 0.304, we fail to reject H_0. There is not statistically significant evidence that male homosexuals show a greater pupillary response to pictures of males than to pictures of females.

c. $t = 3.472$, df $= 8$. Since this is larger than the critical value of 2.306, we reject H_0. There is a differential response of male heterosexuals and male homosexuals to pictures of males and females.

24. As a statistician, you are impressed when you reject H_0 with a small N. The reason is the treatment effect must be large, relative to the standard error of the difference, in order to reject H_0 when N is small. Given a large enough N, virtually all null hypotheses would be rejected. In many cases the effect described would be trivial.

25. a. $t = 4.432$, df $= 43$, $p < 0.05$ **b.** $t = 3.69$, df $= 44$, $p < 0.05$
     c. Baseline: lower limit $= 1.04$; upper limit $= 1.59$. Mescaline: lower limit $= 1.60$, upper limit $= 2.67$

Chapter 15

1. $F = 47.02$; reject H_0.

2. All comparisons are significant at 0.01 level. It is clear that death rates are lowest in summer, next to lowest in spring, next to highest in fall, and highest in winter.

3. $F = 0.643$

4. When we employ the 0.05 level, one out of every twenty comparisons will be significant *by chance*. Thus, a significant difference at the 0.05 level in one of ten studies can be attributed to chance.

5. $F = 0.30$, df $= 3/12$

6. $F = 10.43$, df $= 2/12$, HSD $= 7.16$

7. $F = 12.99$, df $= 5/18$, HSD $= 6.02$

8. If the F-ratio is less than 1.00, we conclude that the groups probably come from the same population.

9.

Source of Variation	Sum of Squares	Degrees of Freedom	Variance Estimate	F
Between groups	1.083	2	0.5415	0.6228
Within groups	13.042	15	0.8695	
Total	14.125	17		

10.

Source of Variation	Sum of Squares	Degrees of Freedom	Variance Estimate	F
Between groups	12.067	1	12.067	3.102
Within groups	108.934	28	3.8905	
Total	121.0	29		

11.

Source of Variation	Sum of Squares	Degrees of Freedom	Variance Estimate	F
Between groups	919.793	3	306.598	6.43
Within groups	954.167	20	47.708	
Total	1873.96	23		

12.

Source of Variation	Sum of Squares	Degrees of Freedom	Variance Estimate	F
Between groups	26.80	2	13.4	9.348
Within groups	17.20	12	1.43	
Total	44.00	14		

13. The only comparison significant at 0.01 level is between Group C and Group A.

14.

Source of Variation	Sum of Squares	Degrees of Freedom	Variance Estimate	F
Between groups	285.431	2	142.716	1.606
Within groups	2843.312	32	88.854	
Total	3128.743	34		

15.

Source of Variation	Sum of Squares	Degrees of Freedom	Variance Estimate	F
Between groups	15.8645	3	5.288	15.57
Within groups	6.7917	20	0.3396	
Total	22.6562	23		

16.

Source of Variation	Sum of Squares	Degrees of Freedom	Variance Estimate	F
Treatment combinations	169.04	8		
A-variable	7.37	2	3.68	0.35
B-variable	161.37	2	80.68	7.64
A × B	0.30	4	0.08	0.01
Within (error)	475.33	45	10.56	
Total	644.37	53		

17.

Source of Variation	Sum of Squares	Degrees of Freedom	Variance Estimate	F
Treatment combinations	95.33	5		
A variable	80.66	1	80.66	17.31
B variable	1.13	2	0.56	00.12
A × B	13.54	2	6.77	1.45
Within (error)	84.00	18	4.66	
Total	179.33	23		

Chapter 16

1. $N_a = 30$

2. Step 1: The value of $\sigma_{\bar{X}}$ is 0.5.
Step 2: The critical value of $\bar{X}$ is 71.165.

Step 3: The critical value of $\overline{X}$ has a z-score in the distribution under H_1 of -1.67.

Thus, the power of the test is 95.25.

3. 28.77%
4. a. (i) 0;   (ii) $\beta = 0.1685$;   (iii) Power $= 0.8315$
    b. (i) α;   (ii) $\beta = 0$;   (iii) The concept of power does not apply.
5. a. 5.26%   b. 10.20%   c. 17.88%   d. 28.77%
6. Since the correlation is so low, we lose the advantage of using correlated samples.
7. It takes time, effort, and money to conduct research. When the power to reject a false null hypothesis is low, we are in effect sending good money after bad. A small increase in time, effort, and funding may sometimes be sufficient to raise the power of a test to levels that justify the risk.
8. Power is the probability of rejecting a false null hypothesis. If the null hypothesis is true, there is no *false* null hypothesis to reject.
9. When the null hypothesis is false, a rejection of the null hypothesis is the *correct* statistical decision. The concept of type I error simply does not apply.
10. a. 80   b. 67   c. 57   d. 50   e. 40
11. Factors affecting power:
    a. Sample size: As N increases, power increases.
    b. α-level: The higher the α-level we set, the greater the power of the text.
    c. Nature of the alternative hypothesis: One-tailed test is more powerful than two-tailed alternative (unless the parameter lies in a direction opposite to the one predicted).
    d. Nature of the statistical test: Parametric tests are more powerful than their non-parametric counterparts (assuming assumptions underlying the use of the parametric test are valid).
    e. Correlated measures: When subjects have been successfully matched on a variable correlated with the criterion, a statistical test that takes this correlation into account is more powerful than one that does not.
    Power may be increased by:
    a. Increasing sample size.
    b. Setting α high (for example, 0.05 as opposed to 0.01).
    c. Employing a one-tailed alternative hypothesis.
    d. Employing parametric tests rather than nonparametric.
    e. Employing correlated measures, if appropriate.

Chapter 17

1. a. $p = 0.070$ b. $p = 0.020$ c. $p = 0.040$ 2. a. $p < 0.0003$ b. $p = 0.0003$
    c. $p = 0.1335$
4. Inflated N 5. $\chi^2 = 6.00$, df $= 3$
6. Binomial test $N = 8$, $\chi = 6$, $P = \frac{1}{3}$, $Q = \frac{2}{3}$; reject H_0 at $\alpha = 0.05$
7. $\chi^2 = 1.941$, df $= 1$
8. $P = 0.20(1/5)$, $Q = 0.80\ (4/5)$, $N = 6$

	6	5	4	3	2	1	0
$(P + Q)^6$	$\dfrac{1}{15625}$ 0.000	$\dfrac{24}{15625}$ 0.002	$\dfrac{240}{15625}$ 0.015	$\dfrac{1280}{15625}$ 0.082	$\dfrac{3840}{15625}$ 0.246	$\dfrac{6144}{15625}$ 0.393	$\dfrac{4095}{15625}$ 0.262

9. $\chi^2 = 2.185$, df $= 1$

10. $f_0 = 5 \quad 15$

$f_e = 10 \quad 10$

$$\chi^2 = \frac{(5 - 10)^2}{10} + \frac{(15 - 10)^2}{10} = 5.00.$$

The value of z^2 is:

$$z^2 = \left(\frac{(5 - 10)}{\sqrt{5.00}}\right)^2 = 5.00 = \chi^2.$$

11. $\chi^2 = 6.00$, df $= 3$ 12. $\chi^2 = 3.60$, df $= 3$

13. $x = 28$, $N = 46$ (Table M), critical value $= 31$; we fail to reject H_0 14. $\chi^2 = 20.452$, df $= 1$

15. $\chi^2 = 12.5$, df $= 2$ 16. $\chi^2 = 3.5$, df $= 2$ 17. $\chi^2 = 7.86$, df $= 5$ 18. $z = 2.108$

19. $\chi^2 = 4.44$, df $= 1$ 20. $\chi^2 = 12.81$, df $= 2$ 21. $\chi^2 = 8.077$, df $= 1$ 22. $\chi^2 = 8.869$, df $= 1$

24. $\chi^2 = 8.763$ Significant at $\alpha = 0.01$. The status with respect to FOS is dependent on the political category to which the person belongs. A greater proportion of radicals and liberals evidence FOS than moderates or conservatives.

25. a. $\chi^2 = 1.2$. When no information was given, there was no statistically acceptable evidence that compliance depended on the size of the request.

b. $\chi^2 = 9.6$ Reject H_0. With placebic information, there was significantly greater compliance when the request was small.

c. $\chi^2 = 12.344$. Reject H_0. With sufficient information, there was also significantly greater compliance when the request was small.

Chapter 18

1. a. sign test $N = 10$, $x = 7$ b. $N = 10$, $T = 10$ c. $U = 23$, $U' = 77$ 2. $U = 9.5$, $U' = 62.5$

3. $U = 18$, $U' = 103$ 4. $T = 11.5$ 5. $T = 48$ 6. $U = 25$, $U' = 75$

7. sign test $N = 10$, $x = 6$; Wilcoxon, $T = -12$ 8. $T = -7.5$ 9. $U' = 89$, $U = 11$

Index

485

NUMBER	FORMULA	PAGE
(9.11)	$z_{y'} = r z_x$	170
(9.16)	$s_{est\ y} = s_y \sqrt{\dfrac{N(1 - r^2)}{N - 2}}$	174
(10.4)	$p(A\ or\ B) = p(A) + p(B)$, where the events are *mutually exclusive*	204
(10.6)	$P + Q = 1.00$ when the events are *mutually exclusive* and *exhaustive*	205
(10.9)	$p(A\ and\ B) = p(A)p(B)$ when the events are *independent*	210
(10.10)	$p(A\ and\ B) = p(A)p(B|A) = p(B)p(A|B)$ when the events are *not independent*	210
(12.8)	$s_{\overline{X}} = \dfrac{s}{\sqrt{N - 1}} = \sqrt{\dfrac{\sum(X - \overline{X})^2}{N(N - 1)}} = \sqrt{\dfrac{SS}{N(N - 1)}}$	254
(12.9)	$t = \dfrac{\overline{X} - \mu_0}{s_{\overline{X}}}$	256
(12.10)	Upper limit $\mu_0 = \overline{X} + t_{0.05}(s_{\overline{X}})$	262
(12.11)	Lower limit $\mu_0 = \overline{X} - t_{0.05}(s_{\overline{X}})$	224
(13.1)	$s_{\overline{X}_1 - \overline{X}_2} = \sqrt{\left(\dfrac{SS_1 + SS_2}{N_1 + N_2 - 2}\right)\left(\dfrac{1}{N_1} + \dfrac{1}{N_2}\right)}$	277
(13.2)	$s_{\overline{X}_1 - \overline{X}_2} = \sqrt{\dfrac{SS_1 + SS_2}{N(N - 1)}}$	277
(13.3)	$t = \dfrac{(\overline{X}_1 - \overline{X}_2) - (\mu_1 - \mu_2)}{s_{\overline{X}_1 - \overline{X}_2}}$	278
(13.4)	$s_{\overline{X}_1 - \overline{X}_2} = \left[\dfrac{(N_1 - 1)s_1^2 + (N_2 - 1)s_2^2}{N_1 + N_2 - 2}\right]\left[\dfrac{N_1 + N_2}{N_1 N_2}\right]$	280
(14.1)	$s_{\overline{X}_1 - \overline{X}_2} = \sqrt{s_{\overline{X}_1}^2 + s_{\overline{X}_2}^2 - 2rs_{\overline{X}_1}s_{\overline{X}_2}}$	295
(14.2)	$t = \dfrac{\overline{D} - \mu_{\overline{D}}}{s_{\overline{D}}} = \dfrac{\overline{D}}{s_{\overline{D}}}$	298
(14.3)	$SS_D = \sum D^2 - \dfrac{(\sum D)^2}{N}$	298
(14.5)	$s_{\overline{D}} = \sqrt{\dfrac{SS_D}{N(N - 1)}}$	298